ARMOUR AND WEAPONS
Volume 1

The Artillery of
the Dukes of Burgundy
1363–1477

ARMOUR AND WEAPONS

ISSN 1746–9449

General Editor
Robert Douglas Smith

Throughout history armour and weapons have been not merely the preserve of the warrior in battles and warfare, but potent symbols in their own right (the sword of chivalry, the heraldic shield), representing the hunt and hall as well as the battlefield. This series aims to provide a forum for critical studies of all aspects of arms and armour and their technologies, from the end of the Roman Empire to the dawn of the modern world; both new research and works of synthesis are encouraged.

Proposals or queries should be sent in the first instance to the publisher, at the address given below; all submissions will receive prompt and informed consideration.

Boydell & Brewer Limited, PO Box 9, Woodbridge, Suffolk, IP12 *3DF*

The Artillery of
the Dukes of Burgundy

1363–1477

Robert Douglas Smith
Kelly DeVries

THE BOYDELL PRESS

First published 2005
The Boydell Press, Woodbridge

ISBN 1 84383 162 7

The Boydell Press is an imprint of Boydell & Brewer Ltd
PO Box 9, Woodbridge, Suffolk IP12 3DF, UK
and of Boydell & Brewer Inc.
668 Mt Hope Avenue, Rochester, NY 14620, USA
website: www.boydellandbrewer.com

A CIP catalogue record for this book is available
from the British Library

Library of Congress Cataloging-in-Publication Data
Smith, Robert D. (Robert Douglas), 1954–
    The artillery of the Dukes of Burgundy, 1363–1477 / Robert Douglas Smith and
Kelly DeVries.
       p. cm. – (Armour and weapons, ISSN 1746–9449)
    Summary: "A major new exploration of the history and development of gunpowder weapons
in the 15th century based on the artillery of the Dukes of Burgundy" – Provided by publisher.
    Includes bibliographical references and index.
    ISBN 1–84383–162–7 (hardback : alk. paper)
    1. Artillery – France – History – 15th century.   2. Burgundy (France) – History – House
of Valois, 1363–1477.   3. Gunpowder – History – 15th century.   4. Military history,
Medieval.   I. DeVries, Kelly, 1956– II. Title. III. Series.
    UF72.B87S65 2005
    623.4'1'094409024–dc22   2005010515

This publication is printed on acid-free paper

Typeset by Pru Harrison, Hacheston, Suffolk
Printed in Great Britain by
Cromwell Press, Trowbridge, Wiltshire

Contents

Acknowledgements

Robert Douglas Smith

First, A.V.B. Norman and, especially, Guy Wilson, both past Masters of the Armouries, consistently supported the research that went into this work. Both gave generously of their time and knowledge and were always ready to advise and help. I must also gratefully acknowledge the generosity of past Trustees of the Armouries in awarding me research time and travel expenses which enabled me to visit most of the important artillery collections around the world in order to compile data and information. In addition, I must thank the British Academy for an additional research grant that enabled me to return to Switzerland and check all the relevant details, and I beg their indulgence that this work has taken so long to appear.

Among my greatest debts are those to two colleagues and friends. Sarah Barter Bailey, for many years the Librarian of the Royal Armouries, fed me a continual diet of books, articles and information as well as being a thorough and probing sounding board for many ideas and theories. Alex Hildred of the Mary Rose Trust has over the years been generous with passing on information, ready to discuss and tease out every minute piece of information, and her boundless energy and enthusiasm have been a constant source of inspiration.

To all the curators and guardians of the various museums and collections around Europe that have allowed me to go through their collections I would like to say thank you.

Finally, and by no means least, my greatest debt is to my wife, Ruth Rhynas Brown – not only for her scholarship, her knowledge and incisive mind, but more especially for her love and trust and for her belief in me.

Kelly DeVries

I would like to begin these acknowledgements with a thanks to my co-author, Robert D. Smith, for collaborating with me on a project which I am not sure that I could have done alone, and also serving as the means for bringing me to the Royal Armouries in Leeds for my sabbatical leave in 1999 during which the research progressed and writing on this volume began. The Royal Armouries itself should also be thanked for providing me with a fine location for research and one of the best, if not the best, library of arms and armour books in the world. Especially singled out for praise in this should be Guy Wilson, past Master of the Armouries, and Philip Abbot, head librarian, at the Armouries. In conjunction with my visit, I want to issue a special note of gratitude to Ruth Rhynas Brown, who is not only Bob's wife, as you read above, but a fine historian and scholar in her own right.

While in Leeds I was hosted, as I have been on a number of occasions, by the Midgley family of Menston. To Mike, Elizabeth, and their children – Edward, Emma, Matthew, Eleanor, and William – I owe you so much for your love and support that I can never repay it. Their hearts are clearly the biggest ever encountered by one constantly-appearing academic.

I must also thank the grant-giving programs which allowed me to spend more than a year of time away from my teaching duties. First, I must thank my academic institution, Loyola College in Maryland, for not only allowing me two semesters of sabbatical leave, but extending it by another semester when a second grant became available, and I must thank my colleagues in the History Department there who obviously picked up the teaching burden which I left them. Thanks, too, to the Dibner Institute for the History of Science and Technology at Massachusetts Institute of Technology which appointed me a Senior Fellow during the school year 1998–99 thus providing me with the funds, office space, scholarly environment, and perhaps the most pleasant staff of any academic institution in which to begin my research on this subject, and to the United States of America's National Science Foundation, Science and Technology Studies division, which provided me with a Professional Development Fellowship which I used to fund my stay and study in the United Kingdom during the last six months of 1999.

Finally, it would be completely wrong of me not to thank my wife, Barbara Middleton, and my children, Beth, Michael, and Catie. It is hard to lose a spouse and father for any length of time for whatever reason, yet without a murmur they have supported my rather lengthy stays away from the household. My wife especially must be praised for raising such a fine family both in my absence and, undoubtedly, in my presence as well. I love you all very, very much.

All photographs © The Board of Trustees of the Armouries
All drawings © Robert D. Smith

Introduction

The modern history of gunpowder weapons was born in the middle of the nineteenth century when the future Emperor, Napoleon III, while imprisoned in Ham castle, undertook an investigation of the origins of artillery. The result, the six-volume *Études sur le passé et l'avenir de l'artillerie* was published in Paris between 1846 and 1871,[1] with the final volume ironically appearing in the year that the Franco-Prussian war ended Louis Napoleon-Bonaparte's reign. In fact, only the first volume was written by Napoleon; an artillery officer of some historical talent, Ildéfonse Favé, continued the work based on the emperor's outline and notes. This magisterial work, based largely on original research, not only introduced the subject to a scholarly world but also set a standard which has seldom been matched over the following hundred and fifty years.

While Napoleon and Favé naturally concentrated on French sources and history, other scholars soon added works based on their own countries' archives and libraries. In England the works of Colonel Henry Brackenbury and R. Coltman Clephan, in Belgium the works of Paul Henrard, and in Germany the works of Bernhard Rathgen, have all contributed significantly to our understanding of the history of gunpowder weapons in the last two centuries of the Middle Ages.[2] The value of these works, like those of Napoleon and Favé, was their strict adherence to contemporary documentary and narrative sources.

In the first half of the twentieth century, when politics began to infect all forms of scholarly inquiry, historical investigations into the history of gunpowder weapons were not immune and began to be influenced strongly by ideologies and nationalism. In

---

[1] Louis Napoleon had trained at the Swiss military academy at Thun and in 1834 was promoted to the rank of Captain of Artillery in the Berne militia. Intriguingly his uncle, the Emperor Napoleon I, also trained as an artillery officer. Louis Napoleon-Bonaparte and Ildéfonse Favé, *Études sur le passé et l'avenir de l'artillerie*, 6 vols. (Paris, 1846–71).

[2] Henry Brackenbury, "Ancient Cannon in Europe. Part I: From their First Employment to A.D. 1350," *Proceedings of the Royal Artillery Institution* 4 (1865), 287–308, and "Ancient Cannon in Europe. Part II: From A.D. 1351 to A.D. 1400," *Proceedings of the Royal Artillery Institution* 5 (1867), 1–37; R.Coltman Clephan, *An Outline of the History and Development of Hand Firearms, from the Earliest Period to about the End of the Fifteenth Century* (London, 1906); "The Military Handgun of the Sixteenth Century," *Archaeological Journal* 67 (1910), 109–50, and "The Ordnance of the Fourteenth and Fifteenth Centuries," *Archaeological Journal* 68 (1911), 49–138; Paul Henrard, *Histoire de l'artillerie en Belgique* (Brussels, 1865), and "Documents pour servir à l'histoire de l'artillerie en Belgique. 1er partie: Les fondeurs d'artillerie," *Annales de l'académie d'archéologique de Belgique* 45 (1889), 237–90; Bernhard Rathgen, "Feuer- und fernwaffen des 14. jahrunderts in Flandern," *Zeitschrift für historisches Waffenkunde* 7 (1915–17), 275–306; (with Karl Heinrich Schäfer) "Feuer- und fernwaffen beim päpstlichen Heere im 14. Jahrhundert," *Zeitschrift für historisches Waffenkunde* 7 (1915–17), 1–15; *Die feuer- und fernwaffen in Naumburg von 1348–1449* (Naumburg, 1921); *Das Aufkommen der Pulverwaffe* (Munich, 1925), and *Das Geschütz im Mittelalter* (Berlin, 1928; rpt. Dusseldorf, 1987).

addition, some of the operators of the artillery which played such a large role in World Wars I and II decided that they too should try their hand at explaining the historical background of the weapons of which they were so proud. The first set of historians manipulated the sources in an attempt to provide evidence of their nations' crucial role in the early developments of gunpowder and gunpowder technology in order to further cement the martial superiority of their armies then marching across Europe.[3] The second group, in their enthusiasm for the subject, but also in their inability to use difficult-to-access historical sources and methodology, substituted secondary sources and their own experiences to provide historical interpretations. Their use of hindsight and assumption in the place of thorough research resulted in the development of many inaccuracies and myths concerning the effectiveness and success of early gunpowder weapon technology.[4] Unfortunately, these historians soon supplanted the earlier, and much finer works, due mainly to their accessibility, and their conjectures and assumptions about early gunpowder artillery quickly replaced the more cautious and circumspect renderings of their earlier counterparts.

A complicating factor was that the two world wars, as well as smaller military conflicts following them, most notably in Korea and Vietnam, produced an environment not conducive to the study of military history, and in particular to the study of military technologies. The resulting dearth of academic interest in the history of early gunpowder weapons during this period allowed those with lesser historical abilities to dominate the interest in this field.

All of this produced by the end of the twentieth century a mixture of bad and good scholarship about the origins and development of early gunpowder weapons. To be certain, some scholars did read the earlier historians on gunpowder weapons and were influenced by their scholarly methodology and caution. These, Howard L. Blackmore, M.G.A. Vale, Philippe Contamine, John S. Guilmartin, and Bert S. Hall, among others, produced investigations based on primary sources although often with conclusions mixed with the romanticism of technological determinism.[5] Others, however,

---

3   A prime example of this sort of scholarship is the translation of *Das Feuerwerkbuch von 1420*, which was edited by W. Hassenstein and was published in Munich in 1941, while several of the articles appearing before World War I and World War II in the *Zeitschrift für historisches Waffenkunde* (which was later renamed *Zeitschrift für historisches Waffen- und Kostümkunde*) also fall into this category.

4   As examples of these historical works see Brigadier O.F.G. Hogg, *English Artillery, 1326–1716* (London, 1963), and *Artillery: Its Origin, Heyday and Decline* (London, 1971); Colonel H.C.B. Rogers, *Artillery through the Ages* (London, 1971).

5   Howard L. Blackmore, *The Armouries of the Tower of London*, I: *Ordnance* (London, 1976); "The Boxted Bombard," *Antiquaries Journal* 67 (1987), 86–96; "The Oldest Dated Gun," *Canadian Journal of Arms Collecting* 34.2 (May 1996), 39–47, and "Master Jacobo's Culverin, 1517," *Journal of the Arms and Armour Society* 12.5 (1988), 312–44; M.G.A. Vale, "New Techniques and Old Ideals: The Impact of Artillery on War and Chivalry at the End of the Hundred Years War," in *War, Literature and Politics in the Late Middle Ages: Essays in Honour of G.W. Coopland*, ed. C.T. Allmand (Liverpool, 1975), pp. 57–72, and *War and Chivalry: Warfare and Aristocratic Culture in England, France and Burgundy at the End of the Middle Ages* (London, 1981); Philippe Contamine, "L'artillerie royale Française à la veille des guerres d'Italie," *Annales de Bretagne* 71 (1964), 221–61; *Guerre, état et société à la fin du moyen âge: Études sur les armées des rois de France, 1337–1494* (Paris, 1972); *La guerre de Cent Ans*, 3rd ed. (Paris, 1977) (translated as *War in the Middle Ages*, trans. Michael Jones (London, 1984)); "La guerre de siège au temps de Jeanne d'Arc," *Dossiers de archéologie* 34 (May 1979), and "Les industries de guerre dans la France de la Renaissance: l'exemple de l'artillerie," *Revue historique* 271 (1984), 249–80; John Francis Guilmartin, "The Early Provision of Artillery Armament

seem to have continued the errors of the less cautious writers of the past, often by repeating their conclusions and assumptions without critical focus on the original sources and their limitations.[6] Some, too, have been influenced by the conjectures of power contained within the early gunpowder weapons, so much so that they have determined that their ownership and use in conflicts created a "military revolution" which led to the growth of modern states and the domination of Europe throughout the early modern world.[7]

One result is that historians who enter the field of early gunpowder weapons as a detail in their syntheses of history in general and military history and the history of technology in particular are forced to use poor modern works which, all too frequently, they use uncritically. These writers then perpetuate the myths and errors about the manufacture, use, and effectiveness of gunpowder weapons, introducing and reintroducing them to an equally uncritical and unsuspecting new generation.[8]

However problematic this might be, there has been much good work over the last two decades on the history and development of early artillery, and this has brought into question many of the long-held ideas and suppositions. For example, it is now clear that wrought iron was used for the manufacture of guns from the fourteenth until well into the seventeenth century. Far from being the inferior material, superseded as soon as was possible by bronze or cast iron, it was evidently seen at the time as a useful and appropriate material for some types of guns. Similarly, breech-loading cannon were not the inefficient, dangerous pieces, as so often stated in modern works; breech loading was used well into the seventeenth century for large pieces and for smaller pieces until the eighteenth century, a period of time which surely argues against this supposition.[9] This recognition of the longevity of many types of gunpowder weapons and their effectiveness has also led to the redating of many existing guns, previously assumed to be fifteenth century or earlier, to the sixteenth or even the seventeenth century.[10] In addition, patterns of gunpowder weapon acquisition and use by late medieval states have been challenged: some powerful political entities, such as France and Burgundy, moved from local to central control of their realm's gunpowder

on Mediterranean War Galleys," *Mariner's Mirror* 59 (1973), 257–80; *Gunpowder and Galleys: Changing Technology and Mediterranean Warfare at Sea in the Sixteenth Century* (Cambridge, 1974), and "Ballistics in the Black Powder Era," in *British Naval Armaments*, ed. Robert D. Smith (London, 1989), pp. 73–98; Bert S. Hall, "The Corning of Gunpowder and the Development of Firearms in the Renaissance," in *Gunpowder: The History of an International Technology*, ed. Brenda Buchanan (Bath, 1996), pp. 87–120, and *Weapons and Warfare in Renaissance Europe: Gunpowder, Technology and Tactics* (Baltimore, 1997).

6 Of particular note here is the work of Adrian B. Caruana, *The History of English Sea Ordnance*, I: *The Age of Evolution, 1523–1715* (Rotherfield, 1994), which is littered with many errors of fact, transcription, and translation.

7 Note, in particular but not exclusively, Geoffrey Parker, *The Military Revolution: Military Innovation and the Rise of the West, 1500–1800* (Cambridge, 1988); Clifford J. Rogers, "The Military Revolutions of the Hundred Years War," *Journal of Military History* 57 (1993), 241–78; David Eltis, *The Military Revolution in Sixteenth-Century Europe* (London, 1995); and Thomas Arnold, *The Renaissance at War* (London, 2001).

8 See, for example, Maurice H. Keen, "The Changing Scene: Guns, Gunpowder, and Permanent Armies," in *Medieval Warfare: A History*, ed. Maurice Keen (Oxford, 1999), pp. 273–91.

9 Robert D. Smith, "Port Pieces: The Use of Wrought-Iron Guns in the Sixteenth Century," *Journal of the Ordnance Society* 5 (1993), 1–10.

10 Robert D. Smith, "Wrought-Iron Swivel Guns," in *The Archaeology of Ships of War*, ed. M. Bound (Oxford, 1995), pp. 104–13.

weapons during the fourteenth and fifteenth centuries, while others, particularly England, followed an opposite pattern, one of central to local control during the same period.[11] Gunpowder weapons have also been recognized as more effective weapons at sea at an earlier period than previously believed,[12] and less effective as siege artillery.[13]

These examples alone show that a reassessment of the earlier history of gunpowder weapons is needed and must be made essentially from the ground up. Early works, such as Napoleon and Favé, established some foundations, especially in methodology, but even these failed to establish a framework from all contemporary sources: narrative, documentary, and artifactual; nor has any subsequent scholarship managed to do so. It is very apparent that in the main these works do no more than scratch the surface of what is a complex and complicated history. This is, in part, understandable as the subject does not yield its secrets easily. Using narrative sources alone as a guide may be confusing because those witnesses, often not trained in the art of military technology were themselves confused by what they saw. These chroniclers and other narrative writers were also obviously influenced by patronage, audience, and personal allegiances, and were only able to use those sources available to them, with their attendant biases. Documentary sources rely on a sort of notarial code, the terminological technicality of which needs to be broken before it can be used. And extant weapons generally do not have accurate provenances, with the result that their type and date are often not known, while their use and effectiveness is misunderstood. At times it seems that the more one investigates, the more confusing the subject becomes: the very complexity of the field often leads those who specialize in its study to conclude that it is not open to analysis and understanding, and that they may never see through the opaque veil.

On the whole previous studies have also tended to either concentrate on one particular period or event or have been part of larger works where the history of artillery has been treated subsidiary to the wider picture. In addition, these works have tended to concentrate on the narrative or documentary sources and have made little or no attempt at relating these to existing guns or types of guns. Some work has been done, notably by François T'Sas on fifteenth-century bombards[14] and similar work on the same field by one of the present authors,[15] but little has been published as a consequence of these works.[16] No studies have attempted to marry all three of the available

---

11　Kelly DeVries, "Gunpowder Weaponry and the Rise of the Early Modern State," *War in History* 5 (1998), 127–45.

12　Kelly DeVries, "A 1445 Reference to Shipboard Artillery," *Technology and Culture* 31 (1990), 818–29, and "The Effectiveness of Fifteenth-Century Shipboard Artillery," *The Mariner's Mirror* 84 (1998), 389–99.

13　Kelly DeVries, "The Impact of Gunpowder Weaponry on Siege Warfare in the Hundred Years War," in *The Medieval City under Siege*, ed. I.A. Corfis and M. Wolfe (Woodbridge, 1995), pp. 227–44, and "Facing the New Military Technology: Non-*Trace Italienne* Anti-Gunpowder Weaponry Defenses, 1350–1550," in *Colonels and Quatermasters: War and Technology in the Old Regime*, ed. Brett Steele (Cambridge, 2004), pp. 37–71.

14　François T'Sas, "Dulle Griet. La grosse bombarde de Gand, et ses souers," *Armi Antiche* (1969), 13–57.

15　In particular, Robert D. Smith and Ruth Rhynas Brown, *Mons Meg and her Sisters*, Royal Armouries Monograph 1 (London, 1989).

16　Although recently Marc Beyaert, "Nieuwe historisch onderzoek van de Dulle Griet bombarde in Gent," *Handelingen der Maatschappij voor geschiedenis en oudheidkunde te Gent*, n.s. 53 (1999), 3–59, and C. Gillet and M. Lefebvre, "Quelle etait la puissance de feu de la 'Mons Meg', bombard Bourguignonne conservée à

source types – narrative, documentary, and artifactual. In light of this, there is a real and pressing need to re-evaluate and re-think the whole history and development of artillery before the sixteenth century.

This book then is an attempt to put together a coherent framework for the development of gunpowder weaponry throughout the fifteenth century from a synthesis of the available evidence: contemporary narrative, documentary sources, and surviving examples. The fifteenth century is particularly rich in narrative sources covering the military events of the period, especially those occurring in France, Burgundy, and the Low Countries, and these provide a background against which a better understanding can be achieved. They are, however, not without their problems, both of interpretation and perspective. The largest and most comprehensive of all the surviving documentary sources on fifteenth-century gunpowder artillery, and perhaps the most important, are the accounts of the dukes of Burgundy: Philip the Bold, John the Fearless, Philip the Good and Charles the Bold. These were extracted, brought together, transcribed, and published, although with very limited analysis, late in the nineteenth century by Joseph Garnier, a Dijonnais archivist.[17] However, despite their enormous value in the understanding of artillery in the fifteenth century, they too are not without their problems, the primary one being difficulties of terminology and the apparent lack of notarial standardization during this period. For example, while several different types of guns are listed, it is not always clear to the modern reader what exactly is being referred to. Finally, and equally important, there are the surviving artifactual examples, and it is here that we are particularly fortunate. In the final wars of the reign of Duke Charles the Bold, the Swiss Confederate forces defeated the duke's armies at the battles of Grandson, Murten, and Nancy and captured, among other things, their artillery. Although greatly reduced in number from those recorded to have been captured, some of these pieces are still preserved in museums in Switzerland, mainly in Murten, La Neuville, and Basel.[18]

This work begins with a synthesis of the history of gunpowder weapons from the earliest times to 1500, followed by three separate sections which provide the detailed evidence to support that synthesis. The first of these tells the military history and events of the dukes of Burgundy, derived largely from narrative and documentary sources, and serves as a back drop for the historical development of artillery. The next section is an analysis of the various types of gunpowder weapons, taken principally from the work of Garnier. This is followed by an illustrated catalogue of the surviving guns.

Edimourg?" *Le musée d'armes* 28.98–99 (Dec. 2000), 2–22, have appeared, so perhaps the trend is beginning to change ever so slightly.

17 Joseph Garnier, *L'artillerie des ducs de Bourgogne d'après les documents conservés aux archives de la Cote-d'Or* (Paris, 1895). One of the problems of Garnier's work is its utter inaccessibility. Very few copies seem to have survived outside of France. The authors have located only one copy in England, one in Canada, and one in the United States.

18 And yet, even these have been little studied, the only catalogue being that in Florens Deuchler's seminal *Die Burgundebeute: Inventar der Beutestucke aus den Schlachten von Grandson, Murten und Nancy 1476/77* (Bern, 1963).

EDITORIAL CONVENTIONS

Note on names of gunpowder weapons

Contemporary names of late medieval arms and armour often have many variant forms and spellings, and gunpowder weapons are no exception, indeed they may be worse. In this book, we have decided to use the following spellings for the most common gunpowder weapons: *bombard, canon, coulovrine, courtau, crapaudeau, hacquebus, mortar, pestereau, serpentine, veuglaire*. However, in quotations from the original language, original spellings will be used. For variant spellings on these gunpowder weapon names, see Part 3 below.

Note on measurements

Before the age of standardization there was a bewildering, to modern eyes, array of different measurement systems throughout Europe. Trying to decide which one was used for the various dimensions given in the contemporary documents is, to say the least, problematic. However the pioneering work in the field by Monique Sommé[19] suggests that for the Burgundian documents, a useful baseline is:

> 1 *piez* = 276mm
> 1 *pouce (polz)* ($\frac{1}{12}$ piez) = 23mm
> 1 *livre* = 490g

These conversion factors have been used throughout this book.

Note on proper and place names

Of necessity in dealing with late medieval sources written in different languages, and the problems caused by modern national boundaries and language borders, place and personal names are often expressed in different forms and spellings. The authors have attempted to standardize and modernize these names wherever possible. The names of the four Valois dukes, following the lead of their eminent biographer, Richard Vaughan, will be expressed in English translation. Place names in the Low Countries and personal names of Low Countries' leaders, which often have French and Dutch equivalents, will be expressed in their most common modern forms.

---

[19] Monique Sommé, "Les mesures dans l'artillerie Bourguignonne au XVe siècle," *Cahiers de metrologie* 7 (1989), 43–53.

1

An Overall History of Gunpowder Weapons during the Fourteenth and Fifteenth Centuries

By the end of the fourteenth century the Ottoman Turks had become a threat to the Christians of the eastern Mediterranean. Whether Catholic or Orthodox, these Christians worried about their future with the rise of this new infidel power. Almost from the initial rise of Ottoman power, Turkish armies spread east and west from their Asia Minor homeland, invading regions of the Byzantine Empire, the Middle East, and southeastern Europe – areas which had not encountered this form of ruthless warfare for at least one hundred years, in the case of the Middle East, or two hundred years, in the case of Byzantium and southeastern Europe. Calls for assistance, in the form of Crusades, spread quickly, and even before the middle of the fourteenth century discussions were held in the courts of western Europe as to how and when to assist these beleaguered people.[1] Of course, nothing could be accomplished by the three strongest western powers, France, England, and Burgundy, enmeshed as they were in their own continuing dynastic struggles which we know as "The Hundred Years War."

Ottoman Turkish invasions continued, with conquests of parts of Macedonia, Greece, Bulgaria, Bosnia, and Serbia. Calls to crusade similarly continued and ultimately pricked the conscience of even those Christian warriors fighting among themselves. Finally, in 1393, when the Hundred Years War was at an ebb, brought about more by fatigue than by any decisive event, those same princes determined to turn their military strength towards the Ottomans in the east. Just as the earlier Crusades had required the efforts of some of the greatest diplomatic minds of Europe to encourage their undertaking, so too did peace between England, France, and Burgundy before this journey to the east could be undertaken.[2] Indeed, it was only after lengthy negotiations that the "*paix impossible*," as a recent article by Françoise Autrand has called it,

---

[1] See Norman Housley, *The Later Crusades, 1274–1580: From Lyons to Alcazar* (Oxford, 1992).

[2] Chief among these diplomats was Philippe de Mézières whose endeavors in this matter were extensive. See N. Jorga, *Philippe de Mézières (1327–1405) et la croisade au XIVe siècle* (Paris, 1896). Among his most important crusading works is a letter written to Richard II pleading for the English king to seek peace in the Hundred Years War. See Philippe de Mézières, *Letter to King Richard II: A Plea Made in 1395 for Peace between England and France*, ed. and trans. G.W. Coopland (Liverpool, 1975).

was made.[3] It included: the restoration of Cherbourg to France; the marriage of Richard II of England to Isabelle, the daughter of Charles VI of France; a truce of twenty-eight years; and an agreement to a Crusade against the Turks in which both kings, as well as Duke Philip the Bold of Burgundy would participate.[4] Originally negotiated in 1393, by 1396 all of the provisions had been accomplished except for the Crusade.

By 1396, although sufficient finances had been raised to support a large army on its journey to the east, the crusading ardour seems to have gone out of all of the main would-be crusaders. Charles VI had pushed his participatory responsibility onto his brother, Louis, duke of Orleans, Richard II had similarly moved his onto his uncle, John of Gaunt, earl of Lancaster, and Philip the Bold onto his son, John the Fearless, count of Nevers. When Louis of Orleans and John of Gaunt also backed out, the Burgundian heir-apparent, John the Fearless, the highest-ranking noble remaining, was left in charge.[5] He left Dijon on 30 April 1396, with a sizeable contingent of French, Burgundian, English, and Low Countries troops. But, as they marched first to Regensburg, then traveled by boat down the Danube, stopping first in Vienna and then in Buda, more and more soldiers from Germany, Austria, and Italy joined them. When the army of King Sigismund I of Hungary and several Knights Hospitallers also joined, the total force had become the largest pan-European army raised in the post-Black Death era. Contemporary sources put it at more than 100,000, with modern historians numbering it between 12,000 and 16,000.[6] Their eastward march eventually brought them to the large, well-populated, and fortified town of Nicopolis, which they began to besiege sometime between 8 and 10 September 1396.[7]

While the crusaders were on their way east, the Ottoman Sultan Bayezid I, who was besieging Constantinople,[8] was kept well informed of their movements by his scouts

---

3   Françoise Autrand, "La paix impossible: les négociations franco-anglaises à la fin du 14e siècle," in Actes du colloque Nicopolis 1396–1996, *Annales de Bourgogne* 68 (1997), 11–22.

4   See Autrand, p. 37; J.J.N. Palmer, *England, France and Christendom, 1377–99* (Chapel Hill, 1972), pp. 142–51, 166–79; and Richard Vaughan, *Philip the Bold: The Formation of the Burgundian State* (London, 1962), pp. 61–62.

5   Vaughan, *Philip the Bold*, pp. 62–63.

6   The numbers of troops at Nicopolis is disputed. While Aziz Suryal Atiya (*The Crusade of Nicopolis* (London, 1934), pp. 66–69, and *The Crusade in the Later Middle Ages* (London, 1938), p. 446) holds to the large numbers given by contemporary western chroniclers, other historians have chosen to lower them. See Housley, *The Later Crusades*, p. 76; Gustav Kling, *Die Schlacht bei Nikopolis im Jahre 1396* (Berlin, 1906), pp. 14–24, 81; Hans Delbrück, *History of the Art of War Within the Framework of Political History*, vol. III: *Medieval Warfare*, trans. W.J. Renfroe, Jr. (Westport, 1984), pp. 476–81; and R. Rosetti, "Notes on the Battle of Nicopolis (1396)," *Slavonic and East European Review* 15 (1936–37), 629–38. The truth is probably somewhere in the middle, modern historians tending to underestimate numbers as much as contemporary historians tend to exaggerate them. For a survey of who claims what in the dispute see Kenneth M. Setton, *The Papacy and the Levant (1204–1571)*, vol I: *The Thirteenth and Fourteenth Centuries* (Philadelphia, 1976), pp. 351–53. Setton himself believes the number to have been between 12,000 and 16,000 on each side.

7   Setton, pp. 347–49, and Vaughan, *Philip the Bold*, pp. 68–69.

8   A narrative of and the sources for this siege can be found in Paul Gautier, "Un récit inédit du siège de Constantinople par les turcs (1394–1402)," *Revue des études byzantines* 23 (1965), 100–17 and N. Necipoglu, "Economic Conditions in Constantinople during the Siege of Bayezid I (1394–1402)," in *Constantinople and Its Hinterland*, ed. C. Mango and G. Dagron (Aldershot, 1995), pp. 157–67.

and spies. His response to the siege of Nicopolis was to break off from his own siege and move to relieve the town. His speed was extraordinary, and, on 24 September, he camped only four miles south of the besieged town, his presence surprising the enemy.[9]

The Turkish army consisted mostly of infantry, with some light cavalry, while the crusaders had a notable contingent of heavy cavalry, containing almost all of the French, Burgundian, English, German, Low Countries, Italian, and Hospitaller soldiers. The Hungarians and other central Europeans (Wallachians, Transylvanians, and some Germans) were mostly infantry. But, while Bayezid and his "officer corps" were veterans, John the Fearless and his officers were not. Sigismund was the only Christian general who had fought against the Ottoman Turks, but the crusading knights, who felt that they had traveled all that way to defend Hungary because the Hungarian king had not been able to do so, were not about to listen to him, no matter how experienced he was.[10] Sigismund recommended that the infantry should lead the other forces into battle and should take up a defensive position to try to provoke the Turks into a charge onto their lines. However, the western Europeans were not prepared to follow this suggestion.[11] Instead French and Burgundian leaders used their influence to counter the Hungarian king's proposal, confident instead in their own traditional method of fighting battles.

Following their plan, the crusader cavalry charged first into their Turkish opponents, who had themselves taken the defensive stance that Sigismund had suggested. At first, this cavalry charge was effective, even driving back the Turkish troops, and a second charge by the crusaders also proved effective. Yet neither attack forced the Turks into a rout, and when Bayezid's remaining soldiers launched their own charge, the western European crusaders could not withstand it and, even though some reinforcements tried to come to their aid, they were soundly defeated.[12] Some managed to flee, but, as so many had committed themselves to the charges, in reality few escaped the massacre.

The tactics of the western Europeans at Nicopolis were not unlike those which had been used throughout most of the Middle Ages: a cavalry charge or charges to cause the

9   Vaughan, *Philip the Bold*, p. 69.
10 The standard secondary accounts of battle are: Atiya, *Nicopolis*, pp. 82–97; Setton, pp. 351–56; Delbrück, pp. 473–81; Kling; Rosetti; Sir Charles Oman, *A History of the Art of War in the Middle Ages* (London, 1905), II:348–53; Gustav Köhler, *Die Entwickelung des Kriegswesens und der Kriegführung in der Ritterzeit von Mitte des 11. Jahrhunderts bis zu de Hussitenkriegen* (Breslau, 1886), II:625–55; Gustav Köhler, *Die Schlachten von Nicopoli und Warna* (Breslau, 1882); Alois Brauner, *Die Schlacht bei Nikopolis, 1396* (Breslau, 1876); and Ferdinand von Šišić, "Die Schlacht bei Nikopolis (25. September 1396)," *Wissenschaftliche mitteilungen aus Bosnia und der Hercegovina* 6 (1899), 291–327.
11 Atiya, *Nicopolis*, pp. 82–84, and Atiya, *Crusade*, p. 447. This comes chiefly from Jean Froissart, *Chroniques*, in *Œuvres de Froissart*, ed. Kervyn de Lettenhove (Brussels, 1867–77), XV:313–14.
12 Atiya, *Nicopolis*, pp. 89–93; Oman, II:351–52; Delbrück, pp. 478–79; and Setton, pp. 352–55. Atiya (*Nicopolis*, pp. 92–93) maintains that there was German and Hungarian reinforcement, even though Johannes Schiltberger (*Bondage and Travels of Johann Schiltberger, a Native of Bavaria, in Europe, Asia, and Africa (1396–1427)*, ed. K.F. Neumann and trans. J.B. Telfer (London, 1879), p. 3) is the only contemporary author to contend that this took place. He was an eye-witness to the battle and may have been taken prisoner in this charge, and this convinces Atiya when *Le livre des fais du bon messire Jehan le Maingre, dit Boucicaut, mareschal de France et gouverneur de Jennes* (Paris, 1985), pp. 110–111, claims that the Hungarians fled without entering the conflict. Setton agrees with Atiya (*Crusade*, pp. 354–55).

rout of a foe. But on that September day in southeastern Europe it was those who charged who were put into disarray and defeated by the well-disciplined and well-led Turkish forces. This also was not that unusual, as infantry forces frequently were able to defeat those who tried to ride them down when they remained steadfast in their lines.[13]

And so the battle of Nicopolis is written in history, as a traditional battle with a traditional result. Yet, in 1396 should this have been a traditional medieval battle? By 1396 gunpowder weapons had been in existence in the west for at least seventy years, and yet the method of fighting and the outcome of the battle indicates that they were not a part of the western European tactical plan, not even of the alternative offered by Sigismund I. Why not?

BEFORE THE VALOIS DUKES OF BURGUNDY

There is little doubt that by 1326 gunpowder weapons were known in western Europe. The two illustrations found in Walter de Milemete's *De notabilibus, sapientiis et prudentiis regum* (Concerning the Majesty, Wisdom and Prudence of Kings) and the *De secretis secretorum Aristotelis* (The Secrets of Secrets of Aristotle), both made in London, cannot be contested. Each shows a large vase-shaped cannon lying on its side. In the Milemete manuscript, a soldier, dressed in armour, is firing the gun, loaded with a large arrow-shaped projectile towards what appears to be a fortification.[14] The Pseudo-Aristotle illustration is similar to the first, but depicts a larger gunpowder weapon (no target is shown), and a squad of four armoured soldiers.[15] In the late 1330s and 1340s references to gunpowder weaponry increase. Guns were included in armouries in Rouen, Bruges, Lille, Lucca, Aachen, Deventer, London, Siena, St. Omer, and Bioule Castle, and elsewhere. They also appeared at the attack of Southampton in 1338, the sieges of Cambrai also in 1338, of Quesnoy, Mortague, Saint-Amand, Marchiennes, and Tournai in 1340, of Calais in 1346–1347, and almost certainly at the battle of Crécy in 1346, where they were used on the battlefield solely "to cause panic."[16] In this early period, in fact, it may have been their sound that was more impressive and important than their effectiveness as weapons; sound is an aspect of military action that should not be underestimated by the modern scholar.

---

[13] For at least the early fourteenth century, this is the thesis of Kelly DeVries, *Infantry Warfare in the Early Fourteenth Century: Discipline, Tactics, and Technology* (Woodbridge, 1996).

[14] Montague Rhodes James, ed., *The Treatise of Walter de Milemete* (London, 1913), p. 140. Recently the Royal Armouries replicated and fired a gunpowder weapon based on that illustrated in the Walter de Milemete manuscript. See Robert D. Smith, The Reconstruction and Firing Trials of a Replica of a 14th-Century Cannon," *Royal Armouries Yearbook* 4 (1999), 86–94.

[15] James, ed., p. 181.

[16] On these engagements see Kelly DeVries, "Gunpowder Weaponry and the Rise of the Early Modern State," *War in History* 5 (1998), 127–45. For a discussion of the gunpowder weapons at Crécy see Alfred H. Burne, *The Crécy War: A Military History of the Hundred Years War from 1337 to the Peace of Bretigny, 1360* (London, 1955), pp. 193–203, and T.F. Tout, "Firearms in England in the Fourteenth Century," *English Historical Review* 26 (1911), 671–73. Even with such seemingly undeniable proof for the existence of guns at Crécy, there are still some who doubt that they were there. See Oman, II:142 n. 2 and Henri de Wailly, *Crecy, 1346: Anatomy of a Battle* (Poole, 1987), p. 91.

Indeed, it may be gunpowder weapons that Walter de Milemete refers to when he writes:

> And before you fight, you should arrange your army in secure positions. Also, the warriors of your army should become accustomed to seeing and knowing the enemy. Furthermore, the enemy should begin to be terrified when they see the battle lines arranged against them. And you ought to terrify and disturb your enemy by throwing blazing objects and [making] horrible sounds, since a large part of victory is terrifying enemies and inducing fear, and this in the extreme when you wish to begin to fight.[17]

For the first fifty years of their existence our knowledge of gunpowder weapons is slight. Some of this can obviously be explained by the paucity of records. Narrative sources of military engagements do not often mention gunpowder weapons explicitly, and when references do occur, there are insufficient details to enable a clear understanding of the practice, operation, or technology of the weapons. Documentary sources are somewhat better, but do not provide enough detail to enable a determination of exactly what is being described. And there are no extant examples or other illustrations, other than those mentioned above, which can be dated securely to this period. This very paucity must lead us to the conclusion that gunpowder weapons were not common or extensively used throughout the first three-quarters of the century.

The reasons for this are not clear to us today. There are a number of interrelated factors that must be considered. Of these the manufacture of powder and, in particular the production of saltpetre, may be the most significant. Knowledge of saltpetre had come from China and the east, possibly via Muslim North Africa and Spain, and was surely known to medieval Europe at the time Roger Bacon was composing his recipes for gunpowder in the middle of the thirteenth century.[18] But whether it was only imported from non-European sources or produced in Europe is still open to question. One thing does seem certain, however: saltpetre was an expensive item, there was not a lot of it around, and, of course, there was no point in acquiring gunpowder weapons if the gunpowder could not be obtained. Therefore, one of the reasons why gunpowder weapons did not immediately proliferate may have been shortage of saltpetre to make powder.[19]

There is also a question over the effectiveness of gunpowder weapons in conflicts: How good were they? and How many was a military leader able to use? Narrative

---

[17]   Cary J. Nederman, ed. and trans., *Political Thought in Early Fourteenth-Century England: Treatises by Walter of Milemete, William of Pagula and William of Ockham* (Tempe, 2002), pp. 58–59.

[18]   On Roger Bacon and his recipes for gunpowder see Kelly DeVries, "Gunpowder and Early Gunpowder Weapons," in *Gunpowder: The History of an International Technology*, ed. Brenda Buchanan (Bath, 1996), pp. 121–23.

[19]   This line of reasoning is provoked by the works of Gerhard Kramer (*Berthold Schwarz: Chemie und Waffentechnik im 15. Jahrhundert* (Munich, 1995) and "*Das Feuerwerkbuch*: Its Importance in the Early History of Black Powder," in *Gunpowder: The History of an International Technology*, ed. B. Buchanan (Bath, 1996), pp. 45–56), and Bert S. Hall ("The Corning of Gunpowder and the Development of Firearms in the Renaissance," in *Gunpowder: The History of an International Technology*, ed. Brenda Buchanan (Bath, 1996), pp. 87–120, and *Weapons and Warfare in Renaissance Europe: Gunpowder, Technology, and Tactics* (Baltimore, 1997). It is in this last work of Hall's that the subject is most completely refined, however there is still much to be done.

sources from the period which mention guns rarely discuss their successes; it appears that they did not kill soldiers or bring down walls of fortifications in any more numbers or with any more speed than traditional medieval weapons. The spear, sword, staff weapon, bow, crossbow, and trebuchet still held sway in the minds of the chroniclers. However, that they did note gunpowder weapons leads inevitably to the conclusion that they were used, but they seem to have been a curiosity, peripheral to the engagement, the "panic-causing noise-makers" of Crécy, for example.

Had these gunpowder weapons proved to be really "revolutionary" in early military engagements, there is no doubt that the early fourteenth-century saltpetre problem might have been overcome, as it would be later in the Middle Ages. It was a cycle, after all: the lack of effectiveness meant that there was not a great demand for gunpowder weapons, the lesser demand for gunpowder weapons did not stimulate the trade or production of saltpetre, while the lack of saltpetre undoubtedly contributed to the ineffectiveness of early gunpowder weapons.

Still, gunpowder weapons must have excited the military minds of the period, enough at least to keep them being made and improved. There was never a period in western European history when the gun was "given up," as scholars have suggested occurred elsewhere.[20] Indeed, there is evidence to suggest that there was royal support for much of the development of gunpowder weapons, at least in England, and for local support, either princely or communal, in France, the Low Countries, and Italy throughout the period.[21] With so little evidence much must remain opaque to us concerning motives, techniques, quantities, and detailed development.

Some rays of light pierce the darkness, however, and lead to the conclusion that some advances had taken place. In 1375, for example, an account exists of the construction of a *grand canon de fer* at Caen. Made for the siege of Saint-Vicomte-le-Sauveur, its construction included both iron and steel, and at its completion, on 3 May, it weighed 2,310 *livres*. It was, therefore, not a small piece, nor inexpensive, costing in all 5,201 *livres* 16 *sous* 2 *deniers tournois*. The lengthy account of the construction of this cannon, transcribed by Ildéfonse Favé, records all the payments for materials – metal, wood, etc. – salaries (for smiths, carpenters, transporters, etc.) – and sundry miscellaneous expenses (candles for working at night, baskets for carrying the charcoal to the forge, and a leather cover for protecting the piece, etc.). It was a massive undertaking, necessitating a large manufacturing workforce, which included five master smiths and their valets, which took forty-two working days to complete.[22]

By 1375, therefore, it is certain that large gunpowder weapons were being made. Still, this account is of the construction of only one piece, which, though impressive, had only four gunstones made for it, two of which were taken during the siege of Saint-Vicomte-le-Sauveur. Does this suggest that gunpowder weapons were still not

---

[20] See, for example, Noel Perrin, *Giving Up the Gun: Japan's Reversion to the Sword, 1543–1879* (Boston, 1979), and David Ayalon, *Gunpowder and Firearms in the Mamluk Kingdom: A Challenge to a Mediaeval Society* (London, 1956). Both of these books should be used with caution, however, as they have their critics.

[21] DeVries, "Gunpowder Weaponry and the Rise of the Early Modern State."

[22] Louis Napoleon-Bonaparte and Ildéfonse Favé, *Études sur le passé et l'avenir de l'artillerie* (Paris, 1846–71), III:97–99 (summarizes the construction); IV: xviii–xxxvi (transcription). [N.B. These volumes were written by Favé himself.]

seen as a significant part of the larger military force? One may conclude that this was the case, as shown by the evidence above; and yet, more than 5,000 *livres* were spent on this single gun, an extraordinary amount in relative terms. Although a ray of light, the 1375 gun still cannot illuminate the entire subject, which must remain obscure.

What does come out of the obscurity, though, is the increasing use of early gunpowder weapons. The Caen gun was constructed, as accounts of payment make clear, for the siege of Saint-Sauveur-le-Vicomte, an English fortification left over from the attacks Edward III had made across the Cotentin and Normandy in 1346. Since then its role had been one largely of providing a fortification from which English soldiers were able to raid the surrounding countryside. In 1372, French forces decided that they would mount an operation against the fortress to end this harassment. Anticipating an easy victory, as those inside the castle had no expectation of reinforcement or relief, the French instead faced a siege that dragged on until 1375. Frustrated at the lack of a submission by traditional siege tactics – negotiation, starvation, etc. – the French eventually brought gunpowder weapons to the siege, one of which was the weapon detailed above.

On 21 May 1375 the fortress of Saint-Sauveur-le-Vicomte surrendered. But did gunpowder weapons effect that surrender? According to Bert S. Hall, they did not. The English defenders do not appear to have had gunpowder weapons of their own, yet they did prepare themselves and their fortification to lessen the damage of the French guns, indicating at least a knowledge of the possible effects. At the same time, the French gunpowder weapons seem to have been unable to shoot in a high trajectory, thus leaving the more vulnerable tops of the walls, and the inhabitants' homes untouched. There were also problems with the supply of gunpowder, which needed to be supplemented from Paris at least once during the final stages of the siege. It was only when the garrison was offered 55,000 gold *francs* that they decided to make a truce and to leave Saint-Sauveur-le Vicomte.[23] So gunpowder weapons did not determine the victory.

Did they not, though? Can one deny that the date of surrender was coincident with the date of the arrival of several gunpowder weapons? The situation is not at all clear. While it is impossible to suggest that guns were "effective" in concluding the siege, it is also impossible to suggest that they did not at least contribute to the surrender of the garrison. None of the original sources describe such a cause-and-effect relationship, and even if they did, the modern historian might doubt this technologically deterministic conclusion. Take for example the 1377 Burgundian siege of Odruik, which will be discussed in detail below. At this fortification, which stood outside Calais, the Burgundian duke fired a number of bolts from his gunpowder weapons. These not only seem to have damaged the walls, but, according to Jean Froissart's account, "because of the power of the discharge, they penetrated the walls . . . [and those

---

23 Hall, *Weapons and Warfare in Renaissance Europe*, pp. 56–57, see also Leopold Delisle, *Histoire du chateau et des sires de Saint-Sauveur-le-Vicomte* (Paris, 1867), I:185. For other gunpowder weapons at the siege of Saint-Sauveur-le-Vicomte, see *Le compte du clos de galées de Rouen au XIVe siècle*, ed. C. Bréard (Rouen, 1893), p. 205.

defending Odruik] surrendered the fortress, to save their lives."[24] So, in this case, there is evidence to suggest that gunpowder weapons effected the taking of the fortress.

Yet, does this mean that a corner had been turned in the development of gunpowder weapons? Or does it simply add to our perplexity in understanding the subject? The siege of Saint-Sauveur-le-Vicomte occurred in 1375, Odruik in 1377, and many other examples of the 1370s and 1380s lead to the simple conclusion that, by the 1370s, it had become common to take gunpowder weapons to sieges.

At the siege of Saint-Sauveur-le-Vicomte the French gunpowder weapons fired stone balls, while at the siege of Odruik the Burgundian guns fired bolts. In a way, this highlights a further obscurity of the history of gunpowder weapons during their first half century. Little is known about the types, shapes, sizes, and materials of either the guns or their ammunition. The earliest illustrations, those in the Milemete and Pseudo-Aristotle manuscripts, portray a vase-shaped gun, probably made of a copper-alloy.[25] Written records confirm that this shape was not fantastical.[26] The guns are shown firing bolts or *garros*, which, again according to written sources, were used throughout the fourteenth century. Use of an arrow-shaped projectile, at least initially, may have derived from the fact that projectile-firing weapons traditionally discharged arrows or bolts. Yet, the fact that gunpowder weapons were still firing bolts at the end of the century, as seen at the siege of Odruik, would indicate that they were still a common gunpowder-propelled projectile. So common, in fact, that when the late fourteenth-century French poet Eustace Deschamps composed a poem attacking arms makers, entitled "De la maledicion sur ceuls qui requierrent a faire armes," in which he records a list of weapons needed for warfare during his time, among those listed are "*canons*," which discharged "stones" and "bolts."[27] One of the earliest trustworthy written sources on gunpowder weaponry, a document written in 1326 in Florence ordering the construction of gunpowder weapons for the defense of the city, directs those constructing these weapons to manufacture not only iron "*palloctas*" (presumably ball-shaped projectiles – the Latin word is vague) but also "*pilas*" (presumably arrow-shaped projectiles) for the same weapons.[28] Of course, as seen at the siege of Saint-Sauveur-le-Vicomte in 1375, balls were being used, and thus from the outset of gunpowder weapons, and at least throughout their earliest period, both balls and bolts were fired.

[24] Jean Froissart, *Chroniques*, ed. S. Luce (Paris, 1869–1975), VIII:249.

[25] The modern historian's inability to be completely sure what contemporary sources mean when they refer to copper-based gunpowder artillery, for example *bronze, arrain, latten, metaille, métal*, among others, has led us to use the modern descriptor "copper-alloy" to describe all non-ferrous gunpowder artillery. It is also unclear whether contemporary metal-smiths used these terms in a precise way.

[26] Kelly DeVries, "A Reassessment of the Gun Illustrated in the Walter de Milemete and Pseudo-Aristotle Manuscripts," *Journal of the Ordnance Society* 15 (2003), 5–17; R. Coltman Clephan, "The Ordnance of the Fourteenth and Fifteenth Centuries," *Archaeological Journal* 68 (1911), 58–61; and J.R. Partington, *A History of Greek Fire and Gunpowder* (Cambridge, 1960; rpt. Baltimore, 1998), pp. 100–02.

[27] Eustace Deschamps, *Œuvres complètes*, ed. Q. de Saint Hilaire and G. Raynaud (Paris, 1878–1903), VII:35.

[28] See Clephan, "The Ordnance of the Fourteenth and Fifteenth Centuries," p. 56; Partington, p. 100; Philippe Contamine, *War in the Middle Ages*, trans. Michael Jones (London, 1984), p. 139; J.-F. Finó, *Forteresses de la France médiévale* (Paris, 1967), p. 290; and Victor Gay, *Glossaire archéologique du moyen âge et de la renaissance* (Paris, 1887, 1928), I:76.

Nothing more than these facts can be concluded by looking at the Milemete and Pseudo-Aristotle illustrations, nor are there any other datable illustrations of gunpowder weapons before the end of the fourteenth century, while the earliest datable extant weapon is 1399. Therefore, further information on the technology of early gunpowder weapons must come from written accounts: narrative, literary, and documentary. From these, all that can be determined with certainty is that guns tended to be small, 200–500 pounds, breech-loading, and mounted on wooden beds.[29] The actual shape of gunpowder weapons is rarely mentioned in these sources, leaving a lingering doubt as to when the transformation from vase- to tube-shaped took place, or even whether they were used simultaneously, as is very likely. Where the material of the weapons is referred to in written sources from this early period of gunpowder weaponry use it is to both copper-alloy and iron; neither predominates.

It must also be said that at some stage during the fourteenth century, perhaps during the period 1326–1375, stone cannonballs became the most commonly used projectile. At some time a further type of ammunition appears, the *plommée* or "lead ball," although, again, exactly when cannot be determined with any accuracy.[30]

While the battle of Nicopolis was certainly a continuation of traditional medieval warfare, by the end of the fourteenth century some military activities were changing. A new military history was beginning. An example of this is the battle of Bevershoutsveld, fought on 3 May 1382 between the Ghentenaars and the Brugeois. A conflict within the larger Ghent War of 1379–85, the battle of Bevershoutsveld would probably not have been noted beyond the Low Countries had it not been for the interesting way in which it was decided. The Ghentenaars had traveled to Bruges not with the idea of fighting a battle, but to lay siege. As had become common in the Ghent War, the Ghentenaars brought with them a large number of gunpowder weapons, Jean Froissart suggesting a tally of three hundred.[31] But the Brugeois were not about to let the Ghentenaars besiege their town. Drunk on alcohol consumed in celebrating the Holy Blood Procession, it has been suggested by contemporary sources, the Brugeois rushed out from their protective walls determined to fight, not only inebriated, but apparently leaderless and disorganized.[32] In response, the Ghentenaars turned their gunpowder weapons on the Brugeois soldiers. They fired these guns "all at the same time," writes

29 The best works containing fourteenth-century gunpowder weaponry records are Clephan, "The Ordnance of the Fourteenth and Fifteenth Centuries;" Henry Brackenbury, "Ancient Cannon in Europe. Part I: From Their First Employment to A.D. 1350," *Proceedings of the Royal Artillery Institution* 4 (1865), 287–308, and "Ancient Cannon in Europe. Part II: From A.D. 1351 to A.D. 1400," *Proceedings of the Royal Artillery Institution* 5 (1867), 1–37; Bernhard Rathgen, "Feuer- und fernwaffen des 14. jahrunderts in Flandern," *Zeitschrift für historisches Waffenkunde* 7 (1915–17), 275–306; and Bernhard Rathgen and Karl Heinrich Schäfer, "Feuer- und fernwaffen beim päpstlichen Heere im 14. Jahrhundert," *Zeitschrift für historisches Waffenkunde* 7 (1915–17), 1–15.
30 J.-F. Finó, "L'artillerie en France à la fin du moyen âge," *Gladius* 12 (1974), 24.
31 Froissart (ed. Luce), X:31–32. Elsewhere Froissart (X:22) uses "two hundred carts full" to express the numbers of gunpowder weapons that were with the Ghentenaars.
32 See *Chronicon comitum Flandriae*, in *Corpus chronicorum Flandriae*, 1, ed. J.J. de Smet (Brussels, 1837), p. 248; Oliver van Dixmude, *Merkwaerdige gebeurtenissen vooral in Vlaenderen en Brabant van 1377 tot 1443*, ed. J.J. Lambin (Ypres, 1835), p. 11; and *Chronique de Flandre*, in *Istore et croniques de Flandres*, ed. Kervyn de Lettenhove (Brussels, 1879–80), II:247.

Froissart,[33] while the *Chronique de Flandre* claims that the "artillery fired a blast with such a furor that it seemed to bring the [Brugeois] line directly to a halt."[34] How many Brugeois were killed in this onslaught is not revealed by these or any of the other contemporary sources. It may not have been many, nor important – medieval engagements never seem to have required large numbers of deaths to be decisive – but the Brugeois broke into rout, attempting to flee back into their town. The gates became so jammed with men that they could not be closed in time and the Ghentenaars were able to enter as well. Chaos and Ghentenaar victory followed.[35]

There was, then, gunpowder artillery after 1326. It was used at a large number of sieges and in some battles. It did not guarantee victory, although sometimes it obviously played an important role and may even on occasion have turned the tide from defeat to victory. Skillful tactics, strong leadership, and good discipline were still the necessary foundations on which military success was built, then as throughout the Middle Ages.

PHILIP THE BOLD AND JOHN THE FEARLESS

It is probable that our understanding of gunpowder artillery in the decades after 1380 would have been very poor had it not been for the four Valois dukes of Burgundy – Philip the Bold, John the Fearless, Philip the Good and Charles the Bold – who reigned from 1363 to 1477. They amassed large quantities of gunpowder weapons, and used them on almost all of their numerous military expeditions. They also supported "research and development" of all aspects of gunpowder weaponry technology and did not allow the technology to remain stagnant. The reason why so much more is known about the subject during their reigns, as opposed to during the period before their rise to power, is that the dukes of Burgundy created a large bureaucracy, one which assiduously recorded every aspect of their various realms' polities. Furthermore, the Burgundian dukes had a fervent belief in their role in history which led to their patronage of chroniclers who recorded all of their actions, especially their military deeds. Using the Valois Burgundians as a case study allows the modern historian to better understand gunpowder weaponry in the period from 1363 to 1477.

Philip the Bold was given the duchy of Burgundy in the early 1360s by his royal father, John II, as a means of the crown securing a loyal duke and duchy for assistance. Instead, what he founded was a dynasty which would continually stand next to, although not always by, France. Sometimes that proximity meant peace and security between the two related rulers and at other times it meant rivalry and war. The relationship between the two was further complicated and strained after Philip began acquiring Low Countries principalities, a practice which was copied by his three successors and one which could not be duplicated by his royal cousin. The Low Countries principalities brought with them immense wealth dependent chiefly on trade with

---

33 Froissart (ed. Luce), X:31–32.
34 *Chronique de Flandre*, II:247.
35 Froissart (ed. Luce), X:33–34; *Chronique de Flandre*, II:247; and *Chronicon comitum Flandriae*, p. 240.

England, especially in wool and cloth, which could not be replaced by either Burgundy alone or by Burgundy and France combined. England, of course, was France's enemy in the Hundred Years War, fought during the period in which the Valois dukes ruled, so the security which John II had hoped for was immediately compromised. Hence, from the beginning of their successive reigns until the very end, the four Valois dukes of Burgundy fought wars: wars against the French, the English, the Holy Roman Empire, the Swiss, and, more often than they would have hoped, against their own subjects.[36] In each and every one of these engagements they used gunpowder weapons.

The first Valois duke of Burgundy, Philip the Bold (1363–1404) can be seen as a conventional military ruler of his time, one whose use of gunpowder weapons was relatively small, especially in comparison with that of his more conventional weapons in his military engagements.[37] Indeed, his enemies, especially the Ghentenaar rebels, seem to have been equal if not superior in their use. Yet, Philip was to become the first member of one of the greatest military and technologically innovative dynasties of the later Middle Ages. Philip's innovation was characterized by the gradual increase in size and wider use of his gunpowder weapons. That he seemed to learn almost in a "line upon line, sequence upon sequence" method is important to recognize. When he was first given his duchy, he had almost no gunpowder weapons; even the addition of Lille, Douai, and Orchies, in 1369 as a wedding gift, did not to add many gunpowder weapons to his arsenal. Yet, scarcely eight years later, in 1377, his cannon forced two fortifications to surrender: one, Ardres, by intimidation, and the second, Odruik, by actually breaching the walls. Philip undertook these engagements to assist his brother, Charles V, in an abortive attempt to recapture Calais.

The sources report that Philip the Bold faced no defensive gunpowder weapons in his successful attacks on these two fortifications. But such could not be said when he faced his next opponent, the Ghentenaars, who, from 1379 to 1385, rebelled against Philip's father-in-law, Louis of Male, count of Flanders (the so-called Ghent War). The Ghentenaars not only possessed their own gunpowder artillery train of enormous size, perhaps the largest of any western European entity at that time, if Jean Froissart's estimate of three hundred guns can be trusted, but they used it both in sieges and in battles. In fighting the rebels, which he did both when assisting his father-in-law and on his own, after Louis of Male's death in 1384, Philip not only used but also faced gunpowder weapons. The Ghent War was a time when he both learned from his own use of gunpowder weapons and from his opponents' use of them. Ultimately, at the siege of Damme in 1385, this knowledge allowed Philip to use his gunpowder weapons so effectively and with such intimidating force that Ghent – a greater prize, the destruction of which would have been economically damaging to the duke – was compelled to negotiate a surrender.

Even more impressive than his use of gunpowder weapons in warfare is Philip the

---

36 On the idea of a separate Valois Burgundy as a power in the later Middle Ages see Richard Vaughan, *Valois Burgundy* (London, 1975). For specific studies on each of the dukes see Richard Vaughan's impressive biographies: *Philip the Bold: The Formation of the Burgundian State* (London, 1962); *John the Fearless: The Growth of Burgundian Power* (London, 1966); *Philip the Good: The Apogee of Burgundy* (London, 1970); and *Charles the Bold: The Last Valois Duke of Burgundy* (London, 1973).

37 Citations for much of what follows can be found in the historical chapter on Philip the Bold below.

Bold's improvements in their manufacture and acquisition. During Philip's reign, many centres of gunpowder weapons' manufacture were established and maintained: Lille, Mons, Dijon, Châlons, and Luxembourg are all mentioned in the records as production sites.[38] Philip also employed more "masters of cannon" than earlier or contemporary military lords, bringing them to these centres from other places, including the newly inherited county of Flanders. These men were responsible not only for operating the Burgundian gunpowder weapons but also, at times, for their manufacture. Jacques and Rollant Mayorques, Joseph Colard, Jacques and Jean Maillorgues, and Pierre Roy all appear as "*maitres de canons*" in contemporary documents.[39] This administrative encouragement was unusual for a sovereign of the late fourteenth century. Though a precedent had been set by Edward III of England, it was unknown of anyone else, including Richard II, Edward's heir.[40] This has led some historians to conclude that Philip the Bold at least "partly centralized" his ducal gunpowder artillery, including guns, ammunition, and gunpowder – something that was to be a characteristic of all four Valois dukes of Burgundy.[41] While this centralization may be difficult to prove from the records available, it seems certain that Philip, at least, encouraged the production of gunpowder weapons and their accessories, with the implied promise of continual acquisition.

It is tempting to view John the Fearless' rule (1404–1419) from the perspective of his two assassination scandals. The first, in 1407, removed his greatest rival, Louis of Orléans, thereby provoking the civil war which led to his own assassination.[42] Such a view surely blinds us to this duke's military leadership and his role in the evolution of gunpowder weaponry during the late Middle Ages. John's prestige as a military leader grew, from the disaster of Nicopolis in 1396 to his victory at Paris in 1418. Though his military career was not always one of success, ultimately his strategy and tactics show his excellent generalship. And these strategies and tactics were successful to a large extent due to his use of gunpowder weapons. John the Fearless seems to have learned how to use his guns both on the battlefield and at siege from others.

On the battlefield the numbers of gunpowder weapons increased, but so too, it seems, did the knowledge of how to fight against them. At Nicopolis, fought in 1396, crusader gunpowder weapons brought for the siege were not used in the battle, the impulsive charge of the French cavalry and the defensive posture of the Ottoman Turks deciding the outcome. At Othée, fought in 1408, both the Burgundians and the Liégeois had gunpowder weapons on the battlefield, and these were discharged at the

---

[38]   Joseph Garnier, *L'artillerie des ducs de Bourgogne d'après les documents conservés aux archives de la Côte-d'Or* (Paris, 1895), pp. 8–15, and Claude Gaier, *L'industrie et le commerce des armes dans les anciennes principautés Belges du XIIIme à la fin du XVe siècle* (Paris, 1963), pp. 155, 287–88.

[39]   Dijon, Archives départementales de la Côte-d'Or, B15, f. 49; Garnier, pp. 8–15, 211; and Vaughan, *Philip the Bold*, p. 124.

[40]   See DeVries, "Gunpowder Weaponry and the Rise of the Early Modern State."

[41]   The quotation is from Vaughan, *Philip the Bold*, p. 124. See also Garnier, pp. 8–15; Gaier, *L'industrie et le commerce des armes*, especially pp. 287–88; M. Guillaume, *Histoire de l'organisation militaire sous les ducs de Bourgogne* (Brussels, 1848); and J. Lachauvelaye, "Les armées des trois premiers ducs de Bourgogne," *Mémoires de l'académie des sciences, arts et belles-lettres de Dijon*, ser. 3, 6 (1880), 19–335, all of which contain the same sentiment.

[42]   Citations for what follows can be found in the chapter on John the Fearless below.

beginning of the engagement, in a role traditionally filled by archery. However, after this, the two armies settled into a traditional tactical posture and encounter not influenced by gunpowder artillery. There was limited battlefield use of guns after this by John the Fearless. Some were probably present at the minor engagements fought at Saint-Cloud in 1411 and at Saint-Rémy-du-Plain in 1412; but this was chiefly due to John's preferred use of the siege as his primary military strategy.

In sieges, this Burgundian duke set new military standards. The use of gunpowder weapons to force a surrender was not original to John the Fearless; in fact, he may have learned the technique from his father or from the Liégeois rebels who used it against Maastricht in 1407–1408. But whereas the Liégeois and Philip the Bold's bombardments never led to surrender, John's almost always did. He would arrive outside a chosen location and unleash the fury of his numerous gunpowder weapons. Fortifications were breached, and destruction of buildings and homes followed. Generally, before too much damage and loss of life occurred, either the town surrendered or negotiations followed from which John the Fearless benefitted both in the acquisition of territory and in political standing within France. Ultimately, this tactic led to the acquisition of the largest French prize: Paris. Interestingly, while John was using his own gunpowder artillery in this manner, King Henry V of England was using his gunpowder artillery train in an entirely different way, its presence alone provoking surrender by intimidation, especially in Normandy.[43]

Yet, even more important than John's use of gunpowder weapons in battles or sieges were his administrative changes dealing with his artillery. John the Fearless was the first of the Valois dukes of Burgundy, and possibly the first medieval ruler of any principality, to systematize and centralize his gunpowder weaponry records. From 1410 to the end of his reign and on into his son's and grandson's, a paper trail of gunpowder weapons, their numbers, types, locations, and condition remains. Some of these records are full and detailed, with information about such aspects as weight, length, calibre, type of projectile, projectile weight, whether chambered or not, numbers of chambers, chamber weight, chamber length, names (separate pieces, generally the larger guns, are sometimes named), carriages, colours (if painted), gunpowder details, and purpose, as well as some miscellaneous information specific to the gunpowder weapons or artillery train being recorded. These records not only indicate that John the Fearless increased the number of these weapons but also show, towards the end of his reign, the beginnings of a greater diversity of gunpowder weapon types, for example the introduction of the veuglaire and coulovrine.[44]

The records further show John the Fearless' interest in gunpowder weapons as an arm of the Burgundian military. He appointed Germain de Givry as master of artillery, and, on 13 May 1415, ordered him to catalogue the ducal gunpowder weaponry holdings and to bring all the gunpowder weapons in Burgundy "not actually in use in his castles" to an arsenal in Dijon, the duchy's capital. It was these that formed the core of

---

43 On the tactics of Henry V's campaign in Normandy, 1417–20, see Richard Ager Newhall, *The English Conquest of Normandy, 1416–1424: A Study in Fifteenth Century Warfare* (New Haven, 1924) and E.F. Jacob, *Henry V and the Invasion of France* (London, 1947).

44 Charles Brusten, *L'armée Bourguignonne de 1465 à 1468* (Brussels, 1953), p. 108.

the artillery train that followed him on his military adventures throughout France, including the capture of Paris.[45] In addition, during John's reign artillery operators were given separate and distinctive "uniforms," including a blue hat, for use in ducal processions.[46] Finally, in his treaty of alliance with England, dated 1407, John excluded makers of gunpowder weaponry, together with makers of more conventional weapons, from a policy of free trade between the two lands.[47]

At his assassination in 1419, John the Fearless passed this interest and these innovations to his son and heir, Philip the Good, who would build upon his father's and grandfather's legacy and become one of the most important gunpowder weapon owners of the fifteenth century.

During the reigns of Philip the Bold and John the Fearless two gunpowder weapon terms predominate: the bombard and the *canon*. The former, unusually for early gunpowder weapons, was always clearly defined: a large gun firing stone shot. It is clear from the sources that the notaries and chroniclers who recorded the gunpowder weapons they were inventorying and writing about understood what feature it was that distinguished a bombard. Yet, from the records alone it is impossible to know exactly what that feature was. The second word, *canon*, seems to have been used for all other gunpowder weapons than bombard. The problem is whether *canon* was the generic name for a multiplicity of types or whether all gunpowder weapons that were not bombards were essentially the same and so carried the same name. If the term referred to a multiplicity of gunpowder weapon types, it may be that there may not have been a need to differentiate between them, for whatever reason. If, however, all *canons* were essentially the same weapon, then the question arises as to why, later in the 1410s and 1420s, different gunpowder weaponry names appear in the records. Is this because new types were developed or were they simply new terms? It is impossible to answer this question from the extant sources from the reigns of the first two Valois dukes, as good as these may be.

Another problem is the definition of the word "large." Bombards were large; every source says so, even exclaiming their surprise and the surprise of those against whom they were used. But what does "large" mean in this context and at this time? Descriptive terms, such as "devils from hell," are also used to define the sounds a bombard produces, as if in so doing the describer can emphasize his impression at hearing such an enormous weapon. On other occasions, bombards are named separately from other weapons in siege descriptions, again showing their ability to impress a medieval witness even in comparison with other gunpowder weapons. Finally, bombards are often given names while *canons* are not. All of these comparative literary devices are governed by the age in which they are written, but one thing does seem to come through to our modern sensibilities, that bombards were large, impressive weapons in the late fourteenth and early fifteenth centuries. However, the size of bombards was not

---

[45] Vaughan, *John the Fearless*, p. 151.

[46] Vaughan, *John the Fearless*, pp. 151, 168, and Brusten, *L'armée Bourguignonne*, p. 108.

[47] Thomas Rymer, ed., *Foedera, conventiones, litterae. et cujuscunque generis acta publica inter reges Angliae et alios quosvis imperatores, reges, pontifices, principes, vel communitates (1101–1654)* (London, 1709), VIII:470. (The entire treaty is printed on pp. 467–76.)

standardized, nor can it often be known, especially from narrative sources, exactly how large they were. It is possible, especially early on, that large was not that large at all!

In the Burgundian documentary sources of the first two dukes the term bombard first appears in 1412, though from other accounts it is clear that the name came into use in northern Europe during the last quarter of the fourteenth century.[48] There are at least thirty-three references to bombards in these documents, although it is clear from the names assigned to some of them that the same gun is being referred to. Almost all of these bombards are named, carrying either place-names, presumably of where they were made (e.g. *d'Auxonne, de Valecon, Compaigne, Dijon*, etc.), or female names (e.g. *Liete, Griete, Senelle*, etc.). Strangely, in comparison with other sources, little detailed information is provided on the Burgundian guns. When specifically mentioned, in just four cases, the bombards are made of copper-alloy, while two other references note not the metal, but that they were cast, implying that they too were made of a copper-alloy. The weight of only one bombard, the *gros bombard d'Auxonne*, of 16,000 *livres*, is stated, while the sizes of three others are indicated by the weight of the ball they fired. These are 12 *livres*, 84 *livres*, and 100 *livres*. The material of the 12 *livres* ball is, unusually, noted as iron, while the 100 *livres* ball is the more common stone. In the six instances where the weight of powder to fire the projectile is given, surprisingly small amounts are recorded, ranging from 1½ to 9 *livres*. To the modern scholar, predetermined as we are to define the material world in measurements, this range of size is confusing: the last two ball weights would be expected in a "large" gun, while the first would not. To the scribes who were inventorying these gunpowder weapons, however, all three of these guns are "bombards." This is a common theme: size was not the defining factor.

Other sources support the description of bombards taken from the documents printed in Garnier. An account of the Burgundian siege train facing the castle of Vellexon in 1409–1410 included a bombard which fired a ball weighing 700 to 850 *livres*.[49] The bombard named *Griete*, reported in several narrative sources, was noted not only for its power, both real and intimidating, and ability to bring about the submission of besieged sites (the castle of Ham for one), but also for shooting stones of enormous weight at the cost of large quantities of gunpowder and much hard and dangerous work on the part of its expert crew. Nearly twenty men were required to handle it. When it was fired the thunderous noise could be heard four miles away.[50]

Canons are mentioned more frequently than bombards in sources which cover the reigns of Philip the Bold and John the Fearless, with 230 listed in the inventories transcribed by Garnier. The majority of these guns were made of iron, two of which are intriguingly noted to be of "cast iron." Using cast iron as a material for making gunpowder weapons was not perfected before the middle of the sixteenth century. References before this time, though not unknown, are unusual at this very early date.

---

[48] It is clear from Italian sources that the term *bombarda* appears in the early fourteenth century as a generic term for gunpowder weapons. See Rathgen and Schäfer. It may be speculated that the term then spread throughout Europe and in so doing was adopted as the name for a specific type of gun.

[49] See pp. 78–9 below.

[50] The partial quote comes from *Chronique du religieux de Saint-Denis*, ed. L. Bellaguet (Paris, 1839–52), IV:652.

Had such a method of manufacture been successful, it is likely that more cast-iron weapons would be seen in the sources and among extant examples; their relative absence leads to the conclusion that cast iron was not an easy material to use in making gunpowder weapons. It must be assumed that those iron pieces not reported to be "cast" were made of the more usual wrought iron. There are only two references to removable chambers among the inventoried *canons*, one which has three chambers and one which is specifically said to be "of one piece."[51]

The weight of only three *canons* are recorded in the Burgundian inventories – 8½, 15, and 18 *livres* – with six more recorded in a 1376–1377 list – 130, 100, 90, 60, 30, and 20 *livres* – although frequently the weight of the ball which they fired is mentioned.[52] This indicates a very wide range in size, from guns firing balls from 5 to 24 *livres*. All the weights recorded are for stone balls, although many canons fired lead shot, *plommées*. This wide range of ball sizes and therefore of the weapon itself again begs the question of terminology and types: could it indicate that there were many different types of gun all called *canons*, or one type of gunpowder weapon made in different sizes. It is unfortunate that so few weights and no lengths of *canons* are recorded, as these, together with the ball size, might help to clarify the issue.

It should also be noted that references to *canons* before and throughout the early reign of Philip the Bold, both in narrative and documentary sources, indicate that bolts were used as ammunition. In 1362, for example, "deux quanons à gitter garroz" (two *canons* to fire bolts) were purchased at Troyes by Jaquemard the Metalworker ("le serrurier") for three florins, and, in 1368, an inventory made by Philip's treasurer, Thévenin Vurry, noted "deux canons et cinq livres et demie de poudre, quatorze garroz et douze plombées d'estain" (two *canons* and five and a half pounds of powder, forty bolts and twelve *plommées* of "tin") to be taken to the siege of the castle of Rochefort-sur-le-Doubs.[53] However, by 1410 no bolts are mentioned in connection with Burgundian *canons*; the normal projectiles were either stone or lead balls.

Veuglaires as a term for gunpowder weapons appears at the very end of John the Fearless' reign. In the Burgundian inventories four are listed in 1417, but there are no further details. What is interesting, however, is that two of these, ordered to be taken from Arras to Flanders by a squire, Andre de Thoulongeon, are said to be "petiz canons appellez veuglaires," and two others, sent by the duchess Margaret of Bavaria to Robert de Longchamp, captain of Nogent-le-Roi, are "vueilglaires appellés canons."[54] If nothing else, this seems to mark the differentiation of the terms for gunpowder weapons. However, again, whether these "*canons* called *veuglaires*" signify the development of a new type of gunpowder weapon is unclear. Nor is the problem clarified by the records of veuglaires in narrative sources covering this period: for example, Enguerran de Monstrelet's record of two medium-sized veuglaires mounted on *ribaudequins* at the siege of Ham in 1411; the same chronicler's reference to veuglaires at the siege of Arras in 1414; or the author of *Le livre des trahisons de France envers la*

---

[51]   See Garnier, p. 47, for quote.
[52]   This inventory, by Simon Lambert, is also found in Garnier, pp. 8–11.
[53]   Garnier, p. 7.
[54]   Garnier, pp. 47–48.

maison de Bourgogne's inclusion of veuglaires in a list of gunpowder weapons at the same siege. None of these provide more information except for the presence of these gunpowder weapons at their respective engagements.

In summary, during the reigns of the first two Valois dukes of Burgundy, especially from 1375 to 1419, gunpowder weapons were used more frequently and in ever greater numbers in military engagements, especially at sieges. Part of this can undoubtedly be laid at the feet of John the Fearless, whose bellicosity against the Liégeois and Armagnacs certainly provided him with more opportunities for warfare than his father, Philip the Bold, had. Of course, one might also conclude that one of the reasons for John's confidence in warfare, and certainly his siege tactics, was his large and powerful gunpowder artillery arsenal. Still, despite the greater number of sieges in which John used his gunpowder weapons, it cannot be said that they alone provided him with any more victories than Philip the Bold won; it was instead John's strategic and tactical leadership in these conflicts that established his military legacy. In the few battles that were fought gunpowder weapons still did not play a determining role.

During this period two main terms describing gunpowder weaponry were used. One, clearly defined in the medieval mind but which is unclear to the modern scholar, was the bombard, while the second, *canon*, was probably given to all other gunpowder weapons whatever their size or form. Over this period, too, there was a shift from some guns firing bolts to one where the projectile was almost exclusively stone or lead balls. By the end of John the Fearless' reign, in the 1410s, one sees the introduction of new terms for gunpowder weapons, a development which would continue during the reign of his son, Philip the Good, and grandson, Charles the Bold.

PHILIP THE GOOD

It may seem somewhat artificial in a history of early gunpowder weapons to break at the death of John the Fearless in 1419. His assassination was obviously political and should, one assumes, not relate to changes in military technology. However, what occurred in the reign of his son, Philip the Good (1419–1467), does indicate a transition in the history of gunpowder weapons between the earlier Valois dukes and their two successors. First, and most important for the modern historian, is the survival of two notarial registers devoted to Philip's arsenal, including his gunpowder weapons. The first of these, which begins during the reign of John the Fearless, in 1411, and ends in 1445, has written at the top: "This is a book of artillery and other munitions delivered into the *Chambre des Comptes* to be placed in the fortresses of the Lord of Burgundy."[55] The second covers the period 1446–1475 and is "the new paper of artillery beginning the first of January 1446 in the time of Phelibert de Vaudrey, master of artillery."[56] Together these registers contain an enormous amount of information on early gunpowder weapons, including weights, lengths, calibres, metal, chambers, projectile material and weight, as well as details of supports and carriages, personnel,

---

[55] Garnier, p. 36.
[56] Garnier, p. 108.

transport, and gunpowder. There are naturally some limitations to understanding this information, primarily due to the difficulty of the translation of fifteenth-century French technical terms. This is compounded by the problem of the meaning of non-standardized terms and the fact that some of the details are incomplete and somewhat erratic.

Second, numerous chroniclers took an interest in the dukes, due to the importance that the Burgundian realm began to have in European politics as a whole, especially in this phase of the Hundred Years War, the historical position which Philip the Good and Charles the Bold held, and undoubtedly also due to the wealth that the dynasty had acquired, leaving a great legacy of narrative material. Many were even patronized and given courtly positions. Consequently, writers, such as Enguerran de Monstrelet, Georges Chastellain, Olivier de la Marche, Jean de Haynin, Philippe Commynes, and Jean Molinet, as well as others, some of whom never recorded their names, have left an unequaled account of all of the military activities of the two final Valois dukes of Burgundy, and as gunpowder weapons were used in all of these military activities, these narrative sources assist in a more complete understanding of their history between 1419 and 1477.

Third, there are extant weapons from the period. Though these mostly come from the closing years of the Valois dynasty, they provide the means to more fully understand the forms and types of artillery through the second half of the century, a situation denied to us for the earlier period when there are few reliably dated examples.

Fourth, there are artistic portrayals of gunpowder weapons, especially in manuscript illuminations, though their exact dating can be problematic. Among their other opulent possessions, the Burgundian dukes acquired a large library, many volumes of which were heavily illustrated, frequently containing military scenes in which gunpowder weapons are present. These, and other artistic representations, in paintings, tapestries, and sculptures, further aid an understanding of the history of late medieval gunpowder weaponry.

Finally, on occasion there are literacy sources where the use of gunpowder weapons and the exploits of gunners are recounted.

During the 48-year reign of Philip the Good he consolidated the Burgundian realm.[57] Most important, he increased the duchy's power by the constant acquisition of territories, by his thorough understanding of the nature of diplomacy and alliance-making, especially by arranging advantageous marriages for all of his kin, and by taking advantage of the political and military environment in which he lived. At the same time, he was more than willing to use force, on land and sea, whenever he felt it was necessary. He fought against the French, English, and Turks, and he was also involved in putting down insurrections in his ducal holdings, principally in the southern Low Countries.

Philip's chief means of fighting wars was the siege. Of course, he was not alone in this tactic; the Hundred Years War of this period could justifiably be called a war of sieges. By this time, siege warfare had come to be based on the attack and, where

---

[57] Citations for much of what follows on Philip the Good can be found in the chapter dedicated to his reign below.

necessary, destruction of walls by gunpowder weapons. But the old tactics still held sway: the surrender of those living within a besieged site was always preferred to the lengthy and costly destruction of its fortifications. However, while submissions were common in the preceding generation, to Henry V and John the Fearless, they were less frequent during the reign of Philip the Good. He waged nearly as many unsuccessful sieges as successful ones. Philip was far more successful in waging sieges against his own rebellious subjects than he was against French or English targets. This in fact may have more to do with his determination to put down rebellions than to fight in the Hundred Years War.

Initially, Philip's military activities, fueled by a desire for vengeance for his father's murder, were directed towards the French. Sometimes they were pursued in alliance with the English and sometimes, especially after the death of Henry V, on his own. French fortifications at Allibaudières, Montereau, Sens, Melun, Saint-Riquier, and Abbeville all felt the force of Burgundian gunpowder weapons in the two years after Philip the Good ascended the ducal throne, and all fell to him, although it is difficult to ascertain whether this resulted from his gunpowder weapons, Philip's resolve and leadership (or that of the English leaders, when present), or some other factor. Undoubtedly, the willingness of the inhabitants and Armagnac garrisons in the towns he besieged, if they were garrisoned by anything more than local militia, to surrender quickly in the face of a Burgundian or Anglo-Burgundian siege must also be accorded a role in the capture of these fortifications.

The years following the death of Henry V in 1422 saw similar Burgundian siege victories, at Guise (1424), Terraisse (1425), Anglure (1431), Coursent (1432), Mussy-l'Eveque (1432), Fortepice (1432), Avallon (1433), Saint-Valery-sur-Somme (1433), Haplincourt (1433), and Belleville (1434), and Anglo-Burgundian siege victories, at Le Crotoy (1423), Landrecies (1423), Saint-James de Beauvron (1425), and Mailly-le-Château (1426), although the narrative sources reporting these engagements are mixed in their opinions of the role played by gunpowder weapons. Landrecies, Coursent, Mussy-l'Eveque, Fortepice, Avallon, Saint-Valery-sur-Somme, Haplincourt, and Belleville seem definitely to have been bombarded into surrender, while at Le Crotoy, Guise, Terraisse, and Anglure, the guns only seem to have aided in their negotiated surrender. But at Saint-James de Beauvron the chroniclers assert that, even though the Anglo-Burgundian gunpowder weapons were fired at the town, this really was not necessary as the Armagnac garrison inside was in such disarray that it would have surrendered anyway, while at Mailly-le-Château the inhabitants surrendered so quickly to the Burgundian besiegers that their gunpowder weapons had not yet arrived on the scene.

At those sieges, it again seems likely that the determination of the besieged to withstand the attacks played as much of a role in the surrender of their fortifications as did the Burgundian gunpowder weapons. Certainly, Philip the Good's gunpowder weapons played a significant role; the amount of destruction they could effect, added to starvation and other depredations that besieged populations were forced to suffer, often prompted a decision to negotiate surrender rather than hold out, especially as the weak dauphin, Charles, was unable to offer any military relief.

It was when opponents decided to hold out against a siege rather than submit that the limitations of gunpowder weapons in this type of warfare began to be recognized. For example, at Zevenbergen, which Philip besieged in 1426 during his long conflict with Jacqueline of Brabant and Humphrey of Gloucester, the Burgundian duke first encountered a population determined to hold out, no matter how many gunpowder weapons he had with him or whatever else he did. Ultimately the town did fall, after the demoralized and hungry citizens overthrew their garrison and opened their town's gates to the besiegers. But it took four months to bring about this result. At Compiègne, besieged by Philip the Good in 1430, there was similar opposition. In this engagement the townspeople were spurred on in their resistance to the Burgundians by Joan of Arc until her eventual capture. Even after she was taken, however, the defenders held out against an extremely large number of gunpowder weapons, and eventually forced a Burgundian withdrawal; Compiègne did not fall.

A similar result followed at Calais in 1436. Philip the Good had abandoned his alliance with the English the year before with his signing of the Treaty of Arras and turned his sights on Calais. The defeat of English-held Calais would have bolstered the duke's reputation at the French royal court, and it certainly would have removed any doubt as to his post-Arras loyalties, but, even more, it would have ensured Burgundian control of the coastline from Friesland to the Somme. Philip gathered what may have been his largest gunpowder artillery train for the expedition, and he used it in its full force against the town's fortifications. But Calais held out, partly as a result of the population's resolve, but mostly because of the failure of the gunpowder weapons, as well as more traditional siege tactics, to bring about a surrender within the fifteen days that the siege was waged. Philip's intention of gaining the town was thwarted also by divisions within his own forces, the Ghentenaars among them receiving the blame. After the Burgundians again failed to defeat the English using similar tactics and another large gunpowder artillery train at Le Crotoy the following year, Philip began to rethink his military operations.

This resulted in two strategic changes. First, Philip withdrew from participating further in the Hundred Years War and did not actively engage again with either the English or the French. In fact, on many occasions he sought to establish peace through trade agreements and alliances with these two states as well as with other principalities and dynastic families. Second, it appears that Philip ceased carrying out offensive campaigns. He reacted rather than acted, choosing only targets that concerned his dynastic interests, either against rebels in his own principalities – Flanders and Holland – or against those who conspired to keep him or his kin from inheriting other principalities – Liège and Luxembourg.

In this dynastic warfare, Philip again used his gunpowder weapons in sieges. In 1443, although most of Luxembourg surrendered to the Burgundians at the very presence of Philip's armies with their large gunpowder artillery trains, he did have to use them to subjugate the towns of Villy and Luxembourg. Once more, though, the situation seems to have been one in which Philip really did not face a population eager to hold out against him. The same can be said about the small Liégeois rebellion of Evrard de la Marck, count of Arembergh, in 1445. On this occasion, Philip used only a small number of gunpowder weapons to bring about the surrender of the count's castles at Agimont and Rochefort. Nor, indeed, was la Marck punished for his insurrection, repaying the favour by becoming one of the duke's most trusted Liégeois allies in the ensuing, larger rebellion of 1465–1468.

In the Ghent War of 1449–1453 Philip faced rebels who were more determined to hold out against him, though the motivations behind this determination are difficult to ascertain from the sources available. What resulted was a more intense conflict characterized by fiercer sieges, more destruction caused by gunpowder weapons, and more ruthless punishment of the garrisons who held out against him. Initially, Philip seems to have reacted with a reluctance to send his full military power against Ghent, perhaps due to his lack of confidence in the force that had let him down against Calais and Le Crotoy earlier, but more than likely the duke simply hoped to limit the need to destroy towns or kill citizens who provided him with a large amount of taxes. However, by mid-1453, when it had become apparent to Philip the Good that these rebels were not likely to submit to his military might without having it displayed against them, he gathered a large gunpowder artillery train and advanced against his Ghentenaar opponents. He did not advance directly against Ghent, though, choosing instead to reduce three outlying fortifications garrisoned by the rebels: Schendelbeke, Poeke, and Gavere Castles. To each of these in turn he sent a large number of his guns and after each successful engagement he executed the garrison. Though cruel, the tactic ultimately proved its worth. For once Schendelbeke surrendered, after two days of bombardment, Poeke after four days, and Gavere after five days (and the battle of Gavere which will be discussed below), Ghent negotiated a peace without a single Burgundian shot being fired at the large town.

Yet, the successes of Philip the Good in his sieges during the Ghent War of 1449–1453 did not mean that he had discovered a means of always waging successful sieges using gunpowder weapons. This would be proven in his last siege experience, that of Deventer in 1455. As had happened previously, despite heavy bombardment of the walls, the town did not fall, and the Burgundian army was forced to withdraw. While the failure of this siege, as with the others earlier in his reign, might be attributed to other factors – in this case poor weather conditions – it still must have been apparent to the duke, even if it has been missed by some modern commentators, that having a large and powerful gunpowder artillery train at sieges did not ensure victory, even against traditional medieval fortifications.

The same observations can be made on the use of Burgundian gunpowder weaponry in battles. The armies of Philip the Good, unlike his ducal predecessors, used gunpowder weapons against opponents in battle who also used gunpowder weapons. This said, it must be recognized how singular the battle of Bevershoutsveld was in 1382, and that it was not until Philip's reign, and even more so his son's, Charles the Bold's, that gunpowder weapons became an integral part of late medieval battles.

In his first battle, at Mons-en-Vimeu, fought on 31 August 1421, there apparently were no gunpowder weapons, as these were busy besieging the fortifications of nearby Saint-Riquier. A far larger battle was fought in concert with the English at Cravant on 31 July 1423, and it included a large force of gunpowder weapons. In this engagement *veuglaires* were fired by especially identified Auxerrois cannoneers at the Armagnac soldiers in the early stages of the battle. They, together with bow and crossbow fire from Anglo-Burgundian archers, seem to have disordered their opponents so that, when a charge of infantry followed, most of the Armagnacs fled in rout.

In the northern Low Countries lands in which Philip the Good and Countess Jacqueline of Hainault chose to wage their war, two battles were fought: Alphen, on 22 October 1425, and Brouwershaven, on 30 December 1425. In the first of these battles the Burgundians were defeated. Although they had gunpowder weapons with them, the original sources do not report if or how they were used, and whether they made any impact on the outcome of the engagement – indeed, the lack of comments is itself perhaps an indication that their role, if any, was limited. At the second battle, a Burgundian victory, gunpowder weapons, operated (it was reported) by Dordrechter cannoneers, did play a role, especially at the beginning when the gunpowder weapons, coulovrines, were fired into the lines of English troops allied with the countess of Hainault. This gunfire preceded the English advance, which was eventually driven back and defeated by the main body of Burgundians, but whether such an advance had been prompted by the gunpowder artillery is not indicated by the chroniclers.

Burgundian armies fought two battles during the 1430s. The first was at Bulgneville on 2 July 1431. This engagement also began with a Burgundian artillery barrage. The Barrois who were marching towards the Burgundians were frightened by their "canons et couleuvres," causing them to stop. When the Burgundian soldiers themselves then charged, the Barrois fled and the battle ended. Thus it seems that at Bulgneville gunpowder weapons were effective in bringing victory to the Burgundians. In the second battle, fought in the market places and streets of Bruges on 22 May 1437, it was mostly the Burgundian opponents who fought with gunpowder weapons, townspeople, not soldiers. The reasons behind such an odd encounter will be described in greater detail below; in short, as Philip the Good and several hundred of his soldiers – the rest had been prohibited from entering their town – marched through Bruges in an attempt to pacify a rebellion, the townspeople began to attack them with whatever weapons they had at hand. Among these were some of the town's gunpowder weapons. The Burgundians responded, but they do not seem to have had their own guns inside the town. Eventually and at great cost, Philip was able to fight his way through Bruges and, aided by an intense gunpowder artillery bombardment of the town's walls by his troops outside Bruges, escaped the townspeople's wrath and, eventually, pacified the rebel furor.

Philip the Good's final battle, at Gavere on 23 July 1453, may have been the most successful of his military career, and it may also have been the only one where gunpowder weapons definitely brought victory. All of the narrative sources, both Burgundian and Ghentenaar, confirm this conclusion. Again, the Burgundians used their gunpowder weapons at the beginning of the battle, during which, for the first time, they received a Ghentenaar gunpowder artillery exchange in return. This continued for a while until it seemed that, all of a sudden, the Ghentenaar gunners fled, taking the rest of the army with them. Only in the Ghentenaar sources is it made clear that this was due to a spark flying into their cannoneers' supply of gunpowder, causing their flight and Burgundian victory.

It can be suggested on fairly conclusive grounds that Burgundian siege warfare during the reign of Philip the Good had come to be fought almost entirely with gunpowder weapons, both against the fortification being besieged and in its defense, and that these weapons played some role in the success of the siege, if it was successful.

However, the same cannot be said in the case of the battles. Gunpowder weapons were used in most of the battles fought by the ducal armies between 1419 and 1465, although in at least one, Mons-en-Vimeu, and perhaps at Alphen, there were no gunpowder weapons. Beyond that, it can only be certain that they were used primarily at the beginning of battles to provoke an enemy charge against the main Burgundian infantry force, in a way that archery had been used in battles a century before.[58] At Cravant and Brouwershaven, gunpowder artillery fire was accompanied by archery, while at Bulgneville and Gavere gunpowder artillery fire alone preceded the battle. In all four battles, this initial bombardment led to a charge, even if the bombardment cannot definitely be said to have provoked the charge, or a rout. In all engagements, the Burgundians were victorious.[59]

Beyond sieges and battles, Philip the Good must be credited among the Valois Burgundian rulers with a further innovation in the use of gunpowder weapons: placing them on Burgundian naval vessels. Shipboard guns were of course not novel when Philip placed them on board his own ships, operating chiefly in the Mediterranean against Ottoman Turkish targets. But the duke seems to have been the first to arm his ships with veuglaires and coulovrines which could be loaded from the rear with inter-changeable chambers. He also may have been among the first to use his shipboard gunpowder weapons to bombard fortifications on land.

Bombard and *canon* were the only terms used for gunpowder weapons prior to the *veuglaire* being introduced at the very end of John the Fearless' reign. After Philip the Good became duke of Burgundy three new terms appear in both the narrative and documentary sources: *bombardelle*, *crapaudeau*, and *couleuvrine*. However, what the medieval scribe meant when he referred to a gunpowder weapon by these terms is difficult to assess and must be approached with caution. In addition, none of these terms replaced the terms *canon* and *bombard*, both of which remained in use.

Bombards are frequently listed in inventories and mentioned in chronicles throughout the whole of Philip's reign. They were still essentially the same weapon: a large gun firing stone shot. However, like all other early gunpowder weapons, their size was not standardized and the reason why a particular gunpowder weapon was called a bombard remains not completely known today. From the registers it is clear that they were made in both iron and copper-alloy. Where weights are noted they are of a large size, ranging from 8,200 to an enormous 30,000 *livres*. Although few lengths are mentioned, these indicate a long weapon of from 12 to 16 *piez*. Their calibres range from 12 to 28 *pouces* and, where ball weights are mentioned, they range widely, from 80 to 600 *livres*. Some bombards are listed with removable chambers, although at least one, dating from 1445, is specifically said to be "of one piece."[60] The picture that emerges, as earlier, in the reigns of Philip the Bold and John the Fearless, is one in which the bombard is essentially a very large gunpowder weapon. This is confirmed in the narrative sources where they continue to be singled out from the other gunpowder

---

[58] See DeVries, *Infantry Warfare*.
[59] It must be recognized that the battle of Bruges, because of its odd character, cannot be used to judge gunpowder weapon effectiveness in battle.
[60] Garnier, p. 111.

weapons in sieges. They also carry on being named: *Bourgoingne, Prusse, Bergiere, Bergier, Griete,* etc.

Two extant bombards, *Dulle Griet* in Ghent and *Mons Meg* in Edinburgh, can be traced through archival sources to Philip the Good's reign. *Dulle Griet* not only carries Philip's coat of arms but was also used at Oudenaarde during the Ghent War of 1449–1453.[61] *Mons Meg* was made in 1449 and subsequently given as a gift to James II of Scotland.[62] By a comparison of their shape and form a third extant bombard, today located in the Historisches Museum in Basel, can be associated with *Dulle Griet* and *Mons Meg* and probably dates from the same period.[63]

In 1431 there is a reference in the Burgundian artillery registers to a *bombardelle.* Three more appear in 1442 and a further one in 1443. Four of these were made of iron, with two said to be cast iron, the fifth carries no metallurgical details. The 1431 bombardelle fired an iron ball weighing six *livres.* Those made in 1442 are indicated to be "all of one piece," while the 1443 bombardelle, named *Bergier,* has a removable chamber. Little further information is provided; a bombardelle may simply be a small bombard, as its name suggests, but there is nothing in the sources to confirm this.

The name *canon* also continues throughout Philip the Good's reign. Those listed in his registers are mostly iron with occasional copper-alloy examples, and two *canons* of 1442 are said to be cast iron. Their size ranges widely: weights from 31 to 4,000 *livres*; lengths from 1 to 9 *piez*; and calibres from 3 to 8 *pouces.* Balls are either stone or lead, with stone shot weighing between 3 and 24 *livres* (lead-shot weight is never given). Most of the guns, when indicated, have removable chambers, although four are made in one piece. Although for the earlier period it is unclear whether *canon* was the name of a type or the term for gunpowder weapons in general, the references to these weapons during the reign of Philip the Good surely indicate by their wide variation in size that the term must refer to gunpowder weapons in general. It would appear that when a notary or chronicler did not know the proper name for a gun, for whatever reason, they used the general term *canon.*

As noted above, the term veuglaire first appears in the last years of the reign of John the Fearless when just four examples were noted; they proliferate under Philip the Good – no fewer than 875 veuglaires are recorded in his artillery registers. Though the great majority of them were made of iron, there are a few of copper-alloy but none of cast iron. Like all the other gunpowder weapons in this period their size was not standardized, with weights varying from 105 to 7,895 *livres,* length varying from 1½ to 8 *piez,* and calibre from 2 to 11 *pouces.* Ball weights, most of which are stone, also vary widely, from 2 to 25 *livres.* Although there is this wide variation in size, there is some evidence that veuglaires were made in three "sizes": small, medium, and large. Small veuglaires weighed up to 300 *livres,* medium veuglaires weighed approximately 400 to 800 *livres,* and large veuglaires weighed over 1,000 *livres.*

---

61 Marc Beyaert, "Nieuwe historisch onderzoek van de Dulle Griet *bombarde* in Gent," *Handelingen der Maatschappij voor geschiedenis en oudheidkunde te Gent,* n.s. 53 (1999), 3–59, and Robert D. Smith and Ruth Rhynas Brown, *Mons Meg and her Sisters* (London, 1989), pp. 23–38. For a description of this gun see below.

62 Claude Gaier, "The Origin of Mons Meg," *Journal of the Arms and Armour Society* 5 (1965–67), 425–31, and Smith and Brown, pp. 1–22. For a description of this gun see below.

63 Smith and Brown, pp. 39–45. For a description of this gun see below.

In 1445 a contract was drawn up with the Dijonnais smith Jehan Quenot for 206 iron veuglaires in which the sizes were specified.[64] This extremely important document reveals that the intention was to purchase veuglaires in a number of specified sizes, ranging from pieces 6½ *piez* in length, firing a stone ball of 12 *livres*, to small pieces 4½ *piez* long, firing projectiles of 2 *livres*. The following year there is a record of the delivery of 28 of these veuglaires to Philibert de Vauldrey, master of the artillery which reveals that the actual weapons were not so rigidly fixed in size.[65] For example, nine of the smallest veuglaires delivered, ranged in length from 3 to 4 *piez* and in weight from 105 to 281 *livres*, while the medium sized pieces ranged from 4 to 4½ *piez* and from 418 to approximately 1000 *livres*. This emphasizes the lack of any standardization and size control at this period and reinforces the view that there was no absolute dimensional rigidity for guns. What is a problem, however, is the definition of what constitutes a veuglaire? Although there are no clearly defined criteria, these lists strongly suggest that this type of gunpowder weapon was short for its calibre. An analysis of the veuglaires delivered by Quenot suggest an approximate calibre-to-length ratio of 13 to 16 for small veuglaires, 8 to 13 for medium-sized veuglaires, and approximately 5 to 8 for the larger veuglaires. Intriguingly, a contract to supply veuglaires by Jehan Cambier in 1446 indicates that a calibre-to-length ratio of 12 was demanded for all sizes of veuglaires.[66]

Almost all of these guns have removable chambers; only a very few veuglaires are made in a single piece. Of note in the documentary sources is a reference in 1449 to removable chambers aboard Burgundian ships which were to fit all the veuglaires, the first sign among these records of interchangeability and a move towards some form of standardization. More interestingly, these veuglaires are also said to be "loaded from the rear," implying a different, possibly new, technique of loading the projectile. Does this indicate that earlier veuglaires were loaded only from the muzzle? Extant examples of gunpowder weapon barrels show that some have an additional internal ring at the breech into which the powder chamber fitted, making it impossible to load them from the rear. The majority of extant gunpowder weapons do not have this feature, and can be loaded from either the breech or muzzle. Perhaps this innovation could be dated from the placing of gunpowder weapons aboard ships where loading from the rear made it easier and safer to fire.

A second new term for gunpowder weapons, *crapaudeau*, appears in Philip the Good's reign. They are first mentioned in 1433 when two copper-alloy and one iron crapaudeau were transported from Flanders to Burgundy while the last reference in the registers is in 1451 – a period of only eighteen years. Paradoxically, within that short period, over 800 crapaudeaux are listed, making it one of the commonest gunpowder weapons during this period. During the 1430s only about 40 are noted, but after 1440 their numbers increase markedly, with, for example, 74 iron and 29 copper-alloy in a 1443 reference, and 120 iron and 50 copper-alloy in a 1445 reference. Interestingly, crapaudeau is not used in narrative or literary sources of the time, and yet it was

[64] Garnier, pp. 166–67.
[65] Garnier, pp. 168–70.
[66] Garnier, p. 113. There is no information given as to whether the guns from Cambier were made or delivered.

seemingly a favorite term among Burgundian notaries. Just why is unclear. Does the term refer to a new development in gunpowder weapons, a new type of gun, or was it a new name for an already existing type, previously referred to under the generic name *canon*?

Unlike all other gunpowder weapons of the Burgundian arsenal, crapaudeaux have the narrowest size range: weights vary between about 100 and 200 *livres*; lengths from 4 to 5 *piez*; and calibres between 1 and 4 *pouces*. Both iron and copper-alloy crapaudeaux appear in the sources, although there are more than twice the number of iron as copper-alloy. Though most fired stone balls, a large number also fired lead. And almost all have removable chambers, with either two or three supplied with each gun.

The large numbers of crapaudeaux in the inventories allows for some simple analysis, with the conclusion that it is a gunpowder weapon which is long in relation to its calibre: essentially it is a long, thin gun with a calibre-to-length ratio of 15 to 30, as opposed to veuglaires where it is 5 to 15. The fact that the name does not appear until the 1430s strongly suggests that it was probably a new type of gun. If correct it marks a turning-point in the history of gunpowder weapon development. From this time, it appears, two types of gunpowder weapons were being made: veuglaires, shorter length and larger calibre, for shorter-range fire (i.e. in sieges), and crapaudeaux, longer with a smaller calibre, for longer range fire (i.e. on the battlefield and on ships).

A final new term for gunpowder weapons appears in Philip the Good's reign, the *coulovrine*. This term, also popular in both narrative and documentary sources, is first noted in the artillery registers in 1420. Perhaps the most interesting aspects of the coulovrine is the number of variant spellings of the word, from *coleuvre* to *coleuvrine*, and that some are indicated to be handheld (*à main*) or having a rest (*à escappe*). Very large numbers are recorded in the registers: more than 1,000 for each of the 1430s and 1440s. These large numbers are also reflected in the narrative sources which often use the adjective "innumerable" to describe the quantities present at a military engagement. Two general sizes of these gunpowder weapons predominate: smaller coulovrines weigh approximately 10 to 15 *livres*, with a length of around 6 *pouces* or ½ *piez*; larger coulovrines weighed 40 to 50 *livres*, with a length of between 2 and 4 *piez*. Coulovrines are made of both iron and copper-alloy.

Where mentioned almost all coulovrines fired lead balls, with only a very small number firing stone. Although some are said to be equipped with removable chambers, several are also mentioned to be "of one piece." Curiously, only two extant hand-held gunpowder weapons are known to be chambered – one in Portsmouth and one in Dublin.[67] Like the shipboard veuglaires two of the shipboard coulovrines in the 1449 inventory are said to have interchangeable chambers and be loaded from the rear.

Frequently, coulovrines are mentioned as "mounted" or "encased" in wood. Although this may be similar to the stocks of later hand-held gunpowder weapons, it is not made clear exactly how the coulovrine was mounted at this time. From illustrations it seems that they could be mounted either with a wood extension or tiller attached to

---

[67] See Joe J. Simmons, "Lidded-breech Wrought-iron Swivel Gun at Southsea Castle, Portsmouth, England," *Journal of the Ordnance Society* 1 (1989), 63–68, and N. St. John Hennessy, "The Dublin Breech-Loading Swivel Gun," *Journal of the Ordnance Society* 3 (1991), 1–4.

the rear, or they could be laid on or encased in the wood. There is never any mention of an attached firing mechanism or lock in the sources, and it may be presumed that these were fired with a hand-held "match."

Finally, judging from the size of gunports dating from this period, coulovrines must have served as the primary gunpowder weapon for defense of fortifications. In this regard they undoubtedly replaced the bow which had served the same function earlier; indeed, bow slits were often altered into gunports as fortifications during the fifteenth century were transformed to face gunpowder weapon bombardment.[68]

Philip the Good reigned for the longest time of any of the Valois dukes of Burgundy, and during this period the first phase of gunpowder artillery development came to an end. At the beginning of his reign, and carrying on from his father, John the Fearless, just bombards, undoubtedly because of their size, were singled out from the other undifferentiated gunpowder weapons which went by the term *canon*. By the end a multiplicity of gunpowder weapon types had evolved and the foundations for the fully developed gunpowder artillery of the early modern period were clearly laid down. Additionally, during Philip's reign gunpowder weapons became fully integrated into the Burgundian military forces. Their constant presence at sieges were beginning to determine strategy and tactics, although not, it must be stressed, always ensuring success. In battles, too, they appear more regularly and began to effect some tactical change, although it is clear that at this stage they were simply added to or replaced traditional projectile weapons, the bow and the crossbow. Finally, they were added to ships.

CHARLES THE BOLD

There were times of peace during the reigns of each of the preceding Valois dukes of Burgundy; even John the Fearless, whose life was cut short during the Armagnac-Burgundian war, did not fight between 1404 and 1408. But in the reign of Charles the Bold it is only 1469 that was free from military engagements, although he spent most of that year planning for his next war.[69] He fought the French, the Liégeois, the Alsatians, the Lorrainers, the Germans, and the Swiss. A brief military summary of his reign is thus simple: Charles the Bold fought everyone all the time! Warfare was the chief characteristic of his reign. It brought him many accolades among contemporary writers, but general disapproval among historians writing today.[70] In the end it cost him his life.

---

68 See Kelly DeVries, "The Impact of Gunpowder Weaponry on Siege Warfare in the Hundred Years War," in *Medieval City Under Siege*, ed. Ivy A. Corfis and Michael Wolfe (Woodbridge, 1995), pp. 227–44, and "Facing the New Military Technology: Non-*Trace Italienne* Anti-Gunpowder Weaponry Defenses, 1350–1550," in *Colonels and Quartermasters: War and Technology in the Old Regime*, ed. Brett Steele, pp. 37–71.

69 Vaughan, *Charles the Bold*, p. 59.

70 Even Richard Vaughan, who serves generally as a cheerleader for the Valois dukes of Burgundy through his biographies of all of them, questions Charles the Bold's military leadership. See, among many others, Jean-Marie Cauchies, "Charles le Hardi à Neuss (1474/75): Folie militaire ou contrainte politique," *Publication*

Charles the Bold's military reputation rests on the number of battles he fought, most of which historians like to point out were unsuccessful. Yet, like his Burgundian predecessors, these were still fewer in number than the sieges. These, too, are recognized to have been largely unsuccessful. Of course, sometimes "success" at a siege is difficult to define. For example, on his first campaign as a Burgundian general, in 1465, two years before the death of his father, Philip the Good, Charles, then count of Charolais, followed victory at the battle of Montlhéry with a siege of Paris. Naturally the city proved too large to encircle, a problem faced by all of its would-be conquerors since the time of the Vikings. So he chose with his allies to focus on the northwestern fortifications of the city, located between Saint-Denis and Conflans. They ordered their gunpowder weapons in protective trenches and field fortifications around the walls and began their by now customary bombardment. But they did not take the city. In fact, they did not seem to have weakened either the fortifications or the resolve of the Parisian or royal defenders. By the first week of October, after a bombardment of two months, the city showed no signs of falling, but Louis XI decided to sue for peace anyway, giving all of the rebel lords, among them Charles, precisely, if not more than, what they had been fighting for. In the case of Charles, this meant suzerainty over former Burgundian-held Picard lands and several royal towns along the River Somme. His guns had thus failed to "capture" Paris, but had they really failed to gain the prize, which in this case was probably not the city?

In his sieges of rebel Liégeois towns between 1465 and 1468, one might accord greater success to the Burgundian ducal gunpowder artillery train. Indeed, at his two greatest siege victories in this war, Dinant and Liège, the destruction caused by gunpowder weapons, both against fortifications and buildings, was extremely heavy. But no more heavy than that caused by the soldiers and, in fact, by Charles himself. At Dinant, which fell in 1466, it is the punishments suffered by the citizens by the order of Charles – the tossing of the town's master of artillery off the cliff behind the church and the tying of 800 townspeople back-to-back and then casting them into the River Meuse to drown – which is remembered both then and now. At Liège, which fell in 1468, it was the systematic looting, burning, and leveling of the town by Burgundian soldiers, compared in contemporary Low Countries chronicles to the troops of the Ottoman Turks, which has brought the greatest amount of disapproval. In these

du centre européen d'études bourguignonnes (XIVe–XVIe siècles) 36 (1996), 105–15, and *Louis XI et Charles le Hardi: De Péronne à Nancy (1468–1477): le conflit* (Brussels, 1996); Werner Paravicini, *Karl der Kühne: Das Ende des Hauses Burgund* (Göttingen, 1976); Bertrand Schnerb, *L'état Bourguignon, 1363–1477* (Paris, 1999); and the numerous works by Charles Brusten, especially, *L'armée bourguignonne de 1465 à 1468* (Brussels, 1954), "La bataille de Morat," *Publications du centre européen d'études burgundo-médianes* 10 (1968), 79–84, "Les campagnes Liégeoises de Charles de Téméraire," in *Liège et Bourgogne. Actes de colloque tenu à Liège les 28, 29 et 30 Octobre, 1968* (Liège, 1972), pp. 81–99; "Charles le Téméraire et la camp de Lausanne, mars-mai 1476," *Publications du centre européen d'études burgundo-médianes* 14 (1972), 71–81; "Charles le Téméraire et la campagne de Neuss, 1474–75," *Publications du centre européen d'études burgundo-médianes* 13 (1971), 67–73; "Les compaignies d'ordonnance dans l'armée Bourguignonne," *Revue internationale d'histoire militaire* 40 (1978), 112–69; "La fin des compaignies d'ordonnance de Charles le Téméraire," in *Cinq-centième anniversaire de la bataille de Nancy (1477): Actes du Colloque organisé par l'institut de recherche régionale en sciences sociales, humaines et économiques de l'Université de Nancy II (Nancy, 22–24 septembre 1977)* (Nancy, 1979), pp. 363–75; and "A propos des campagnes bourguignonnes, 1475–78," *Publications du centre européen d'études burgundo-médianes* 9 (1967), 79–87.

engagements, the destructive role played by Burgundian gunpowder weapons was just a part of Charles the Bold's overall plan for dealing with those rebelling against him.

On the other hand, a conclusion of siege warfare success based on Charles the Bold's demeanor and not his gunpowder weapons creates problems when used to explain the duke's failure in all his other major sieges. For the period 1469–1477 small towns in his wars with France, Alsace, Lorraine, Guelders, and Switzerland readily fell to the Burgundians and their gunpowder weapons, but larger locations did not, the most notable being Beauvais and Neuss. Victory or defeat in the latter engagements seems to have been decided more by the determination of the inhabitants to withstand Charles, than his determination to gain their towns. At Beauvais, the siege of which began on 27 June 1472, Philippe de Commynes contends that he could easily have breeched the fortifications of the town "had he come with that intention."[71] Charles could not fully surround the walls allowing the besieged citizens to be continually supplied with victuals, men, and armaments, including gunpowder and gunpowder weapons. The Burgundian forces grew weary and hungry for lack of supplies, and after twenty-five days they retreated to Burgundy. While at Neuss, the siege of which lasted almost a year, from 30 July 1474 to 13 June 1475, during which time its walls were constantly bombarded by the Burgundian gunpowder artillery, Charles was also never able to force the inhabitants to surrender. Nor was the duke able to breech the fortifications. Midway through the siege the gates and walls of the town lay in ruins, but only twice were Burgundian soldiers able to enter the town and on both occasions they were beaten back and their further entry blocked. Finally, late in May 1475 a German relief force approached Neuss and Charles, influenced by the fatigue of his soldiers, dissatisfaction among his subjects paying for the siege at home, and, of course, the rumblings of revolt in the Low Countries, was forced to seek a truce and to raise his siege.

Charles the Bold also fought a large number of battles, many more than his Burgundian ducal predecessors. In each of these engagements, as had become normal by his time, Charles used gunpowder weapons, and at least in his earlier battles, at Montlhéry and Brustem, as again had become common, he seems to have used them to initiate combat in an attempt to provoke a charge onto his lines.

At Montlhéry, fought on 16 July 1465, while Charles was fighting as part of the League of Public Weal, the French charge, prompted by the Burgundian *serpentine* fire, broke through their lines, capturing some of Charles' guns and nearly driving his soldiers into a rout. Indeed, it was only the tenacity of the Burgundian soldiers which finally stopped the French and forced them back. At this point, a gunpowder artillery duel between both sides took place, ultimately decided in the favor of the Burgundians, although its outcome was so uncertain that Louis XI also claimed victory.

At Brustem, fought on 28 October 1467, Charles the Bold, now duke of Burgundy, fought the rebellious Liégeois. Again the Burgundian gunpowder artillery opened the battle, this time with the guns from Liège responding. Both sides had many of these weapons, but neither was able to get the advantage of the situation, as both the Liégeois and the Burgundian projectiles flew harmlessly over the heads of their opponents. Nor

[71] Philippe de Commynes, *The Memoirs of Philippe de Commynes*, ed. Samuel Kinser, trans. Isabelle Cazeaux (Columbia, 1969), I:236.

did any charge from either side follow. Fearful that the oncoming night might cause the Liégeois to try to slip away or attempt a surprise attack, Charles decided to send a unit of archers and men-at-arms in a flanking manoeuvre through the village of Brustem. At the same time, a Burgundian cavalry charge directed at the center of the Liégeois line led by Charles' half-brother, Baudouin, was successfully turned back. Yet, it distracted the rebels long enough for the Burgundian flanking archers and men-at-arms to chase the Liégeois from the field, leaving behind their guns. While gunpowder weapons played no discernable role, the generalship of Charles and the determination of his army won the battle.

But it was the last time Charles the Bold was to taste victory in a major battlefield engagement. In little more than two years, between November 1474 and January 1477, the Burgundian army fought four battles against the Swiss and Lorrainers and lost each one. The first, the battle of Héricourt, fought on 13 November 1474, was a rather small engagement, and Charles was not himself present, being at Neuss at the time. There were no large gunpowder weapons present, although both sides seem to have had them at their disposal – the Swiss, who had been besieging the castle of Héricourt had left theirs at the siege, while the outnumbered Burgundian troops were caught retreating to their encampment and had no guns with them. However, a large number of coulovriniers were on both sides in what may have been one of the first battles fought with units of hand-held gunners. Within a short time, the Burgundians suffered an incredible number of casualties – 1,617 dead – and were forced to flee.

Charles was present at the next three battles, Grandson, Murten, and Nancy, but his presence did not bring success. The battle of Grandson was fought on 2 March 1476. In response to the Burgundian duke's occupation of several castles and towns in Switzerland, including the recently captured castle of Grandson, the Swiss mustered an army and decided to meet the Burgundians in battle. Unlike at Héricourt, on this occasion the Burgundians were armed with serpentines and other larger gunpowder weapons; like Héricourt they also had a large number of hand-held coulovrines. The field artillery was mostly set up in a field fortification which Charles had built along the shore of Lake Neuchâtel, facing the path that he anticipated the Swiss troops would travel. The coulovriniers seem to have been set up below but facing the same direction. However, the Swiss did not come that way. Instead, they first provoked some movement from Charles' position with a diversionary attack on a nearby Burgundian-held castle and then, using the confusion this caused, marched unseen along the mountain side and through the dense forest, out-flanking the surprised Burgundians. Rather than encountering their powerful gunpowder artillery, the Swiss clashed with infantry and cavalry units of Burgundians. In the midst of this, Charles seemed to have tried a "feigned retreat," which instead drew the rest of his army into a full-fledged rout. The Burgundian guns, field and hand-held alike, never had a chance to fire into the charging Swiss without hitting their own soldiers. Most of Charles' gunpowder artillery train was lost, part of the fabulous and renowned *Burgunderbeute* (Burgundian Booty).

Less than four months later, on 22 June 1476, a second Swiss-Burgundian battle was fought, outside the town of Murten. Charles the Bold was besieging the well-fortified town when the Swiss, buoyed by their victory at Grandson, and accompanied by their Lorrainer allies, led by their duke, René II of Anjou, decided to raise the siege. All contemporary evidence suggests that Charles was aware of the Swiss-Lorrainer intention, and that on 21 June he positioned his troops between their camp and the main siege batteries on the south side of the town. But, for some unexplained reason, when these troops were not attacked that day, the Burgundian leader disbanded and sent his army back to their tents where they huddled against the rain of that night and the next morning. It was in fact around midday of that day that the Swiss-Lorrainers launched their attack, completely surprising the Burgundians. A unit of artillery and English archers was able to halt the charge, but only briefly as it was soon overrun. As at Grandson, by the time most of the Burgundian artillerymen, either those manning the field guns or the coulovrines, were able to prepare their weapons, their opponents were among them. Once again the use of gunpowder weapons at this battle was largely insignificant due to the speed and surprise of the attack. The Burgundians were soundly defeated, the only route of escape for many being the lake beyond the town, a three kilometer swim to the opposite side; several thousand were killed, and even more Burgundian gunpowder weapons were captured by the Swiss.

Charles the Bold's final battle was fought at Nancy on 5 January 1477. Again, as at the other engagements which the Burgundians had recently fought, gunpowder weapons had little or no effect on the outcome, although they were certainly present, especially in the form of hand-held guns. After the losses they had suffered at Grandson and Murten, where the Burgundian army and artillery had been decimated, Charles was left with too few troops either to besiege the town or to fight a battle, leaving open the question as to why he did both. His opponents, composed of all his enemies, the Swiss, Germans, Lorrainers, and French, greatly outnumbered the Burgundians, by as many as three or four to one. There was no need for the surprise attack which had been so effective in the two previous battles. Charles knew that his opponents were coming, and he ordered his troops behind a fortified defensive position bordered on three sides by streams and rivers. He should, of course, have withdrawn.

The Burgundians still had some gunpowder artillery and these presented a threat to a direct charge on their position, so the enemy generals decided on a flank attack. The weather was cold and snowy, and the allies used this to cover their advance. Before they knew what was happening, the allied soldiers were among the Burgundian right flank leaving no time to change the direction of their gunpowder weapons or for an effective use of their coulovrines. It did not take long for the flank to fail, and it collapsed onto Charles' artillery positions and troops in the centre. Those not immediately killed or captured were run down as they tried to flee, including Charles the Bold, whose mangled and frozen corpse lay undiscovered for two days on the battlefield. Such was the ignoble death of the last Valois duke of Burgundy.

Despite Charles the Bold's short reign, which lasted only a decade, more new terms for gunpowder weaponry appear in the sources than previously: *courtau*, *hacquebus*, *serpentine*, *mortar*, and *pestereau*. In addition, *canon* as a term for a type of gunpowder weapon disappears from the middle of the 1460s, and becomes the generic term for non-personal guns from then down to the present day in phrases such as *cannon*, *cannonballs*, *poudre à canon*, etc.

During his reign, bombards are rarely mentioned in the Burgundian registers, but are obviously still popular and mentioned frequently in the narrative, literary, and other documentary sources. However, it is clear that the numbers of bombards have declined by Charles the Bold's time, only two appear in 1474, and they are accorded less status. *Dulle Griet*, for example, captured from Oudenaarde by the Ghentenaars in their rebellion against Philip the Good is never again used in warfare, staying in the arsenal there and later placed on display in the town.[72] It clearly had become more important as a trophy to the Ghentenaars than as a working gunpowder weapon. Indications are that this was not unusual throughout western Europe from the later fifteenth century when the use of bombards as a predominant gunpowder weapon begins to decline. Only in armies relatively new to gunpowder weapons, i.e. the Ottoman Turks and Scots, do bombards continue being used into the sixteenth century.

Bombardelles also seem to have declined in use and are mentioned less in the sources through Charles' reign and later. A few continue to appear in the documentary sources,[73] but, never a popular gunpowder term for chroniclers, it does not appear with any frequency in narrative sources. By the end of the fifteenth century it had disappeared.

In 1474 there is a single reference to courtau in the Burgundian artillery registers, when two copper-alloy courtaux firing stone balls were taken by sixteen horses to the siege of Neuss. Other records indicate, however, that these were not the only courtaux in the Burgundian gunpowder artillery arsenal of the 1470s, and they continue to be mentioned in the sources after Charles' death. Based on somewhat circumstantial, but convincing, evidence this large gun may be the successor to the bombard, although such a statement is difficult to fully justify. First, it is a large gunpowder weapon, able to fire a large stone projectile. Second, although smaller than the bombards they replaced, there is some evidence that developments in gunpowder technology would have meant that it was no less powerful Third, there is a probable link from the courtau to the *perrier*, a gunpowder weapon developed at the very end of the fifteenth century and which continued in use throughout the sixteenth century, and in England at least, until the 1630s. This progression shows that even though the bombard disappears, there was a need for large calibre guns. Fourth, there is an extant Burgundian weapon that probably must be identified as a courtau. Dated on the barrel to 1474 and attributed by inscription to Jehan de Malines, it is a long (217 centimeters) copper-alloy gun capable of firing a large stone ball from its 23 centimeter calibre muzzle. While there is obviously some speculation in naming this piece a courtau, contemporary sources do refer to Jehan de Malines as a maker of copper-alloy courtaux.[74]

The last veuglaire mentioned in the artillery registers collected by Joseph Garnier comes from a 1467 reference to one received at Fouvent Castle "for its defense."[75] However, other contemporary sources definitely indicate that they continued in use

---

[72] See Beyaert.

[73] Although these are found not in the records preserved in Garnier but in the *Inventaire sommaire des archives départementales antérieures à 1790. Nord. Série B*, ed. A. le Glay et al. (Lille, 1863–1906), VIII:248–62.

[74] *Inventaire sommaire des archives départementales du Nord*, VIII:254.

[75] Garnier, p. 82.

and popularity well into the 1470s. They do not seem to have changed in character, with the same size and features common to those found earlier. Yet, after Charles the Bold's death, as the Burgundian gunpowder weapons find their place among Maximilian of Austria's arsenals, they begin to be named less and less. Whether this means that they stop being made, change their name, or evolve into an entirely new gunpowder weaponry type cannot be determined from the sources or from extant artillery pieces.

Unlike the bombard, bombardelle, and veuglaire, the coulovrine does continue to appear frequently and in large numbers in Charles the Bold's artillery registers. These differ little from their earlier counterparts, except that a number are now listed as having a hook (*à croucher*). This feature is also found on a large number of extant hand-held gunpowder weapons which are traditionally dated to the end of the fifteenth century.[76] These may be the same as the gunpowder weapon known as the hacquebus which appears in the Burgundian records in the 1470s. Nine of these guns are listed, five being made of iron and four without metallurgical details. The iron hacquebus weighs on average 44 *livres*, corresponding to the larger size of coulovrine. As in all hand-held gunpowder weapons, where noted, these fired lead balls. There seems little doubt that the hacquebus served as the forerunner of the early modern *arquebus* and musket.

The most numerous and prominent new gunpowder weapon of Charles the Bold's reign was the serpentine. It appears in narrative sources during Philip the Good's reign, but only in the of Charles the Bold does it become perhaps the most widely used non-hand-held artillery piece in battles and on ships, and its use in sieges was not unknown. These were gunpowder weapons weighing around 500 *livres*, although at least one *gros* serpentine from 1474 weighed 1,549½ *livres*. The length of only one serpentine is also indicated, at 5 *piez*. They were made of both iron and copper-alloy and, where indicated, fire lead balls, are said to have removable chambers, and were mounted "on iron wheels."

It is tempting to connect the rise of the serpentine with the decline of the crapaudeau. There certainly seems to be continuity in the dates of the two and also a great similarity in their sizes, shapes, and quantity. Both the crapaudeaux and the serpentines were long guns in relation to their calibre, and both seem to have been produced in large numbers.

The term *mortar* does not appear in the documentary records for Charles the Bold's reign gathered by Garnier, but is in other sources, both documentary and narrative. In the narrative sources of siege warfare mortars are prevalent, in the way bombards were earlier in the century. A mortar also was adopted as an heraldic symbol of Lodewijk (or Louis) de Gruuthuse, a prominent Burgundian administrative official whose family's lack of previous nobility allowed him to place a gunpowder weapon on his coat of arms and throughout his palatial mansion in Bruges.[77]

---

[76] See R.T.W. Kempers, "Haakbussen uit Nederlands bezit," *Armamentaria* 11 (1976), 75–97; trans. "Haquebuts from Dutch Collections," *Journal of the Arms and Armour Society* 11 (1983–85), 56–89.

[77] Jean de Haynin specifically indicates that Lodewijk van Gruuthuse's heraldic symbol was a "*mortar*" (*Mémoires*, ed. R. Chalon (Mons, 1842), I:68. See also L. Van Praet, *Recherches sur Louis de Bruges: Seigneur*

Finally, the *pestereau* appears in documentary sources after the death of Charles the Bold, but may have been included in the ducal arsenal earlier. Certainly some extant gunpowder weapons said to be booty taken from the defeated Burgundian forces after 1476–1477 can probably be identified as pestereau. These are very short guns of large calibre made in both forged and cast iron, similar in many respects to mortars. Two extant examples still retain parts of their original mount which show that pestereaux were mounted on wooden beds to which fixtures could be attached allowing the weapon to be raised or lowered easily. Unfortunately, the limited amount of source material about these gunpowder weapons means that it is impossible to make any firm conclusions. Strangely, all surviving examples come from Swiss/Burgundian provenances of limited chronology which might indicate a parallel development with the mortar which proved ultimately to be the more successful weapon.

AFTER THE VALOIS DUKES OF BURGUNDY

The direct line of the Valois dukes of Burgundy died with Charles the Bold at Nancy on 5 January 1477. He had no male heirs and the duchy passed instead to his daughter, Mary. By this time she was engaged to Duke Maximilian of Austria, the Habsburg heir who, later, became Holy Roman Emperor. Mary continued to rule the shrinking Burgundian lands on her own. The transition was not peaceful, and it was quickly apparent that the enemies of her father and grandfather were prepared to take advantage of the situation. Most active among these were Louis XI and René II of Anjou. René immediately followed his success at Nancy with a reconquest of the parts of Lorraine which he and his ancestors had lost to the dukes of Burgundy over the preceding seventy years. Louis XI did the same with Picardy and the towns along the Somme which he lost to Charles in the War of the Public Weal in 1465 and which had been the targets of so much fighting since. These fell so rapidly to him that his armies then moved into Artois and Burgundy itself. In these campaigns the French king was so successful that not only did he push back the borders of northern France to essentially where they are today, but he even captured Dijon.[78] The Swiss, the third member of the alliance which defeated Charles at Nancy, seem to have been satisfied with having removal the Burgundians from the Vaud and from Switzerland.

Mary of Burgundy had always considered the southern Low Countries her "homeland," and while military adventures were made against her French and Burgundian lands she had taken refuge there. For the moment, the Low Countries were supportive of her rule or at least as supportive as any of these frequently rebelling principalities and towns usually were. This support did not last long, at least for the Flemings and Liégeois, and much of Mary's resources both before and after her marriage to Maximilian were expended to keep these rebellions at bay.

de la Gruythuse (Paris, 1831), and Jan Pieter Puype, "Het embleem van Lodewijk van Gruuthuse," in *Lodewijk van Gruuthuse: Mecenas en europees diplomaat, ca. 1427–1492*, ed. Maximiliaan P.J. Martens (Bruges, 1992), pp. 93–108.

[78] See Paul Murray Kendall, *Louis XI: ". . . the Universal Spider . . ."* (London, 1974), pp. 315–22, and Edouard Perroy, "L'artillerie de Louis XI dans la campagne d'Artois," *Revue du Nord* 26 (1943), 171–96, 293–315.

Once Maximilian became her spouse, on 19 August 1477, things began to look up for Mary, at least politically and militarily. She would never regain the lands lost immediately after her father's death, but once her realm had been bolstered by the powerful forces, political and military, of Maximilian, the attacks on her remaining lands stopped. In addition, Maximilian would take a similar ruthless stance as had Charles in putting down the Low Countries rebellions, and when it came to defending those lands against incursions from outside, such as against Louis XI in 1477–1479, the duke of Austria was diligent.[79] The Burgundian Low Countries stayed completely intact until 1492, with most of them forming the base of Charles V's power in the early sixteenth century.

There is no doubt that the numerous Burgundian gunpowder artillery holdings had been severely decimated by the losses at Grandson, Murten, and Nancy. Further losses followed with Louis XI's capture of Picardy, Artois, and the duchy of Burgundy. Many of these guns were integrated into the artillery trains of the victors, although some captured by the Swiss had greater value as symbols of victory than as machines of war. However, some of these surviving gunpowder weapons have been altered or modified, suggesting perhaps that they were in fact used by the Swiss. It should also be noted that of the hundreds of gunpowder weapons which were captured in these engagements only twenty-five or so survive, indicating perhaps that many of the others were used in later warfare by them.

The few gunpowder weapons left to Mary by her father, mostly in the Low Countries, became part of Maximilian's arsenal; more importantly, Maximilian adopted the Ordinances concerning gunpowder weapons that had largely been established by Philip the Good and developed by Charles the Bold. This, combined with the Burgundian military administration which Maximilian also adopted, formulated much of the Habsburg military machine which dominated central Europe throughout the end of the fifteenth century.

By the end of Charles the Bold's reign, the Burgundians no longer led the way in gunpowder weapon production and numbers. The Swiss, Lorrainers, and French who faced him during the last two years of his life certainly had as many gunpowder weapons, both field and hand-held pieces, and demonstrated better tactical use of them. In the case of all of these powers, but especially in the case of France, there had been a long-term and parallel development although one outshone by the Valois duke of Burgundy. During the reign of Charles VII the work of the Bureau brothers, Jean and Gaspard, who reorganized the administration and tactical use of the French gunpowder artillery train during the latter stages of the Hundred Years War, was particularly important. So influential were they in French military circles that Jean Bureau rose to lead the entire army of France at the battle which ended this War, Castillon, fought in July 1453, the first "master of artillery" to have done so.[80] However, the "revolution" attributed by modern historians to the Bureau brothers, for

---

79 Gerhard Benecke, *Maximilian I (1459–1519): An Analytical Biography* (London, 1982), pp. 32–35.
80 See Michel de Lombarès, "Castillon (17 juillet 1453), dernière bataille de la guerre de Cent Ans, première victoire de l'artillerie," *Revue historique des armées* (1976), 7–31. As Lombarès shows, there is little doubt that Jean Bureau's previous experience as Master of the French gunpowder artillery aided his victory in this battle.

example the introduction of iron cannonballs and the standardization of gunpowder weapons, cannot be substantiated from the evidence.[81]

Louis XI inherited the French gunpowder weapon administration and arsenal from his father. Although its power was not realized in his first engagement with Charles the Bold in 1465, at the battle of Montlhéry, it was certainly much in evidence during the king's campaigns in Picardy, Artois, and Burgundy in 1477.[82] It is clear that he had done much in the twelve years between these events to increase the numbers of his gunpowder weapons. He also seems to have understood, as had so many competent medieval military leaders, that the effective use of his guns was not so much determined by the force they could deliver but, equally, by the willingness of those whom he faced to withstand that force. In his 1477 campaigns few wanted to hold out against him, preferring to avoid death and destruction by switching allegiance. It was a lesson that his son, Charles VIII, was also to learn.

The development of gunpowder weapons through the fourteenth and fifteenth centuries came to fruition in the closing decades of the fifteenth century. It had been a slow development – a natural progression as it were – characteristic of the changes in gunpowder weapons during the next four centuries. It had been a long time since the Milemete manuscript of 1326 and its depiction of a vase-shaped gunpowder weapon. For almost 100 years after this, though our knowledge is very limited, it appears that developments were slow. Gunpowder weapons became larger and more numerous as the new weapon and its technology were better understood. However, in the fist two decades of the fifteenth century, and certainly by 1420, one can be sure that the first real significant changes had taken place which led, step by step, to the fully developed artillery of the very end of the fifteenth century.[83] From the early bombard and *canon*, the development of the veuglaire, the crapaudeau, and coulovrine led to the evolution of the courtau, serpentine, and hacquebus, leading to the four types of later "classic" gunpowder weapons: the cannon perrier, the cannon, the culverin, and the arquebus. To use these new weapons effectively and successfully, new mounts and carriages were developed which enabled them to be used in all warlike situations from sieges and the battlefield to the sea. And as new metallurgical technologies were developed, cast-iron projectiles, heavier per unit volume, were introduced.

Charles VIII's excursion into Italy in 1494–1495 has long been attributed as the campaign which changed the medieval into the early modern world.[84] There is no

---

81   H. Dubled's article, "L'artillerie royale Française à l'époque de Charles VII et au début du règne de Louis XI (1437–1469): Les frères Bureau," *Memorial de l'artillerie Française* 50 (1976), 555–637, has influenced a number of historians, including Contamine, Vale, Hall, and Keen, who have accepted this work uncritically. However, it is poorly referenced and difficult to follow, and therefore should be used with caution, especially when Dubled makes these rather remarkable conclusions about the Bureau brothers' influence on the history of gunpowder weapons.

82   See Edouard Perroy, "L'artillerie de Louis XI dans la campagne d'Artois," *Revue du Nord* 26 (1943), 171–96, 293–315.

83   Robert D. Smith, " 'All Manner of Peeces': Artillery in the Late Medieval Period," *The Royal Armouries Yearbook* 7 (2002), 130–38.

84   See, for example, Geoffrey Parker, *The Military Revolution: Military Innovation and the Rise of the West, 1500–1800* (Cambridge, 1988); Theodore Ropp, *War in the Modern World*, 2nd ed. (New York, 1962); and William H. McNeill, *The Pursuit of Power: Technology, Armed Force, and Society since A.D. 1000* (Chicago, 1982).

doubt that the march which he made to Naples with his gunpowder artillery marked the beginning of a change in the political and military affairs of Europe over the next half century, when Italy became the battlefield on which the Habsburg Empire faced the Valois French Kingdom. It was a relatively easy campaign; a fact which Francesco Guicciardini claimed, in a passage which has become ubiquitous, was the result of the French gunpowder weapons:

> The French brought a much handier engine made of brass, called cannon, which they charged with heavy, iron balls, without comparison with those of stones made use of hitherto, and drove them on carriages with horses, not with oxen, as was the custom in Italy; and they were attended by such clever men, and on such instruments appointed for the purpose that they almost ever kept pace with the army. They were planted against the walls of a town with such speed, the space between each shot was so little, and the balls flew so quick, and were impelled with such force, that as much execution was done in a few hours, as formerly in Italy, in the like number of days. These rather diabolical than human instruments, were used not only in sieges, but also in the field, and were mixed with others of a smaller size. Such artillery rendered Charles' army very formidable to all Italy.[85]

Unfortunately, this quote, in the words of Simon Pepper, "has assumed enormous authority."[86] It is clear that Guicciardini was comparing the French gunpowder weapons to those which he had seen in Italy which seem from this comparison to have been significantly outdated and inferior. Notwithstanding the problems that such a statement might present to the Italian military historian, to those who study gunpowder weapons his astonishment at the sight of the French guns is rather surprising, if taken at face value. His statement is simply incorrect!

As Simon Pepper has recently shown, Charles VIII's success rested far less on his gunpowder weapons than has always been assumed. When Charles was forced to fight and used his guns to do so, his success was due more to other factors, not the least of which was the unwillingness of the Italians to fight against him. Only at Castel dell'Ovo were the defendants bombarded into surrender, while at Monte San Giovanni, he did indeed succeed in breeching the walls although one source says that this may have been a small gateway. Most of his other successes, however, were due to intimidation, political negotiation, fortunate accidents – as when a ball broke a drawbridge chain, lowering the bridge and letting the French troops in or the explosion of an opponent's gunpowder magazine.[87]

The mistake Guicciardini made, which has been followed by all those who have relied on his statement to explain the beginning of the Italian Wars, was to attribute French success to revolutionary types of gunpowder weapons, iron cannonballs, and

---

85 Francesco Guicciardini, *The History of Italy*, trans. Chevalier Austin Parke Goddard (London, 1754), I:148–49, as quoted in Simon Pepper, "Castles and Cannon in the Naples Campaign of 1494–95," in *The French Descent into Renaissance Italy, 1494–95: Antecedents and Effects*, ed. D. Abulafia (Aldershot, 1995), p. 263.

86 Pepper, p. 263.

87 Pepper, pp. 263–93.

light, fast, moveable carriages drawn by horses.[88] In fact, none of these were new or revolutionary in 1494. The French gunpowder weapons were the same as those which had been in existence for almost half a century; iron cannonballs in significant quantities had been around since the 1460s; and light, fast, moveable carriages may have been in use for as long, and perhaps longer.

GENERAL BURGUNDIAN ARTILLERY

The above study has focused on a chronological development of gunpowder weapons, and their western European use and technology down to the end of the fifteenth century, with the Valois dukes of Burgundy as a guide from 1363. There are other aspects of this development that have been omitted so far. Some of these topics cut across this period, while others are more difficult to define chronologically. These include: materials and metallurgy; surface treatment, colours, and marks; gunpowder and projectiles; loading, aiming, and firing; carriages, mounts, protection, and transportation; and personnel.

Gunpowder artillery in this period, as throughout the later centuries, was made from copper-alloy, wrought iron, or cast iron. It seems likely that the methods of manufacturing copper-alloy gunpowder weapons came from the casting industry already in existence by the early fourteenth century, especially bellfounding. There is at least one example of this when Philip the Bold employed Joseph Colard, a Dinantais gun-caster, who also made for the duke bronze art objects, including bells, chandeliers, bronze eagles for lecterns, and columns to support angels for an altar.[89] Copper-alloy gunpowder weapons were made by pouring molten metal into a pre-fashioned mould in which a core had been placed to form the bore. The mould was then broken up to extract the gun. Few if any analyses of pre-sixteenth-century western European copper-alloy gunpowder weapons have been carried out. An analysis of the large Turkish gun in the Royal Armouries collections, dated to 1464, shows that the metal contained 93% copper and 4.2 % tin. Similar analyses of sixteenth-century English gunpowder weapons vary between 85% and 95% copper and from 1% to 4% tin, with up to 6% zinc in at least one example, and small amounts of lead and other trace elements.[90] Copper-alloy has always been a valuable metal and has always been remelted and reformed into either new guns or other artifacts. Consequently, there are few surviving copper-alloy gunpowder weapons.

Wrought iron cannot be heated to a high enough temperature to make it molten so that wrought-iron gunpowder weapons were made by building up the shape of the gunpowder weapon from smaller pieces of iron which the smith formed and hammer-welded together as and where necessary. The barrel was made of long iron staves bound together with iron hoops and bands while the powder chambers could be made in the same way or from smaller pieces of wrought iron hammer welded

---

[88] See, for example, Parker, *The Military Revolution*, and Ropp.
[89] Garnier, pp. 14–15, and Vaughan, *Philip the Bold*, p. 203.
[90] Howard L. Blackmore, *The Armouries of the Tower of London*, I: *Ordnance* (London, 1976), pp. 408–09.

together.[91] It was, consequently, relatively easy to repair them, as several extant gunpowder weapons show. There are also frequent references to wrought-iron gunpowder weapons which were "*rompue*" (broken), indicating possibly that they were waiting to be repaired. But it was difficult to always reuse the material and this, coupled with the fact that wrought-iron cannon continued to be made and used into the eighteenth century, has resulted in the survival of many examples. Unfortunately, the basic technology did not change throughout this long period making them difficult, if not impossible, to date accurately. This also proves conclusively that gunpowder weapons made in wrought iron were not primitive or inferior to those made in copper-alloy.

Cast iron, like copper-alloy, could be heated to the molten state and poured into a mould. However, before the sixteenth century the use of cast iron for making cannon was rare, primarily due to the fact that the gunpowder weapon which resulted could be brittle and prone to fracture, causing injury to its operating crew. Yet, the fact that some gunpowder weapons are listed as cast iron in the Burgundian artillery registers indicates that they were able to use the material, although how they managed to make safe guns before the problems were solved in the mid-sixteenth century is a mystery.

An interesting area revealed by the Burgundian sources is the use of surface treatments to protect gunpowder weapons. When this is mentioned it is frequently to note that iron guns were painted red or white, treated with a varnish (*vernissié*), or covered in grease.[92] There is also a reference to an iron coulovrine covered with tin (*étain*).[93] Obviously this would have afforded these weapons protection from water and the elements. It is also recorded in the Burgundian documents that guns carried marks usually consisting of lines or simple geometric forms. These were probably marks for identification, makers or owners, although most are indecipherable. Only on the fine copper-alloy courtau from 1474 extant in the Historisches Museum, Basel, is the name of the founder: Jehan de Malines. It and other copper-alloy cannon were also decorated with coats of arms and shields. Wrought iron gunpowder weapons were occasionally decorated with simple line and dot patterns, and sometimes they might carry a larger design, such as the coat of arms found on *Dulle Griet* or the shield mark on the iron gun in Basel. Unfortunately, few of these decorations or marks can be identified.

References to gunpowder throughout the fourteenth and fifteenth century are numerous. The three elements of gunpowder remained the same throughout the period – saltpetre, charcoal, and sulphur. There are frequent payments in the records for saltpetre and sulphur, but rarely charcoal. Gunpowder was shipped ready-made, but it could also be transported as separate components. At some time in the first half of the fifteenth century a distinction was made between cannon powder (*poudre à canon*) and handgun powder (*poudre de coulovrine*), although what that distinction was is never made clear.

The history of gunpowder has yet to be written. Its properties depend on several factors, not only on the materials from which it is made and their purity, but also on

---

[91] Robert D. Smith, "The Technology of Wrought-Iron Artillery," *Royal Armouries Yearbook* 5 (2000), 68–79.
[92] Garnier, pp. 82, 43, 184.
[93] Garnier, p. 80. This may refer to a coating of a lead-tin mixture.

the proportions in which they are mixed and the final physical state of the powder itself. While charcoal and sulphur are relatively straightforward for the early period, current debate centres on the composition of the saltpetre used and whether this was calcium nitrate or potassium nitrate or, more probably, a mixture of the two. Numerous recipes for gunpowder survive, each varying in detail as to exact proportions of the constituents; current research indicates, however, that as long as the saltpetre content is relatively high, over about 50%, the overall composition does not seem to have mattered. What is more important is the physical state of the powder: whether it is a simple dry mixture of the finely ground ingredients or formed into larger pieces. The latter was produced by wetting the finely ground mixture – vinegar, alcohol, or urine, are frequently cited as wetting agents – which was then shaped while damp into balls of a fixed size (referred to as "corns") or large cakes, which were crumbled into smaller pieces for use, and then dried. Both in contemporary and modern sources, it is usually stated that "corned" powder is more powerful, but quantifying the difference in the power of caked, "corned," or dry powder has not been sufficiently investigated. That dry powder continued to be made and used throughout the later Middle Ages and early modern period must mean that corned powder was not the revolutionary development that some have asserted it to be. More important for this study, the changes in gunpowder technology have not been satisfactorily dated so that it remains impossible to determine whether they had any effect on the development of gunpowder weapons. That it must have done is self-evident, as the co-existence of *canon powder* and *coulovrine powder* in the records proves; however, until further work is carried out the relationship between the guns and its propellants will continue to be obscure.

Transportation of gunpowder and the tools which would be used to prepare it are mentioned in the original sources. Sieves, pestles, and mortars, occasionally mentioned, were obviously the tools for making the gunpowder, while a variety of containers are named, ranging from wooden barrels and casks to leather sacks.

There is also evidence that the cost of powder fluctuated during the period, and may in fact have declined as the production of saltpetre increased. However, as this period also saw the greatest fluctuation in currency values, it is impossible to quantify this with any precision. One interesting fact does present itself in the inventories. On several occasions when prices of gunpowder or its constituents are mentioned, more than one price is indicated, for example in 1476–1477 when 12,140 *livres* of saltpetre is purchased at 10 and 12 *francs* per hundred weight and sulphur is purchased at 4, 6, and 10 *francs* per hundred weight.[94] This would suggest that there was no fixed price and each purchase was the subject of a barter process and/or quality affected the price.[95]

Gunpowder weapons of the later Middle Ages fired numerous types of projectiles, including bolts, stone balls, lead balls, cast iron balls, and *fusée*. Bolts were essentially long, thick arrows. They were made of wood, sometimes oak, with an iron tip, and

---

[94] Garnier, p. 41.

[95] That different qualities of gunpowder and saltpetre were available for purchase is made clear by the frequent references to means of deciding quality and purifying saltpetre found in the *Feuerwerkbuch*, written in the beginning of the fifteenth century and existing in numerous manuscripts copied throughout the century. See Gerhard W. Kramer, ed., and Klaus Leibnitz, trans. "The Firework Book: Gunpowder in Medieval Germany (Das Feuerwerkbuch, c. 1440)," in *Journal of Arms and Armour Society* 17 (Mar. 2001), 31–33.

were mostly flighted with copper-alloy "feathers," nailed to the wooden shaft. Some-times the ends of the bolts which fitted into the gunpowder weapon were wrapped in leather, presumably to ensure a tight fit.[96] Bolts were used in gunpowder weapons throughout the fourteenth and into the early fifteenth centuries, sometimes side by side with cannonballs. However, by the late fourteenth century it is clear that their use was diminishing.

Stone balls were by far the most common form of gunpowder weapon projectile. Used in all sizes and types of gunpowder weapons, even occasionally in hand-held guns, their presence at sieges, on the battlefield, and at sea is verified by all sources, narrative, documentary, literary, and artistic. There are also numerous extant stone cannonballs throughout Europe, although few can be dated with any certainty, a problem made more difficult as stone shot continued to be purchased for gunpowder weapons as late as the middle of the seventeenth century. Stone balls were made in all sizes and were carefully cut to the right size by masons; documents attest to their presence with the gunpowder weapons, as well as their tools, hammers, chisels, and gauges. A common assumption among modern historians is that stone balls were primitive and less effec-tive than metal shot. A second assumption, tied to the first, is that stone balls were so expensive that when cheaper cast iron became available it quickly superseded stone.[97] In fact, although cast-iron shot did appear in the early fifteenth century, it was not until the 1470s that it was common, and it does not appear to have replaced stone in all circumstances until well into the early modern period. Nor can it be proven that stone was any less effective than metal balls in its use against fortifications, ships, or men.

The importance of cast-iron balls for gunpowder weapons came not in its use or effectiveness in military engagements, but the fact that its higher density meant that a similar weight of projectile as stone could be fired from a much smaller gunpowder weapon.[98] That not many cast-iron balls appear in the records until the 1460s and 1470s would suggest that the technology for making cast iron was not properly devel-oped until then, and after that it is clear that gunpowder weapon manufacturers took full advantage of them.

Lead was the usual projectile for smaller gunpowder weapons, including most hand-held guns. It is obvious that the reason for this is that smaller shot could not easily be cut from stone by masons. As such, lead, a metal which has a low melting point, making it easy to melt and pour into a mould, was less costly and more suitable for these small guns. The melting point of lead was also not extraordinarily high so that, if needed, lead shot could be made to the required size on site, as evidenced by the exis-tence of moulds, ladles, and other lead-casting tools in Burgundian artillery trains.[99]

---

96 See Smith, "The Reconstruction and Firing Trials of a Replica of a 14th-Century Cannon," pp. 92–93. An account for making bolts in Saint-Omer in 1342 is published in Napoleon and Favé, III:77–78, n. 1 (volume by Favé alone). Recently Wilfried Tittmann, published an article on several large bolts found in Burg Eltz in Germany which he dated to 1331/2 and identified as bolts for use in gunpowder weapons. See Wilfried Tittmann, "Die Eltzer Büchsen pfeile von 1331/2," *Waffen- und Kostumkunde* 36 (1994), 117–28; 37 (1995), 53–64.
97 Contamine, *War in the Middle Ages*, p. 145.
98 A cast-iron ball weighs almost three times more than a stone ball of the same size.
99 See Garnier, pp. 126, 141, 154.

There are also a few references in the artillery registers to what today is called composite shot, lead cast around an iron *billet* or cube or lead cast around stone.[100]

Fusées were a further, although infrequent, projectile used in gunpowder weapons of the fifteenth century. Appearing in the sources as early as 1412, when 25 *fusées* were taken to the siege of Chinon by John the Fearless, they appear again on and off throughout the century. Most often these are said to be fired to throw "Greek Fire," at an enemy. This undoubtedly means that a *fusée* was a type of artillery "shell" which was filled with an incendiary mixture. Although it is not clearly stated what they were made of, they are indicated to be "cast," which by inference means that they were likely made in copper-alloy. No sizes are given, but they appear to be quite expensive in comparison to other projectiles of the same date. Greek Fire in its own right is a confusing weapon, with no standard formula known in western Europe for its composition. Nor does it seem to have mimicked the Greek Fire of Byzantium or the Middle East. One reference to *fusée* found in the Burgundian artillery registers and dated to 1431 lists the following ingredients for making the Greek Fire: "two *onces* of camphor, one *livre* of *eau de vie*, two *livres* of powder, two *livres* of saltpetre, four *livres* of sulphur, and an *ell* of fustian."[101] It should also be noted that during the siege of Neuss by Charles the Bold in 1474–1475 letters were "delivered" between the inhabitants of the town and certain relieving soldiers of Cologne by firing them from gunpowder weapons, possibly using empty *fusées*.[102]

The problems with transportation devices and mounts are that though there is an enormous amount of information from the written sources, many of the words used to describe these are difficult to translate, for instance *symosour* or *ortours*. Even if one might translate the words, it is not always possible to discover how all the parts of the devices fitted together, especially if the items are listed without further explanation.

Carts were used to transport gunpowder weapons. Sometimes a cart might carry a single gun or many smaller pieces; at times, for the very large gunpowder weapons, especially bombards, two carts might be required, one for the powder chamber and one for the barrel. Although the size of carts is not mentioned, sometimes the number of horses necessary to pull a particular cart with its weapon (or weapons) loaded is noted.[103] For example, in 1433, to transport one *gros bombard*, known as *Bourgoingne*, and its necessary equipment from Dijon the following carts and horses were required: 1 very large cart for the chamber drawn by 32 horses; 1 very large cart for the barrel with 34 horses; 2 carts for 12 stone balls drawn by 9 horses each; 1 cart for the "engine" and other munitions for the bombard with 8 horses; and 1 cart for a large barrel carrying the ropes and 3 casks of powder drawn by 8 horses, a total of 6 carts and 100 horses.[104] Another inventory in Charles the Bold's reign of a gunpowder artillery train to be taken to the siege of Neuss in 1474 lists all of the carts and horses necessary: 16 horses to pull two courtaux; 23 horses to pull 5 medium and 4 small serpentines; 24 horses to pull 6

---

[100] Garnier, pp. 126, 194.
[101] Garnier, p. 74.
[102] Vaughan, *Charles the Bold*, pp. 330–31.
[103] See Appendix 6.
[104] Garnier, pp. 99–100.

carts each carrying 5 barrels of gunpowder; 20 horses to pull 5 carts each carrying 40 stone balls for the courtaux; and 6 horses to pull 1½ carts to carry the lead projectiles for the 9 serpentines.[105]

In this last record, and unlike the reference in 1433 to a *gros bombard*, there is no mention of carts on which the courtaux and serpentines were being transported, although there are carts mentioned for the gunpowder and ammunition. This probably indicates that the guns were being moved on their own wheeled mounts.

Although most frequently gunpowder weapons and their munitions traveled by land, occasionally they could also be transported by water. In 1452 the Burgundians sent their "great *bombard* of Courtrai" by water to the siege of Schedelbeke,[106] and gunstones were delivered by barge from Bruges to the siege of Poeke.[107] Some idea of comparative costs between land and water transport comes from a 1431 reference when the bombard *Prusse* and its munitions were taken from Dijon to Saint-Jean-de-Losne, a journey of approximately 28 kilometers which cost 20 *francs* 4 *gros* and from there to Chalon on the River Saone, which cost 9 *francs* 4 *gros*, a distance of roughly 60 kilometers, making land transport some seven times more costly.[108]

It does not appear that bombards always had their own specific pre-made beds or mountings for firing, especially in the early period. They were laid on the ground or on timber, and a wooden framework built around them. Occasionally, and especially later, these large gunpowder weapons do seem to have a framework to which they were attached, although they also may have been built on site.

The barrels of breech-loading gunpowder weapons were usually mounted on a wooden bed with a space behind in which the removable powder chamber was inserted so that the neck of the chamber fitted into the rear of the barrel. A transverse or vertical wedge, secured if necessary in an iron frame, was then hammered into place to secure the chamber and barrel tightly together for firing. This wooden bed could then be mounted on a pair of wheels and, with the attachment of shafts and horse harnesses, the whole gunpowder weapon could be easily transported. This form of mount in all its variations is shown frequently in illustrations dating to the second half of the fifteenth century, indicating its ubiquity and popularity. Non-chambered pieces were also frequently mounted on a bed of wood in a similar fashion. When trunnions were developed is not known for certain, the first dated gunpowder artillery piece with them being the Jehan de Malines courtau in Basel (1474). As early as 1437, however, some wooden beds are said to "turn on pivots," presumably affording the same manoeuverability that trunnions would later give the barrel itself.[109]

Contemporary illustrations show a huge variety of mounting systems – mounts, beds, and carriages – ranging from the fanciful and fantastic to the simple and practical. It is clear that in the fifteenth century there were many means of mounting gunpowder

[105] Garnier, p. 179. See also Appendix 6.
[106] Archives Départementales du Nord, B.2012, f. 217v, as found in M.G.A. Vale, *War and Chivalry: Warfare and Aristocratic Culture in England, France and Burgundy at the End of the Middle Ages* (London, 1981), pp. 131–32.
[107] Archives Départementales du Nord, B.2012, f. 219r, as found in Vale, *War and Chivalry*, p. 132.
[108] Garnier, p. 53.
[109] Garnier, pp. 121–22.

weapons, but that, once again, there was no standardization. It is also clear that, unlike claims by some modern historians,[110] gunpowder weapons were, on the whole, easily moved and manoeuvered. They were transported effectively and relatively quickly to an engagement, set up, and moved around easily. There were of course some limits. Very heavy guns, such as bombards, were always less maneouverable and easy to transport. For example, in 1436 at Châtillon in Burgundy, the passage of heavy cannon en route to the siege of Calais badly damaged a bridge on the main road,[111] and in 1452, even though Philip the Good reinforced the bridges over which his gunpowder weapons traveled on their way to Flanders for the Ghent War, one of his large bombards, borrowed from the town of Mons, still fell into a ditch and took two days to be removed.[112] Still, it is important to note from the above incident that military leaders recognized the potential problems and sought ways to solve them; it must also be remembered that the moving of any army, with or without gunpowder weapons, at this time was difficult and slow. Monique Sommé, analyzing the transportation of gunpowder weapons to the siege of Calais in 1436 has calculated that three convoys which included bombards, as well as other gunpowder weapons, traveled from 11½ to 20 kilometers a day;[113] this was not significantly slower than the pace set by sixteenth-century Spanish armies not "hindered" by such large weapons which Geoffrey Parker estimated averaged between 19 and 22 kilometers per day.[114]

Bad weather could also be a serious factor. After heavy rain or snow, muddy fields and roads would have bogged down any wheeled vehicle, with heavier loads being more badly affected, though, of course, this problem was not one for late medieval gunpowder artillery trains alone. Weather played a vital part in Charles the Bold's final battle fought in the snow at Nancy on 5 January 1477. Finally, fast moving actions at a siege or in battle might influence the ability to manoeuvre or remove gunpowder weapons. This was the situation after the siege of Compiègne in 1430 and Calais in 1436 and, especially, the battles of Grandson and Murten in 1465 when the dukes of Burgundy lost large numbers of gunpowder weapons left behind by fleeing troops, or at the battle of Montlhéry on 16 July 1465 when some of Charles the Bold's serpentines were captured as their positions were overrun. But this was not because of the weight or "lack of manoeuverability" of these weapons.

The term *ribaudequin* has frequently been commented on by late medieval military historians, most of whom have interpreted it to be a type of gunpowder weapon.[115] However, from most of the evidence it appears that it was not the weapon itself but a type of "carriage" on which one or more gunpowder weapons were mounted.[116] For example, in a 1414 reference, four small copper-alloy cannon are indicated to be "for

110　See Vale, *War and Chivalry*, pp. 131–32, and Gaier, *L'industrie et le commerce des armes*, p. 95.
111　Vaughan, *Philip the Good*, p. 79.
112　Vale, *War and Chivalry*, p. 131.
113　Monique Sommé, "L'armée Bourguignonne au siège de Calais de 1436," in *Guerre et société en France, en Angleterre et en Bourgogne XIVe–XVe siècle*, ed. P. Contamine et al. (Lille, 1991), pp. 197–219.
114　Geoffrey Parker, *The Army of Flanders and the Spanish Road, 1567–1659* (Cambridge, 1972), pp. 96–98.
115　See, for example, Hall, pp. 44, 45, 47, 49, 54, etc.
116　A.V.B. Norman was one of the few who made the same conclusion see, "Notes on Some Early Representations of Guns and on Ribadekins" *Journal of the Arms and Armour Society* 8 (1975), pp. 234–7.

ribaudequins,"[117] while a 1446 inventory reports that "55 chariots of wood called *ribaudequins*" were "furnished with shafts, wheels, beds, pavises, and other things appertaining there."[118] Though these citations seem self-evident, however, confusion has arisen with other references, for example in 1474 when four chambers are said to be "for the two *ribaudequins*,"[119] implying that these ribaudequins were gunpowder weapons. Yet, this is likely to be notarial "short-hand" for chambers being for the guns mounted on the ribaudequins. Even taking into account these occasional contradictory references, all the evidence points to these being the gunpowder weapon mountings rather than the gunpowder weapons themselves.

What made ribaudequins different from other carts or carriages for gunpowder weapons? The assumption has always been that they carried more than one weapon, and this assumption is verified by the sources. However, there are numerous documentary references and contemporary illustrations which portray two or more gunpowder weapons sharing the same mount.

Illustrations of gunpowder artillery emplacements in siege and battle often show protective screens around them. From these and written sources it can be determined that there were three types of these defenses: mantlets, gabions, and pavises. Mantlets were wooden frames supporting wooden screens which could be raised when firing the gunpowder weapon or lowered to protect its operators while loading. Their size varied, of course, depending on the gunpowder weapon which they protected, but one early fifteenth-century source describes them as being quite large. Christine de Pisan, in her *Book of Deeds of Arms and Chivalry*, gives the following dimensions: "fashioned on an axle with support, each of them 10 or 12 feet wide, 30 feet long and a hand's-breadth thick."[120] These devices could be built on site, but records show that they were more often simply assembled there from prefabricated pieces.[121] That they were effective defenses can be seen in the comments of the chroniclers who discuss the death of Jacques de Lalaing at the siege of Poeke in 1453. While Adolph of Cleves and the bastard of Burgundy who stood under the mantlet protecting a bombard were not hurt, he stood under the less protective pavise (see below) and was killed.[122]

Gabions, large, circular wicker drums filled with earth, had been used as field defenses before the advent of gunpowder weapons. In protecting gunpowder artillery and gunners they were set up in groups to form a wall behind which guns, their operators, and other soldiers could stand. Though not mentioned in the documentary sources, they are quite numerous in contemporary illustrations. Pavises, large wooden shields, were used to protect gunners in the later Middle Ages as well as archers and crossbowmen. Smaller than mantlets and gabions, these could be held in place by soldiers, but more commonly were set up with an iron or wooden strut. Using each of

---

117 Garnier, p. 58.
118 Garnier, p. 112.
119 Garnier, p. 79.
120 Christine de Pisan, *The Book of Deeds of Arms and of Chivalry*, ed. Charity Cannon Willard, trans. Sumner Willard (State College, 1999), p. 119.
121 See, for example, Sommé, "L'armée Bourguignonne," p. 203, and, Robert D. Smith, "Good and Bold: A Late 15th-Century Artillery Train," *The Royal Armouries Yearbook* 6 (2001), 100–01.
122 See below p. 131.

these protective devices on its own or in combination, sometimes with other fencing and the natural terrain, defensive field fortifications could be built which would protect the valuable gunpowder weapons and personnel from attack.

There is so much information on so many areas of the history of gunpowder weapons that it is quite curious that on the actual operation of the guns themselves there is almost nothing. As noted, bombards are frequently mentioned as being loaded onto and off their carriages using an "*engin*," but there is nothing about how the very heavy stone ball, weighing as much as 400 to 800 *livres*, was loaded into the barrel of this weapon. Presumably smaller balls could be loaded by hand into their gunpowder weapons, whether at the front or the rear, but larger balls would definitely need some form of crane or lifting device, though these are not indicated in the sources nor are there any illustrations of the loading process for these large weapons.

Loading the gunpowder is another issue, and for this there is more information, although certainly not as much as one would wish. In gunpowder weapons made "all in one piece" the gunpowder would have to be loaded into the muzzle, as in later centuries. For this ladles would be used, and there are references to these in the artillery registers, "made of black iron for loading the powder."[123] Pictorial evidence from the 1470s shows pre-prepared, pre-measured bags of powder to make the loading procedure both safer and easier.[124]

Many types of gunpowder weapons during this time have removable chambers which would be filled with powder, and there is evidence to show that this powder would then be sealed with a wooden plug or tompion hammered into place. Extra chambers would be pre-loaded with powder and rotated during military action to maintain a constant, high rate of fire. Frequently, modern historians describe breech-loading guns as "primitive" and "dangerous" and that they were superseded by muzzle-loading, one-piece guns. This is blatantly false, as breech-loading guns with removable chambers were used until the mid-eighteenth century, especially on shipboard, proving that this technology was safe and reliable.[125]

On aiming there is no information in the written sources. However, extant gunpowder weapons frequently have rudimentary sights. These range from a simple pointed protrusion at the muzzle to more complex sighting systems. On one long gunpowder weapon (almost three meters in length) for instance there is a sight consisting of three raised squares pierced with a single slot which the operator would have lined up on the target.[126] There are many contemporary illustrations of gunpowder weapon mounts which show a variety of devices for raising and lowering the barrel. These range from a simple lug and cross-pin device to more complex screw or ratchet systems; some of these may be fanciful, as they occur in courtly engineering

---

[123] Garnier, p. 96.

[124] Walter Muschg and E.A. Gessler, ed. *Die schweizer Bilderchroniken des 15/16 Jahrhunderts* (Zurich, 1941), ill. 16.

[125] See Robert D. Smith and Kelly DeVries, "Breech-Loading Guns with Removable Chambers: A Long-Lived Military Technology," in *Gunpowder, Explosives, and the State: A Technological History*, ed. Brenda Buchanan (Aldershot, 2005) and Robert D. Smith, "Wrought-Iron Swivel Guns," in *The Archaeology of Ships of War*, ed. M. Bound (Oxford, 1995), pp. 104–13

[126] This gun is in La Neuville (catalogue 16).

treatises, but as they appear in such great numbers in these and other sources, and the technology for making them is so simple, it seems certain that some must actually have been constructed.[127]

The operator of a late medieval gunpowder weapon had to light the gunpowder in order to fire the weapon. Illustrations, such as the Walter de Milemete gun, appear to depict a match being used to ignite the gunpowder charge, but there is no written evidence to support this as the sole or even the main method of firing these early guns. Indeed, several methods may have been used, including a match, a lighted taper, or a hot iron, although the latter would certainly require a fierce fire close to the gun.

As with modern gunpowder weapons, fourteenth- and fifteenth-century guns were crewed by several men. However, how many were assigned to each gunpowder weapon cannot be determined from the written sources. Illustrations generally show two men operating each large gunpowder weapon – one loading the ball and the other firing it – with smaller guns and coulovrines being loaded and fired by a single man. A Burgundian gunpowder artillery train inventory dating from 1475 lists the following artillery personnel: 6 master bombardiers for 6 bombards; 6 other cannoneers or bombardiers for 6 bombardelles; 6 cannoneers for 6 mortars; 20 cannoneers for 9 courtaux and 15 large serpentines; 40 cannoneers for 90 serpentines; 50 coulovriniers for 200 hacquebusses; and 14 cannoneers' and bombardiers' aides.[128] Why there is not one gunner per gunpowder weapon is not explained in the source.

But the gun crew were only a few of the personnel attending a gunpowder artillery train. The same inventory of 1475 also mentions: 1 master mason and 6 assistant masons; 3 founders of lead shot; 1 master carpenter and 103 other carpenters, some on foot and some on horseback; 2 master farriers and 4 farriers; 1 master carter and 20 other carters; 400 sappers; 50 miners; 1 master joiner, 4 other joiners, and 2 assistants; 224 tent erectors; 45 armorers; 8 sailors; 4 millers; and 74 other servants and assistants, making a total of 953 men.[129] The masons and founders were obviously there to make projectiles for the gunpowder artillery, while the carpenters must have been responsible for building and maintaining all the woodwork, including the mounts, carriages, and mantlets. This artillery train also included over 5,000 horses and a great number of carts, perhaps as many as 1,000, which explains the presence of so many farriers and carters. Miners and sappers not only dug under the walls of a besieged fortification, if required, but would also have erected earthen field fortifications and repaired and maintained roads. All of these men needed housing, the responsibility of the joiners and tent erectors, while the millers may either have prepared flour or gunpowder. Armourers might have repaired the gunpowder weapons; the sailors helped when crossing rivers. Finally, the servants and assistants did the cooking, cleaning, and odd-jobs. Other gunpowder artillery trains included smiths and founders to maintain

---

[127] See the numerous examples in Bertrand Gille, *Engineers of the Renaissance* (Cambridge, 1966).

[128] The original of this inventory is in *Inventaire sommaire des archives départementales du Nord*, VIII:160–61. See also Smith, "Good and Bold," p. 100. The entire artillery train inventory is transcribed and translated in Appendix 2.

[129] Again, see the original inventory in *Inventaire sommaire des archives départementales du Nord*, VIII:160–61; Smith, "Good and Bold," p. 100; and Appendix 2.

and repair damaged gunpowder weapons, using pre-fashioned rings and bars and portable forges taken with them.

Early in the history of gunpowder weapons the title "master of artillery" appears. The men who first held this title seem simply to have been responsible for every aspect of gunpowder weapons, from their manufacture to their use, their loading and firing. However, as the proliferation and use of gunpowder weapons increased late in the fourteenth and throughout the first half of the fifteenth century, masters of artillery begin to take on more of an administrative role. Leaving the battlefield behind, these officials became responsible for all contracts – both for construction and/or purchase – of gunpowder weapons, for the purchase of powder, ammunition, and other necessities, for staffing, and for the storage of the weapons, or perhaps more accurately for knowing what gunpowder weapons were in the stores, so that they could be gathered quickly and conveniently should the duke need them for his campaigns. By the end of the reign of the Burgundian dukes, there seem to have been several masters of artillery, all with their administrative staff, which included not only gunners and other personnel, as noted above, but notaries as well.

2

The Military Careers of the Dukes of Burgundy

PHILIP THE BOLD

Gunpowder artillery was first found in Burgundy before the duchy's acquisition by the Valois dukes, in the transitional years between the death of Philip de Rouvres, who died without an heir in 1361, and Philip the Bold's acquisition of the duchy two years later when, amid a record of non-gunpowder weapons' purchases, "deux quanons à gitter garroz" (two cannon to fire bolts) were purchased at Troyes by Jaquemard the Locksmith ("le serrurier") for three florins. However, whether it was Philippe de Rouvres or the transitional governors who were responsible for these guns, cannot be determined from the evidence.[1]

This is not particularly early in the early history of European gunpowder weapons, compared to the much earlier use of these weapons in France, England, Italy, and the Low Countries. In France, by the middle of the fourteenth century, not only had the king a supply of gunpowder weapons stored in his royal fortifications, but nearly every large town and noble domain had its own supply. These included, among others, the town of Rouen which acquired gunpowder weapons in 1338, Lille in 1339–40, Saint-Omer in 1342, Bioule Castle in 1347, Paris in 1351, Tours in 1358–59, Ponthieu in 1368–69, Arras in 1369, and Harfleur in 1369.[2] Lille also had a "master of cannon" in 1341.[3] French guns were used at the French attack of Southampton in

---

1 Joseph Garnier, *L'artillerie des ducs de Bourgogne d'après les documents conserves aux archives de la Côte d'Or* (Paris, 1895), pp. 6–7.
2 For Rouen, see Victor Gay, *Glossaire archéologique du moyen âge et de la renaissance* (Paris, 1887), I:76; for Lille, see A. Fromont and A. de Meunynck, *Histoire de canonniers de Lille*, 2 vols. (Lille, 1892), 28; for Saint-Omer, see J.R. Partington, *A History of Greek Fire and Gunpowder* (Cambridge, 1960), p. 100; for Bioule, see "Règlement pour la défense du château de Bioule, 18 mars 1347," *Bulletin archéologique* IV (1846–47), pp. 490–95; for Paris, see Philippe Contamine, *Guerre, état et société à la fin du moyen âge: Études sur les armées des rois de France, 1337–1494* (Paris, 1972), p. 123 n.185; for Tours, see J. Delaville le Roulx, ed., *Registres des comptes municipaux de la ville de Tours* (Tours, 1878), I:55; for Ponthieu, see Philippe Contamine, *War in the Middle Ages*, trans. Michael Jones (London, 1984), p. 146; for Arras, see R. Coltman Clephan, "The Ordnance of the Fourteenth and Fifteenth Centuries," *Archaeological Journal* 68 (1911), p. 63; and for Harfleur, see A. Merlin-Chazelas, ed., *Documents relatifs au clos des galées de Rouen*, Collection de documents inédits sur l'histoire de France, Section de philologie et d'histoire jusqu'a 1610 (Paris, 1977), I:205.
3 Contamine, *War in the Middle Ages*, p. 139.

1338; at Poitiers in 1369, when the fortress was defended by local militias using gunpowder and non-gunpowder artillery; and at the battle of La Rochelle in 1372, when gunpowder weapons were used on board Spanish ships hired by the French.[4] Finally, anti-gunpowder defensive measures began appearing in France early in the fourteenth century, gunports being built in the town wall of Mont-Saint-Michel and at the castles of Blanquefort and Saint-Malo by the time that the duchy of Burgundy acquired its first guns.[5]

In the southern Low Countries, lands which would come under the control of the Valois dukes of Burgundy over the next century, there were even more early and mid-fourteenth-century gunpowder weapons than in France. They were found in arsenals in Bruges in 1346 and 1362, in Mons in 1349, in Binche in 1362–64, and in Valenciennes in 1363.[6] A "master of cannon" is noted at Mechelen in 1365.[7] And guns were used by local Low Countries militias in conjunction with English gunpowder artillery at the sieges of Quesnoy, Mortagne, Saint-Amand, Marchiennes, and Tournai in 1340.[8]

So the acquisition of gunpowder weapons only two years before Philip the Bold obtained the duchy seems to indicate either no interest or a late interest in this new technology by Philippe de Rouvres, the previous Burgundian leader. More importantly, and more historically certain, it indicates that there were few gunpowder weapons in the Burgundian arsenal at the start of Philip's reign. This is important primarily because it shows the innovative military nature of this first Valois duke of Burgundy compared to his predecessor. Indeed, perhaps no ruler of the time was more interested in acquiring gunpowder weapons than Philip.

The Burgundian records of the time though sparse, do show that in the first few years of his Burgundian rulership Philip begun to build an impressive gunpowder

---

4   On the attack on Southampton see Kelly DeVries, "A 1445 Reference to Shipboard Artillery," *Technology and Culture* XXXI (1990), pp. 819–20 and L. Lacabane, "De la poudre à canon et de son introduction en France," *Bibliothèque de l'école de chartes* 2nd ser., I (1844), pp. 36–38. On the defense of Poitiers see Jean Froissart, *Chroniques*, ed. S. Luce (Paris, 1869–1975), VII:160–61. And on the battle of La Rochelle see Froissart, *Chroniques*, VIII: 36–43.

5   On the gunports at Mont-Saint-Michel see Contamine, *War in the Middle Ages*, p. 202. On those at Saint-Malo see Michael Jones, "The Defence of Medieval Brittany: A Survey of the Establishment of Fortified Towns, Castles and Frontiers from the Gallo-Roman Period to the End of the Middle Ages," *Archaeological Journal* 138 (1981), p. 174. And on gunports at Blanquefort Castle see M.G.A. Vale, "Seigneurial Fortification and Private War in Late Medieval Gascony," in M. Jones, ed., *Gentry and Lesser Nobility in Late Medieval Europe* (Gloucester, 1986), p. 141. See also Kelly DeVries, "The Impact of Gunpowder Weaponry on Siege Warfare in the Hundred Years War," in I.A. Corfis and M. Wolfe, eds., *Medieval City Under Siege* (Woodbridge, 1995), p. 234.

6   On Bruges, see Clephan, "The Ordnance," pp. 61, 65; on Mons, see Gonzalès Decamps, *L'artillerie montoise, ses origines* (Mons, 1906), pp. 2–3, 8–9; on Binche, see C. Roland, "L'artillerie de la ville de Binche, 1362–1420," *Bulletin de la société royale paléontologique et archéologique de l'arrondissement judiciaire de Charleroi* 23 (1954), pp. 30–32; on Valenciennes, see Gay, I:171. On fourteenth-century Low Countries gunpowder artillery in general, see Bernhard Rathgen, "Feuer- und fernwaffen des 14. jahrunderts in Flandern," *Zeitschrift für historisches Waffenkunde* 7 (1915–17), pp. 275–306 and Paul Henrard, *Histoire de l'artillerie en Belgique* (Brussels, 1865).

7   Clephan, "The Ordnance," p. 62.

8   On these actions see Froissart, *Chroniques*, II:14, 64, IV:166, 194–95, V:11, VIII:244, XI:61, 248–49, XII:13, 238, XIII:139.

weaponry arsenal.[9] These guns were used in 1368 when Philip besieged the castle of Rochefort-sur-le-Doubs, held by Louis de Chalon, a man whom Philip had, rightly, connected with mercenary routiers' attacks on his lands. According to an inventory made by Philip's treasurer, Thévenin Vurry, on this expedition the duke took "deux canons et cinq livres et demie de poudre, quatorze garroz et douze plombées d'estain" (two cannon and five and a half pounds of powder, forty bolts and 12 *plombées* of "tin"). Evidently these cannon could fire both bolts and balls.[10] Not much is known about the siege and Philip's use of cannon in it, other than it seems that he captured the castle and thereby stopped its use as a base for raids into his territory.

The numbers of Philip the Bold's gunpowder weapons increased drastically both in real and potential terms on 19 June 1369 when, after lengthy negotiations, he married Margaret of Flanders, the heir of her father, Louis of Male, count of Flanders.[11] In real terms due to the gift of the towns and dependencies of Lille, Douai, and Orchies from the French king, Charles V (Philip's brother), these, once southern Low Countries towns, had become French after numerous failed Flemish rebellions.[12] From later records it is clear that Douai and Orchies had a fledgling, locally controlled gunpowder weaponry arsenal, although how many and what types of guns these were cannot be ascertained.[13] More easily determined is the gunpowder weaponry of Lille where the records of gunpowder weapons of the Confrérie de Sainte-Barbe (Confraternity of Saint-Barbara), which has existed since the Middle Ages, are more complete and clearer. These show, not only the early dates of Lille's earliest gunpowder weapons mentioned above, but also the town's continuous increase in gunpowder weapons from the middle of the fourteenth century.[14] In 1363, six years before Philip's marriage, the town's arsenal contained "seven cannons with many quarrels to be used by them, plus a *thonnel* of saltpeter," as well as numerous non-gunpowder artillery pieces.[15] Gunpowder was being manufactured in the town, and a store of it had been established in a small tower attached to the twelfth-century chapel named, somewhat ironically, the Notre-Dame des Ardents. It is clear, too, that gunners had also been recruited and trained who as previously mentioned were led by a master of cannon whose annual salary was six *livres*.[16]

In potential terms, Philip the Bold was to acquire the Flemish gunpowder weaponry holdings when his wife inherited the county on her father's death, an event which was ensured by the time of the marriage, although it did not occur effectively until 1384.

---

9   Garnier, p. 6.
10   Garnier, p. 7. For this Philip paid handsomely, 4 *livres* and 10 *sols*, to Parrenin du Pont (perhaps making him the earliest Du Pont to be in the gunpowder business).
11   On the marriage and its negotiations see Richard Vaughan, *Philip the Bold: The Formation of the Burgundian State* (London, 1962), pp. 4–7.
12   For these towns Philip the Bold was to pay the French king a tribute of 10,000 *livres* annually.
13   See Henrard.
14   An analysis of these records can be found in A. de la Fons-Meliococq, *De l'artillerie de la ville de Lille aux XIVe, XVe et XVIe siècles* (Lille, 1854); M. Scrive-Bertin, "Les canonniers Lillois avant 1483," *Bulletin de la commission historique du departement du Nord* 19 (1890), 119–91; and A. Fromont and A. de Meunynck, *Histoire de canonniers de Lille*, vol. 1 (Lille, 1892).
15   Fromont and Meunynck, p. 30.
16   Fromont and Meunynck, pp. 30–32. See also Scrive-Bertin, pp. 125–26.

The gunpowder weaponry arsenal of the county of Flanders may have been the richest in all Europe in 1369, and was, perhaps, even more so in 1384.[17] But the possession of the county of Flanders did not come without problems. Perhaps the reason why no region possessed more gunpowder weapons than Flanders is that no region in the fourteenth century was more rebellious than this relatively small, very urban and well populated county.[18]

Philip had direct experience of this when, in 1379, ten years after his marriage, the most prosperous Flemish town, Ghent, led a rebellion against its aging count, Louis of Male, and his son-in-law heir. Both sides used gunpowder weapons during this rebellion, which lasted into Philip's reign as count, not ending until 1385. Perhaps in anticipation of a rebellion such as this, by the time this "Ghent War" began, Philip had already increased his gunpowder weaponry supply many times. A Burgundian inventory from 1376–77 made by Simon Lambert provides the costs of manufacture and materials of a forged "cannon of iron" weighing around sixty *livres*. The total cost of the weapon was 38 fr. 10½ gros, including the expense to different suppliers for the iron, the charcoal for the forge, the labor for forging the weapon, the gunpowder to fire it, the wood for its carriage, the carpentry to build the carriage, and rent on a cart and two horses to take the weapon, its accessories, and "two round stones weighing 120 *livres*" from Chalon to Dijon. Also included in the same inventory, with similar manufacturing details, are five other iron cannon, weighing 130 *livres*, 100 *livres*, 90 *livres*, 30 *livres*, and 20 *livres* respectively.[19] Further evidence suggests that, in Philip the Bold's Burgundian realm, Chalon was not unique in its ability to organize and manufacture gunpowder weapons.[20] Thus, by the 1370s, Philip the Bold had at his disposal several different sized gunpowder weapons. At the same time, he was organizing and funding the production of gunpowder weapons and the materiel needed for their operation, including powder and projectiles.

In 1377, in an attempt to take advantage of the death of his long-reigning English royal enemy, Edward III, King Charles V decided to attack the town of Calais and its English-held environs. He asked Philip the Bold for military assistance, especially for his gunpowder artillery train.[21] In response, Philip not only supplied those gunpowder weapons that he had in stores throughout his duchy, including the guns from Chalon, mentioned above, but he also brought into his employ two "fondeurs de canon reputes," Jacques and Rolant Mayorque, commissioning them to make gunpowder

---

[17] See Kelly DeVries, "Gunpowder Weaponry and the Rise of the Early Modern State," *War in History* 5 (1998), 133–35.

[18] For a history of this see Henri Pirenne, *Histoire de Belgique*, vol. 2: *Du commencement du XIVe siècle à la mort de Charles le Téméraire* (Brussels, 1903), and David Nicholas, *Medieval Flanders* (London, 1992). For an analysis of these rebellions see Kelly DeVries, "The Rebellions of Southern Low Countries' Towns during the Fourteenth and Fifteenth Centuries" (forthcoming).

[19] Garnier, pp. 8–11. Two different types or iron are indicated in this inventory, "fer au pois" and "taulles de fer." These may indicate that some raw iron was delivered in balls and some in bars by the ironmonger, whose name, Jehan Pourterat, a bourgeois of Chalon, is also indicated in the inventory.

[20] See Claude Gaier, *L'industrie et le commerce des armes dans les anciennes principautés Belges du XIIIme à la fin du XVe siècle* (Paris, 1963), p. 155, 287, for other examples.

[21] Vaughan, *Philip the Bold*, pp. 9–10; Garnier, pp. 11–12; and John Bell Henneman, *Olivier de Clisson and Political Society under Charles V and Charles VI* (Philadelphia, 1996), p. 81.

and to build seven new cannon for use in this campaign. One of these was a very large weapon, firing a stone cannonball of 450 *livres*, which took nine people ninety days to complete, although it eventually failed to work.[22]

This campaign was relatively short, at least in comparison to others of the Hundred Years War, and it was not successful, if Charles V's purpose was the reconquest of Calais. But the combined French and Burgundian armies were successful in conquering a number of English castles near Calais. At two of these Philip the Bold's gunpowder weapons were especially influential in the their capture. At the siege of Ardres, according to Jean Froissart, the inhabitants of the castle negotiated a surrender in the face of the duke's gunpowder weapons.[23] While at the siege of Odruik Castle a short time later, Philip's guns actually breached the walls, thereby causing its defeat. Again, Froissart narrates the scene:

> The castle of Odruik was situated on a motte, surrounded by a ditch filled with very large spikes, which was not easy to defeat . . .Then the duke of Burgundy set up his cannons and fired maybe five or six quarrels in order to provoke a surrender. These quarrels were such that, because of the power of the discharge, they penetrated the walls. When those in the castle saw the strength of the artillery which the duke had, they doubted themselves more than ever before . . . and the duke fired from his cannons two hundred quarrels in number, which penetrated the walls . . . [and those defending Odruik] surrendered the fortress, to save their lives, and they were led by the duke of Burgundy all the way to Calais.[24]

By the end of 1377, then Philip the Bold was used to fighting with gunpowder weapons, although it seems from the sources of the Calais campaign that neither his nor the French king's forces faced gunpowder weaponry in opposition; there were guns in Calais at the time,[25] but apparently not in the surrounding fortifications. In facing the Ghentenaars, led by Philip van Artevelde, and their allies in the "Ghent War," however, this would not be the case. The rebellious Flemings had numerous guns and were not afraid to use them. Indeed, the first military strike of this war,[26] on 7 October 1379, against the French and French-allied garrison in the Flemish town of

---

22   Garnier, pp. 12–14, and Gaier, *L'industrie et le commerce des armes*, p. 288. Interestingly, the testing of this flawed weapon was halted by another "master of cannon," Aymery de Traispièce, out of concern for those firing it. After this incident, the Mayorques continued in Philip's favor, and at least Jacques served him in numerous other engagements during the Ghent War.

23   Froissart, VIII:244–47. See also Garnier, pp. 12–13.

24   Froissart VIII:249. Garnier (p. 12) calls this castle Arduic, while the contemporary notary, Amiot Arnaut, writes the name as Audruit (Garnier, pp. 12–13). None of the spellings of this castle's names–Odruik, Oudruich, Arduic, or Audruit–can currently be found, indicating that this castle and its place-name has ceased to exist.

25   See T.F. Tout, "Firearms in England in the Fourteenth Century," *English Historical Review* 26 (1911), 666–702; rpt *Firearms in England in the Fourteenth Century* (London, 1968).

26   The initial blow of the Ghentenaars against the count of Flanders came on 5 September 1379 when they murdered his bailiff to the town, Rogier van Outrive. Following this, a popular government was immediately installed in the town, and legates were sent to the other regions of the county announcing the rebellion of Ghent and asking others to join the independence movement. See Nicholas, *Medieval Flanders*, p. 228, and Maurice Vandermaesen and Marc Ryckaert, "De Gentse opstand (1379–1385)," in *De Witte Kaproenen: De Gentse opstand (1379–1385) en de geschiedenis van de Brugse Leie*, ed. M. Vandermaesen, M. Ryckaerts, and M. Coornaert (Ghent, 1979), pp. 12–14.

Oudenaarde, was a siege using gunpowder weapons in what may have been one of the earliest sustained gunpowder artillery bombardments in Europe. Froissart claims that the Ghentenaars "fired and fired their cannons against those in the town." So intense was this bombardment, with many of the projectiles passing over the walls, that the inhabitants of Oudenaarde were forced to cover their houses with dirt to protect their roofs from fire.[27]

Count Louis of Male was not in Oudenaarde at the time, but instead had sought refuge in the nearby town of Dendermonde which was also attacked, possibly with gunpowder weapons, although their use there is not recorded as it is at Oudenaarde. Both of these engagements forced Louis to seek respite and some succor. He sued Philip van Artevelde for peace, asking his son-in-law, Philip the Bold, to be the mediator in this dispute with the Flemings.[28] This was a sly choice on the count of Flanders' part, for he knew that once the duke of Burgundy had been brought into the engagement, with his obvious interest in preserving baronial authority over the rebellious Flemish townspeople, he would be forced to intercede militarily.

A peace treaty, extremely favorable to the Ghentenaars, was signed on 1 December 1379, but Louis clearly never meant to abide by its provisions, although it did buy him some time to regroup and build his forces. In the following summer the count went to war against the rebels, recapturing Ypres and occupying Courtrai, both important rebel towns. Furthermore, the more important, but until then non-aligned town of Bruges, decided to side with the count against their economic and, often, political adversary, Ghent. This allowed Louis, in autumn 1380, to besiege Ghent itself. Frequent gunpowder artillery duels followed, which Froissart – the best authority for the Ghent War because of his interest in his native southern Low Countries – attests "killed and wounded many." Ultimately, however, Louis of Male did not prove to have sufficient forces to effectively besiege the town, the second largest in northern Europe, and with his supplies dwindling and winter approaching, he was forced to raise the siege and again agree to peace.[29]

Of course, this peace did not hold for very long either. Throughout 1381 and into 1382 the two sides fought several fruitless engagements, with the rebels directing their military activity from Ghent against Bruges, and the comital forces responding from Bruges against Ghent.[30] It was not until 3 May 1382 that a more significant battle was fought, at Bevershoutsveld, outside of the town of Bruges.[31] Ghent, the contemporary

---

27 Froissart, IX:196–201. See also Vaughan, *Philip the Bold*, p. 21; Vandermaesen and Ryckaert, pp. 14–15; and David Nicholas, *The Van Arteveldes of Ghent: The Varieties of Vendetta and the Hero in History* (Ithaca, 1988), p. 141

28 Vaughan, *Philip the Bold*, pp. 21–22; Vandermaesen and Ryckaert, p. 15; Pirenne, pp. 191–92; Nicholas, *Medieval Flanders*, p. 228; and Edouard Perroy, *The Hundred Years War*, trans. W.B. Wells (London, 1951), pp. 188–89.

29 Froissart, X:60–63; Vaughan, *Philip the Bold*, pp. 22–23; Vandermaesen and Ryckaert, p. 15; and Pirenne, pp. 192–93.

30 Vaughan, *Philip the Bold*, p. 23. Froissart (X:63–218) concerns himself much with the travels made and skirmishes fought by the two sides. But in the final reckoning of the greater Ghent War these engagements meant very little.

31 The following is a synopsis of Kelly DeVries, "The Forgotten Battle of Bevershoutsveld, May 3, 1382: Technological Innovation and Military Significance," in *Armies, Chivalry and Warfare: Harlaxton Medieval Studies, VII*, ed. Mathew Strickland (Stamford, 1998), pp. 280–94.

chroniclers record, was suffering from severe hunger at the beginning of 1382.[32] The Flemish harvests had been destroyed by the constant warfare of the preceding three years, and what little food was available in 1382 had gone to Bruges which had the support of Count Louis of Male.[33] Therefore, it was expedient that the Ghentenaars attack and defeat Louis and Bruges to try and free their town from hunger. At least that is the rationale given by the southern Low Countries chroniclers.[34]

The Ghentenaar force was not large; contemporary chroniclers estimate that their numbers were only between four and eight thousand men.[35] However, a large number of gunpowder artillery pieces accompanied the force, with Jean Froissart recording the presence of two hundred carts full of this type of weaponry.[36] These guns seem to have been brought by the Ghentenaars in anticipation of a siege of Bruges. The Brugeois and their army were not prepared for battle. Why this was so can only be guessed at. However, there is some indication that the Brugeois, together with whatever soldiers were there to protect the count and the town, were celebrating the Holy Blood Procession, a most important and still practiced local holiday.[37] Those who went to fight, almost all of the chroniclers declare, were drunk, because, in the words of Oliver van Dixmude, "they had been drinking all day."[38] On the other side, the Ghentenaars were in high spirits and were well organized.[39]

In this way the two armies prepared for battle: the Ghentenaars enthusiastic, organized, and prepared to fight and die for their town; the Brugeois disorganized; lacking both leadership and morale and undoubtedly inebriated and fatigued by the celebrations of the day. Still, the Brugeois went out of the town to fight with the Ghentenaars and in the end were defeated. But why did they have to fight a battle at all when it is likely that the Ghentenaars, extremely low on supplies, could not have won a lengthy siege against their town, especially as such a siege would certainly have brought a relief force from the French king in support of his faithful lord? The Ghentenaars had brought their gunpowder weapons with them in order to shorten the length of any siege which they might have to fight, and without question this is the reason for their presence among their forces. Obviously from his attack of Oudenaarde in 1379 it can

32 See Froissart, X:1–3; *Chronicon comitum Flandriae*, in *Corpus chronicorum Flandriae*, i, ed. J.J. de Smet (Brussels, 1837), p. 240; *Rijmkroniek van Vlaenderen*, in *Corpus chronicorum Flandriae*, iv, ed. J.J. de Smet (Brussels, 1865), p. 869; and Oliver van Dixmude, *Merkwaerdige gebeurtenissen vooral in Vlaenderen en Brabant van 1377 tot 1443*, ed. J.J. Lambin (Ypres, 1835), p. 10.
33 Froissart, X:5–8.
34 Against this reason for the attack are the contemporary French chronicles: *Chronique des quatre premiers Valois (1327–1393)*, ed. S. Luce (Paris, 1862), p. 302; *Chronique du religieux de Saint-Denis*, ed. L. Bellaguet (Paris, 1839), I:351; and Jean Juvenal des Ursins, *Histoire de Charles VI*, ed. M. Michaud, in *Nouvelle collection des memoires pour servir à l'histoire de France depuis de xiiie siècle jusqu'à la fin du xviiie siècle*, vol. 2 (Lyons, 1851), p. 351.
35 For estimations of the Ghentenaar numbers at Beverhoutsveld see Froissart, X:22; Oliver van Dixmude, p. 10; and *Chronique de Flandre*, in *Istore et croniques de Flandres*, ed. Kervyn de Lettenhove (Brussels, 1879–80), II:246.
36 Froissart, X:22.
37 *Chronicon comitum Flandriae*, p. 248.
38 Oliver van Dixmude, p. 11: ". . . want zy al den dach ghedronken hadden." See also *Chronicon comitum Flandriae*, p. 240, and *Chronique de Flandre*, II:247.
39 Froissart, X:26–27.

be surmised that Philip van Artevelde believed in using these weapons for sieges, and he would employ his guns again against Oudenaarde following his victory at Bevershoutsveld.[40] But van Artevelde did not use his guns against the walls of Bruges, the Brugeois left them to do battle on the plain outside the town. Instead, he used them in another, much less conventional way.

As the Brugeois exited from their town, they faced a Ghentenaar army arrayed in well ordered lines. Seeing this array may have caused some of the Brugeois to lose face and retreat, but the majority of troops seems to have remained to fight. This group, still larger than the Ghentenaar army, moved forward. It is here that Philip van Artevelde decided to use tactics different from those common in these types of conflicts. Instead of waiting to receive the Brugeois attack, he fired his guns into their oncoming force. Then, he wheeled his troops on an axis, to where the sun shone in their opponents' eyes, and attacked the approaching Brugeois troops. Jean Froissart describes this action:

> The Ghentenaars placed themselves on a hill and they gathered themselves all together. Then they fired more than three hundred cannon all at the same time. And then they turned around on a hub and ordered themselves, placing the Brugeois with the sun in their eyes which distressed them greatly. Then they attacked them crying "Ghent!" At the moment that the Brugeois heard the voices of the Ghentenaars and the firing of the cannon and saw that they were about to be brutally attacked, they, like cowards and villains, opened their lines and allowed the Ghentenaars to enter among them without putting up any defense. And they flung down their weapons and fled.[41]

The *Chronique de Flandre* confirms what Froissart writes:

> The Ghentenaars moved themselves and their artillery forward. Which artillery fired a blast with such a furor that it seemed to bring the [Brugeois] line directly to a halt.[42]

The Brugeois fled in rout, rushing for the safety of their town. The Ghentenaars pursued them, showing little mercy,[43] and were able to enter the town where their slaughter of the count's adherents continued.[44] However, the chief prize, Louis of Male, was not found among the dead or captured, as he had successfully escaped from his enemies.[45]

But without the Flemish count's capture, there was to be no end to the Ghentenaar rebellion, even though they now had Bruges and soon would have Ypres and Courtrai back in their control. They now began a siege of Oudenaarde using large numbers of gunpowder weapons.[46] Among "de engiens, de canons, de bombardes, de truies et de

---

[40] Froissart, X:57–62. See also DeVries, "The Impact of Gunpowder Weaponry," p. 229.

[41] Froissart, X:31–32.

[42] *Chronique de Flandre*, II:247.

[43] Froissart, X:31–32; Jean Juvenal des Ursins, p. 351; and *Chronique du religieux de Saint-Denis*, I:168.

[44] Froissart, X:33–34; *Chronique de Flandre*, II:247; *Rijmkroniek van Vlaenderen*, pp. 870–71; and *Chronicon comitum Flandriae*, p. 240.

[45] There are several versions of Louis' escape from Bruges. For a recounting of these see DeVries, "The Forgotten Battle of Bevershoutsveld."

[46] Froissart, X:247–49.

moutons" which the Ghentenaars used against the walls of Oudenaarde was one which Jean Froissart describes as:

> a marvelous great bombard . . . which shot quarrels of marvelous size, large and heavy, and when this bombard fired, which one could hear from five leagues away and during the night from ten leagues, it made such a great noise with the discharge that it seemed that all the devils of hell were making the sound.[47]

Still, despite such artillery, the garrison and townspeople of Oudenaarde refused to surrender, hoping that they would be rescued.

Louis of Male traveled quickly to Paris where he petitioned his son-in-law, Philip the Bold, and Philip's nephew, the recently crowned Charles VI – Charles V had died in 1380 – for aid against the rebellion. The French king could hardly refuse such a petition, especially after Philip the Bold convinced his nephew that to allow Flanders to rebel without punishment would fuel the already hot fires of independence in his own towns. The king was further convinced when he received word that the Flemish rebels had violated French territory and attacked several small villages around the French-allied town of Tournai.[48]

Charles VI and Philip the Bold gathered their armies and moved north towards the southern Low Countries. The Flemings put up some relatively small and futile resistance at Commines using "*bonbardes portatives*" (portable gunpowder weapons) which fired large quarrels against the Franco-Burgundian army as they crossed the River Lys;[49] but Ypres surrendered without a fight.[50] Before the Franco-Burgundians could move on to Bruges, however, scouts reported that a Flemish force had amassed between Ypres and Bruges near West Rosebeke. Philip van Artevelde, perhaps confident due to his recent, relatively simple victory over the Brugeois, believed it was to his advantage to meet his enemy in open battle. He selected an advantageous terrain, brought his gunpowder weapons, and awaited the arrival of the Franco-Burgundian forces.[51] Philip the Bold must also have brought some guns, as Jacques Mayorque was present at Rosebeke,[52] but the chroniclers only mention the Ghentenaar gunpowder weapons and not those of the Franco-Burgundians. The battle of Rosebeke was fought on 26 November 1382, but this engagement would not be a victory for the rebels.

---

[47] Froissart, X:248. See also Jean Juvenal des Ursins, pp. 351–53; *Chronique du religieux de Saint-Denis*, I:170–72, 180–82, 186–88; and *Chronographia regum Francorum*, ed. H. Moranville (Paris, 1891–97), III:40.

[48] On the petitions of Louis to Philip the Bold and Charles VI see Vaughan, *Philip the Bold*, p. 16; Pirenne, p. 197; Françoise Autrand, *Charles VI: La folie du roi* (Paris, 1986); p. 124; and J.J.N. Palmer, *England, France and Christendom, 1377–99* (Chapel Hill, 1972), p. 20.

[49] The quote comes from Froissart, XI:13–14. See also *Chronique du religieux de Saint-Denis*, I:192–96; Jean Juvenal des Ursins, pp. 353–54; *Chronographia regum Francorum*, III:41–42; *Chronique des quatre premiers Valois*, pp. 305–06; *Chronique du bon duc Loys de Bourbon*, ed. A.-M. Chazaud (Paris, 1876), pp. 167–69; *Chronique des règnes de Jean II et de Charles V*, ed. R. Delachenal (Paris, 1910–20), IV:24–26; and Autrand, *Charles VI*, pp. 126–28.

[50] *Chronique des règnes de Jean II et de Charles V*, IV:27–30; Jean Juvenal des Ursins, p. 354; *Chronique du religieux de Saint-Denis*, I:200–02; *Chronique du bon duc Loys*, pp. 169–70; *Chronographia regum Francorum*, III:41–42; *Chronique de Flandre*, II:214; and Autrand, *Charles VI*, pp. 129–30.

[51] Autrand, *Charles VI*, p. 131.

[52] Garnier, p. 14.

At Rosebeke Philip van Artevelde was not able to repeat his successful gunpowder weapon tactics. Although he had chosen the battlefield and had ordered his lines "very subtly and in good order," according to the *Chronique de Flandre*, with one line interspersed with "canons et engiens,"[53] it seems that he was unable to discharge these in the face of the enemy's attack, as he had at Bevershoutsveld. Perhaps this was because the Franco-Burgundian soldiers came onto the rebel lines too quickly, in better order and without the disadvantage of being drunk. This more ordered advance is certainly attested to in numerous narrative sources.[54] In such an engagement, certainly the seemingly more experienced, better organized and trained, and better armed and armored Franco-Burgundian soldiers would and did have the upper hand. Jean Froissart describes the meeting of these two armies:

> The [Franco-Burgundian] men-at-arms knocked down the Flemings with all their power, and some had very sharp battle-axes which burst helmets and split open heads, and some had iron maces which gave such great blows that they knocked everything to the ground . . .The clattering on the helmets, on the swords and axes, on maces and on armor and weapons was so great and so loud that nothing could be heard above the noise. And it is said that if all the armorers of Paris and of Brussels were gathered together working at their trade, they would not have made such a great noise as the combatants made on these helmets . . . There was a mountain and a mass of dead Flemings, very large and very high.[55]

But there is another possible explanation as to why the Ghentenaar rebels did not discharge their gunpowder weapons at Rosebeke as they had at Bevershoutsveld. Some chroniclers, Froissart included, claim that there was a dense fog which hung over the battlefield on the morning of 26 November, so dense, in fact, that visibility was severely limited. The Franco-Burgundians advanced on the Flemings under cover of this fog, which did not lift until just before the two armies encountered each other. The *Chronique du religieux de Saint-Denis* reports:

> With such a density of clouds the sky was covered for six days before [the battle], so that the hostile army directly in front of them was scarcely to be seen, and, what is more, with the air continually dark with an almost tangible fog, it was such that those who followed with difficulty held to the paths of those preceding them, and those who went before with difficulty were able to discern their location by casting stones in front of them.[56]

Froissart attributes this to the French unfurling of the sacred *Oriflamme*, a banner which was normally kept in the Basilica of Saint-Denis and only taken out in most dire circumstances. Most historians, modern and contemporary, including Froissart,

53 *Chronique de Flandre*, II:214, 251.
54 Jean Juvenal des Ursins, p. 355; *Chronique du religieux de Saint-Denis*, I:218; *Chronicon comitum Flandriae*, p. 242; *Chronique de Flandre*, II:215; *Chronique du bon duc Loys*, pp. 170–73; and *Chronique des quatre premiers Valois*, p. 306.
55 Froissart (Kervyn de Lettenhove, ed.), X:170–2.
56 *Chronique du religieux de Saint-Denis*, I:214. See also *Chronique du religieux de Saint-Denis*, I:175–76, 214; Jean Juvenal des Ursins, p. 352; Olivier van Dixmude, p. 15; and *Chronique de Flandre*, pp. 215, 252.

believe that the *Oriflamme* was only to come out at times when the French were fighting heretics, which in this case they were as the Ghentenaars supported a pope, Urban VI, which the French deemed was a heretical substitute for the true pope, Clement VII. However, the French had always taken the *Oriflamme* from its ecclesiastical setting when fighting the Flemings in the fourteenth century, even before this papal schism.[57] Jean Froissart writes:

> . . . the Oriflamme was displayed, which Sir Pierre de Villiers carried . . . Again its virtue was demonstrated there, for all the morning there was a great fog and so thick that with difficulty could one see another. But as soon as the knight displayed the Oriflamme which he carried and which on a lance was raised high, the fog lifted into the sky and dispersed. And the sky was so pure and clear, and the air was more clear than it had been for more than a year. And the lords of France rejoiced much when they saw that a bright day had come and that the sun had shone, and that they could see on both sides and to the front and back.[58]

It is possible that the Flemish gunners simply could not see the enemy troops clearly enough to warrant firing their gunpowder weapons. And in the close combat which followed, the Ghentenaars were simply no match for their foes.

The battle of Rosebeke was a resounding defeat for the Ghentenaars and other Flemish rebels, and among the dead on the battlefield lay Philip van Artevelde. The remnants of his forces fled to the safety of Ghent and nearby towns. The rebel siege of Oudenaarde was raised, and Bruges submitted again to the authority of the count.[59] Ghent refused to surrender, even after being offered amnesty, though at a high cost in reparations. However, the Franco-Burgundians were unable to proceed against the still rebellious city as winter was approaching. As a parting gesture, however, they marched on Courtrai, which had sided with Ghent in this rebellion, burned the town, and returned to France with the armor and golden spurs which had hung in the town's Notre Dame church since their capture at the battle of Courtrai eighty years previously.[60]

His victory at Rosebeke established Charles VI's military legacy early in his reign, something that his contemporary biographers would later remember during the king's bouts of mental instability.[61] It also confirmed Philip the Bold's growing reputation for military leadership, which ultimately gave him a military as well as political legitimacy when he took over Flemish comital responsibility two years later. But it did not end the rebellion. The Ghentenaars still held out. More important, though in the end of little consequence as the military intervention was entrusted to an imbecilic military leader,

57 For the best study on this very interesting French military symbol see Philippe Contamine, *L'oriflamme de Saint-Denis aux XIVe et XVe siècles* (Nancy, 1975).
58 Froissart, XI: [?]. See also *Chronique du religieux de Saint-Denis*, I:216, and Jean Juvenal des Ursins, p. 352.
59 *Chronique de Flandre*, II:216–17, 266–67; Olivier van Dixmude, p. 16; *Chronicon comitum Flandriae*, p. 242; *Chronique des règnes de Jean II et Charles V*, p. 31; and Autrand, *Charles VI*, 134–35.
60 Froissart, XI: [?]; *Chronique du religieux de Saint-Denis*, I:228–29; Jean Juvenal des Ursins, p. 356; Olivier van Dixmude, p. 16; and *Chronique de Flandre*, II:217–18.
61 See especially Jean Juvenal des Ursins, p. 353; *Chronique du religieux de Saint-Denis*, I:188, 218, 230; and Christine de Pisan, *Le livre des fais et bonnes meurs du sage roy Charles V*, ed. S. Solente (Paris, 1936–40), II:25–26.

the Bishop of Norwich, is that the Ghentenaar loss at Rosebeke provoked an English response.

To be certain, such a response had been talked about in England since Charles V's and Philip the Bold's 1377 attacks on the fortifications around Calais. But they had resulted in nothing of significance.[62] The Ghentenaars had also sought English intervention on their side since the beginning of the Ghent War, even reiterating their allegiance to the English king, now Richard II, as sovereign of France, and consequently of Flanders.[63] But such requests before 1382 had fallen on deaf ears. As modern biographers of Richard II are quick to point out, this grandson of Edward III and son of Edward, the Black Prince, possessed none of the military qualities or bellicose urges of his ancestors.[64] Even after the rebel defeat at Rosebeke, only a meager expedition led by Henry Despenser, the bishop of Norwich, could be organized. In addition, the reason given for this expedition was not the preservation of economic, political, or military ties with Flanders, but religious. The bishop of Norwich's campaign was to be a Crusade against those believers in Pope Clement VII, the French, in favor of those believing in Pope Urban VI, the Flemings.[65]

It took some time for the bishop to assemble his army, and acquire the necessary funding, and weaponry, including what seems like some, although not a great number of gunpowder weapons. He withstood numerous parliamentary debates and other obstacles, but in the end he was able to interest the participation of two very experienced English military leaders, Sir Hugh Calveley and Sir William Elmham. Unfortunately, he was not able to recruit many soldiers with the result that his Crusade was woefully undermanned.[66]

The English landed at Calais some time before 17 May 1383. It seems apparent that, before his arrival on the continent, the bishop had no definite plan. Most historians suggest that he planned to attack nearby French, and thereby Clementine, holdings, perhaps even the fortifications lost in 1377. Instead, at Calais he met with representatives from Ghent who convinced him to direct his campaign into Flemish lands lost after Rosebeke, in other words against Urbanist supporters![67] On 17 May he

---

62 Palmer, pp. 32–38.

63 Palmer, pp. 44–45.

64 See, for example, Anthony Steel, *Richard II* (Cambridge, 1941), and Nigel Saul, *Richard II* (New Haven, 1997).

65 A detailed military history of the Bishop of Norwich's Crusade needs to be written. In the meantime, see Norman Housley, "The Bishop of Norwich's Crusade, May 1383," *History Today* 33 (1983), 15–20; George M. Wrong, *The Crusade of 1383 Known as That of the Bishop of Norwich* (London, 1892); Edouard Perroy, *L'Angleterre et le grand schisme d'occident: étude sur la politique religieuse de l'Angleterre sous Richard II (1378–1399)* (Paris, 1933), pp. 166–209; and F. Quicke, *Les Pays-Bas à la veille de la periode Bourguignonne, 1356–1384: Contribution à l'histoire politique et diplomatique de l'Europe occidentale dans la seconde moitié du XIVe siècle* (Brussels, 1947), pp. 341–55. The best contemporary sources are two from the southern Low Countries, Jean Froissart's *Chroniques* and the *Chronique de Flandre*, and two from England, Thomas Walsingham's *Historia Anglicana* (ed. H.T. Riley (London, 1863–64), and *The Westminster Chronicle, 1381–1394* (ed. and trans. L.C. Hector and Barbara F. Harvey (Oxford, 1982)).

66 On this Wrong is especially good. See also James Magee, "Sir William Elmham and the Recruitment for Henry Despenser's Crusade of 1383," *Medieval Prosopography* 20 (1999), 181–90.

67 This thesis is played out further in Kelly DeVries, "The Reasons for the Bishop of Norwich's Attack on Flanders in 1383," in *Fourteenth Century England III*, ed. W.M. Ormrod (Woodbridge, 2004, pp. 155–65).

disembarked from Calais, directing his campaign northeast along the coast toward Flanders, and on19 May he captured Gravelines without conflict and began a siege of Bourbourg.[68] Leaving a few troops behind to continue that siege, which ended successfully a few days later, the bishop of Norwich captured Dunkirk, again without any conflict, and on 25 May had his first real engagement with enemy troops a few kilometers up the coast, outside Dunkirk. This was an English victory, but it slowed their advance and cost the lives of several soldiers.[69] At this point the bishop turned east, towards Ypres, besieging the town from 9 June.[70]

As the English were making this progress, the Ghentenaar army marched towards Damme, outside Bruges, and, again, towards Oudenaarde. Damme, without a protective garrison, fell quickly, and so, surprisingly due to its previous history, did Oudenaarde. The Ghentenaars also moved on to Ypres, arriving a short time after the English. So far, it looked like a successful campaign, although certainly not the Crusade against the Clementines anticipated by some of the English, including Sir Hugh Calveley.[71] But Ypres did not surrender, as was clearly expected. For whatever reason, the Yprois decided to put up an active defense. So the English and Ghentenaars began the by now customary gunpowder artillery bombardment of the town's fortifications. Almost all of the contemporary chronicles of this siege recount the heavy bombardment and its destructive results. "Many were killed by [the English and Flemish] artillery," writes Jean Froissart.[72] The *Chronique de Flandre* agrees, however adding the story of "one stone shot from a cannon at night [which] fell among three houses on the *rue de Boesingues*. And this stone fell onto the roof of a woman who was asleep on her bed. But because she was a woman of God, she was not hurt." The anonymous chronicler concludes, "Thus God saved the people of Ypres."[73] This sentiment is still somewhat held by the Yprois who have continued to revere a statue of the Madonna, now mounted above the entrance to the post-World War I reconstructed Cloth Hall, as influential in saving the town from the English siege of 1383.

Despite the intensive bombardment, the fortifications of Ypres seem to have held. This may have been because of the large water-filled moats around the town which almost all the chroniclers refer to.[74] Many of the shots fired from the besieging weapons may have missed the walls or gates of the town, while many others, based on the story above, may have gone over them into Ypres itself. Evidence for this comes from the fact that when most of the artillery-related destruction is reported in the contemporary

---

68 Froissart, XI:95–7; *Chronique de Flandre*, II:285, 293, 307; Thomas Walsingham, II:88–90; and *Westminster Chronicle*, pp. 38–39. On the siege of Bourbourg an interesting study is Gustave Monteuuis, "Le siège de Bourbourg en 1383," *Annales du comité flamand de France* 22 (1895), 259–313.

69 Froissart, XI:97–99, 102–03; *Chronique de Flandre*, II:285–86, 293, 307; Thomas Walsingham, II:90–93; and *Westminister Chronicle*, pp. 38–41.

70 Froissart, XI:107–08; *Chronique de Flandre*, II:281, 283, 286–91, 293–320; Thomas Walsingham, II:95–96; and *Westminister Chronicle*, pp. 44–47.

71 Froissart (XI:93–94) has Calveley vocalize his disagreement with the Bishop's change in plans at Calais, before the actual campaign begins.

72 Froissart, XI:121: "et que mout perdoient de leur artillerie." See also *Chronique de Flandre*, II:294, 298, 309, 311–12, 317.

73 *Chronique de Flandre*, II:298.

74 Froissart, XI:121, and *Chronique de Flandre*, II:288–89, 297, 312.

sources, it is almost entirely in the town and among the inhabitants and their homes and not the fortifications. This may explain why, after two months and one final assault, on 10 August, the bishop of Norwich abandoned his participation in the siege – leaving behind his gunpowder weapons and other military materiel, according to Henry Knighton.[75] The bishop and his army retreated to Calais, and by the middle of September, he had given up Bourbourg, Dunkirk, and Gravelines.[76] By the beginning of October he had returned to England, where he was tried for abusing indulgences, misusing funds, and personally profiting from his willingness to retreat across the Channel without doing battle with Charles VI or Philip the Bold – it seems that the bishop had negotiated his retreat with these two enemy leaders, personally benefitting financially from it.[77] Thus ended one of the most poorly planned and executed English campaigns of the Hundred Years War.

Throughout the bishop of Norwich's campaign and the siege of Ypres Charles VI and Philip the Bold had been conspicuously absent. After the battle of Rosebeke, Charles had returned to Paris, and Philip, together with his army, had remained south of Ypres in Picardy. He gave assistance to Louis of Male, in the form of soldiers and financial support. He may also have given his father-in-law gunpowder weapons, although there are no records in support of this assumption. But he left Louis to deal with Ypres on his own, and the count of Flanders chose to do nothing.[78] Interestingly, this tactic, if it was a planned one, worked, as the Ghentenaars continued their siege of Ypres for only a short time after the English retreat, raising it by 10 September.

But a simple explanation for Louis' inaction may be the fact that he was ill – he died shortly afterwards, on 30 January 1384. Of course, Philip the Bold succeeded him as count of Flanders,[79] and almost immediately began to deal more aggressively with the Ghentenaar rebels. Fearing that what happened at Oudenaarde might also occur at Dendermonde, the other fortified town which had remained faithful throughout the entire conflict to Louis of Male, Philip reinforced the garrison there. He also set about building and strengthening his other castles surrounding the rebel-held territory: the castle at Lille was repaired and parts rebuilt, and construction of a new castle at Sluys began.[80] He also asked for and received funds from Charles VI to increase the size of and improve his army.[81]

In more active military terms, on 25 May 1384 one of Philip's newly allied nobles, Arnould de Gavre, lord of Escornay, set about reacquiring Oudenaarde on his own. In a very daring, apparently single-handed operation, Gavre, through some heroic chicanery, was able to gain entrance into the rebel town with some wagons, ostensibly filled with provisions, but filled instead with armed men, who overpowered the small

---

[75] Henry Knighton, *Knighton's Chronicle*, ed. and trans. Geoffrey Martin (Oxford, 1995), pp. 326–29; Froissart, XI:120–1; Thomas Walsingham, II:98–99.

[76] Froissart, XI:126–37; *Chronique de Flandre*, II:290–91, 320; and Thomas Walsingham, II:102–04.

[77] Margaret Aston, "The Impeachment of Bishop Despenser," *Bulletin of the Institute of Historical Research* 38 (1965), 127–48.

[78] Vaughan, *Philip the Bold*, pp. 29–30.

[79] Vaughan, *Philip the Bold*, pp. 31–32.

[80] Vaughan, *Philip the Bold*, p. 33.

[81] Vaughan, *Philip the Bold*, pp. 33–34.

garrison of troops inside and recaptured the town.[82] It was an embarrassing episode in the Ghent rebellion, but accurately reflected what their uprising had become. They knew by this time that there was little hope left. The English had proved of little help, and their own military adventures, though frequently victorious had not effected any enduring success. Now only Ghent remained in rebel hands, and the new, more militarily astute and powerful count led the forces against them, one who could bring an equal number of gunpowder weapons to bear against them as they had been able to bring against their earlier enemies. It was only a matter of time.

That time came on 21 July 1385. Provoked by a surprise attack from Ghent which struck the fortified towns of Damme and Aardenburg, taking the first but failing to capture the second, Philip the Bold, together with the recently married French king, marched north from Amiens, where the wedding had taken place four days previously, to retake Damme and march on Ghent. Philip's previous attitude of negotiating a surrender with the Ghentenaar rebels to protect this very important source of tax revenues had now turned to military action. With him were a number of gunpowder weapons which he ordered to be fired against the walls of Damme. The town held out for a little more than a month. Ultimately, it was the presence of these gunpowder weapons, combined with the lack of relieving reinforcements, which caused the rebels in Damme to surrender. Jean Froissart writes:

> On the 27 September 1385 the town of Damme surrendered to the king of France and the French. I will tell you by what manner. When the French had been led by the king of France to besiege the town for around one month, and because both their artillery was weakening the town and there was no relief which appeared on any side, they began to become fatigued.[83]

Surrender soon followed.

Before the end of the siege of Damme both Charles VI and Philip the Bold petitioned for a Ghentenaar surrender. By the end of that siege they were willing to do so. Terms were quite lenient. Although financial exactions were required, as well as some other provisions, such as the dismantling of some of the town's fortifications, most of the participants, even many of the leading rebels, were given amnesty for their treasonous crimes. The town of Ghent and its inhabitants were in quite dire straits, having been unable to conduct business, the basis of their wealth, for the past six years. Starvation and deprivation were certainly apparent, although it was perhaps the fatigue of carrying out a sustained rebellion which was most telling on the townspeople. Although their sovereignty would be severely limited under this new count, the provisions of the peace treaty allowed them to continue to live in peace and prosperity. The loss of sovereignty remained an issue; of course, and, as will be seen, this was not the last time the town of Ghent rebelled against its Burgundian count. The treaty ending the Ghent War was signed in Tournai on 18 December 1385, and on the following

---

[82] Vaughan, *Philip the Bold*, p. 34.
[83] Froissart, XI:244. Froissart (XI:244–45) then describes at length the negotiations among the garrison as to whether they would surrender. In the end, they chose to do so, with only the leader, Francis Ackerman, being executed for the rebellion.

4 January, Philip the Bold, with all the pomp and wealth which his positions and possessions gave him, entered the town.[84]

The remaining years of Philip the Bold's life, after the conclusion of the Ghent War, were peaceful ones and he died on 27 April 1404 in the Stag Inn at Halle, near Brussels. The Hundred Years War was in abeyance, with the Truce of Paris, finally signed in 1396 between the English and French after years of negotiation, actually holding both sides in the conflict from military action until well into the fifteenth century.[85] In addition, the county of Flanders, as well as Philip's other holdings, remained peaceful and willing to abide by his rule.[86]

This did not mean, however, that the Burgundian duke remained militarily inactive. Indeed, during times of peace, especially, it seems that he and his Valois successors sought to build up their military, including their gunpowder weaponry, arsenal. In December 1385, for example, during Philip the Bold's visit to the defeated Ghent, he employed a man from Dinant, Joseph Colard, as a ducal "cannonier," paying him well to move his southern Low Countries workshop to Dijon. There he served for several years not only as a caster of bronze cannon, but also as the maker of bronze art objects which adorned the ducal Charterhouse, including the convent bell, chandeliers, bronze eagles for lecterns, and columns to support angels on the altar.[87] He and other Burgundian cannon-makers greatly increased the numbers of gunpowder weapons available to the duke.[88]

[84] Vaughan, *Philip the Bold*, pp. 37–38.
[85] On these negotiations and the treaty itself see Palmer.
[86] Vaughan, *Philip the Bold*, pp. 35–38, is especially detailed in his discussion of the various ways Philip used to control his widely diverse towns and people.
[87] Garnier, pp. 14–15, and Vaughan, *Philip the Bold*, p. 203. Vaughan indicates the name as Colart Joseph.
[88] Garnier, pp. 14–15.

JOHN THE FEARLESS

Neither John the Fearless' life nor his reign was long. Born on 28 May 1371, he was almost thirty-three years old when he ascended the ducal throne. He was assassinated on 10 September 1419, an assassination which he had provoked both by his attempts at political and military control over the kingdom of France, and by his assassination of one of his chief opponents, Louis, duke of Orléans.

For more than a decade before John ascended to the Burgundian leadership he had been included in the governance of his father's lands. However, due largely to the peace in these areas, little of this had been militarily experienced. He had been too young to serve with Philip the Bold in the Pas-de-Calais in 1377 or in the Ghent War of 1379–85, and, while he did accompany the Burgundian contingents, led by his father, in a French campaign against the duke of Guelders late in 1388, there was actually little fighting, and none in which the young Burgundian heir participated.[1] This is perhaps why, when the opportunity for military leadership arose in the Nicopolis Crusade in 1396, Philip sought to include his son. John the Fearless was put in command of the forces which suffered one of the most disastrous defeats of the later Middle Ages. His army was defeated by the Ottoman Turks at the siege and battle of Nicopolis in September 1396. Only twenty-three years old at the time, John's command came not from any superior military experience or skill. Rather, as was common at the time with allied armies put together as a "crusading" force – which is perhaps the easiest way to describe the Western Christian Anglo-Burgundian-Franco-German-Teutonic Knight-Hungarian-Wallachian-Transylvanian contingent which fought against the Ottomans that day[2] – John's noble rank placed him in charge. Of course, John was not alone in the decision-making leadership of this army. He was surrounded by other great and noble military leaders, in particular, the Franco-Burgundian generals, Philip of Artois, the Constable of France, Jean II le Meingre dit Boucicault, the Marshal of

---

[1] On John's activities before he led the Nicopolis crusade, see Richard Vaughan, *John the Fearless: The Growth of Burgundian Power* (London, 1966), pp. 2–6.

[2] On the composition of the crusader army see David Nicolle, *Nicopolis, 1396: The Last Crusade* (London, 1999), pp. 19–23; Aziz Suryal Atiya, *The Crusade of Nicopolis* (London, 1934), pp. 33–49; Aziz Suryal Atiya, *The Crusade in the Later Middle Ages* (London, 1938), pp. 437–43; Hans Delbrück, *History of the Art of War within the Framework of Political History*, vol. III: *Medieval Warfare*, trans. W.J. Renfroe, Jr. (Westport, 1984), pp. 437–39; R. Rosetti, "Notes on the Battle of Nicopolis (1396)," *Slavonic and East European Review* 15 (1936–37), 629–38; J.J.N. Palmer, *England, France and Christendom, 1377–99* (Chapel Hill, 1972), pp. 185–204; Henry L. Savage, "Enguerrand de Coucy VII and the Campaign of Nicopolis," *Speculum* 14 (1939), 423–42; Charles L. Tipton, "The English at Nicopolis," *Speculum* 37 (1962), 528–40; Richard Vaughan, *Philip the Bold: The Formation of the Burgundian State* (London, 1962), pp. 59–78; and the articles in Jacques Paviot and M. Chauney-Bouillot, eds., "Nicopolis, 1396–1996: Actes du Colloque international," *Annales de Bourgogne* 68 (1996). On the battle itself, the best works are Nicolle, and Atiya, *The Crusade of Nicopolis*.

France, Jean de Vienne, the Admiral of France, Guillaume de la Trémoille, the Marshal of Burgundy, and Enguerrand de Coucy VII.[3]

Unfortunately, the young and inexperienced John listened to these leaders over others accustomed to fighting against the Ottoman Turks – none of the Franco-Burgundians had ever fought against this enemy before – especially the Hungarian king, Sigismund I. At Nicopolis, once the Ottoman army appeared to raise the Crusader siege of the city, Sigismund recommended that his and the other central European troops, almost entirely infantry, should be in the vanguard, there to meet the irregular infantry of the Turks who stood in the van of their own army. The Christian infantry would take a defensive stance and try to provoke the Turks into a charge which would either be defeated at the contact of the two infantry forces or could be reinforced by the strong Franco-Burgundian cavalry ordered in the rear. This, John the Fearless ultimately refused to do.[4] Philip of Artois used his influence and constabulary office to counter the Hungarian king's proposal. According to Jean Froissart, he replied with these words:

> Yes, yes, the king of Hungary wishes to gain all the honor of the day. He has given us the vanguard, and now he wishes to take it away, that he may have the first blow. Let those who will believe what he sends to us, but for my part I never will . . . In the name of God and Saint George, you shall see me this day prove myself a good knight.[5]

So on 25 September 1396, John the Fearless followed the tactical traditions of at least a century of western military leaders:[6] with a flurry of pride and enthusiasm the Franco-Burgundian cavalry rode head-long into their Turkish opponents, safely positioned behind a line of stakes. Initially, the horsemen were successful, breaking through the stakes and pushing the Turkish infantry back. A second attack by the crusaders also achieved some success. But the Turks did not break into flight, and when the counter-attack came from the Ottoman regular troops, cavalry, infantry, and archers, the impetus of the crusaders had been spent and, even though some Germans and Hungarians rushed to reinforce them, they were routed.[7] Those who could, tried

---

3   On the Franco-Burgundian leadership of the crusaders see Atiya, *Crusade*, pp. 438–40; Vaughan, *Philip the Bold*, pp. 61–62; and Savage, pp. 423–42. Other notables in the crusader army include: the Count Palatine Ruprecht Pipan, Count Herman II of Cilly, Burgrave John III of Nuremberg, John Holand, earl of Huntingdon, John Beaufort, Philibert de Naillac, Grand Master of Rhodes, and Nicholas Kanizsay, archbishop of Gran. But none of these seem to have held much power in the tactical planning of the battle, and most may have stayed in the rear with Sigismund and the Hungarian, Wallachian, and Transylvanian troops.

4   Atiya, *Nicopolis*, pp. 82–84; Atiya, *Crusade*, p. 447; and Savage, pp. 434–35. This comes chiefly from Jean Froissart, *Chroniques*, in *Œuvres de Froissart*, ed. Kervyn de Lettenhove (Brussels, 1867–77), XV:265–68.

5   Froissart (ed. Kervyn de Lettenhove), XV:268.

6   On this tradition see Kelly DeVries, *Infantry Warfare in the Early Fourteenth Century: Discipline, Tactics, and Technology* (Woodbridge, 1996).

7   Atiya, *Nicopolis*, pp. 89–93; Delbrück, pp. 478–79; Charles Oman, *A History of the Art of War in the Middle Ages* (London, 1905), II:351–52; and Kenneth M. Setton, *The Papacy and the Levant (1204–1571)*, vol I: *The Thirteenth and Fourteenth Centuries* (Philadelphia, 1976), pp. 352–55. Atiya (*Nicopolis*, pp. 92–93) maintains that there was a German and Hungarian reinforcement, even though Johannes Schiltberger (*Bondage and Travels of Johann Schiltberger, a Native of Bavaria, in Europe, Asia, and Africa (1396–1427)*, ed. K.F. Neumann and trans. J.B. Telfer (London, 1879), p. 3) is the only contemporary author to contend that

to flee, but the River Danube blocked their path and few were actually able to leave the scene of what had become a slaughter-house. Following the defeat, Franco-Burgundian soldiers who surrendered to their opponents were slain. Only after the capture of John the Fearless were prisoners accepted, and even then several hundred more Christian troops were summarily executed. A mere three hundred western European soldiers, from a total of perhaps as many as 6,000 who had been involved in the fighting, were eventually spared.[8] Their ransom paid, an amount of more than 200,000 ducats, they returned home some nine months later.[9]

Were there gunpowder weapons at Nicopolis? Aziz Suryal Atiya is emphatic that they were not: "It is beyond question that firearms were not used in the siege or the battle which ensued."[10] To support this declaration, Atiya notes the use of mines made by the Hungarians during the siege, which he reasons came from the fact that the besieging crusaders, according to the anonymous chronicler of *Le livre des fais du bon messire Jehan le Maingre, dit Bouciquaut*, had few "balistas, catapults and other siege machines";[11] he also asserts that there is no mention of gunpowder weapons in the Nicopolis campaign except for the *Chronique du religieux de Saint-Denis*' reference to "missiles" fired at the siege of Rahova (or Rachowa) undertaken earlier in September.[12] Furthermore, Atiya claims that, as gunpowder weapons were not needed in the Lithuanian crusades of the same period, they were unlikely to have been needed on the Nicopolis crusade as well: "Thus if the crusaders had no need for gunpowder in pagan Lithuania, it was thought that they would hardly want it in infidel 'Turkey.' "[13]

Atiya is certainly correct that the original sources which narrate the details of the battle are largely silent on the matter, but this may be because those from the west, more numerous than their Ottoman counterparts, were all written after the event, and were obviously interested more in the action of the charge and its failure than in unused military materiel or preliminary skirmishes where the weapons may have been used. Moreover, other evidence suggests that Atiya is correct in noting that the Ottomans did not possess gunpowder weapons at the time of the battle and would not have had them at Nicopolis.[14] But the westerners certainly did have gunpowder weapons; they were present in the Lithuanian crusades;[15] and they were used in conjunction with mining efforts.[16] In addition, as seen in connection with Philip the Bold, the

---

this took place. He was an eye-witness to the battle and may have been taken prisoner in this charge, and this convinces Atiya when *Le livre des fais du Mareschal de Bouciquaut* (*Le livre des fais du bon messire Jehan le Maingre, dit Bouciquaut, mareschal de France et gouverneur de Jennes* (Paris, 1985), pp. 110–11) claims that the Hungarians fled without entering the conflict. Setton (pp. 354–55) agrees with Atiya.

8   Atiya, *Nicopolis*, pp. 94–97 and Setton, pp. 355–56.

9   On the ransom for John of Fearless and other captives and how it was raised see Vaughan, *Philip the Bold*, pp. 71–78.

10   Atiya, *Nicopolis*, pp. 61–62 (quote is from p. 61).

11   *Le livre des fais du Mareschal de Bouciquaut*, pp. 100–111.

12   *Chronique du religieux de Saint-Denis*, II:494–97.

13   Atiya, *Nicopolis*, p. 62.

14   See Kelly DeVries, "Gunpowder Weaponry at the Siege of Constantinople, 1453," in *War, Army and Society in the Eastern Mediterranean, 7th–16th Centuries*, ed. Yaacov Lev (Leiden, 1996), pp. 351–54.

15   See, for example, Volker Schmidtchen, *Die Feuerwaffen des deutschen Ritterordens bis zur Schlacht bei Tannenberg 1410* (Lüneberg, 1977).

16   Not only were gunpowder weapons used at Oudenaarde and Damme with mines during the Ghent War, but

Burgundians, at least, were accustomed by this time to use them in all engagements. The 1396 Crusade, too, was initially conceived as a siege of Nicopolis, and as such must have meant that the Crusaders would have taken gunpowder weapons. Finally, the fact that there were several Hungarian vessels anchored in the River Danube on which some of the defeated forces made their escape provides evidence that guns could have been easily transported to the battlefield. Yet, the tactics used by the crusaders at Nicopolis certainly prohibited their use in the battle itself, although they certainly could have used them before the initial charge. Of course, the issue will remain in dispute until more evidence as to whether gunpowder weapons were used there or not is forthcoming. What is not in dispute, however, is that the battle of Nicopolis was one of the numerous late medieval military engagements which signaled the end of conventional medieval warfare and the domination of cavalry over infantry, replacing it with a style of fighting in which infantry and artillery might easily defeat those who relied on an intimidating cavalry charge for victory.

Perhaps because of the defeat of Nicopolis and the dishonor it brought to its leaders and participants, or perhaps because he did not reign as duke of Burgundy on his own until 1404, it was almost another decade before John the Fearless once again undertook military action and an association with gunpowder weapons. In 1406, at a time of peace between the French and English in the Hundred Years War, John, like his father before him, attempted to retake the English stronghold of Calais. There had been an active Burgundian military presence around the town since the capture of the surrounding fortresses by Philip the Bold in 1377. Yet, perhaps held in check by truce and perhaps by action elsewhere, the Burgundians had not made an attack of the actual town since that time. In 1406 this changed. Jean de Waurin claims that early that year John asked for and received permission from the French king, Charles VI, to attack Calais. He made "machines of war" and gathered large numbers of gunpowder artillery – 21 iron cannon from Bruges alone – transporting them to Saint-Omer in preparation.[17] However, before such an attack could be launched, the king withdrew his permission and asked the duke to send him the gathered siege machines and artillery for his own military action against the castle of Renty, then being threatened by the English king, Henry IV. John reluctantly sent the requested equipment to Charles. This incident, which the Burgundian chroniclers, Jean de Waurin and Enguerran de Monstrelet, recalled later with disdain, certainly affixed the conclusion in John the

Henry V also used the same tactical formula at his siege of Harfleur in 1415. See Alfred H. Burne, *The Agincourt War: A Military History of the Latter Part of the Hundred Years War from 1369 to 1453* (London, 1956), pp. 42–46.

[17] Jean de Waurin, *Récueil des croniques et anchiennes istories de la Grant Bretaigne*, ed. W. and E.L.C.P. Hardy (London, 1864–91), II:105–07, and Enguerran de Monstrelet, *Chronique*, ed. L. Douet-d'Arcq (Paris, 1857–62), I:136. On the number of gunpowder weapons being sent from Bruges see Claude Gaier, *L'industrie et le commerce des armes dans les anciennes principautés Belges du XIIIme à la fin du XVe siècle* (Paris, 1963), p. 120. According to M. Guillaume, *Histoire de l'organisation militaire sous les ducs de Bourgogne* (Brussels, 1848), p. 77, more than 1,200 gunpowder weapons were gathered by John to besiege Calais, but, judging from the archival sources analyzed below, this is probably an exaggeration. John may have planned to besiege Calais the year before asking permission of the king as the Burgundian duke had sent gunpowder to the count of Saint-Pol in 1405 which, Waurin notes, was to be used in a siege of the town (Waurin, II:99).

Fearless' mind that Charles VI was being misled by his advisers and ultimately may have led to the events of the following year.

The next year, in 1407, war broke out on two fronts for John the Fearless. First, in importance if not chronology, civil war arose in France due to the mental illness of French king, Charles VI. The result was an unstable government in which a number of nobles vied for power, among whom John the Fearless was one of the two most important, the other being Louis, duke of Orléans. The dukes of Burgundy and Orléans both were cousins to the king, which of course made them cousins to each other. But their family ties did not bring them to an accord, and for almost the rest of John the Fearless' reign, these two factions, typically known as the Burgundians and Armagnacs, utilized every means, including warfare, against each other. Still, there had been little more than words between the two parties before 20 November 1407, when Louis of Orléans was cruelly assassinated in Paris. John was quickly implicated, and the kingdom of France was divided between the two parties, the Burgundians, led by John, and the Armagnacs led at that time by Louis' son, Charles of Orléans, and his son-in-law, Bernard, the count of Armagnac.[18]

There seems little doubt among historians or among his contemporaries that John had planned this assassination with the intention of taking advantage of the then weakened Armagnacs to extend his own lands and political power, although his initial claim was that it came about "through the intervention of the devil."[19] Later, he paid a master in theology at the University of Paris, Jean Petit, to write a *Justification* for the murder, claiming that it was done only to put a stop to Louis of Orléans' "tyrannicide."[20] Such maneuvers were able to convince or pacify some French nobles, but not all, and, as John must have known before his opponent's murder, the Burgundians ultimately were going to have to fight against the Armagnacs.[21]

But before they were able to do so, a second military front opened that forced John the Fearless to take military action outside French borders: the prince-bishopric of Liège. At this point, this prince-episcopality had not yet come under direct control of the dukes of Burgundy – this happened later in the century – but their influence there was significant. The rebellion which eventually brought John the Fearless into the fray had been growing for several years. Indeed, it could be said that the prince-bishopric of Liège had been one of the most rebellious of all medieval localities throughout the two centuries prior to Burgundian domination.[22] This particular rebellion actually began in 1390 when John of Bavaria, the seventeen-year-old brother-in-law of John the

---

18   Edouard Perroy, *The Hundred Years War*, trans. W.B. Wells (Oxford, 1951), pp. 226–27; Vaughan, *John the Fearless*, pp. 43–48; Bertrand Schnerb, *Les Armagnacs et les Bourguignons: La maudite guerre* (Paris, 1988), pp. 67–76; and Bernard Guenée, *Un meutre, une société: L'assassinat du Duc d'Orléans, 23 novembre 1407* (Paris, 1992).

19   Perroy, p. 227; Vaughan, *John the Fearless*, pp. 46–48; and Schnerb, *Les Armagnacs et les Bourguignons*, pp. 78–83.

20   Perroy, pp. 228–29, and Vaughan, *John the Fearless*, pp. 68–74. Part of the *Justification* is translated in Vaughan, *John the Fearless*, pp. 70–72. The full document is quoted in de Monstrelet, I:177–242.

21   Perroy, pp. 229–30, and Schnerb, *Les Armagnacs et les Bourguignons*, pp. 93–97.

22   See Fernand Vercauteren, *Luttes sociales à Liège, XIIIe et XIVe siècles*, 2nd ed. (Brussels, 1946), and Kelly DeVries, "The Rebellions of Southern Low Countries' Towns during the Fourteenth and Fifteenth Centuries," (forthcoming).

Fearless, was named prince-bishop of Liège. By 1394, the Liégeois had revolted against his, in the words of Richard Vaughan, "vigorous if rash attempts to establish and maintain his authority."[23] This rebellion was initially quelled, but it resumed in 1402 and continued to grow in the ensuing years. Eventually, in August 1407, John of Bavaria was forced to call on his Burgundian relative who responded by mustering his army to come to the prince-bishop's aid.

Beyond the obvious desire to be away from his French problems, John the Fearless may also have seen in the Liégeois conflict the means of establishing his own military skill in the face of growing tensions with the Armagnacs. There seems to be little doubt that he increased his knowledge about fighting wars, especially about fighting wars with gunpowder weapons, in putting down the rebellion. However, the first thing he learned came not from a direct confrontation with the rebels, but from an engagement which occurred before John himself became involved: the siege of Maastricht. Although most of the other towns of the prince-bishopric had joined the rebellion, Maastricht remained loyal and gave refuge to John of Bavaria. Thus, at the end of September 1407, the rebels besieged Maastricht.[24] But this was a siege like none fought previously. The rebels decided that they had neither the time nor the soldiers to undertake a siege of any length, and, anticipating Burgundian reinforcements, the Maastrichters were not likely to surrender without putting up an enduring defense. So, after fighting a few skirmishes, the rebels turned to a relatively novel tactic: gunpowder artillery bombardment.

At Maastricht, the rebels did not use just a few guns, but many, perhaps their towns' entire arsenal. From 24 November 1407, when the bombardment began, to 7 January 1408, when the siege was raised, Maastricht received 1514 large bombard balls – an average of thirty per day.[25] A further siege with yet a second bombardment followed in July, but even though it, too, included a lengthy, heavy gunpowder bombardment, it too was unsuccessful; and, by August 1408, John the Fearless was marching on Liège, the main rebel town, with his Burgundian army, forcing the rebels once again to raise the siege of Maastricht. But, though the siege was a military failure, as shall be seen below, John learned a valuable tactical lesson from the besiegers which he would put into practice in the fight against his more powerful foes, the Armagnacs.

First the Liège situation had to be dealt with. Negotiations between the rebels and John the Fearless, brokered by the French crown, halted activities until the middle of September, during which time the Burgundian forces grew larger and better armed. Finally, on 20 September, John broke from the negotiations and determined to fight the rebels. Three days later and after beginning a siege on Tongeren, one of the leading

23 Vaughan, *John the Fearless*, p. 50.
24 The best account of this siege, which deserves a more complete treatment, is Vaughan, *John the Fearless*, pp. 52–54.
25 On the numbers of gunshot fired into Maastricht see Gaier, *L'industrie et le commerce des armes*, pp. 94–95; Philippe Contamine, *War in the Middle Ages*, trans. Michael Jones (London, 1984), pp. 200–01; and Alain Salamagne, "L'attaque des places-fortes au XVe siècle à travers l'exemple des guerres anglo et franco-bourguignonnes," *Revue historique* 289 (1993), 87. See also Jean de Stavelot, *Chronique latine*, in *Chroniques Liègeoises*, 1, ed. S. Balau (Brussels, 1913), p. 117, and Erich Wille, *Die Schlacht von Othée, 23 septembre 1408* (Berlin, 1908), pp. 17–18.

rebel towns, with "many" gunpowder weapons,[26] he met his enemy nearby in the battle of Othée.[27] At this battle, John was not to repeat the mistakes of Nicopolis. He could not count on numbers or the technological strength of his gunpowder weapons to carry him to victory. Instead, he had to "out-general" his opposition, to tactically defeat the rebels. In his own words – via a letter which the duke sent to his brother, Anthony – he tells how this was accomplished:

> When we had ridden forward about half a league, we saw them plainly . . . and they saw us. At this point my brother-in-law [John of Bavaria was also present] and I, together with our people, dismounted in a fairly advantageous position, thinking that they would come and attack us there. We placed all our troops in a single mass in order to resist more effectively with shock and charge which the Liégeois were likely to give us; and we formed two wings of bowmen and men-at-arms. Soon, they approached us to within about three bowshots, concentrating somewhat towards the right . . . There they stopped, drawn up in excellent order, and immediately opened fire on us with their cannons.
>
> After we had waited a little and seen that they were not going to move, my brother-in-law and I, with the advice of the good captains and knights in our company, decided to advance in good order and attack the enemy where they were. [We also decided that], to break up their array and throw them into confusion, we should need 400 mounted men-at-arms and 1,000 stalwart infantrymen to strike at their rear, while we engaged them [in frontal assault] . . . One hour after midday we marched to attack [the enemy] in the name of God and of Our Lady, in handsome and excellent order, joining battle with them and attacking them in such a way that, with the grace and help of Our Lord, the day was ours.[28]

With this victory, the rebellion ended.

John the Fearless' tactics at Othée duplicated none of the disastrous campaign of Nicopolis. His patience in the 1408 engagement was obvious. He initially ordered his troops in a single massive infantry formation and prepared to defend against an attack. After an archery and artillery exchange, and after determining that his enemy was not going to rush foolishly onto the Burgundians, he consulted with his "good captains and knights" (note John's emphasis). Then his army marched in a "good order" towards the rebels, at the same time assisted by a attack on their rear by horse and foot. In that same "good order," the Burgundians met the Liégeois and defeated them. There was no proud charge of disordered cavalry, as there had been at Nicopolis, only a strong,

---

26 John the Fearless' letter to his brother, Anthony, recounts this. See note 28 below.

27 Vaughan, *John the Fearless*, pp. 51–66; Claude Gaier, *Art et organisation militaires dans la principauté de Liège et dans le comté de Looz au moyen âge* (Brussels, 1968), pp. 306–20; Claude Gaier, *Grandes batailles de l'histoire Liegéoise au moyen âge* (Liege, 1980), pp. 133–49; and Wille. The sources of this battle are most recently discussed in Hubert Carrier, "*Si vera est fama*: Le retentissement de la bataille d'Othée dans la culture historique au XVe siècle," *Revue historique* 305 (2001), 639–70.

28 This letter can be found in U. Plancher, *Histoire générale et particulaire de Bourgogne* (Dijon, 1793–81), III:260, and *Régestes de la cité de Liège*, ed. E. Fairon (Liège, 1933–40), III: no. 657. With only a few changes, I have followed the translation found in Vaughan, *John the Fearless*, pp. 60–62. Other contemporary sources attest to the veracity of John the Fearless' account: Enguerran de Monstrelet, I:365; *Chronique du religieux de Saint-Denis*, ed. L. Bellaguet (Paris, 1839–52), IV:168, 170; de Waurin, I:119–20; and *Chants historiques et populaires du temps de Charles VII et de Louis XI*, ed. L. Roux de Lincy (Paris, 1857), p. 13.

well-led advance. John the Fearless' leadership at Othée is particularly singled-out by the contemporary Burgundian chronicler Enguerran de Monstrelet:

> There is no need to expatiate on the bravery and coolness of the duke of Burgundy; nor to explain at length how, at the start of the battle, he moved on a small horse from one part of the army to another, exhorting and encouraging his men; and how he bore himself, until the end of the battle. In truth, his conduct was such that he was praised and honored by all the knights and others of his company; and although he was frequently hit by arrows and other missiles, he did not, on that day lose one drop of blood. When he was asked, after the defeat, if they ought to cease from killing the Liégeois, he replied that they should all die together, and that he had no wish for them to be taken and ransomed.[29]

How many gunpowder weapons were there at Othée? John refers to those used against the Burgundians by the Liégeois rebels, but does not mention any of his own. However, other sources indicate that there were quite a large number of Burgundian guns at the battle, even with some presumably left to continue the siege of Tongeren.[30] Waurin counts 1,200 carts filled with "artillery, victuals, and war habiliments;" these included "ribaudequins and coulevrines." According to Monstrelet, who also insists that the Burgundians opened the battle by firing them "very strongly," these fired "many shots," but seem to have only played a minor role in determining a victory clearly won by John the Fearless' tactics.[31]

Othée was the last battle John the Fearless undertook, although large skirmishes were later fought by his forces at the bridge of Saint-Cloud, near Paris, on 9 November 1411, and at Saint-Rémy-du-Plain, on 10 May 1412. Nevertheless, as revealed in a rare extant plan of battle written by John the Fearless on 14 September 1417 and published by J.F. Verbruggen in 1959, this duke of Burgundy was prepared to do battle with his enemies any time such an engagement presented itself. This plan also established the defensive infantry tactics of Othée as John the Fearless' chosen means of fighting battles.[32]

With the rebellion of Liège quelled, John was ready to take on a larger target: Armagnac France. However, once again, the Burgundian duke had to contend with a rebellion before trying his military leadership skills against the Armagnacs. This time it was against one of his lesser nobles, Count Henri IV of Blamont, who seems to have counted on John's stay in the southern Low Countries to distract the duke from

---

[29] Monstrelet, I:365. See also Vaughan, *John the Fearless*, p. 62.

[30] There is also the possibility, as there is no evidence to the contrary, that the Burgundians withdrew all of their cannons from Tongeren and took them to the battlefield of Othée.

[31] Waurin, II:119, and de Monstrelet, I:359–62. See also *Le livre des trahisons de France envers la maison de Bourgogne*, in *Chroniques relatives à l'histoire de la Belgique sous la domination des ducs de Bourgogne (textes Français)*, ed. Kervyn de Lettenhove (Brussels, 1873), p. 37; Guillaume, p. 77; Salamagne, pp. 71, 73; and Paul Henrard, *Histoire de l'artillerie en Belgique* (Brussels, 1865), p. 15. For a more complete discussion of the role of gunpowder weapons at Othée see Wille, pp. 46–53, although even he must conclude that they "probably had little effect on the battlefield" (p. 52).

[32] J.F. Verbruggen, "Un plan de bataille du duc de Bourgogne (14 september 1417) et la tactique de l'époque," *Revue internationale d'histoire militaire* 20 (1959), 443–51. See also Bertrand Schnerb, "La bataille rangée dans la tactique des armées Bourguignonnes au début du 15e siècle: essai de synthèse," *Annales de Bourgogne* 61 (1989), 5–32.

noticing that he had retained the strong fortress of Vellexon when directed to surrender it. But John the Fearless' stay in Liège was not long, nor did it distract him from Blamont's treason. In 1409, he ordered his leading general, Jehan III de Vergy, the Marshal of Burgundy, to capture Vellexon. John the Fearless had learned the lesson of Maastricht well: Vergy's siege train was filled with gunpowder artillery of all sizes – the largest bombard able to fire a stone weighing between 700 and 850 *livres*, masons to make stone balls for ammunition, horsemen to transport the guns, carpenters to build mounts for the guns, and ropemakers, to bind the guns to their mounts. The bombardment of the fortifications began in September 1409 and lasted until 22 January 1410, when it fell. As contemporary documents report, the artillery fire was relentless and destructive, but it could not breach the castle's walls. Nor did it cause the inhabitants of Vellexon to surrender. However, the bombardment concealed the mining of the walls, and eventually this, together with the artillery fire, breached the fortifications.[33]

During both the engagements against Vellexon and against the Liégeois rebels, the Armagnacs had been busy working against John the Fearless and his adherents. Many French nobles and commoners continued to support the Burgundians, while the success of John's military endeavors also brought him much propaganda value. So, despite the Armagnac blockade on John the Fearless' governmental power in France from 1407 to 1410, his popularity increased rather than decreased. Several even accepted the Burgundian leader's *Justification* for the assassination of Louis of Orléans, as penned by Jean Petit. Especially in Paris was the duke of Burgundy welcome.[34]

In response, in the summer of 1411 the Armagnac forces began to attack Burgundian locations, while Burgundian forces, which, for more than a year, had been gathering men and arms, including a large number of gunpowder weapons,[35] began to attack Armagnac locales. This was not difficult to do, especially in the region of Picardy, north of Paris. There a Burgundian town often stood only kilometers away from an Armagnac town. So, it was that within a few days John the Fearless acquired the Armagnac town of Saint-Quentin, on the River Somme, but, at the same time, lost Ham, further up the river. This would not do, especially not for someone who had recently become used to crushing his opposition, not trading equal blows. Therefore, while under the pretense of seeking a truce, he gathered his army and his artillery train

---

33 Contemporary documents of the siege of Vellexon can be found in Plancher, III: 291–97, but see also Joseph Garnier, *L'artillerie des ducs de Bourgogne d'après les documents conservés aux archives de la Côte-d'Or* (Paris, 1895), pp. 17–30, and J. Bertin, "Le siège du château de Vellexon en 1409," *Bulletin de la société d'agriculture, science, commerce et arts du département de la Haute-Saône*, 3rd ser. 31 (1900), 1–190 (also published as *Le siège du château de Vellexon en 1409* (Vesoul, 1901)), both of which also contain some documents. For secondary accounts of and references to the siege see J. Bertin; Vaughan, *John the Fearless*, pp. 175–76; Salamagne, pp. 71, 73; P. Camp, *Histoire d'Auxonne au moyen âge* (Dijon, 1961), pp. 23–26; and Pierre Bertin, "Le siège du château de Vellexon dans l'hiver 1409–1410," *Revue historique des armées* 27 (1971), 7–18.

34 On this period of the Burgundian-Armagnac conflict see Vaughan, *John the Fearless*, pp. 67–87.

35 For example, see Garnier, pp. 37–42; Henrard, p. 15; J. de Laborde, *Les ducs de Bourgogne. Études sur les lettres, etc.* (Paris, 1849–52); I:22–23; Paul Fredericq, *Essai sur le rôle politique et social des ducs de Bourgogne dans les Pays-Bas* (Ghent, 1875), p. 159; A. Fromont and A. de Meunynck, *Histoire de canonniers de Lille* (Lille, 1892), pp. 35–36; M. Scrive-Bertin, "Les canonniers Lillois avant 1483," *Bulletin de la commission historique du departement du Nord* 19 (1890), 127; and Jules Huyttens, "Recherches sur l'organisation militaire de la ville de Gand au moyen-âge," *Messager des sciences historiques*, 6th ser., 26 (1858), 445.

and advanced against the Armagnac holdings. By the end of August, the duke had both besieged Rougemont with, among other gunpowder artillery, "the great bombard of Burgundy," and achieved a rapid victory in the reconquest of Ham.[36] According to *Le livre des trahisons de France envers la maison de Bourgogne*, at the latter siege three shots were fired from the bombard known as *Griette*, a gunpowder weapon which had been made earlier that year in Saint-Omer and tested in the presence of the duke himself.[37] The first passed over the town's castle and fell into the Somme; the second hit the ground in front of the castle, but still had enough power that it began to destroy a tower and two adjacent walls; and the third shot, which also struck the ground, made a breach in the wall itself. Before a fourth shot could be fired, the town capitulated.[38] Enguerran de Monstrelet however claims that the town fell by gunfire from several sources, especially from the numerous ribaudequins on each of which were mounted at least two medium-sized veuglaires which "fired night and day against the town [and] which greatly tormented their adversaries."[39] Other Armagnac towns soon followed suit, Péronne, Nesle, and Roye all fell to the duke before 22 September. Only at Montdidier did John meet substantial opposition, and when anticipated reinforcements failed to appear, gave up his effort there and withdrew first to his more secure northern lands and later to Paris for the winter.

Though 1412 found John the Fearless at the height of his French popularity, this did nothing to quell his opponents' enthusiasm to fight. John decided to strike directly at one of the strongest power-bases of the Armagnacs. The town of Bourges was not only the capital of the province of Berry but also the home of one of the most influential Armagnac leaders in France and John the Fearless' uncle, Jean, duke of Berry. Jean de Berry, in his eighties at the time, was not a prominent military leader, but his economic and political acumen was recognized by all Armagnacs, and, evidently, by John the Fearless. John's plan was to attack Bourges in an attempt either to capture it, thereby depriving Jean de Berry of his primary financial source, or to cause enough destruction to demoralize the duke and his colleagues. The town was also well inside the kingdom of France, a good distance from Burgundian territory. An attack of Bourges, especially with a heavy gunpowder artillery bombardment, would show the Armagnacs that he could reach and cause damage to any of their lands or towns. On 11 June, again with the bombard *Griette* in tow, the duke of Burgundy laid siege to Bourges. A monk of Saint-Denis was an eyewitness to the bombardment at Dun-le-Roi, a suburb of the town, and left this account:

> [The besiegers] . . . caused a cannon called *Griette*, which was bigger than the others, to be mounted opposite the main gate. It shot stones of enormous weight at the cost of large quantities of gunpowder and much hard and dangerous work on the part of

36 Monstrelet, II:172–75; *Chronique des Pays-Bas, de France, d'Angleterre et de Tournai*, in *Corpus chronicorum Flandriae*, 3, ed. J.J. de Smet (Brussels, 1856), p. 342; Schnerb, *Les Armagnacs et les Bourguignons*, p. 111; Salamagne, pp. 71, 80, 93, 110; and Camp, p. 59.
37 M.G.A. Vale, *War and Chivalry: Warfare and Aristocratic Culture in England, France and Burgundy at the End of the Middle Ages* (London, 1981), p. 141.
38 *Livre des trahisons*, p. 96.
39 Monstrelet, II:172–75 (quote is on p. 175). See also Guillaume, p. 77.

its expert crew. Nearly twenty men were required to handle it. When it was fired the thunderous noise could be heard four miles away, and terrorized the local inhabitants as if it were some reverberation from hell. On the first day, the foundations of one of the towers were partly demolished by a direct hit. On the next day this cannon fired twelve stones, two of which penetrated the tower, thus exposing many of the buildings and their inhabitants. At the same time, other batteries at the siege were also making breaches in other parts of the wall.[40]

The defenders of Bourges fought back, using their own gunpowder weapons, providing one of history's earliest gunpowder artillery duels; death and destruction was significant on both sides.[41] However, Bourges did not fall. On August 22 1412, at Auxerre, peace between both parties was signed. One of the provisions of this peace treaty was the granting of a pardon for the assassination of Louis of Orléans to John the Fearless and any others not directly responsible for the actual murder.[42]

Seemingly, John the Fearless had won the war between the Burgundians and the Armagnacs. However, Hundred Years War peace treaties were notoriously brittle, and the Treaty of Auxerre's provisions were not heeded for long. Throughout the remainder of 1412 and all of 1413, Armagnac factions worked to undermine John the Fearless' victories, while a popular rebellion in Paris – known as the Cabochien revolt – broke out against the duke.[43] Ultimately, before the end of the summer 1413, the Burgundian leader was forced to flee from Paris itself, surrendering it to Armagnac control.[44]

The military impetus now turned to the Armagnac forces which, in May 1414, began taking the war into Burgundian territory. Richard Vaughan has suggested that this was done "with an aim of crushing John and conquering or confiscating his territories."[45] Such a conclusion however seems to ignore the fact that the Armagnacs did not have the military might, nor the desire, to occupy all of the Burgundian-controlled towns of Picardy, let alone to capture Burgundy, Artois, and the Low Countries. Moreover, the targets of the Armagnac campaign, Compiègne, Soissons, Bapaume, and Arras, the capital of Artois, seem to display a wiser strategy: to nibble away at more vulnerable Burgundian sites. Compiègne, Soissons, and Bapaume all fell quite rapidly.[46] Arras did not. Although not previously attacked, the inhabitants of Arras had not been idle in their military preparations. Enguerran de Monstrelet writes:

> The people of Arras, who were daily expecting to be besieged by all the power of the king, made great preparations to resist them and to defend themselves against their

---

40 *Chronique du religieux de Saint-Denis*, IV:652. See also Monstrelet, II:273–74, 281–82; Vaughan, *John the Fearless*, pp. 95–96; Schnerb, *Les Armagnacs et les Bourguignons*, p. 112; Garnier, pp. 14–15; and Salamagne, pp. 71, 93.

41 Monstrelet, II:281–82, and Guillebert de Lannoy, *Œuvres*, ed. C. Potvin (Leuven, 1878), p. 19.

42 Vaughan, *John the Fearless*, pp. 96–98.

43 See Vaughan, *John the Fearless*, pp. 98–102; A. Coville, *Les cabochiens et l'ordonnance de 1413* (Paris, 1888); and Schnerb, *Les Armagnacs et les Bourguignons*, pp. 127–43.

44 On 23 August 1413.

45 Vaughan, *John the Fearless*, p. 197.

46 *Chronique du religieux de Saint-Denis*, V:293; Monstrelet, II, 466, III:6–7; Jean le Fevre, *Chronique*, ed. F. Morand (Paris, 1876), I:160–63; and Schnerb, *Les Armagnacs et les Bourguignons*, pp. 149–51.

adversaries. They endeavored to make *boulevards* before their gates, of large oaks planted in the earth . . . and also barriers and ditches in many and diverse places, so that no one would be able to approach them. In these *boulevards*, on the towers and walls, and put all around their town, they placed more large cannons, veuglaires, and other instruments of war to torment their enemy.[47]

Thus, when the Armagnacs began their siege, they encountered strong defenses and a determined populous. Again, an artillery duel ensued. Despite, "firing their bombards, cannons, veuglaires, and colleuvres, which were discharged incessantly day and night," according to the anonymous author of *Le livre des trahisons de France envers la maison de Bourgogne*, the numerous Armagnac gunpowder weapons and siege machines were useless, and their mines were continually and effectively counter-mined.[48] In the meantime, the Armagnac army outside the walls of Arras was beset by dysentery.[49]

In order to end the siege and perhaps to allow him time to regroup and reinforce his military forces, John the Fearless resorted to diplomacy, asking his brother-in-law, the duke of Brabant, and his sister, the countess of Holland and Hainault, to negotiate another peace treaty. This treaty, the Peace of Arras, was almost the exact opposite of the one signed at Auxerre the year previously. It clearly condemned the duke of Burgundy for all of his actions in France since 1407, including the murder of the duke of Orléans, and commanded him to make territorial, financial, and spiritual reparations.[50]

It would be folly to think that John the Fearless ever intended to keep this treaty; as already noted, the status of peace treaties and negotiations during the Hundred Years War was more to stop current fighting than to prevent future warfare. However, it was events outside of the Burgundian-Armagnac conflict – principally the 1415 landing of King Henry V of England in Normandy, his successful siege of Harfleur, and his even more successful battle at Agincourt – that effected what occurred next.[51] John the Fearless was not among the French forces at Agincourt, although he seems to have intended to be, putting aside his animosity for the Armagnac military leaders who were present. Nor was he immediately able to take advantage of the defeat and death of his opponents there. Although many of his supporters styled these as Armagnac defeats,[52] the English threat for the moment seems to have superseded French politics and the Armagnacs stayed in power, even after the leading Armagnac leader, the dauphin,

---

47 Monstrelet, III:22. See also Salamagne, pp. 71, 98.

48 *Livre des trahisons*, p. 127; Monstrelet, III:22–31; *Chronique du religieux de Saint-Denis*, V:370–75; Jean le Fevre, I:184; Vaughan, *John the Fearless*, pp. 197–98; Schnerb, *Les Armagnacs et les Bourguignons*, pp. 151–52; and A. d'Héricourt, *Les sièges d'Arras* (Arras, 1844).

49 Monstrelet, III:29–30. See also *Journal d'un bourgeois de Paris, 1405–49*, ed. A. Teutey (Paris, 1881), p. 56.

50 See Vaughan, *John the Fearless*, pp. 198–203; J. Finot, *La paix d'Arras, 1414–15* (Nancy, 1906); and, most recently, Nicolas Offenstadt, "Le paix d'Arras, 1414–15: un paroxysme rituel?" in *Arras et la diplomatie européenne, xve–xvie siècles*, ed. Denis Clauzel, Charles Giry-Deloison, and Christophe Leduc, Centre de Recherches Historiques: "Des Anciens Pays-Bas à l'Eurorégion" (Université d'Artois–Arras) (Arras, 1999), pp. 65–80.

51 There are numerous accounts of these events, but few connect them with what was happening in the French Civil War, despite the obvious military relationship.

52 Vaughan, *John the Fearless*, pp. 207–08.

Louis of Guienne, died in December 1416, his replacement being the very capable Count Bernard of Armagnac.[53]

It was only in 1417, with the return of Henry V and the beginning of his successful conquest of Normandy, that John the Fearless was once again able to make military inroads against his Armagnac enemies. Because he had not regained the leadership of France since Agincourt, the Burgundian duke sought an alliance with Henry V. Following a secret meeting with the English king at Calais on 11–16 October 1416, a pact was consolidated, which, at the very least, seems to have given John foreknowledge of the 1417 English invasion.[54] With this intelligence, John the Fearless was able to coordinate his campaign against Armagnac holdings in Picardy and the Ile-de-France with Henry's against Normandy. His first target was Montdidier, the town which had held out against him so often before; it fell in June. In July, he captured, among others, Nogent-sur-Seine and Troyes; in August, Doullens, Amiens, Rheims, and Beauvais; in September, Beaumont-sur-Oise, Senlis, Pontoise, Vernon, Mantes, Provins, and Poissy; and in October, Montlhéry and Chartres. Most of these were either intimidated into surrender – John would show up outside the town walls with his large gunpowder artillery train in tow and threaten death and destruction if the inhabitants did not surrender[55] – or bombarded into submission. Those locations which did try to defend themselves held out for little more than a few days.[56]

John the Fearless' strategy in 1417 was simple: he sought to encircle Paris with Burgundian acquisitions in order to make a coordinated attack of the capital city. Since John's forced departure in 1413, the Parisians had been split on whether to give their allegiance to the Burgundians or to the Armagnacs. Before Agincourt, when the dauphin, Louis of Guienne, or one of his Armagnac military leaders, Charles of Orléans, Louis of Anjou, or Bernard of Armagnac, had been in the city, the inhabitants had favored their side, but when not present, and especially after Agincourt, their commitment to the Burgundians had increased. During 1416–17, several small Parisian rebellions had even tried to force the city to accept John the Fearless' rule. These had always been harshly quelled by the Armagnacs. The Armagnacs also built up defenses in and around Paris, preparing the city for a Burgundian assault. The *religieux de Saint-Denis* reports that passages over the rivers Oise and Seine were fortified and that bombards were placed on the wall ramparts.[57]

But when Burgundian soldiers – so numerous that, Monstrelet claims, the Parisians thought their large number of tents "was a good sized city"[58] – stood outside the city in late 1417 and early 1418, firing their cannon and other gunpowder weapons onto the

53 Charles of Orléans had been captured at Agincourt.

54 See *Chronique des cordeliers*, in Enguerran de Monstrelet, *Chronique*, ed. L. Douet-d'Arcq, vol. 6 (Paris, 1857–62), p. 235; *Gesta Henrici quinti*, ed. B. Williams (London, 1850), pp. 103–04; and Vaughan, *John the Fearless*, pp. 213–15.

55 For example, Monstrelet (III:218–19) claims that the inhabitants of Montlhéry, "thinking that they had no succor" from the French king, made a treaty with John the Fearless once he arrived outside the town with his gunpowder artillery train.

56 Monstrelet, III:218–91; *Livre des trahisons*, pp. 127–57; *Chronique des cordeliers*, pp. 243–44; and le Fevre, I:320–24.

57 *Chronique du religieux de Saint-Denis*, VI:85.

58 Monstrelet, III:216.

walls and into the city, the intensity of these rebellions increased. During one of them the chief Armagnac leader, Count Bernard of Armagnac, was even murdered. Finally, on 29 May 1418, the citizens of Paris, being attacked from without and within, opened their town's gates to John the Fearless' troops.[59] A massacre of Armagnac supporters ensued, with more than two thousand killed, and the mentally unstable King Charles VI and his queen, Isabeau of Bavaria – she was already in the custody of and friendly to the Burgundians – welcomed John the Fearless as the governor and "protector" of France.

In the year following the capture of Paris, and while continuing his attacks of Armagnac locations, in particular Roye, which was besieged in the by now traditional Burgundian fashion of harsh artillery bombardment from a large number of gunpowder weapons,[60] John the Fearless tried to put together a governing coalition of Burgundians and Armagnacs. In a treaty signed in early September 1418, he even made sure that the last remaining son of Charles VI and Isabeau, the dauphin, Charles, received the lands of Dauphiné, Touraine, Berry, and Poitou as an appanage, and he continued to recognize him as heir to the French throne. He also allowed Charles, now the *de facto* Armagnac leader, to name one of the three officials who would handle the state's finances. In addition, John seems to have been interested in halting any further English advance into France and, perhaps, to regain some of those lands already lost to them. However, John was never able to carry out this plan, for on 10 September 1419, in meeting with the dauphin on the bridge at Montereau under a writ of "safe passage," he was set upon and murdered by Armagnac adherents.[61]

59 *Chronique du religieux de Saint-Denis*, VI:85, 127–29; Monstrelet, III:216; Jean Juvenal des Ursins, *Histoire de Charles VI*, in *Nouvelle collection des mémoires relatifs à l'histoire de France*, 2, ed. M. Michaud (Paris, 1857), pp. 537–38; Vaughan, *John the Fearless*, pp. 221–27; and Schnerb, *Les Armagnacs et les Bourguignons*, pp. 180–93.
60 See Monstrelet's description of this siege (Monstrelet, III:367–68).
61 Vaughan, *John the Fearless*, 263–86; Schnerb, *Les Armagnacs et les Bourguignons*, pp. 194–207; and Paul Bonenfant, *Du meurtre de Montereau au traité de Troyes* (Brussels, 1958), pp. 1–16. For an analysis of the sources on this assassination see P. Cockshaw, "L'assassinat du duc Jean de Bourgogne à Montereau: Études des sources," in *Les Pays-Bas bourguignons: Histoire et institutions. Mélanges André Uyttebrouck*, ed. J.-M. Duvosquel, J. Nazet, and A. Vanrie (Brussels, 1996), pp. 145–62.

PHILIP THE GOOD

When the assassins' blows felled John the Fearless on Montereau Bridge that 10 September 1419, his son and heir, Philip (the Good) of Charolais, was of majority, aged twenty-three. Yet, his father had included him in very few of his military engagements; nor does it seem that the new Burgundian duke had been included in his father's strategic and tactical planning sessions. He therefore had little combat experience, a mistake which he would not repeat with his own son, Charles the Bold. However, Philip would learn the art of warfare quickly, and throughout his long reign of forty-eight years he frequently put this knowledge to work. And every time he did so, he used his impressive gunpowder weaponry train, one which he had inherited at his father's death, but one also which he strengthened both numerically and in its overall power and diversity throughout his reign. Indeed, Philip the Good's use and development of this military technology is the reason why so many modern historians studying military history at the end of the Middle Ages, in particular those studying the Burgundian armies of the four Valois dukes, have determined that their gunpowder artillery was "the strongest of Europe".[1]

In military affairs, Philip was almost always his own man. However, it did not start out that way. John the Fearless' death not only thrust him into ducal leadership, but, as the assassination quickly was tied directly to the French heir to the throne, the Dauphin Charles,[2] Philip had no choice but to continue John's fight against the Armagnacs, no matter what he personally thought about the civil war for which his father was largely to blame.[3]

Perhaps even more important, the slaying of John the Fearless thrust Philip the Good into an alliance with the English. This was both bad and good. The English forces which occupied a large part of France in 1419 really had no justifiable reason for their success. After all, England was a far less-populated kingdom than was France. Comparative demographic figures show a disparity of more than 300 percent.[4] This of

1   The quotation is from Florens Deuchler, *Die Burgunderbeute: Inventar der Beutestucke aus den Schlachten von Grandson, Murten und Nancy 1476/77* (Bern, 1963), p. 302, but a similar sentiment is found in M. Guillaume, *Histoire de l'organisation militaire sous les ducs de Bourgogne* (Brussels, 1848); J. Lachauvelaye, "Les armées des trois premiers ducs de Bourgogne," *Mémoires de l'academie des sciences, arts et belles-lettres de Dijon* ser. 3. 6 (1880), 19–335; Claude Gaier, *L'industrie et le commerce des armes dans les anciennes principautés Belges du XIIIme à la fin du XVe siècle* (Paris, 1963); and Charles Terlinden, *Histoire militaire des Belges* (Brussels, 1931).

2   On this point see the sources discussing the murder mentioned in the chapter above. See also Richard Vaughan, *Philip the Good: The Apogee of Burgundy* (London, 1970), pp. 4–5.

3   Vaughan, *Philip the Good*, pp. 3–8, indicates a belief that Philip was not enthusiastic about pursuing this war, except for the fact of his father's assassination.

4   Edouard Perroy's tallies of 10–12 million French inhabitants and 3½ million English inhabitants (*The Hundred Years War*, trans. W.B. Wells (London, 1951), pp. 36, 50–51) are pre-Black Death numbers (1328). However, there is no indication in his work, or in anyone else's, that the population disparity ninety years later was any different.

course meant that the potential number of soldiers from England was much smaller than that from France. Calculations of the number of English soldiers in France by Anne Curry, based on expeditions sent from England to France between 1415 and 1419, show an incredibly small number of troops to protect all of the occupied regions of France, as well as to carry on further offensive military operations.[5]

But then there was King Henry V. In the year of John the Fearless' death the English king had made great military strides, which, while not geographically large, included the most important regions of France ever to fall to the English. He began the year 1419 by capturing Rouen, on 19 January, and as had happened so frequently before, there was little French reaction to this conquest. As in Normandy earlier, opposing garrisons and militias of the many castles and towns between Rouen and Paris which Henry attempted to capture were small, and they seemed to have had little desire to fight or endure a siege against him. None of them even held out beyond the exhaustion of their food supply. Arques (later known as Arques-la-Bataille), Lillebourne, Vernon, Mantes, Neufchâtel, Dieppe, Gournay, Eu, Fécamp, Tancarville, and Honfleur, all surrendered to the English before the end of February 1419; Gisors, Ivry, La Roche-Guyon, Pontoise, Meulan, Poissy, Saint-Germain, and Château Gaillard, all held out only a little longer, but were still captured by the end of the year.[6] By September 1419, Henry V entered Burgundian-held Paris and was wooing Catherine of Valois, the daughter of the mentally incompetent King Charles VI and Isabeau of Bavaria, who were willing to do whatever they could to preserve their lives and to bring peace to their kingdom. Later, such desperation was to bring ignominy to Isabeau's name and legacy.[7] As it happened, Philip the Good's wife, Michelle of France, was Catherine's sister. Although Michelle of France died on 8 July 1422, the close personal ties to Henry V undoubtedly strengthened Philip's resolve to be allied to him even above his desired revenge against those who had killed his father.[8]

On 21 May 1420, the Treaty of Troyes was signed between Henry V and Charles VI.[9] This treaty in all its intricacy can be reduced essentially to one provision: it made Henry V heir to the throne of France. Charles VI was still recognized as king, but should he die, and he was ill almost all of the time, then Henry V would assume his throne. Charles' own son, the Dauphin Charles, whose complicity in the murder of John the Fearless had been firmly proven, was effectively disowned. Henry was also to

---

5   Anne Curry, "English Armies in the Fifteenth Century," in *Arms, Armies and Fortifications in the Hundred Years War*, ed. A. Curry and M. Hughes (Woodbridge, 1994), p. 45. This citation refers to a chart which lists the numbers of troops sent each year to France between 1415 and 1450. Curry's entire article (pp. 39–68) is devoted to the calculation of English soldiers serving in France during the fifteenth century.

6   Alfred H. Burne, *The Agincourt War: A Military History of the Latter Part of the Hundred Years War from 1369 to 1453* (London, 1956), pp. 133–34; Richard Ager Newhall, *The English Conquest of Normandy, 1416–24: A Study in Fifteenth Century Warfare* (New Haven, 1924), pp. 123–32; and E.F. Jacob, "The Collapse of France, 1419–20," *Bulletin of the John Rylands Library* 26 (1941–42), 307–26.

7   See, for example, Rachel Gibbons, "Isabeau of Bavaria, Queen of France (1385–1422): The Creation of an Historical Villainess," *Transactions of the Royal Historical Society*, 6th ser., 6 (1996), 51–73, and Marie-Véronique Clin-Meyer, *Isabeau de Bavière, La reine calomniée* (Paris, 1999)

8   Vaughan, *Philip the Good*, p. 8.

9   The Treaty of Troyes is recorded in Eugène Cosneau, ed., *Les grandes traités de la guerre de cent ans* (Paris, 1889), pp. 100–15.

serve for the time being as regent of the crown, which placed him effectively in charge of the government. Finally, Henry V would marry Charles VI's youngest daughter, Catherine, their eldest son to be heir to both the French and the English kingdoms. The marriage took place less than a month later, on 2 June 1420, in Troyes Cathedral.[10] From this treaty it seems that Philip the Good received nothing, although he did gain some revenge for the assassination of his father in the knowledge that the man who was responsible for his father's death had been disinherited. He probably also recognized that there was little likelihood that Henry would have been in this position except that he and his father had placed him there. Finally, Philip may have believed that, should he so desire, he could remove Henry at any time.

In 1420, even before the Treaty of Troyes was signed and Henry and Catherine's marriage solemnized, the Burgundian armies of Philip the Good were on the move against Armagnac targets. Of course, the Armagnacs did not accept the Treaty of Troyes and considered the legitimate heir of the throne to be their leader, the dauphin. However, despite the murder of their greatest enemy, John the Fearless, and maybe a little bit because of it, they were weak. It appears that their numbers in 1420 were smaller than ever before, and there was very little chance of their summoning the strength to take advantage of what was, for only a brief moment, a loss of leadership on the Burgundian side. Although certainly restless, their plan seems to have been to fall back to more secure lands and try to regroup. It was to become a position in which they would grow increasingly more comfortable and from which they would be less willing to move.

Neither the English nor the Burgundians intended to let them follow this plan, and both allies continued to wage war against their common enemy over the next two years. Sometimes they acted together, and sometimes separately, but, almost always, they were successful. However, what Philip the Good's military role was during this period is disputed. Richard Vaughan, the accomplished biographer of the duke, taken by Philip's humble opinion of the time that he was "as yet but slightly equipped" with the necessities of military leadership takes the position that this Burgundian duke was primarily interested in protecting his lands and boundaries and not carrying forth a conflict which had gained his father little but his own murder.[11] He writes:

> For the Burgundian chroniclers, and perhaps for the participants, Philip the Good's French campaigns of the years after 1420 seemed of paramount interest. But for us, viewing the whole long reign in the perspective of history, these military activities assume a secondary importance. It was the diplomatic system . . . which ensured the peace and security of Philip's lands in these years, not the battles and sieges.[12]

Yet, throughout the decade of the 1420s, Philip did not have this "perspective of

---

[10] Perroy, *The Hundred Years War*, pp. 243–44; Burne, *The Agincourt War*, pp. 139–44; Paul Bonenfant, *Du meurtre de Montereau au traité de Troyes* (Brussels, 1958); Christopher T. Allmand, *The Hundred Years War: England and France at War c. 1300–c. 1450* (Cambridge, 1988), pp. 29–32; Christopher T. Allmand, *Henry V* (Berkeley and Los Angeles, 1992), pp. 136–50.

[11] Vaughan, *Philip the Good*, pp. 6–11. The quotation comes from *Inventaire sommaire des archives départementales antérieures à 1790. Nord. Série B*, ed. A. le Glay et al. (Lille, 1863–1906), I.2:272.

[12] Vaughan, *Philip the Good*, p. 10.

history"; what he did have was a desire for revenge and an English alliance. So, it is hard to ignore what the chroniclers describe as an extremely active ducal participation in carrying forth the Armagnac-Burgundian civil war.

Philip's first Armagnac target seems to have been Montereau, both as an effort to obtain his father's remains and to punish the town for its role in John the Fearless' death. But along the way from Burgundy to Montereau stood the Armagnac-held town of Allibaudières in Champagne, which had been very well fortified, including the recent additions of anti-gunpowder weapon boulevards. Here was Philip the Good's first chance to see what his gunpowder weapons could do. The town was surrounded and battered from every direction with continual bombardments of what must have been a sizeable gunpowder artillery train. Eventually, according to Enguerrand de Monstrelet and Jean de Waurin, all of the gates, towers, and walls were destroyed and the town surrendered.[13]

After Allibaudières, Philip met up with his allies, the English, and, at their insistence added his forces and gunpowder weapons to the siege of Sens. It fell in six days.[14] Then the two armies proceeded to Montereau. Montereau was a much smaller location than either Allibaudières or Sens, and it may not have been very well fortified – none of the original sources mention stone walls. But it had been the scene of John the Fearless' assassination and, at least in Philip's mind, warranted some punishment for the crime, whether the inhabitants were complicit in it or not. So, together with a large number of English troops, and with a large amount of gunpowder artillery, the Burgundians bombarded the town into surrender, disinterred the corpse of his father, and sent it, spiced and salted, back to Dijon in a lead coffin.[15]

The Anglo-Burgundian attack of Montereau was to satisfy the duke of Burgundy. Melun, the next target of 1420, was primarily for the English. So large were the forces of both princes that they were able to surround this substantial walled town. Both Philip the Good and Henry V were present. Enguerran de Monstrelet and Georges Chastellain, the two best chroniclers of this siege, write that the Anglo-Burgundians fired bombards and other machines of war in an attempt to hit and destroy the walls. Night and day these gunpowder weapons were fired into the town, the bombards causing much damage to the walls, while mortars did much damage to the houses inside. However, despite "many being killed by coulovrine shot," the inhabitants within were undaunted in the defense of their town: When the gunpowder weapons destroyed their walls, they reinforced the breaches with large quantities of earth and Anglo-Burgundian mines were countermined. The result was a siege lasting eighteen weeks. Still, the besiegers were determined. There was no relieving Armagnac army, and the Anglo-Burgundian camp was well outside the range of the town's guns.[16] In

---

[13] Enguerran de Monstrelet, *Chronique*, ed. L. Douet-d'Arcq (Paris, 1857–62), III:382–84, and Jehan de Waurin, *Récueil des croniques et anchiennes istories de la Grant Bretaigne*, ed. W. and E.L.C.P. Hardy (London, 1864–91), II:301–02.

[14] Vaughan, *Philip the Good*, p. 11, and Burne, *The Agincourt War*, p. 148. Few of the original sources give much attention to Sens, probably in light of its weak defense.

[15] Monstrelet, III:405; Georges Chastellain, *Œuvres*, ed. Kervyn de Lettenhove (Brussels, 1863–66); and Vaughan, *Philip the Good*, p. 11.

[16] Chastellain, I:153–56; Monstrelet, III:410–13; and Waurin, II:326–27. Chastellain's mention of mortars

fact, Monstrelet comments on the amount of music and frivolity in this camp, a sure sign of relaxation in their task.[17] Even an Armagnac attack and bombardment of the Burgundian-held Pont-Saint-Esprit à Rosnes, meant as a diversion to dislodge Philip the Good's force from Melun, failed to achieve its goal.[18] The Anglo-Burgundians stayed put, and eventually the town surrendered.

The campaign year of 1421 began with a similar fervor among the Anglo-Burgundian forces. Little is known about what transpired in the June conference between Henry V and Philip the Good at Calais, where the two met after a winter and spring stay of the English king and the Burgundian duke in their own homelands.[19] However, the military actions which progressed following this meeting seem to indicate that the two armies were to strike at separate Armagnac targets closer to their own lands. Vaughan claims that this was a defensive measure, at least on Philip's part,[20] but if so then the Burgundian duke certainly performed it in a very offensive manner, in a manner very imitative of his father, as his target in these engagements was the same Picardy which John the Fearless had spent so many years trying to acquire.

Philip's first attack was against Saint-Riquier, a town near the region's Armagnac capital of Abbeville. The Burgundians began the siege using "bombards and cannons," which contemporary narratives report "greatly damaged" the walls, gates, and houses of the town. But the town did not immediately fall; indeed, the inhabitants responded by firing their own "engines" – which undoubtedly included the town's arsenal of gunpowder weapons – into the Burgundian attackers.[21] An Armagnac army marching from Compiègne to relieve the siege, meant that Philip the Good had to turn his attention to the battlefield, and on 31 August he fought his first battle, at Mons-en-Vimeu. Although a relatively minor engagement, it apparently included no gunpowder weapons as these had been left to batter the walls of Saint-Riquier, and the duke himself performed valiant feats of arms on the field, even after the disintegration of many of his own forces; but by the end it was a Burgundian victory.[22] Following this, Saint-Riquier surrendered, as did Abbeville after a significant bombardment of its walls using many gunpowder weapons – Chastellain notes especially those which had come from Mechelen, Bruges, and Beaurevoir.[23]

Henry V was having more difficulties in the south. His attempted siege of Meaux, situated thirty miles outside Paris, was not going smoothly. This town, like so many previously, did not simply negotiate a surrender when an Armagnac army did not show up to relieve it. More importantly, even though it was continually bombarded by

---

may reflect his own time more than that of the 1420s, as no contemporary confirmation of the existence of this type of weapon is found until later.

[17] Monstrelet, III:412–13.

[18] Monstrelet, III:407.

[19] Vaughan, *Philip the Good*, p. 12.

[20] Vaughan, *Philip the Good*, p. 12. Vaughan also claims that Philip left Henry "to conduct the main offensive against the dauphinists" which seems to be a very narrow-minded and somewhat pro-English view of looking at the engagements of 1421. The weakening of Armagnac control in the north was every bit as important to the Hundred Years War at this stage as doing so in the center of France.

[21] Monstrelet, IV:53; Waurin, II:371; and Chastellain, I:250–51.

[22] See Monstrelet's account (IV:59–63) which has been translated by Vaughan, *Philip the Good*, pp. 12–14.

[23] Chastellain, I:275–77. Chastellain also notes that one of the Beaurevoir cannons had been "rebuilt."

English gunpowder weapons, the thickness of the medieval walls, built as they were on strong Roman foundations, held throughout the autumn and winter.[24] The armies of the duke of Clarence and the earl of Salisbury, however, were having more success in Maine and Anjou. Ultimately, this led to the English victory at the battle of Baugé, although at the cost of Clarence's life.[25] Still, the victory at Baugé brought little boost in morale for the English forces, nor did the fall of Meaux, which eventually surrendered on 2 May 1422,[26] for Henry V was stricken with an illness, generally thought to have been dysentery, at the siege, and on the last day of August he was dead, predating by less than two months the death of his father-in-law, Charles VI, the elderly and ailing man whom Henry had sought to replace by the Treaty of Troyes.[27]

The death of Henry V left many crises unresolved. The most famous, and undoubtedly the most important, of these were the inheritance problems. The Treaty of Troyes had named Henry V as heir to the throne of France after the death of Charles VI. But as Henry V's death had preceded that of Charles VI, who was to be the heir to the throne of France? Was it to be Henry's newborn son, Henry VI? Or was it to be the Dauphin Charles, disinherited by his royal parents, at his mother's behest, but not by many of his countrymen? This crisis would not be solved entirely until 1453 and the end of the Hundred Years War.

A lesser crisis brought about by the death of Henry V was the future of the Anglo-Burgundian alliance. So far, the alliance had proven to be only of slight benefit to the duke of Burgundy, providing him with some vengeance against the assassins of his father, but little more. However, it had been a costly endeavor. In letters written on 7 January 1421 addressed to the officers in charge of collecting funds throughout his realm, Philip writes that

> owing to the very heavy military expenses we have had to meet since the death of our . . . father . . . especially for the sieges of Sens, Montereau and Melun, which we undertook in person with large forces of men-at-arms and archers, as well as those of Roye in Vermandois and Allibaudières in Champagne, which were very costly, we cannot find the money from our rents and revenues. Instead, we must of necessity borrow on the security of some of our jewelry and gold and silver plate, and mortgage certain parts of our domain.[28]

Additionally, Henry's death had also been preceded on 8 July 1422 by that of Philip's wife, Michelle of France, and so there was absolutely no familial connection left between the Burgundian duke and Henry's widow or young heir, Henry VI.[29] So, Philip the Good might be excused had he reckoned that the Anglo-Burgundian alliance was finished.

Instead, the alliance appears to have thrived for the rest of the decade. In July 1422

---

24 Monstrelet, IV:71. See also Desmond Seward, *Henry V as Warlord* (London, 2001), pp. 182–86.
25 On this battle see Burne, *The Agincourt War*, pp. 151–63.
26 Monstrelet, IV:83; Burne, *The Agincourt War*, 169–77; and Seward, pp. 186–95.
27 Burne, *The Agincourt War*, pp. 177–78; Allmand, *Henry V*, pp. 169–74; and Seward, pp. 209–16.
28 A translation of this letter, found in the Archives départmentales du Nord, Lille, B1602, f. 149v, is in Vaughan, *Philip the Good*, p. 30.
29 Vaughan, *Philip the Good*, p. 8.

English assistance was sent by the dying Henry V to Philip the Good at Cosne in the person of John, the duke of Bedford, the brother whom Henry put in charge of his armies in France and the regency of Henry VI.[30] And, in 1423, the two armies fought together at Le Crotoy, Landrecies, and Cravant. In the first conflict, a siege of this strong site at the mouth of the Somme, a gunpowder weapon bombardment of the town and castle of Le Crotoy, eventually led to a negotiated surrender by the inhabitants which allowed them to leave the castle with all their gunpowder, crossbows, and arrows, except for nine veuglaires, two casks of gunpowder, 23 crossbows, and 9 coffers of arrows, which were to be surrendered to the Anglo-Burgundians.[31] The second conflict, the siege of Landrecies, was accomplished more quickly when an Anglo-Burgundian force led by Jean of Luxembourg, count of Ligny, who had become Philip the Good's chief lieutenant, reduced the town to submission with gunpowder weapons.[32]

Finally, the third conflict, the battle of Cravant, was one of the greatest achievements of the Anglo-Burgundian alliance. According to the anonymous author of *Le livre des trahisons de France envers la maison de Bourgogne*, an incredibly detailed source for the encounter but one which unfortunately has not been used by many modern historians,[33] the battle began as a siege of Burgundian-held Cravant, "a small town, but strong and well situated because it sits below a mountain one bow shot from the Yonne River," by an Armagnac force strengthened by Scottish and Lombard mercenaries. The citizens of Cravant immediately sent letters to their patron, the dowager duchess of Burgundy, Philip's mother, pleading for an intercession with her son on behalf of their town. This the duchess did, promising to sell all of the horses on her lands to pay for the relief of the town, if necessary.[34]

Other sources indicate that this prompted a war-planning session between the Burgundians and English at nearby Auxerre Cathedral at the end of July 1423. As the people of Cravant had been reduced to near starvation, there was some urgency in the discussions, and the following agreement was quickly written up:

1. They [the Anglo-Burgundian leaders] would set out with their men at 10:00 a.m. the next day, Friday (30 July 1423) and advance towards Cravant.
2. Two marshals were appointed to look after the troops, the lord of Vergy for the Burgundians and Gilbert Halsall for the English.
3. English and Burgundians to be ordered to live together in amity and not to quarrel, on pain of punishment at the discretion of the captains.
4. They would all ride together, but 120 men-at-arms, sixty English and sixty Burgundians, with as many archers, were to be sent ahead.

---

30 Vaughan, *Philip the Good*, p. 14.

31 Monstrelet, IV:157–67.

32 Monstrelet, IV:164.

33 Neither Alfred H. Burne (pp. 181–95) nor Charles Oman (*A History of the Art of War in the Middle Ages* (London, 1905), II:390–91) make any use of this source for their battle narratives. Vaughan (*Philip the Good*, p. 15 n.1) does refer to *Le livre des trahisons de France envers la maison de Bourgogne* as a source for the battle of Cravant, but does not discuss the battle itself.

34 *Le livre des trahisons de France envers la maison de Bourgogne*, in *Chroniques relatives à l'histoire de la Belgique sous la domination des ducs de Bourgogne (texts Français)*, ed. Kervyn de Lettenhove (Brussels, 1873), p. 169.

5. It was agreed that, when they arrived at the battlefield, they would all dismount promptly on the word of command. Those who refused to be put to death. The horses to be led half a league to the rear. Any found nearer were to be confiscated.

6. Each archer to provide himself with a pole, sharpened at both ends, to fix in front of him as necessary.

7. No one, of whatever rank, may take prisoners during the battle until victory is completely assured. Any prisoners thus taken to be executed, along with their captors.

8. Everyone must provide himself with food for two days. The citizens of Auxerre to be asked to send provisions to the army which will be paid for.

9. On pain of death, no one is to ride in front or behind of his appointed place without leave of the captains.

10. Tonight, everyone is to pray as devoutly as possible, while awaiting life or death next day according to the grace of God.[35]

This list shows, perhaps because of the Burgundian problems at Mons-en-Vimeu, that English tactics were adopted, though with the addition, again according to *Le livre des trahisons de France envers la maison de Bourgogne*, of carts carrying between thirty and forty Burgundian veuglaires, which were to be operated by the Auxerrois. The same source also numbers the Anglo-Burgundians at 500 English men-at-arms and 2000 archers, with 1000 Burgundian men-at-arms, or more, and crossbowmen and pioneers "without number."[36]

About half a league from their enemy the Anglo-Burgundian forces halted for a day, ostensibly to reform the army, but the following day, 31 July, Thomas Montagu, the earl of Salisbury, the general of the Anglo-Burgundians, tried to outflank the Armagnacs only to come face to face with them lined up solidly across the River Yonne. The battle began a while later when the Scots along both wings of the Armagnac army began to shoot arrows into the Anglo-Burgundians. Their response was for the Auxerre cannoniers to fire the veuglaires, together with an archery barrage by the English and Burgundian archers and crossbowmen, leading to a "large amount of death." Seeing the Armagnacs disturbed and disordered by the artillery and archery attack, Salisbury executed a decidedly unEnglish tactic: he charged straight across the shallow river into the more numerous Armagnacs. As *Le livre des trahisons de France envers la maison de Bourgogne* recounts: "The enemy saw 1500 men or more all in view in the water up to their chain, their lances and pommels." This charge clearly surprised the Armagnacs and some, including the Lombards, quickly broke into rout, although the Scots, whose anger at the English often kept them fighting when others were fleeing, stood their ground. Soon, they, too, were overrun, "cut apart, and killed." The town of Cravant was relieved.[37]

35 The original list is printed in Monstrelet, IV:159–60; in Waurin, III:64–66; and, in part, in Jean le Fevre, *Chronique*, ed. F. Morand (Paris, 1876–81), II:77–78. This translation comes from Vaughan, *Philip the Good*, p. 15.

36 *Le livre des trahisons de France envers la maison de Bourgogne*, p. 169.

37 *Le livre des trahisons de France envers la maison de Bourgogne*, pp. 169–70. See also Monstrelet, IV; Waurin, III:55–60; *Liber de virtutibus sui genitoris Philippi Burgundiae ducis*, in *Chroniques relatives à l'histoire de la*

In the years following their combined victory at Cravant, the Burgundians and English largely fought separately, apart from each other, but again this should not be seen as a division of purpose in the way that Richard Vaughan reckons.[38] On the French side, the dauphin, Charles, showed less and less interest in seeking combat with the Anglo-Burgundians after a defeat at the battle of Cravant in 1423, followed by a defeat against the English at the battle of Verneuil the next year.[39] The result was a two-front campaign by the two allied armies against the geographically diverse Armagnac holdings that can only be seen as military activity pursued for a common purpose against a common enemy. Thus in 1424–1426, as the English pushed towards the River Loire towns and castles supporting the Dauphin, several Burgundian armies marched in separate directions against their enemy. First, in 1424, the Burgundians took a huge gunpowder artillery train against Guise – which resulted in the capture of the town[40] – and into the Maconnais – which meant the recapture of many Burgundian villages and lands of the region which the Armagnacs had taken following the death of John the Fearless. Among the gunpowder weapons used by Philip in the Maconnais were the bombards named *Griete*, *Katherine*, *Cambray*, and *l'Ecluse*, as well as several veuglaires and ribaudequins.[41] Next, in 1425, Philip the Good directed Jean of Luxembourg to take his army and artillery against the Guise castle at Terraisse which fell to a similar negotiated surrender as Guise had the year before.[42] This was followed by the siege of Saint-James de Beauvron, at which Jean Chartier insists that the Burgundians, who seem to have been assisting the English on this occasion, used their "bombards and artillery" without necessity as the Armagnacs inside the town were in such disarray that they would have surrendered without such an attack.[43] Finally, in 1426, the Burgundians began a siege of the fortification of Mailly-le-Château, near Auxerre, although the garrison of this castle so quickly negotiated a surrender that the Burgundians guns had not yet arrived.[44]

Yet, there is little doubt that relations between the two allies were becoming strained. Even though the leaders of the two armies seemed to get along, their soldiers had very different attitudes and allegiances. This can be seen clearly in several provisions of the Cravant war-plan listed above which pushed towards harmony and unity between the two armies. Furthermore, Philip the Good, who had been able to push a

Belgique sous la domination des ducs de Bourgogne (texts latins), ed. Kervyn de Lettenhove (Brussels, 1876), pp. 19–20; and Burne, *The Agincourt War*, 188–95. The *Liber de virtutibus sui genitoris Philippi Burgundiae ducis* also discusses the fortifications of the town of Cravant.

38   Vaughan, *Philip the Good*, p. 15.

39   This battle did not include Burgundian troops. See Burne, *The Agincourt War*, pp. 198–215. For a novel view of this battle see Michael K. Jones, "The Battle of Verneuil (17 August 1424): Towards a History of Courage," *War in History* 9 (2002), 375–411.

40   Monstrelet, IV:204. Interestingly, Monstrelet writes that in surrendering Guise, the garrison was allowed to take all their "cannons, artillery, engines, machines of war" and other material with them as they left the town.

41   Joseph Garnier, *L'artillerie des ducs de Bourgogne d'après les documents conservés aux archives de la Côte-d'Or* (Paris, 1895), p. 93.

42   Waurin, III:177, and *Le livre des trahisons de France envers la maison de Bourgogne*, p. 172. In both this and the above Guise engagement, there is a record of some English troops among the Burgundian force.

43   Jean Chartier, *Chronique de Charles VII*, ed. Vallet de Viriville (Paris, 1858), I:50.

44   See Garnier, pp. 94–95.

large amount of his military expenses for 1420–22 onto King Charles VI of France, began to think about charging the English for his participation in what he began to think of more and more, as a conflict that was more beneficial to them than to himself. Although for the moment, Philip did not press this issue with the English, in 1429 and 1430 when his allies were in the midst of failures against Joan of Arc, he did require the English to pay for his military services.[45]

But perhaps the most important reason for the strain in relations between Philip the Good and the English was the situation which arose in the counties of Hainault, Zeeland, and Holland. The extension of Burgundian interests in the Low Countries had been pursued by the Valois dukes since the beginning of their reigns. Flanders and Namur had already come under direct Burgundian rule, while the duchy of Brabant, the counties of Hainault, Zeeland, and Holland (then ruled by the same count), and the prince-bishopric of Liège had been associated with the Burgundian realm by marriage or kinship as early as the reign of Philip the Bold. In 1417, after the deaths of the leaders of the principalities of Brabant, Hainault, Zeeland, and Holland, John the Fearless had arranged for his nephew, the young male heir of the duchy of Brabant, John IV, to marry his niece, the young female heir of the counties of Hainault, Zeeland, and Holland, Jacqueline. Two years later the two were married. However, in the county of Holland, succession was far from settled. John of Bavaria, the prince-bishop of Liège and brother-in-law to John the Fearless, made a claim to the comital throne. John the Fearless, too involved in his own civil war with the Armagnacs, had allowed the situation in Holland to remain unresolved. Initially at least, Philip the Good also played little role in solving the inheritance problem, although at times he did step in as arbitrator when it appeared that open warfare might result.[46]

Finally, in 1420, John IV decided to resolve the problem on behalf of his wife, and, for the payment of a large mortgage, he surrendered Holland and Zeeland to John of Bavaria. This, however, turned out to be far from what Jacqueline had wanted, and she abandoned her husband, fleeing from Brussels, the Brabant capital, to England, where she met and married Humphrey, duke of Gloucester and uncle to Henry VI.[47] Among the things which Gloucester promised Jacqueline was the return of her Zeeland and Holland counties.

On 6 April 1424 the plot thickened when the childless John of Bavaria made Philip the Good his heir. Thus when Gloucester landed in Calais with an army reputed to be going to Holland but reported to be traveling only to Hainault, which was still in Jacqueline's hands, Philip interceded by forbidding the English duke from marching

---

[45]   Vaughan, *Philip the Good*, pp. 17–18. This ducal dissatisfaction seems to have arisen especially in the wake of the English capture of Le Crotoy in 1423 and Compiègne in 1424, when the Burgundians were pressed by the English to allow them to occupy these sites.

[46]   The best account of this is in Vaughan, *Philip the Good*, pp. 31–34.

[47]   There are all sorts of difficulties in understanding the history of this event. Most historians suggest that there was some incompatibility, sexual or otherwise, between John IV and Jacqueline which is not explained fully in the original sources, with the mortgage of Holland and Zeeland to John of Bavaria as simply the "last straw." See Vaughan, *Philip the Good*, p. 34. Jacqueline's first marriage was annulled not by Pope Martin V in Rome, but by Pope Benedict XIII in Peñiscola. Martin V would later claim that this marriage should not have been annulled.

through Flanders and only allowed him to cross Artois with an escort. As this was happening, John of Bavaria died in Holland. This meant, technically, that the mortgaged lands of Holland and Zeeland should have reverted to the control of Duke John IV of Brabant and Countess Jacqueline of Hainault. Of course, with Jacqueline married to Gloucester, and Philip the Good John of Bavaria's heir, the technicality of the issue bore little weight. Early in March 1425 a Burgundian-Brabantese army crossed into Hainault and besieged Braine-le-Comte, which according to Jean de Waurin, was garrisoned by Gloucester's Englishmen. Within a few days, and after a lengthy gunpowder weapon bombardment – by gunpowder weapons "without number," writes Waurin – the town fell and the garrison surrendered.[48]

It is clear that Philip the Good did not like the brash English duke, no matter to whom he was related and communication between the two verged from provocation to open warfare, Philip put an end to this when, following the conquest of Braine-le-Comte, he challenged Duke Humphrey to single, personal combat as a means of averting further bloodshed. The duel was accepted and the date set for 23 April 1425. But as the combat drew near, Gloucester fled back to England, without his wife, Jacqueline – although with one of her ladies-in-waiting, Eleanor Cobham, in tow –[49] who was captured by Philip and put under house arrest in Ghent.

Jacqueline, abandoned by her erstwhile protector, and with few friends in Hainault, escaped from Ghent "dressed as a man" and made her way to Holland where she was able to inspire some opposition to the Burgundian occupation of the county. In September 1425, despite the conflict with the Armagnacs in France, Philip the Good marched to war against Holland and Zeeland.[50] Many towns, including Rotterdam, Amsterdam, Haarlem, and Leiden, were faithful to him, while other, mostly smaller towns, including Gouda, Oudewater, and Schoonhoven, were loyal to Jacqueline. Still, Holland was not like Flanders, Liège, or France, with large populated urban centers which had to be dealt with; Holland's economy revolved around agriculture and fishing, and Jacqueline seems to have gathered her most numerous adherents from the villages and hamlets which supported these economies. This made her quite confident, even against the formidable Burgundians. In the first engagement, the battle of Alphen (22 October 1425), Jacqueline not only took the initiative against the duke, by attacking a Burgundian force largely made up of urban militias from Haarlem, Amsterdam, and Leiden who were marching towards Gouda, but she also defeated him.[51]

After this defeat, Philip the Good rode north to Leiden to take control personally of the situation. But he had first to engage a force of English soldiers sent to assist Jacqueline by her estranged husband, Humphrey, the duke of Gloucester. This occurred on

---

48 See Waurin, III:165. On the events leading up to Braine-le-Comte see Vaughan, *Philip the Good*, pp. 34–37.

49 Vaughan, *Philip the Good*, pp. 38–39, and E.F. Jacob, *The Fifteenth Century, 1399–1485* (Oxford, 1961), p. 225. It certainly seems on his part that Philip was serious about this risky endeavor. See le Fevre, II:106–07.

50 Philip's first attack into the county did not however occur until the following month.

51 Vaughan, *Philip the Good*, pp. 41–44. From the original sources there appear to have been no gunpowder weapons used in this battle.

30 December 1425 at Brouwershaven in Zeeland. In a letter written following the battle, Philip tallies the forces to more than 4,000 on each side. Unfortunately, he recounts little of the battle itself, except that:

> By the grace of God, they were defeated. A good many were put to flight, and we chased these into the sea, so that few escaped. This in spite of the fact that, at the moment when battle was joined with the English, only about two-thirds of our people had got to shore. For the English advanced to attack us, and began to fight us, before all our men had disembarked.[52]

Further information from *Le livre des trahisons de France envers la maison de Bourgogne* also indicates that, as Philip said, the Burgundians had not completely disembarked, but adds that their gunners had. These gunners had come from Dordrecht, and, records the anonymous author of this work, held the same reputation as gunpowder weapons' operators as the Ghentenaars had in Flanders. They even wore special uniforms which included hats banded in red and white. At the beginning of the battle these gunners played an important role, firing their coulovrines into the English lines. The English advanced in order, where they were met by crossbow fire to which they responded with their own longbow archery fire. Initially, this pushed the Dordrechters back, but then Philip and his heavily-armored cavalry appeared to strengthen the line, seemingly impervious to the English archers who only dented and damaged their armor. Eventually, the English soldiers were themselves driven back, along the dikes and into the water where "they were either drowned or else cut down as they tried to climb out of the water."[53] No further English troops would come to the aid of Jacqueline of Hainault.

Still, the war continued. The defeat of the English at Brouwershaven had done little to convince the Hollanders to come over to Philip's side, although it does appear that he secured most of Zeeland with this victory. In fact, the opposite seems to have happened: some towns and villages, such as Utrecht, Amersfoort, Alkmaar, and the Kennemerland, actually joined Jacqueline after the battle; and she continued to lead her troops with some success against Burgundian strongholds. On 30 April 1426 Jacqueline won a second victory at Alphen and, at the same time, laid an impressive siege against Haarlem.[54] Once more, Philip the Good was forced to personally lead a Burgundian army into Holland.

In the autumn of 1426, Philip began to besiege the island town of Zevenbergen, a town loyal to Jacqueline that sheltered her fleet, enabling it the freedom of pirating Burgundian ships and pillaging Burgundian locations. Even with gunpowder weapons, besieging an island was not an easy task, as the English had discovered at Mont-Saint-Michel which they had been unsuccessfully besieging since 1417. It took four months of continual gunpowder weapon bombardment of Zevenbergen, a

---

52   The original of this letter is in the Archives départementales de la Côte-d'Or, Dijon, B11942, no. 48. The translation I have used is in Vaughan, *Philip the Good*, pp. 42–43.

53   *Le livre des trahisons de France envers la maison de Bourgogne*, pp. 181–83. See also Vaughan, *Philip the Good*, pp. 43–44.

54   Vaughan, *Philip the Good*, p. 44.

bombardment which Jean de Waurin insists became increasingly heavy as the days rolled on, before the town fell, and even then this came about only because the hungry townspeople revolted against the town's military garrison and opened their gates to the besiegers.[55]

Philip's patience had won out at Zevenbergen. Still, the war was not over, as it had not been over after Brouwershaven. Philip clearly understood this. His patience would prove to be wise once more after Easter when, again according to *Le livre des trahisons de France envers la maison de Bourgogne*, the Burgundian duke sailed to Amsterdam from Flanders. There he gathered his officials and instructed them to make a "*bolewerc*" (the Middle Dutch word for *boulevard*) sixty feet long and thirty feet wide along the seaward side of the town. For protection it was covered by pavises "all the way to the water" fastened "to the tops of the wall with a mortar made of tar and flax," and this strengthened the walls "so that no handgun (*canon à main*) could damage them." The walls rose sixteen feet above the water and were "sufficiently" machicolated. In the sea next to this boulevard, the Amsterdamers were to add "a force of floating barges" to barricade goods from being shipped up river to Utrecht and Amersfoort. Such a defensive structure, which also obviously played a significant offensive role, had rarely been built before. No doubt by its construction, Philip the Good not only wanted to stop supplies, and especially, English troops, from getting through to Jacqueline's strongholds, but it was also meant to impress those in Holland still standing against him – he was not likely to be kept from his goal, their domination.[56]

By late spring 1427 the war in Holland had begun to swing in Philip's favor. What quick military actions had not accomplished in the years prior to this seemed to have been achieved by the duke's more patient campaigning of the last several months. Philip even went so far as to declare the war over and won in May 1427. But Jacqueline fought on, even gaining a few significant victories, against Burgundian fortifications along the shores of Zeeland, in the months following Philip's declaration. The war dragged on into 1428 with both armies still fighting, although the conflicts had been reduced largely to skirmishes. Ultimately, however, abandoned by the English, and beset by Burgundian military might, even though her subjects, especially in Gouda and Utrecht, would have fought forever, it seems, to keep her in power, Jacqueline was forced to surrender. In signing the Treaty of Delft, on 3 July 1428, she was able to retain her title as countess of Hainault, Holland, and Zeeland, but essentially ceded those principalities to Philip the Good.[57]

John of Bedford, the commander of English forces in France, tried to remain out of the Gloucester-Jacqueline affairs and the war in Holland. Humphrey, duke of Gloucester, was his younger brother, but Bedford's wife, Anne of Burgundy, was the sister of Philip the Good, and this relationship, coupled with the much more powerful role Philip had been playing in the English conquest of France, kept Bedford from assisting

---

[55] Waurin, III:210. See also Vaughan, *Philip the Good*, p. 45.
[56] *Le livre des trahisons de France envers la maison de Bourgogne*, pp. 194–95.
[57] Vaughan, *Philip the Good*, pp. 47–50. The actual transference of these counties did not come, however, until 1432 when Jacqueline, found to have violated the agreements of the Treaty of Delft by marrying Frank van Borselen, was forced to abdicate the thrones in favor of Philip.

his brother's interests in the Low Countries.[58] Bedford may even have gone so far in his support of Philip that he informed the Burgundian duke of Gloucester's return and intentions in 1424 and also of the English army's arrival in Zeeland which allowed Philip to fight them without their Hollander allies at Brouwershaven in 1425.[59] In addition, during the years which Philip fought in Holland and Zeeland the Earl of Salisbury rolling up numerous victories against the Armagnacs between Paris and the Loire.[60] Bedford wisely reckoned that he might, once again, need to call upon his brother-in-law to supply men and gunpowder weapons.

That time came in 1429 when a young peasant woman, ironically born and raised in Burgundian territory, appeared saying that she had received a mission from God to free occupied France from its English occupiers. To the Burgundians, Joan of Arc posed little problem. Their encounters with her during her early career were minimal. She was born and raised in Burgundian territory, and in fact in July 1428 Philip the Good seems to have sent troops into her birthplace, Domrémy, after word got out that she had visited Robert de Baudricourt, the Captain and Governor of nearby Vaucouleurs – who was not an ally of Philip – with a fantastic story of having a mission from God to rid the French kingdom of English and crown the Dauphin as its king. This Burgundian raid accomplished little as the villagers seem to have known of its coming and fled to the safety of nearby Neufchâteau. Ironically, though, it may have given Baudricourt reason to invite Joan to a second meeting – perhaps Baudricourt felt guilty about not defending the village, or perhaps he reasoned that if the duke of Burgundy accepted the possibility of Joan's mission there might be something in her story – after which she was able to get his blessing to visit the dauphin in Chinon.[61]

But, while she caused few initial difficulties to the Burgundians, the same could not be said of the English. Joan of Arc menaced them. It is true that she had to pass certain tests of the Dauphin Charles after she had arrived at Chinon, but once he realized her worth in the conflict against the Anglo-Burgundians, she made rapid military strides. Less than a week after she had arrived at Orléans, she had relieved the English siege of that town, an incredibly difficult task considering that they were in control of the forti-fied bridgehead across the Loire, the Tourelles. A month later, she removed the remaining English forces from their Loire strongholds – at Jargeau, Meung-sur-Loire, and Beaugency – and had won the battle of Patay. Then, shortly after, she led an army to Rheims, capturing towns along the way, where Charles the Dauphin was crowned King Charles VII of France.[62] Only the fact that she had marched the dauphin through largely undefended Burgundian territory to Reims and that there were Burgundian soldiers among those who defeated her attempt to take Paris (and who, among others, fired cannon and coulovrines at the attackers, according to Enguerran de Monstrelet

---

58 Jacob, *The Fifteenth Century*, pp. 225–26.
59 Vaughan, *Philip the Good*, p. 42.
60 For these campaigns see Burne, *The Agincourt War*, pp. 196–249.
61 Kelly DeVries, *Joan of Arc: A Military Leader* (Stroud, 1999), pp. 31–43. Robert de Baudricourt did not immediately send her to Chinon, however. First, he had her visit Count René of Anjou, and once that meeting was successful, sent her to the Dauphin (DeVries, *Joan of Arc*, pp. 42–43).
62 DeVries, *Joan of Arc*, pp. 54–121.

and Perceval de Cagny[63]), directly affected the Burgundian duke and then, it seems, only marginally.[64] On the other hand, Joan herself, perhaps due to where she had been born and raised, constantly wished that the Burgundians return to the "French" fold. This shows in the only remaining letter of several that she wrote to the duke, which was written on the day of the coronation of Charles VII:

> *Jhesus Maria*
>
> High and dread prince, duke of Burgundy, the Maid calls upon you by the King of Heaven, my rightful and sovereign Lord, to make a firm and lasting peace with the king of France. You two must pardon one another fully with a sincere heart, as loyal Christians should; and if it pleases you to make war, go and wage it on the Saracens. Prince of Burgundy, I pray you, supplicate, and humbly request rather than require you, make war no more on the holy kingdom of France. Withdraw at once and swiftly those of your men who are in certain places and fortresses of the aforesaid holy kingdom. As for the gentle king of France, he is ready to make peace with you, saving his honor, if it has to do with you alone. And I must make known to you from the King of Heaven, my rightful and sovereign Lord, for your good and for your honor and upon your life, that you will win no more battles against loyal Frenchmen and that all those who wage war against the aforesaid holy kingdom of France are warring against King Jesus, King of Heaven and of all earth, my rightful and sovereign Lord. And I pray you and call upon you with hands joined not to seek any battle nor war against us, neither you nor your men nor subjects, and believe firmly that no number of men that you bring against us will win, and that there will be great pity for the battle and the bloodshed there of those who come against us.[65]

After his coronation, Charles VII also made entreaties for peace towards the duke.[66]

What Joan of Arc and Charles VII did not offer Philip the Good, however, John, duke of Bedford, did: money. By the end of 1429, Bedford was desperate for Burgundian assistance. The reverses suffered by the English at the hands of Joan of Arc in that year were more significant than any the last fifty years. He needed to halt their progress before the English lost any more territory. So, Bedford needed Philip and, when the Burgundian duke demanded payment in return for services, he was forced to ensure that the Burgundians would get it. And, indeed, Philip the Good did: by the end of 1431 he had been paid £150,000, although he was still owed £100,000.[67] Obviously, money was a more important incentive to the Burgundian duke than Joan of Arc's or Charles VII's prospect of peace or French unity.

With this settlement, the Anglo-Burgundian alliance was once again in force. A detailed and intricate military plan was agreed on, indicating how those lands currently

---

63 Monstrelet, IV:355, and Perceval de Cagny, *Chronique des ducs d'Alençon*, in Jules Quicherat, ed., *Procès de condamnation et de réhabilitation de Jeanne d'Arc dite la Pucelle* (Paris, 1841–49), IV:26–27.

64 DeVries, *Joan of Arc*, pp. 122–34.

65 This letter is preserved in the Archives du Nord in Lille. It is edited in Quicherat, ed., *Procès de condamnation et de réhabilitation de Jeanne d'Arc*, V:126–27, and Régine Pernoud and Marie-Véronique Clin, *Joan of Arc: Her Story*, trans. and rev. J.D. Adams (New York, 1998), pp. 253–54. I have used the translation found in Pernoud and Clin, pp. 67–68. See also DeVries, *Joan of Arc*, p. 139.

66 Vaughan, *Philip the Good*, pp. 20–22.

67 Vaughan, *Philip the Good*, p. 17.

held were to be apportioned and by whom governed, and what new military targets were to be undertaken.[68] The Burgundian army then set out against its first objective, Compiègne. Compiègne, like several ungarrisoned French towns, had joined with Charles VII after he had been crowned. Yet, despite staying in the town for several days before Joan of Arc's attack on Paris – Compiègne held a royal castle – Charles retreated to his River Loire following Joan's failure to take Paris, abandoning Compiègne and the other towns in the region which had joined him.[69]

Philip the Good may have thought that as Compiègne had gone over so easily to Charles, it might just as easily leave him, especially as he had, it seems, so quickly abandoned the town. However, Compiègne was not going to abandon the French king. The people of the town received news in March 1430 that Philip was planning to lay siege to Compiègne and decided that they would not surrender to him. They chose to remain French even though that meant that they would have to resist attempts to capture their town. The citizens of Compiègne began to stockpile supplies and weapons. Such bravery inspired Joan of Arc who felt that she had been held back from military engagements since the beginning of the year. Eventually she joined the townspeople in the defense of their town, arriving there before the Burgundians.[70]

Philip had amassed a large army and an impressive artillery train. At this date, there was perhaps no power with a stronger or more numerous gunpowder weaponry arsenal than the Burgundians, and almost all of it was directed at Compiègne. Contemporary chroniclers report the existence of at least five large bombards, two veuglaires, one large and one small, innumerable couloverines, and two "*engins*" among the besieging Burgundian army;[71] other sources record the transportation of at least 17,000 lb of gunpowder with the artillery train.[72] Extant artillery *comptes* for the Burgundian forces have shown that these tallies are far too low.[73] But this show of military technology did not intimidate either Joan of Arc or Guillaume de Flavy, the governor of Compiègne and leader of its defense effort. The fortifications of the town were very strong. The town walls were tall and thick; indeed, several still stand today as impressive examples of medieval defensive power. More than 2,600 meters long, they surrounded a town of 53 hectares. A large number of towers had been built along these walls, no fewer than forty-four of them along the River Oise. This river served as a "moat" on one side of Compiègne, while its waters also filled a wide and deep ditch surrounding the rest of the walls. A rampart, made from the material taken from the ditch, added to the town's

---

[68] This plan is in the Bibliothèque Nationale, MS fr. 1278, ff. 12–14. It is edited in part in Pierre Champion, *Guillaume de Flavy: Captaine de Compiègne: Contribution à l'histoire de Jeanne d'Arc et à l'étude de la vie militaire et privée au XVe siècle* (Paris, 1906), no. 30, and translated in part in Vaughan, *Philip the Good*, pp. 22–24.

[69] DeVries, *Joan of Arc*, pp. 153–54.

[70] DeVries, *Joan of Arc*, pp. 166–70.

[71] Waurin, III:362; Monstrelet, IV:418–19; Chastellain, II:53; and Antonio Morosini, *Chronique: Extraits relatifs à l'histoire de France*, trans. and ed. L. Dorez (Paris, 1898–1902), III:319–23. See also DeVries, *Joan of Arc*, pp.169–70, and Gaier, *L'industrie et le commerce des armes*, p. 111.

[72] Philippe Contamine, "La guerre de siège au temps de Jeanne d'Arc," *Dossiers de archéologie* 34 (May 1979), 16.

[73] As transcribed in Champion, 174–83. See also Alain Salamagne, "L'attaque des places-fortes au XVe siècle à travers l'exemple des guerres anglo et franco-bourguignonnes", *Revue historique* 289 (1993):78–79.

defenses as a counterscarp outside the moat. Should these defenses be breached, there
was also the large royal castle, modelled after the Louvre in Paris, located within the
walls. The only weak defensive points seem to have been the numerous gates into the
town – these were protected by large gatehouses – and the single bridge over the Oise,
450 feet long and built on ten or eleven arches. This bridge was lined with houses, with
a large fortified gate at the town end, and on the shore opposite the town a boulevard.[74]
Additionally, the defenders of Compiègne had their own gunpowder weaponry
arsenal, and they had prepared their defenses to use it by destroying any superfluous
fortifications which might hinder gunfire.[75] These guns would prove very effective,
particularly, as reported by an anonymous eyewitness, "the great number of small
engines, called coulovrines, which were made of bronze and which fired lead balls." He
even boasted that these balls were able to penetrate the armor of a man-at-arms.[76] This
was not going to be a quick siege, but the Burgundian leaders, especially Jean of
Luxembourg, felt that they could still achieve a victory, even against such a fortified
location and even against Joan of Arc.

The actual defeat of Joan was accomplished quite easily. Not accustomed to stand
behind walls in a defensive posture, on 23 May 1430, with a small group of soldiers,
she decided to ride out of the town and strike into the Burgundian army. What she
hoped to accomplish with this misguided tactic, no one has adequately explained, for
it was unsuccessful. At her trial, she gave the following testimony to what happened
next:

> She crossed over the bridge and through the French boulevard and went with a
> company of soldiers manning those sections against the lord of Luxembourg's men
> whom she drove back twice, all the way to the Burgundian camp, and a third time
> half way back. And then the English who were there cut her and her men off, coming
> between her and the boulevard, and so her men retreated. And withdrawing into the
> fields on her flank, in the direction of Picardy, near the boulevard, she was
> captured.[77]

Her capture proved to be worth 10,000 *livres tournois* to Jean of Luxembourg, whose
men had captured her, the sum the English paid for her ransom. A little more than a
year after she had been captured, on 30 May 1431, Joan of Arc was burned to death as a
heretic in the market-place of Rouen.[78]

However, the capture of Compiègne was quite another matter. In fact, it never
occurred. Despite the large number of gunpowder weapons which Philip the Good
had at the siege, and the constant bombardment against the town, its walls, gates, and
inhabitants, the town did not capitulate. All contemporary narrative sources record
that the Burgundian guns were very powerful and very destructive. Monstrelet
describes a siege where the Burgundians built a large bastille or boulevard of earth, a

[74] See DeVries, *Joan of Arc*, pp. 170–71, and Pernoud and Clin, p. 232.
[75] Champion, p. 48.
[76] Quoted in Champion, p. 49 n.10.
[77] Joan of Arc, in Quicherat, I:207–08. See also DeVries, *Joan of Arc*, p. 176.
[78] DeVries, *Joan of Arc*, pp. 176–82.

bow-shot from the town in which they set up their gunpowder weapons. These were aimed against Compiègne "which, because of the continuation of large stones which they fired, disrupted and breached the gates, bridge, mills, and boulevard of the town in many places." The mills ceased to mill; and one gunshot even killed Louis de Flavy, the brother of the governor, Guillaume. Mines also were attempted and failed.[79] Still, Guillaume de Flavy continued to diligently defend the walls and the boulevard. And, according to both *Le livre des trahisons de France envers la maison de Bourgogne* and Jean de Waurin, the gunpowder weapons of the townspeople seemed to have been as effective as those of the Burgundians, with "one cannon mounted on the wall" killing ten or twelve besiegers.[80]

Throughout the summer the siege of Compiègne went on. The joy of capturing Joan of Arc was soon forgotten, and the plodding of the constant conflict must have worn on the soldiers. Surprisingly, little fatigue seems to have afflicted the besieged; who seem to have been well provided for, despite being encircled by hostile forces. No contemporary source even mentions hunger being a problem inside the town, thus missing a narrative *topos* so prevalent in accounts of other Hundred Year War sieges. On the other hand, the besieged were both fatigued and tormented by their inability to conquer the site. Suddenly, and really without an adequate explanation in any of the original sources, the Burgundians abandoned the siege. In fact they abandoned it so quickly that they left behind their numerous gunpowder artillery pieces which the inhabitants of Compiègne quickly captured and brought within the gates. What actually happened is truly one of the biggest mysteries of the Hundred Years War. Monstrelet claims that it was a decision made by Jean of Luxembourg, the Burgundian general at the siege, the count of Hontiton, and "many other notables in their company." But, if this was the case, why did they leave with such speed that they abandoned "a very large number of large bombards, cannons, veuglaires, serpentines, coulovrines, and other artillery which were left in the hands of the French, their adversaries?" Monstrelet ends his account: "This artillery was the duke of Burgundy's!"[81] Jean de Waurin is equally confused and offers the same surprise at the abandoning of "a large quantity of large bombards, cannons, veuglaires, serpentines, and other artillery which fell into the hands of the enemy."[82] The author of *Le livre des trahisons de France envers la maison de Bourgogne* professes that it was the defensive gunfire which "convinced them to retreat."[83] Still, this can hardly be the sole or even the primary reason for such a quick withdrawal.

Modern authors are equally befuddled at the Burgundian retreat. Richard Vaughan suggests only that the Burgundians "were forced" to leave;[84] Pierre Champion praises

[79] Monstrelet, IV:390–91. See also Waurin, III:361–63, 385–89; Chastellain, II:53, and Morosini, III:319–23.

[80] *Le livre des trahisons de France envers la maison de Bourgogne*, p. 176. See also Waurin, III:388–89.

[81] Monstrelet, IV:418–19.

[82] Waurin, III:389–90. There is perhaps an irony in the fact that almost immediately after this Waurin reports the English capture of French gunpowder artillery at Clermont that same year (Waurin, III:392–93).

[83] *Le livre des trahisons de France envers la maison de Bourgogne*, p. 176.

[84] Vaughan, *Philip the Good*, p. 24.

the inhabitants of Compiègne and especially their governor and military leader, Guillaume de Flavy, whose reputation he was trying to rehabilitate from one who "gave up" Joan of Arc;[85] most do not even record the siege, except for its relationship to the soon-to-be martyred Saint Joan.[86] Yet, the failure of the Burgundians to capture Compiègne, with its attendant loss of gunpowder artillery, was of enormous importance both to the next phase of the Hundred Years War and, especially, to the relationship between the Burgundians and the English, at whose behest the duke of Burgundy was undertaking the siege. Although Monstrelet reports that Jean of Luxembourg was condemned for his actions by Philip the Good,[87] the duke himself felt that blame for the military debacle should be laid firmly at the feet of the English. In a letter written 4 November 1430 by Philip to Henry VI, he clearly makes this known:

> Most redoubted lord, I recommend myself to you in all humility. I imagine that you and your councillors remember that it was at your urgent request that I took part in your French war. For my part, I have so far accomplished everything that I agreed to and promised in the indenture made between . . . the cardinal of England [Henry Beaufort], acting in your name, and myself. It is a fact that, as a result, all my lands both in Burgundy and Picardy have been and are at war and in danger of destruction . . . Moreover, it was at your request and command that I undertook the siege of Compiègne, though this was contrary to the advice of my council and my own opinion. For it had seemed to us better for me to advance towards Creil and Laon, as appears in the recommendations drawn up on this and sent to Calais by our secretary Master Jehan Milet.[88]
>
> It is also true, most redoubted lord, that, according to the agreement drawn up on your part with my people, you ought to have paid me the sum of 19,500 francs of royal money each month for the expenses of my troops before Compiègne,[89] as well as the cost of the artillery; while my good cousin the earl of Huntingdon with his company ought to have remained with me before the said town of Compiègne . . . It was under the impression that this would be done on your part, and especially that the said payment would be made without fail, as agreed, that I had my men stationed before Compiègne all the time.
>
> But, most redoubted lord, these payments have not been kept up by you, for they are in arrears to the tune of two months. The same goes for the artillery, for which I myself paid out over 40,000 *saluts* . . . Likewise, my good cousin of Huntingdon has been unable, according to him, for want of payment, to keep his forces in the field any longer . . .
>
> My redoubted lord, I cannot continue these [military operations] without adequate provision in future from you . . . and without payment of what is due to me, both on account of the two months abovementioned, and for the artillery. Thus most redoubted lord, I ask and entreat you most humbly to see that the said sums are

---

85   Champion, pp. 42–58, 162–82.
86   See, for example, Burne; Oman; and Ferdinand Lot, *L'art militaire et les armées au moyen-âge en Europe et dans le proche orient* (Paris, 1946).
87   Monstrelet, IV:419.
88   Recommendations made in the Anglo-Burgundian plan of war mentioned above.
89   This was the sum agreed to by the duke of Bedford before the siege.

paid over at once to my people at Calais who have been waiting there for this purpose for some time . . .[90]

The Anglo-Burgundian relationship, perhaps never an entirely solid one during the reign of Philip the Good, may have been irreparably damaged at Compiègne.

Philip also probably blamed himself somewhat for the Compiègne loss. He had not been able to be at the siege itself. 1430 had been a busy year for him. He had taken another, and final, wife, Isabel of Portugal, and to celebrate the occasion, he originated what would come to be Europe's most exclusive chivalric order, the Order of the Golden Fleece.[91] At the same time, both the Flemings and Liégeois presented problems which required his military attention. The situation in Flanders – a small peasants' uprising – was soothed quickly and without bloodshed,[92] but the Liégeois problem – a flair-up of a long-term feud between two towns, Dinant and Bouvignes, lying across the Meuse from each other – took the threat of military action by the duke of Burgundy before a very tentative truce with the Liégeois was agreed to.[93] Threats of war from Duke Frederick of Austria and an alliance based on a potential marriage between him and Charles VII, although minor in their results, further complicated matters for the duke of Burgundy that year.[94] Then there was the defeat of another Burgundian general, Louis de Chalon, prince of Orange, on 11 June 1430 in a French ambush at Anthon in the Dauphiné, which the prince had rather foolishly, and with far too few troops and very little wisdom, decided to invade; Louis of Chalon did escape, but only just.[95] Finally, the call for Philip the Good to lead a Crusade against the Hussites, something which had been made repeatedly over the recent years and something which the duke truly wished to do, intensified in 1430, adding to the reasons keeping him from military leadership at Compiègne.[96]

However Philip the Good may have felt about his own involvement in the failure at Compiègne, or perhaps because he felt embarrassed by what had happened there, the years following the failed siege, until 1436, were all filled with warfare against the French king and his allies. Sometimes in conjunction with the English, as if the alliance was still thriving, but mostly on his own and in his own interests.

And act quickly, strongly, and violently he did. In 1431 Burgundian armies struck

[90] This letter is edited in *Letters and Papers Illustrative of the Wars of the English in France during the Reign of Henry VI*, ed. J. Stevenson (London, 1861–64), II.1:156–64. The partial translation I am using comes from Vaughan, *Philip the Good*, pp. 24–25.

[91] On the negotiations, arrangements, and ceremonies of the marriage, and on the establishment of the Order of the Golden Fleece see Vaughan, *Philip the Good*, pp. 54–58. See also Pierre Cockshaw and Christiane Van den Bergen-Pantens, ed., *L'ordre de la Toison d'or, de Philippe le Bon à Philippe le Beau (1430–1505): Idéal ou reflet d'une société?* (Brussels, 1996).

[92] Vaughan, *Philip the Good*, pp. 57–58.

[93] Vaughan, *Philip the Good*, pp. 58–62. The best source on this brief war is *Le livre des trahisons de France envers la maison de Bourgogne*, p. 201.

[94] Vaughan, *Philip the Good*, pp. 64–65.

[95] Vaughan, *Philip the Good*, p. 62. A recent work on this battle, little more than an ambush and rout, is Philippe Gaillard, *La bataille d'Anthon: 11 juin 1430* (Annecy-le-Vieux, 1998).

[96] Vaughan, *Philip the Good*, pp. 69–70. See also the original documents charting the Burgundian proposals and preparations for a Crusade against the Hussites contained in Thomas A. Fudge, ed. and trans., *The Crusade against Heretics in Bohemia, 1418–1437: Sources and Documents for the Hussite Crusades* (Aldershot, 2002), pp. 268–75, 282–84.

out into the lands of René of Anjou, duke of Bar and titular king of Naples, with, Monstrelet writes, "16–20 wagons and carts with victuals, cannons, artillery, and other war materiel."[97] René of Anjou had tried to stay neutral in the Hundred Years War, his lands bordering both those of the king of France and duke of Burgundy. But the recent events concerning Joan of Arc – he had supported her mission to the Dauphin – and a succession crisis in the duchy of Lorraine between himself and Anthony of Lorraine, count of Vaudémont, allowed the military entry of Philip the Good into René of Anjou's affairs and lands. Philip's army was not large; it appears that the duke did not think of his incursion as anything very substantial. Monstrelet even calls the expedition a "chevauchée," a raid through the Barrois countryside meant more for terror than for battle. Perhaps Philip felt that René would not try to counter his invasion into Bar, being willing instead to face the loss of a little territory and a few fortifications as punishment for his allegiance to France rather than face the terrible force of the Burgundian army, led by the Lord of Barbazan, and its artillery. If this was Philip's plan, it did not work out that way; but the way it did work out greatly benefitted the Burgundian duke.

Barbazan's initial action was to besiege the Barrois fortification at Anglure. A short artillery exchange between the defending guns of the inhabitants and the larger, more numerous ones of the Burgundian troops ended with Anglure's surrender.[98] Maybe this defeat spurred René of Anjou into action, for he gathered his army and, on 2 July 1431, marched against the small Burgundian force. Although Philip the Good may not have expected this move, Barbazan had anticipated it. The Burgundians were able to choose the battlefield, between the towns of Bulgnéville and Vaudoncourt, and prepare it for battle. Among these preparations was the expert placement of "*canons et couleuvres*" by the ducal cannoneer assigned to the expedition, Jean Maréchal. Monstrelet reports what happened next: "And when they saw that the Barrois were near to them, twelve to sixteen *destres* away, they shot with fire from their cannons and couleuvres all at the same time and then gave out a large shout. At the discharge of the cannons, large numbers of the Barrois dove to the earth and were very afraid."[99] Following this gunfire, the Burgundian archers fired and the Burgundian men-at-arms charged. The Barrois broke in rout, with most eluding capture, except for René of Anjou. He would not be free until 1445. Bulgneville stands out as one of the few battles of the later Middle Ages decided almost chiefly by gunpowder weapons.[100]

Although Joan of Arc was burned in 1431, French interest in carrying forth the Hundred Years War against the English and Burgundians did not die with her. Indeed, the new military leadership which took over the French armies after Joan's martyrdom

---

[97] Monstrelet, IV:460.

[98] Monstrelet, IV.440–41, and Waurin, II:395–96.

[99] Monstrelet, IV:464. See also Vaughan, *Philip the Good*, p. 26, and Bertrand Schnerb, *Bulgnéville (1431): L'état bouguignon prend pied en Lorraine* (Paris, 1993). Schnerb's book presents a very complete examination of this battle. The payment record for Jean Maréchal's services on this expedition (including compensation for the loss of his horse) can be found in Schnerb, *Bulgnéville*, p. 138.

[100] Schnerb agrees with this assertion: "En juin 1431, Antoine de Toulongeon ne manqua pas d'emmener en Barrois des 'canons et couleuvres' qui allaient jouer un rôle non négligeable sur le champ de bataille de Bulgnéville" (*Bulgnéville*, p. 69).

– Jean, the Bastard of Orléans, and later Count Dunois; Jean, duc d'Alençon; Etienne de Vignolles, called La Hire; Poton de Xaintrailles; and Arthur III de Richemont, who replaced the overly cautious royal advisor, Georges de la Trémoille – were those who had fought by her side. In 1431, a small French army made a *chevauchée* from Beauvais to Rouen, meeting with and losing against a similar-sized English force at the battle of Savignies,[101] while another struck at the southern Burgundian town of Sancenay, although this siege failed when faced with the 24 stone-firing and 15 lead-firing gunpowder weapons of the garrison, including the bombard *de Prusse*.[102]

Neither of these conflicts was a French success, but their very occurrence in the year of the death of their saintly female leader, an action which the Anglo-Burgundians felt would demoralize and defeat the French, was no doubt surprising. The conflict was far from over. To counter this, both John of Bedford and Philip the Good decided to go on the offensive. In 1432, some 8,000 Anglo-Burgundian troops, led by Bedford in person, besieged Lagny-sur-Marne, a town ten miles from Paris which had submitted to the French at the time of the crowning of Charles VII.[103] The besiegers, accompanied by a large gunpowder artillery train, including several bombards, tried to accelerate the fall of the town by using these weapons. Monstrelet writes: "many engines, large and small, were placed against the gates and walls, which in many diverse places breached and battered them." Apparently, the townspeople had few, if any, of their own gunpowder weapons, but in the end, even though the Anglo-Burgundian guns "gave them great tribulation and mischief," they refused to surrender. After eight days in extremely hot weather, and increasing illness among the besieging army, the Bastard of Orléans relieved the siege and Bedford and his Anglo-Burgundian troops were forced to retreat to the safety of Paris.[104]

The next year, Philip the Good again mustered his soldiers and artillery. Monstrelet claims that this was because the duke anticipated a French attack of Burgundy or the Low Countries.[105] But this assertion rings false, for after Philip gathered "chariots, artillery, and other war materiel" from the Low Countries at Arras,[106] he proceeded to attack French towns and fortifications along his borders. His first target, the castle of Coursent, fell after eight days of bombardment from the large number of Burgundian "*canons et bombards*."[107] A second target, Mussy l'Eveque, lasted longer, but also fell to the Burgundian gunpowder weapons which breached the town's gates and walls,[108] and, a third target, the castle of Fortepice (or Forte-Espice) also fell to the Burgundians, flattened, it was said, by only a single large bombard, named *Bourgoigne*.[109]

Several more Burgundian sieges followed in 1433. Avallon was attacked for more

[101] Burne, *The Agincourt War*, p. 272.
[102] Gaier, *L'industrie et le commerce des armes*, pp. 94–95, and Garnier, p. 52.
[103] On the submission of Lagny see DeVries, *Joan of Arc*, pp. 139–40.
[104] Monstrelet, V:29–30. See also Waurin, IV:24–25, and Burne, *The Agincourt War*, p. 273.
[105] Monstrelet, V:63.
[106] Monstrelet, V:63–65.
[107] Le Fevre, II:277.
[108] Monstrelet, V:65, and Garnier, pp. 98–99.
[109] Garnier, pp. 98–99.

than three weeks by the main Burgundian army, "during which time," Jean le Fevre writes, "the town and wall was much worked and damaged by bombards and cannons, and many of the people were killed or wounded, as many by artillery attack as by other means." In desperation the French garrison and townspeople tried to slip out of the postern gate and make a surprise attack on the Burgundians; it too failed, and Avallon became Burgundian.[110] Also Saint-Valery-sur-Somme was besieged by Burgundian lieutenant, Philip of Luxembourg, the count of Saint-Pol. It, too, fell to the constant bombardment of Burgundian gunfire.[111] At nearly the same time, his brother, Jean of Luxembourg, captured Haplincourt, to the north of Saint-Valery, after a combined attack of gunpowder artillery and Burgundian soldiers.[112]

Buoyed by his successes in 1433, the following year Philip the Good spent a lot of time gathering more artillery and men as well as promises of the same. Among these, it is recorded that Annon Laure of Bruges sold 56 bronze coulovrines to the duke.[113] Philip also made an alliance with the prince-bishop of Liège, Jean de Heinsberg, under which the town of Liège would provide the Burgundians gunpowder artillery whenever the duke of Burgundy requested it.[114] Yet, the only military action of 1434 was a siege of the town of Belleville. This town was quite small and otherwise insignificant but a contemporary biographer of Philip, whose name is now unfortunately lost, has left a detailed description of the operation of the Burgundian artillery there:

> A siege was undertaken at Belleville. . . . Towers and fortifications were destroyed by stone-firing cannons and other machines. Small stone-firing weapons, called coulovrines, were placed at medium range, and large stone-firing weapons, called bombards, were placed at longer range. These leveled the towers of the town to their foundations. These weapons were mounted on a strong wood, which was called an "*escandis*". There was then added a sulphuric powder, compressed by hand, and having been touched off by fire from a hooked piece of iron, large, round stones, which were called "*pierre de bombard*," were discharged with much fire and smoke. And part of the walls shook with the horrible shock of the stone, and they were brought down by this shaking. The walls were breached.[115]

Perhaps it was his military successes of 1433–1434, achieved without any assistance from the English, which provoked Philip the Good to question his allegiance to the alliance which he had made with them in 1420. By 1435 sixteen years had passed since the assassination of Philip's father, John the Fearless, and thirteen years since the death of Henry V. The loss of John had provoked the Anglo Burgundian alliance, but the death of Henry foretold its end. In the time since, during the reign of the infant Henry VI and the Hundred Years War leadership of his uncle, the duke of Bedford, there had been continuing problems with the alliance. The English military leadership were certainly at the source of these problems. Field leaders, such as John Fastolf, John

110 Le Fevre, II:282. See also Monstrelet, V:70.
111 Monstrelet, V:71.
112 Monstrelet, V:76.
113 Gaier, *L'industrie et le commerce des armes*, p. 120.
114 *Régestes de la cité de Liège*, ed. E. Fairon (Liège, 1933–40), II:296.
115 *Liber de virtutibus sui genitoris Philippi Burgundiae ducis*, pp. 35–36. See also le Fevre, II:302.

Talbot, Thomas Scales, and William de la Pole, had produced more defeats than successes, especially after the death of the earl of Salisbury on the Loire campaign, while Bedford always saw himself as more of a political leader than a military one. It is small wonder that Philip the Good felt that his leadership was greater than that of his allies.[116]

In January 1435 Philip the Good met with Valois French officials, Archbishop Regnault de Chartres and Arthur de Richemont, in Nevers. No English representative was present. This was an unusual occurrence for the Burgundian duke, for never, since the assassination of his father, had Philip sought relations with the French. The two sides signed truces at this meeting, but Philip was reluctant to push further for peace without the presence of the English.[117] Still, as Philip discovered later, the mere presence of all sides at peace negotiations, as would happen at Arras in July 1435, would not alone sort out the problems between England and France.

When all three of the warring parties met at Arras, in the Burgundian county of Artois, little was accomplished. One of the chief problems which stalled any progress in the talks at Arras, and one which particularly troubled Philip the Good, was the bickering of the two sides over who held title to the French throne. So fiery did the rhetoric become over this issue that the Burgundians eventually determined to make a truce with the French without English consent or participation. To the English this was an abandonment of the Treaty of Troyes, and, in disgust, they left Arras on 6 September. Fifteen days later, at four minutes after 7 p.m., on 21 September 1435, after a lengthy discussion in the ducal council, Charles VII and Philip the Good signed the Treaty of Arras. Philip had effectively left the English side in the Hundred Years War.[118]

Two questions always rise in the wake of Philip the Good's signing of the Treaty of Arras: first, why did he want to make peace with the French; and, second, did it profit him? The first question is easier to answer than the second, if only because of the chronological circumstances of the Congress. The Burgundians had certainly defeated the French army in numerous engagements in the few years prior to the meeting in Arras, but these military accomplishments had in fact gained him very little, and had undoubtedly cost far more than they achieved. More importantly, while pursuing these attacks into France, political problems for the Burgundian duchy appeared in two other theaters. The first occurred in the relations between Burgundy and its neighbor, the Holy Roman Empire. In December 1434, Sigismund, Holy Roman Emperor, who had been named such only the year before, and King Charles VII signed a truce. This agreement not only ensured economic ties between the two states, bypassing the duchy

---

116 A perfect example of this comes from their respective reactions to Joan of Arc: the English feared and lost to her on every occasion of military meeting; some may even have come to wonder about and perhaps even accepted the validity of her "divine mission" claims. In contrast, the Burgundians seemed to have lacked any fear of this French military leader, capturing her in their first direct conflict.

117 This is the version of the story given by Burne, *The Agincourt War*, p. 275, and Jean Favier, *La guerre de cent ans* (Paris, 1980), p. 537. Joyceline Gledhill Dickinson, *The Congress of Arras, 1435: A Study in Medieval Diplomacy* (Oxford, 1955) is less certain about the duke's allegiance to England at this time.

118 Dickinson remains the authority on the Congress and Treaty of Arras. Other secondary sources include: Vaughan, *Philip the Good*, pp. 98–107; Burne, *The Agincourt War*, pp. 272–78; Perroy, *The Hundred Years War*, pp. 290–96; and Favier, pp. 535–42. The Treaty is found in Cosneau, ed., pp. 102–07.

of Burgundy, but also insisted that the Emperor declare war against Philip the Good within six months.[119] Although no war actually occurred, the threat of such surely pushed the duke of Burgundy to seek for peace between himself and his French royal cousin at Arras.

The other theater was much more of a persistent problem for the Burgundians, and one which Philip the Good correctly foresaw would become more of a problem after the Congress of Arras: the towns of the Low Countries. As witnessed during both Philip the Bold's and John the Fearless' reigns, urban rebellions and uprisings throughout the Low Countries happened quite frequently, certainly more frequently than elsewhere in those dukes' realms, even, it might be argued, than elsewhere in Europe.[120] Thus far in his reign, Philip the Good had not suffered a major Low Countries rebellion, depending on how one defines Jacqueline of Hainault's military activity. Yet, dissatisfaction among some urban institutions and social classes had begun in the 1430s. Both Geraardsbergen and Ghent suffered revolts among the lower classes who opposed ducal monetary policies and local manipulation of public finances in 1430 and 1432 respectively. For the moment, the town aristocracies had not sided with their less wealthy urban counterparts, but should they do so, and this had definitely been the case in past insurrections, the Burgundian duke would have to put more resources into the quelling of such rebellions.[121]

Of course, there is also the possibility that Philip the Good had become fatigued by the constant warfare of his reign and sought, in Richard Vaughan's words, "a 'general peace' to bring to an end all hostilities between England, France and Burgundy."[122] Fatigue certainly must have been a factor, and perhaps the duke might have wanted to participate in his once promised Crusade against the Hussites. Philip may even have relished his role as a peacemaker between the other two warring powers. The validity of such judgments can only be guessed at, however, as the second question raised above must first be answered: did the Congress and Treaty of Arras profit the Burgundians, and in particular Philip the Good? Vaughan is hostile to the conclusion that Philip the Good profited from the Treaty of Arras. He uses the term "duped" to express his impression that what was signed at Arras did not profit the duke of Burgundy. Philip had to give up too much, Vaughan claims, ceding his territorial possessions of Péronne, Montdidier, Roye, Auxerre, Bar-sur-Seine, Mâcon, Saint-Quentin, Amiens, Abbeville, and the county of Ponthieu. In return, the French paid 400,000 gold crowns, apologized for the murder of John the Fearless, and promised expiatory religious foundations in the assassinated duke's name. At the same time, Charles VII bribed the ducal counsel to ensure their support and manipulated the negotiations at Arras by including among the officials there Charles, the duke of Bourbon, and Arthur de Richemont,

---

119 Vaughan, *Philip the Good*, pp. 71–72.
120 See Kelly DeVries, "The Rebellions of the Southern Low Countries' Towns during the Fourteenth and Fifteenth Centuries," *Power and the City in the Netherlandic World, 1000–2000*, ed. W. TeBrake and W. Kibler (Leiden, forthcoming).
121 Wim Blockmans and Walter Prevenier, *The Promised Lands: The Low Countries under Burgundian Rule, 1369–1530*, ed. Edward Peters, trans. Elizabeth Fackelman (Philadelphia, 1999), p. 96.
122 Vaughan, *Philip the Good*, p. 99.

two of Philip the Good's brothers-in-law.[123] Thus there could be no "general peace" between the warring parties. The Hundred Years War was far from over.

The continuing warfare that followed the Congress of Arras seems to justify what Vaughan asserts. But this may be because he is led to this conclusion from a modern Anglo-French Hundred Years War historical perspective. In planning his military participation throughout this conflict, Philip the Good had only thought of his and his realm's benefits or costs, and the fact that seems evident in Philip's thinking leading up to and during his negotiations at Arras was how little the alliance with England had profited the Burgundians during the sixteen years prior to the Treaty of Arras. Problems in the alliance greatly outweighed the benefits, of which the only notable one was revenge for his father's death. As can be seen by the military course Philip followed in the next few years, he obviously placed little esteem on English military capabilities and may well have believed that it was he and his armies alone which had preserved the English position on the continent. Especially in view of his gunpowder weapons' arsenal and manufacture, Burgundian numbers far exceeded English ones. Alone the English were not going to win the war; the only question was how long they would linger. In Philip's mind, it might have been better to finish off the English and then work on the French. If nothing else was achieved by Arras, the removal of Burgundy from the English side turned the tide of the Hundred Years War.

In 1436 Duke Philip the Good of Burgundy proved beyond any doubt that the Anglo-Burgundian alliance was at an end when he directed his largest army and artillery train yet assembled to attack Calais. This important coastal town had since 1347 been securely held in the hands of the English. Its symbolism may even have outweighed its strategic significance. Had Philip successfully besieged Calais, following so closely on the heels of their diplomatic defeat at the Congress of Arras, the English would surely have changed their strategic plans for the future of the Hundred Years War. Instead, the siege of Calais was a resounding defeat for the Burgundians and their large gunpowder artillery train.

Philip began to formalize his plan in January 1436. Because of logistical problems, whenever a leader needed to gather a large number of gunpowder artillery pieces, as the siege of Calais required, a longer planning time was necessary. In this case the Burgundians had no central artillery arsenal, and thus had to amass his gunpowder weapons from smaller, local armories. Most of the guns used at the siege of Calais were supplied from the Low Countries, especially from the counties of Flanders, Holland, Picardy, and Artois. There were also four hundred ships, not including additional smaller vessels, "stuffed with the most strong ordnance and all other materiel of war that any man had ever heard of," which sailed from the harbors of Sluys, Beirvliet, and Rotterdam.[124] One convoy from Holland included a large veuglaire with eight removable chambers, two crapadeaux with six chambers, one hundred bronze coulovrines, and bombard gunstones weighing between 180 and 350 *livres*, not to mention a large

---

[123] Vaughan, *Philip the Good*, pp. 99–100.

[124] This quote comes from a document written by an English spy (Archives départementales du Nord, B10401, f. 29) with a complete transcription in Vaughan, *Philip the Good*, pp. 75–80.

number of lances and crossbows.[125] Notarial documents at the Archives de la Côte-d'Or record the following numbers and types of Burgundian gunpowder weapons at the siege of Calais:

3 Iron *Gros* Bombards and 3 other *Gros* Bombards from Holland
2 Iron Bombards from Picardy
3 Bronze Bombards from Burgundy
2 Iron and 1 other Bombard from Abbeville
2 Bronze Bombards, named *Pruce* and *Bergiere*, and 1 Iron Bombard from the Saint-Bertin Monastery in Saint-Omer (indicated in other documents to have been brought there as a central site)
1 Bronze Bombard chamber for the *Bourgoinge* from the Saint-Bertin Monastery
7 *Gros* Veuglaires taken from naval vessels
4 Iron and 1 other *Gros* Veuglaires from Saint-Bertin Monastery
2 Iron and 3 other *Gros* Veuglaires (no site mentioned)
2 *Gros* Veuglaires from Gravelines
1 *Gros* Veuglaire from Damp
17 Iron and 13 other Veuglaires from Sluys
23 Veuglaires from Bruges or Sluys
11 Veuglaires from Holland
14 Iron and 9 other Veuglaires (no site mentioned)
6 Iron Veuglaires from naval vessels
1 Veuglaire, named *Anvers*, and 2 other Veuglaires from Abbeville
2 Iron Veuglaires from Avennes
2 Veuglaires from Bruges
23 *Petit* Veuglaires (no site mentioned)
2 *Petit* Veuglaires from Abbeville
4 Veuglaire Chambers from Sluys
23 Cannons or Veuglaires from Sluys
2 *Petit* Cannons from Abbeville
12 Iron Crapaudeaux (site not mentioned)
5 Iron Crapaudeaux from Gravelines
3 Iron Crapaudeaux from Abbeville
2 *Petit* Crapaudeaux (site not mentioned)
48 (or 52) *Gros* Coulovrines
200 Bronze Coulovrines
40 Iron Coulovrines
3 Other Coulovrines
2 Bronze Coulovrines *a escappe*[126]

It is also recorded that Burgundian and Low Countries carpenters made carts, wagons, and mantlets for the large- and medium-sized gunpowder weapons; masons carved stone cannonballs; and cannoneers purchased saltpeter and made gunpowder.[127]

125 Monique Sommé, "L'armée Bourguignonne au siège de Calais de 1436," in *Guerre et société en France, en Angleterre et en Bourgogne XIVe–XVe siècle*, ed. P. Contamine et al. (Lille, 1991), p. 203.
126 See the documents preserved in Garnier, pp. 151–63.
127 Sommé, "L'armée Bourguignonne," p. 203.

The size and presence at Calais of this incredibly large gunpowder artillery train is commented on by all of the chroniclers who discuss the siege. As a whole they are impressed with what the duke of Burgundy was able to deliver to the walls of the English town. Enguerran de Monstrelet describes the "large number of *ribauds* carrying *canons* and other large *engins*" to the siege.[128] Jean de Waurin writes that the Philip the Good had "a large number of bombards, cannons, ribaudequins, and large serpentines."[129] And Jean Chartier notes that one of the Burgundian bombards was so large that it required 50 horses to pull it, another 36 horses, and others 26 horses each, not including the large number of other various sized guns which accompanied those larger weapons.[130] This artillery force was so large, it seems, that to utilize the numerous gunpowder weapons, the Burgundian army not only placed them at weak spots around the walls, but also constructed their own earth-and-wood artillery fortifications, boulevards and artillery towers around Calais and filled them with guns.[131]

The result of all of these gunpowder weapons at the siege of Calais, which began in earnest on 9 July 1436, was an intense bombardment of the town. Day and night cannonballs fell on the walls and flew over them to land on the buildings inside. The most cinematic portrayal of this comes from a Middle English poem written at the time of the siege. First, the anonymous author of this poem describes the weapons which the duke had brought to Calais:

> With gonnes grete and ordinance,
> That theyme myght helpe and avance,
> With many a proude pavis;
> Gailly paynted and stuffed wele,
> Ribawdes, armed with Iren and stele,
> Was neuer better devyse.

Then the cannoneers began to attack the town:

> Gonners began to shew thair art,
> Into the tovn in many apart,
> Shot many a full grete ston.

But, fortunately, the townspeople were preserved from the terror that these weapons delivered, preserved by God, Mary, and, interestingly, the patron saint of cannoneers, Saint Barbara:

> Thanked be god, and marie mylde,
> They hurt neither man, woman, ne childe.
> Houses thogh they did harme;

---

[128] Monstrelet, V:240. See also Oliver van Dixmude, *Merkwaerdige gebeurtenissen vooral in Vlaenderen en Brabant van 1377 tot 1443*, ed. J.J. Lambin (Ypres, 1835), p. 150.

[129] Waurin, IV:160. See also *Le livre des trahisons de France envers la maison de Bourgogne*, p. 211, and *Liber de virtutibus sui genitoris Philippi Burgundiae ducis*, pp. 62–63.

[130] Chartier, I:242.

[131] See Waurin, IV:175; Thomas Basin, *Histoire de Charles VII*, ed. C. Samaran (Paris, 1933–44), I:243–44; and *The Brut, or the Chronicles of England*, ed. F.W.D. Brie (London, 1906–08), II:578.

"Seynt Barbara!" than was the crie,
Whan stones in the tovn flye,
They cowde noon other charme.[132]

Yet, these Burgundian gunpowder weapons, despite their power and numbers, were not successful in breaching the walls or causing the town's capitulation. For fifteen days they fired on the town, but without success. This might be credited to the defensive gunpowder weapons which were inside the town which, at least according to the English chronicle, *The Brut*, were very effective in the defense of the town, with one Calaisien gunshot even piercing Philip the Good's tent.[133] However, most contemporary chroniclers give no credit to the town's defensive weapons in relieving the siege. Indeed, they note that neither the offensive or defensive gunfire was effective. While the Burgundian forces were easily able to conquer smaller nearby fortifications, such as Oye, Marck, and Balinghem, by placing their guns near the walls and battering them down, when it came to the larger and better defended walls of Calais, they were incapable of breaching them, even if, as Monstrelet claims, these gunpowder weapons "strongly damaged" the walls of the town.[134]

On the other hand, how effective can a bombardment lasting only fifteen days be? The military history of the fifteenth century showed that, if the inhabitants desired to withstand a siege, strong fortifications generally took a very long time to be defeated, even when faced with the constant bombardment of gunpowder weapons. Indeed, it seems that only when there was no desire to withstand a siege was there a quick capitulation, such as those gained by Henry V in Normandy and Joan of Arc along the coronation route to Rheims. At all other times sieges either failed or dragged out until fatigue or privation on one side or the other brought about victory or defeat. Yet, on some occasions, and ever more frequently during the mid-fifteenth century, military leaders simply gave up when their combatants and artillery were unable to bring about a victory either from intimidation at the sight of the large number of gunpowder weapons facing a site or the increased fear of destruction after a few days of gunpowder weaponry bombardment. Such can only be the reason for Charles VII's unwillingness to pursue the attack of Paris after only one day in 1429[135] and perhaps may also be the reason why Philip the Good raised his siege of Calais after little more than two weeks in 1436.

Richard Vaughan raises other possibilities. He cites the failure of the Burgundian

---

132 The version of this poem used is Ralph A. Klinefelter, ed., " 'The Siege of Calais': A New Text," *Publications of the Modern Language Association* 67 (1952), 888–95. The quotes which appear in the text above are found on pp. 891–93. Another version can be found in Rossell Hope Robbins, ed., *Historical Poems of the XIVth and XVth Centuries* (New York, 1959), pp. 78–83. See *The Brut*, II:578, for the people also crying "Saint Barbara."

133 *The Brut*, II:578. Monstrelet (V:245) confirms this, adding that while the cannonball did not kill the duke, it did kill a trumpeter and three knights who were with him. See also Olivier van Dixmude, pp. 154–55.

134 Monstrelet, V:243, 245. See also Waurin, IV:175; *The Brut*, II:577–79; the *Liber de virtutibus sui genitoris Philippi Burgundiae ducis*, p. 63; and Vaughan, *Philip the Good*, p. 79. The fortifications of the nearby castle of Guines also held out during the siege.

135 See DeVries, *Joan of Arc*, pp. 152–54.

fleet, raised largely among Flemish and Dutch coastal towns, to arrive at Calais at the same time as the army, appearing only after fatigue and discouragement had begun to inflict their toll on the besieging troops. Before they arrived, English ships had sailed in and out of Calais, and there was no evidence of distress among the besieged inhabitants. Once the Burgundian fleet arrived, it did little to change the situation, proving as Edward III had discovered in 1346–47 when he conquered the town, that it was extremely difficult for a blockade of any size to cut off all relieving maritime traffic to the stricken inhabitants.[136]

In the meantime, rivalry between two of the larger factions of Flemish troops, the Brugeois and Ghentenaars, had begun to affect the morale of the Burgundian troops. Unwittingly, the Calaisiens played on this rivalry. On 26 July, the day after the Burgundian ships' arrival at Calais, they made a sortie from the Boulogne gate, surprising a unit of Brugeois troops, which at the time also included Philip the Good. This defeat was met by jeers and mockery from the Ghentenaars. On 28 July, another group of English inhabitants of the town attacked a wooden artillery tower manned by Ghentenaar troops again by surprise. It was now the Brugeois soldiers' turn to respond with their own derision. The Ghentenaars had reached their breaking point, and as fear, and rumors of other attacks, spread throughout their camp, they fled during the night. The next morning, the Brugeois joined them. The rest of the Burgundian soon followed suit.[137] The defeat was made even more serious by the abandonment of many of the Burgundian gunpowder weapons to hasten the retreat. *The Brut* indicates that the Brugeois tried to bury some of their guns in the sand in an effort to keep them from falling into English hands, but most seem simply to have been left behind.[138] The failure of the siege of Calais adds to a growing list of Hundred Years War engagements at which gunpowder weapons were not decisive.

Whether the Flemings were to be blamed entirely for this military debacle is debatable. Certainly the English felt so, with poems such as "The Englishman's Mocking Song against the Flemings" and "An English Ballad against the Flemings" becoming so prevalent that they found their way into accounts of *The Brut*.[139] In these there is little doubt that the Flemings were to blame for the defeat:

> Remembres now, ye Flemmynges, vpon youre owne shame;
> When ye laide seege to Caleis, ye wer right still to blame;
> For more of reputacioun, ben Englisshmen þen ye,
> And comen of more gentill blode, of olde antiquitie;
> For Flemmynges come of Flemmed men ye shal wel vndirstand,
> For fflemed men & banshid men enhabit first youre land.
> ("The Englishman's Mocking Song against the Flemings"[140])

136 Vaughan, *Philip the Good*, p. 79. On the problems of Edward III's siege in 1346–47 see Kelly DeVries, "Hunger, Flemish Participation and the Flight of Philip VI: Contemporary Accounts of the Siege of Calais, 1346–47," *Studies in Medieval and Renaissance History*, n.s 12 (1991), 129–81.
137 Vaughan, *Philip the Good*, pp. 79–80. See also Waurin, IV:186.
138 *The Brut*, II:581, 583. See also Vaughan, *Philip the Good*, p. 80. Jean de Waurin (IV:188–89) claims that the Flemings did take their best gunpowder weapons with them.
139 *The Brut*, II:582–84, 600–601.
140 *The Brut*, II:583–84.

Vndyr a veyle of fals decepcioun,
Record of Flaundrys, whiche falsly dothe malygne.
What hast thou wonne with al thy bysinesse
And alle thy tentys to Caleys caryed doun,
Thyn ordynauncys, whiche cost gret rychesse,
Bastyle, and cartys of fagot gret foysoun,
Of thy gounnys the dredful noyse and soun?
("An English Ballad against the Flemings"[141])

The loss of their gunpowder weapons is especially highlighted as cowardly:

As ferd as þe Flemmynges, with hertes full of sorowe.
Ye lost there your ordynaunce, of gunnes that was cheff :
To you & to al Pycardis, shame and gret repreff.
("The Englishman's Mocking Song against the Flemings"[142])

Thy cowardly flyght, cokeney of a chaumpyoun,
Whyche darst not fyght, and canst so wel malygne.
("An English Ballad against the Flemings"[143])

The English poets made no distinction as to which of the various groups of Flemings were to blame for the Burgundian failure at Calais; Philip the Good accused the Ghentenaars alone. In a letter written a few days after the siege by the duke to his brother-in-law, Charles, the duke of Bourbon, Philip writes:

Dearest and well-loved brother, you know how I called up and assembled my army, consisting of my people and subjects of the Four Members of Flanders, as well as some of my nobles, vassals, and loyal soldiers from Picardy, with the aim of laying siege to my town of Calais, which is part of my ancient patrimony and inheritance, in order to wrest it from the hands of the king of England, inveterate enemy of my lord the king and of us.

To carry out our plan, we arrived outside the said town with our army, and camped in two groups, the men of Ghent and its castellany with us in one place, and the men of Bruges, Ypres, the Franc of Bruges their followers and some of our nobles in another place. . . .

Because the spot where we and our people of Ghent were lodged was unsuitable for fighting a pitched battle when the enemy came, we asked them to withdraw with us and the noblemen in our company to a certain place quite near their encampment . . . which was said to be the best, most suitable and most advantageous position to await the enemy in battle order, and they agreed to do this . . .

Nevertheless, on Saturday 28 July late at night, these people of Ghent, considering neither our honour nor their own, regardless of the promises which they had that very day renewed, and at a time when we were expecting the enemy to arrive on the following Monday or Tuesday, came to tell us that they had decided to decamp that night and to withdraw to a place near the town of Gravelines in Flanders, which is

---

141 *The Brut*, II:601.
142 *The Brut*, II:583.
143 *The Brut*, II:601.

three leagues from Calais. There, they would await events, having put the river [Aa] at Gravelines between themselves and the enemy. And at once, without listening to our requests or waiting for our advice, they departed that night, together with the men from the castellany of Ghent, and withdrew to the above-mentioned position near Gravelines. Moreover, not content with this, they persuaded the men of Bruges, Ypres, and the Franc of Bruges, who would willingly have stayed to carry out our wishes, to withdraw likewise. Since the contingent of noblemen we had with us was too small to do battle with the enemy . . . we were forced to depart and withdraw to Gravelines with the Flemings, abandoning what we had begun with the utmost.[144]

Blame for the defeat at Calais was not the only Flemish problem of the mid-1430s. Immediately following the flight from Calais, Humphrey, duke of Gloucester, who had succeeded to the leadership of the English troops in France after the death of his brother, John of Bedford, the previous year, and who had arrived to take command at Calais only to see the flight of the besiegers, led his own raid into western Flanders. Taking advantage of the Burgundian confusion after Calais, Gloucester burned several villages south of Dunkirk and around Ypres. The English fleet also raided along the Flemish coast as far north as the Zwin estuary and the island of Cadzand before both army and navy returned to Calais.[145]

There is little doubt that for several years the townspeople of Bruges had been showing signs of dissatisfaction with the Burgundian rule. Philip the Bold and John the Fearless had always favored Bruges over Ghent, so the Brugeois favored Burgundian rule and had done whatever they could to support the dukes in their military action. But Philip the Good seemed to show no such favoritism toward Bruges; his taxation and other policies directed at the Low Countries had displayed more equanimity. Neither did the blame placed on Ghent by Philip in the wake of the Calais failure, and his excusing of the Brugeois for their own flight as those "who would willingly have stayed to carry out our wishes" in the letter noted above, seem to restore faith in their Burgundian overlord. By the end of 1436, led by their militia returning from Calais, the inhabitants of Bruges had begun an open rebellion against Philip the Good.[146]

Initially, at least through to the end of 1436, Philip left the Brugeois alone in their rebellion, and by the end of the year it seems as if this strategy was working, as the revolt began to run out of steam. Philip even spent Christmas in Bruges without difficulty or danger. But by April 1437 things had begun to worsen once again. In that month one of the town's leaders, Morissis van Varsenare, and his brother, Jacop, were murdered because, as Jan van Dixmude reports, "he worked with the prince to keep down the common people of Bruges."[147] In addition, the rebellion seemed to be spreading

---

144 A translation of this letter is found in Vaughan, *Philip the Good*, pp. 81–82. The original is edited in Marie-Rose Thielmans, ed., "Une lettre missive inédité de Philippe le Bon concernant le siège de Calais," *Bulletin de la commission royale d'histoire de Belgique* 115 (1950), 285–96, although she mistakenly has Philip the Good sending the letter to his other brother-in-law, Arthur de Richemont.

145 Vaughan, *Philip the Good*, pp. 82–84.

146 The best work on this rebellion is the recently published Jan Dumolyn, *De Brugse opstand van 1436–1438* (Courtrai-Heule, 1997). See also Vaughan, *Philip the Good*, pp. 86–92, and Blockmans and Prevenier, pp. 98–99.

147 Jan van Dixmude, *Kronyk*, in *Corpus chronicorum Flandriae*, 3, ed. J.J. de Smet (Brussels, 1856), p. 176, as quoted in Vaughan, *Philip the Good*, p. 87.

throughout the county, with riots in April also occurring in Ghent. Philip the Good could not risk further inaction. In May 1437 he decided to intimidate the rebels by marching his army (numbering 3,000–4,000 soldiers) and artillery north from Lille towards Sluys and Holland. Initially, he planned not to march into the town of Bruges, only close by, in an effort to frighten the inhabitants into compliance with his sovereignty and policies.[148]

But if this was Philip's initial plan, it soon changed. Instead of just marching past Bruges, on 22 May the Burgundian leader decided to make camp for the majority of his force at the comital castle of Male, three miles to the east of the town, while he and a contingent of soldiers, including, it seems, many archers and some of his gunpowder artillery train, would spend the night in Bruges itself. Trouble between this group of Burgundian soldiers and the rebellious townspeople was bound to occur, and it is difficult to understand what Philip intended with such a maneuver. Perhaps the duke felt that this show of force would be the final incentive for the rebels to sue for peace. In fact, the opposite happened. As Philip the Good and his troops began to enter the town, after a delay of three or four hours, they met a number of rebels armed with both personal arms and "cannons and guns and other weapons of war all prepared."[149] After allowing a few of Philip's contingent into the town – Dumolyn numbers them at 500[150] – the Brugeois rebels succeeded in closing the barbican gate and raising the drawbridge, cutting off the entry of the majority of Philip's troops. This minor achievement further incited the rebels, while it made those Burgundians who had successfully entered the town very nervous of what might happen to them. Leading these troops, Philip the Good threatened the town leaders with violence unless the rebellion cease and the town submit to him. Before the threat could even be acted on, however, violence between the two sides broke out. The Fleming, Jan van Dixmude, claims that this was begun by the unprovoked firing of Burgundian archery into an unarmed crowd gathered on the town's Vrijdagsmarkt (Friday Market) and in houses which lined the public square, during which "numbers were wounded, and some 300 arrows remained stuck in the dormers, gables and tiles of the houses."[151] Philip the Good, does not agree with the assertion of this Flemish chronicler, ascribing the initiation of the Vrijdagsmarkt violence to the citizens of Bruges.[152] Whomever was to blame became irrelevant as the conflict soon escalated. The battle soon spread to the nearby Cattle Market square, where Philip the Good himself was stationed, "armed, holding a drawn sword in his hand, sitting on his horse while his men either shot at the common people of Bruges or laid about them with the swords," according to Jan van Dixmude.[153] The Brugeois fought back. Again, as recorded by Jan van Dixmude:

---

[148] This is Vaughan's contention, drawn from a letter by Philip the Good and the narrative of Jan van Dixmude (*Philip the Good*, pp. 87–91).

[149] This is Philip's assertion (see his letter translated in Vaughan, *Philip the Good*, pp. 90–91), but it is confirmed in Jan van Dixmude's chronicle (Jan van Dixmude, pp. 76–80). The original of Philip's letter is found in *Hanserecesse: Die Recesse und andere Akten der Hansetage von 1431 bis 1476*, ed. G. von der Rupp (Leipzig, 1876–92), II:106–09.

[150] Dumolyn, pp. 225–27.

[151] Jan van Dixmude, p. 78, as translated in Vaughan, *Philip the Good*, p. 89.

[152] In Vaughan, *Philip the Good*, pp. 90–91.

[153] Jan van Dixmude, p. 78, translated in Vaughan, *Philip the Good*, p. 89.

When the common people of Bruges saw that people were being killed, and heard the cry "Kill them all! Town won!", they rushed back to their houses to arm themselves, and some of the gilds brought small cannons to the Noordzandbrugge and Zuidzandbrugge [two bridges over the River Dijver running through the town], and fired wooden missiles at the Frenchmen and the prince's people, who turned and fled back towards the Boeveriepoort [the town gate through which the Burgundians had entered]. But they found it closed.[154]

A fierce battle ensued, with the Burgundian soldiers now taking more casualties than they inflicted, including the deaths of at least 72 as well as Jehan de Villiers, the lord of l'Isle, a man whom Philip described as "our well loved and loyal knight, councillor, chamberlain and brother of our Order [the Golden Fleece]."[155] Only after the Burgundians broke open the Boeveriepoort gate, using tools acquired from the night watchman's house, was Philip and his remaining troops able to escape.[156]

There are of course a number of interesting points which should be investigated in this 1437 encounter at Bruges, but for this study only two need to be emphasized. The first is the fact that despite the losses of Brugeois communal gunpowder weapons at the siege of Calais, it seems that the townspeople and gilds still had quite a number. Second, these weapons may have been old fashioned, at least that might be one conclusion drawn from the curious account of Jan van Dixmude that these guns "fired wooden missiles." Should this account be trusted, it can only mean that the Brugeois gunpowder weapons fired bolts, something which had not been recorded in original sources since the turn of the fifteenth century.

Surprisingly, Philip the Good's close-call at Bruges did not result in a harsh reprisal. Indeed, according to Enguerran de Monstrelet the only retaliation for the May 1437 attack of the duke and his troops was an expedition of troops and artillery against Bruges made in latter part of the year. In this expedition were a large number of troops and "ribaudequins and other military machines" which the Burgundians used against the walls and domiciles of the Flemish town. The townspeople were unable to resist these gunpowder weapons, and eventually the Burgundian attackers overran the gate where their enemies were assembled and gained access to the town.[157] In February 1438 leaders of Bruges were forced to kneel, bare-headed and bare-footed, before the duke at Arras and accept his rather lenient terms of surrender and obedience.[158]

While Philip the Good was waging war against the rebels in Bruges, another of his armies, led by his capable general, Jean of Luxembourg, tried again to capture an English-held coastal site. In the wake of Arras, the fortunes of the English had been mixed: they had held on to Calais despite Philip the Good's attacks and were able to regain Pontoise, but had lost the arguably more important Paris to Charles VII. Now

---

[154] Jan van Dixmude, p. 79, translated in Vaughan, *Philip the Good*, pp. 89–90.

[155] In Vaughan, *Philip the Good*, p. 91. See also Jan van Dixmude, pp. 79–80, and Dumolyn, pp. 228–29. Of the Brugeois, 150 were captured with 22 of these later publically executed.

[156] Jan van Dixmude, p. 80.

[157] Monstrelet, V:284–88.

[158] Mostly these were financial exactions weighed on the townspeople, although forty of the leading rebels were imprisoned and ten beheaded. On these terms see Dumolyn, pp. 267–99; Vaughan, *Philip the Good*, pp. 93–94; and Blockmans and Prevenier, p. 99.

that the English had two enemies in the Hundred Years War, these attacks would naturally continue.

In 1437 this was to be Jean of Luxembourg's siege of Le Crotoy. Le Crotoy was a strategic site located on the northern side of the "*Baie de Somme*," the estuary of the River Somme. Occupation of it, even without holding Saint-Valery-sur-Somme, on the southern shore, controlled much of the riverine access to north-central France. No doubt Philip the Good saw the town's capture as a defensive strategy, similar to how he viewed Calais, a means of protecting his own northern French lands once the Treaty of Arras had determined the English to be his enemies.

Late in 1437, with his Flemish problems in decline, Philip directed Jean of Luxembourg to besiege Le Crotoy. As at Calais, the duke's plan was simple: he hoped that his large and impressive gunpowder artillery train, which numbered according to contemporary records 4 *gran* veuglaires, 3 *gros* veuglaires, 2 veuglaires, 4 *petit* veuglaires, 3 veuglaire chambers, 2 canon, 16 crapadeaux, 59 bronze coulovrines, 75 iron coulovrines, and 54 other other coulovrines,[159] would either force the garrison to surrender or bring down the walls of the fortifications – Le Crotoy had both town walls and a castle. In order to facilitate this, Philip the Good ordered a large fortified tower to be made, filled with gunpowder weapons. This may even have been pre-fabricated, transported to the siege, and there reconstructed.[160] From this tower the Burgundians bombarded the town and its walls. But Le Crotoy, again like Calais, did not surrender, and by the first week of December the inhabitants' perseverance was rewarded when John Talbot, the earl of Shrewsbury, arrived with a relief army of 5,000 men. The Burgundian soldiers fled, with the Flemings again carrying the major part of the blame, leaving behind arms, cannon, and munitions.[161]

The two years following the Congress of Arras had been difficult ones for the duke of Burgundy. But the experiences seem to have taught Philip much. In military terms, there were of course few victories. Neither attack on English holdings proved successful despite the large artillery train employed by the Burgundians against each town. And, while the Brugeois rebellion was eventually put down, it proved costly not only in men lost but also in terms of prestige. It is small wonder that over the remainder of his reign, and that of Charles the Bold, his son, Philip's greatest threat came not from France, England, or any outside political entity, but instead from the inhabitants of his own realm, in particular those from the Low Countries. However, this was not the only lesson learned by Philip during these two years. He also had to face the fact that his seemingly invincible army could be defeated by less able military forces. For most of the remainder of his reign the duke was far more cautious than he had been before 1437. Instead of attacking the English and French, the duke tried to steer a course of peace with and between the two of them. For example, in 1439, Philip allowed a trade agreement to be set up between Burgundy and England which enabled the free trading

[159] Garnier, pp. 139–45.
[160] Waurin, IV:229–30. The account of this tower's construction by Jean de Waurin does not state when and where it was made.
[161] See Waurin, IV:230–38; Garnier, pp. 139–40; Vaughan, *Philip the Good*, p. 89; and Burne, *The Agincourt War*, pp. 284–86. Garnier (pp. 144–45) includes contemporary documents which list the gunpowder weapons left and recovered by the Burgundians.

between the two powers of all goods, excluding armor, artillery, cannon, gunpowder, etc.[162] The following year, when Charles VII asked for the a loan of Flemish and Tournaisien gunpowder weapons to be used by his troops against the rebel participants of the *Praguerie*, Philip had few qualms about lending them to him.[163] In fact, the Burgundian duke was so successful in maintaining this peace with his former allies following 1437 that his once most trusted general, Jean of Luxembourg, in the fear of having to face either the French, English, or even the Burgundians, felt the need to strengthen and to add gunpowder weapons to his fortifications in order "to defend them should some one or other wish to attack him."[164]

Philip the Good, not content with peace between himself, France, and England during this part of his reign also sought alliances with many other leaders, both from regions near to Burgundy and some also quite far away. Many of these alliances came through dynastic marriages with his children, nieces, nephews, and other family relations. Most historians would also agree that, in Philip's case, far more was given up – in terms of land and wealth – than was acquired by him. One of the most interesting of these marriages came about in 1449 when Philip the Good married his grand-niece, Mary of Guelders, to King James II of Scotland. However, this marriage was not noteworthy solely because of who was marrying whom – although many later observers have wondered why the king of Scotland took a wife of such "lowly status" when he surely could have made a far more significant dynastic match – but because of the dowry which Philip provided the married couple. For not only did this dowry contain all of the usual monetary payments, in this case 60,000 crowns plus all wedding expenses, it also contained a large quantity of weapons which the duke of Burgundy, Philip the Good, sent to Scotland from his own extensive stores. Within this shipment, among the traditional arms and armor – body armor (brigandines), helmets (salades), shields (pavises), lances, polearms, crossbows, bows, bolts, arrows, and caltrops – were:

22 Iron Veuglaires and 64 chambers for those veuglaires
46 Iron Coulovrines
5 barrels of powder, as much for coulovrines as for veuglaires
4 barrels of Antwerp rope
16 winches
400 stones for the veuglaires

All in all, it was quite a dowry and one which greatly enriched the arsenal of Scottish gunpowder weapons.[165] These were not the only Burgundian gunpowder weapons acquired by Scotland at this time, the bombard *Mons Meg*, and sent to Scotland in

[162] Marie-Rose Thielmans, *Bourgogne et Angleterre: relations politiques et économiques entre les Pays-Bas Bourguignonnes et l'Angleterre, 1435–1467* (Brussels, 1966), pp. 443–53.
[163] Monstrelet, V:461–64. On the *Praguerie* see Favier, 549–56.
[164] Waurin, IV:244–45.
[165] See Kelly DeVries, "A 15th-Century Weapons Dowry: The Weapons Dowry of Duke Philip the Good of Burgundy for the Marriage of Mary of Guelders and James II of Scotland in 1449," *The Royal Armouries Yearbook* 6 (2001), 22–31. See also Appendix 5 for a transcription and translation of the complete weapons dowry.

1457, being the most famous.[166] Gunpowder weapons were also sent by Philip to the prince of Orange and the king of Portugal.[167]

The relative peace of the late 1430s and 1440s allowed Philip the Good to pursue what seems to have been one of his greatest desires, to fight the foes of Catholicism. His first choice in fulfilling this goal had been a Crusade against the Hussites. But this had gone unfulfilled, as the duke had been required to concern himself with the military affairs of Compiègne, among others. By 1438 a Crusade against the Hussites was no longer necessary. On their demise, the Ottoman Turks had taken their place as the non-Christian enemy *du jour*, and Philip took an interest in fighting against them. But in the early 1440s no organized western European plans were being made for a Crusade against the Ottomans. The Hungarian army, led by the famous general, János Hunyadi, had been able to defend its lands quite capably, at least prior to its defeat first at the battle of Varna in 1444 and then at the battle of Kossovo in 1448.[168]

On the sea in the eastern Mediterranean, the Ottomans had met with some success in capturing several islands previously held by Byzantine or western Christian powers. One of their chief targets had always been the island of Rhodes, then under the control of the Sovereign Military Order of the Hospital of St. John of Jerusalem, better known as the Knights Hospitallers. Since the rise of the Ottomans in Asia Minor, the Hospitallers had been asking for assistance from the Christian kingdoms, but, after the failure of the allied western armies at Nicopolis in 1396, little aid had come to them. In 1443 Philip the Good decided he would change that. Although not holding any Mediterranean ports, the dukes of Burgundy had long operated ships in the Mediterranean, primarily, it seems, to protect Levantine trading vessels destined for or coming from Burgundy, northern France, or the Low Countries.[169] Several of these were warships, which in 1443 Philip directed to attack Ottoman ships near Rhodes. Jean de Waurin reports that these ships were armed with two cannon on the poop deck which sailors used to damage the Turkish ships, while they used crossbows against personnel on those same vessels.[170] However, a document dated 1445 reveals that Waurin's description of the Burgundian shipboard gunpowder weapons may have been incomplete or that over the two years between the Rhodes engagement and the document's date these

166   See Robert D. Smith and Ruth Rhynas Brown, *Mons Meg and Her Sisters* (London, 1989), pp. 1–22, and Claude Gaier, "The Origin of Mons Meg," *Journal of the Arms and Armour Society* 5 (1965–67), 425–31.

167   Garnier, pp. 97, 127, and Gaier, *L'industrie et le commerce des armes*, p. 171. That these gunpowder weapons sales came earlier than the period mentioned here suggests a willingness by the duke of Burgundy to trade these weapons to allies throughout his reign.

168   On this defense of Hungary see Kelly DeVries, "The Lack of a Western European Military Response to the Ottoman Invasions of Eastern Europe from Nicopolis (1396) to Mohács (1526)," *Journal of Military History* 63 (1999), 555–59. On János Hunyadi and Hungarian military history of the period see Joseph Held, *Hunyadi: Legend and Reality* (Boulder, 1985); Pál Engel, "János Hunyadi: The Decisive Years of his Career, 1440–1444," in *War and Society in Eastern Central Europe*, vol III. *From Hunyadi to Rákóczi: War and Society in Late Medieval and Early Modern Hungary*, ed. J.M. Bak and B.K. Király (New York, 1982), pp. 103–23; L. Kupelweiser, *Die Kämpfe Ungarns mit den Osmanen bis zur Schlacht bei Mohács*, 2nd ed. (Vienna, 1899); and F. Szakály, "Phases of Turco-Hungarian Warfare before the Battle of Mohács," *Acta orientalia academia scientia Hungarensis* 33 (1979), 65–111.

169   For a comprehensive look at the naval history of Burgundian dukes see Jacques Paviot, *La politique navale des ducs de Bourgogne, 1384–1482* (Lille, 1995).

170   Waurin, V:35–36.

shipboard guns had evolved into weapons that had developed a difference in technology than their counterparts on land. This document records the gunpowder weapons of a Burgundian galley operating in the Mediterranean as five veuglaires, two mounted coulovrines ("coulovrines pour tirer sur chevalez"), and twelve hand-held coulovrines ("coulovrines pour tirer à main"). What is interesting about these gunpowder weapons is not only their large number or diverse types but also that the veuglaires and mounted coulovrines are described as having removable chambers which fit into all of their respective weapons ("lesdites chambres servans aussi bien à l'ung des veuglaires que à l'autre and chacune chambre [des veuglaires] servant autant à l'ung qu'à l'autre") and that the stone projectiles of the veuglaires were able to be loaded from the rear ("et se boutera la pierre par derrière").[171] With these shipboard guns, the Burgundian ships were able to help the Hospitallers of Rhodes to defend successfully their island against the Ottoman attackers.[172] These Burgundian ships remained in the eastern Mediterranean for the next few years, using their gunpowder weapons further against Ottoman ships and fortifications – on one of these latter occasions, against the Turkish fortress of Giurgevo, Jean de Waurin writes that a Burgundian shipboard bombard became overheated and burst, causing the gunners on board to abandon their attack.[173]

In 1454, the year after the Ottoman Turks had successfully conquered Constantinople, Cardinal Aeneas Silvius Piccolomini (later Pope Pius II) approached Philip the Good to call this very wealthy and pious western European leader to participate in a Crusade against the Ottomans in the eastern Mediterranean.[174] 1454 was a good time for the Cardinal to approach the Burgundian duke. The English had lost Normandy in 1450 and Gascony in 1453, and for the first time since the beginning of Philip's reign there was a relative peace among the major combatants of the Hundred Years War. Also in 1453 the latest Low Countries rebellion, that of Ghent (which will be investigated below), had ended ostensibly, and again for the moment only, bringing domestic peace to his lands. All this made the Burgundian duke interested in accepting the call to Crusade delivered by Piccolomini. In Lille, on 17 February 1454, Philip convened what would become known as the Feast of the Pheasant. In the manner of the great feasts of the day, this was a banquet rich with food, symbolism, and celebrity. Nobles

171 Garnier, pp. 175–76. For a discussion of this document see Kelly DeVries, "A 1445 Reference to Shipboard Artillery," *Technology and Culture* 31 (1990), 818–29. See also Appendix 3. Although Garnier does contain other inventories of gunpowder weapons that were able to be loaded from the rear, in "the new fashion" according to one 1443 reference, none of these or any other gunpowder weapons in the Burgundian archives are said to be able to be loaded with interchangeable removable chambers except for these 1445 naval veuglaires and mounted coulovrines.

172 Waurin, V:35–37.

173 Waurin, V:92–96. See also Kelly DeVries, "The Effectiveness of Fifteenth-Century Shipboard Artillery," *The Mariner's Mirror* 84 (1998), 393. The *Liber de virtutibus sui genitoris Philippi Burgundiae ducis* (p. 69) mentions another occasion around the same time when a Burgundian ship used its gunpowder weapons against a Muslim-controlled eastern Mediterranean fortification. Although the narrative of this engagement is not well detailed in this account, the anonymous author of this chronicle did name the captain of this ship as Petrus de Moroges.

174 On Philip the Good's promise to go on Crusade in 1454 see Kelly DeVries, "The Failure of Philip the Good to Fulfill His Crusade Promise of 1454," in *The Medieval Crusade*, ed. Susan Ridyard (Woodbridge, 2004), pp. 157–70.

and courtiers throughout the Burgundian lands were attended. But, the central purpose for the Feast of the Pheasant was for the members at the banquet to swear a promise to go on Crusade against the Ottoman Turks.[175] There was great enthusiasm by those in attendance – most of whom took similar vows – and by those who subsequently heard of the Feast and what was undertaken there. Later in the year, on 23 April 1454, at the Diet of Regensburg, and present at the invitation of the Holy Roman Emperor, Frederick III, Philip again promised to go against the Ottomans.[176] Plans were made to set a date of the following year for the commencement of this crusade.[177]

Philip returned from Regensburg full of enthusiasm for participating on the crusade. Also infected was his son and heir, Charles, the count of Charolais. By the end of the year, Charles had written in the name of his father to every major lord and town in the Burgundian realm, especially those in the Low Countries, urging any with military experience to join the campaign to be launched the following year. Reporting the recent problems which the Ottoman Turks had caused, including the defeat of Constantinople, Charles wrote:

> My lord [the Duke of Burgundy] has written to me about this and informs me that, in accordance with the decision of the congress of Frankfurt and to accomplish his vow, he for his part resolved, determined and decided, with the help of our blessed creator . . . to undertake and carry out by recruiting as many troops as he can find, both from those who have made a vow for the aid and defense of our said christian faith, and from among those who are resolved to go. And he himself intends to set out next spring in person on this journey.[178]

In 1454, Philip also showed a willingness to subject his entire, war machine to the

---

175 A translation of this Crusade oath can be found in Vaughan, *Philip the Good*, p. 297. The original Crusade promise can be found in *Deutsche Reichstagsakten*, ed. J. Weizsäcker et al. (Munich, 1867–), XIX:150. Several recent works have been devoted to the Feast of the Pheasant: Agathe Lafortune-Martel, *Fête noble en Bourgogne au XVe siècle. Le banquet du Faisan (1454): Aspects politiques, sociaux et culturels* (Montreal,1984); Marie-Thérèse Caron, "17 février 1454: le Banquet du Voeu du Faisan, fête de cour et stratégies de pouvoir," *Revue du nord* 78 (1996), 269–88; and the numerous articles in Marie-Thérèse Caron and Denis Clauzel, ed, *Le Banquet du Faisan* (Arras, 1997). Other studies on Philip the Good and his Crusade promise include: Paviot, *La politique navale*, pp. 105–52; Heribert Müller, *Kreuzzugspläne und Kreuzzugspolitik des Herzogs Philipp des Guten von Burgund* (Gottingen, 1993; Jean Richard, "La croisade bourguignonne dans la politique européen," *Publications du centre européen d'études burgundo-médianes* 10 (1968), 41–44; Johanna Dorina Hintzen, *De Kruistochtplannen van Philips den Goede* (Rotterdam, 1918); Jules Finot, "Projet d'expedition contre les Turcs préparée par les conseillers du duc de Bourgogne Philippe le Bon," *Mémoires de la société des sciences de Lille*, 4th ser. 21 (1895), 161–206; Jules Finot, *Projet d'expédition contre les turcs préparé par les conseillers du duc de Bourgogne Philippe-le-Bon (janvier 1457)* (Lille, 1890); and Yvon Lacaze, "Politique 'Méditerranéenne' et projets de croisade chez Philippe le Bon: De la chute de Byzance à la victoire chrétienne de Belgrade (mai 1453–juillet 1456)," *Annales de Bourgogne* 41 (1969), 81–132.
176 Pius II's account of the Diet of Regensburg (which Piccolomini identifies as Ratisbon) is found in *The Commentaries of Pius II*, trans. F.A. Gragg (Northampton, 1937, 1940, 1947, 1951, 1957), pp. 69–71. See also Vaughan, *Philip the Good*, pp. 298–302, and Müller, pp. 64–71.
177 Pius II's account of this Diet is found on pp. 71–74. See also Vaughan, *Philip the Good*, pp. 358–59, and Müller, pp. 71–80.
178 This is from the letter written by Charles to the sovereign-bailiff of Namur on 20 December 1454. It is translated in Vaughan, *Philip the Good*, pp. 359–60. The original can be found in *Analectes historiques*, iii, ed. L.P. Gachard, in the *Bulletin de la commission royale d'histoire*, ser. 2, 7 (1855), 141–43.

effort against the Ottoman Turks. In existence is an incredibly intricate and detailed plan which shows not only the Duke's desire to participate on this crusade, but also, true to his character, his seriousness in ensuring that all contingencies were to be prepared for, so that the endeavor would not fail. Among other things, this campaign plan included the number of men Philip wished to have on the journey and who was to lead them, including clerical and notarial staff – among whom were two secretaries knowledgeable in Latin and German and two Latin, French, and Dutch. It also contained "advice" on the route, on "raising troops and what they will cost," on "the shipping which will be needed if the route is via Italy," and on how the army should act in Germany if the route was overland. Most impressive in the plan is the attention that Philip paid to the acquisition and transportation of gunpowder weaponry. Perhaps influenced by the reports of Mehmed's guns at Constantinople,[179] Philip insisted early in his plan that there needed to be "Five or six hundred gunners, carpenters, masons, smiths, pioneers, miners, workmen . . . with their tools, armed and equipped with pikes, ready to fight if necessary, to have the same wages as archers". Furthermore, these gunners were to be placed "between the vanguard, the main division and the rear-guard" when the army was on the march, and they were to be commanded by the Burgundian master of artillery.[180]

But the Crusade was not undertaken in the spring of 1455. Nor was it undertaken on the rescheduled date of summer 1456. Philip the Good, his son, Charles, nor their large number of soldiers never left for a Crusade against the Ottoman Turks. While the dukes of Burgundy had a great desire to go on Crusade, in actuality they knew that they could not trust the French kings, Charles VII and Louis XI, to respect their lands' boundaries or their Low Countries inhabitants to respect their governance should they be a continent away fighting non-Christians. Events of the mid-1450s and later proved them right!

From 1436 until the end of Philip's, and even Charles', reign, the population of the Burgundian-controlled Low Countries had certainly given their sovereigns reason not to trust them. The Brugeois rebellion of 1436–38 described above was but one chapter in the history of Low Countries rebellions against the Burgundian dukes. In 1443 another occurred in Luxembourg.

Luxembourg had never "legally" been the dukes of Burgundy's land. However, it was part of their family's land-holdings; until his death at Agincourt in 1415, John the Fearless' brother, Anthony, duke of Brabant, had been the leader, or *mambour*, of Luxembourg, having married Elizabeth of Görlitz, the duchess of Luxembourg. She had received the duchy from her father, Emperor Charles IV of Bohemia, as a dowry at the time of their marriage. After the death of Anthony of Brabant, Philip the Good enjoyed the duchess of Luxembourg's allegiance, even after she remarried John of

---

179   See Kelly DeVries, "Gunpowder Weaponry at the Siege of Constantinople, 1453," in *War, Army and Society in the Eastern Mediterranean, 7th–16th Centuries*, ed. Yaacov Lev (Leiden, 1996), pp. 343–62.

180   A copy of this plan is printed in translation in Vaughan, *Philip the Good*, pp. 360–65. The original is printed in Jules Finot, *Projet d'expédition contre les turcs préparé par les conseillers du duc de Bourgogne Philippe-le-Bon (janvier 1457)* (Lille, 1890), pp. 24–35. Although this copy was written on January 19, 1456 at The Hague, the ideas on which this was made, if not the entire plan itself, originated previous to this later date and come from 1454–55.

Bavaria, the ex-bishop of Liège and ruler of Holland, who died in 1425. Several of her sons and nephews, Jean of Luxembourg, Jacques of Luxembourg, and Philip of Luxembourg, also served the Burgundian duke as leaders of his military forces.[181]

But in 1443 an inheritance crisis over Luxembourg developed. Elizabeth of Görlitz was aging – although she would not die until 1451 – and she was being pressured to return the duchy to her family, in particularly to the child, Ladislas Posthumus, titular king of Bohemia and last surviving male member of the Luxembourg family. The other viable claimant was her nephew, Philip the Good, who felt that he held the duchy not only through his family ties but also because he had negotiated his rights over the principality of Luxembourg with Elizabeth for many years. Indeed, his latest negotiation with the duchess, which resulted in the Treaty of Hesdin, signed on 4 October 1441, had named the duke of Burgundy as *mambour* of Luxembourg and recognized him as heir to the ducal throne. (The duke, in turn, had to pay Elizabeth of Görlitz 7,000 florins per year.)[182]

Still, several Luxembourg nobles were unwilling to agree to Philip the Good's dominion over their lands and duchy, and they sought to defy the Treaty of Hesdin, hoping by doing so to gain Holy Roman Imperial assistance and favor. Instead, they gained Philip's army and artillery. In August 1443 Philip the Good marched into Luxembourg in an effort to put down the rebellion by his newly acquired subjects. His strategy seems to have been the same as that followed at Calais and Le Crotoy, but on this expedition it was successful. His gunpowder artillery train was again large and impressive, although sources indicate that it was smaller than that used before, which might reflect the losses of gunpowder weapons at those two defeats, but might only mean that on this campaign Philip did not feel that such a large number of gunpowder weapons were necessary or feasible. It included:

1 Iron Bombard
1 Iron Bombardelle, named *Bergier*
1 Bronze *Gros* Veuglaire
1 Iron *Gros* Veuglaire
4 *Gros* Veuglaires
8 Bronze Veuglaires
12 Iron Veuglaires
4 Veuglaires
3 Bronze *Petit* Veuglaires
2 Bronze Crapaudeaux
4 Crapaudeaux
4 Iron Cannons
7 *Petit* Cannons
1 *Petit* Cannons *à main*
1 Bronze *Gros* Coulovrine
25 Iron *Gros* Coulovrines

---

181 On the history of early fifteenth-century Luxembourg and its relation to Burgundy see Vaughan, *Philip the Good*, pp. 274–78.
182 Vaughan, *Philip the Good*, pp. 278–79.

25 Iron *Moyen* Coulovrines
8 Bronze Coulovrines
37 Iron Coulovrines
17 Coulovrines[183]

On encountering the Burgundian army and this artillery, most of the rebellious Luxembourg nobles surrendered without putting up much, if any, resistance. Only at the fortifications of Villy and Luxembourg was it necessary for Philip to employ his gunpowder weaponry. At Villy the Burgundian artillery did much "strong damage" to the walls, to use Waurin's phrase, before the occupants surrendered.[184] At Luxembourg, though, the guns proved to be ineffective, at least the walls were judged to be too strong to be breached by them. Instead, the Burgundians tried a more stealthy approach. During the night of 21–22 November, around one hundred chosen Burgundian soldiers scaled a weak part of the town's walls using specially constructed ladders – silk scaling ladders with iron hooks on one end, affixed to the top of the wall by a series of sticks fitting into each other. These lightly armed and armored troops broke open the locks on the gates and posterns and, at two o'clock in the morning, the Burgundian army entered the town and captured it with little bloodshed.[185] The duchy of Luxembourg was Philip the Good's.

As during the reign of John the Fearless, the principality of Liège was also prone to political upheaval. Since 1408, however, most of the problems in Liège tended to be settled by the various factions – pro-Burgundian and anti-Burgundian – without the need for intervention from the duke of Burgundy. Mostly this was because those towns in support of the duke of Burgundy were able to hold their own against those who were against his rule. Sometimes, however, being on the side of Philip the Good could have disastrous results. For example, the Liégeois town of Poilvache, a thriving walled town, protected by a castle, with a prosperous economy and its own mint, and allied to Duke Philip the Good, virtually ceased to exist following its 1430 siege by the rebellious Prince-Bishop of Liège, Jean de Heynsbergh, and an estimated army of 30,000 Liégeois, Dinantais, and Hutois. The devastation was so complete following this attack, that a short time later the town was almost completely abandoned.[186] Yet, after this devastating raid, and probably because Philip's interest and military strength were set on the siege of Compiègne, and perhaps also because Jean de Heynsbergh's forces retreated to their homes without further warfare, there was little Burgundian punishment against the rebels.

Only on one occasion before 1465 and the breaking out of a more wide-scale

---

183 These are recorded in Garnier, pp. 124–35.

184 Waurin, V:85. Gaier (*L'industrie et le commerce des armes*, pp. 94–95) asserts that only a few guns were present at Villy, a single battery of 17 artillery pieces, and that they only fired 2–3 balls a day. Nevertheless, he agrees that such a small number did cause the castle's surrender. If what Gaier claims is accurate, it must mean that Philip had split his force on this campaign, which cannot be verified from the original sources.

185 Olivier de la Marche, *Mémoires*, ed. Henri Beaune and J. d'Arbaumont (Paris, 1883–88), II:40. See also Vaughan, *Philip the Good*, pp. 280–82.

186 Vaughan, *Philip the Good*, p. 323; Édouard Gérard, *Analectes pour servir àl'histoire de la ville de Dinant* (Namur, 1901), pp. 119–20; and Raoul Libois, Jacques Jeanmart, and Philippe Jaumin, *Houx (Yvoir) en zijn middeleeuws kasteel van Poilvache*, 2nd ed. (Everhailles-Yvoir, 1993), pp. 17–18.

rebellion did Philip the Good feel the need for military intervention in Liège, and on this occasion, in 1445, it was probably more because the duke and his army was not busy elsewhere than that the crisis warranted military intervention. It was also not the bishop of Liège, still Jean de Heynsbergh, who was in revolt, but a local magnate, Evrard de la Marck, count of Arembergh, who opposed the duke. In response to la Marck's rebellion, Philip sent a contingent of troops and some gunpowder artillery, under the command of his lieutenants, Anthoine de Croy and Philip the Good's illegitimate son, the Bastard of Cornille, to enforce his political will. Few gunpowder weapons accompanied this expedition, only three bronze and four iron coulovrines are listed in the inventory preserved in the Archives de la Côte-d'Or, although the large amount of gunpowder and numbers of stones, as well as lead to make coulovrine shot, mentioned in the same inventory might indicate the addition of a number of gunpowder weapons not listed.[187] However, two of Evrard de la Marck's castles, Agimont and Rochefort, surrendered and Bishop Jean de Heynsbergh raised an army and pacified the rebellious count without further Burgundian intervention.[188] Apparently the Liégeois at this time were not prepared to oppose Philip's military might; that rebellion would come later.

Without a doubt, the largest and longest rebellion faced by Philip the Good was that fomented by the Ghentenaars. Called the "Ghent War" by most historians – although it should be more properly known as the Second Ghent War after that faced by Louis of Male and Philip the Bold in 1379–85 – it began in 1449 and lasted four years, ending in July 1453 with relative decisiveness by Burgundian military victory at the battle of Gavere. The townspeople of Ghent had always been closely observed by the duke and his ducal administrators. Ghent was so populous and produced so much in tax revenue that Philip the Good could not afford to dissatisfy the townspeople; but, at the same time, he could not give up too much of his dominion over the town for fear of setting a precedent which could then spread to other Burgundian urban areas. It can honestly be said that, from 1419 when Philip assumed the ducal throne until 1449, he and the town of Ghent danced a very cautious dance of mutual tolerance.

The proverbial "straw that broke the camel's back" in 1449, according to most contemporary sources was a request for a new tax on salt made by Philip the Good in January 1447. After two years of heady negotiations between the duke and the town the Ghentenaars refused to accept the tax, and once this was made known, other populous Flemish towns followed their lead.[189] From 1449, then, the town of Ghent was in open rebellion against the Burgundians. Although Philip did his best to keep the peace

---

187 Found in Garnier, p. 138. See also Charles Brusten, *L'armée bourguignonne de 1465 à 1468* (Brussels, 1954), pp. 116–17.

188 Vaughan, *Philip the Good*, p. 222. An interesting footnote follows the conquest of Agimont and Rochefort castles: A 1452 letter from a magistrate of the pro-prince episcopal town of Dinant to the chapter of Saint-Lambert in the town of Liège reports that he had two bombards which had belonged to those castles defeated seven years previously and was intending to "surrender" them and other artillery by boat to Liège as soon as possible. See *Régestes de la cité de Liège*, III:406–07.

189 See Vaughan, *Philip the Good*, pp. 306–11. Only Thomas Basin (*Histoire de Charles VII*, II:204–06) differs from this conclusion, believing that there was insufficient evidence to see the salt tax as the cause of rebellion.

between himself and this most populous town in his lands, the Ghentenaars had tasted self-rule and, despite the illogic of such a decision, intended to follow the rebellion to its fruition.[190] When several Burgundian partisans in the town, individuals who had promoted peace with Burgundy, were imprisoned and executed in late 1451, Philip the Good recognized that there was little option open to him than war. In turn, the Ghentenaars sought the help of the other Flemish towns and the king of France. Only the small town of Ninove, economically dependent on Ghent, agreed. Everyone else in Flanders remained firmly allied to Philip and the Burgundians, while the king of France and his allied northern French towns chose to remain neutral. On 31 March 1452, Philip the Good declared war against the Ghentenaar rebels.[191]

The Ghentenaars made the first moves in the conflict. They captured Biervliet in December 1451, and, in mid-April 1452, marched down the River Schelde against Oudenaarde and Espierres and down the River Dender against Aalst and Geraardsbergen. At Oudenaarde, the frequent target of the rebellious Ghentenaars during the 1379–85 War, the attackers first burned the suburbs and then began to besiege the town from both sides of the River Schelde. The Ghentenaars had their own large gunpowder artillery train which they employed against the walls of Oudenaarde. The author of *Le livre des trahisons de France envers la maison de Bourgogne*, writes:

> The Ghentenaars came to lay siege to the town of Oudenaarde, and they transported by water [the River Schelde] many pieces of artillery, such as bombards, cannons, veuglaires, serpentines, pavises, and other war materiel needed for a siege, by which they battered the town . . . and the bombards and canons were fired night and day.

Still, this bombardment was not decisive and Oudenaarde held out. *Le livre des trahisons de France envers la maison de Bourgogne* continues: "But they toiled in vain, because Sir Simon de Lalaing was there and many other noble leader well provided with soldiers and supplies to hold the large town." Among the supplies which Simon de Lalaing was "well provided with" was a large number of gunpowder weapons which he used to defend Oudenaarde's fortifications. For twelve or thirteen days this siege produced one of the largest artillery duels known at that time.[192]

While the siege of Oudenaarde was going on, Philip the Good mustered the main Burgundian army at Geraardsbergen, which had held off its own Ghentenaar attack. Another Burgundian force, under the leadership of Jean de Bourgogne, the count of Étampes, had mustered in Seclin. Both prepared their troops to relieve the siege of Oudenaarde and then to attack Ghent itself. Jean de Bourgogne marched first. Philip the Good wrote to the townspeople at Mechelen about Jean's success and what followed immediately afterwards:

---

[190]   How can the town of Ghent, as rich and populous as it was, pretend to defy the Burgundian war machine? See DeVries, "The Rebellions of the Southern Low Countries' Towns." On the attempts by Philip the Good to keep the peace see Vaughan, *Philip the Good*, pp. 311–12, who contends that the participation in the rebellion by the lower social classes in Ghent prohibited this peace being made.

[191]   Vaughan, *Philip the Good*, pp. 312–17. Philip's declaration of war is translated in its entirety on pp. 313–17.

[192]   *Le livre des trahisons de France envers la maison de Bourgogne*, p. 223. See also la Marche, II:227–31; Waurin, V:200–01; Mathieu d'Escouchy, *Chronique*, ed. G. du Fresne de Beaucourt (Paris, 1863–64), I:387; and Vaughan, *Philip the Good*, pp. 319–20.

It is a fact that, last Friday, 21 April, those who held the bridge at Espierres on the Schelde on behalf of the town of Ghent, our enemies, rebels and disobedient to us, were defeated by our cousin the count of Étampes and those of our troops in his company, and the passage of the said river Schelde was cleared and opened, and Helchin, which they likewise held, was recovered. The Monday following, 24 April, my said cousin and his men raised the siege of Oudenaarde on the far side of the Schelde, and defeated the besiegers, and my cousin entered the town with his men. As to the Ghentenaars encamped on this side of the Schelde, as soon as they heard the news of the defeat of their people on the other bank, they evacuated the place and fled towards Ghent, abandoning their baggage and artillery. As soon as we received this news in our town of Geraardsbergen, we went after them in pursuit with all the troops we had with us. During this pursuit, which continued right up to our town of Ghent, a large number of Ghentenaars were intercepted and struck down.[193]

Among those gunpowder weapons taken by the count of Étampes were "many bombards, veuglaires, and crapaudeaux," according to Mathieu d'Escouchy, which "he then took into the said town of Oudenaarde."[194]

Between 1 and 15 May Ghent was attacked by both Philip the Good and Jean de Bourgogne. But the town's fortifications, assisted by its defensive artillery, held against the duke's own artillery attacks. Philip pulled back to Oudenaarde, Dendermonde, and Aalst. For the next few months the two sides in the conflict fought back and forth. Several Ghentenaars and Burgundians were wounded and killed, including Philip's illegitimate son, the Bastard of Cornille.[195] By July, the Burgundians had gained the upper hand in the conflict, controlling almost all of Flanders east of Ghent, and Duke Philip the Good had secured the neutrality of other potentially rebellious Flemish towns. Philip planned a concerted attack of the rebellious town. However, before doing so, King Charles VII of France intervened and induced the warring parties to agree to a six-week truce. Philip decided to withdraw from Flanders and, after strongly garrisoning Aalst, Dendermonde, Oudenaarde, and Courtrai, returned to Burgundy for the winter.[196]

The Ghent rebels had no intention of withdrawing to their town for the winter. Almost immediately after the Burgundians' left Flanders, the Ghentenaars started raiding the countryside earlier controlled by Philip's forces. They even harassed those towns which held Burgundian garrisons, burning their suburbs, before unsuccessfully attacking the towns themselves.[197] On one occasion, the rebels even made a sortie against Lille in an attempt to destroy the duke's gunpowder and gunpowder artillery, which had been put into storage there for the winter. They failed, but just barely, Jean

---

193 I have used the translation of this letter found in Vaughan, *Philip the Good*, altering it only slightly. The original is found in P.J. van Doren, *Inventaire des archives de la ville de Malines* (Mechelen, 1859–94), III:94–96, and *Collection de documents inédits concernant l'histoire de la Belgique*, ed. L.P. Gachard (Brussels, 1833–35), II:112–13. See also *Le livre des trahisons de France envers la maison de Bourgogne*, p. 223; la Marche, II:231–42; and Waurin, V:198–201.

194 Escouchy, I:395.

195 Waurin, V:202–06; Chastellain, II:301–07; and Vaughan, *Philip the Good*, pp. 320–21.

196 Vaughan, *Philip the Good*, pp. 321–26. See also Escouchy, I:400–01; la Marche, II:282–83; and Waurin, V:210–11; and Chastellain, II:330–32.

197 La Marche, II:283–99; Waurin, V:213–23; and Vaughan, *Philip the Good*, pp. 326–27.

de Waurin reports, when "someone went into the cellar [of the tower where the gunpowder was kept – the gunpowder artillery being stored above] at the time when the fuse (*les cercles dune queve*) to the powder was burning" and put it out.[198]

Throughout this period Philip personally had stayed away from the Ghent War. Indeed, it appears from all the contemporary sources that during the winter and spring of 1452–53 neither he nor any of his forces attempted to counter any of the Ghentenaar raids or maneuvers. Why this was the case cannot be easily understood, although Richard Vaughan suggests that during this time Philip the Good was attempting to end the rebellion by negotiation rather than by war.[199] Certainly, that may have been the case, given the difficulty of capturing the town of Ghent as well as the value of a Ghentenaar tax-base pacified by diplomacy rather than bloodshed. Yet, by mid-1453, Philip realized that these peace negotiations were not working, and, in fact, that the Flemish military victories which had come in the meantime, however small, were giving a morale boost to the rebels. He decided to march his entire army towards Ghent-held Flanders while his navy set sail in an effort to blockade the rivers leading into the rebel town.[200]

On 18 June 1453, Philip began the final campaign in the Ghent War. While his navy sailed from Sluys and Antwerp towards Ghent, Philip the Good began the march north from Lille. His strategy was simple: his army was to attack three smaller Ghentenaar fortifications before advancing on the rebel town itself. The first target was the castle at Schendelbeke, which lay south of Ghent near Geraardsbergen; the second was Poeke Castle, west of Ghent; and the third was Gavere Castle, which lay on the River Schelde between Ghent and Oudenaarde.[201] All three of these fortifications, as with Ghent itself, were to be heavily attacked by large gunpowder artillery forces, gathered from the store at Lille and from allied towns earlier that year.[202] Although the actual size of this artillery force is not indicated in any contemporary inventory, from the numerous narrative sources which record the campaign, it can be estimated to have been large indeed.

Schendelbeke fell quickly, on 27 June, after less than two days of siege and gunpowder weaponry bombardment. Georges Chastellain writes:

> The artillery was set up and aimed, and the place was so battered by the cannons and bombards that those Ghentenaars there lost heart, so much that they surrendered to the will of the duke, who commanded that they all be hanged and strangled.[203]

The whole garrison of 104 rebels soldiers was executed.

The Burgundians, who had suffered no casualties in this first engagement, then

---

[198] Waurin, V:223.

[199] Vaughan, *Philip the Good*, p. 327.

[200] Vaughan, *Philip the Good*, p. 327.

[201] Adrien de Budt, *Chronique*, in *Chroniques relatives à l'histoire de la Belgique sous la domination des ducs de Bourgogne (texts latins)*, ed. Kervyn de Lettenhove (Brussels, 1870), p. 344. See also Vaughan, *Philip the Good*, p. 327.

[202] For example, two of the duke's requests for gunpowder weapons and for their operators from Mechelen, dated 6 April and 29 May 1453, can be found in *Collection de documents inédits*, II:125–28.

[203] Chastellain, II:357–58. See also Escouchy, I:82–83, and Vaughan, *Philip the Good*, pp. 327–28.

marched to Poeke, arriving at the castle on 2 July. Their gunpowder artillery bombardment began immediately. At this site, Olivier de la Marche reports,

> the artillery, large and small, was trained on one part of the wall between two towers,
> which part of the wall was built a hall and two other chambers, and was seen clearly
> by the windows there that this wall was not able to withstand much force. And also at
> this place the land was good to place artillery on while marshes surrounded the other
> sides, and there would be only a short time before the towers and walls weakened.[204]

For four days and three nights the gunstones flew back and forth – there were also
many defensive guns inside of the fortification. Indeed, one of the chief leaders of the
Burgundians was killed by a veuglaire firing from within the Poeke Castle defenses, Sir
Jacques de Lalaing, called the "bon chevalier" by the Burgundian chroniclers who
report the attack at Poeke, all of whom remark on and mourn his death, one of the few
members of the elite Burgundian chivalric order, the Golden Fleece. Georges
Chastellain records what happened:

> The renown and celebrated Sir Jacques lighted from his horse, as he had been
> wounded slightly in one arm, and he went to look at a bombard which the duke was
> firing in order to damage and destroy the wall of the castle of Poeke, that is to say
> between the gate and a tower which was very strong, and also other gunpowder
> weapons, mortars, and veuglaires, as well as small cannons.

After advising on the better sighting of these guns and discussing certain matters of the
Order of the Golden Fleece with Adolph of Cleves, the Seigneur of Ravenstein, and the
bastard of Burgundy, probably Anthony, another illegitimate son of Philip the Good,
the three leaders decided to watch the continuing bombardment of the castle:

> The Seigneur of Ravenstein, the bastard of Burgundy, and Sir Jacques de Lalaing
> went to watch the destruction being done by the bombard against the wall of the
> fortress of Poeke and all three were well covered against projectiles coming from that
> place. But Sir Jacques de Lalaing was outside the mantlet of the bombard but under
> the cover of a pavise watching the action. At that time there was a cannoneer placed in
> one of the towers of the said fortress who had aimed a veuglaire at the mantlet of the
> bombard, which was discharged at this evil time, so that once fired, the stone from
> this veuglaire hit the pavise behind which was Sir Jacques de Lalaing. And a splintered
> piece of wood which had come from the right side of the pavise was carried into his
> head, just under the ear, so that a corner of his head and a part of his brain was blown
> away. And he fell to the ground without any movement of his feet or arms.[205]

Finally, on 5 July the castle walls had become so battered and weakened that the
garrison was forced to surrender. To a man, it, too, was executed.[206]

---

[204] La Marche, II:308–09.
[205] Because of the prominence of Sir Jacques de Lalaing, all contemporary Burgundian sources on the Ghent
       War report on his death. The quotes above come from Chastellain, II:360–62, but see also la Marche,
       II:309–11; Escouchy, II:84–85; Waurin, V:226–27; *Livre des trahisons de France envers la maison de
       Bourgogne*, p. 225; Basin, *Histoire de Charles VII*, II:213; and Jacques de Clercq, *Memoires*, in *Collection
       complète des memoires relatifs à l'histoire de France*, 11, ed. M. Petitot (Paris, 1826), 94–95.
[206] Chastellain, II:360–65; la Marche, II:309–13; Escouchy, II:84–85; Waurin, V:226–27; *Livre des trahisons*

The last small target for the Burgundians before advancing on Ghent was the castle at Gavere. It also looked to pose no significant threat to the duke's gunpowder weapons. Duke Philip arrived there on 18 July and immediately began his bombardment of the site. For five days the Burgundian guns shot their projectiles against Gavere Castle.[207] As the fortification began to weaken, records Jean de Cerisy, the secretary of Jean de Bourgogne, and an eyewitness to the campaign,

> the captain and some of the others with him to the number fifteen . . . escaped from the said castle secretly over the draw-bridge and slipped through the army wearing St. Andrew's crosses and using the password "Burgundy". They crossed the River Schelde in a boat which was moored near the castle for the duke's foragers to cross over in to get forage for their horses, and in doing this they wounded some of the duke's men. These people went to Ghent, where they arrived about 5:00 a.m., and worked on the Ghentenaars to such an extent that that morning, which was Monday 23 July, they set out from the town of Ghent in force, with 30,000 men or more, to bring help to those defending the castle of Gavere by raising the duke's siege.[208]

In response to the requests from those who had escaped the siege of Gavere Castle, the rebel Ghentenaars decided that, rather than waiting until Philip the Good had conquered Gavere and then moved on Ghent, they would take the conflict to the duke, traveling with "a large number of cannons, veuglaires, serpentines, coulovrines, and other weapons," according to the *Chronique des Pays-Bas*.[209] Their timing could not have been worse. Unable to communicate with their troops in the Gavere Castle, the relieving troops did not realize that on the morning of 23 July, as they left Ghent on their way south, the remaining garrison of Gavere – numbering only 28–30 persons – was surrendered to their Burgundian besiegers. This garrison, too, was executed by hanging.[210]

The Ghentenaars arrived later that morning, not to relieve the castle, but to fight a battle. The duke's scouts had seen the approach of the Ghentenaars, marching towards the castle along the River Schelde, and Philip was able to order his forces on his chosen battlefield north of the castle. The Ghentenaars did the same, ordering their numbers "inside and in front of a wood." After some brief skirmishing between the two armies, an artillery barrage began. Jean de Cerisy's report continues:

> As soon as the Ghentenaars saw the duke's vanguard and his above-mentioned patrols [those involved in the skirmishing] they opened fire with the ribaudequins and coulovrines which they had brought with them, and also with crossbows and

---

de France envers la maison de Bourgogne, p. 225; Basin, *Histoire de Charles VII*, II:213; Clercq, pp. 94–95; and Vaughan, *Philip the Good*, p. 328. According to Waurin, the garrison was executed because of Lalaing's death, but that hardly seems correct as Schendelbeke's garrison was executed although the Burgundians suffered no casualties.

207 Waurin, V:227; Chastellain, II:366–671; Escouchy, II:86–89; and la Marche, II:313–15.

208 This document is translated in its entirety in Vaughan, *Philip the Good*, pp. 329–30. The original manuscript, which is not edited, is Bibliothèque Nationale, MS. fr. 1278, fols. 161b–163b. See also Waurin, V:228–29; Chastellain, II:367–68; and la Marche, II:314–15.

209 *Chronique des Pays-Bas, de France, d'Angleterre et de Tournai*, in *Corpus chronicorum Flandriae*, 3, ed. J.J. de Smet (Brussels, 1856), p. 517.

210 Cerisy in Vaughan, *Philip the Good*, p. 329.

longbows, without leaving the wood. Likewise, the said patrols, which comprised valiant knights, experienced in deeds of arms and battles, engaged the Ghentenaars hotly, firing veuglaires, ribaudequins, coulovrines, and longbows at them. Several coulovrines belonging to the town of Valenciennes, and some others, did excellent work.[211]

According to Olivier de la Marche, because "the Ghentenaar artillery fired with such great force . . . [the duke of Burgundy] was advised to transport his light artillery forward among his first companies."[212]

These guns did the trick. As the ducal gunfire fell upon the Ghentenaars, according to the Burgundian chroniclers, the rebels started to weaken and become demoralized. Within a very short time many broke rank and fled. Seeing this, the Burgundian vanguard charged forward on those remaining in the rebel lines. The rout of Ghentenaars continued; those who did not flee were killed. Some rebels tried to regroup in small units to fight on and one Ghentenaar was even able to threaten the duke, Philip the Good having entered the fighting in this later stage of the battle, wounding him in the process. These troops fought fearlessly until Burgundian archers were able to disperse them. Other rebels tried to swim the Schelde to safety, but many drowned. Casualties among the rebels ranged from sixteen to twenty thousand, according to most contemporary narratives.[213]

But why did the Ghentenaar lines break and flee after being only slightly engaged in combat? The Burgundian chronicles have no answer, except to trumpet Philip the Good's military prowess and that of the Burgundian army. A different story is found in one of the Ghentenaar narrative sources, the *Kronyk van Vlaenderen*. That chronicle reports that the rebels broke ranks and fled because one of their cannoneers allowed a spark into an open sack of gunpowder which burst into flames. All the nearby cannoneers panicked and ran. When others saw this, they also took flight.[214]

By the time the remnants of rebel troops reached Ghent in full flight, panic set in among the citizens. Quickly they understood the significance of their soldiers' defeat and the large number of casualties. The remaining townspeople immediately gave up their rebellion and submitted to the duke. To his credit, and perhaps again recognizing the implications such submission had to his tax rolls, he did not march into or plunder the town. Instead, he placed relatively minor, highly symbolic, and mostly financial punishments, on the Ghentenaars: a total of 350,000 riders were to be paid as reparations.[215]

---

[211] Cerisy in Vaughan, *Philip the Good*, pp. 329–30. See also Waurin, V:230–31; Chastellain, II:369–73; Escouchy, II:89–90; la Marche, II:314–21; and *Chronique des Pays-Bas*, pp. 518–19. Two modern studies of the battle are V. Fris, "La bataille de Gavre," *Bulletin de la société d'histoire et d'archéologie de Gand* 18 (1910), 185–233, and Luc De Vos, "La bataille de Gavere le 23 juillet 1453. La victoire de l'organisation," in *XXII. Kongreß der Internationalen Kommission für Militärgeschichte*, Acta 22: *Von Crécy bis Mohács Kriegswesen im späten Mittelalter (1346 1526)* (Vienna, 1997), pp. 145–57.

[212] La Marche, II:320–21.

[213] Cerisy in Vaughan, *Philip the Good*, p. 330; Waurin, V:231–32; Chastellain, II:373–76; la Marche, II:321–25; Escouchy, II:90–91; and *Chronique des Pays-Bas*, pp. 519–20.

[214] *Kronyk van Vlaenderen van 580 tot 1467*, ed. P. Bloomaert and C.P. Serriere (Ghent, 1839–40), II:194. See also Vaughan, *Philip the Good*, p. 34, and Kelly DeVries, "Gunpowder and Early Gunpowder Weapons," in *Gunpowder: The History of an International Technology*, ed. Brenda Buchanan (Bath, 1996), pp. 121–36.

[215] Escouchy (II:92–111) reprints the agreement made between Philip the Good and the Ghentenaars. Several

As a year, 1453 may stand as the turning point in the history of gunpowder weapons, as it was a time when throughout all of Europe, from the farthest east in the Mediterranean, at Constantinople, to the shores of the Atlantic Ocean, at Castillon, gunpowder weapons were proving their worth in warfare. The role of gunpowder weapons in the Ottoman Turks' victory at Constantinople has been well and frequently presented, and even those at the French victory at Castillon have received their due;[216] however, the Burgundian gunpowder weapons and their role in the Ghent War have largely been ignored. Only V. Fris has determined that their use by Philip the Good at Gavere was important, and his conclusions, written in 1910, have not found their place in general histories of gunpowder weapons.[217] Yet, it is in the Ghent War that the Burgundian artillery arsenal, built up over eighty years during the reign of three Valois dukes, was able to play its part in some of the greatest of Burgundian victories. Undaunted by their failures in so many sieges in the past, in 1453 Philip decided to employ a strategy in attacking the castles of Schendelbeke, Poeke, and Gavere that was almost exclusively depended on his gunpowder weapons. All three fell to him in relatively short time. Then when the Ghentenaars forced him into a battle outside the walls of Gavere, the Burgundian duke used his gunpowder weapons effectively there as well. In fact, in looking at all of the narrative sources of the battle, and depending on how trustworthy the *Kronyk van Vlaenderen* is on its details, it might be said that the capable use of gunpowder weapons by the Burgundians or the incapable use of their guns by the Ghentenaars determined victory and defeat at Gavere.

Before his reign was over there would be other Low Countries revolts, but only one of which Philip the Good personally took charge. (The others, primarily that fought against the Liégeois in 1465–68, were fought by Philip's son and heir, Charles the Bold, and will be discussed in the chapter below devoted to his military leadership and reign.) This took place further north in the Low Countries in 1455–56, and, despite using the same strategy as far as his military technology was concerned, ultimately it was not at all successful.

The rebellion in this case was over who was to fill the vacant seat of Bishop Rudolf von Diepholz of Utrecht. Philip the Good's candidate for this episcopal seat was his own illegitimate son, David, then serving as bishop of Thérouanne, while Duke Arnold of Guelders supported a German candidate, Stephen of Bavaria, and the Utrechters themselves supported the local provost of their cathedral, Gijsbrecht van Brederode. Of course, there really was never any doubt who would succeed to the bishopric: Philip the Good was simply too powerful. He also had the support of the pope,

---

diplomatic documents on the peace negotiations can also be found in V. Fris, ed., "Oorkonden betreffende den opstand van Gent tegen Philips den Goede (1450–53)," *Handelingen der Maatschappij voor Geschiedenis en Oudheidkunde te Gent* 4 (1901–1902), 55–146. On the end of the rebellion see Chastellain, II:376–90; Waurin, V:232–38; la Marche, pp. 327–35; and Vaughan, *Philip the Good*, pp. 331–33.

216 On guns at Constantinople see DeVries, "Gunpowder Weaponry at the Siege of Constantinople, 1453," pp. 343–62, and Steven Runciman, *The Fall of Constantinople, 1453* (Cambridge, 1965). On the use of gunpowder weapons at Castillon see Burne, *The Agincourt War*, pp. 331–45, and Michel de Lombarès, "Castillon (17 juillet 1453), dernière bataille de la guerre de Cent Ans, première victoire de l'artillerie," *Revue historique des armées* (1976), 7–31.

217 Fris, "La bataille de Gavre."

perhaps still hoping that the duke might fulfil his promise of going on a crusade against the Turks. On 12 September 1455, Pope Calixtus III transferred Bishop David from Thérouanne to Utrecht. In response, the following year both Utrecht and Guelders rebelled. (In technical terms, as Guelders was not an "actual" part of the Burgundian duke's land-holdings, it was not in rebellion; although as the duchy had signed a number of treaties with Burgundy, Philip certainly regarded their uprising against him as treason.) In return for a bribe of 50,000 gold lions, Gijsbrecht van Brederode and the townspeople of Utrecht backed down from their military stance and accepted Philip's very powerful and obviously wealthy authority.[218] But in Guelders, there was no such surrender. Philip responded by besieging the town of Deventer, on the border between the bishopric of Utrecht and the duchy of Guelders. However, this siege did not last long, nor was it a victory for the duke of Burgundy. Despite an extremely heavy bombardment of the town's walls by the ducal gunpowder weapons, as autumn brought rainfall, the conditions of the besiegers worsened more than those of the besieged, and ultimately Philip was forced to raise his siege and return south to Brussels and then Dijon.[219]

The siege of Deventer was the last military engagement that Philip led himself. By the time of his defeat there the duke had turned sixty and for over thirty-seven years he had been at war both in and out of his extended duchy. He had not always been successful. Indeed, it seems that most of his military engagements, including many in which gunpowder weapons had played a large part, had proved unsuccessful. Only in the Ghent War had Philip the Good see victories determined in part, if not in whole, by his gunpowder artillery train.

After 1456 the third Valois Burgundian duke seems to have retired from both the siege and the battlefield. This did not mean that he ceased to build up his gunpowder weaponry arsenal. On the contrary, records exist which show that Philip was continually adding to his gunpowder weapon stockpile. For example, in January 1457 two merchants of Cologne traveled to Brussels to furnish gunpowder weapons to the duke, including 100 hand-held bronze coulovrines and one bronze serpentine weighing 300 pounds.[220] Later that year, Philip acquired a large iron bombard from the gunsmith, Jehan van de Velde.[221] The duke also reaffirmed his interdiction against gunpowder weaponry trade with England in 1458,[222] although in 1463, his son, Charles of Charolais, did authorize the loan of gunpowder weapons to Henry VI for his use during the

218 Chastellain (III:129) contends that the bribe worked only once Philip showed up with his gunpowder artillery, "large serpentines, veuglaires, cannons," had been brought to Utrecht's walls and were discharged a few times.

219 No historian has yet undertaken a study of this unsuccessful siege, leaving the student of Philip's life to guess from the meager original sources why it failed. Georges Chastellain, the ducal chronicler and friend to Philip, claims that it was not the conditions at Deventer but rather the unexpected arrival of Louis, the Dauphin of France, with his problems with his father, King Charles VII, against whom he sought Philip's assistance, which caused the raising of this siege (Chastellain, III:69–80, 98–106). See also Waurin, V:370–72. Vaughan's account of the engagement (*Philip the Good*, pp. 228–30) is uncharacteristically weak.

220 Gaier, *L'industrie et le commerce des armes*, p. 163, n. 151.

221 Gaier, *L'industrie et le commerce des armes*, p. 120.

222 Thielmans, *Bourgogne et Angleterre*, p. 246.

Wars of the Roses,[223] and in 1464 Philip himself promised to send gunpowder artillery to Marseilles for assistance against a possible conflict against the Venetians.[224] Finally, Philip the Good also understood the need for new defensive structures to counter the effects of gunpowder weapons. Under his direction, in 1461, François de Surienne devised a flanking fire defense for the town fortifications of Dijon,[225] and about the same time a similar "artillery fort" with flanking fire was constructed near Dijon at Posanges.[226]

Philip could be confident in retirement primarily because Charles, count of Charolais, Philip's eldest legitimate son, had proven to be quite a good military leader. Born on 10 November 1433, he became involved in his father's military activities while still a teenager. His role in the Ghent War was quite prominent; on one occasion during the height of the fighting, Jean de Waurin writes, Philip even tried to remove his son to the safety of Lille, but Charles, having discovered his father's intentions, refused to go, staying with the army and witnessing his father's close but ultimate triumph at Gavere.[227] He was also present in Holland and probably at Deventer three years later. During the period of peace that followed those engagements, the count continued to hone his political and military skills. By the time war broke out again, in 1465, Charles of Charolais was completely in charge of the Burgundian armies and artillery trains, although his father lived for two more years.

---

223 Thielmans, *Bourgogne et Angleterre*, p. 395.
224 Thielmans, *Bourgogne et Angleterre*, p. 404.
225 Jean Richard, "Quelques idées de François de Surienne sur la défense des villes à propos de la fortification de Dijon (1461)," *Annales de Bourgogne* 16 (1944), 36–43. See also Kelly DeVries, "The Impact of Gunpowder Weaponry on Siege Warfare in the Hundred Years War," in *Medieval City Under Siege*, ed. Ivy A. Corfis and Michael Wolfe (Woodbridge, 1995), p. 243.
226 G. Vedrès, *Chateaux de Bourgogne* (Paris, 1948), pp. 47–48. See also Kelly DeVries, "Facing the New Military Technology: Non-*Trace Italienne* Anti-Gunpowder Weaponry Defenses, 1350–1550," in *Colonels and Quartermasters: War and Technology in the Old Regime*, ed. Brett Steele, pp. 37–71.
227 Waurin, V:229–30.

CHARLES THE BOLD

In 1465, two years before Philip the Good died, Charles, count of Charolais, Philip's son and heir, endeavored to fight two wars. History is silent as to what Philip thought of these military endeavors. He was, of course, still the ruler of the duchy of Burgundy and all its vast land holdings, but at sixty-nine years of age he seems to have been, or at least thought himself, incapable of leading his troops in the manner he had for so many years of his reign, fighting beside and among them. This role was now filled by his son, Charles, who at his father's death would become the fourth Valois duke of Burgundy and would be assigned the name Charles the Bold, or Charles the Rash depending on how one translates the sobriquet *le Téméraire*. Charles gained this nickname, no matter the translation, due to his method of military leadership. He chose, like his father had, to lead by fighting beside and among his men in nearly every military engagement he was involved in – and there were many – during his relatively short reign of less than ten years, plus the two years of warfare which he participated in prior to Philip's death. However, unlike his father, this method of military leadership, after many close calls, would eventually cost Charles his life at the battle of Nancy on 5 January 1477.

The reason why it is difficult to know how Philip the Good felt about the Burgundian involvement in these two campaigns of 1465 is that one was an offensive campaign against the kingdom of France, the so-called War of the Public Weal (*Guerre du Bien Public*), sometimes known as the War of the League of Public Weal; the second was an expedition to put down a rebellion fomented by urban elements within one of his Low Countries principalities, a "Liège War," and hence proved strikingly similar to the numerous Low Countries rebellions which Philip himself had involved the Burgundian army in during his younger days. Based on his own past performance, Philip surely would have approved of Charles of Charolais' military action against Liège. But Philip had not been at war with France officially since 1435, although such warfare had been a staple of his younger years, when vengeance for his father, John the Fearless' death, was almost his sole military purpose. Moreover, since 1435 the French military had become increasingly more powerful and certainly more victorious. Between 1435 and 1453, the tide of the Hundred Years War had turned, almost universally, towards French victory.[1] Without Burgundian allegiance, the English had clearly suffered militarily. Outnumbered in almost every engagement, it was only time

---

1   There were several English victories after the Treaty of Arras, but they tended to be minor in the larger scheme of the Hundred Years War, far less important than Alfred H. Burne (*The Agincourt War: A Military History of the Latter Part of the Hundred Years War from 1369 to 1453* [London, 1956], pp. 279–303) or Michael K. Jones ("The Relief of Avranches (1439): An English Feat of Arms at the End of the Hundred Years War," in *England in the Fifteenth Century: Proceedings of the 1992 Harlaxton Symposium*, ed. N. Rogers [Stamford, 1994], pp. 42–55, and "John Beaufort, Duke of Somerset and the French Expedition of 1443," in *Patronage, the Crown and the Provinces in Later Medieval England*, ed. Ralph A. Griffiths [Gloucester, 1981], pp. 79–102) would like them to be.

before Paris fell (in 1436), then the Ile-de-France (in 1442), Normandy (in 1450), and Gascony (in 1453).

One of the areas in which the French military had improved markedly was in gunpowder weaponry technology. Generally this is attributed to the involvement of the Bureau brothers, Jean and Gaspard, royal *artillieurs*, with Jean's rise to command the entire French army at the battle of Castillon in 1453 and his use of gunpowder weapons as a determining tactic as evidence for these brothers' effective change of France's strategy and tactics.[2] Other theories attribute France's victory in the Hundred Years War to changes in French military organization,[3] its changes in tactics,[4] or to England's inability to continue fighting a foreign war, deprived of sufficient manpower, military leadership, economic strength, or a willingness to continue to fight a war over issues, such as land or crown, not as tangible as they once had been.[5] Given all of this, the less "rash" Philip the Good might not have been as willing to seek war with France as his son was in 1465.[6]

For France since 1435, the Burgundian duke had always remained a problem. Philip the Good had made peace with Charles VII, it is true, and in doing so he had broken his alliance with the English which had proven so detrimental to the French crown since even before the assassination of John the Fearless in 1419, but could he, or any Valois duke of Burgundy, be trusted to keep that peace, or to keep from revisiting the earlier alliance?

The latter question had been partially answered by the defeat of the English at Castillon in 1453, which had forced them from the continent, hanging on only to the smallest of their former French landholdings, Calais. The Burgundians had not come to aid the English then, when their former allies needed them most, although that may have been due only to Philip's need to fight against his Low Countries rebels in the Ghent War. In addition, since 1453 the English had certainly desired to return to France and resume the war, although quite frankly their own civil war, the War of the Roses, had prohibited them from mounting anything more than rhetorical expeditions. The English and Burgundians had kept in constant negotiations, resulting in numerous agreements, although most of these were economic without any discussion of military affairs. Nor were these unique, as Philip the Good made similar negotiations and agreements with any number of foreign states.[7] But in 1465, England's

2 H. Dubled, "L'artillerie royale Française à l'époque de Charles VII et au début du règne de Louis XI (1437–1469): Les frères Bureau," *Memorial de l'artillerie française* 50 (1976), 555–637. On the use of gunpowder weapons at the battle of Castillon see Michel de Lombarès, "Castillon (17 juillet 1453), dernière bataille de la guerre de Cent Ans, première victoire de l'artillerie," *Revue historique des armées* (1976), 7–31.

3 See Philippe Contamine, *Guerre, état et sociéte à la fin du moyen âge: Études sur les armées des rois de France, 1337–1494* (Paris, 1972).

4 Kelly DeVries, *Joan of Arc: A Military Leader* (Stroud, 1999), pp. 186–89.

5 See M.G.A. Vale, "The Last Years of English Gascony, 1451–1453," *Transactions of the Royal Historical Society* 5th Ser., 19 (1969), 119–38.

6 M. Guillaume, *Histoire de l'organisation militaire sous les ducs de Bourgogne* (Brussels, 1848), p. 88, for one does believe that Philip was in support of Charles' participation in the War of the Public Weal, although he does not indicate why he believes this.

7 Richard Vaughan's *Philip the Good: The Apogee of Burgundy* (London, 1970) is filled with discussions of these types of economic negotiations. For a specific case study see Jacques Paviot, ed., *Portugal et Bourgogne au XVe siècle: Recueil de documents extraits des archives bourguignonnes* (Lisbon and Paris, 1995).

domestic political situation had become more stable, under the rule of King Edward IV, and the Burgundian heir, Charles of Charolais, had shown an interest in returning to an Anglo-Burgundian alliance, an interest which would become even more tangible when, within a few weeks after the death of his second wife, Isabel of Bourbon, Charles was negotiating for his own marriage to Margaret of York, Edward's sister, and the marriage of Edward's brother, George, the duke of Clarence, to Mary of Burgundy, Charles' daughter.[8] The former marriage would occur, the latter would not.

The question of whether the French could trust the Burgundians after 1435 was even more difficult to answer. Although there had been no direct military activity between the Burgundians and the French in the two decades following the Treaty of Arras, most of this might be accounted for by the divergent military activities under-taken by the duke and the king. The truth was that the Burgundians always posed a threat to the French, and vice versa. This "mutual threat" among related late medieval powers often produced "close-calls" if not outright warfare. One example occurred in 1456 when Philip the Good was used by Louis, the French dauphin and later King Louis XI, as a mediator in a familial squabble between himself and his royal father, Charles VII. Although no military action resulted from this situation, the danger of such was present.[9]

Still, all had remained peaceful between France and Burgundy since 1435. So, why did the two sides fight the War of Public Weal starting in 1465? Richard Vaughan, whose fervent support of the other Valois dukes does not extend to the fourth, blames Charles the Bold:

> . . . Charles had built up a political organization of his own in the last few years of his father's reign. He possessed his own revenues and financial organization. He sought *aides* for himself from the Estates of his father's territories. He had created a veritable system of foreign alliances of his own. He had elbowed his way into power at court and then led his father's armies into battle in France in 1465 . . .[10]

No doubt, there is great merit in what he says. In the declining health of a father who had gained a reputation as a great general, despite proving reluctant to engage in mili-tary affairs for several years, Charles certainly saw an opportunity of gaining some mili-tary legitimacy for his own reign in fighting the War of the Public Weal.

However, Charles was not the only one with such a goal. King Louis XI of France seems to have had a similar ambition. He had assumed the French throne only a short time before the War of Public Weal, in 1461. His father, Charles VII, had also not been militarily active during his final few years, but before that time had secured a great military reputation for his defeat of the English in the Hundred Years War. Louis XI also sought a military legitimacy to secure his own rule. For him, the Burgundians, and other members of the League of Public Weal, proved a perfect target.

Louis' interaction with the Burgundians is an interesting topic for examination, but one that, it must be said, produces little in the way of clear results. It seems that he had a

---

8   Richard Vaughan, *Charles the Bold: The Last Valois Duke of Burgundy* (London, 1973), pp. 45–46.
9   See Georges Chastellain, *Œuvres*, ed. Kervyn de Lettenhove (Brussels, 1863–66), III:195–96.
10   Vaughan, *Charles the Bold*, p. 3.

good relationship with Duke Philip the Good, both as dauphin and as king. The 1456 example above is but one of many in which Louis and Philip discussed affairs, during which discussions they almost always agreed.[11] Louis also seems to have taken advantage of this friendship, doing things that otherwise might have infuriated (or even mocked) the Burgundian duke, such as finishing the purchase of and frequently visiting Picardy, a land which before the Treaty of Arras had been Burgundian,[12] or siding with the Lancastrians during the English Wars of the Roses, while Philip's, and later Charles', allegiances were with the Yorkists.[13]

But Louis' relationship with Philip's heir, Charles the Bold, was not at all like his relationship with Charles' father. Louis did not like Charles and vice versa. This hatred had been growing for quite some time, perhaps even while the two were young – when Charles may have resented Louis' closeness to Philip – but since Louis had become king, it had especially festered. Charles would not ignore Louis' Picardian activities, and he did not like the French courting of the enemies of his brother-in-law, Edward IV of England.

The War of the Public Weal began with a squabble between Louis and his younger brother, and then heir, Charles, duke of Berry. Although Louis seems to have always been close to his younger sibling, by 1465 Charles had begun to distance himself from his royal brother, complaining about his pension and responsibilities. He also began to seek out the company and advice of those French princes who opposed Louis. These included: René II, duke of Lorraine; Jean, duke of Bourbon; Francois II, duke of Brittany; Jacques d'Armagnac, duke of Nemours; Jean, duke of Calabria; Jean V, count of Armagnac; Louis of Luxembourg, count of Saint-Pol; Jean, the Bastard of Orléans, count of Dunois; Antoine de Chabannes, the count of Dammartin; and, of course, Charles the Bold, the count of Charolais.[14] On 5 March, under the pretension of going hunting, Charles of Berry slipped away from the royal entourage at Poitiers and rode to Brittany.

Charles the Bold was not with the duke of Brittany and the other rebellious princes at the arrival of Charles of Berry. Initially there may even have been some doubt as to whether he would join with the others. No doubt Louis XI hoped to keep him from the conflict when he wrote to Philip the Good: "I beg you, my uncle, that you will not allow [the count of Charolais] nor any others to do anything against me."[15] But Philip could not, or perhaps would not – the record is unclear – keep his son from entering

---

[11] See other examples in Vaughan, *Philip the Good*, and Paul Murray Kendall, *Louis XI: ". . . the Universal Spider . . ."* (London, 1974).

[12] Kendall, pp. 121–22, 126–28.

[13] Kendall, pp. 120–21, and Vaughan, *Charles the Bold*, pp. 45–48, 61–67. For one thing, Louis XI spurned a marriage offer of Edward IV's sister-in-law, Bona of Savoy (Kendall, p. 127), while, as mentioned, Charles married Edward's sister, Margaret (Vaughan, *Charles the Bold*, pp. 43–56).

[14] There are very few works on the War of the Public Weal, which is in need of a more detailed survey. For a very cursory look see Kendall, pp. 140–86, although relevant chapters in Henri Stein, *Charles de France, frère de Louis XI* (Paris, 1919) are still valuable. Some of these lords would eventually join the king against his brother in the war.

[15] *Lettres de Louis XI roi de France*, as translated in Kendall, p. 143. This plea may also have included the count of Saint-Pol as well, as he was also under the duke's sovereignty.

the rebellion. By May 1465, Charles had assembled his army and artillery in the region of Péronne; after waiting for his gunpowder weapons from the main arsenal at Lille, he departed for the south on 2 June.[16]

Louis XI was already on the march; on 23 April he had left Tours, where he had mustered his forces, including his own impressive artillery train, within which according to Johanne Petro Panigarola, an ambassador from Milan who was with Louis on this journey, the king had "many good artillery pieces, large bombards and very impressive instruments of war, which seemed unable to be numbered," as well as 800 men-at-arms and 10,000 franc-archers. So large was the train that it "stretched out more than six leagues on the road with twelve hundred horses required to pull it."[17] Louis' army marched quickly and, at least in the beginning, effectively through the county of Berry towards the duchy of Bourbon. He captured Montluçon, Herrisson, Saint-Pourçain, and Varennes, but was stopped outside Moulins by the duke of Bourbon and the count of Dammartin. Knowing by then that Charles the Bold was marching to join the others, the king pressed for peace with Bourbon; however, Bourbon, too, had also heard the news of the Burgundian march and refused to meet with the king's emissaries. Louis moved forward, taking Riom and marching toward the Ile-de-France.[18] The rebels had far fewer successes than the king; their hope lay in the armies of Charles the Bold.

As Charles the Bold journeyed south to confront the king, several towns and castles, seeing his power, simply surrendered: Bray-sur-Somme, Nesle, Roye, Montdidier.[19] Indeed, only on three occasions was the count of Charolais forced to stop his march. First, he met with his own military leaders at Honnecourt, holding a council of war and adding their troops and guns to his own. Jean du Clercq describes the mustering of Charles' gunpowder artillery train there:

> for 236 carts loaded with *bombards, mortars, veuglaires, serpentines,* and other *canon* had passed through the town of Arras, having been brought from the castle at Lille; and a great deal of artillery from Brussels and Namur was said to have passed through Cambrai, and it was assembled in the count's army at Honnecourt.[20]

This meant that Charles' gunpowder artillery train numbered between 700 and 800 carts full, according to the author of *Le livre des trahisons de France envers la maison de*

---

16 Colonel Charles Brusten has tracked all of Charles the Bold's movements on this campaign in "Les itinéraires de l'armée Bourguignonne de 1465 à 1478," *Publications du centre européen d'études burgundo-médianes* 2 (1960), 55–67. On Lille being the arsenal for Burgundian gunpowder weapons see *Inventaire sommaire des archives départementales antérieures à 1790. Nord: Archives civiles, série B*, ed. J. Finot (Lille, 1895), VIII:160–61.

17 *Dépêches des ambassadeurs Milanais en France sous Louis XI et Francois Sforza*, ed. B. de Mandrot and C. Samaran (Paris, 1916–23), III:130. See also Kendall, pp. 147–48.

18 Kendall, pp. 147–51.

19 Jean de Waurin, *Récueil des croniques et anchiennes istories de la Grant Bretaigne*, ed. W. and E.L.C.P. Hardy (London, 1864–91), V:473–74.

20 Jacques du Clercq, *Mémoires*, ed. J.A.C. Buchon, in *Choix de chroniques et mémoires relatifs à l'histoire de France: Jacques du Clercq, Mémoires* (Paris, 1875), p. 263, as translated in Vaughan, *Philip the Good*, p. 381. See also de Waurin, V:469–70, and Guillaume, pp. 89–90.

Bourgogne.[21] Inventories of the artillery sent to Montlhéry suggest that this latter number is not an exaggeration; in fact, it may actually be too low.[22] The artillery train also included a large number of gunners, coulovriniers, and other men needed to operate these gunpowder weapons, commanded by a master of artillery whom Jean de Haynin, himself a leader of the Burgundian forces, describes as "capable."[23] Counting these, as well as the more traditional infantry and cavalry troops, as many as 20,000 Burgundians may have attended the count of Charolais on this military expedition.[24]

The second stop was at Beaulieu, a town held in support of King Louis XI. There Charles' guns did great damage to the walls, with mortars also firing incendiaries over the walls and into the town. Quickly, Beaulieu submitted to its Burgundian besiegers.[25]

A third stop was outside Paris near Saint-Denis. Here, Jean de Waurin writes, Charles the Bold fired two or three rounds from his serpentines, medium-sized guns generally mounted on their own carriages which could be relatively quickly prepared and fired. Their fire was directed toward the anti-gunpowder weaponry devices which had been outfitted to the older medieval walls of the city, and they killed some Parisians. But the Burgundians did not make a full attack of Paris at this time.[26] It was 8 July and Charles learned that both his allies and his enemies were still quite far from him. Should he stay at Paris and pursue its capture or push on to fight against the king? Some grumbling among his soldiers at the failure of his allies to join with them at Paris forced Charles the Bold's decision to leave Paris and take the war to Louis;[27] action rather than inaction gave his soldiers more satisfaction in their tasks. On 10 July, the Burgundians captured the bridge over the River Seine at Saint-Cloud and passed by Paris. They would stop at Montlhéry.

In the meantime, some rebel armies had begun to march north to join the Burgundians. Louis XI also moved north, seemingly confident in his recent victories that he could defeat the armies of his rebel opponents. On 15 July he stopped his troops and prepared for battle. He and his generals celebrated masses with their soldiers and then discussed the situation: if the Burgundians were blocking the road to Paris, the French would have to fight him. But that would work in their favor, affirmed the king, as he believed that "the omnipotent God and the most glorious Virgin, Mother

[21] *Le livre des trahisons de France envers la maison de Bourgogne, in Chroniques relatives à l'histoire de la Belgique sous la domination des ducs de Bourgogne (texts Français)*, ed. Kervyn de Lettenhove (Brussels, 1873), p. 238.

[22] Jules Finot, *L'artillerie bourguignonne à la bataille de Montlhéry* (Lille, 1896). See also Paul Henrard, *Histoire de l'artillerie en Belgique depuis son origne jusqu'au règne d'Albert et d'Isabelle* (Brussels, 1865), p. 96.

[23] Jean de Haynin, *Mémoires*, ed. R. Chalon (Mons, 1842), I:10. See also Waurin, V:469–70.

[24] This is Kendall's number (p. 161). Guillaume (p. 88) numbers the Burgundian army at no more than 15,000.

[25] Waurin, V:476, and *Le livre des trahisons de France envers la maison de Bourgogne*, p. 239. On the use of mortars discharging incendiaries see Charles Brusten, *L'armée bourguignonne de 1465 à 1468* (Brussels, 1954), p. 113.

[26] On the firing of two or three rounds from serpentines see Waurin, V:476. On the use of these weapons to attack the anti-gunpowder weapons see Haynin, I:22. And on the deaths of some Parisians by these weapons see Jean de Roye, *Chroniques*, in *Collection complète des mémoires relatifs à l'histoire de France*, 13–14, ed. M. Petitot (Paris, 1820), I:277.

[27] Kendall, p. 155. Guillaume (p. 89) blames this on the inexperience and disorganization of the Burgundian troops, especially the archers.

Mary" would support his cause. He would "break [the Burgundians] and put them to total rout."[28] The French lords were not so certain of victory, but in the end they agreed with the king. They would fight the Burgundians the next day, Tuesday, 16 July 1465.[29]

The Burgundians had been at the battlefield for several days before the French arrived. During that time they had prepared their defensive positions and planned their lines. Among these were Charles the Bold's artillery positions. Gunpowder weaponry had not been used successfully in battle too often, but, when it had, such as at Gavere in 1453, a battle in which Charles fought, the gunpowder weaponry had been set up prior to the engagement and the battle had then been directed to the advantage of the artillery. At Montlhéry Charles attempted the same tactic. Johanne Petro Panigarola describes one of the Burgundian artillery positions on the battlefield: "fortified behind a ditch and entrenched with springards, *bombards*, and many other artillery pieces."[30] Charles also "positioned four or five *serpentines* before his archers and men-at-arms," according to Jean de Haynin. These were there, the general claims, to keep the French army at bay until the other artillery could be set up.[31] One of these serpentines were also fired as the "first salutation" from the count of Charolais, "which was followed by the others." These surprised and astonished the oncoming French, although they quickly rallied. More importantly, the Burgundian leader now knew the distance of the French troops, something which was difficult to do, Haynin recalls, as the Burgundians were on the lower ground, in a *vallée*, while Louis had ordered his men along the ridge, on *la montaigne*, and the trees which lay between the two armies "always changed the sight."[32]

The fire of these serpentines signaled the arrival of the French army. This was the vanguard of Louis' forces, with, according to Burgundian scouts, a large gunpowder train following them.[33] As the numbers of French increased, Charles the Bold's gunpowder weapons continued to fire into them. Before too long, Jean de Haynin recalls, these troops broke from their lines and charged down onto the Burgundian positions.[34] Such a result was certainly expected, based on past experience, and it generally meant that the Burgundians could control the flow of the battle. Unfortunately for Charles and the Burgundians, they seem not to have been able to control this phase of the battle, for their offensive lines did not halt the charge, as was obviously hoped for. Haynin reports that the French even overran the Burgundian lines. In doing so, they also captured the Burgundian guns there, which were cumbersome and could not be quickly moved out of the way of the charging Frenchmen; the French soldiers

---

[28] The quotes are those found quoted from original sources in Kendall, p. 157. Unfortunately, Kendall's book rarely contains citations to the sources from which he quotes.

[29] Kendall (pp. 157–58) describes this meeting and the discussion which was far from unanimous in its support for Louis' strategy.

[30] *Dépêches des ambassadeurs Milanais*, III:256. Charles would build a similar field fortification at Grandson.

[31] Haynin, I:29. See also Waurin, V:481.

[32] Haynin, I:29–30.

[33] Haynin, I:32, 34.

[34] Haynin, I:36.

returned with them to their lines and camp as booty.[35] Perhaps even more importantly, these charging French soldiers had given their own artillery train time to arrive and set up on the ridge.

Charles was understandably upset at the changing flow of the battle. Olivier de la Marche claims that he approached his master of artillery and "instructed" him to "gain and recover" the lost Burgundian guns.[36] This would require a charge of the Burgundian soldiers, during which at least some of the Burgundian guns were recaptured and returned to Charles. Bombardment of each others' lines continued, somewhat effectively according to eyewitnesses. On one occasion, Panigarola writes that a rumor even went through the French army that Louis XI had been killed by a Burgundian cannonball;[37] while de Haynin reports that French serpentine fire killed many on his side and even came close to hitting Charles the Bold, striking the *salade* (helmet) of his squire.[38] Eventually, the Burgundians drove the French back with the fire of their gunpowder weapons,[39] causing Louis XI and his soldiers to flee "so hastily" that they left their artillery behind and Charles was able to capture it. Other French gunpowder weapons were taken by the counts of Berry and Brittany.[40] The battle of Montlhéry had been won by the League of Public Weal, those rebelling against the French king; although, as Louis after the battle would retreat past the Burgundians and enter Paris, he also claimed victory.[41] But, as everyone knew that day, the true victor of Montlhéry was the young heir of Burgundy, Charles of Charolais.

But had his gunpowder artillery train determined his victory at the battle of Montlhéry? The above version of the story, taken primarily from Jean de Haynin's eyewitness leadership of the conflict, with other contemporary accounts added, especially from Panigarola, another eyewitness, gives one the unmistakable impression that the Burgundian gunpowder weapons brought victory to their side on 16 July 1465. However, this has not been the interpretation of all modern historians of the struggle. Claude Gaier claims that the field artillery at Montlhéry was basically mediocre, able to discharge only ten salvos before they were captured.[42] Paul Murray Kendall's version of the battle contains very little about the gunpowder weaponry used in it, Burgundian or French, let alone crediting it with any role in victory or defeat.[43]

In contrast, Colonel Charles Brusten regards Charles the Bold's purpose in using his gunpowder weapons as one not for the determination of victory, but only to find the range of his enemy, which they did, and to provoke a French charge, which they also

[35] Haynin, I:36–37. See also Waurin, V:481–82.
[36] Olivier de la Marche, *Mémoires*, ed. Henri Beaune and J. d'Arbaumont (Paris, 1883–88), II:238.
[37] *Dépêches des ambassadeurs Milanais*, III:239.
[38] Haynin, I:40–41.
[39] Roye, I:283.
[40] Haynin, I:41. See also Vaughan, *Philip the Good*, p. 388.
[41] This is apparent in the letters which Louis XI wrote following the battle, a sampling of which are found in Louis XI, *Lettres choises*, ed. Henri Dubois (Paris, 1996), pp. 129–32. See also Vaughan, *Philip the Good*, p. 386.
[42] Claude Gaier, *Art et organisation militaires dans la principauté de Liège et dans le comté de Looz au moyen âge* (Brussels, 1968), p. 95. Although with this claim he may only be counting the serpentine fire at the beginning of the battle and not all of the Burgundian artillery during the entire battle.
[43] Kendall, pp. 155–69. Kendall's account of the battle is a rather fanciful retelling.

did. Hence, they were an "effective" if not entirely a "determining" factor at Montlhéry.[44] Richard Vaughan is more certain of the role of Burgundian gunpowder weapons in determining victory, by emphasizing not only their use by Charles the Bold in the battle, but also their use by him in the celebration of his victory. At the end of the battle, Charles fired off his guns to impress the dukes of Brittany and Berry. The victorious Charles of Charolais would only have done this, Vaughan implies, because of the importance he felt that this military technology had in gaining the field of Montlhéry.[45]

It is an importance not missed by eyewitnesses either. Johanne Petro Panigarola, observing from the French side, wrote to the leaders of Milan that "My lord of Charolais . . . opposed the king strongly with the smell of powder, smoke of *bombard*, and furor of battle."[46] Charles himself reported to his mother, Isabel of Portugal, through his aide, Guillaume de Torcy, that he opened fire "with great effect, so that they [the French] ceased to advance and 1,200 or 1,400 of the king's people were killed with a large number of horses."[47] So there seems little doubt that gunpowder weapons were a significant, if not a determinant cause, of victory and defeat at the battle of Montlhéry.

Royal forces still held Paris, and even if the battle of Montlhéry had not been a victory for the king, it seems to have halted the Burgundians long enough for Louis XI and the remnants of his army to be able to evade his enemy and to enter the city on the afternoon of 18 July. Once there, Louis set about to rebuild his forces and his reputation. Many new troops – Kendall numbers them at 12,000 – and a large artillery train were added to his forces.[48] He also prepared the Parisians for what he correctly predicted would be an ensuing siege. As it happened the city had only about two weeks to prepare. The rebel armies met together after Montlhéry at the nearby town of Étampes, and did not depart from there until 31 July.[49] To slow their advance across the River Seine, Louis sent a small force to intercept them. The Burgundian guns from across the river easily chased these soldiers away.[50] But they were able to tell the king that the rebels were on the way to Paris.

So far the War of the Public Weal had gone pretty well the way that the rebels had hoped it would. Louis XI had won some victories, against smaller, minor rebel targets, but when faced with the prospect of a larger conflict, at Montlhéry, the king had failed when confronted by Burgundian military and technological might. Yet, Paris would be a different matter completely. The few times that this largest city in northern Europe fell during the fifteenth century had been because Parisians inside the walls sided with the city's conquest, and even though gunpowder weapons were involved in each of these conquests, they had also been involved in the more frequent fifteenth-century failures to take the city. It is easy to conclude that Paris was not likely to fall unless its

---

44 Brusten, *L'armée bourguignonne de 1465 à 1468*, pp. 116–27.
45 Vaughan, *Philip the Good*, p. 388.
46 *Dépêches des ambassadeurs Milanais*, III:243.
47 As quoted in Vaughan, *Philip the Good*, p. 387.
48 Kendall, p. 175. Kendall does not indicate how he arrived at this figure.
49 Kendall, pp. 170–71.
50 Vaughan, *Philip the Good*, p. 389.

citizens felt it advantageous to do so. In late summer/early autumn 1465, the Parisians were determined to stay with the king.

Even though he may have lost some gunpowder weapons at Montlhéry, Charles of Charolais still had an enormous artillery train outside Paris when he directed his gunfire at the city in August–September 1465. And it appears to have been accurate and destructive. Several eyewitnesses testify to this: Jean de Roye reports on the Burgundian gunpowder weapons which targeted the English and Saint Antoine's Gates into Paris. These fired "many shots of *canons, serpentines*, and other artillery";[51] on one occasion, Roye remarks that a Burgundian serpentine even decapitated a Norman *gentilhomme* fighting on the king's side.[52] Philippe de Commynes, yet another witness, although not recalling it until years later when he composed his *Memoires*, agrees with Roye on the effect of the Burgundian artillery: "the king's men . . . would not dare to emerge from the ditch [in which they entrenched themselves] for fear of the artillery."[53] However, on this occasion, the Burgundians received the same or better gunfire in return. Commynes recollects the effective royal gunpowder artillery in Paris as well:

> The king had a large train of artillery mounted on the walls of Paris, and they fired several shots which reached as far as our army; this is no small distance, for it consists of two leagues; but I believe that the muzzles were raised very high. The noise made by our artillery made those on both sides believe that an important undertaking was taking place.[54]

Indeed, this artillery of Louis' "killed many [Burgundian] men," two shots even coming close, again, to hurting Charles the Bold; they entered the room where he was staying and "killed a trumpeter on the stairs as he was bringing up a dish of meat."[55] Commynes could only exclaim: "I have never seen so much shooting in such a few days."[56]

Charles the Bold's strategy was simple, again in Commynes' words: "for our part, we expected to drive them out by dint of our artillery."[57] But it did not work; and as September moved on with no change in status for either the royal or rebel armies, peace became a more appetizing option. No doubt this was driven by the news that reached the Burgundian leadership that the Liégeois had once more taken advantage of the absence of a nearby Burgundian army to rebel, and by a rumor spreading throughout the Public Weal camp that Louis XI was recruiting more soldiers and manufacturing a large number of serpentines and other guns and would soon be much more powerful than those opposing him.[58] In addition, the fatigue of an ongoing siege and the

---

51   This quote appears on Roye, I:312, but see Roye, I:303–15, for his account of the siege.
52   Roye, I:303–04.
53   Philippe de Commynes, *The Memoirs of Philippe de Commynes*, ed. Samuel Kinser, trans. Isabelle Cazeaux (Columbia, 1969), I:128.
54   Commynes (trans. Cazeaux), I:133.
55   Commynes (trans. Cazeaux), I:127.
56   Commynes (trans. Cazeaux), I:127.
57   Commynes (trans. Cazeaux), I:127.
58   Waurin, V:522. Waurin does not say where these troops or guns were expected to come from.

increasing lack of supplies certainly added to the need for seeking a quick end, especially if it could be seen as advantageous to those supporting Count Charles of Berry. Therefore on 5 October 1465 the Peace of Conflans was agreed on. It was certainly favorable to the rebels: in particular, the count of Berry received his desired principality of Normandy and Charles the Bold received Montdidier, Roye, and the Picard lands previous held by his father, as well as all royal lands north of the River Somme. With these acquisitions, Burgundian territory stretched to within eighty kilometers from Paris.[59]

With peace established to his liking, Charles the Bold, together with his soldiers and large artillery train began to march home. But they would not stop there. Instead, the decision was made to journey with this same army and gunpowder artillery against the rebellious Liégeois. It would be an error in historical judgement to suggest that this Liège War was a new or unique rebellion in 1465. Although defeated soundly in their initial rebellion against the Burgundian dukes, in 1407–1408, the seeds of rebellion seem always to have been present in Liège and the Liégeois-allied countryside. Towns favorable to Burgundian dominion were always opposed by those in favor of self-rule or rule by the prince-bishop of Liège – which, in terms that towns such as Tongeren or Dinant recognized, amounted to the same thing. Take, for example, the story of Bouvignes, a town lying less than five kilometers up but on the opposite side of the River Meuse from Dinant. It also lay on the opposite side of the Dinantais politics, with Dinant firmly allied with the Liégeois and Bouvignes on the side of the duke of Burgundy. During the period from 1430 to 1465, the town of Bouvignes never recovered its vibrancy in the wake of numerous enemy Liégeois and Dinantais attacks and gunpowder artillery bombardments.[60] Yet, on these occasions the Liégeois had been attentive enough of Burgundian events to plan their anti-Burgundian activities when the duke had other, more important military obligations elsewhere, such as in 1430 when the Dinantais attack of Poilvache[61] and Bouvignes was shadowed by the Burgundian siege of Compiègne. If there was a Burgundian military response to the Liégeois rebellions at that time, and frequently, such as in 1430, there was none, the Liégeois were generally able to appease Burgundian anger with apologies, symbolic gestures and ritual, and sometimes reparations. Only in 1445, with the rise of Count Evrard de la Marck of Arembergh, did Philip the Good respond to a Liégeois rebellion promptly by attacking the count's castles at Agimont and Rochefort, and on this occasion the Liégeois disavowed the rebellion and actually mustered their military forces against la Marck and fought on the side of the duke of Burgundy.[62]

---

59 These conditions are reported in a letter by Charles to his father, Philip the Good: *Collection de documents inédits concernant l'histoire de la Belgique*, ed. L.P. Gachard (Brussels, 1833–35), II:225. See also Kendall, pp. 178–83.

60 See Kelly DeVries, "The Rebellions of Southern Low Countries' Towns during the Fourteenth and Fifteenth Centuries" (forthcoming); Vaughan, *Philip the Good*, pp. 59–61, 396–97; Gaier, *Art et organisation militaires*, p. 324; Henri Pirenne, *Histoire de Belgique*, vol. 2: *Du commencement du XIVe siècle à la mort de Charles le Téméraire* (Brussels, 1903), pp. 257–58, 280; and Édouard Gérard, *Analectes pour servir à l'histoire de la ville de Dinant* (Namur, 1901), pp. 38–39.

61 See above p. 126.

62 See above p. 127.

But in the 1465 Liégeois rebellion there was to be a Burgundian response, and this would be a response more violent and harsh than ever previously seen. The Burgundian response came not because the Liégeois political acumen had declined or even because the leaders of the rebellion misjudged Burgundian involvement in the War of the Public Weal.[63] Indeed, it seems to have had little to do with the Liégeois at all, but was instead the result of the ability of Philip the Good, who was not with his son in France, to muster enough troops, gunpowder artillery, and military leadership from his subjects not involved in the War and to send them against the Liégeois.

The rebels may also have been pushed prematurely into conflict with Burgundy by an agreement they had made with Louis XI on 17 June 1465.[64] The result of several months of negotiations between the French king and the governors of Liège, the bene-fits of such an agreement for the French can easily be seen, especially in the wake of the War of the Public Weal. Less certain are the benefits for the Liégeois. There were provi-sions in the agreement for military assistance, especially in artillery, including saltpeter, and men, including two "good masters of artillery." However, even if they did materi-alize, and there is no evidence of this, they proved insufficient to assist the Liégeois in any measurable way during their rebellion.

In late fall/early winter 1465, as Charles of Charolais marched slowly north after Montlhéry and Paris, the Liégeois soldiers set out to attack several Burgundian sites along their borders: the duchy of Limburg, and the towns of Maastricht and Dinant. The inhabitants of those sites, all forewarned of the rebels' intentions, prepared for these attacks.[65] Limburg was the first to be targeted.

Perhaps because of the absence of the main Burgundian army or perhaps because of their alliance with the French king, the Liégeois were rather self-assured of their endeavor, as the following letter to Philip the Good and Charles of Charolais declaring war on 28 August 1485 indicates:

> Resplendent prince, Lord Philip, duke of Burgundy, of Brabant and of Limburg, count of Flanders, of Artois, of Burgundy, of Hainault, of Holland, of Zeeland and of Namur, and of Charles of Burgundy, count of Charolais, lord of Chastelbain and of Béthune, lieutenant, etc., we, Marc, by the grace of God margrave of Baden, administrator-postulate of the church of Liège, governor and regent of the lands of Liège, of Bouillon, of Looz, of Clermont, of Franchemont, etc., we . . . make it known to you that we are reliably informed of various injuries and oppressions perpe-trated by you and yours . . . to the very great harm, prejudice and damage of our said lands. These we can no longer suffer nor tolerate since we, by the pleasure of almighty God, have been elected governor and regent as mentioned above, and since we and our said lands have an obligation towards the most excellent prince and lord, Lord Louis, most christian king of France, our very dear and beloved lord, against whom you are waging open war. So much so that, for the above-mentioned reasons and

---

63 This is the view of Gaier, *Art et organisation militaires*, pp. 335–36.
64 This agreement is printed in *Régestes de la cité de Liège*, ed. E. Fairon (Liège, 1933–40), IV:139–43, and *Collection de documents inédits concernant l'histoire de la Belgique*, II:197–205. See also Vaughan, *Philip the Good*, pp. 392–93, and Gaier, *Art et organisation militaires*, p. 335.
65 For Maastricht see *Régestes de la cité de Liège*, IV:157–59, and for Dinant see *Régestes de la cité de Liège*, IV:163–64.

others, we prefer a royal master to you. Because of this we, with our lands and subjects, wish to be your enemies and the enemies of your lands and subjects.[66]

The letter was sent by the Liégeois in the name of Marc, the margrave of Baden, whose leadership they clearly preferred over Louis de Bourbon, the Burgundian prince-bishop, and the "royal master" they preferred was equally clearly Louis XI. Marc von Baden had bolstered the Liégeois force on 1 August with his own army of three counts, 400 knights, numerous infantry, and a huge bombard, but his presence with them did not last long, as he and his German soldiers abandoned the rebellion in the beginning of September and returned home.[67] The sources do not say why this occurred. As neither Philip's nor Charles' Burgundian armies had come to blows with the Liégeois rebels, fear of the Burgundians cannot have been the reason for von Baden's departure. There may have been some disagreements in leadership or military planning, or possibly the Germans simply lacked the bellicose enthusiasm of their rebel allies.

With Marc von Baden's desertion from the rebellion and Louis XI's above-mentioned assistance apparently not materializing, it would seem that the Liégeois enthusiasm for war against their Burgundian lords would decline. Certainly Louis was worried about this possibility, and his ambassadors to the city and its inhabitants were kept busy encouraging their rebellious activities. The French king, although from a distance, did likewise. He even went so far as downplaying the peace treaty he had signed with Charles of Charolais following their Montlhéry and Paris combat, the signing of which obviously meant the freeing of the main Burgundian army from the fighting of the War of the Public Weal, while at the same time binding the French king from actively assisting the Liégeois in their rebellion, as he had earlier promised.[68] Maybe such ambassadorial and royal cheerleading was effective, or maybe the Liégeois were simply too immersed in their rebellion and confident of its results to be persuaded by the result of events happening south of them, for they did not sway or falter in their desires to go to war against the very powerful Burgundian duke and his son.

In the meantime, the old warlord, Philip the Good, unable to be certain of the new warlord, Charles' quick victory in France, mustered what troops were still available to him in his lands and sent them to defend Limburg. This should not be thought of as having been an easy task. Although from the original sources it cannot be ascertained exactly how many potential soldiers there were in Burgundian lands, numbers were no doubt depleted by those serving with Charles in the south. Nor does it seem to have been a shift in Philip's policy at this time to completely denude certain parts of his realm of soldiers in order to defend against a rebellion in another part – better not to risk uprisings elsewhere, especially in the Low Countries, if forces were spread too thinly. In addition, there was the problem of the necessary speed required to put down the Liégeois rebellion: Philip did not have the luxury of bringing troops from too far afield, nor to take the time to muster and arm his sometimes unreliable urban militias. Still, while not as formidable nor as numerous as his son's army, those who marched to

66 The original of this letter can be found in the *Chronique* of Adrien d'Oudenbosch (ed. C. de Borman [Liège, 1902]), pp. 273–74. This translation is from Vaughan, *Philip the Good*, pp. 393–94.
67 Vaughan, *Philip the Good*, p. 394, and Gaier, *Art et organisation militaires*, p. 338.
68 Vaughan, *Philip the Good*, pp. 394–95, and *Lettres de Louis XI*, III:1–2.

the relief of Limburg in September and October 1465 put on an impressive display of arms and artillery, for, yes, they were also outfitted with a number of gunpowder weapons, although it is clear that the largest number of those in the Burgundian arsenal were with Charles.[69]

When and where the Liégeois first learned that they would face a Burgundian army of some size and strength is not known. If it was in mid to late October, their reluctance to break from their ill-advised attacks into Limburg could be justified. However, if it was in September or early October, one might think that such knowledge would have sent the rebels home, but it did not seem to dampen the enthusiasm of the Liégeois for rebellion. This may be because the leaders were confident in their numbers, some 3,000–4,000 in total, mostly infantry, and opted to press the attacks against the small number of Burgundian troops recently raised by Philip the Good to face them.[70] Jean de Haynin, for one was impressed by the rebels: "the most strong, the most valiant and the most difficult to fight in all the land."[71] Perhaps, too, the lure of Brabantese booty may have outweighed the more customary Liégeois caution, especially with Raes de Lyntre, the lord of Heers, and new leader of rebel forces predicting that the Liégeois would be able to march all the way to Brussels.

All of this came to a head outside the walled village of Montenaeken on 20 October 1465 when the Burgundian army sent by Philip the Good encountered the main force of 2,000–3,000 Liégeois rebels, and it appears from the original sources that the Burgundians may actually have surprised the Liégeois as they were preparing to launch attacks into Brabant.[72] Still, the Burgundians themselves probably did not exceed the numbers of the Liégeois, maybe numbering only 1,800, although many of these were cavalry.[73] More importantly, while the Burgundians were well organized, well led, and more accustomed to fighting, the Liégeois were a mix of urban rebels from Liège, Dinant, and other towns, and rural militias from the prince-bishopric of Liège and the counties of Looz and Hesbaye, characterized by contemporary countrymen, Henri de Merica and Jean de Looz as "an enormous mass of burghers and peasants, but few warriors."[74] It is this lack of unity, discipline, and experience which would ultimately cost the Liégeois the battle.

As the Burgundians approached Montenaeken, the rebels withdrew behind and barricaded the walls of the town. Recognizing the impossibility of attacking such a stronghold by force, or even the probability of reducing it to starvation by siege due to their small numbers and lack of time, the Burgundian military leaders decided to try and draw the Liégeois out of the town by ravaging the surrounding countryside. This

---

69 Gaier, *Art et organisation militaires*, pp. 338–39, seems quite impressed with the aged duke's accomplishment here, while Vaughan, *Philip the Good*, pp. 392–96, is surprisingly quiet about it.

70 This according to Jean de Looz, *Chronicon*, in *Documents relatifs aux troubles du pays de Liège sous les princes-évêques Louis de Bourbon et Jean de Horne, 1455–1505*, ed. P.F.X. de Ram (Brussels, 1844), p.29. See also Gaier, *Art et organisation militaires*, p. 339.

71 Haynin, I:119. Gaier (*Art et organisation militaires*, p. 339) correctly dismisses this as "unbelievable."

72 This is Claude Gaier's conclusion (*Art et organisation militaires*, p. 340).

73 This is the number given by Henri de Merica, *De cladibus Leodensium*, in *Documents relatifs aux troubles du pays de Liège sous les princes-évêques Louis de Bourbon et Jean de Horne, 1455–1505*, ed. P.F.X. de Ram (Brussels, 1844), p. 151.

74 Merica, p. 151, and Looz, p. 29. See also Gaier, *Art et organisation militaires*, p. 339.

was an old but almost always successful tactic, especially in the face of a non-military population not solidly in support of the rebellion; and such were the Montenaekenais and their neighbors. It was an organized rape of the countryside, with seemingly the entire Burgundian army taking place. In fact, perhaps too many of them took part. As a Burgundian unit of 300–500 cavalry returned to their camp from a raid, they were surprised by a unit of Liégeois soldiers, probably their entire force, lined up between "two hills (*tumuli*)," which protected their flanks. Also among the Liégeois troops were an unspecified number of gunpowder weapons. However, rather than retreating from their more numerous foes, this contingent of Burgundian cavalry charged the Liégeois. This charge was met and stopped by a Liégeois artillery barrage. Again the Burgundians charged the rebel army, and again they were met by gunpowder artillery fire. After this, writes Jean de Haynin, they "began to be disorganized and to become disordered."[75]

Uttering a cry, "Saint Denis et Saint Lambert," representing their allegiance to France and Liège, the rebel soldiers broke from their line and charged after the Burgundian cavalry. However, these horsemen were not as "disorganized" as the Liégeois had considered them to be. Regrouping quickly, the Burgundians turned and charged back into the Liégeois, causing panic and flight among them. The Burgundians pursued those fleeing without mercy, riding down and killing all who could not escape – contemporary Liégeois chronicler Jean de Looz puts the number at 1,200 killed.[76] The result of the battle of Montenaeken was a total rout of the Liégeois army, and not even the entire Burgundian army had taken part! The following day, the Burgundians entered the town of Montenaeken, now abandoned by its population, and destroyed the fortified church and some of the walls.[77] (The Montenaekenais later returned, presumably under the promise of safe-passage given by the Burgundians leaders, but on the way they were ambushed by their "protectors," suffering many casualties, thus setting the stage for later punishments meted out against even passive participants in this rebellion.)

On 22 October 1465, the siege of Limburg, which had been laid by the rebels for twenty-one days, was raised. Thus the Burgundian contingent put together quickly by Philip the Good in the wake of Charles of Charolais' participation in the War of the Public Weal had certainly done more than had been expected of them, defeating the Liégeois rebels at the battle of Montenaeken and raising the siege of Limburg, let alone putting the entire rebellion in check until the arrival of Charles' army from France late in November.

The day following the battle of Montenaeken also saw the end of the Franco-Liégeois alliance. Likely determined by his defeat at the battle of Montlhéry and the Peace of Conflans negotiated with Charles of Charolais during the ensuing siege of Paris, yet probably not influenced by the defeat of Liégeois rebels – although it

---

[75] Haynin, I:122. That the Liégeois had a fairly formidable gunpowder artillery arsenal at Montenaeken can be found in *Le livre des trahisons de France envers la maison de Bourgogne*, p. 251. See also Claude Gaier, "Le rôle des armes à feu dans les batailles Liègeoises au XVe siècle," *Publication du centre européen d'études Bourguignonnes (XIVe–XVIe s.)* 26 (1986), 31–37.

[76] Looz, p. 29.

[77] Gaier, *Art et organisation militaires*, pp. 340–41.

certainly is possible that news of the battle had reached him in Paris within a day of the conflict – Louis XI turned his back on the Liégeois. In a letter dated 21 October 1465 and addressed to "our old and particular friends," Louis announces the abandonment of his alliance with them along with the following advice and warning:

> . . . We are well content with the way you have conducted yourselves in this matter, by employing yourselves in our favor against those who opposed us. We are eternally obliged to you and we thank you most warmly. Nevertheless, because of the treaty between us and the above-mentioned [princes], especially in so far as fair uncle of Burgundy and brother-in-law of Charolais are concerned, and because you are comprised in the said treaty as our special good friends, we ask you, just as we have asked all our other allies and supporters, to desist from and stop waging the war you have begun in the lands of our said uncle and brother-in-law. If you do not do this, since hostilities here have now ceased and treaties have been made between us and the above-mentioned [princes], it is likely that a large and powerful army will fall on your lands, perhaps with dire consequences, for it would be difficult for you to resist and for us to help you. Therefore you should take good advice about this and, for your part, accept the said treaty.[78]

The peace treaty, signed at Saint-Trond (Sint Truiden) on 22 December 1465, made to end the rebellion, in fact only delayed its continuation for a few months.[79]

On their part, the Liégeois seem to have attempted to pursue a peaceful settlement with the Burgundians, but the bellicose heir to the Burgundian throne, Charles of Charolais, who of course had been left out of fighting the rebellion, would have little of peace. Although Charles disbanded his War of Public Weal army following their return from Paris – probably less from his willingness to do so and more out of his soldiers' dismay at the lack of action, provisions, and timely pay[80] – he sought a reason to make his own assault against the erstwhile rebels. His target on this occasion, was Dinant. Charles, it seems, had a special hatred for the Dinantais. Undoubtedly, this was the result of the townspeople's equal hatred of Charles, most recently manifest by their hanging the count of Charolais in effigy while he was fighting in France and by their spreading the preposterous rumor of his illegitimacy, being the offspring not of Duke Philip the Good but of the adulterous affair of the previous hated bishop of Liège, Jehan de Heinsberg, with the Burgundian duchess, Isabel.[81]

It is also important to note Dinant's location and, especially, its geographical proximity to Bouvignes, the cross-Meuse urban rival with whose townspeople the inhabitants of Dinant were almost constantly in conflict. Situated on a bend in the River Meuse, Dinant is squeezed in between a cliff of considerable size and the wide river. In premodern times, this location provided the town with tremendous protection, even without considering the walls that documents also report ringing the town, although archaeology has yet to confirm their extent – it is possible that the walls only blocked the narrow passages above and below the town, the only non-riverine approaches, and

78   *Lettres de Louis XI*, III:1–2. The translation I am using is Vaughan, *Philip the Good*, pp. 394–95.
79   On this peace of Saint-Trond see Looz, pp. 30–31, and Merica, pp. 152–53.
80   This is suggested by Vaughan (*Philip the Good*, pp. 395–96), but without substantiation.
81   Merica, pp. 148–49. See also Vaughan, *Philip the Good*, p. 396.

the bridgehead.[82] The town itself is not large; even today it is comprised of only about three or four streets. Although it now has extended across the River Meuse, during the Middle Ages the major urban growth took place between the river and the cliff, with only a few inhabitants living in suburbs across the river; however, how much this growth progressed within or beyond the town's current limits is again impossible to ascertain without further archaeological research. In the fifteenth century a bridge crossed the river to near where the cathedral that has existed since that time stands. Much smaller than the modern traffic bridge that crosses further down the river, its wooden remains have been located in the Meuse, although neither of the likely fortified bridgeheads have been excavated.[83]

Dinant's greatest problem in the later Middle Ages was its competition with Bouvignes. Bouvignes lies about a kilometer (two bow shots in medieval terms) north and on the opposite side of the Meuse from Dinant. Unprotected by the natural terrain of its competitor, Bouvignes was surrounded by large walls, the remnants of which still impress the visitor today, and by an earlier built medieval castle which peered over the town from a nearby mountain top but may not have taken part in its defense during this period, as no record of support in the ensuing conflict has been found.[84] As suggested above, Dinant's rivalry with Bouvignes had always been vibrant, but never so much so, it seems, as in the course of the 1465 Liégeois rebellion. Already on 16 July of that year, in a letter written to Duke Philip the Good complaining of "hostilities" committed by Burgundian officials against their town, the Dinantais had suggested that the Bouvignois had violated their previous peace treaty by constructing fortifications between the two towns, in particular a gate and a number of ditches, and that they had fired "many shots" from their *canons*, veuglaires, and bombards at Dinant, "without any preceding cause."[85] (Interestingly, this letter may provide a clue as to the range of these various gunpowder weapons, with complaints against the firing of the *canons* and veuglaires separated from the bombards: the *canons* and veuglaires only hit the gates of Dinant, while the bombards threatened the people inside the walls of the town.[86])

These complaints, and a second, similar entreaty sent on 24 September 1465,[87] went unheeded by the duke. Still, this does not adequately seem to be reason enough for the Dinantais to undertake an attack of their rival town in the spring of 1466. This seems however to have been moderately successful, at least in terrorizing the Bouvignois if not in actually conquering the town; according to Philippe de Commynes, the Dinantais "cannonaded [Bouvignes] continually with two *bombards* and other large pieces of artillery, shattering the houses of the town of Bouvignes and

82 There are only a few general histories of Dinant and no histories of medieval Dinant. For a discussion of the town's situation during the late fifteenth century, see Gérard, *Analectes pour servir à l'histoire de la ville de Dinant*; Édouard Gérard and Gabrielle Gérard, *Histoire de la ville de Dinant* (Dinant, 1988); and Henri Hachez, *Histoire de Dinant* (Brussels, 1932).
83 Some of these timbers are currently on display in the later citadel built on the cliff above Dinant.
84 Although an edited cartulary of medieval Bouvignes does exist, Jules Borgnet, ed., *Cartulaire de la commune de Bouvignes*, 2 vols. (Namur, 1862), as of yet no history of the town for that period has been written.
85 This letter is reprinted in *Collection de documents inédits*, II:205–09.
86 This is found in *Collection de documents inédits*, II:208.
87 This is found in *Collection de documents inédits*, II:223–24.

forcing the poor people to take refuge in the cellars and to remain there."[88] But, what could they have hoped to obtain by such attack? The townspeople of Dinant must have known of the special animosity held by Charles of Charolais against them. Perhaps they felt that he was taken up with the affairs of the Burgundian realm and his place in it, as his father faced his last few weeks of life, and thus was too busy to concern himself with such a small, local matter; or perhaps they felt that the count would be reluctant to muster his army so soon after their fighting at Montlhéry, Paris, and Montenaeken; or perhaps they were simply being used by their Liégeois masters to provoke further rebellion? The reasons behind the attack are not revealed in contemporary sources. What is known is the response by Charles the Bold, who seems to have been completely willing to leave the court, completely willing to remuster his army, and more than pleased to be able to "justly" march against the town of Dinant.

It took a bit of time for Charles to gather his army and march against Dinant, although obviously not as long as the Dinantais would have hoped or wanted. By 18 August 1466 he was ready to set out from Namur, his site of mobilization, and the next day he arrived at and established his siege of Dinant. Contemporary sources claim a Burgundian siege train of more than 30,000 men, outfitted with a large number of artillery pieces, but the number of men is obviously too large, and at the same time would not have been necessary to undertake such a military engagement.

On the other hand, it would certainly have been in character for Charles the Bold to have appeared before such a hated foe with such a formidable and intimidating force. And the number of gunpowder weapons at just such a siege could never have been too many. Indeed, the destruction made by the Burgundian guns at Dinant indicates that Charles had truly brought a very large number with him.[89] Some even identify the types of pieces, with Jean de Haynin reporting that the Burgundians fired two large bombards, one courtau, one mortar, and other "*engins*" against the walls of Dinant and Jean de Brusthem increasing this number to four bombards, two veuglaires, one *canon*, one courtau, and two mortars.[90] Neither of these mentions what may have been the mainstay of the Burgundian artillery train, the serpentines, which Claude Gaier numbers at 120 and which Thomas Basin indicates fired iron balls.[91] This artillery was chiefly set up across the Meuse, in suburbs of Dinant destroyed by the Burgundians, and aimed principally at the town's comparatively more vulnerable gates, although Jean de Brusthem insists that Charles of Charolais' mortars also fired over the walls at the inhabitants of the town.[92]

---

88   The translation of this text is from Commynes (trans. Cazeaux), I:149.
89   A very large number of original sources discuss the siege of Dinant including la Marche, II:257–58; Haynin, I:65–69; Waurin, V:526–32; Roye, I:345–48; Jean de Brusthem, *Chronique*, in *Chronique Liègeoises*, 2, ed. S. Balau (Brussels, 1931), pp. 113–27; and Thomas Basin, *Histoire de Louis XI*, ed. C. Samaran (Paris, 1963–72), I:273–76.
90   Haynin, I:69, and Brusthem, p. 127.
91   Claude Gaier, *L'industrie et le commerce des armes dans les anciennes principautés Belges du XIIIme à la fin du XVe siècle* (Paris, 1963), pp. 94–95, and Basin, *Histoire de Louis XI*, I:274–75. Gaier calculates that these serpentines fired 502 balls measuring between 7 and 16 inches during the 19–25 August siege.
92   Brusthem, p. 113. On the setting up of Burgundian guns across the River Meuse from Dinant see Waurin, V:527. On their being directed principally at the gates see la Marche, II:257–58.

The siege lasted for only eight days. The Burgundian bombardment was heavy and merciless, so heavy Olivier de la Marche remarks that "those in the town did not dare to raise their heads about the walls or gates";[93] many in the town were killed.[94] Initially, the Dinantais were able to repair the damage caused by the Burgundian guns. At the same time, their own gunpowder weapons, which they had used so effectively againt Bouvignes to incite this engagement, kept up their own regular bombardment of the besiegers. This return fire may even have been the cause of the explosion of some gunpowder in the count's camp which, Jean de Waurin reports, "killed or wounded thirty-two men and shocked many others who were near to it."[95] Eventually, however, the Dinantais gunpowder weapons ceased to be a factor in the defense of their town. Simple attrition may have been the reason for this, although Jean de Haynin gives credit to a child who accidently set off the supply of gunpowder used by the besieged to fuel their weapons.[96]

Still the Dinantais refused two entreaties to surrender, one, again according to de Waurin, delivered by an adult messenger from Bouvignes, who was rapidly beheaded, and a second by a child, who met the same fate.[97] Perhaps they expected relief from Liège, although one suspects their bellicose stubbornness might have resulted more from their fear, justified as will be seen, of what punishments awaited their surrender.

Ultimately, eight days after they had begun the siege – certainly not a long time by medieval standards, although few sieges before this time had witnessed such a fierce gunpowder artillery bombardment – the Burgundians marched into the conquered Dinant. Thomas Basin credits this to their intense artillery fire, a judgement held by most of the other contemporary chroniclers;[98] Jean de Waurin was the sole exception, as he gives credit for the victory to a final assault by Burgundian troops against the battered walls and gates of Dinant brought about by a warning from the prince-bishop of Liège that he was sending a relief army numbering between 30,000 and 40,000 to the besieged town.[99] The town was quickly given over to pillaging by the victorious soldiers, an indignation that Charles the Bold did nothing to stop, perhaps expressing his wrath against townspeople who had so openly defied his and his father's rule. An even more infamous expression of this wrath came when the count of Charolais decided to punish the citizens of Dinant for their rebellion by tying 800 of them back-to-back and then casting them into the River Meuse to drown. A different fate awaited the town's master of artillery, who was taken to the mountain above Dinant's cathedral and thrown down into the town. Punishment must certainly have been expected. However, its severity and harshness could not have been: it inspired no fewer

---

[93] La Marche, II:258.

[94] Waurin, V:529.

[95] Waurin, V;529–30. See also Haynin, I:65.

[96] Haynin, I:65. The veracity of Haynin's contention here is put in doubt however by the claim of Waurin that the Burgundians captured a large amount of gunpowder when they took the town (Waurin V:532). Haynin, unlike other engagements during Charles' reign, does not claim to have been at Dinant.

[97] Waurin, V:528.

[98] Basin, *Histoire de Louis XI*, I:276. See also la Marche, II:258; Haynin, I:69; Roye, I:346; and Brusthem, p. 127.

[99] Waurin, V:529–30.

than three poems written at the time[100] and is still remembered in Dinant today.[101] In the aftermath of the siege and pillage, the town burned and its walls and gates were pulled down.[102]

The siege and destruction of Dinant brought about another peace treaty, the Treaty of Oleye, signed between the Burgundians and the Liégeois on 10 September 1466, and confirmed on 8 December 1466 in Huy. Still, no one witnessing the death of Philip the Bold on 15 June 1467 and the inheritance of the ducal throne by his son, Charles, held any illusions as to this peace holding for very long.[103] In fact, even before the year was out the Liégeois were again in rebellion, this time striking out against the Burgundian-allied town of Huy.

Once more it is difficult to understand the motives of the rebels in this uprising, only to conclude that yet again the once politically cautious Liégeois seem to have thrown sanity to the wind in estimating that they could either count on Burgundian inaction or, even more impossible in light of recent events, defeat them. Of course, one must consider this to be merely a continuation of the rebellion that had been fought since 1465 – news of the death of Philip had brought celebration instead of sorrow throughout the prince-bishopric of Liège.[104] The fact of the matter is that the Liégeois had never been truly defeated, not at Montenaeken nor at Dinant, but the idea that they did not deem these defeats to be significant still poses a problem for the historian.[105]

Part of the answer may be that Huy was besieged by a large group of Liégeois rebels known as the Company of the Green Tent (*Verte Tente*). Sounding as if they were an unruly mob of inexperienced, underarmed, and poorly led rebels, the Company of the Green Tent was instead a formidable force of rebel soldiers, several with military experience, armed with numerous gunpowder weapons, and capably led by Raes de Lyntre, lord of Heers. Raes de Lyntre, who in modern terms one might describe as an "extreme nationalist," had been in control of Liège for several months by the time of

---

[100] See Claude Thiry, "Les poèmes de langue Française relatifs aux sacs de Dinant et de Liège," in *Liège et Bourgogne. Actes du colloque tenu à Liège les 28, 29 et 30 Octobre 1968* (Liège, 1972), pp. 101–27. Most are edited in *Chants historiques et populaires du temps de Charles VII et de Louis XI*, ed. L. Roux de Lincy (Paris, 1857). All of these poems were written from the Burgundian perspective, so that although they report the destruction of Dinant, the anonymous poets always see it as justified. (Indeed, the first of these poems is actually entitled "Justice de Dynant.")

[101] Waurin, V:531. See also Gérard, *Analectes pour servir à l'histoire de la ville de Dinant*, p. 40.

[102] Waurin, V:531–32. Waurin claims however that this fire was of "mysterious" origin, and that it was only when Charles could not get control of it that he ordered the rest to be burned and the walls and gates destroyed.

[103] On the peace treaty see Charles Brusten, "Les campagnes Liégeoises de Charles de Téméraire," in *Liège et Bourgogne. Actes de colloque tenu à Liège les 28, 29 et 30 Octobre, 1968* (Liège, 1972), p. 85. On the death of Philip the Good and the inheritance of Charles the Bold see Vaughan, *Charles the Bold*, pp. 1–5.

[104] Vaughan, *Charles the Bold*, p. 12. Vaughan translates one chronicle, the *Gesta pontificum Leodiensium* of S. Petri (S. Petri, *Gesta pontificum Leodiensium a Joanne de Bavaria usque ad Evrardum a Marcka*, ed. J. Chapeaville, in *Gesta pontificum Leodiensium*, iii [Liège, 1616], p. 167), which reports that the inhabitants of Beringen "beat on kitchen utensils by way of mock bells for his obsequies and yelled out insultingly that the old devil had died." It was an affront that later caused the town's destruction.

[105] This question is further developed in Kelly DeVries, "The Rebellions of the Southern Low Countries' Towns during the Fourteenth and Fifteenth Centuries," in *Power and the City in the Netherlandic World, 1000–2000*, ed. W. TeBrake and W. Kibler (Leiden, forthcoming).

the attack on Huy, even though he had shown no military fortitude in the earlier 1465 warfare, in between then and September 1467 he had endeared the Liégeois towns-people to him by dressing his followers in red tunics with the words "Long Live Liège!" embroidered on the sleeves and by having a large bombard, which he named *Liégeois*, constructed and fired throughout the town. Even after the bombard blew up during one of its firing demonstrations, it still seems to have impressed the citizens of Liège.[106] Most important, however, was Raes' defiance of Burgundian rule of Liège, and of the ducal-appointed prince-bishop, Louis de Bourbon, and his lieutenant, Count Evrard de la Marck. Huy just so happened to be the current residence of these two hated leaders, hence the target of the Company of the Green Tent on 16–17 September 1467.

In less than a day Huy fell, although this may have been due less to the gunpowder artillery fire of the rebels against the town – which Georges Chastellain reports was nevertheless quite heavy[107] – than to its abandonment by Louis de Bourbon. Still, Evrard de la Marck did remain behind with the town's inhabitants to defend them-selves against the Liégeois, but this quickly proved to be in vain as the small town had no adequate fortifications.[108]

No doubt the occupation of Huy helped to provoke the following moves by Charles the Bold. But it alone cannot be blamed for initiating the duke's response. Even without the attack on Huy, Charles seems to have been planning to move against the Liégeois. Already on 29 July 1467 Bishop Louis of Bourbon had transferred his authority to the Burgundian duke to settle the rebellion of his people against him, by whatever means possible.[109] From this time on the duke began preparing a military expedition into Liège, mustering soldiers, especially from the other southern Low Countries, and gathering gunpowder weapons. In fact, the only thing that the fall of Huy may have actually provoked was the launching of this attack, which occurred on 19 October. The real size of the whole force is not known, although the payment accounts which survive put it at 35,000–45,000 men; contemporary sources claim only that it was the largest army ever assembled, gathered from throughout the Burgundian realm, with several mercenary soldiers as well, including a contingent of English longbowmen.[110]

Clearly the Liégeois rebels were going to be dealt with by the Burgundian ruler, once and for all. Such a large force allowed Charles the Bold to spread out, striking at several targets at once in an effort not only to capture a very large amount of land in a short amount of time but also undoubtedly to intimidate any possible recruits for the rebels. On 22 October one large contingent of Burgundian soldiers attacked Huy, while another besieged Saint-Trond, quite a distance to the north, beginning on 27 October. Neither of these adventures was to be successful on its own, however. Indeed, the attack of Huy turned out to be a miserable failure. Fortunately for historians, Jean de

[106] Vaughan, *Charles the Bold*, pp. 12–14.
[107] Chastellain, V:334–36.
[108] Looz, pp. 51–52, and Merica, p. 162.
[109] Vaughan, *Charles the Bold*, p. 15.
[110] Vaughan, *Charles the Bold*, pp. 16–18. See also Guillaume, pp. 184–85, and Brusten, *L'armée bourguignonne*, pp. 60–70.

Haynin was among that Burgundian force and has left a relatively lengthy account of their failed effort. He recounts a disorganized and poorly led assault which not only failed to surprise the rebellious defenders of the town – its stated purpose – but also aided their own demise by being caught under the town's walls within range of the defenders' archery, serpentine, and coulovrine fire. Several of the Burgundians were killed or wounded. Those still outside of this range chose to remain there, while the unlucky ones closer to the walls fought on, ultimately without success. Jean de Haynin writes:

> The men who had gone [down to the walls] attacked them and skirmished for at least an hour or thereabouts and clearly saw that they were laboring in vain, for they had neither a single ladder to scale the walls, nor a pick-axe nor a hook to remove stones, nor any device for cutting or breaking down the gate, nor any artillery and, though some of the men from Namur said: 'They are fleeing and we'll dine and drink good wine again at night inside the town,' the contrary was the truth, because they were not fleeing at all . . . So everybody climbed back up the hill and got back to their horses as fast as they could, and so returned without having achieved anything else.[111]

The siege of Saint-Trond was unsuccessful for an entirely different reason. It was actually not even allowed to be undertaken let alone completed, for on 23 October, aroused by the invasion of their principality and, at the same time, bolstered by news of the defense of Huy, Raes de Lyntre led a large army of rebels from Liège against the Burgundians.[112] The two armies met in battle at Brustem, thirty-five kilometers southeast of Saint-Trond.

The battle of Brustem is one of the most important but least studied of late medieval battles,[113] this despite having two eyewitness accounts, one from the Burgundian military leader, Jean de Haynin, with a second, much shorter report found in a letter written nine days following the battle on behalf of the duke by one of the magistrates from the nearby village of Saintron signed simply as Hautain.[114] Substantial accounts of the engagement also appear in the chronicles of Olivier de la Marche, Jean de Waurin, Philippe de Commynes, Jean de Brusthem, Adrien d'Oudenbosch, Henri de Merica, Diederick Pauwels, and Peter of Bethlehem, with references to it in more than a half dozen other contemporary works.[115] These report that both armies arrived at the

---

111   Haynin, I:75–83 (the quote appears on p. 83). The translation is mostly from Vaughan, *Charles the Bold*, p. 20–21. See also Oudenbosch, pp. 177–78.

112   On the rebel march from Liège and some of the problems attached to the study of it see Vaughan, *Charles the Bold*, pp. 21–22. On the siege of Saint-Trond see Guillaume, p. 107.

113   There are very few discussions of more than a cursory reference. These include: Gaier, *Art et organisation militaires*, pp. 342–48; Guillaume, pp. 107–08; Paul Henrard, *Les campagnes de Charles les Téméraire contre les Liégeois (1465–1468)* (Brussels, 1867), pp. 50–65; G. Kurth, *La cité de Liège au Moyen Age* (Brussels, 1910), III:262–67; and J. Daris, *Histoire du diocèse et de la principauté de Liège pendant le XVe siècle* (Liège, 1887), III:419–21.

114   Haynin, I:83–93, and Hautain, in *Collection de documents inédits*, I:168–70.

115   La Marche, II:276–77; Waurin, V:553–54; Commynes (ed. Calmette and Durville), I:105–15; Brusthem, pp. 113–15; Oudenbosch, pp. 178–79; Merica, pp. 166–67; Diederick Pauwels, *De rebus actis sub de ducibus Burgundiae* in *Chroniques relatives à l'histoire de la domination des ducs de Bourgogne (texts latins)*, ed. Kervyn de Lettenhove (Brussels, 1876), pp. 196–97; and Peter of Bethlehem, *Chronica*, in *Chroniques relatives à l'histoire de la Belgique sous la domination des ducs de Bourgogne (texts latins)*, ed. Kervyn de Lettenhove

battlefield at about the same time on the day and night before the battle was to commence, and that as such the next morning their leaders were able to organize the two forces in opposition to each other without the one side holding the advantage over the other – Haynin writes that for the Burgundians at least their organization and battle order had been drawn up by the duke of Burgundy himself the night before the engagement.[116] In addition, both the Burgundians and the Liégeois were well outfitted with gunpowder weapons, the fire from which heralded the beginning of the conflict.[117] "The air resounded with the sounds of these machines of war," writes Peter of Bethlehem,[118] but, evidently, to no appreciable effect. Throughout the morning the two sides exchanged gunfire, but, poorly aimed it seems, the shot of both the Burgundian and Liégeois gunpowder weapons flew harmlessly over the heads of their enemy, crashing instead into the trees above and bringing down large branches on top of them, but otherwise doing little damage.

Failing to cause any movement with this tactic, with the afternoon drawing on, and fearing an attack in the night should the engagement not be brought to a conclusion, Charles the Bold dismounted his archers,[119] including the English longbowmen, and marched them forward towards the Liégeois lines. Their task, however, was not to loose their arrows into these, at least not yet. Instead they were to find a path through the marshy, hedge- and ditch-filled fields to the village of Brustem for the mounted men-at-arms who were following closely behind them.[120] From there the Burgundian cavalry, led by Baudouin, a bastard son of Philip the Good, launched its attack on the rebels. Initially, the Liégeois soldiers successfully turned back this charge, which had difficulty carrying its impetus through the mostly natural barriers protecting the rebel lines. Liégeois resistance was also quite strong, and eventually the cavalry was forced to retreat and regroup behind their archers in the village.

The Liégeois artillery renewed its bombardment, this time targeting the village, and this time also seemingly more effective, as two Burgundian leaders were hit by some of the gunfire. In response the Burgundian archers let loose their own barrage of air-borne projectiles which was followed by "a great cry" and their own charge at the Liégeois. Other Burgundian troops followed; quickly the "courage of the Liégeois began to fail while the Burgundians fought more ardently, and soon they began to fall and die,"[121]

(Brussels, 1876), p. 429. Citations to the shorter contemporary accounts can be found in Gaier, *Art et organisation militaires*, p. 343 n. 2.

116 Haynin, I:85–86.
117 Haynin (I:86) indicates this to be from serpentines only, those gunpowder weapons, as at Montlhéry, beginning to take on their more modern artillery function in battles. See also Gaier, "Le rôle des armes à feu dans les batailles Liègeoises," pp. 34–36.
118 Peter of Bethlehem, p. 429.
119 Haynin (I:86) remarks that their horses, used only for transportation as there is no indication that these were mounted archers in the traditional sense, were to be taken to the rear, and that one man was to guard seven or eight horses.
120 On the terrain see Brusthem, p. 113, who must have known it if he indeed did come from the village as his name suggests. See also, Gaier, *Art et organisation militaires*, p. 345. Unfortunately, this battlefield cannot be studied now as it lies in the middle of a secure modern Belgian military base.
121 Haynin, I:86–87. Both Haynin and Hautain (I:169) are insistent on the decisive role of the archers at Brustem.

perhaps as many as 3,000–4,000.[122] Even a countercharge by their own cavalry failed, and the rebels were forced to flee from the battlefield. Nightfall saved the lives of many, including Raes de Lyntre, although Hautain claims that the Burgundians chased them for more than "a league and a half" and for "two hours after night fall,"[123] but all of the Liégeois gunpowder weapons, carts, tents, and provisions were captured by the Burgundians – who also, to the chagrin of Jean de Haynin, robbed the corpses[124] – an outcome of the battle remarked on at length by all the contemporary sources. Of the gunpowder artillery, a letter from Louis van den Rhyne to the magistrates of Ypres describes the haul which included: "*serpentines, veuglaires, ribaudequins, courtaux,* as many as 52 carts full." Furthermore, each of the Liégeois guns were outfitted with "a pavise painted with the arms of Liège which were also on the carts," an odd inclusion by den Rhyne, indicating perhaps more the symbolic defeat of the rebellion at Brustem than the physical capture of these large shields.[125] On 2 November Saint-Trond, abandoned by its citizens, was taken and its gunpowder weapons' arsenal captured.[126]

It is quite difficult for the historian studying the sources of the battle of Brustem to conclude that the gunpowder weapons played any significant role there, although their presence and amount of fire is certainly remarked on by all contemporary writers. Paul Fredericq does suggest an effectiveness of the gunfire,[127] being influenced perhaps by the overall psychological effect that such a bombardment would have on the morale of the soldiers engaged in the battle, something certainly noticed by the contemporary Jean de Brusthem.[128] However, most historians see little resulting from the gunpowder weapons in this battle, although suggesting that this was due to their mediocre use, as Claude Gaier does, is a bit harsh.[129] As at Montlhéry, their presence was surely important, but other, less technological factors seem to have carried the day, in this case the Burgundian archers whose leadership and bravery led other Burgundian troops to push on to victory.

Building on a confidence brought by their victory at Brustem, the Burgundians marched quickly on the headquarters of the rebellion, Liège, arriving there on 11–12 November. Along the route the Liégeois allied towns of Wellen, Looz, and Tongeren were captured and ransacked or burnt. The army also stopped at Othée, scene of John the Fearless' victory against the Liégeois rebels of 1408. However, perhaps nothing was more significant to Charles the Bold than when his army burned down the castle and village of Heers on 2 November; owned by his rival in the Liégeois rebellion, Raes de

---

[122] See the discussion in Gaier, *Art et organisation militaires,* p. 347 n. 1.

[123] Hautain, I:169.

[124] Haynin, I:87. See also Paul Herard, *Histoire de l'artillerie en Belgique depuis son oringe jusqu'au règne d'Albert et d'Isabelle* (Brussels, 1865), p. 53.

[125] This letter is contained in the *Régestes de la cité de Liège,* IV:240–42. Three other letters/documents in the *Régestes de la cité de Liège* (IV:234, 236, 239–40) confirm the severity of this loss to the Liégeois.

[126] Again, the capture of Saint-Trond is remarked on by all contemporary writers, with Louis van den Rhyne reporting the capture of its artillery to the Yprois magistrates (*Régestes de la cité de Liège,* IV:240–42).

[127] Paul Fredericq, *Essai sur le rôle politique et social des ducs de Bourgogne dans les Pays-Bas* (Ghent, 1875), p. 156.

[128] Brusthem, pp. 113–16.

[129] Gaier, *L'industrie et le commerce des armes,* p. 95.

Lyntre, the destruction of this location must have brought a certain revengeful satisfaction.[130]

Being abandoned by Raes de Lyntre and other radical leaders of the rebellion, who had fled at the approach of the Burgundians, and, perhaps more importantly, being threatened with a Burgundian bombardment "day and night,"[131] the more moderate inhabitants of Liège quickly negotiated a surrender. Surprisingly, Charles' punishments were not severe, comprising mostly of the destruction of Liège's walls and towers and the confiscation of the town's remaining gunpowder weapons – a not inconsiderable prize, as remarked on by several contemporaries, including Charles the Bold himself.[132] Perhaps the reason for this leniency is that the Burgundian duke hoped that defeat at Brustem might mean that he would not have to destroy Liège, the value of which was much greater as an economic entity. On the other hand, Colonel Brusten surmises that with the advent of winter and the rainy season the Burgundian army could not afford to carry out a lengthy siege of the town, quoting the following description of the situation from Philippe de Commynes: "we are in great need of victuals and money, and the army is almost completely destroyed."[133] So leniency may have been called for out of necessity more than polity. No doubt it was welcomed by the Liégeois – although that Charles the Bold forced 340 of the leading citizens to grovel before him wearing nothing except their shirts and socks cannot have endeared the duke to the recently conquered townspeople[134] – but neither the lenient punishments nor the defeat at Brustem convinced the Liégeois to give up their rebellion.

Diplomatic negotiations between the Burgundians and Liégeois continued throughout the end of 1467 and into 1468; even Pope Paul II became involved, sending his legate Onofrio de Santa Croce, bishop of Tricarico, to act as mediator between the two sides. Ultimately, as shall be seen, his tireless efforts on behalf of peace would fail, but Onofrio's presence in the process allowed him to leave one of the most important "outside" sources of what was to happen when these negotiations failed and Charles the Bold's wrath reached its vengeful peak.[135] In these negotiations the Burgundians seemed to have been flexible enough to recognize some of the desires of Liégeois sovereignty, but only so far as these were able to function under the leadership of Charles the Bold's choice of prince-bishop, Louis de Bourbon, and his ducal representative, Guy de Brimeu, lord of Humbercourt. Yet, this the Liégeois seem to have been entirely unable or, perhaps better put, unwilling to do. They openly refortified their walls, although mostly only with earthen ramparts, and sought to acquire new gunpowder weapons, borrowing as many as they could from nearby towns, including

---

130   On the progress of the Burgundian army towards Liège following Brustem see Vaughan, *Charles the Bold*, p. 23.

131   This threat is recorded in the *Régestes de la cité de Liège*, IV:236–38.

132   Charles' comments, really a bragging about the number of gunpowder weapons that his army had captured in Huy, Tongeren, and Liège, were made in a letter to the magistrates of Ypres (*Régestes de la cité de Liège*, IV:247). See also Haynin, I:95, 99, and Waurin, V:557.

133   Brusten, "Les campagnes Liègeoises de Charles de Téméraire," p. 91. The quote comes from Commynes (ed. Calmette and Durville), I:112.

134   Vaughan, *Charles the Bold*, p. 23.

135   Onofrio de Santa Croce, *Mémoire*, ed. S. Bormans (Brussels, 1885).

Aachen, and, when these did not prove to be sufficient to defend their town, melting down their numerous church bells to make others.[136] Both of these actions completely violated the treaty of peace made between themselves and the Burgundians only a few months before and were tantamount to declaring a renewed rebellion. But still Onofrio persisted to push for peace.

Finally, at the beginning of September 1468 the Burgundian leadership in Liège decided that it would take no more effrontery to their rule. Gathering the army put at his disposal by the duke for just such a situation, on 1 October Guy de Brimeu, accompanied by Bishop Louis de Bourbon, marched into the principality, and by 9 October it had reached Tongeren. There, once again, Onofrio tried to stem Burgundian bellicosity, warning Guy that the fight was not yet out of the Liégeois. In fact, this the ducal representative discovered more quickly than he expected, for as these negotiations were being made, a small force of rebels snuck into Tongres, and under the very eyes of the surrounding Burgundian soldiers, kidnapped Guy, Louis, and Onofrio; leaving Guy behind to tell the tale, they returned to Liège with Louis and Onofrio.[137]

As this had all been happening, Charles the Bold had been playing politics. During the early days of October the duke of Burgundy had been meeting with the king of France, Louis XI, at Péronne.[138] Situated on the borders of their two realms, at Péronne the two princes had been discussing peace between France and Burgundy and had been making great headway in doing so. Thus removing a potentially troublesome ally from Liège, Charles ordered a larger Burgundian army to march against the rebels.[139] By 12 or 13 October this force had reached Tongres. Again Onofrio tried to intercede, for ten days appealing to the Burgundian military leaders to turn back. However, one more time rebel activity proved to end any negotiations. On 22 October a rebel cavalry unit, riding on horses that Onofrio claimed had been captured from the Burgundians earlier at Tongres, attacked a small contingent of Burgundians outside the village of Lantin. It was virtually annihilated.[140]

On 26 October the Burgundians camped outside Liège. The duke, accompanied by Louis XI, whom he had convinced to join him as a gesture of their alliance, arrived on 27 October. Onofrio had spoken prophetically: despite the presence of their seemingly

136 On the acquisition of new gunpowder weapons from other towns see Pauwels, p. 286; on the melting of church bells to construct others see Basin, *Histoire de Louis XI*, I:316.
137 Vaughan, *Charles the Bold*, p. 29.
138 On this meeting between Charles and Louis see Vaughan, *Charles the Bold*, pp. 29–30, 53–58; Kendall, pp. 209–14; and Jean-Marie Cauchies, *Louis XI et Charles le Hardi: De Péronne à Nancy (1468–1477): le conflit* (Brussels, 1996), pp. 21–33.
139 Onofrio blames this army on the 9 October incident in Tongres (Onofrio, pp. 108–09). However, there is no way that Charles, at Péronne, would have been able to receive news of what occurred there, had then been able to issue the order to mobilize the army, at that time in Namur and Hainault, and finally have that army march to Tongres, all in the space of three or four days. Basing his conclusions on the chronicle of Jean de Haynin (I:123–26), who was with this army, and the letter of Anthoine de Loisey, also present, written after the sack of Liège (in Philippe de Commynes, *Mémoires*, ed. Dupont [Paris, 1840–47], II:70–71), Vaughan (Vaughan, *Charles the Bold*, pp. 29–30) correctly suggests that Charles had begun the process of sending this army against the Liégeois earlier. Guy de Brimeu's troops may only have been the vanguard of this larger army, or perhaps the duke merely wanted to determine his relationship with Louis XI before he chose to commit to such a military adventure.
140 Vaughan, *Charles the Bold*, pp. 30–31.

inadequate fortifications and supply of gunpowder artillery and the large Burgundian army, the Liégeois were determined to fight on. Several times groups of armed rebels ventured out to attack contingents of Burgundians, but only rarely were they successful beyond gaining anything more than small victories and symbolic booty. One attack, made on the night of 29–30 October, by a body of "picked men," according to the sources tried to capture or kill both the duke and the king, but only made it so far as the ducal lodgings before they were discovered and defeated. However, they had come so close to fulfilling their quest – Ludwig von Diesbach, a Bernese noblemen attending Louis XI at the time, claims that his life was only just saved, with his tent catching fire, while Charles the Bold needed the protection of his bodyguards to stave off the attack[141] – that Charles was determined to end the conflict once and for all.[142]

The following morning, 30 October 1468, the final Burgundian attack of Liège began, signaled to start, claims Jean de Haynin, by the firing of a large bombard.[143] The attack lasted ten hours.[144] Initially, the Liégeois fought well, resisting strongly the assault of the Burgundians. Pauwels writes:

> The citizens gathered their arms and everywhere strenuously resisted them with *bombards*, crossbows, and slings, and they defended their city strongly for some time. Yet, so horrid was the sound of both the powerful blasts of the *bombards* and the continuous blowing of the trumpets there that no one could hear anything. At the same time, so many projectiles (*jacula et tela*) were continually and thickly fired into the sky from both sides that the air seemed to be darkened, as if night had fallen.[145]

But their resistance was futile. Fighting was house to house and the Burgundians were merciless in their attacks and indiscriminate in their use of weapons and targets. Philippe de Commynes reports: "Our men [the Burgundians], who were close by, had four good pieces of artillery; they fired two or three major shots along the main street and killed many people."[146] The Liégeois, no matter how badly they wanted to defend their homes and families, simply could not withstand this type of warfare for long. Soon their resistance began to give way as they sought refuge from the destruction.

Fighting gave way to pillage, and what had once been the site of very proud rebels was soon engulfed in thievery and fire. The *Chronijk der landen van Overmaas en der aagrenzende gewesten* indicates that "there remained no chalice, no book, no cassock, and no vestment" in any church following the sacking of the town. Supported by other narrative and non-narrative sources, the anonymous chronicler of this *Cronijk* compares Charles the Bold's army to that of the Ottoman Turks in their destruction, claiming that anyone encountered in the town was killed, some 30,000–40,000

---

141 Ludwig von Diesback, *Chronik und Selbstbiographie*, in *Schweizerische Geschichtsforscher* 8 (1830), 161–215. See also Looz, pp. 59–60, and Vaughan, *Charles the Bold*, pp. 31–32.

142 Pauwels (p. 286), contends that the duke was noticeably shaken by the Liégeois attack and vowed by St. George that he would avenge it, "even if he lost half his army." See also Vaughan, *Charles the Bold*, p. 32.

143 Haynin, I:141. See also Pauwels, p. 291, and la Marche, II:287–88. Pauwels records that all the Burgundian bombards were fired and that this noise was accompanied by the blowing of trumpets and the unfurling of banners.

144 The time is from Haynin, I:141.

145 Pauwels, p. 291. See also Merica, p. 166.

146 Commynes (trans. Cazeaux), I:182.

according to most sources, a tally that is probably too high, but indicative of contemporary opinion. The town centre was gutted and most houses were damaged, if not completely destroyed. Different quarters of Liège were assigned to different units of the Burgundian army, and all soldiers profited enormously from the collection of booty.[147]

The duke of Burgundy did try vainly to retrieve the ecclesiastic booty taken by his troops, but otherwise seemed to relish in the destruction. These were people who had defied his rule, his army, and his gunpowder weapons for long enough and, though he had given them many opportunities to submit, they had continued to rebel. His feeling was no doubt mirrored by this contemporary description of the Liégeois given by Henri de Merica, "having more presumption than fortitude, less power than arrogance."[148]

Besides, the king of France, Louis XI, had ridden next to him at Liège, witnessing the destruction of the town that had tried to choose his reign over that of the duke. Whatever allegiance the king had with the Liégeois had been brutally severed when Louis, adorned with the cross of St. Andrew, Charles the Bold's insignia, had spurred on the Burgundians by shouting "Long live Burgundy!"[149] The two had once been enemies, but were they now friends? Georges Chastellain perhaps put it best when he wrote: "there was always rancor between these two princes; there could never be truce, friendship between them for their personalities and habits of mind were incompatible, and they invariably disagreed."[150] The source of the rancor for Louis, at least in 1468–70, was the territories he had lost to the Burgundian duke in the War of the Public Weal, as well as those that he perceived were his but had been lost over the century to the Valois dukes of Burgundy. The towns along the River Somme and in Picardy – Saint-Quentin, Corbie, Amiens, Abbeville, Doullens, Saint-Riquier, Crèvecoeur, Arleux, Mortagne, Péronne, Roye, and Montdidier – all should be French and not Burgundian.[151] And the fact that he had to meet with Charles in one of these locations, and there sign a agreement of peace with the Burgundian duke, only thereafter to be present at the destruction of a town that he had promised to assist in their rebellion against the Burgundians, surely did not help the situation any.

Then there was the marriage of Charles the Bold to Margaret of York, sister of King Edward IV of England, on 3 July 1468, which was a further insult to the French throne, binding the Burgundians once more to the English. An institutional memory of the pre-1435 Anglo-Burgundian alliance which had separated the two Valois realms from each other for so long; in a way the current "civil war" could still be blamed on it. So, the uniting of the Burgundians with the English, even if the English throne was in

147 *Chronijk der landen van Overmaas en der aagrenzende gewesten*, ed. J. Habets, in *Publications de la société archéologique et historique dans le duché de Limbourg* 7 (1870), pp. 27–30 (quote is on p. 28). See also Looz, p. 61, and the poetic and prose works by Mathieu Herbenus in "Deux écrits de Mathieu Herbenus sur la destruction de Liège par Charles-le-Téméraire," ed. E. Bacha, in *Bulletin de la commission royale l'histoire de Belgique* 76 (1907), 385–90. Vaughan, *Charles the Bold*, pp. 32–37; and Pirenne, *Histoire de Belgique*, II:286–89.
148 Merica, pp. 168–69. Looz (pp. 60–61) has a similar opinion but couches it amid numerous ecclesiastical comparisons. See also Gaier, *Art et organisation militaires*, p. 348.
149 Pauwels, p. 290, and Haynin, I: 141.
150 Chastellain, V:455–56. The translation is from Vaughan, *Charles the Bold*, p. 41.
151 Vaughan, *Charles the Bold*, p. 42.

the hands of a different branch of the family, could not have been a welcome one. Indeed, Louis XI had tried everything in his power to stop it from taking place, sending ambassadors to both Charles and Edward to express his dismay over the union, even going so far as to petition the pope not to grant the dispensation needed for the marriage and spreading rumors of the bride's previous sexual indiscretions.[152] Still, the wedding had taken place, and Louis now had to contend with the fact that an alliance between the English and the Burgundians was not likely to be broken. Of course, this was made somewhat easier by the fact that, in England in 1468–71, a question hung over who was actually on the throne, the Yorkists or the Lancastrians, and Louis could always hope that the situation might play into his favor.

Still, there had been Louis' witness to the armed might and technological strength of the Burgundian army at Liège which obviously influenced any further military decision which the French king might make concerning Burgundy. Such a display of power and ferocity must have made him nervous about any possibility of facing Charles in combat. Although Charles the Bold certainly could not have planned that the king be intimidated by his presence at the destruction of Liège – after all, what would have happened had the Burgundians lost or been forced into agreeing to a relatively non-punishing peace – that Louis XI was intimidated by such a show of military force must be the explanation as to why there was no significant action between France and Burgundy until 1471. Charles Brusten has surely described it correctly when he calls the period a "*guerre froid.*"[153]

This is not to say that either Charles the Bold or Louis XI ceased to prepare for war during the period. Contemporary records suggest that the Burgundians were especially active during these years in building up their gunpowder weapons' arsenal. Jean de Roye's *Chroniques*, for example, reports that in 1470 English sailors visiting the ports of France had described seeing Burgundian ships "strongly furnished with food, and artillery, and men of war."[154] In addition, Charles purchased the services of Portuguese vessels, caravels, to sail with the Burgundian fleet, all possessing a large number of gunpowder weapons.[155]

Of course, there were other concerns besides the Burgundians' military might and technology that kept Louis XI from pursuing his goal of northern French reconquest. The old League of the Public Weal still technically existed, at least many of the major parties that had provoked the war in 1465 were still alive, among them Francois II, duke of Brittany, Louis of Luxembourg, count of Saint-Pol, and Charles, duke of Berry, the brother of the French king. They also had to be appeased before Louis could think of fighting against the Burgundians. And during the "*guerre froide,*" Louis did what he could to befriend his old enemies, frequently bribing them with lands and

---

[152] Vaughan, *Charles the Bold*, p. 48. At twenty two, Margaret was older than most dynastic brides. A discussion of the arrangements for the marriage and of the festivities held at the time of the celebration – at which Jean de Haynin was present and of which has left a wonderful description – see Vaughan, *Charles the Bold*, pp. 45–53.

[153] Brusten, "Les itinéraires de l'armée Bourguignonne," p. 55.

[154] Roye, I:399.

[155] See, for example, Jacques Paviot, ed., *Portugal et Bourgogne au XVe siècle: Recueil de documents extraits des archives bourguignonnes* (Lisbon and Paris, 1995), no. 420, pp. 443–446.

titles – Saint-Pol became Louis' constable, while Charles became the duke of Guienne. Often this also included blackening Charles the Bold's character and slandering his right to rule. Charles did his best to counter these moves, but in effect after 1465 he found it difficult to count on the support of his old allies.[156]

Then, in 1470 something occurred that neither Charles the Bold nor Louis XI could have anticipated, something that would not only weaken the Burgundian duke that year but also left him substantially weaker for the rest of his reign: Edward IV lost his throne in England. Escaping by sea for Burgundy in April 1470, his exile there proved to be rather short, as he returned to the throne for good only a year later, in April 1471, defeating his foes, including King Henry VI, first at the battle of Barnet, fought on 13 April, and then at the battle of Tewkesbury, on 4 May.[157] Charles the Bold welcomed his brother-in-law during the months they were together. He even tried to assist him on occasion by sailing his fleet against English ships traveling in the English Channel. But he had never been very successful. He certainly must have wanted to restore Edward to the kingship of England, but even when this feat occurred, the duke of Burgundy must have known that the alliance with England would never be as beneficial to him as it once was, that Edward IV would always be more concerned with his security in his kingdom than with what was happening on the continent, even if he did continue to claim the French crown.

Indeed, evidence for this was recognized even before the Yorkist king left Burgundy, in January 1471. Thinking correctly that Charles the Bold was without allies of much use to him militarily, Louis XI launched his campaign to regain his lost northern towns and countryside. Assembling a large army and artillery – the fact that these could be mustered so quickly during the winter months must indicate a lengthier plan than historians generally accord the king[158] – and using the submission of the citizens of Saint-Quentin to French authority – at the urging of the constable, Louis of Luxembourg[159] – as an excuse, Louis broke the peace with the Burgundians and marched his army north. Charles, unprepared for what seemed like an inevitable possibility, could not quickly counter Louis' strategy, and the French king soon occupied not only Saint-Quentin, but also Amiens, Corbie, Roye, and Montdidier. Almost everywhere the king went the townspeople threw open their gates to receive him and his troops, probably more out of fear of his gunpowder artillery than in any innate desire to be ruled by the French king.[160] Only at Abbeville was there any Burgundian defense, and

---

156   Vaughan, *Charles the Bold*, pp. 59–60; Kendall, pp. 225–28; and Cauchies, *Louis XI et Charles le Hardi*, pp. 35–47.

157   So many works have been written on the Wars of the Roses that it would be folly to try and list all of them here. The best military histories may be Anthony Goodman, *The Wars of the Roses: Military Activity and English Society, 1452–97* (London, 1981), and Philip A. Haigh, *The Military Campaigns of the Wars of the Roses* (Stroud, 1995). On the battles of Barnet and Tewkesbury see P.W. Hammond, *The Battles of Barnet and Tewkesbury* (New York, 1990). On Louis XI's support for the Lancastrians see Kendall, pp. 228–36.

158   Vaughan (*Charles the Bold*, p. 68) and Kendall (p. 237) both seem surprised at the speed of Louis' action. Cauchies (*Louis XI et Charles le Hardi*, pp. 42–44), on the other hand, seems to indicate a more lengthy preparation.

159   Waurin, V:613–14; Vaughan, *Charles the Bold*, p. 68; Kendall, pp. 237–38; and Cauchies, *Louis XI et Charles le Hardi*, pp. 43–44.

160   Vaughan, *Charles the Bold*, pp. 68–69; Kendall, pp. 237–38; and Cauchies, *Louis XI et Charles le Hardi*, pp. 43–44.

that only after the leader of the garrison, Philippe de Crèvecoeur, lord of Esquerdes, threatened the citizens and confiscated all their weapons.[161]

It was not until mid-February that Charles the Bold was able to try and regain the lost towns along the River Somme. Knowing that they would not so easily surrender to him as they had to Louis, the Burgundian duke headed straight towards the biggest prize in the region, Amiens.[162] Arriving there on 24 February, Charles immediately set about attacking the cathedral town and nearby villages. Jean de Haynin, again an eyewitness, writes that the Burgundians had a large number of serpentines and coulovrines, as well as non-gunpowder weapons, with them. These the duke used to successfully capture the bridge, village, and castle of Picquigny, along the Somme northwest of Amiens – aiming not at fortifications but at the houses near the castle and walls (Charles may have used this tactic because he saw the citizens of the region as treasonous and thus, like the Dinantais and Liégeois, justifiable targets for his warfare), but when he tried the same tactic against both the northern and, then later, southern walls of Amiens he met defeat.[163]

Having lost face and, after a daring French raid captured sixty carts of Burgundian supplies, some badly needed "victuals, armors, and artillery,"[164] but not giving up on his attack of Amiens, Charles the Bold opened a second front against the also recently lost town of Corbie. Here, too, according to Jean de Haynin, the Burgundians fired many large stones from the bombards, mortars, and serpentines into the town and against the town walls.[165] But they were not successful against this location either. Into March Charles attacked these two towns, but to no avail. Richard Vaughan believes that this was because the duke did "not seriously [press] home" his attack; nor did Louis XI "press home his attack on Charles."[166] But this was hardly the case. Both sides dearly wanted to defeat the other. Perhaps they felt that a battle would decide the matter; and on 14 March when the two forces did collide in battle, at Buxy, they fought the entire day, using gunpowder weapons on both sides, as well as hand-to-hand combat, with numerous casualties and both claiming a victory that neither had actually earned.[167] That Charles and Louis began negotiating for a peace two days following the battle of Buxy must be seen as a result of a hard fought, albeit short war.

However, this peace, as in all other matters between the two sovereigns, was built on very shaky ground. Now it was the duke of Burgundy's turn to want to recapture the towns along the Somme. In the following few weeks, the town of Nesle was defeated and sacked by the Burgundians; Roye and Montdidier were attacked and fell quickly.[168] But then Charles seemed to change his strategy, deciding not to take on

161 Vaughan, *Charles the Bold*, pp. 68–69.
162 On Charles the Bold's army and its artillery see Waurin, V:619.
163 Haynin, II:164–73. See also de Waurin, V:620–24.
164 Waurin, V:623. A later raid captured even more Burgundian supplies. See Waurin, V:626.
165 Haynin, II:185. See also Waurin, V:624.
166 Vaughan, *Charles the Bold*, pp. 69–70.
167 Vaughan, *Charles the Bold*, p. 70, and, J. Robert de Chevanne, *Les guerres en Bourgogne de 1470 à 1475* (Paris, 1934), pp. 52–56.
168 Vaughan, *Charles the Bold*, pp. 77–78; Kendall, pp. 248–49; and Cauchies, *Louis XI et Charles le Hardi*, p. 53.

Amiens and Corbie again, but instead to launch an attack fairly deep into French territory, against a site, the town of Beauvais, the loss of which would surprise if not intimidate the French king. Perhaps, although it is not written anywhere, once he captured this important town, he merely wanted to use it to bargain for the return of his own lost towns. Richard Vaughan does not think so, as he feels that the duke of Burgundy was instead trying to link up with his ally, Duke François II of Brittany, who was about to go to war with Louis XI in Normandy.[169]

The siege of Beauvais began on 27 June 1472 and lasted for twenty-five days. It was not one of Charles' successes, although not because Louis came to the rescue of his town. Nor in fact did the townspeople seem to have many gunpowder weapons with which to defend their fortifications, which were however quite strong. Even more important in this siege, though, seems to have been the ardent defensive spirit displayed by the citizens of Beauvais. Gaining special mention in almost all sources, contemporary and modern, are the women of Beauvais, who, led by the Jeanne Laisné, later known as Jeanne Hachette, gained so much renown for their defensive energy that Louis XI suspended the sumptuary laws of the time and allowed the Beauvais towns' women to dress in whatever clothing they liked and to precede the men in the yearly municipal processions to commemorate the victory.[170] They were not about to submit to the Burgundian army, no matter what technological power was displayed against them.

But how powerful was the Burgundian technological display? The narrative sources are somewhat split on the issue. Thomas Basin, for example, seems to indicate that Charles the Bold delivered his usual strong bombardment of the town for the entirety of the siege, that his "bombards and other gunpowder weapons battered the walls and towers with stone balls" continually.[171] While the *Discours sur le siege de Beauvais* is impressed both by the number and the size of the projectiles which they were able to fire: "And very often in many places they fired their stone balls; some with as large a calibre as the bottom of a cask, others with the roundness of a large bowl, others of cast iron weighing 20 or 30 pounds, and others of lead and of iron the size of a fist and a palm."[172] On the other hand, Philippe de Commynes issues this rather contemptuous denial of the duke's abilities:

> My lord of Cordes [Charles the Bold] . . . had two *canons* which were fired only twice through the gate and made a large hole in it. If he had had more stones to continue firing he would have certainly taken the town. However, he had not come with the intention of performing such an exploit and was therefore not well provided.[173]

This has led to an equal confusion among modern commentators. Paul Murray

169 Vaughan, *Charles the Bold*, p. 79.
170 Kendall, pp. 250–51, and Vaughan, *Charles the Bold*, pp. 79–80. A recent, particular folkloric biography of the woman who, it should be admitted, very little is known about, is Sylvie Binet, *Jeanne Hachette: l'héroïne de Beauvais* (Paris, 1995).
171 Basin, *Histoire de Louis XI*, II:126. See also *Légende Bourguignonne*, in *Recueil de pièces historiques imprimées sous le règne de Louis XI*, ed. E. Picot and H. Stein (Paris, 1923), p. 78.
172 *Discours du siège de Beauvais en 1472*, quoted in Guillaume, p. 145.
173 Commynes (trans. Cazeaux), I:236.

Kendall, for one, sides with Basin: "Day and night Beauvais was hammered by Burgundian artillery, which, planted on high ground, smashed streets and houses as well as fortifications."[174] While, Jean-Marie Cauchies accepts Commynes' testimony: "The duke laid siege to Beauvais (27 June), without great preparation nor ample matériel, it seems."[175]

It should be remembered that neither Basin nor Commynes were eyewitnesses to the siege. Jean de Haynin was, and his chronicle is filled with account after account of failed assault against the town's walls with hardly any discussion of the gunpowder weapons used there, quite a different recounting for a military leader so taken by the use of these arms elsewhere during Charles' reign. And Olivier de la Marche, while not an eyewitness was the ducal secretary and his chronicle thus better informed than either Basin's or Commynes'; his narrative, after simply reporting that the siege was laid and that "nothing was gained there," discusses no tactics at Beauvais but instead recalls the numerous Burgundian deaths suffered, naming some of the more prominent ones.[176] From these sources then might be derived a more accurate story of the siege, one where the Burgundians met their match in powerful walls and a determined population. As such one realizes that both Charles the Bold's gunpowder weapons needed to be as powerful in their offensive force as the walls of Beauvais were in their defensive strength and the determination of his soldiers needed to be as strong as was that of the townspeople. Neither were, something that the Burgundian duke discovered less than a month into the siege, when he decided to break it off and return home.

Yet, despite the defeat of his rival at Beauvais, Louis XI was unable to take advantage of the situation. Beset as he was with François II in Brittany, he could not himself pursue the retreating Burgundian army nor even recover Nesle, Montdidier, or Roye. He was able to send word to the Grand Master of his Household, Anthoine de Chabannes, to "strike some good blow against the duke of Burgundy," to which Chabannes responded by leading 3,000 French troops in a raid on the unfortified small town of Prischies in Hainault.[177] This force was outfitted with "*engins* and *serpentines*," according to Jean de Haynin, and these were used to make "a strong assault against the good men and women of the town who refused to surrender." Eventually, however, the serpentines did bring down the town's church, where the townspeople had taken refuge – "by the force and the medium of the *serpentines* the door of the church was blown apart and entered."[178]

For the rest of 1472 the Burgundians and French continued to trade blows in the region of the River Somme. The Burgundians accepted the surrender of Eu and

174 Kendall, p. 250. As for Commynes' comment, Kendall seems to relegate this to a single attack on a single gate which "the citizen-defenders fought like demons, blocking the shattered gate with their swords and their bodies, pouring down a hail of archery and crossbow fire, stones and lead from the walls" (Kendall, p. 250).

175 Cauchies, *Louis XI et Charles le Hardi*, p. 53.

176 Haynin, II:198–200, and la Marche, II:292–93. The contemporary *Discours du siège de Beauvais en 1472* (ed. L. Cimber, in *Archives curieuses de l'histoire de France*, I [Paris, 1834], pp. 111–35, and in *Album historique et paléographique beauvaisien* [Beauvais, 1913]), tells a similar story from the French perspective.

177 Vaughan, *Charles the Bold*, p. 80. The original directive to Anthoine de Chabannes is in *Lettres de Louis XI*, V:5, 20.

178 Haynin, II:200.

Saint-Valery and destroyed the unprotected Aumale, Poix, and Gamaches. The French in turn raided Artois and tried, in vain, to retake Montdidier. At sea, French ships pirated the Flemish and Dutch coasts. Ultimately, with winter approaching and both armies needing to regroup and restock, the war simply fizzled out.[179]

Surprisingly, what treaties could not do, ennui and fatigue did. Despite having no peace treaty or even active negotiations towards one in winter 1472–73, Louis XI and Charles the Bold would not fight against each other the next year, nor would they fight against each other ever again. At least initially Louis had other priorities, primarily bringing his other rebellious princes in line. For his part, Charles turned his armies elsewhere.

In 1473 that elsewhere was Guelders. Guelders had never been a part of the Burgundian Low Countries, either through marriage or through conquest. Nor does it appear that the Valois dukes had ever shown desires to bring it within that fold. On the other hand, as the duchy and its dependent county, Zutphen, bordered against Burgundian Low Countries principalities, and the economy of these entities and the four largest towns – Arnhem, Nijmegen, Roermond, and Zutphen – relied largely on Burgundian trade, Guelders and Burgundy were incontrovertibly interlinked. Thus it seems rather odd that since the mid-1450s, during the reign of Philip the Good, the duchy of Guelders had begun to create political problems between itself and the duchy of Burgundy.

Relations between the two dukes had been tense since that time. Only the greatest patience kept Burgundian troops from invading Guelders, for example, at the over-throw of the legitimate duke, Arnold of Egmond, by his son, Adolf, in 1465, or during the war between Guelders and Cleves – a duchy controlled by Arnold's brother – which followed, in 1466–69. The Burgundians had chosen to remain as mediators in these conflicts, although not very effective ones, rather than military participants, but by 1473 the situation had changed and Charles the Bold had Duke Adolf of Guelders captured and imprisoned, restoring his father to the throne. When Arnold of Egmond died in February 1473, having no heir except for the son who had tried to overthrow him, then languishing in Burgundian custody, he left his duchy to Charles in his will. But this transfer of sovereignty to the Burgundian duke was rejected both by the Estates of Guelders – the council of nobles – and by the towns of Nijmegen, Arnhem, and Zutphen. Charles was left with little option than military enforcement of his rule over Guelders.[180]

Charles' army set out from Maastricht on 9 June 1473. His army seems not to have been large, but it did contain a contingent of English archers, and, of course, gunpowder weapons.[181] Traveling along the River Meuse, the Burgundian force was soon in Guelders. No resistance was met. Indeed, many towns sent delegates who surrendered to the duke as he approached their suburbs; the citizens of Roermond, one

[179] Vaughan, *Charles the Bold*, pp. 80–83.
[180] Vaughan, *Charles the Bold*, pp. 112–18, and W. Jappe Alberts, "De eerste Bourgondische bezetting van Gelre, 1473–7," *Bijdragen van het Instituut voor middeleeuwsche geschiedenis der Rijksuniversiteit te Utrecht* 27 (1954), 49–82.
[181] On the artillery train and its personnel which accompanied the Burgundian army to Guelders see Guillaume, pp. 146–49, and Henrard, *Histoire de l'artillerie en Belgique*, p. 62.

of the four primary towns, submitted to him even before he left Maastricht. The Burgundian army did have to stop for a few days outside the "most fortified town" of Venlo, but, as Willem van Berchen writes, "after the besieged had been harassed for four days and nights by terrible *bombards* and other diverse machines of war they obtained a surrender."[182]

No other fighting took place until the Burgundians reached Nijmegen on 28 June. This town, the most ardent of those who opposed Charles the Bold, was not about to surrender without putting up a valiant effort. Perhaps the townspeople believed that what had happened at Beauvais would repeat itself a year later at their town, in this putting great faith in the strength of their fortifications. Of course, Charles was looking to duplicate his victories in Liège. Again, the Burgundians sat back and let their gunpowder weapons batter the town walls. They were joined in this endeavor by soldiers from Cleves and after three weeks were successful. Willem van Berchen once more writes: "those from Burgundy and Cleves having fired their innumerable *bombards* and *serpentines* and other diverse instruments of war horribly throughout the entire day and night against the towers and walls of the city, they shook and partly destroyed them."[183] Thomas Basin agrees, suggesting that it was this destruction which brought about the town's surrender, and with this surrender the submission of the rest of Guelders.[184]

Throughout this period Charles the Bold was also reforming his military forces. Most changes were administrative, organizational, and disciplinary in nature, but show a certain desire of the Burgundian duke to improve his military forces. The first of these reforms was the Military Ordinance of July 1468. In this Ordinance the Marshal of Burgundy was commanded to review and pay the troops and to march them against the town of Liège – as seen above these troops destroyed that rebellious town later, in October of that year – and to refrain from any other warfare unless attacked by the French once they were underway. Other provisions set out who was required to serve in the military and also what arms and horses were to be brought by each soldier. Of special importance is that the Marshal was to be accompanied by a gunpowder artillery train of twelve serpentines, each with 100 cannonballs, four cannoneers, each with an assistant, a dozen carpenters, a dozen masons and their tools, eighty pickaxes, eighty axes, lances, ropes, and other equipment.[185]

182 Willem van Berchen, *Gelderse kroniek*, ed. A.J. de Mooy (Arnhem, 1950), p. 131. See also Basin, *Histoire de Louis XI*, II:168, and Vaughan, *Charles the Bold*, p. 119.
183 Berchen, pp. 132–33 (quote is on p. 132).
184 Basin, *Histoire de Louis XI*, II:170, and Vaughan, *Charles the Bold*, pp. 119–20.
185 Vaughan, *Charles the Bold*, pp. 205–06. This Ordinance is printed in *Mémoires pour servir à l'histoire de France et de Bourgogne* (Paris, 1852–64), II:283–85. In general, on the military ordinances which follow see Guillaume, pp. 118–50; J. de Lachauvelaye, "Mémoire sur la composition des armées de Charles le Téméraire dans les deux Bourgognes d'après les documents originaux," *Mémoires de l'academie des sciences, arts et belles-lettres de Dijon* 3rd ser., 6 (1880), 139–369, and Charles Brusten's articles: "Les compaignies d'ordonnance dans l'armée Bourguignonne," *Revue internationale d'histoire militaire* 40 (1978), 112–69; "L'armée Bourguignonne de 1465 à 1477," *Revue internationale d'histoire militaire* (1959), 452–66, and "La fin des compaignies d'ordonnance de Charles le Téméraire," in *Cinq-centième anniversaire de la bataille de Nancy (1477): Actes du Colloque organisé par l'institut de recherche régionale en sciences sociales, humaines et économiques de l'Université de Nancy II (Nancy, 22–24 septembre 1977)* (Nancy, 1979), pp. 363–75.

A second military Ordinance is known as the Abbeville Ordinance as it was delivered at Abbeville on 31 July 1471.[186] In this ordinance Charles organized 1,250 lances of permanent mercenaries into what he called "troops of the ordinance." Each lance was to contain a man-at-arms, his mounted page, a mounted swordsman, three mounted archers, a crossbowman, a coulovrinier, and a pikeman, the latter three on foot. The ordinance also specified the arms and armor each of these soldiers was to have, as well as their livery or uniform (ducal colors emblazoned with the cross of St. Andrews). In addition, command positions and hierarchy were established.

This was followed by the Ordinance of 1472 which was issued on 13 November 1472 and hence seems to have been very much influenced by the defeat at Beauvais. In many ways this was a repetition of Charles the Bold's ordinance of the year previously, except that the number of troops in each category, still organized in lances, were to be reduced in overall numbers. Of the 8,400 "troops of the ordinance" mandated by this ordinance, 600 were to be coulovriniers. More detail was given on personal armament, on discipline – each soldier was to take a loyalty oath – and training – including the institution of a roll call for the first time in the history of Burgundy – while bureaucratic "paperwork" was also increased for each captain and other officer. All of these new provisions can be seen as attempts by the duke to tighten his control over his army and its officers in an effort to prevent what occurred at Beauvais from ever happening again.[187]

Finally, in the fall of 1473 Charles issued the final Military Ordinance of his career. It, too, spoke to the numbers, organization, and leadership of the Burgundian army: chiefly this was the establishment of companies composed of four squadrons, each containing a captain (*chief d'escadre*) and four *chambres* comprised of a *chief de chambre* (officer) and five men-at-arms. As each man-at-arms was still responsible for a *lance* of himself, his page, three mounted archers, a pikeman, coulovrinier, and crossbowman, the numbers of each company would actually be quite large. Disciplinary changes forbade swearing, blaspheming, or playing dice. Individual women camp-followers would also no longer be permitted, although each company would be allowed to have up to thirty women in common to perform cleaning and other services for them. Finally, all units were to be drilled and exercised in the use of arms. This included: "to practice charging with the lance, keeping in close formation while charging, [how] to charge briskly, to defend their ensigns, to withdraw on command, and to rally, each helping the other, when so ordered, and how to withstand a charge." They were also to

---

186 This is Vaughan's name for it (Vaughan, *Charles the Bold*, pp. 206–07). He admits also that it is possible that other military ordinances might have been delivered between that of 1468 and 1471. It, too, is printed in *Mémoires pour servir à l'histoire de France et de Bourgogne*, II:285–94. See also David S. Bachrach, "A Military Revolution Reconsidered: The Case of the Burgundian State under the Valois Dukes," *Essays in Medieval Studies* 15 (1999), 9–17.

187 Vaughan, *Charles the Bold*, 207–08, and Bruno Scherff, "Die Ordonnanz Karls des Kühnen von Burgund aus dem Jahre 1473," *Militärgeschichtliche Mitteilungen* 57 (1998), 319–31. The number of troops is as follows: 1,200 men-at-arms; 3,000 mounted archers; 600 crossbowmen; 1,000 foot archers; 2,000 pikemen; 600 coulovriniers. See also Charles Brusten, "Les compaignies d'ordonnance dans l'armée Bourguignonne," in *Grandson 1476: Essai d'approche d'une action militaire du XVe siècle*, ed. D. Reichel (Lausanne, 1976), p. 131.

practice shooting their bows from horses and other archery skills, and to use the pike in conjunction with the bow.[188]

Any of the types of soldiers who were to fill the requirements of these Ordinances could have been mercenaries. Charles the Bold was not against hiring such troops, nor to hiring captains who provided such troops; the most notable of these were Italian and English.[189] Yet, it seems that most coulovriniers were drawn from Burgundian-controlled lands. That said, recruitment never completely met the Ordinances' guidelines, with numbers of men-at-arms, mounted archers, and pikemen seeming to meet their goals, but foot archers and coulovriniers falling far short. The numbers of coulovriniers appears especially low. In 1471, for example, a year when Richard Vaughan suggests that soldiers were recruited "so labouriously," of the three strongest companies, that of Olivier de la Marche only had raised 48 of 100 coulovriniers, with those of Jacques de Harchies and Jehan de la Viefville recruiting only 34 and 36 out of 100 respectively.[190] Why the lack of coulovriniers can perhaps be explained by a number of reasons: lack of experienced coulovriniers; lack of training of new coulovriniers; real and perceived dangers of the weapon, etc. What cannot be a reason, it seems, is that there were too few coulovrines. As will be seen below, in the numerous military engagements fought by the Burgundian army during the last few years of Charles' reign, narrative sources always comment on the large numbers of coulovrines and, it should be noted, coulovriniers in both the Burgundian forces and those which they face.

The campaign against Guelders in 1473 was to be one of the last successful military adventures of Charles the Bold, although he fought almost continually throughout the rest of his reign, 1474–77. How he became involved in the political turmoil that brought this downfall is quite intricate and confusing and as such will not be detailed at any length here. But in short, the catalyst was the revolt of Alsace which, after the 9 May 1469 Treaty of Saint-Omer, became controlled by Burgundy, mortgaged to Charles by Duke Sigmund of Austria-Tirol. The seeds of this rebellion began with the appointment of Peter von Hagenbach as bailiff of Upper Alsace later that year, on 20 September. In this role Hagenbach especially alienated his Swiss neighbors, threatening them with military invasion should they not follow policies favorable to Burgundy. He also threatened to occupy the border town of Mulhouse. In response the Swiss successfully sought alliances with Louis XI and several German principalities.[191] Charles the Bold immediately tried to make peace, but his sincerity may be doubted as,

---

[188] Vaughan, *Charles the Bold*, pp. 208–10 (quote is on pp. 209–10). See also Brusten, "Les compaignies d'ordonnance," p. 131. This ordinance is edited in Guillaume, pp. 191–202.

[189] Vaughan, *Charles the Bold*, pp. 211–118, and Bertrand Schnerb, "Troylo da Rossano et les Italiens au service de Charles le Téméraire," *Francia* 26 (2000), 103–28. Interestingly, at a time when English recruiters were having difficulty raising longbowmen Charles seems to have had no problem doing so. See B. Mark Allard, "An Expedition of English Archers to Liège in 1467, and the Anglo-Burgundian Marriage Alliance," *Nottingham Medieval Studies* 34 (1990), 152–74, and Louis-Edouard Roulet, "Présence et engagement des combattants Anglais à Grandson et à Morat," in *L'Angleterre et les pays Bourguignons: Relations et comparaisons (XVe–XVIe siècles* (Neuchâtel, 1995), pp. 107–22.

[190] Vaughan, *Charles the Bold*, p. 212.

[191] Vaughan, *Charles the Bold*, pp. 261–66.

at the same time, he was also seeking how militarily to face this new enemy.[192] The Swiss, too, seemed to realize the situation and never completely trusted Burgundian ambassadorial promises.

Problems intensified at the end of March/beginning of April 1474 with the establishment of the League of Constance by Charles the Bold's enemies, including not only several Swiss towns or cantons – Zurich, Bern, Luzern, Uri, Schwyz, and Unterwalden – but also his former ally, Sigmund, and several other German princes and towns. Finally, a group of Alsatian towns also joined the League. Their primary purpose was simple: in the words of Johann Knebel, they were "to consider the peace of the land and how to extricate it from the tyranny of the duke of Burgundy and his wicked bailiff Peter von Hagenbach."[193] Although there were other elements in the foundation of the League of Constance, its main one directed at Charles the Bold was that he must return Alsace to Sigmund. Indeed, at the 6 April meeting of the League, the duke of Austria even reported that he had repaid the mortgage and was retaking the county.

In mid-April certain elements of the League of Constance also initiated military action against the all too few Burgundian forces in Alsace. Most bellicose of these was Strasbourg, the townspeople of which believed that they had been especially harassed earlier by Hagenbach. Moving quickly to take advantage of the confusion brought about by the establishment of the League, the Strasbourgers soon recaptured a number of Alsatian strongholds, including Ortenberg Castle, which had been lost to Hagenbach three years previously, and in doing so chased all the remaining Burgundians from Alsace.[194] Strasbourg and other League members also began preparing to extend the war beyond Alsace into other Burgundian territories. In an effort to calm their belligerence, Charles the Bold reluctantly allowed the arrest of Hagenbach, his former bailiff of the region, who was then imprisoned, tortured, tried, and executed, in essence the scapegoat for his duke's policies.[195]

It was Charles' turn to act. Determined to avenge his honor against Sigmund and Strasbourg, and at the same time regain Alsace, the duke of Burgundy decided to aim his military might at the county and town of Montbéliard. Again, the reasons for targeting Montbéliard are convoluted and confusing, as the town was not part of the League of Constance nor did it have obvious connections with Charles' enemies; the targeting also seems to defy strategic logic, a similar accusation to that made against Charles' choice of Neuss as a military goal later that year.[196] In part this was due to the, "albeit forced," signing of a deed to the county by its then Burgundian-imprisoned Count Henry. In part it must also have been because the Burgundian duke thought that he could simply march a small contingent of his army into the town and thereby control it. Neither reason is really relevant, as the captain of Montbéliard refused either to recognize Count Henry's right to transfer the county and town to the Burgundians or to surrender it to the armed force sent to receive the submission of the town, despite

---

[192] Vaughan, *Charles the Bold*, pp. 267–73.
[193] Vaughan, *Charles the Bold*, pp. 277–83. The quote is translated on p. 278.
[194] Vaughan, *Charles the Bold*, p. 284.
[195] Vaughan, *Charles the Bold*, pp. 284–86.
[196] Vaughan (*Charles the Bold*, p. 287) tries to make sense of this choice, but is not entirely able to do so.

the fact that the Burgundians had the count with them and threatened to behead him outside the town unless they did surrender. Neither in fact happened.[197]

Charles the Bold's next military endeavor, also unsuccessful – indeed, perhaps his most disastrous defeat because of what it cost the duke both in money and reputation – was his lengthy siege of the town of Neuss, waged from 29 July 1474 to 13 June 1475. One of the most widely recorded of medieval military events, so much so that the modern historian is almost able to reconstruct a daily diary of the conflict,[198] the origins of the siege of Neuss are, like so many other of Charles' actions in the 1470s, not at all clearly understood. There is no doubt that Charles the Bold had a desire to acquire some of the land belonging to his neighbor, the archbishop of Cologne, a desire which he shared with his father, Philip the Good. But, even if that was the case, taking the military action that he did against one of the archbishop's towns, Neuss, in 1474, when he seemed to have so many other political and military problems, none of which involved the archbishop, simply defies all logic.

In trying to understand the siege, Richard Vaughan dates the origin of the conflict to 1465 and the beginning of negotiations between Philip the Good and the archbishopric of Cologne over the inheritance of the archepiscopal throne at the death of its former inhabitant, Dietrich von Moers. Philip, in keeping with his tradition of acquiring lands by placing relatives in dynastic marriages and important ecclesiastic positions, of course wished for one of his nephews to succeed to the seat. In this endeavor Philip failed; but, despite this, or maybe because of it, the Valois dukes continued to yearn for the archbishop's lands. Another chance to take some of these

---

[197] The best source for this odd event is la Marche, III:207–08, who was one of the generals sent to take over Montbéliard. See also Johann Knebel, *Diarium*, ed. W. Vischer and H. Boos, in *Basler Chroniken*, II–III (Leipzig, 1880, 1887), II:82; Diebold Schilling, *Die Berner-Chronik, 1468–1484*, ed. G. Tobler (Bern, 1897, 1901), I:170–71, 194–95; and Vaughan, *Charles the Bold*, pp. 287–88.

[198] Naturally the chroniclers so active in the rest of Charles' reign continue to report on this siege: Haynin, II:251–62; la Marche, II:293–300; Basin, *Histoire de Louis XI*, II:201–22; Commynes, I:252; Chastellain, VIII:262–63; and Roye, II:7. These are joined by Knebel, II:108–260; *Légende Bourguignonne*, pp. 77–82; Jean Molinet, *Chroniques*, ed. G. Doutrepont and O. Jodogne (Brussels, 1935), I:30–105; *Magnum chronicon Belgium, 54–1474*, ed. B.G. Struve, in *Rerum germanicarum scriptores*, III (Regensburg, 1726), pp. 441–56; Jean de Margny, *L'aventurier*, ed. J.R. de Chevanne (Paris, 1938), pp. 57–61, 83–85, 99–100; W. von Schaumberg, *Die Geschichten und Taten*, ed. A. von Keller (Stuttgart, 1859), pp. 18–27; Konrad Stolles, *Thuringische-Erfurtische Chronik*, ed. L.F. Hess (Stuttgart, 1854), pp. 80–81; J. Unrest, *Oesterreichische Chronik*, ed. K. Grossmann, Monumenta Germaniae Historica Scriptores (new series), XI (Weimar, 1957), pp. 53–61; Continuation of Henri de Merica, *De cladibus Leodensium*, in *Documents relatifs aux troubles du pays de Liège sous les princes-évèques Louis de Bourbon et Jean de Horne, 1455–1505*, ed. P.F.X. de Ram (Brussels, 1844), I:314–16; C. Wierstrait, *Historij des belegs van Nuys*, ed. K. Meisen (Bonn, 1926); Hans Erhart Tuesch, *Chronique rimée des guerres de Bourgogne*, in *Recueil de pièces historiques imprimées sous le règne de Louis XI*, ed. E. Picot and H. Stein (Paris, 1923), pp. 129–84; Conrad Pfettisheim, *Chronique rimée des guerres de Bourgogne*, in *Recueil de pièces historiques imprimées sous le règne de Louis XI*, ed. E. Picot and H. Stein (Paris, 1923), pp. 103–06; Letter from Jehan Baugey to the mayor and echevins of Dijon, in *Correspondance de la mairie de Dijon*, ed. J. Garnier (Dijon, 1868), I:143–48; Letter from Philippe de Croy, count of Chimay, to Georges Chastellain, in Chastellain, VIII:261–68, and in Jean de Haynin, *Mémoires*, ed. R. Chalon (Mons, 1842), pp. 273–75; and several letters written by Johanne Petro Panigarola. Surprisingly, however, not many modern studies of the siege have been written. The most accessible may be: Vaughan, *Charles the Bold*, pp. 312–344; Joseph Lange, "Pulchra Nussia: Die Belagerung der Stadt Neuss, 1474/75," in *Neuss, Burgund und das Reich* (Neuss, 1975), pp. 9–190; and F. Schmitz, *Der Neusser Krieg, 1474–75* (Bonn, 1896).

came in 1473 when a rebellion broke out against the current archbishop, Ruprecht. This archbishop appealed to Burgundy for assistance, gaining a promise of protection, while his rebels signed a military alliance with a rival German prince, Henry, landgrave of Hesse. Following the exchanging of threats and resistance to negotiation, and judging that Cologne was too large a target to take on in a military expedition, in the summer of 1474 Charles the Bold led his army in a siege of one of the archbishop's chief towns, Neuss.[199]

Vaughan's effort is valiant and certainly goes far in trying to suggest that the Burgundian duke was following a sound political and military strategy. He is not alone in his analysis; in fact, Jean-Marie Cauchies would say that he has not gone far enough in defending Charles' decision to attack Neuss. Cauchies, who dates the origin of conflict even earlier than Vaughan, to the acquisition of Luxembourg in 1447, sees the Burgundian strategy in 1474 as a *contrainte politique*, one which was made to "demonstrate the power" of the duke of Burgundy, and that this military action was a legitimate move. Indeed, Charles the Bold was practically required to attack Neuss, based on his political position in relation to his own lands, his ally – England – his enemies – Alsace, the bishops of Strasbourg and of Bâle, Duke Sigimund of Austria, and René II, duke of Lorraine – and his potential enemies – Emperor Frederick III of Germany and King Louis XI of France.[200]

Both of these authors give somewhat convincing arguments. Yet, one must still question the sagacity of Charles the Bold's strategy in military terms, if not in political ones. With the exception of his Guelders' campaign, when virtually no one opposed him, the duke of Burgundy had certainly not shown stellar military achievements in a very long time. His victory at the battle of Montlhéry and the siege of Liège were by this time distant memories, while losses in Beauvais and Alsace had proven that the tactics which he used to bring Dinant and Liège down, intensive bombardments by large gunpowder artillery trains, had not done the same against defenders who were more determined, better fortified, and better armed with their own gunpowder weapons. Moreover, the potential involvement in this conflict of the emperor and other German principalities and towns, which certainly could not allow a military engagement against their neighbors by a foreign foe, again calls such a military decision into question. In essence, Charles was creating an imperial enemy where there had not been one before. As a military strategy it was a failure.

It is also important to note that this was not a sudden decision made by Charles the Bold. He had been mustering troops and gathering gunpowder weapons for much of 1474 prior to his march into Germany.[201] Soldiers came from all of his domains, with mercenaries from Italy and England also joining the Burgundian force; Jean-Marie Cauchies suggests a total number of 20,000.[202] Charles' gunpowder artillery train

---

199   Vaughan, *Charles the Bold*, pp. 313–19, and Cauchies, *Louis XI et Charles le Hardi*, pp. 88–89.

200   Jean-Marie Cauchies, "Charles le Hardi à Neuss (1474/75): Folie militaire ou contrainte politique," *Publication du centre européen d'études bourguignonnes (XIVe–XVIe siècles)* 36 (1996), 105–15, which he repeats in *Louis XI et Charles le Hardi*, pp. 83–102.

201   An example of this gathering of gunpowder weapons, found in Garnier, pp. 178–79, has been translated in Appendix 6.

202   For English and Italian mercenaries, see, especially, the letter of Baugey. The Italians, generically called

again impressed contemporaries. Jean de Haynin, who would fight alongside them at Neuss, remarked that Charles the Bold's gunpowder weapons were "very fine and very large," counting eight serpentines, one small bombardelle, an untold number of hacquebusses and coulovrines, powder and saltpeter, traveling with his military unit alone, while Jean Molinet numbers two *gros* bombards, one bombardelle, many courtaux, and many serpentines, along with a very large number of coulovrines; both accounts are echoed by Philippe de Commynes, Thomas Basin, and Jean de Roye.[203] The anonymous author of the *Légende Bourguignonne*, writing from the enemy perspective of a Strasbourger, agrees with those assertions, reporting that the Burgundians took "many *canons*, large and small," with them to Neuss.[204] And Olivier de la Marche, also an eyewitness to the siege, reckons that the Burgundian gunpowder weapons certainly exceeded in number those of the Germans defending the town.[205]

Yet, at Neuss these gunpowder weapons faced a fairly formidable task. Jean Molinet spends a great deal of space describing the town's impressive walls and other defenses:

> Neuss is notably towered of granite stone, strongly walled, of great strength, tall and thick and reinforced by strong belts, finely composed of stone and brick, and in many places, all in earth, were defensive towers, a marvelous artifice to repel the assailants. Between these and the walls were very wide moats and rock-lined below the belts other large moats of extreme width, some channeled and filled with water in large amounts.

The water for these moats was supplied by a number of rivers which ran around the town, most notably the River Rhine. In addition, the most vulnerable spots of many towns, their gates, seem not at Neuss to have been weak at all. Molinet continues:

> Four principal gates together of the same type and some postern gates and sally ports were decorated and strongly fortified with a limestone enclosure, because each of them had in front of them a boulevard, in the manner of a bastion, large, strong, and defensible, filled with all machines of war, and filled with much ammunition and powder.[206]

Breeching these walls, with even the most numerous gunpowder artillery train was not going to be easy. But Charles the Bold had accomplished such a feat before and undoubtedly felt that he could do so again. Almost immediately after establishing his positions surrounding Neuss, including setting some up on islands in the Rhine, the duke began his bombardment of the town. Again contemporary chroniclers are impressed, all agreeing that the Burgundian guns not only seemed constant in their fire on the defenses of Neuss, but also destroyed many of these. Gunshot also fell on the

---

Lombards, are singled out for recognition in several of the sources: Letter of Croy; *Légende Bourguignonne*, p. 79; la Marche, II:293–94; and Tuesch, pp. 130–36. Cauchies, *Louis XI et Charles le Hardi*, p. 90, and Guillaume, pp. 154–56.

203 Haynin, II:249, 251; Molinet, I:34–35; Commynes, I:252; Basin, *Histoire de Louis XI*, II:220–22; and Roye, II:7.

204 *Légende Bourguignonne*, I:251.

205 La Marche, II:295.

206 Molinet, I:31. See also Tuesch, p. 131.

houses within the town, causing destruction there as well.[207] Jehan Baugey, writing from Neuss to the mayor and echevins of Dijon on 16 September, details what had happened since the siege began:

> It is a fact, most honoured and redoubted lords, that six weeks ago last Saturday my most redoubted and sovereign lord, Monseigneur the duke of Burgundy, arrived and established his camp of honour before the town of Neuss. Since he began his siege in this way he has fired against the said town with about ten *bombards*, six *mortars*, and a large number of *coulovrines*, *serpentines*, and other pieces of artillery, so that the town has been badly damaged in places. My lord has established six sieges around the town . . . Since then the town has been bombarded as well as possible and the duke has enclosed his entire army [with siegeworks][208]

While the siege works Baugey refers to were no doubt static structures, Jean de Haynin does describe "a bulwark of wood, placed on large wheels" which Charles the Bold had constructed so that "one hundred men were able to be behind it," with their artillery pieces.[209] Jean Molinet also discusses such a siege machine, which he more clearly seems to describe as a siege tower, although he calls it an *engin* and claims that it was twenty feet long, twenty feet wide, and sixty feet high and moved on four wheels. It also could also hold more men, 300 more, than Haynin claims.[210]

According to Baugy, the siege seemed to have been going well for Charles the Bold at this point, not quite two months into it. The Neussers had defended themselves well, and they had support of the townspeople of Cologne who had sent contingents of their military forces – which Baugy claims numbered 4,000 soldiers – to assist the besieged. But, so far, these attempts at assistance had failed to hinder the Burgundians, such as one night, when the letter writer reports:

> . . . the Cologners sent a few people in boats down the Rhine, bringing with them a large boat loaded with wood, grease, oil, and gunpowder and, when they were near the duke's army they set fire to this boat and let it go with the water, intending that it should run up against and burn the bridge which the duke had made to cross into [an island in the Rhine]. As soon as the said bridge was burned the Cologners planned to attack the 300 lances on the island, the duke being unable to help them since the bridge would have been burned. But thanks be to God, and because of the good watch kept by the people in boats and ships (about 50 of them) which the duke had brought up the Rhine from Holland, whose duty it was to prevent the Neussers leaving by water and see that no help or provisions could reach them, the said boat was anchored in the Rhine and it burned there without doing much harm to the bridge.[211]

---

[207] See, for example, Haynin, II:252–58; la Marche, II:296; Commynes, I: 252; Basin, *Histoire de Louis XI*, II:201; Roye, I:70; Margny, pp. 83–84; Continuation of de Merica, I:315; Stolles, pp. 80–81; *Légende Bourguignonne*, pp. 78–79; Pfettisheim, p. 105; and Tuesch, pp. 130–36.

[208] Letter of Baugey, I:143–44. I have used the translation of this letter in Vaughan, *Charles the Bold*, pp. 322–23, with some alterations.

[209] Haynin, II:253.

[210] Molinet, I:45.

[211] Letter of Baugey, I:144–45. Again the translation is Vaughan's (*Charles the Bold*, pp. 322–23), with some alterations.

Still, Baugy could see some problems beginning to appear among the besiegers, among these especially problems with the English: several of the English soldiers wished to leave the army and then quarreled over "a wench," an argument which almost led to the duke's death when he was shot at by English archers who, "as they claimed," mistook his approach to quell the argument as an attack from the town.[212]

This is, of course, the most significant problem for any general at a prolonged siege, the boredom that sets in among his troops. Almost the only relief from such tedium was military action, but the only appreciable Burgundian attempt in the siege of Neuss at the time Baugy was writing had been an assault of the town, actually led by the Italians, against one of the boulevards built in front of one of the town gates. However, it had been successfully beaten back, with Baugy reporting: "it was pitiful how the *coulovrines* were fired at them thicker than rain, and hot water, great stones, and other things [thrown at them], so that in the four hours our people were in front of the fortification they achieved nothing and were forced to withdraw."[213]

Finally, at the end of his letter Baugy shows some concern about the possible arrival of the Emperor and his forces. As expected, at least by all contemporary discussants of the siege, if not by Charles the Bold himself, only a couple of days after the siege began the Emperor, together with several other German lords and towns, had declared war against the Burgundians and had begun amassing troops and artillery. The Cologners tried desperately to let the defenders of Neuss know of this, but, Baugy reports, at least one of these messengers, who tried to swim the Rhine "to take letters to the town in a wooden bottle, stating that the Emperor and his son were at Cologne and instructing the Neussers to hold firm as the Emperor was coming to attack the duke," was captured by the Burgundians. Intercepting this news made Charles determined "to bombard the town again more thoroughly than it has been, and it is planned to throw fire into it with some *engins* which are in the army."[214] Interestingly, when these efforts failed, the Cologners tried a more "modern" means of delivering word of the Emperor's approach to the besieged, inside a hollowed-out cannonball. Many messages seem to have been sent into Neuss this way – Jean de Margny maintains that one even set fire to some of the town[215] – with at least one received and read by the townspeople who answered the Cologners using a similar gunpowder-propelled delivery system. This latter message, or a later one sent the same way, survives: written 18 March 1475, it reports what had been already lost to the Burgundians – "one fortification after another, with moats too" – and that this had led to despair among the townspeople and their leaders, leaving them to exclaim "unless we are relieved soon and powerfully and with utmost expedition we are bound to report to you that we shall suffer a complete disaster."[216]

212 Letter of Baugey, I:145–46.
213 Letter of Baugey, I:145, again translated by Vaughan, *Charles the Bold*, p. 323. See also Molinet, I:42–44. Although Baugy claims that this was not an assault, "because the attack was in one place only and without ladders," Vaughan has suggested that "this attack on 10 September was described by some of the German sources, and has been accepted since, as a major assault on Neuss" (*Charles the Bold*, p. 323, n. 1).
214 Letter of Baugey, I:147–48, translated in Vaughan, *Charles the Bold*, pp. 324–25.
215 Margny, p. 59.
216 The original letter is edited in E. Kuphal, ed., "Der Neusser Kugelbrief von 1475," in *Aus Mittelalter und Neuzeit: Festschrift Gerhard Kallen* (Bonn, 1957), pp. 155–57. Translation is in Vaughan, *Charles the Bold*, pp. 330–31.

Although Baugy thought that the Emperor would be arriving at Neuss the Monday after he wrote his letter,[217] in fact it took him quite a long time to prepare and set out with his relief force. Defense of their town was left up to its citizens, and they seem to have done very well at it, bringing admiration from all contemporaries who commented on the siege. This began even before the siege began, Jean Molinet writes, when the mayors of Neuss, Jehan de Herprode and Rembault Keyebisch, hearing that the siege of their town by the Burgundians was imminent, had the townspeople stock up on essential items they would need to withstand a prolonged siege. These included sulphur, saltpetre, serpentines, coulovrines, and hacquebusses.[218] (The townspeople of Cologne also made gunpowder weapons for the Neussers which they sent to the town before the siege began.[219]) The same determination continued throughout the siege. Continually the townspeople fired their own gunpowder weapons at the besiegers, and as the walls and gates of Neuss became battered, they tried quickly to rebuild or repair them.[220] Burgundian mines were also effectively countermined.[221] Twice Burgundian sorties even gained a foothold inside the gates of the town, but on both occasions these were fought back by the town's defenders.[222] Additionally, on several occasions, Neussers conducted their own attacks on the Burgundians, almost always bringing back supplies of food, and gunpowder,[223] while Jean Molinet reports that once five hundred Cologners were able to sneak into the town undetected to reinforce the besieged.[224] (His encirclement of the town was obviously not as tight as Charles the Bold would have liked it!)

The defense of Neuss began to take such a toll on the Burgundians that when Philippe de Croy, the count of Chimay, wrote his letter to the chronicler Georges Chastellain at the end of 1474, almost six months after the beginning of the siege, it had a decidedly different tone from that of Baugey earlier:

> The works we are engaged in are more like those which Hannibal endured crossing the Alps than he experienced in Capua. The thunder of the two *bombards* and their fumes in which we are cured are not musical instruments nor do they make a cordial syrup. Shot from *haquebusses* and *coulovrines* flies at us thicker than arrows in an English battle. Imagine that our icy and snow-covered pavilions are German baths; that the feathers of our beds are Dutch down; or the pavements of our roads where we are in mud to our knees, are the market at Valenciennes! Where is the dinner ushered in with the sound of a bell? Alas! Where are women to entertain us, to inspire us to do well, to provide us with undertakings, devices, desires and wimples? The chemists' and jewellers' shops and banks of Bruges are far away from us.

Still, Charles the Bold was very energetic, working to make certain that the town would fall to his army:

217 Letter of Baugy, I:148.
218 Molinet, I:32.
219 Basin, *Histoire de Louis XI*, II:202–03.
220 Haynin, II:261.
221 See the letter of Johanne Petro Panigarola in Vaughan, *Charles the Bold*, p. 331.
222 Vaughan, *Charles the Bold*, p. 329.
223 Molinet, I:46–49, and Vaughan, *Charles the Bold*, p. 329.
224 Molinet, I:53–54.

We have a duke who moves about more than a swallow. One moment he is in the Italians' quarters, another moment in those of the English. He visits the Hollanders, the Hainaulters, and the Picards. He commands troops of the ordinance. He gives orders to the feudal forces; and I can assure you that he does not keep his household troops and those of his guard in idleness. He is always on his feet, never rests, and manages to be everywhere. One day he pierces the ground with mines and trenches. On another, he climbs up on piles and causeways. He alters watercourses and has dried up a river more than 800 feet wide and deeper than a pike or lance could measure, which had such an impetuous current that no boat could ascend it. He has altered a river which was formerly a small stream so that it is now so deep and wide that it is without a bank or ford and seems to the judgement of men to have been navigable for all time . . .[225]

However, despite such energy shown by their commander, the Burgundian soldiers' boredom with the siege began to affect their attitude:

I am lodged in an abbey, in its dormitory, where there are small rooms and lodgings for religious people of other profession than those who used to converse there. In this place I can daily experience a great many of the abuses of the world, because in some [rooms] here an excess of money games and gambling go on all day long and in others, in default [of money], there is only dinner. Some sing and play flutes and other instruments; others weep and regret their dead relatives or even their own infirmity. On one side I hear the cheery cry "A right royal drink!"; on the other "Jesus", to encourage those who are in the last agony of death. There are whores in some rooms; in others the cross which leads the lifeless body to the grave. To God alone who knows the cause of these diversities, these and other things must be referred.[226]

The siege went on, as did the heavy Burgundian bombardment of the town, so much so that it seems to have picked up almost a folklore of its own. The gunpowder-delivered message shot into Neuss mentioned above is one such story repeated by Jean de Margny, for his poetic autobiography, *L'aventurier*. A second example written by the same author tells the story of two brothers who were hit successively by *canon* shot: "The one man was hit by a *canon* [shot]. His brother saw this and ran to him . . . The brother who had run over to the first started to return [to where he had been previously] but before he had walked four steps, a *canon* [shot] hit him and he died in that place."[227] On another occasion, Charles' half-brother, Anthony, the bastard of Burgundy, who was used mainly by the duke as an ambassador to the English and French courts, stopped by the siege and, according to Jean Molinet, advised that "two *serpentines* be mounted in such a place that they fired extremely well against the town."[228]

---

[225] Molinet also refers to this (I:40–42).
[226] Letter of Chimay. I have used the translation in Vaughan, *Charles the Bold*, pp. 327–28, with some alterations.
[227] Margny, pp. 83–84.
[228] Molinet, I:63. See also Stolle, p. 82. The Bastard was not the only visitor of rank to come by the siege; these included, among others, King Christian I of Denmark, King Ferdinand of Sicily and Aragon, King Alfonso V of Portugal, and King Ferrante of Naples. See Molinet, I:62–63, and Vaughan, *Charles the Bold*, p. 236.

But still the town did not fall. As the *Légende Bourguignonne* puts it: "Many *canons*, large and small, [were fired] against the town of Neuss, which almost destroyed it, against the towers, the walls, and the gates, which were built so well that they were not penetrated."[229] By the time the Milanese ambassador, Johanne Petro Panigarola, wrote from Charles' camp to the duke of Milan, on 19 March 1475, it seems that the Burgundians were no closer to taking the town than nearly eight months earlier when they began the siege. He writes:

> To tell the truth, my lord, this undertaking at Neuss is a difficult thing and, according to people expert in the art of war, it will take a long time to have it by force. The place is strong in its site and because of the river. It is well defended, with perhaps over 3,000 stout defenders within it, with good artillery – one person exhibits a hat that has been shot off. It is necessary to work underground in tunnels which, as they are made, so likewise the [enemy] makes theirs, assembling inside to defend them, and they defend themselves so valiantly that anyone wishing to do battle with them will send a whole crowd of men to the butcher's shop.

Still, Panigarola has many compliments for Charles the Bold and his soldiers, although he may be exaggerating their numbers:

> This is a very fine camp, in which there are more than 30,000 combatants and a mass of artillery. There have been even more people here than there are now, but there is no need [for them]. This lord could have the place on terms but he does not want this; he wants it at discretion. He is in close touch with the Emperor and the lords of Germany concerning an agreement. In any case, whether by honourable agreement in his own way or otherwise, he says he is resolved not to leave until he achieves his aim. His lordship is most diligent, by day and by night he inspects the *bombards* and excavations as if he were the least person in the camp, and he takes the utmost trouble.

However, he remains rather skeptical about the enterprise:

> What will happen I am unable to tell yet though I would have liked to have advised your lordship of the limits of the place . . .[230]

Yet, a month later, on 25 April, when Panigarola wrote the duke of Milan again, nothing of significance had changed, on the surrender of the town or on the negotiations with the German Emperor, although the Milanese ambassador was concerned that the entry of Louis XI into the affair might alter matters.[231]

In the meantime, in the spring 1475, Frederick III and the German relief force had begun to march to Neuss. It was a slow advance, fraught with difficulties in supplying the troops and paying for goods consumed along the way, but on 6 May 1475 the army left Cologne bound for Neuss. It then took him seventeen days to arrive at the besieged town. Why so long? Richard Vaughan proposes that the Emperor really had no desire

229 *Légende Bourguignonne*, p. 79.
230 The translation of this letter is found in Vaughan, *Charles the Bold*, pp. 331–32.
231 Letter of Panigarola in *Dépêches des ambassadeurs Milanais*, I:106–09.

to fight the Burgundians.[232] On the other hand, Charles the Bold had no desire to leave Neuss without taking it.[233] Negotiations between the two leaders had been constant, but they had resulted in no peace agreements.[234] Moreover, Charles tried several times to disrupt the Germans during their lengthy relief march, even going so far as to send an expedition to capture the imperial town of Bonn on 12–13 May; it failed either to capture the town or to interrupt the emperor's progress. He also tried unsuccessfully to keep them from setting up camp when they arrived at the siege on 23 May.[235] However, during the following six days, with the threat of warfare between the two sides ever-present, negotiations continued. Finally, a truce was agreed to, with both forces willing to withdraw from the town. But the Burgundians did not just retire the three miles set by the truce; they kept going, burning their camp on 8–9 June and sending their gunpowder artillery down the Rhine – although five of the boats laden with guns were captured by the Cologners in the process which delayed the Burgundian withdrawal until they were returned.[236]

Charles the Bold left Neuss on 27 June. Although he tried hard to call the siege a victory, as he had gained some concessions from the emperor in the peace negotiations, the cost of the siege, in money, men, equipment, and time, certainly defined it as a defeat – a major one! The contemporary Strasbourger Hans Erhart Tuesch claims a loss of 6,000 Burgundian soldiers, with 19 standards and 12 "good *coulovrines*" captured by the Germans, against 800 Neussers killed.[237] A German report written for the Emperor on 16 June, no doubt more accurate, tallies Burgundian losses at over 3,000 men and 12,000 horses, with an estimated 100,000 *florins* worth of gunpowder shot.[238]

No doubt Vaughan is technically correct in writing that at Neuss, "[Charles the Bold] had been checked but by no means decisively defeated."[239] Still, it is quite difficult to see his lack of success at the siege of Neuss as anything more than the proverbial "beginning of the end," or perhaps more correctly as "one more step toward the end." Charles' military failure there was recognized as such by everyone, and it would be added to those suffered also at Beauvais and in the revolt of Alsace. The Burgundian military, with its vaunted gunpowder artillery, had lost its formidability. Gunpowder artillery had again proven insufficient on its own to bring down the walls of medieval fortifications backed by a determined populace.

Most immediately the effects of Neuss were felt in Charles the Bold's own lands. With the army and its duke away for a year at the siege, Burgundy and Burgundian holdings were left fairly bereft of defending forces. Guillaume de la Marck, lord of Aremberg, following his father's example, led his own forces and those of Liégeois

232 Vaughan, *Charles the Bold*, p. 342.

233 This is asserted by several contemporaries beyond Panigarola (see note 225 above), including Haynin, II:262; Commynes, I:252; and *Légende Bourguignonne*, p. 79.

234 See Vaughan, *Charles the Bold*, pp. 335–41.

235 Vaughan, *Charles the Bold*, p. 342.

236 Margny, pp. 59–61, and Vaughan, *Charles the Bold*, p. 344.

237 Tuesch, p. 136.

238 See Vaughan, *Charles the Bold*, p. 345. This report is edited in *Die Eidgenössischen Abscheide aus dem Zeitraume von 1421 bis 1477*, in *Amtliche sammlung der älteren Eidgenossichen Abscheide*, II, ed. A.P. Segresser (Luzern, 1863), p. 546.

239 Vaughan, *Charles the Bold*, p. 345.

exiles, such as Raes de Lyntre, on raids of Luxembourg and Stavelot; and René II of Lorraine, who had declared war against the Burgundians in May 1475, also tried to invade Luxembourg that June.[240] However, most aggressive in his bellicosity toward Charles the Bold had to be Louis XI who, immediately after his truces with the Burgundian duke lapsed on 1 May 1475, made several sorties with his army against Burgundian lands, his army attacking many of Charles' Somme towns and invading Artois, Hainault, and the two Burgundies, while his navy also harried the coast of the northern Low Countries. By mid-1475, the towns of Montdidier, Roye, Corbie, Jonvelle, and Jussey were under French control, while Saint-Riquier, Hesdin, Doullens, Arras, Bavay, Avesnes, and Valenciennes all received damage. So, too, did the principalities of Franche-Comté, Maconnaise, Charolais, Artois, Hainault, Picardy, Luxembourg, and, even, Burgundy itself.[241]

But it might have been the entry of the Swiss into war with Charles the Bold that had the most lasting effect on the ultimate demise of the Valois dukes of Burgundy. Like the others mentioned above who took advantage of the duke of Burgundy's preoccupation with the siege of Neuss, the Swiss, led by the townspeople of Bern, also decided to declare their military dislike for the Burgundians. This they did officially by declaring war against Charles on 29 October 1474, and unofficially by joining with German soldiers to attack Burgundy the following month. Their goal was the border castle of Héricourt. Amassing a large army – Vaughan contends that there may have been as many as 18,000[242] – and outfitted with a large number of gunpowder weapons, including a large bombard from Strasbourg known as *der Strauss*, the ostrich, which was pulled by eighteen horses – Conrad Pfettisheim writes that "it buzzed freely and did a horrible dance, when it was full of powder it laid hard eggs[243] – the Swiss army arrived at Héricourt on 5 November. Firing this artillery, the Swiss soon caused Héricourt castle significant damage. However, laying a siege on a remote castle in the dead of winter began taking its toll on the besiegers, who likely might have abandoned the siege had the issue not been decided by what in hindsight was undoubtedly an unwise battle.

On 13 November a Burgundian force led by Henry de Neuchâtel, the lord of Châtel-sur-Moselle, Blamont, Héricourt, and Neuchâtel, decided to relieve his castle. Mustering a mainly cavalry army, far smaller than that of the Swiss – although Tuesch claims a total of 9,000 cavalry and 5,000 infantry – Henry de Neuchâtel faced the besiegers, whom he initially surprised but then gave enough time to form their battle-lines. At that time, seeing that he was so greatly outnumbered, Neuchâtel seems to have turned around and fled, only to be caught by the pursuing Swiss near the Burgundian campsite. A "last-stand" effort to defend their camp failed, and the Burgundians were quickly routed, taking at least 1,617 casualties, many among the coulovriniers, and losing five standards. The castle surrendered a short time later.[244] It

240   Vaughan, *Charles the Bold*, pp. 345–46. On René II's political struggle with Charles the Bold see René Taveneaux, *Histoire de Nancy* (Toulouse, 1978), pp. 94–95.

241   Vaughan, *Charles the Bold*, pp. 346–47; Kendall, pp. 285–95; and Cauchies, *Louis XI et Charles le Hardi*, pp. 104–06.

242   Vaughan, *Charles the Bold*, p. 295.

243   Pfettisheim, p. 107.

244   On the siege and battle of Héricourt see Pfettisheim, pp. 106–07; Schilling, I:177–87; Tuesch, pp. 160–62; and Vaughan, *Charles the Bold*, pp. 295–96.

was the first loss of Burgundians against the Swiss; more, of course, would follow.

In order to block further military action by the French king, and perhaps also to focus his own military energies on smaller tasks, such as the Swiss and Lorrainers, Charles the Bold's initial reaction to the loss at Neuss was to negotiate a peace with Louis XI. This was made by the Treaty of Soleuvre, signed the 13 September 1475. It established an almost *status quo* border, with the return of a few, but not all, of the most recently French-captured Burgundian towns, and a land and naval peace for the space of nine years. It is quite fair to say that no one really expected the peace to hold between Burgundy and France, but it did hold, at least until the death of Charles the Bold, less than a year and a half later.[245]

One of the seemingly lesser concessions awarded Charles in the Treaty of Soleuvre was the return of the duchy of Bar. However, Louis XI was not in control of Bar at the time. It was, instead, held by René II of Lorraine, a one-time ally of the Burgundian duke, who, however, in 1475 was an enemy.[246] Just the past May René had declared war against Charles the Bold, and the following month he had attacked his lands; now he "held" one of these lands illegally, according to the Treaty of Soleuvre. Even before meeting with Louis XI, the duke of Burgundy had wanted to avenge the earlier slights, and now he had his provocation.

The Burgundians began their march on Lorraine almost immediately after the Treaty had been signed.[247] Within days Charles the Bold's army had split into two and was advancing both into the north of Lorraine – with Charles himself in charge – and in the south – with Anthony, the Bastard of Burgundy and Charles' half-brother, in the lead. Several small towns had quickly fallen to them – Bulgnéville, Châtillon-sur-Saône, Lamarche, Darney, Monthureux-sur-Saône, Passavant-la-rochère, and Pont-à-Mousson – when Anthony, fearing a Swiss attack against his small force, halted. Charles, however, kept advancing and, bypassing Nancy, continued to capture more small towns – Laneuveville, Bayon, Charmes, Vézelise, Mirecourt, Dompierre, Épinal, and Vaudémont. Nowhere did he meet any resistance, which may have come as a result of the threat of his now-accustomed brutality against the inhabitants; indeed, René of Lorraine himself, seemed to be hiding from the Burgundians, his allies sending little assistance. Returning to Nancy on 24 October, Charles began to besiege it in the manner that was now traditional for him: using a heavy bombardment of the town and its fortifications from his large gunpowder artillery train.[248] That this train was such is indicated in documents from the *Archives départementale du nord* where an extremely large number of guns are noted coming just from the arsenal of Lille:

[245] *Dépêches des ambassadeurs milanais*, I:225; la Marche (ed. Beaune and Arabeaumont), III:214–34; Molinet, I:115–27; Commynes; Roye, I:341–46; Basin, *Histoire de Louis XI*, II:252–58; Vaughan, *Charles the Bold*, pp. 351–52; and Cauchies, *Louis XI et Charles le Hardi*, pp. 113–20. Basin is especially critical about the treaty and skeptical about its longevity.
[246] Vaughan, *Charles the Bold*, p. 352.
[247] This campaign into Lorraine is covered in Basin, *Histoire de Louis XI*, II:260–64; Molinet, I:111–14, 127–30; Schaumberg, pp. 27–30; and *Chronique de Lorraine*, ed. L. Marchal, in *Recueil de documents sur l'histoire de Lorraine*, V (Nancy, 1859), pp. 160–85. For a modern interpretation of this 1475 war see Vaughan, *Charles the Good*, pp. 353–56. René of Anjou had encouraged this surrender as he was unable in any way to assist the resistance of Nancy's townspeople.
[248] On the strength of the bombardment see Molinet, I:127–29.

6 bombards, as many of iron as of copper alloy
6 bombardelles
6 mortars
the serpentine *Lambillon*
10 courtaux
10 large serpentines
3 serpentines *de l'hotel*
2 serpentines of *Jacquin*
a serpentine of *Montlhéry*
36 medium serpentines
48 small serpentines
200 *arquebuses*.[249]

Unlike that at Neuss, on this occasion the siege was quickly successful, with its citizens surrendering on 30 November. Charles the Bold had himself inaugurated as duke of Lorraine on 18 December.

During the winter of 1475–76 the townspeople of Strasbourg panicked. Thinking they were the next target of Burgundian military aggression, the Strasbourgers began to accumulate foodstuffs and military equipment, including gunpowder weapons and powder, and to strengthen their fortifications, including the digging of a large and deep moat and the destruction of houses – 620 – and monasteries – 5 – around the walls to form a two-mile perimeter of flat land in front of the moat.[250] However, the townspeople of Strasbourg need not have worried, for the following year Charles the Bold chose not to march on their town, but instead to strike out against another persistent, although recent, enemy, the Swiss.

It is difficult to understand exactly why relations between Burgundy and the various Swiss cantons had never been peaceful. There is little to indicate a desire by Charles the Bold to invade Switzerland or to acquire Swiss lands, his much greater interest being clearly in occupying Alsace, Lorraine, and parts of the archepiscopate of Cologne. Of course, some of these lands bordered on Switzerland and this gave the cantons an excuse for being nervous about Burgundian military activity, but it certainly does not explain satisfactorily why the Swiss chose to enter on the side of the enemies of Burgundy in each of those engagements, Neuss alone being the exception. Richard Vaughan side-steps the need for giving an explanation, simply labeling the "motives behind the mounting aggression" of the Swiss "complex and . . . not necessarily shared by all of her citizens."[251] This may be because Vaughan, as most other historians of the Swiss-Burgundian Wars, looks at the issue almost solely from the Burgundian perspective and not from that of the Swiss. Swiss historians, Louis-Edouard Roulet, Hans-Rudolf Fuhrer, and Benjamin Geiger, observing the issue from the Swiss side,

---

[249] This document is originally translated and published as part of Robert D. Smith, "Good and Bold: A Late 15th-Century Artillery Train," *The Royal Armouries Yearbook* 6 (2001), 98–105. The original is transcribed in *Inventaire sommaire des archives départementales du Nord*, VIII:160–61. The complete artillery train inventory is found transcribed and translated in Appendix 2.

[250] Vaughan, *Charles the Bold*, p. 357.

[251] Vaughan, *Charles the Bold*, p. 360. Vaughan is actually discussing the Bernese in this sentence, but it is clear that this "complexity" is also shared by the other Swiss cantons.

suggest that, instead of seeing the military moves of the cantons in the mid-1470s as a reaction to the expansion of Burgundy, one should look at the desires of the Swiss Confederation to expand their territories and influence. This desire had been growing since 1450, but had become especially active since 1467; the lands of Burgundy lay in the path of this expansion, and therein lies the reason for Swiss bellicosity against Burgundy. The Swiss Confederation, led by Bern, saw the opportunity to join the League of Constance and, later, the Lower Union not only as a means of weakening the duchy's power, but also, perhaps, in continuing their expansion.[252]

That this is the reason certainly can be confirmed by the action that most immediately was the cause of the Swiss-Burgundian War beginning in 1476. Ths Swiss attack of the Vaud, beginning with victory in the battle of Héricourt late in 1474, had continued after 14 October 1475, spreading quickly and with little resistance throughout the region. By the end of October the Vaud was under the control of the Swiss Confederation. Charles the Bold had naturally been preoccupied initially with his siege of Neuss and later by his conquest of Lorraine and, beyond some minor attempts to sow insurrection among the Swiss, had not previously tried to avenge his army's defeat at Héricourt or to recapture lost lands.[253] However, after the conquest of Lorraine had been successfully completed late in 1475, he turned his interest, and his army, towards Switzerland.

Charles the Bold began his invasion preparations early, far earlier than was traditional for a medieval military leader and also earlier than he had done for his Neuss campaign. From 22 January to 6 February he began to muster soldiers at Besançon, from where he expected to launch the invasion. He also ordered provisions and gunpowder artillery to be delivered to him, declaring any of the towns which rejected his request as rebellious and subject to military punishment. As he wrote to the Dijonais, his goal was,

> with the help of God and St. George, to deliver our lands and subjects of Burgundy and those of the house of Savoy from the Swiss, Valaisans and other Germans who, up to now, have interfered in order to cause them various injuries, oppressions and damages.[254]

He then informed his Savoyard ally, Geneva, to prepare for an invasion in which he would attack "the Bernese, Zürichers and their allies, your enemies and ours."[255]

---

[252] Louis-Edouard Roulet, "Formation de la Suisse," in *Actes du Ve centenaire de la bataille de Morat* (Fribourg and Berne, 1976), pp. 163–69; Louis-Edouard Roulet, "La route Berne-Genève et les guerres de Bourgogne," *Publication du Centre européen d'études burgundo-médianes* 23 (1983), 43–51; and Hans-Rudolf Fuhrer and Benjamin Geiger, *Les guerres de Bourgogne*, trans. Christophe Eck, 2nd ed. (Zurich, 1996), pp. 5–8. Fuhrer and Geiger also suggest that what the Confederation acquired through warfare against and diplomacy with the Burgundians prior to these Wars was *insignifiants* (p. 11). See also Cauchies, *Louis XI et Charles le Hardi*, pp. 122–23. To be sure, Vaughan (*Charles the Bold*, p. 360) also discusses the desire for expansion of Bern, but does not see it as the reason for the Swiss and Burgundian Wars quite the way the Swiss historians do.

[253] Vaughan, *Charles the Bold*, pp. 359–64.

[254] *Correspondence de la mairie de Dijon*, I:181–82., translated in Vaughan, *Charles the Bold*, p. 366.

[255] *Registres du conseil de Genève*, ed. E. Rivoire et al. (Geneva, 1900–40), II:481–82. See also Vaughan, *Charles the Bold*, 366.

Buoyed by his success in Lorraine, and forgetting his travails at Neuss, Charles was quite confident in his prospects against the Swiss. Realizing that they would be without Imperial or French help, as he had negotiated a treaty of peace with both powers, he compared himself to Hasdrubal going over the Alps against Rome, forgetting obviously that Hasdrubal had not succeeded in capturing Rome once he had actually entered Italy. On the other hand, the Swiss, who knew all of Charles' moves against them, were equally confident, claiming that they did not need the Empire or France, and that should they need to, they would gladly fight them along with the Burgundians.[256]

On 13 February the Burgundians marched out of Besançon intending ultimately to attack the Swiss castles at Yverdun and Grandson which lay on the Lake Neuchâtel. The Swiss army – primarily Bernese, Fribourger, and Züricher troops – marched out to counter this attack two days later. Arriving at Yverdun on 18 February, Charles found that the Swiss garrison had abandoned it, preferring to make a stand in the better fortified Grandson Castle.[257] The following day, the Burgundians began their attack on the town and castle of Grandson.[258] The town of Grandson, with very few fortifications of its own, quickly surrendered. But the castle of Grandson was another thing entirely. The castle seems today every bit as majestic as it no doubt appeared to the Burgundians. Built as a far different defensive structure initially in 1050, the castle had been rebuilt and added to in each of the three centuries preceding its 1476 siege.[259] At that time it was manned by several hundred Bernese who, one would think, could hold off their attackers for a long time, especially, one would also think, as they must have known that a relief army was on its way. Yet, they did not hold out for long, surrendering to the Burgundians on 28 February, after only nine days of siege. Why for only such a short time? The Bernese chronicler Diebold Schilling suggests that this was because some in Charles' army, most notably the German mercenaries, convinced the garrison that Fribourg had already been captured with all of its inhabitants massacred, and that, should they wish to avoid a similar fate, they should surrender the castle.[260] However, Schilling here may simply have been trying to rationalize what essentially amounted to cowardly behavior on the part of the garrison, especially as he, writing in hindsight, knew the results of the battle that followed. The answer may instead lie in the ferocious bombardment that the castle had undergone in those few days, with two escapees from the castle informing the Swiss military leadership that during that time the battlements of the fortification had been entirely shot away, and that their own gunpowder had been destroyed by fire and their master of artillery slain.[261] That

---

256 Vaughan, *Charles the Bold*, pp. 366–68.

257 Hans-Rudolf Kurz, "Grandson – 2 Mars 1476 – le déroulement de la bataille," in *Grandson 1476: Essai d'approche d'une action militaire du XVe siècle*, ed. D. Reichel (Lausanne, 1976), p. 201.

258 Kurz, p. 202, and Fuhrer and Geiger, p. 12.

259 *Le Château de Grandson* (Colmar, 1980), Fuhrer and Geiger, p. 34.

260 In Fuhrer and Geiger, p. 34. Johan Knebel (II:352) claims that Charles agreed to grant the garrison their lives should they surrender, then broke his promise and slew them.

261 *Narratio de morte Caroli ducis Burgundiae*, in *Chroniques relatives à l'histoire de la Belgique sous la domination des ducs de Bourgogne (texts latins)*, ed. Kervyn de Lettenhove (Brussels, 1876), p. 484; *Entreprises du duc de Bourgogne contre les Suisses*, ed. A. Schnegg (Basel, 1948), pp. 109–10; Vaughan, *Charles the Bold*, p. 370; and Kurz, p. 202. On the gunpowder weapons taken by Charles to Switzerland see *Légende Bourguignonne*,

Charles hanged or drowned the entire garrison after the castle's surrender, something that even this bloodthirsty duke would not have done had terms of surrender been negotiated, seems to confirm this.[262]

While Charles had been besieging Grandson, his other generals, principally Jaques de Savoie, count of Romont, had been busy attacking other sites in the Vaud with much of it falling to their troops.[263] Only Neuchâtel and Murten remained under Swiss control. In the meantime, Swiss soldiers had been gathering at Neuchâtel, and by the day that Grandson Castle was surrendered, 28 February, they felt strong or perhaps desperate enough to meet the Burgundians in battle. Why a battle, one might ask? The answer seems quite simple, actually. The Swiss were confident in their ability to meet and defeat the Burgundians on the battlefield. Still, as Monthléry and Brusthem had shown, Charles the Bold had never lost such a battle, although a small contingent of his army had been defeated by some of these same Swiss troops at the battle of Héricourt the previous year. Of course, the latter example might in itself be the answer to the question: while Charles the Bold had never lost a battle, the Swiss had never lost to the Burgundians. They also knew the terrain and, as their actions would show, planned to surprise the Burgundians by using this knowledge.

On his part, the duke of Burgundy was not entirely unaware of the Swiss amassing an army at Neuchâtel and, even before Grandson Castle had fallen, believed that a relief army would try to interfere with his plans of regaining the Vaud. But he reckoned that the only route the Swiss could travel would be on the ancient Roman road along the lakeshore.[264] After all, that would be the only route his army, encumbered by their artillery pieces and supply wagons, could have traveled. So he positioned his army in that direction, even going so far as building a platform or boulevard from which larger gunpowder artillery, "large and small," according to the *Légende Bourguignonne*,[265] could fire on the approaching Swiss troops. This platform still stands on the battlefield, evidence of what was to become a failed tactic.

On 2 March the Swiss began attacking the recently lost Vaumarcus Castle, further up the lakeshore towards Neuchâtel. Ultimately such a move must be seen as a diversion, meant perhaps to draw the Burgundians from their fortified positions, even though Richard Vaughan maintains that "the allies had no further moves planned out, and, in particular, by no means expected Charles to march out of his Grandson camp."[266] But why then make such a vain attempt at this castle, especially doing so with only a portion of their army? Moreover, Charles did move out of his positions,

p. 84; Brusthem, II:123; Roye, II:32–33; Kurz, p. 207; and Brusten, "Les compaignies d'ordonnance dans l'armée Bourguignonne," pp. 114–15, 125.

262 Vaughan (*Charles the Bold*, p. 370) disagrees with this, believing instead "that this atrocity seems characteristic of Charles." On the brutality and violence of this and other acts throughout the Burgundian-Swiss wars see Albert Lynn Winkler, "The Swiss at War: The Impact of Society on the Swiss Military in the Fourteenth and Fifteenth Centuries", unpublished dissertation (Provo, Brigham Young University, 1982), pp. 178–211. See also Cauchies, *Louis XI et Charles le Hardi*, pp. 125–26.

263 Vaughan, *Charles the Bold*, pp. 370–72.

264 Kurz, p. 203.

265 *Légende Bourguignonne*, p. 84. On this field fortification see Kurz, p. 203. On the Burgundian gunpowder weapons at Grandson see Henrard, *Histoire de l'artillerie en Belgique*, pp. 64, 96, 154–55.

266 Vaughan, *Charles the Bold*, p. 373. Kurz (p. 204) sees the attack as a diversion.

planning to reestablish and refortify them nearer to Vaumarcus, some eleven kilometers from Grandson.[267] Indeed, the vanguard of this force even arrived at the new position and had started to set up their tents and artillery when they were met by another, larger force of Swiss soldiers, which had secretly made its way through the woods and completely surprised these Burgundians, whom they soundly and quickly defeated.[268]

Moving toward the main Burgundian army, this Swiss force, made up of pikemen, halberdiers, crossbowmen, coulovriniers, and cavalry, although greatly outnumbered, instead of establishing their lines and waiting for more soldiers, charged into them.[269] Quickly regrouping his army, Charles the Bold and his soldiers successfully withstood this charge and began to fire their gunpowder weapons at the Swiss, for the moment giving him the upper hand in the conflict.[270]

From that time forward, Charles should have patiently used his gunpowder artillery advantage and whittled away the Swiss lines. But he did not. Instead, he seems to have tried to feign a retreat using some of his forward troops, at least this is what the Burgundian chroniclers suggest. The Milanese ambassador, Johanne Petro Panigarola, who was at the battle but not close to the fighting, claimed that the manoeuvre was Charles' attempt to draw the Swiss toward the fire of his gunpowder artillery.[271] However, these soldiers may have simply been fleeing from the combat they were encountering, especially as the Swiss army had grown throughout the conflict as more of their troops, also coming through the woods, joined the small, initial contingent.[272] Whatever may be the case, other seemingly uninformed Burgundian troops saw this "feigned retreat" as a flight and began their own, not so feigned retreat. Ultimately, all of the Burgundians began fleeing from the battlefield, and the Swiss claimed victory.

Burgundian deaths were few, despite Haynin's claim that many Burgundians "of note" had been killed.[273] Of the reputed 20,000 Burgundian soldiers present at the battle of Grandson, only a few hundred were killed, probably fewer than the number of Swiss casualties for the same-sized force.[274] However, all of the Burgundian gunpowder weapons were lost, save those hand-held guns which were carried out by their operators: and not just the medium-sized gunpowder weapons were lost on the battlefield, but also the larger siege guns which had remained in the camp.[275] So

---

267 Knebel (II:352) suggests that Charles was in fact moving his camp from Grandson Castle to Vaumarcus Castle. See also Fuhrer and Geiger, p. 14.

268 Knebel, II:352, and Kurz, p. 205.

269 On the types of Swiss soldiers and their weapons see de Haynin, I:44; *Légende Bourguignonne*, p. 84; Kurz, p. 207; and Contamine, *Guerre, état et société à la fin du moyen âge*, p. 308. Olivier de la Marche (ed. Beaune and Arbaumont, II:239), who was ill and therefore not at Grandson suggests that this initial charge was delivered by the cavalry against a Burgundian force made up chiefly of Ghentenaars. On the fact that the Swiss attacked very well see Haynin, II:295; *Légende Bourguignonne*, p. 84; and Kurz, pp. 206–07.

270 Fuhrer and Geiger, pp. 14–15.

271 This assessment is found in a report on the battle written by Panigarola to the Milanese duke following his own flight from the battlefield on 4 March 1476 (*Dépêches des ambassadeurs Milanais*, I:316).

272 Kurz, pp. 208–09.

273 Haynin, I:295, and Fuhrer and Geiger, pp. 15–16.

274 Vaughan, *Charles the Bold*, pp. 374–76. The number of Burgundians is Charles the Bold's estimate and thus suspicious, the number of Swiss is Vaughan's and is based on far stronger evidence. See also Fuhrer and Geiger, p. 13.

275 See *Dépêches des ambassadeurs Milanais*, pp. 315–18; Knebel, II:352–53; and Kurz, p. 213. According to a

quickly had the flight at Grandson occurred and so quickly had it come back upon its own camp, that those who had remained there, including the Milanese embassy, were forced to abandon everything and join those fleeing from the battlefield – booty from this battle became legendary, even today producing a large catalogue of extant goods.[276] This left only the small Burgundian garrison in the Grandson Castle behind to bear the brunt of Swiss anger when they saw the bodies of their countrymen hanging from the trees outside; each was thrown to his death from the battlements of the castle.[277] The captured guns were taken to Nidau and divided among the cantons.[278] These captured Burgundian gunpowder weapons were not inactive for long, however, as they would be needed shortly after Grandson at the battle of Murten, fought between the Swiss and Burgundians on 22 June 1476.

Charles the Bold's retreat after his defeat at Grandson stopped in Lausanne. There he set about recovering from the battle, reinforcing his numbers and, especially, recouping his lost gunpowder weapons. For the latter he wrote to all of the lords and towns in his lands asking them to send him their guns. Ultimately, his call for troops would give him between 10,000 and 18,000 men.[279] His plea for gunpowder weapons resulted in a train of at least 50 serpentines and 3 large bombards and mortars.[280]

While at Lausanne, from 14 March to 27 May, Charles the Bold also began to plan his next strategy. Still wishing to rid the Vaud of its Swiss attackers, the duke of Burgundy determined that he would have to attack Murten or Fribourg to do so. In his estimation, either site should run the Swiss out of this land, the former by capturing a key spot that would threaten Bern, and the latter by removing a key part of the alliance. Charles also sent out urgent requests for alliance with anyone who might be able to help him. He seems to have offered almost anything to acquire allies at this time, including the promise of his daughter, Mary's, hand in marriage; ultimately, on 6 May, she became engaged to the son of Frederick III, Maximilian. Other alliances were also made, or continued, between the Burgundians, Milan, Hungary, and England.[281]

During this time, the Swiss had been launching small attacks against Burgundian holdings and fortifications. While not successful in sending Charles the Bold back to Burgundy, these attacks had nonetheless shown the Swiss determination to continue

inventory of gunpowder weapons captured at Grandson now found in the Bienne archives, the total number of gunpowder weapons taken by the Swiss was 419: 350 serpentines, 60 *pierriers*, and 9 bombards of huge calibre (*Dépêches des ambassadeurs Milanais*, pp. 319–20, n. 16).

276 Florens Deuchler, *Die Burgundebeute: Inventar der Beutestucke aus den Schlachten von Grandson, Murten und Nancy 1476/77* (Bern, 1963). See also Knebel, II:352–53; Kurz, pp. 209–10; and Fuhrer and Geiger, pp. 36–37.

277 Knebel, II:352.

278 Vaughan, *Charles the Bold*, pp. 376–77, and Kurz, p. 210

279 Vaughan, *Charles the Bold*, pp. 384–85; Guillaume, pp. 156–57; and Charles Brusten, "Charles le Téméraire et la camp de Lausanne, mars-mai 1476," *Publications du centre européen d'études burgundo-médianes* 14 (1972), 71–81. Judging from the records of Charles' *Trésorier des Guerres*, his army on paper numbered no more than 9,748.

280 These figures come from one of the letters sent by the Milanese embassy to their duke on 30 March 1476 (*Dépêches des ambassadeurs Milanais*, II:16) and probably indicates only one delivery of guns and not the entire Burgundian gunpowder artillery train. See also Molinet, I:143–44; Thomas Basin, *Histoire de Louis XI*, II:286–89; and Henrard, *Histoire de l'artillerie en Belgique*, p. 99.

281 Vaughan, *Charles the Bold*, pp. 281–82.

to fight the war against him. Hence, no negotiations between the armies were attempted.[282]

On 27 May 1476 the Burgundian army marched out of Lausanne towards the target that Charles had decided on, Murten. Although planning for a siege of the town, there is little doubt that the ultimate desire of the duke was a battle through which he might drive the Swiss Confederation out of the Vaud, thereby protecting his subjects not only there but throughout the Burgundian realm. However, there was also the question of honour: Charles the Bold wanted to avenge his loss at Grandson. As he told the Milanese embassy on 4 June while en route to Murten, "he could not live with the disgrace of having been defeated by these bestial people."[283]

Arriving at Murten a week later, on 11 June, the Burgundian army set up camp on the hills south of but overlooking the walled town. Units blocked roads leading to Fribourg, but they did not, or rather did not try to, encircle the town itself. Trenches were dug and filled with bombards and other siege weapons, which began immediately to bombard the walls of the town. Some attacks of Murten by small units of Burgundian soldiers were also made, while messages sent into Murten promised the townspeople the same brutality which the Burgundians had perpetrated elsewhere should they not surrender. They did not surrender.[284]

Most modern commentators see these actions not as acts of siege but as attempts by Charles the Bold to provoke the Swiss Confederation into battle. This is further emphasized by the apparent formation of his troops in battle array on 21 June, after the Swiss force had arrived, although no attack took place that day.[285] Yet, if he had prepared so for battle, then how could Jean de Margny and Johann Petro Panigarola, two eyewitnesses to the battle, say that Charles the Bold and his army were surprised when it finally came, on 22 June?[286] This is of course the important question of the battle of Murten, and one which the numerous studies on the conflict have all tried to answer.[287] Could the duke of Burgundy have known that his army was going to be

---

[282] Vaughan, *Charles the Bold*, p. 379.

[283] *Dépêches des ambassadeurs Milanais*, II:216. See also Vaughan, *Charles the Bold*, p. 387.

[284] Schilling, II:34; *Dépêches des ambassadeurs Milanais*, II:282; Molinet, I:144; *Légende Bourguignonne*, p. 85; *Narratio de morte Caroli ducis Burgundiae*, p. 485; Vaughan, *Charles the Bold*, pp. 387–89; and Fuhrer and Geiger, pp. 17–19. The *Légende Bourguignonne* (p. 85) attests to the resistance of the inhabitants of Murten. On the other hand, this resistance really did not have much of an opportunity to be tested, the Swiss army relieving the siege before it had gone on too long.

[285] This is attested to by eyewitness Johann Petro Panigarola, whose frequent dispatches provide perhaps the best account of the battle. The dispatch recording this manoeuvre is found edited in P. Ghinzoni, "La battaglia di Morat," *Archivio storico lombardo*, 2nd ser., 9 (1892), 102–09, with a translation into English in Kendall, pp. 436–39. See also Molinet, I:144–45.

[286] Panigarola, in Ghinzoni, pp. 102–09, and de Margny, pp. 65–66. Thomas Basin (*Histoire de Louis XI*, II:290–91) wrote that Charles had arrayed his troops on the morning of 22 June, for about six hours, before he dismissed them for dinner, after which the Swiss attack came. Although this account has been followed by some modern historians of the battle, as it obviously clears up some of the controversy surrounding the Burgundian lack of preparation for such an attack, as all of the eyewitnesses suggest that the Burgundian army did not line up that day, Basin's version of events must be disregarded. See Vaughan, *Charles the Bold*, p. 392.

[287] See, for example, Charles Hoch, *Morat et Charles-le-Téméraire, 1476–1876* (Neuchatel, 1876); G.F. Ochsenbein, *Die Akten der Belagerung und Schlacht von Murten* (Freiburg, 1876); Hans Wattelet, *Die Schlachten bei Murten: historisch-kritische Studie* (Freiburg, 1894); and P.E. de Vallière, *Morat: Le siège et la*

attacked on 22 June, especially as he had seemingly so diligently prepared for such an assault for several days prior to this one? Richard Vaughan provides the following rationale: "Perhaps it was the heavy rain during the night of 21–22 June and in the early morning of 22 June that convinced Duke Charles that the enemy would not attack him . . ."[288]

Still, while the weather might explain why the Burgundians did not return to their battle lines on 22 June – less why Charles the Bold felt that the Swiss would not do battle, however – it certainly cannot explain why the Burgundian duke compounded the mistake of such a miscalculation by choosing on that very day to pay his troops. This process, begun at 10:00 a.m., caused quite a lot of disorder, as all 8,000 soldiers attempted to collect their pay. The report of Charles' military treasurer survives and describes the problems that this action caused for the Burgundian army:

> While my said lord the duke was at the siege of Murten on 22 June 1476, at about 10:00 a.m. in the presence of Lyonnel Donguieres, his *maître d'hôtel*, and of Maître Thibault Barradot, his secretary, he ordered the said *trésorier des guerres* to pay his troops immediately . . . which three contingents could amount to about 8,000 men. To this the treasurer replied that it would be impossible to do this in detail. Nonetheless my lord the duke said that he must do it and that he would assign some people to help him and proclaim at the sound of the trumpet in all parts of the camp that everyone should report to his captain, *conduictier* or *centenier*. This he did, and at once the said treasurer assembled as many clerks as he could to help him . . . [He] could not make these payments because the battle came an hour after the money had been given to him . . .[289]

Could the Swiss surprise then simply be the product of bad generalship on the part of Charles the Bold who held fast to the idea that the Swiss would not attack that day, as suggested by Hans-Rudolph Fuhrer and Benjamin Geiger: "the comportment of the duke is a typical example of the fatal consequences in the persistence of a preconceived belief; that is a very great danger for a responsible commander?"[290] Such seems to agree with the account written by Panigarola:

> On Friday the 21st the [Swiss] enemy crossed a bridge . . . and quartered themselves near a village about half a mile from the bridge in a countryside so full of marshes, woods, and the customary thick hedges made of interwoven branches, that their forces could not be attacked. The aforesaid lord [Charles the Bold], in full armor, had spent the day with his whole army in a fine high open place above his camp, where he

bataille, 1476 (Lausanne, 1926); Charles Brusten, "La bataille de Morat," *Publications du centre européen d'études burgundo-médianes* 10 (1968), 79–84; and George Grosjean, *La bataille de Morat selon trios enluminures d'anciennes chroniques suisses* (Zurich, 1975); George Grosjean, "Die Murtenschlacht: Analyse eines Ereignisses," in *Actes du Ve centenaire de la bataille de Morat* (Fribourg and Berne, 1976), pp. 35–90.
288 Richard Vaughan, "500 Years after the Great Battles," *Bijdragen en mededelingen betreffende de geschiedenis der Nederlanden* 95 (1980), 385.
289 This report, found in the Archives générales du royaume, Brussels, CC25543, f. 196r–v, has never been edited. The translation used here is in Vaughan, *Charles the Bold*, pp. 392–93.
290 Fuhrer and Geiger, p. 21. For a counter to this see Louis-Edouard Roulet, "Le Téméraire à Morat: plaidoyer pour une rehabilitation," *Publication du centre Européen d'études Bourguignonnes (XIVe–XVIe s.)* 26 (1986), 39–56.

had arranged the battle stations of his squadrons and units. On learning of the arrival of the enemy, he decided to go see where they were lodging. I went also, saw the camp and the enemy, who merely made motions of skirmishing, not issuing from the woods, and fired some hand-held gunpowder weapons. Forming his judgment by the size of their encampment, which could not clearly be seen because it was spread out on low-lying ground, the aforesaid lord conceived the idea that but few troops were there and that they had come in order to encourage the Swiss besieged within Murten to hold out and to cause his lordship to raise the siege and reassemble his forces, and had not come to give battle since they were insufficient in numbers.

After he had so assessed the situation, Charles proceeded to call his generals together and discuss his decision to dismiss most of his soldiers from their array on the following day:

> . . . it was decided that that night about two thousand foot and three hundred lances should be left on the plateau where we were, with some horsemen stationed on the perimeter to keep guard. The remainder of the army would retire to the camp to rest, for the men had spent the whole day armed and mounted.

Of course, Panigarola, who had been present at this council, wanted it known that he opposed this decision, predicting instead what eventually happened:

> At this council of war, everyone gave his opinion, and I had the great satisfaction of saying . . . what seemed best to me – namely, that a strong force on watch was good but it was necessary to guard against the possibility that the enemy's apparent desire to avoid combat was only a trick and that since they were so near, less than a mile from our forces, an attack could be expected from hour to hour because they were seeking to catch the troops unprepared for battle – as indeed they did – through the advantage they possessed of being able to approach through the woods. I therefore proposed that even before daybreak the whole army, in battle array, should take position on the plateau to await the enemy, and even lodge there if necessary.

But Charles refused to budge from his command decision, "being firmly convinced that the enemy were only making a demonstration." This was further confirmed for the duke when the Swiss did not attack during the night or early the next morning:

> [Charles] not only concluded that his estimate of the situation was sound but took it as an absolute truth, being obstinately set in the opinion that the enemy would not come. The idea became all the more firmly fixed in his head when it was reported that the Swiss were discharging their guns and *canon*, which they were doing because their powder was damp from the rain and slow to burn – but they recharged their guns, as the event would prove.

Charles the Bold was decidedly wrong, however, as Panigarola asserts that the Swiss had, throughout the night, been marching towards the Burgundians. These movements were reported to the duke, but he refused to believe them: "he was willing to stake all that they would not come, saying that these reports were made so that he would raise the siege which he would never do, and that those who made them were French traitors, etc." Only after his half-brother, Anthony, sent similar reports did Charles begin to believe them. But by then it was too late:

At this moment the rain ceased. Immediately there began to emerge from the woods above the plateau the front of a unit of Swiss with long slender pikes, all of them on foot and handgunners ahead of them. Then [on the Burgundian left] farther down toward the flat land appeared a second unit, with fewer men. Between the two units were around four hundred horsemen, who, after they had moved forward a little, halted to await the advance of the foot units, which displayed many banners. From the moment the Swiss issued from the woods, our men fired guns and mortars; but the Swiss, in their close-packed formations, continued to move forward foot by foot if not yard by yard.

The Burgundians were slow to respond to this attack. The duke sent out a call to arms, but, completely unprepared and with many soldiers still chasing after their pay, they were slow to respond, as was he himself: "he took so long in mounting his horse that by the time he arrived on the plateau our forces were already turning their backs." The speed of the Swiss was also extraordinary, which among other things did not allow the Burgundian gunpowder weapons any role in the fighting.[291] The battle was short, with victory going quickly to the Swiss Confederation:

> The Swiss, seeing our forces arriving in drops and driblets on the plateau and strug-gling to form a battle line, and seeing [on the Burgundian left] toward the town that [Francesco] Troylo [one of Charles' mercenary Italian captains] had already assem-bled some three thousand men on a small hill, began at a distance of more than three arrow flights to fire their hand-held gunpowder weapons; and thus it was that the Burgundian foot were beginning to turn in flight, because they realized themselves to be so few in the face of such ferocity. Taking positions behind a small hedge, some Burgundian men-at-arms made a stand to bar the enemy's advance. The Swiss . . . cast themselves on the reins of the horses, their arms shielding their faces from the lances of the men-at-arms. The Swiss cavalry immediately charged and with the Burgundian foot breaking into flight, the men-at-arms also turned their backs on the enemy. Seeing this, the units arriving on the plateau . . . likewise turned and fled. In such manner was it that the whole army was broken in less time than it takes to say a *Misere*, and it happened with most of the Burgundians neither fighting nor even showing face to the enemy.

Panigarola determined what caused such a debacle, Charles the Bold's poor leadership, although he actually – or diplomatically – removes ultimate blame from the duke:

> Had the Burgundian army been assembled on the plateau and stood fast, it would have taken at least three days, they letting themselves be killed, to cut their throats. In sum, because of being taken unprepared, the army had been defeated and crushed. Never did I see this lord confused of mind and not knowing what to do except at the time he was arming himself and afterward when mounted. Since he is usually acute in his thinking and vigilant, I attribute his state to divine judgment or else to the decree of the fates. If the enemy had attacked the day before, when the army was drawn up on the plateau in battle order there would have ensued a most cruel spectacle, such would have been the bloodshed on both sides.[292]

---

[291] See also Molinet, I:146.

[292] Panigarola, in Kendall, pp. 436–38 (with several small modifications to military and military technological

As the Burgundians fled from the battlefield, they left all they could not carry behind. This included even some of the money to have been paid to the troops.[293] The Burgundians knew that, if they did not flee quickly, they would be killed, as the brutality of this war had so determined; those who were unable to get away from Murten were executed. Many others were drowned in the waters of the lake trying in vain to get away. Several thousand of those who fought with Charles were killed, including some of his military leaders and a number of his Italian mercenaries.[294]

Charles the Bold's losses at Murten also included most of his gunpowder weapons, especially those that had been brought to bombard the walls of the Murten. In doing so, the Burgundian army lost even more of its once famed gunpowder artillery arsenal.[295] Panigarola gives a tally: "All the artillery is lost, so that between this defeat and the previous one the enemy have taken, what with *bombards*, *mortars*, and guns, around two hundred pieces, sufficient ordnance to accomplish great things."[296] In little more than five months, Charles' battlefield defeats had resulted in a sizeable reduction in the number of gunpowder weapons which he was once so easily able to call on. Desperation to replace these lost gunpowder artillery pieces can be seen in the letter written on 14 December from the siege of Nancy, Charles' next and final military venture, and sent to Claude le Neuchâtel, lord du Fay:

> Dearest and loyal cousin and dearest and well loved, you know that in other letters of ours we wrote some time ago and very expressly commanded that, immediately on reading them, in accordance with the instructions we verbally gave you . . . when you left us, you should bring to us all the cash, gunpowder, and artillery now in our town of Luxembourg, with as many troops, mounted and on foot, as could be found and raised promptly in our land of Luxembourg. Nonetheless we have heard nothing from you about this and we still cannot ascertain that in this affair you have applied any dispatch, duty, or diligence. Considering the instructions on this we have given you, we are astounded, and we have no reason to be content with you since, because of the lack of the said money, powder, and artillery, we have been and are daily in danger of receiving irreparable damage. Because, dearest and loyal cousin and dearest and well loved, it is necessary for us to have the said money, powder, and artillery immediately and without delay, we are writing to you and we order and command you very expressly, and on [the strength of] your desire to obey and serve us, that as soon as you read this, all excuses ceasing, you . . . with the best and the largest number of troops that can be found, bring and escort to us our said money and artillery, especially, so far as the artillery is concerned, all available gunpowder, bows, arrows, pikes, and pole-arms [*vouges*], all with the best possible security and diligence and so that we have news of this from you shortly.[297]

terms). Margny's account (pp. 65–66), although neither as long nor as detailed, essentially tells the same story, emphasizing also the speed and stealth of the Swiss attack. See also Molinet, I:146.

293   As attested to in the Treasurer's Report, in Vaughan, *Charles the Bold*, p. 393. See also Molinet, I:146–47.

294   Molinet (I:146–47) numbers the losses at between 6,000 and 7,000, Guillaume (p. 158) making a modern tally of 8,000–10,000. See also Pfettisheim, p. 111; Vaughan, *Charles the Bold*, pp. 393–94; and Fuhrer and Geiger, p. 24.

295   See Panigarola, in Kendall, pp. 438–39; Thomas Basin, *Histoire de Louis XI*, II:292–93; and Roye, II:38.

296   Panigarola, in Kendall, p. 439. See also Henrard, *Histoire de l'artillerie en Belgique*, pp. 96–97, 127.

297   The original of this document is edited in "Recueil de choses advenues du temps et gouvernement de très

The loss at Murten, however, was not decisive. The duke of Burgundy, Charles the Bold, refused to admit that he had been defeated, and he would not return home to rebuild his army or its gunpowder artillery train. Throughout the rest of 1476 Charles amazed those around him by his positive attitude in the face of what they thought should be despair. On 3 July the Milanese embassy reported to Duke Galeazzo Maria Sforza that Charles ". . . laughs, jokes, and makes good cheer," something that unnerved them so near to the disaster at Murten that they had themselves witnessed. They also indicated that the Burgundian duke continued to believe that God was on his side and that he could raise as many men and artillery as was needed to achieve all of his military goals, even those in which he had recently suffered setbacks.[298]

In fact, this may be the core of Charles' problems in this last year of his life, if not for the whole of his reign: his confidence that he was destined to own a large empire and to wield great political and military power meant that he could not perceive any error in his military judgment, either strategic or tactical. Consequently, he never viewed his defeats on the battlefield or in sieges as defeats in a way a non-sovereign military leader might. He simply would not define them as defeats. It was almost as if he thought he had a "divine right" to victory, that this would come eventually, and that he – and, by extension, his people – must give everything they owned, as well as their lives, to see him achieve it. So on 3 July, less than two weeks after Murten, he was laughing and joking, and on 21 July, less than three weeks after that, he was preparing another onslaught of Lorraine, Germany, and even Switzerland.[299] In the meantime, even if he could not recognize them as such, Charles the Bold's enemies were taking advantage of his defeats. The two principalities that he had hoped to acquire by his adventures against the Swiss, Savoy and the Vaud, were now fully outside of his control, while his rule over Lorraine began to weaken.[300]

There seems to be little doubt that Charles wished to seek revenge against the Swiss soldiers who had defeated him at Grandson and Murten. All of his preparations throughout July, August, and September 1476 seem to indicate such. However, these plans changed when, on 6 October, the Burgundian garrison at Nancy was forced to surrender the town to its rebel Lorrainer besiegers, led by their duke, René II.[301] This

haulte mémoire feu Charles, duc de Bourgogne, estant le seigneur du Fay gouverneur au pays de Luxembourg," in *Publications de la Société pour la recherché et la conservation des monuments historiques dans le Grand-Duché de Luxembourg* 3 (1847), 85–153. The English translation I have used is in Vaughan, *Charles the Bold*, pp. 423–24. Still, despite this, Vaughan (*Charles the Bold*, pp. 412–15, and "500 Years after the Great Battles," pp. 387–88) contends that the Burgundian duke was not short of funds for the carrying on of his 1476–77 warfare. That Charles still had a large number of gunpowder weapons is asserted by Conrad Pfettisheim, p. 112.

298 *Dépêches des ambassadeurs Milanais*, II:342.

299 On 21 July he threatened the mayor of Dijon that should he not send more money, men, and artillery, he and his townspeople would be considered rebels and traitors. See *Correspondance de la mairie de Dijon*, I:189–90, and Vaughan, *Charles the Bold*, pp. 394–95.

300 Vaughan, *Charles the Bold*, pp. 394–97.

301 Pierre Marot, "Le Duc de Lorraine René II et la Bataille de Nancy dans l'historiographie et la tradition lorraines," in *Cinq-centième anniversaire de la bataille de Nancy (1477): Actes du Colloque organisé par l'institut de recherche régionale en sciences sociales, humaines et économiques de l'Université de Nancy II (Nancy, 22–24 septembre 1977)* (Nancy, 1979), pp. 83–126. René II had also fought at the battle of Murten. See Louis-Edouard Roulet, "Le duc René à la bataille de Morat," in *Cinq-centième anniversaire de la bataille de*

was not a sudden capitulation, however. René quickly took advantage of the Burgundian losses by laying siege to his recently lost capital, Nancy. Initially, this siege had very limited success, no doubt due to the reluctance of the duke of Lorraine to use gunpowder artillery against his town, an attitude well understood by the besieged Burgundians and English garrisoned inside it. But, by the end of September, as Charles the Bold had made no attempts to relieve the siege, a mutiny arose among the English, who abandoned the town; the remaining Burgundians could only hold out for a few more days.[302]

Charles arrived outside Nancy on 11 October, a few days too late to relieve the siege of his garrison there, but at the same time confident that he could quickly regain the town with a siege of his own. His army was not as large as those he had fielded earlier in the year, but still probably numbered as many as 2,000–8,000.[303] But these soldiers seem to have had little experience and were poorly led, especially at unit level. They also had few gunpowder weapons, certainly in comparison with those fielded at Grandson and Murten, but they did have some, and they began to fire on the town shortly after the Burgundians completed setting up their siegeworks on 22 October. Unlike René, Charles was more than willing to bombard Nancy; after all, once they had surrendered to the Lorrainers, the inhabitants had become traitors to him.[304]

Throughout winter the siege continued. Attempts by the Pope and Emperor to broker a peace failed to make any headway. Charles the Bold had no intention of leaving Nancy without retaking it, while those in besieged town, including, of course, Duke René, were not willing to submit again to the governance of the Burgundians. The weather, too, became quite harsh and all contemporary sources – and there are far fewer which concern themselves with Nancy than had with Neuss, Grandson, or Murten[305] – remarked on how cold and fierce the conditions were. Such weather was obviously hard on the besiegers, who after all were not well-sheltered; however, it also seems to have kept René's allies from attempting to reinforce him.[306] Still, it is reported that the besiegers suffered more than the besieged, with 400 soldiers frozen to death,

Nancy (1477): Actes du Colloque organisé par l'institut de recherche régionale en sciences sociales, humaines et économiques de l'Université de Nancy II (Nancy, 22–24 septembre 1977) (Nancy, 1979), pp. 415–28.

[302] Vaughan, *Charles the Bold*, pp. 418–19.

[303] Thomas Basin (*Histoire de Louis XI*, II:336–46) provided the larger number, which is reduced to 4,000 by Philippe de Commynes (ed. Calmette and Durville, II:148–53), and to 2,000 by Olivier de la Marche (III:239–41). Vaughan (*Charles the Bold*, pp. 427–28) calculates a total of 5,387.

[304] Haynin, II:297; *Légende Bourguignonne*, p. 88; Molinet, I:154–55; and Taveneaux, pp. 100–02. Vaughan ("Quelques observations sur la Bataille de Nancy," p. 26) is of the opinion that Charles "had a very good chance of taking the town before René could hope to obtain a relief army."

[305] Richard Vaughan, "Quelques observations sur la Bataille de Nancy," in *Cinq-centième anniversaire de la bataille de Nancy (1477): Actes du Colloque organisé par l'institut de recherche régionale en sciences sociales, humaines et économiques de l'Université de Nancy II (Nancy, 22–24 septembre 1977)* (Nancy, 1979), p. 28. There are also far fewer modern commentaries on the battle. See Vaughan, "Quelques observations sur la Bataille de Nancy," p. 24.

[306] Molinet, I:165–67; Knebel, III:90–104; and *Chronique de Lorraine*, pp. 291–310. See also Vaughan, *Charles the Bold*, pp. 421–22, and Vaughan, "Quelques observations sur la Bataille de Nancy," p. 27. The *Légende Bourguignonne* (p. 88) does, however, claim that the inhabitants of Nancy were suffering hunger enough to eat dogs, cats, and the "flesh of horses."

and a knight hanged for imprudently and, evidently, seditiously suggesting that Charles the Bold should be shot into the besieged town from one of his bombards.[307]

By the middle of December the cold weather broke enough for a Swiss army to march towards Nancy, arriving on its outskirts by 31 December. Communication between the Swiss and the Lorrainers seems to have been quite easy, which may indicate the weakness of the Burgundian siege lines, and a plan for combined military action on 4 January was hatched. Further confirming this weakness was the fact that on that date Duke René of Lorraine marched out of Nancy without facing any opposition to unite his forces with those of the Swiss at Saint-Nicolas-du-Port, a bridge over the River Meurthe. The next morning, this combined army faced the Burgundians in battle.[308]

Since the beginning of the siege, Burgundian soldiers and artillery had been entrenched surrounding but, as seen by actions of the besieged and their relievers, not tightly surrounding Nancy.[309] To face the enemy, Charles brought all of his own forces together in a fortified position to the southeast of the town between two streams along the main road to Saint-Nicolas. These streams protected his front and rear, while his left flank lay on the banks of the Meurthe and his right was bordered by a forest. But he was greatly outnumbered by his opponents, who may have numbered between 19,000 and 20,000, at least 800 of whom were coulovriniers;[310] this numerical disparity was made even greater by the defection of many of Charles' Italian mercenaries a few days before the final battle.[311] Perhaps even more importantly, the Lorrainers and Swiss were anxious to fight, while the Burgundians were not; they were exhausted, cold, and unpaid, and they had little faith in their leader, Charles the Bold.

Reports of the battle by eyewitnesses[312] describe the fall of heavy snow on the morning of 5 January 1477 as the Lorrainers and Swiss marched toward the Burgundian position. Stopping unseen in the village of Jarville across the stream from their opponents for a council of war, and having the Burgundian positions described to them by two captured soldiers, the Swiss and Lorraine military leaders decided to turn left and approach the Burgundian fortified position from the woods and rough terrain on its right flank. This manoeuvre was meant to keep the Burgundian gunpowder weapons

307 That these reports come from two chronicles written in Strasbourg – J. von Königshoven, *Chronicke*, ed. J. Schiltern (Strasbourg, 1698), pp. 379–80, and *Straszburgische Archiv-Chronik*, ed. L. Schneegans and A. Strobel, in *Code historique et diplomatique de la ville de Strasbourg* (Strasbourg, 1843), I.2:202 – make them likely apocryphal. Also see Vaughan, *Charles the Bold*, p. 422.
308 Vaughan, *Charles the Bold*, pp. 424–25.
309 On the entrenching of the Burgundian gunpowder weapons see Tuesch, pp. 204–05.
310 These numbers are based on those supplied by Duke René II of Lorraine. See Vaughan, *Charles the Bold*, p. 428; Vaughan, "Quelques observations sur la Bataille de Nancy," p. 28; and Cauchies, *Louis XI et Charles le Hardi*, p. 137. The coulovriniers so numbered were held in reserve. There may have been more who fought with the Lorraine and Swiss troops.
311 Cauchies, *Louis XI et Charles le Hardi*, p. 137, and G. Soldi-Rondinini, "Condottieri italiens au service de Charles le Hardi, pendant les guerres de Suisse (1474–1477)," *Publication du Centre européen d'études burgundo-médianes* 20 (1980).
312 These include la Marche, III:239–41; Margny, pp. 69–70; Schilling, II:111–23; the anonymous author of the *Chronique de Lorraine*, pp. 291–310; and Peterman Etterlin, *Kronica von der loblichen Eydtgnoschaft* (Basel, 1507). See also Vaughan, *Charles the Bold*, pp. 429–32; Vaughan, "Quelques observations sur la Bataille de Nancy," pp. 29–31; and Taveneaux, pp. 103–05.

from effectively firing on the attacking soldiers, but as it, too, was unseen by Charles the Bold and his troops, it also provided his enemy with the same advantage that each of his recent opponents had over him, surprise.

Again, one must marvel at the tactical ignorance of the duke of Burgundy. How is it possible that he did not prepare for an attack by patrolling the land surrounding his position? It seems that he anticipated the possibility of an attack by amassing his troops in one fortified location, but then he allowed his forces to once again be surprised in battle by not providing even the most basic vigilance! Thus around noon Lorraine and Swiss soldiers burst from the woods onto the surprised Burgundian flank. As at Grandson and Murten, the speed of their attack was impressive, its quickness again preventing Charles from firing his gunpowder weapons at them before both armies were fighting hand-to-hand. As the contemporary Strasbourger Hans Erhart Tuesch writes: "Neither *canon* nor *pierrier* could halt them. And even though the *coulovrines* were turned against them, they were not able to be used in the attack, as time did not permit it."[313] Taking advantage of chaos spreading throughout the Burgundian army after the initial attack, another unit of Swiss-Lorrainers first "fired their *haquebusses* and *coulovrines à main*," according to Jean Molinet, and then charged onto their front, quickly overrunning the gunpowder weapons lined up to protect against such a tactic and falling on the main body of Charles' troops.[314] Soon all were in flight; only those who could reach Metz, fifty kilometers away, found safety. Charles the Bold was not so lucky. He had been slain sometime during the short battle, by means and person unrevealed by eyewitnesses, although where his body was found indicates that he was killed in the fight. It was two days before his frozen, stripped, and mangled body could be identified by its scars and long nails.[315]

With Charles' death at the battle of Nancy, the reign of the Valois dukes of Burgundy came to an end. It had lasted only for a short time as dynastic regimes go, from 1363 to 1477, but it had had an incredible effect on the political, military, economic, and technological history of Europe. When it began, with the acquisition of the relatively small duchy by Philip the Bold, gunpowder weapons were still in their infancy, likely less than fifty years old. In fact, the duchy of Burgundy seems to have been slow in the acquisition of guns and, at the time of Philip's ascension to the dukedom, may only have had a very few. However, he, like his three successors, seemed to quickly grasp their military importance. And, as the Burgundians were then taking part in one of the major conflicts of the Middle Ages – the Hundred Years War – the acquisition of more, and constantly improving, gunpowder weapons became an immediate priority.

This importance increased for the Burgundian dukes as their lands grew in size. Given a few towns in northern France as a marriage present, Philip the Bold was to inherit the very wealthy, although not always loyal, county of Flanders at the death of

---

313 Tuesch, p. 204. See also Vaughan, "Quelques observations sur la Bataille de Nancy," p. 29.
314 Molinet, I:166. See also Vaughan, "Quelques observations sur la Bataille de Nancy," p. 29.
315 Of course, Charles the Bold's death was very important news and every chronicler reports it. See, for example, Molinet, I:167; Commynes (ed. Calmette and Durville), II:152–53; and *Légende Bourguignonne*, pp. 88–89. See also Vaughan, "Quelques observations sur la Bataille de Nancy," p. 31.

his father-in-law, Louis of Male, in 1384. Between then and the ascension of Charles the Bold in 1467, the duchy's size and consequent political and military strength had continually increased, sometimes through inheritance or marriages, sometimes through military acquisition. Even Charles the Bold added territory – Guelders and Lorraine – although he is chiefly known for losing dynastic lands, especially with his premature death in 1477. Such territorial increase, unequaled in Western Europe since the death of Charlemagne, also required a military presence, to protect against both outside and inside enemies, and again the Valois dukes of Burgundy tied this to the acquisition of gunpowder weapons. These new lands were to be protected by Burgundian guns, and the citizens usually paid for them by taxes paid into the ducal coffers. In addition, those lands with large urban areas, also provided the industry and skill that produced gunpowder weapons.

In a sense, Charles' death at Nancy put an end to this. For, although his lands, remaining guns, and armies passed to his daughter, Mary, and her husband, Maximilian, old Burgundian foes, René of Lorraine and Louis XI, quickly took advantage of the situation: René retook the rest of Lorraine and began to march into nearby Alsatian and Burgundian lands, while Louis XI spared little time marching his armies into Picardy and Artois.[316] Eventually, the French king would enter the duchy of Burgundy itself and even capture Dijon.[317]

Maximilian, not yet Holy Roman Emperor, was unprepared for the death of his wife's father and initially could do little to defend her inheritance. Only in 1479 did he respond with military force; mustering his Flemish urban militias and adding them to his rather smaller German force, in an effort to protect the southern Low Countries from the ravaging their southern neighbors had witnessed, he met and defeated the French army at the battle of Guinegate on 7 August.[318] This brought only slight relief, however, as Louis continued to press for greater occupation of the southern Low Countries, ultimately forcing Maximilian to sign the Treaty of Arras in 1483, a year after it had been agreed to by the French king and several local Low Countries governors and magnates.[319] Louis gained legal recognition of his occupation of Burgundy and Artois; Maximilian gained peace enough to build up his military and political power. This he did without Mary of Burgundy, who had died in 1482, after a fall from her horse. It took a while, but eventually this duke of Burgundy was able to recover control over the Low Countries and Artois. The Treaty of Senlis was signed in 1493 between Maximilian and the new French king, Charles VIII, his father, Louis XI, having died a decade earlier. 1493 was also the year that Maximilian became Holy

---

[316] See Pierre Champion, *Louis XI*, trans. Winifred Stephens Whale (London, 1929), pp. 263–68, and Edouard Perroy, "L'artillerie de Louis XI dans la campagne d'Artois," *Revue du Nord* 26 (1943), 171–96, 293–315.

[317] Champion, pp. 269–72; André Leguai, "La conquête de la Bourgogne par Louis XI," *Annales de Bourgogne* 49 (1977), 7–12; and André Leguai, "Dijon et Louis XI," *Annales de Bourgogne* 17 (1945), 16–37, 103–15, 145–69, 239–63.

[318] The best study of this battle is J.F. Verbruggen, *De slag bij Guinegate, 7 augustus 1479: De verdediging van het graafschap Vlaanderen tegen de koning van Frankrijk, 1477–1480* (Brussels, 1993).

[319] See several of the articles in Denis Clauzel, Charles Giry-Deloison, and Christophe Leduc, eds., *Arras et la diplomatie européenne, xve–xvie siècles* (Arras, 1999).

Roman Emperor, a title he would pass on to his own grandson, Charles V, in 1519.[320] Those Burgundian lands that he still held became part of the Holy Roman Empire. Never again would the duchy of Burgundy have its old power, sovereignty, or military technological prowess.

[320] Gerhard Benecke, *Maximilian I (1459–1519): An Analytical Biography* (London, 1982).

3

Analysis of the Documentary Sources for the Gunpowder Weapons

INTRODUCTION

By far the largest, easily available contemporary source of information about guns in the fifteenth century are the transcripts of archives of the artillery of the Valois dukes of Burgundy published by Joseph Garnier in 1895.[1] Garnier, an archivist in Dijon in the second half of the nineteenth century, brought together and published transcriptions of the ducal archives on artillery, most notably those contained in two account books, the first covering the period from 1411 to 1445 and the second from 1446 to 1475. They include all the artillery and other munitions delivered into the *Chambre des Comptes* of the last three Valois dukes, John the Fearless, Philip the Good and Charles the Bold. Though these two registers form the nucleus of his work, Garnier includes a number of other transcriptions from the archives extending back to Philip the Bold and providing additional material all through the period. Together, the transcriptions of these documents are an unparalleled source of information about artillery in the period from the end of the fourteenth to the closing decades of the fifteenth century, providing as they do not only details of the types and numbers of pieces of artillery but also about the changes with time that occur. They are not without their problems however – as with all contemporary material about artillery there are difficulties of interpretation and frequent seeming contradictions in the information provided.

The following is drawn largely from Garnier's transcripts. The methodology has been to first take from the archives as much information as possible about each type of artillery and use this to make a reasoned summary of the primary characteristics of that piece as well as its other features. Among the many problems in using any fifteenth-century source is that of names and their spelling so a standard terminology has therefore been used: *bombard, canon, coulovrine, courtau, crapaudeau, hacquebus, mortar, pestereau, ribaudequin, serpentine*, and *veuglaire*. However original spellings have been used in all quotations. In addition to the details about the actual gunpowder weapons, there is a great deal of other information in these archives and this has been brought together to yield details of their metallurgy and manufacture, surface treatment, marks,

---

[1] Joseph Garnier, *L'artillerie des ducs de Bourgogne d'après les documents conservés aux archives de la Côte-d'Or* (Paris, 1895). This work is now very rare and few copies are known to survive.

gunpowder, ammunition, carriage beds and mounts, loading and aiming, the personnel involved, and finally, ship's artillery.

BOMBARD

Summary

Bombards are, perhaps, the easiest of all medieval gunpowder weapons to identify and recognise. They were the largest of the available types of gunpowder artillery, both in their weight and their bore, ranging in size from the relatively small to huge monsters weighing in excess of 20 tonnes, though most were in the range of 5–10 tonnes. Bombards first appear in the Burgundian registers in 1412 and are relatively common until the middle of the century when references to them decrease quite drastically. However, they are a type of gunpowder weapon which is frequently mentioned in a wide variety of other sources – written, narrative and artistic – not only of the Burgundian dukes, but throughout Europe as a whole.[2]

Bombards always fired stone balls, they were muzzle or breech loading, with a separate powder chamber, and made from either iron or copper alloy. They were transported on carts and commonly supplied with a "gin," or "engin" for lifting them on and off their transport and generally moving them around. The frequent references to their being taken to sieges confirm that they were used primarily to batter and destroy fortifications, castle and town walls. That they were also regarded as special, probably due to their large size and cost, is indicated by the fact that so many were given names. Often these names came from the place where they were made – *Bourgogne, Auxonne, Luxembourg* – but frequently and surprisingly were given female names – *Gueriette, Fille Gueriette, Katherine, Liete*, etc.

There are extant examples of bombards including the Burgundian example now preserved in Basel and, closely related to this piece, two similar bombards, *Dulle Griet* in Ghent and *Mons Meg* in Edinburgh. *Dulle Griet* has a bore of 640 mm (25 in.) and would have fired a stone ball weighing in the region of 320 kg (700 lb). Mons Meg is slightly smaller and was ordered to be made by Philip the Good in 1449 before being given to James II of Scotland in 1454.[3] These examples are muzzle loaders; but a piece in the Museo del Ejército in Madrid which, though broken at the muzzle, is clearly a breech-loading bombard. Though no powder chambers survive for this piece, there are examples in collections throughout Europe of removeable powder chambers which, by their size, must have been for bombards.

Whether the *bombardelle* was just a small size of bombard is not clear from the records that exist, and it is possible that the bombard and bombardelle were different in some way which is simply not apparent today and were dissimilar types. From the surviving sources, however, the bombardelle would appear to be just that, a smaller

---

2　It is worth noting, however, that the name *bombard* occurs in other sources well into the sixteenth century and, unlike many other types of early artillery, it is obviously to the same basic type of gun.

3　Robert D. Smith and Ruth Rhynas Brown, *Bombards: Mons Meg and her Sisters* (London, 1989).

bombard. However there is significant overlap and a small bombard could be smaller than a bombardelle. These differences could merely be in our interpretation in a period when such definitions were not hard and fast.

Supporting evidence

Name variants   Bombard, gros bombard, grant bombard, petit bombard, bombard-elle, petit bombardelle, bombard barrel, grant canon bombard.
Several of these variant names must, of course, refer to size. *Gros* and *grant* bombard are larger in the same way that *petit* bombard must be a smaller size. It is very clear that size is relative and not absolute in the way used today. The name bombardelle appears to refer to a smaller size of bombard and *petit* bombardelle to something even smaller. Similarly just what the name *grant canon* bombard means is not at all clear.[4]

Date range   References to bombards appear in the Burgundian registers from 1412 to 1474 though the majority date from before 1445 with only one later reference, in 1474. It is likely that after this date bombards were becoming increasingly less common though they do not disappear entirely from inventories and other records until the latter part of the sixteenth century. By the late fifteenth century they were not used so much and after 1500 references to them in use virtually vanish.[5] Their demise has been attributed to a number of factors – among them being their unwieldy and bulky size, the problems of transport, and the increasing use of iron shot.

Size   The references to weights of bombards are, on the whole, for pieces of considerable size, for example the following dimensions are listed for 1445:

> Two great iron *bombards* which J. Cambier made weighing about 60,000 livres firing stones of 22 *polces.*
> Item three other iron *bombards* one called *Bergier*, the other coming from the young lady Jacques (de la Marches) and the other which the said Jehan Cambier delivered to Namur, which weighs about 24,000 *livres* firing stones of 13 to 14 *polz* and another of copper from the said young lady Jaques.
> Item two other *bombards* called *Le damp*, each with three chambers which weigh about 22,000 *livres* firing stones of 12 *polz.*[6]

---

4   Again though it is not at all precisely clear it would seem likely that the word *canon* refers to both a type of weapon as well as a generic name for guns in general. The phrase *canon bombard* might just be the way a particular clerk or scribe referred to what others just called a bombard. For further discussion, see below under *canon.*
5   However, bombards were used in the later fifteenth century. See Appendix 2.
6   Deux grosses bombardes de fer que J. Cambier a faites qui pevent peser environ 60,000 livres de fer portant pierres de 22 polces.
   Item trois autres bombardes de fer l'une nommée Bergier, l'autre venant du doioiseau Jacques (de la Marche) et l'autre que ledit Jehan Cambier a derrièrement livrée à Namur; qui pevant peser environ 24,000 livres portant pierres de 13 à 14 polz et une autre de cuivre venant dudit damoiseau Jaques.
   Item deux autres bombardes nommées Le damp, chacune a trois chambers qui pevent péser environ 22,000 livres portant pierre de 12 polz. (Garnier, p. 171).

The sizes of guns are frequently given by the size of the ball fired or by the weight of powder used. For example, in 1436 the bombard *Griete* fired a stone ball of 400 *livres* and two others fired shot of 120 *livres*.[7]

A list of 1413 also gives the quantities of powder used by a number of bombards:

> For the *bombard* of *Valecon*, 36 *livres*
> For *Gueriette*, 28 *livres*
> For *Liete*, 24 *livres*
> For the *bombard* called *Fille Gueriete* and for her companion, each 18 *livres*
> For *Senelle*, 36 *livres*
> For ten *canon* with three chambers, 30 *livres*.[8]

A *gros* bombard appears to have been of larger size and this is reflected in their weights. In 1431 a *gros* bombard fired a ball of 600 *livres* while another piece from 1431 weighed an enormous 30,000 *livres*. It would be wrong, however, to state that this difference was always adhered to as a *gros* bombard noted in 1445 weighed just 8,200 *livres*. Lengths are rarely noted, but in 1447 the barrel of a bombard was stated as 12 feet and its chamber 7 feet and a *gros* bombard in 1446 had a barrel of 10 feet with a 6 foot chamber.

Type and material   Where noted there are approximately equal numbers of iron and copper alloy pieces, and while bombards are referred to as being made "in one piece," others have separate barrels and powder chambers. While it is clear that for most gunpowder weapons with removeable chambers the two parts were made from the same material, an interesting entry for 1443 refers to a bombard called *Bourgoingne* that had a copper-alloy chamber together with an iron barrel.

Makers and suppliers   Several persons are referred to as either making, re-making, or repairing bombards. In 1445:

> Two great iron *bombards* which J. Cambier made which weigh about 60,000 *livres* of iron throwing stones of 22 *polces*.[9]

In 1447:

> To master Anthoine Frichier *bombardier* living at Metz by the said Phelibert, by the command and ordonance of my said seigneur, the sum of 2,400 *livres* 8 *sols*, for twenty two thousand [weight] of metal called bronze, to make and cast the chamber of the barrel called *Luxembourg*, which was cast at Luxembourg. The barrel must be

---

[7]   Garnier, pp. 72, 157.
[8]   Pour la bombarde de *Valecon* (Dijon), 36 livres
Pour *Gueriette*, 28 livres
Pour *Liete*, 24 livres
Pour la bombarde dite: *Fille Gueriete* et pour sa compaigne, chacune 18 livres
Pour *Senelle*, 36 livres
Pour dix canons a trois chambers, 30 livres. (Garnier, pp. 57–8).
[9]   Deux grosses bombardes de fer que J. Cambier a faites qui pevent peser environ 60,000 livres de fer portant pierres de 22 *polces*.

12 *piez* in length to fire a stone of 28 *polz* and the chamber seven *piez* in length of ten *polz* of *tampon* [bore] and eleven *polz* from the *tampon* to the rear.[10]

More illuminating is an account of 1430:

> In the year 1430, the 11th day of August, in the Chamber of Accounts of M the duke of Burgundy at Dijon, there were MM of the said accounts, the Receiver General of Burgundy and Germain de Givry, keeper of the artillery of my said seigneur. These men made a contract and agreement with Martin de Cornuaille, maker of *bombards* and *canons*, to remake the *bombard Prusse* belonging to my said lord, which is broken and was shown to him and he has seen and visited it, which he promised to remake whole and sure for the price and sum of 40 *francs*. And to him should be acquired and delivered only as much good metal as is needed and whatever extra he do and deliver all at his [own] charge, mission and expense: that is to say workers, iron, earth, wood, charcoal, iron wire, to bury and dig up the said *bombard* and to deliver it perfect before the following 8th day of September. And the *bombard* will be tested and fired three or four times to prove that it is whole and satisfactory, and in the case that it breaks, he will be held to remake it at his expense.[11]

It was not uncommon to either repair or remake parts of guns.

Transport The usual way to transport bombards was on carts. For example in 1414:

> Another *bombard* called *Cenelle*, with a large iron cart on which it is loaded.
> Two other *bombards* called *Liete* and her companion, loaded on a great iron cart.[12]

The carts were pulled exclusively by horses and there are many references to the numbers of horses necessary to pull them and to carters, for example, in 1424:

---

10 De maistre Anthoine Frichier bombardier demourant à Mez par ledit Phelibert, par le commandement et ordonnance de mondit s[r] et paié par Martin Cornille conseiller et receveur général de toutes les finances de mondit seigneur, la somme de 2,400 livres 8 sols, pour vingt-deux milliers de mitaille nommée arain, pour faire et fonder la chamber de la volée nommée *Luxembourg*, qui a esté fondue audit Luxembourg. Et doit avoir ladite volée douze piez de long et la Pierre de 28 polz et doit avoir ladite chamber sept piez de long de dix polz de tampon et onze poulz depuis ledit tampon en derrière.

11 L'an 1430, le 11e jour du mois d'oust, en la Chamber des Comptes de M. le duc de Bourgogne à Dijon, où estoient MM. desdits comptes, le Receveur général de Bourgoigne et Germain de Givry, garde de L'artillerie de mondit seigneur a esté par les dessus dis nommés, marchandé traicté et accordé avec Martin de Cornuaille, ouvrier de bombardes et canons, de refaire la bombarde de *Prusse* appartenant à mondit seigneur, laquelle est despicée et lui a esté monstrée et icelle a veue et visitée, lequel a promis de la refaire bonne et seure pour le pris at somme de 40 frans. Et lui soignera et livrera bon métail tant seulement et le surplus il fera et livrera tout à ses frais, missions et despens; c'est essavoir ouvriers, fer, terre, bois, charbon, fil de fer, enterrera et desterera icelle bombarde et la rendra parfaite dedans le 8e jour de septembre prouchainement venant. Et sera icelle bombarde essayée et gectée [trois] ou quatre fois pour aprcuver quelle soit bonne et souffisant, et au cas quelle rompe, il sera tenu de la rarefie à ses despens (Garnier, p. 68). To "bury and dig up" the bombard implies that the mould into which the copper-alloy was poured was buried in the ground and needed to be dug up once the casting had cooled. The later technique for casting copper-alloy cannon has been published – see Carel de Beer, ed., *The Art of Gunfounding: The Casting of Bronze Cannon in the Late Eighteenth Century* (Rotherfield, 1991); its similarity to what is referred here in the early fifteenth century is intriguing.

12 Item une autre bombarde apellée *Cenelle*, avec ung gros cher ferré sur lequel elle est chargée.
    Item deux autres bombardes appellées *Liete* et sa compaigne, chargées sur un gros char ferré (Garnier, p. 38).

Paid 108 f. to four carters, four valets and sixteen horses who attended for 24 complete days, from 3 September, to take the *bombards*, *Griete*, *Katherine*, a large *veuglaire*, four small *ribaudequins*, and a quantity of powder, stones, and other artillery from Dijon to the siege of Buxière and back to Chalon.[13]

However at times, bombards could also be moved by water, as in 1431:

The *bombard Prusse*, her munitions, the pickaxes, mattocks, etc., were taken from Dijon to St-Jean-de Losne and embarked on the river Saone for Chalon. The transport by land cost 20 fr. 4 *gros*, and by water 9 fr. 4 *gros*.[14]

Additionally, the sheer weight and size of bombards meant that they were unwieldy and were not easy to move about. Getting such large guns onto and off their transport carts was done by means of portable cranes or "*engins.*" In 1414:

Item a wooden *engin* to load the said *bombards*.[15]

Also in 1414:

To Girard Morelot, for taking the wooden *engin* to mount the *canons* on its cart with three horses and its carter, as well as two horses and another carter, 2½ fr.[16]

However, the current assumption that they were close to impossible to move and extremely slow at the best of times, is not borne out by the historical record. From the frequent refereneces to the taking of bombards to sieges and other engagements, it is clear that they were made and widely used – if they were that difficult to use it is unlikely that so many would have been made and their use so common. That they were not easy to move must have been true and, by our modern standards of speed, extremely slow, but their extensive use points to the conclusion that this does not seem to have caused undue problems. The speed of any operation, especially one as complex and difficult as moving an army of men, supplies, materiel, etc. in this period was always slow.

Monique Sommé has calculated the speed at which large bombards were brought to the siege of Calais in 1436.[17] She quotes three separate examples. The first, for a convoy consisting of, among other warlike stores, "two great *bombards*, *canons*, veuglaires and other artillery," travelled at the rate of 12 km per day. The second convoy, which

---

[13] Payé 108 f. à quatre voituriers, quatre valets et seize chevaux qui ont vacqué 24 jours entiers, à partir du 3 Septembre, à mener de Dijon au siege de la Buxière et remené à Chalon les bombardes, Griete, Katherine, un gros veuglaire, quatre petis ribaudequins et une certaine quantité de poudre, de pierres et s'autre artillerie (Garnier, p. 93).

[14] La bombarde de *Prusse*, ses munitions, les pics, pioches, etc., furent menés de Dijon à St-Jean-de Losne et embarquées sur la Saône pour Chalon. Le transport coûta par terre 20 fr. 4 gros et par eau, 9 fr. 4 gros (Garnier, p. 53).

[15] Item ung engin de bois pour charger lesdites bombardes (Garnier, p. 38).

[16] A Girard Morelot, pour avoir amené à l'engin de bois à drecier ces canon sur son char à trois chevaulx et son charretier, outré deux chevaux et un autre charrelier, 2 fr. ½ (Garnier, p. 38).

[17] Monique Sommé, "L'armée bourguignonne au siège de Calais de 1436", in *Guerre et société en France, en Angleterre et en Bourgogne XIV–XV siècle*, ed. P. Contamine, C. Giry-Deloisin, M. Keen (Lille, 1991), pp. 197–219.

included "three *bombards*," the largest of which was transported on a cart pulled by 10 horses, covered an average of 20 km per day. The third, and largest of the three, which included a large amount of stores and equipment and three bombards, covered a distance of some 570 km at a rate of 11½ km per day. The smallest bombard required a cart pulled by 18 horses, a second one needed a cart pulled by 30, while the last, *Bourgogne*, was carried in two parts; the barrel on a cart pulled by 48 horses and the chamber pulled by 36 horses. These were truly enormous guns and their transport was carefully planned and executed; bridges were reinforced and the way made good wherever necessary. These examples make it plain that this sort of operation was not thought at the time to be impossible nor so slow as to be not worthwhile. Actual figures for the rate of an army on campaign are hard to come by. Parker has calculated that in the late sixteenth century it was possible for a regiment to travel 700 miles in about 7 weeks, "if everything was in order." This is in the region of 14 miles (22 km) a day. He goes on to say that "the normal speed of armies using the [Spanish] 'Road' seems to have been about 12 miles [19 km] a day."[18]

Carriages and mounting   In actual use bombards were probably either laid directly onto the ground and a wooden structure built around them or, sometimes, they had specially prepared beds, probably called "*affusts*," which were reinforced by a separate wooden frame. These constructions, which were not the same as the carts on which bombards were transported, not only supported the gun and prevented recoil but could also include protection from enemy fire. Illustrations of bombards usually show a wooden structure, a mantlet, built over them to shield the operators, and these are commonly listed in the sources when referring to bombards. For example an inventory of 1474 lists:

> To take to Burgundy a *bombard* to Dijon and to take it [the gun itself] requires no less than 24 horses.
> To take a manteau which serves it requires ten carts pulled by 40 horses.
> To take an *affust*, 4 horses.
> To take no less than one hundred stone balls for the said *bombard* at ten stones per cart with 4 horses requires 40 horses.[19]

Ammunition   Where referred to, the shot fired by bombards is always stone. An inventory of 1431 includes:

> An iron *bombard* called *Griete* throwing 400 *livres* of stone, sound and complete.[20]

Loading and firing   There is little, if any, information about the actual loading and firing of bombards. They were probably complicated and time consuming both to load

---

[18] Geoffrey Parker, *The Army of Flanders and the Spanish Road 1567–1659* (Cambridge, 1972), pp. 96–98.

[19] Prendre en Bourgogne une bombarde a Dijon et pour mener celle convient di moins avoir 24 chevaulx.
Pour mener ung manteau servant icelle, convient dix charriots qui font 40 chevaulx.
Pour mener ung affusts, 4 chevaulx.
Pour mener du moins cent pierres servans a ladite bombards a dix pierres, ung charriot a quatre chevaulx, font 40 chevaulx (Garnier, p. 180).

[20] Une bombarde de fer nomme *Griete* portant 400 livres de Pierre, sainne et entière (Garnier, p. 72).

and to fire. For muzzle loading bombards, such as the example in Basel, the powder was loaded from the front, by means of a ladle.

> Paid 13 f. 8 gr. to he who is responsible for the transport of the *bombards*, for the purchase of rope to pull the carriage, for two sheets of black iron to take the powder to load the *bombards*.[21]

And again:

> Gillet du Cellier bought two sheets of black iron to make the ladles to load powder into the *canon*s and *bombards*, *3 gros*.[22]

Surviving Burgundian bombards   A single gunpowder weapon from the surviving *Burgunderbeute*, the wrought iron piece now in Basel, can, with confidence, be called a bombard. This large calibre muzzle-loading gun has been the subject of recent research and can be dated, with a high degree of confidence, to the middle years of the fifteenth century. Its great similarity to *Mons Meg*, now in Edinburgh Castle and known to have been made by Jehan Cambier of Mons, has further led to the assumption that this piece was also made by Cambier. The small armorial shield on the powder chamber has been identified as that of the d'Auxy family. However, the simplicity of the decoration of the shield, an alternating pattern of punch-decorated and plain squares, is not sufficient for a definite identification, though it is, of course, likely. Jehan IV, lord of Auxy, was one of the principal members of Charles the Bold's household and made a member of the order of the Golden Fleece in 1445.[23]

This piece has commonly been said not to have formed part of the original gunpowder weapon train taken to Switzerland by Charles the Bold, but to have been supplied later when he was becoming desperate for replacement pieces for those lost at the battle of Grandson. The implication is that this type of gun, the bombard, was obsolete by this time and Charles would not have used it in his original campaign when he took only the best and most up-to-date guns. This seems very unlikely as there are accounts of the use of bombards in the Burgundian accounts well into the 1470s.[24] It is very clear from the sources that Charles the Bold took a very wide range of equipment, including bombards, on his military expeditions.[25] The fact that this gun was captured after the battle of Murten would indicate that it was not included in his original artillery train but this does not mean that it was "old-fashioned." Similarly, the argument that this type of gun was too large and unwieldy to be taken on long campaigns simply does not hold up to close scrutiny. As noted above, it is clear that the rate for the transport of large artillery pieces, such as bombards, in the fifteenth century was not exceptionally slow and was probably close to, if not the same as, the rate at which the whole

---

[21]   Payé 13 f. 8 gr. au comptable du charroi des bombardes, pour achat de cordes à trait de fut, de deux feuilles de fer noir, pour prendre la poudre et charger les bombardes (Garnier, p. 94).

[22]   Gillet du Cellier vendit deux feuilles de fer noir, pour faire des cuillers à entonner pouldre dedans les canons et bombardes, 3 gros (Garnier, p. 96).

[23]   Smith and Brown, pp. 39–45.

[24]   See Garnier, p. 180, and Robert D. Smith, "Good and Bold: A Late 15th-Century Artillery Train," *The Royal Armouries Yearbook* 6 (2001), 98–105.

[25]   See for example the artillery train in Appendix 2.

army travelled. There is then no reason to suppose that Charles would not have taken large guns with him in the campaigns of the 1470s because they were too difficult to transport, nor that they were obsolete by this date.

CANON

Summary

The term *canon* occurs in the registers from 1410 to 1465 though most references are found in the first decade of this period. It is very unclear as to whether the name refers to a specific type of artillery or was merely a generic term for gunpowder weapons. From the available sources, it is clear that up to the first decade of the fifteenth century gunpowder weapons were somewhat undifferentiated – only the names bombard and *canon* are used. *Veuglaire* appears in 1417 but is not commonly used until the 1430s, while *coulervrine* appears in 1420. This suggests that early in the century all gunpowder weapons, except for the bombards, were referred to as *canons* and it is only later that other names came to prominence. Whether this was a consequence of the increasing sophistication and diversification of artillery types is not clear though it is very probable. A possible explanation is that in the early period there was no vocabulary to describe guns – the various names only evolving with time – though it might be that there were few types of artillery at this early period and that the development of different types of guns for different purposes only occurred in the first decades of the fifteenth century. However, the evidence is unclear and the following is based on the assumption that the *canon* was a separate type of gun.

The evidence from the sources indicates that *canons* were, in the main, relatively small and fired shot of up to 26 *livres*. Though usually made from iron, there are references to both copper alloy and to cast-iron examples. Stone shot was the usual ammunition but some *canons* fired *plommées* – lead shot – implying that they were comparatively quite small, as lead was only used for small calibre guns. References to whether they were breech or muzzleloaders are scarce, making it difficult to be sure what form they took, though there is evidence to suggest that some were muzzleloaders.

Supporting evidence

Name variants   Canon, gran canon, gros canon, petit canon, canon veuglaire.
The name *canon* is a problematic one. Does it refer to a particular type of gunpowder weapon, a *canon*, or is it a general name for gunpowder weapons in general? The answer is probably both. Early on it was the term for all gunpowder weapons except for bombards while later, as other terms were introduced, it was used in a similar way as today, as a general term for gunpowder weapons.

Date range   The name canon in the Burgundian registers is first noted in 1410 and continues to be used until 1465 though it is most commonly found in the early period.

Size The sizes of *canons* are most frequently given by the weight of the ball fired rather than by the actual sizes of the weapons and range from 3 to 26½ *livres*. Occasionally where weights are stated, these, too, indicate a wide size range – from very small pieces weighing just 30 or 31 *livres* right up to one enormous piece weighing 4000 *livres*, measuring 9 *piez* long and firing a ball 8 *polz* in diameter. Lengths also vary considerably ranging from 1 to 9 *piez*. For example, in 1413:

> Ten varnished iron *canons* throwing stone of 7 to 20 *livres*, 2 hundred [weight] of saltpetre, 1 hundred [weight] of sulphur.[26]

And in 1411:

> Item bought from J Manus, cannoneer, 27 iron *canons*, that is to say 4 *canons* each throwing 20 *livres* of stone. Item 4 other *canons* throwing each 12 *livres* of stone. Item 12 *canons* throwing 5 *livres* of stone and 7 *canons* for *plombée*.[27]

It is, however clear that *gros canon* were, on the whole, large pieces. In 1446:

> A large iron *canon* furnished with two chambers, throwing stone of twenty *livres*, each chamber containing eight *livres* of powder, weighing together twelve hundred *livres*, at fifteen *deniers* per *livre*, valued at 72 *livres*.[28]

However, *petiz canons* could also be quite large, as in1413:

> Three *petiz* iron *canons*, one throwing stone of 17 *livres*, the other of 10 *livres* and half, the other of 7 *livres* and a half.[29]

Yet, some *canons* were very small, for example in 1422:

> Two iron *canons* weighing together 120 *livres*, each throwing stone of three *livres* and which cost 30 *francs*.[30]

This very large range in size seems difficult to explain. A possible reason is that the name did not refer to a specific type of gunpowder weapon.

Type and material Where noted the greater number of *canon* were made from iron though there are references to pieces made from copper alloy.[31] Intriguingly a small number are made of cast iron – *fer de fondue*. For example in 1417:

---

[26] Dix canons de fer vernissiez gectans pierre de 7 à 20 livres, 2 cent de salepestre, 1 cent de souffre (Garnier, p. 42).

[27] Item ont esté achetées de J Manus, canonier, 27 canons de fer, c'est assavoir 4 canons chascun gectant 20 livres Pierre. Item 4 autres canons gectant chascun 12 livres Pierre. Item 12 canons gectant 5 livres Pierre et 7 canons à plombée (Garnier, p. 37).

[28] Ung gros canon de fer garny de deux chambers, portant pierre de vint livres, contenant chacune chamber huit livres de pouldre, pesant ensemble douze cent livres, à quinze deniers la livre, valent 72 livres (Garnier, p. 115).

[29] Trois petiz canons de fer, l'ung gectant pierre de 17 livres, l'autre de 10 livres et demie, l'autre de 7 livres et demie (Garnier, p. 40).

[30] Deux canons de fer pesant ensemble 120 livres, gectant chacun trois livres de pierre et qui ont couté 30 francs (Garnier, p. 41).

[31] Garnier, p. 67.

A cast-iron *canon*, throwing stone of about 20 *livres*.[32]

It is clear that this is definitely a different material from the normal iron used to make guns, for example in 1415:

Two cast-iron *canons*, two other iron *canon*, throwing stone weighing 8 *livres* and a half; a barrel of powder weighing 267 *livres*, four *canons* of *plombée*.[33]

In 1422:

Two copper-alloy *canons* throwing stone of 6 and 7 *livres* and 50 *livres* of powder.[34]

And in 1422:

. . . six *canons* of copper alloy cast for the price of sixty six *ecus*.[35]

The very few references to either breech-loading *canons* supplied with removeable chambers or to *canons* made all in one piece makes it impossible to know which was more normal. In 1443:

Item two other iron *canons* of one piece about two *piez* long, each stocked in wood and another about one and half *pié* long stocked in wood.[36]

In 1413:

For ten *canons* with 3 chambers, 30 *livres*.[37]

And in 1437:

Two *canons* firing stone each with two chambers.[38]

Carriages and mounting   There is little information on the mounting of *canons*, but where it is mentioned it is clear that they were mounted on wood. For example, in 1443:

Item a small iron *canon* one *pié* long and mounted in wood.[39]

In 1415:

. . . eleven *canons* mounted, of which there are two throwing each 15 *livres* weight and the others 18 *livres*.[40]

---

[32] Un canon de fer de fondue, gectant pierre pesant environ 20 livres (Garnier, p. 40).

[33] Deux canons de fer fondue, deux autres canons de fer, gectans Pierre pesant 8 livres et demie; une quaque de poudre pesant 267 livres, quatre canons à plombée (Garnier, p. 51).

[34] Deux canons de mitaille portant de 6 et 7 livres de pierre et 50 livres de poudre (Garnier, p. 41).

[35] . . . six canons de mitaille de fondue pour le pris de soixante six ecus (Garnier, p. 67).

[36] Item deux autres canons de fer d'une pièce d'environ deux piez de long, chacun enfusté en bois et ung autre d'environ ung pié et demi de long enfusté en bois (Garnier, p. 129).

[37] Pour dix canons à trois chambers, 30 livres (Garnier, p. 58).

[38] Deux canons gettans pierre chacun à deux chambres . . . (Garnier, p. 143).

[39] Item ung petit canon de fer d'un pié de long enfusté en bois (Garnier, p. 129).

[40] . . . onze canons amplotez, desquels iy y a deux gettans chacun 15 livres pesant et les autres 18 livres (Garnier, p. 51).

Ammunition   *Canons* fired stone shot or else a type of shot called *plombée*, lead balls. In 1411:

An iron *canon* for *plombée*.[41]

And again in 1411:

Three iron *canons*, two for *plombée*, one throwing stone of 5 *livres*.[42]

COULOVRINE

Summary

A type of gun that appears in the registers from 1420 to 1465 and which, as it had a very large number of variant names for which there is no modern equivalent, the commonest form, *coulovrine*, has been used for the group as a whole.[43] Evidence of their size and the fact that many coulovrines are referred to as *à main* makes it clear that they were handguns. Although made in a variety of sizes, the coulovrine was always fired by hand, with or without the use of a stand or crutch. Some are noted as having hooks and many were mounted on, or in, wood. They fired lead shot, *plommées*, and were usually breech loading. They were also supplied with chambers – usually between one and three with each barrel – though muzzle-loading examples are also noted. Like most other types of gunpowder weapons during this period, their size was not fixed. The majority, where weights or lengths are noted, which is not often, weigh less than 20 *livres* and were quite short. However, there is some evidence that *coulovrines* were made in two different sizes. The smaller ones were roughly 140 mm (5.5 in.) long, while the longer ones were anything from 550 mm (21.5 in.) to 1100 mm long (43 in.). Although there is no evidence to correlate length and weight, it would seem likely that the shorter examples correspond to pieces of roughly 10–15 *livres* while the longer pieces would be those weighing 40 to 50 *livres*. Interestingly, the smaller pieces are noted as being mounted in groups, two to a stock. Finally, about equal numbers of iron and copper alloy examples are listed.

Supporting evidence

Name variants   Coleuvre, coulovrine, coleuvrine, colevrine, colovrine, colouvrine, coulouvrine, couleuvre, couleuvrine, coulevre, coleuvre à main, colevrine à crochet, colevrine à main, colouvrine à main, colovrine à croucher.

There are a great many variants of the name of this type of gunpowder weapon, but all are very similar. As there is no modern equivalent, the commonest form, coulovrine, has been used for the group as a whole.

---

[41] Un canon de fer à plombée (Garnier, p. 40).
[42] Trois canons de fer, deux à plombée, un gectant pierre de 5 livres (Garnier, p. 39).
[43] From the late fifteenth century and thereafter the name *culverin*, and variants spellings such as *culverine* and *culveringe*, came to mean a completely different type of gun: a long bronze muzzle-loading piece firing a cast-iron shot of about 18 lb weight.

Date range   The first mention of this type of gunpowder weapon, a *coulevre*, is in 1420 while the last is in 1465 with large numbers especially noted in the 1430s and 1440s. Between 1430 and 1439, there are 1,113 references while between 1440 and 1450 there are a further 1,182, indicating that, perhaps, the duke of Burgundy, after purchasing such large quantities in these two decades, thereafter used his stock without needing to purchase more.

Size   It is clear that this type of gun was small, essentially a hand gun. It was often, but not always, hand held though several types are noted as having hooks or are mounted on or in wood. The majority, where weights or lengths are noted, which is not often, are less than 20 *livres* in weight and quite short. For example, in 1430:

> . . . six coleuves each weighing 12 *livres*.[44]

An account from 1430–31 gives a lot more details of weights:

> Account of Mahieu Regnault, receiver general of Burgundy,
> Paid to J. Mareschal, cannoneer living at Dijon, the sum of 64 *francs*, that is:
> 12 fr. for the making of eight *coleuvres* weighing together 117 *livres*, at 13 *gros* each.
> 12 fr. for eight other *coleuvres*, weighing altogether 105 *l.* for the same price.
> 24 fr. for sixteen others weighing together 239 *livres*.
> 12 fr. for eight other *coleuvres* weighing together 108.
> 4 for the remainder for making of eight others.[45]

The average weights of the various *coleuvres* listed are 14.6 *livres*, 13.1 *livres*, 14.9 *livres*, and 13.5 *livres*.
Again in 1430:

> Item of 26 iron *coleuvres* weighing 372½ *livres* made by Jehan Mareschal.[46]

The average weight of these pieces is 14.3 *livres*.
However, some guns of this type were larger, for example in 1433:

> . . . four *colovrines* weighing together 202 *livres*. . .[47]

This gives an average weight of 50.5 *livres*. This, larger weight, is confirmed by a list of 1474:

> Item a copper alloy *colovrine à croucher*, weighing 44 *livres*

---

[44]   . . . six coleuves chacune du poids de 12 livres . . . (Garnier, p. 68).
[45]   Compte de Mahieu Regnault, receveur général de Bourgogne
    Paiement à J. Mareschal, canonnier demeurant à Dijon, de la somme de 64 francs, savoir:
    12 fr. pour la façon de huit coleuvres de fer pesant ensemble 117 livres, à 13 gros chaque.
    12 fr. pour huit autres coleuvres pesant ensemble 105 l. au même prix.
    24 fr. pour seize autres pesans ensemble 239 livres.
    12 fr. pour huit autres coleuvres pesant ensemble 108.
    4 pour reste de façon de huit autres (Garnier, p. 56n).
[46]   Item de 26 coleuvres de fer pesant 372 livres ½ faites par Jehan Mareschal (Garnier, p. 64).
[47]   . . . quatre colovrines pesant environ 202 livres . . . (Garnier, p. 42).

Item a copper alloy *colovrine à croucher*, weighing 41 *livres*
Item a copper alloy *colovrine à croucher*, weighing 37 *livres*
Item a copper alloy *colovrine à croucher*, weighing 47 *livres*.[48]

Although few lengths are given, it is again clear that there seems to be two different sizes. The smaller size is noted in 1436:

Two hundred copper alloy *coulovrines* about a half *pié* long and are to be mounted two on a stock.[49]

However most were somewhat longer. In 1444:

Three iron *coulevrines* each of three *piez* and three *doiz* long, each furnished with three chambers, each chamber of half *pié* long and the said coulovrines mounted in wood.[50]

Again in 1444:

Two iron *coulovrines* each two *piez* and three *doiz* long, mounted in wood and each furnished with three chambers, each chamber half *pié* long, 50 *livres* of lead to make *plombées*.
Two iron *coulovrines* each two and a half *piez* long, mounted in wood, furnished with three chambers. Item eight *livres* of powder and 24 *livres* of lead to make *plombées*.
An iron coulovrine two *piez* long, furnished with three chambers, two *livres* of cannon powder and 10 *livres* of lead to make *plombées*.
Two iron *coulovrines* each two and a half *piez* long, mounted in wood and each furnished with three chambers 10 *livres* of lead to make *plombées* and 4 *livres* of powder.[51]

In 1465:

Returned to the castellan of Luzy four *coulovrines*, two white ones 2 and a half *pieds* long and two red of two *piez* in length, with some crossbow bolts.[52]

---

[48] It. une colovrine de métail à croucher, pesant 44 livres
It. une colovrine de métail à croucher, pesant 41 livres
It. une colovrine de métail à croucher, pesant 37 livres
It. une colovrine de métail à croucher pesant 47 livres (Garnier, p. 187).

[49] Deux cent coulovrines de cuivre d'environ demi pié de long et sont pour enmenchier deux en ung baston (Garnier, p. 152).

[50] Trois coulevrines de fer chacune de trois piez et trois doiz de long, garnies chacune de trois chambres, chacune chambre de demi pié de long et icelles coulovrines enchassillées en bois (Garnier, p. 78).

[51] Deux coulovrines de fer chacune de deux piez et trois doiz de long, enchassillées en bois et garnies chacune de trois chambres, contenant chacune chambre demi pié de long, 50 livres de plomb pour faire plombées.
Deux coulovrines de fer chacune de deux piez et demi de long, enchasillées en bois, garnies chacune de trois chambres. Item huit livres de pouldre et 24 livres de plomb à faire plombées.
Une coulovrine de fer de deux piez de long, garnie de trois chambres, deux livres de pouldre de canon et 10 livres de plomb pour faire plombée.
Deux coulovrines de fer chacune de deux piez demi de long, enchassillées en bois et garnies chacun de trois chambres 10 livres de plomb à faire plombées et 4 livres de pouldre (Garnier, p. 79).

[52] Elle remet au chatelain de Luzy quatre coulovrines, deux blanches de la longeur de 2 pieds et demi et deux rouges de deux piez de long, avec des traits d'arbaletes (Garnier, pp. 81–82).

In 1472:

> Four large *coulovrines à croichés* of four *piez* long and 50 *livres* of powder.[53]

Types and material   Approximately equal numbers of iron and copper alloy coulovrines are listed. Most are breech loading and supplied with between one and three chambers each, though one coulovrine has four. For example, in 1445:

> Item five copper-alloy *coulovrines*, each with two chambers.[54]

Similarly:

> Item two copper-alloy *coulovrines* encased in wood each furnished with a chamber.[55]

However, some were all of one piece. In 1436:

> Four large iron *coulovrines*, each of one piece.
> Fourteen smaller iron *coulovrines* of one piece.
> Twenty-four large iron *coulovrines* of one piece.[56]

In 1445 there are clear references to coulovrines being hand guns:

> Item 12 iron *coulovrines*, to fire by hand.[57]

There is also reference to coulovrines being used with a crutch. In 1448–49:

> Three iron *coulovrines* of which one is on a stand and the others to fire by hand.[58]

Makers and suppliers   The major suppliers of coulovrines were J. Mareschal, Martin de Cornuaille, and Jehan Cambier.

Carriage and mounting   Coulovrines are frequently noted as being encased or mounted in wood. While this may have been done in a similar fashion to the stocks of later guns, it is never made clear in the early sources how this was done. A number of different words and phrases are used, *emmanchées de bois, enfustées en bois* or *enchassillées en bois*. While it is never possible to know exactly what these terms meant at the time, it is likely that they refer to different ways of mounting a gun barrel. *Emmanchées* is similar to fitting a piece of wood at the rear of a barrel, in the manner of adding a tiller or handle – many extant examples have a socket at the rear for this purpose. *Enfustée* might possibly mean that the piece was set into a channel as in a modern gun stock. And *Enchassillées* is possibly similar to *enfustée*. In addition, there are frequent references to a mount called a *baston*, for example:

---

[53] Quatre grosses coulovrines à croichés de quatre piez de long et 50 livres de pouldre (Garnier, p 79)
[54] Item cinq coulovrines de cuivre, chacune à deux chambres (Garnier, p. 172).
[55] Item deux coulovrines de cuivre enfustées en bois chacune garnie d'une chamber (Garnier, p. 127).
[56] Quatre grosses coulovrines de fer, chacune d'une piece.
Quatorze coulovrines de fer plus petites d'une piesce.
Vingt quatre grosses coulovrines de fer d'une piece (Garnier, p. 152).
[57] Item 12 coulovrines de fer, à tirer à la main (Garnier, p. 139).
[58] Trois coulovrines de fer dont l'une est à potence et les autres à traire à main (Garnier, p. 131).

> Four *coulovrine* mounted each on a *baston*.
> Item another *coulovrine* on a *baston* with four chambers.[59]

Just exactly what a *baston* was is never made clear, but it must have been a stock of some sort. Some typical references are, in 1436:

> Item 33 copper-alloy *coulovrines* mounted on 17 *bastons* by the two ends.[60]
> Item eight copper-alloy *coulovrines* mounted on four *bastons* by the two ends.[61]
> Item two coulovrines mounted on two *bastons*.[62]
> Item four small copper-alloy *coulovrines* mounted on two *bastons* by the two ends.[63]

In some cases several, usually two, coulovrines were mounted on a single stock, although quite what *par les deuz bouts* refers to is not clear.
There are also a few individual references to slightly different mountings:

> Item three large copper-alloy *coulovrines* turning on *chevalés* [trestles] of wood.
> Item two small copper-alloy *coulovrines* encased in wood.
> Item eight copper-alloy *coulovrines* without housing.[64]

In summary, coulovrines were then usually, but not always, mounted in or on wood either singly or in groups.

Ammunition   The ammunition of the coulovrine was almost always *plommées* – lead shot. As in 1430:

> Six iron *coleuvres* to fire *plommées*.[65]

Unfortunately there is no information about just how big the shot for coulovrines was – sizes are never given.

Loading and firing   It is clear from the registers that coulovrines were normally loaded with specific powder, called *coulovrine powder*, as opposed to cannon powder. For example:

> Item *coulovrine powder*, a hundred *livres*.[66]

Though coulovrines are sometimes listed with cannon powder this need not necessarily be the powder to be used with the weapon, for example:

---

[59] Quatre coulovrine estant chacune sur un baston. Item une autre coulovrine sur un baston à quatre chambres (Garnier, p. 121).
[60] Item 33 coulovrines de cuivre enfustées en 17 bastons par les deux bouts (Garnier, p. 161).
[61] Item huit coulovrines de cuivre enfustées en quatre bastons par les deux bouts (Garnier, p. 162).
[62] Item deux coulovrines enfustez en deux bastons (Garnier, p. 162).
[63] Item quatre petites coulovrines de cuivre enfustées en deux bastons par les deux bouts (Garnier, p. 162).
[64] Item trois grans coulovrines de cuivre tournans sur chevalés de bois.
   Item deux petites coulovrines de cuivre emmanchées de bois.
   Item huit coulovrines de cuivre sans mance (Garnier, pp. 127–28).
[65] Six couleuvres de fer a getter plommées (Garnier, p. 45).
[66] Item pouldre de coulovrine, cent livres (Garnier, p. 129).

Three large iron *couleuvrines* and 4 *livres* of cannon powder at 4 *gros* the *livre*.[67]

Surviving Burgundian coulovrines Although it appears from the narrative sources and archival records that the Burgundian army would have been widely equipped with handguns, there are only two examples associated with the *Burgunderbeute*. The small bronze piece now in Basel (catalogue no. 3) mounted on a small wooden carriage and frequently referred to as a larger gunpowder weapon, is, in fact, a bronze handgun. An examination of the piece reveals that it has been converted from a handgun, possiby a coulovrine *à crochet* or a coulovrine *à croucher*, by the removal of the hook, the addition of trunnions, and the filling in of the socket at the rear, into which the wooden stock was secured. Unlike many of those listed in the accounts, this piece is muzzle, not breech, loading, and fits into the larger size category identified above as it is 985 mm (38¾ in.) long with a bore of 29 mm (1.1 in.).

The second piece is a short gunpowder weapon mounted on a wooden stock and now in the collections of the *Musee de l'Armée* in Paris (catalogue no. 2). This gun fits into the smaller type of coulovrine noted above – it is 390 mm (15.3 in.) long with a barrel bore of 130 mm (5.1 in.). Whether its wooden stock is original is open to question, but it does appear to fit the criteria given above and probably represents the appearance of this type of coulovrine in the middle of the fifteenth century.

COURTAU

Summary

Courtaux are a type of gunpowder weapon that only occurs very late in the Burgundian records, so that there are few references to them in Garnier, making it difficult to be certain of their exact form. Those noted in the registers were made of copper alloy, fired stone shot, and were probably quite large, as they needed 8 horses for the transport of a single piece.

Supporting evidence

Name variants Courtaulx, courtant.
With so few references these are the only names used.

Date range References to courtau begin in the later fifteenth century, from about 1474, and continue to the end of the century when the name largely disappears.

Type and material There is very little information in the Burgundian registers about courtaux, but from the few references it seems clear that they were quite large. For example, in 1474:

---

[67] Trois grosses couleuvrines de fer et 4 livres de poudre de canon à 4 gros la livre (Garnier, p. 44).

From my said lord it was ordered to be brought two copper alloy *courtaulx* being presently at Luxembourg and for which is needed to bring them here, 16 horses.[68]

Carriages and mountings   The few references to courtaux in the registers indicate that they were mounted on a form of wheeled carriage, as in 1478–79:

For six large pairs of wheels, to serve the *courtaulx* of the artillery, two pairs of wheels for the great *coleuvrines*.
A pair of shafts and the *almons* and the *falectes* of one of these pieces.
Two pairs of shafts serving the carriages of these same pieces.[69]

Just what these specialised terms refer to is not clear but they were certainly parts of the wheeled carriages on which courtaux were mounted.

Ammunition   Courtaux were always loaded with stone shot. In 1474:

To take two hundred stone shot for *courtaulx* at the rate of 40 shot to each cart with four horses making 20 horses.[70]

And in an inventory of 1475 from the town of Lille:

10 *courtant*, 2,000 stone shot the said *courtants*.[71]

Surviving Burgundian courtaux   Among the surviving gunpowder weapons in the *Burgunderbeute* there is a large copper-alloy piece, captured at the battle of Grandson, which is probably a courtau. It is dated 1474, was made by Jean de Malines, and is marked not only with the Burgundian coat of arms, but also with the initials of Charles the Bold (catalogue no. 4). It is justly famous as the earliest known gunpowder weapon to have trunnions and, there can be little doubt about its origins. It has a bore of 23 cm and probably fired a shot of approximately 14 kg (30 lb). The *Zeughaus Books* of Maximilian I, Charles the Bold's son-in-law and successor, include a piece called *Burgunderin* which appears to be identical to this piece and may possibly be a pair to the gun in Basel.[72]

68 A mondit seigneur ordonné estre méné deux coutaulx de métal estans presentement à Luxembourg et convient pour iceulx mener, 16 chevaux (Garnier, p. 179).
69 Pour six grosses paires de roes, pour servir es courtaulx de L'artillerie, des paires de roes pour les grosses coleuvrines.
Une paire de lymons et les almons et les falectes d'une de ces pièces.
Deux paires de lymons servants es affusts de ces mêmes pièces (Garnier, p. 199).
70 Pour mener deux cent pierres de courtaulx à compter 40 pierres sur chacun (charriot) à quatre chevaulx font 20 chevaulx (Garnier, p. 179).
71 10 courtaux, 2,000 pierres pour lesdits courtaux (*Inventaire sommaire des archives départementales antérieures à 1790. Nord. Série B*, ed. A. le Glay et al. (Lille, 1863–1906), VIII:160).
72 Vienna, Oesterreichische Nationalbibliothek, Cod. 10824.

CRAPAUDEAU

Summary

From the available evidence in the Burgundian registers it is clear that *crapaudeaux* were long, breech loading, small calibre gunpowder weapons. Strangely, the name only appears for a relatively short period – from 1433 to 1451 – but, intriguingly, a very large number of pieces are listed in this period. 43 crapaudeaux are noted during the 1430s while in the 1440s there are almost 850 references which decreases again to only 12 in the 1450s. The reasons why this gunpowder weapon name appears and then disappears so suddenly are unclear, as is the fact that the name is confined, almost exclusively, to the registers of the Burgundian dukes. Several explanations are possible. It may be that it is the name for a new type of gunpowder weapon which then disappears from the arsenals or, more likely, its name was changed. It could be that it was a new name for an existing type of weapon, though why it disappears so suddenly is not clear. It may also be a notarial idiosyncrasy used for a period by a Burgundian clerk or clerks, which then disappeared when they died or were replaced.

   Although, as with most other types of artillery at this period, their size was not fixed, the majority were relatively long, small calibre pieces, 1200–1800 mm (48 to 72 in.) in length with a bore of around 50–100 mm (2 to 4 in.) and weighing 45–90 kg (100–200 lb). They fired stone or lead balls and, though most were made from iron, copper-alloy pieces are also listed. They were frequently mounted in groups on some form of carriage or mount, often called a *ribaudequin* (see below).

Supporting evidence

Name variants   Crapaudeau, crappaudeau, crapaudeaux, crapaudeaulx, crappaudeaulx, crapaudine, grans crappaudeaulx, petits crappaudeaulx, pesan crappaudau.

Date range   The first reference to crapaudeaux in the Burgundian registers is in 1433 and the last in 1451, making this one of the shortest date ranges of any type of gunpowder weapons in these records. However, within this very short time there are records of just over 800 pieces, making it one of the most common types of gun.

Size   Crapaudeaux, unlike many other types of gunpowder weapons during this period, are more generally of a similar size, in the region of 50 mm (2 in.) in calibre, 1200–1500 mm (48–60 in.) long and weighing 45–90 kg (100–200 lb). However, it is clear that there was still no specific size for crapaudeaux and that they came in a variety of sizes, although these variations are not as large as in many types of weapon during this period. Many pieces are listed as firing stone shot of 2 *polz* diameter or 2 *livres* in weight. For example, in 1440:

> Twelve iron *crappaudeaulx* each with two chambers carrying stone of two *polz* across and of four *piez* long chamber and barrel together.[73]

---

[73] Douze crappaudeaulx de fer garnis chacun de deux chambers portant pierres de deux polz en croix et de quatre piez de long chamber et volée ensemble (Garnier, p. 132).

And, from the mid-1440s:

> To him for fifteen *crappaudeaulx* of various sizes, each furnished with two chambers carrying stone of two *livres*, weighing together sixteen hundred *livres* at 15 *deniers* the *livre*, valued at 102 *livres*.[74]

In 1446:

> Item 24 long *crapaudaux* each with two chambers and carrying stone of two *potz* across of . . . *piez* long, barrel and chamber at the said price weighed together.
> Item 87 smaller *crappaudeaulx* each with two chambers carrying stone of two *polz* across and five *piez* long, chamber and barrel at the said price weighed together.[75]

However it is clear that they could range quite widely in size, as in 1451:

> Item 36 large *crappaudeaulx* of various sorts, each with two chambers, firing 6, 5, 4, 3, 2½ and 2 *polz* all encased in wood.[76]

The weight of individual pieces is rarely, if ever, stated, but there are many references where the total weight of many guns together is given enabling an average to be calculated. Of course, average weights be used with care as there may have been a considerable variation from gun to gun. For example, in 1445:

> Item three iron *crappaudeaulx* weighing 525 *livres* of iron, one taken to the said Montaigle, another to the castle of Lembourg and the other to Kerpen.
> Item two iron *crappaudeaulx* with two chambers, weighing together 264 *livres* and given as a gift to my lord J. de Croy.[77]

These two entries give average weights of crapaudeaux as 175 and 132 *livres* respectively. These figures are confirmed by two further entries. In 1445 120 crapaudeaux weighed 23,000 *livres*, giving an average of 191 *livres* per gun, and again in 1445 50 crapaudeaux weighed 7,000 *livres*, giving an average of 140 *livres* per gun.[78]

Type and material   Both iron and copper alloy pieces are noted in the registers, though the greater numbers are made from iron, and most pieces were supplied with chambers – usually 2, though occasionally 3, per weapon. For example, in 1445:

---

[74] A lui pour quinze crappaudeaulx de diverses moisons, garnis chacun de deux chambres portant Pierre de deux livres, pesant ensemble seize cent livres à 15 deniers la livre, valent 102 livres (Garnier, p. 115). The date of this folio is missing, but it is set amid several other folios all dating from the middle of the 1440s.

[75] Item 24 longs crapaudaux garnis chacuns de deux chambres et portans Pierre de deux potz en croisière de . . . piez de long, volée et chamber audit pris pesans ensemble.
Item 87 plus petis crappaudeaulx garnis chacun de deux chambres portans Pierre de deux polz en croisière et cinq piez de long, chamber et volée audit pris, pesant ensemble (Garnier, p. 115).

[76] Item 36 gros crappaudeaulx de plusiers sortes, chacun à deux chambres, tirans de 6, 5, 4, 3, 2½ et 2 polz tous enfustés en bois (Garnier, p. 132).

[77] Item trois crappaudeaulx de fer pesant 525 livres de fer, l'un mené audit Montaigle, l'autre au chastel de Lembourg et l'autre à Kerpen.
Item deux crappaudeaulx de fer garnis de deux chambres, pesans ensemble 264 livres et donnés en don à messire J. de Croy (Garnier, p. 137).

[78] Garnier, p. 17.

That is to say for 120 iron *crapaudeaulx* to put on *ribaudquins* of four and a half *piez* long carrying stone of two *poulces* across and each with three chambers . . . serving all the said *ribaudequins*.[79]

Makers and suppliers   Few makers of crapaudeaux are noted, but in 1445 Jean Cambier, the well-known Mons arms supplier, was providing crapaudeaux as well as many other ordnance supplies.[80]

Carriage and mounting   There are many references to crapaudeaux being mounted, either in wood or on ribaudequins. For example, in 1437:

Item a *crappaudeaux* mounted on wood, set on a small trestle.[81]

In 1443:

Item forty *ribaudequins* all mounted and complete, furnished with one hundred and three *crappaudeaulx*, of which there are 74 of iron and 29 of copper together with 202 iron chambers and 52 chambers of copper and 126 iron chains, each chain containing of eleven *toises* [a *toise* = 6 *pieds*] and fifty-eight *esses* [S-shaped links].
Item 25 keys to put behind the said crappaudeaulx in the manner of a bed.
Item 1,280 stone shot for the said *crappaudeaulx*.[82]

It was common for several crapaudeaux to be mounted together, either on a ridaudequin, as above, or in a bank:

Item a bank to two crappaudeaulx of two chambers.[83]

Ammunition   Crapaudeaux were loaded either with stone shot or else with *plommées*. In 1437:

Item a hundred [weight] and a half of lead, 200 *plommées* for *crappaudeaux*.[84]

Surviving Burgundian crapaudeaux   There are five pieces in the *Burgunderbeute* that conform to a greater or lesser extent to the parameters for crapaudeaux as above, and these are tabulated below:

---

[79] C'est assavoir pour 120 crapaudeaulx de fer à mettre sur ribaudequins de quatre piez et demi de long portans Pierre de deux poulces en croisière et garnis chacun de trois chambers . . . servans à tous lesdiz ribaudequins (Garnier, p. 110).

[80] Garnier, pp. 110, 152.

[81] Item ung crapaudeau enfusté en bois, assis sur ung chevalet (Garnier, p. 142).

[82] Item quarante ribaudequins touz montés et estoffez, garnis de cent et trois crappaudeaulx, dont il a 74 de fer et 29 de cuivre garnis de 202 chambres de fer et de 52 chambres de cuivre et de six vingt-une chaines de fer, chacune chaine contenant onze toises et cinquante huit esses.
Item 25 clefs pour mettre derrier lesdiz crappaudeaulx en manière d'affut.
Item 1,280 pierres servant esdiz crappaudeaulx (Garnier, p. 130).

[83] Item ung banc à deux crappaudeaulx à deux chambres (Garnier, p. 121).

[84] Item un cent et demi de plomb, 200 plommées pour crappaudeaux (Garnier, p. 143).

In Part 4 below	Length		Bore		Booty status
	mm	in.	mm	in.	
Cat. no. 8	1080	42	69	2.70	Grandson
Cat. no. 9	1580	62	70	2.75	Grandson
Cat. no. 11	1400	55	70	2.75	Grandson
Cat. no. 12	2190	86	70	2.75	Grandson
Cat. no. 13	1390	54	35	1.40	Murten

Of these the first three are very close to the dimensions given in the registers, though the figures given here are for the barrel only without a powder chamber so that they would have been longer when mounted for use. The final two pieces may not be crapaudeaux though the variation in sizes which occur in the original documents means that this cannot be ruled out. These would have been mounted in wooden beds into which the powder chamber would also have been secured before firing.

HACQUEBUS

The usual name for hand guns in the Burgundian archives is, as noted above, *coulovrine*, but there are a few uses of the term *hacquebus* at the end of the reign of the Burgundian dukes – obviously also a hand-held gunpowder weapon. For example in 1474–75:

> Five iron hacquebuses, for the defense of the said castle.[85]

Similarly in 1473–74:

> Four hacquebuses.[86]

With so few references it is impossible to know precisely the form of this weapon.

MORTARS

There is almost no mention of *mortars* in the Burgundian sources before 1450 and none in Garnier's transcription until 1485 when a single reference appears, not to a mortar but to a gunpowder weapon like a mortar:

> Item a small *canon* firing stone shot of eight *poulces* in height and two *pieds* in length in the fashion of a *mortar*.[87]

That mortars were known in the latter half of the fifteenth century is certain,

---

[85] . . . cinq hacquebuches de fer, pour la deffense dudit chastel (Garnier, p. 85).
[86] . . . quatre hacquebuses (Garnier, p. 185).
[87] Item ung petit canon portant pierre de huit polces de hault et de longeur deux pieds en facon d'ung mortier (Garnier, p. 229).

though why there is no mention of this type of gun in the Dijon archives is unclear. There are numerous references to them in the narrative sources, especially mentioned together with bombards and serpentines and recorded to be used at sieges almost exclusively. In addition, Lodewijk de Gruuthuse (Louis de Bruges), one of Philip the Good and Charles the Bold's leading councillors, adopted as his personal emblem what the chronicler Jean de Haynin – who should know as he served as one of Charles the Bold's military leaders – calls "a *mortier*."[88] A likely explanation may be that although this gunpowder weapon type was known and called by the name *mortar* or *mortier* in some areas, in other areas and by other individuals it was called something else, possibly *pestereau* (see below) or possibly *bombardelle*.

PESTEREAU

Summary

Unfortunately, there are very few references to this type of gunpowder weapon making it hard to form a clear picture of the type as a whole. However, taken altogether these references do yield enough information to, at least, suggest what type of piece it may have been: basically a very short gun made from either wrought or cast iron and firing stone shot. A single reference to calibre confirms that they may have been like mortars, short pieces of large calibre. No chambers are mentioned for pestereaux, and there is a reference to a gun made in one piece, leading to the conclusion that they were muzzle loaders. A reference to a piece "in the fashion of a mortar" perhaps holds the key to its form, a weapon in which the barrel length was approximately equal to its bore.

Supporting evidence

Name variants   Pottereaul, pestereaulx.

Date range   Pestereaux only appear for a short period at the very end of the century, in the 1480s and 1490s. Like crapaudeaux, the name only appears in the Burgundian registers, and why this is so is again unclear and the same comments as above apply. One other possible explanation may be that the pestereau was a parallel development with the mortar but, for some reason, was not successful, so that the mortar became the preferred type of weapon.

Size   Pestereaux were very short weapons, approximately 400–700 mm (15–27 in.) in length, and of large calibre. For example, in 1480–85:

> Item a small iron *canon* called a *pottereaul*, of one *pié* and a half long all of one piece.

---

88 Jean de Haynin, *Mémoires*, ed. R. Chalon (Mons, 1842), I:68. For a discussion of this emblem see Jan Piet Puype, "Het embleem van Lodewijk van Gruuthuse," in *Lodewijk van Gruuthuse: Mecenas en europees diplomaat, ca. 1427–1492*, ed. Maximiliaan P.J. Martens (Bruges, 1992), pp. 93–108.

Item a small *canon* firing stone shot of eight *poulces* in height and two *pieds* in length in the fashion of a *mortar*.[89]

And again in 1496:

Item two small wrought-iron *canon*s called *pestereaux* firing stone shot.
Item three other small *petereaulx* each about two *piez* and a half long firing stone shot.
Item another small *canon* of cast iron in the fashion of a mortar.
Item thirteen wrought-iron *petereaulx* with long handles which were taken to Talent.[90]

Type and material   The examples of pestereaux in the Burgundian registers were made from either wrought or cast iron. No powder chambers are mentioned, and one reference specifically states that the gun is all of one piece.

Ammunition   All the examples in the inventories fired stone shot.

Surviving Burgundian pestereaux   An easily identifiable group of guns among those preserved in Swiss museums and elsewhere have been called short muzzle loaders – relatively short, large calibre pieces.[91] These unusual pieces are difficult to date and little is known about them except that most, if not all, have provenances that link them directly, or indirectly, with the Burgundian wars of the 1470s in Switzerland.

The surviving pieces can be divided into two very distinct groups: the first made from wrought iron, while the second, and in many ways the more interesting, group are made from cast iron. They are summarised below:

In Part 4 below	Material	Overall length mm	Bore, barrel mm
Cat. no. 18	Wrought iron	535	150
Cat. no. 19	Wrought iron	440	155
Cat. no. 20	Wrought iron	490	130
Cat. no. 21	Wrought iron	625	210
Cat. no. 22	Wrought iron	735	210
Cat. no. 25	Wrought iron	805	180
Cat. no. 23	Cast iron	480	160
Cat. no. 24	Cast iron	480	165

Both groups have the same form: the barrel, which has comparatively thin walls, is only slightly longer than its bore, while the powder chamber is of much smaller diameter. In appearance they are very like a mortar. Although the evidence is limited it is perhaps tempting to identify these surviving pieces as pestereaux.

[89] Item ung petit canon de fer appellé Pottereaul, d'un pié et demi de long tout d'une piece.
Item ung petit canon portant pierre de huit polces de hault et de longeur deux pieds en facon d'ung mortier (Garnier, p. 229).
[90] Item deux petiz canons de fer forgié appellées pestereaulx portant boulets de pierre.
Item trois autres petiz petereaulx chacun de deux piez et demy ou environ portans boulets de pierre.
Item ung autre petit canon de fer fondue en facon d'ung mortier.
Item trieze petereaulx de fer forgié à longue quehue qui furent amenez de Talent (Garnier, p. 233).
[91] Robert D. Smith, "Towards a New Typology for Wrought Iron Ordnance," *International Journal of Nautical Archaeology and Underwater Exploration* 17 (1988), 5–16.

SERPENTINE

Summary

There are few references to serpentines in these accounts though from other sources it is clear that this type of gun was more common towards the end of the fifteenth century, especially on board ships.[92] From the information during the earlier period, serpentines were breech-loading pieces weighing in the region of 227 kg (500 lb). They were made from either iron or copper alloy and usually fired stone or lead balls. From the evidence we have the likely form of these guns is shown in an illustration dating to the end of the fifteenth century by Israel von Mechenen. In this illustration the barrel is mounted on a wooden bed with two large diameter iron-shod wheels, part of an elaborate carriage which includes a simple method of raising and lowering elevation. Behind the barrel the bed is cut to take the separate powder chamber which is held in place by means of a wedge, shown attached to a length of iron chain to prevent it being lost. A large hammer, evidently for making the wedge fast and for removing it once the gun has been fired is shown in the foreground.

Supporting evidence

Name variants Serpentine, grosse serpentine, moïennes serpentine.

Date range Serpentines are only mentioned in the main Burgundian archives in 1473–74, but Garnier also makes reference to them in a note dated to 1466–67.[93] However, from Burgundian narrative and other sources it is clear that this was a common type of gunpowder weapon in the late fifteenth century and early sixteenth century.[94]

Size Serpentines were slightly larger than crapaudeaux, weighing, in general, around 300 to 500 *livres*. For example:

> Paid to P. Douhet merchant of Dijon, the sum of 41½ f. for the sale of two iron serpentines weighing together 664 *livres* at the price of 3 *blancs* the *livre*.[95]

In 1473–74:

> Item a copper-alloy *serpentine* weighing 559 *livres* with its carriage of iron bound wheels, chests and shafts.
> Item another *serpentine* weighing 547 *livres*.

---

92 Robert D. Smith, "Wrought-Iron Swivel Guns," in *The Archaeology of Ships of War*, ed. M. Bound (Oxford, 1995), pp. 104–6.

93 Garnier, p. 82, note.

94 See Smith, "Wrought-Iron Swivel Guns," pp. 104–13, and *Inventaire sommaire des archives*.

95 Payé à P. Douhet, marchand à Dijon, la somme de 41 f. ½ pour la vente de deux serpentines de fer pesant ensemble 664 livres au prix de 3 blancs la livre (Garnier, p. 185).

Item 200 lead *plommées*, some of which have iron inside, for the said *serpentines*, the said *plommées* weighing 505 *livres*.[96]

Slightly later, in 1476–77, the weights of six serpentines are given:

Paid to B. Marion, marshal, 217 f. 11 *gros* 1 *blanc* for making seven iron *serpentines* weighing:

The first	506 *livres*
The second	488 *livres*
The third	520 *livres*
The fourth	552 *livres*
The fifth	500 *livres*
The sixth	492 *livres*

These six *serpentines* were taken to the siege of Vesoul in the month of March 1476/77 with 220 *plommées*.
The seventh with two chambers, 492 *livres*.
In all 4,487 *livres* at 3 *bl.* each.[97]

However, as with all gunpowder weapons at this date, the size of serpentines was not consistent and they could also be much larger:

A large copper-alloy *serpentine* weighing 1,549½ *livres*, with its carriage and cart on 4 iron-bound wheels and shafts.[98]

Type and material   Serpentines were made from both iron and copper alloy and where mentioned most serpentines had chambers. For example, in 1473–74:

To have reforged and newly made the barrels of two small iron *serpentines* of the chateau of Arc in Barrois.
For a new chamber for a *serpentine* of Talaut.
For an iron wedge for the said *serpentine*.[99]

---

[96] Item une serpentine de metail pesant 559 livres garnie de son affust de roes ferrées, coffres et lymonneure.
Item une autre serpentine pesant 547 livres.
Item 200 plommées de plomb esquelles a du fer deans, servans esdites serpentines, lesdites plommées pesans 505 livres (Garnier, p. 187).

[97] Payé a B. Marion, mareschal, 217 f. 11 gros 1 blanc pour la facon de sept serpentines de fer pesans:

La première	506 livres
La seconde	488 livres
La troisième	520 livres
La 4ᵉ	552 livres
La 5ᵉ	500 livres
La 6ᵉ	492 livres

Ces six serpentines furent menées au siège de Vesoul au mois de mars 1476/7 avec 220 plommées.
La 7ᵉ garnie de deux chambres, 492 livres.
En tout 4,487 livres à 3 bl. chacune (Garnier, p. 190).

[98] It. une grosse serpentine de metail pesant 1,549 livres ½, garnie de son affust et chariot à 4 rouhes ferrees de lymonneures (Garnier, p. 187).

[99] Pour avoir reforgé tout à neuf les volées devant des deux petites serpentines de fer du chateau d'Arc en Barrois
Pour une chambre neuve à une serpentine de Talaut
Pour ung coing de fer servant à ladite serpentine (Garnier, p. 186).

Transport   Serpentines were mounted on carriages pulled by horses, as in 1474:

> Item to transport five medium *serpentines* and four small ones it is necessary to have for the medium *serpentines* three horses and for the small ones two: making 23 horses.[100]

Two or three horses per serpentine appear to have been the norm. For example:

> Paid 16 *gros* to a carter attending two days with his four horses to take back from Gray to Dijon the great *serpentine* of the Duke. June 1474.
> Paid 2 f. to another whose six horses also took back three of the Duke's *serpentines*.[101]

In 1477:

> Eighteen horses, grouped in threes and a driver, drawing the six white and red *serpentines*.[102]

Carriages, mountings, etc.   As can be seen from the quotes above, there is quite a lot of information about carriages for serpentines. From these it is clear that serpentines are almost always mounted on their own wheeled carriages, although much detail is obscure and difficult to interpret. Added to these is this example, in 1476–77, after Charles the Bold's death:

> Cart on two *chers* of six large pieces of elm with which to make the carriages of the six *serpentines* last made by Marion, 4½ f.[103]

Ammunition   Most serpentines fired *plommées* – some it seems filled with iron – though there is a single mention of iron shot in 1474:

> . . . and for 450 iron shot for great coulovrines, *serpentines* and other *battons* . . .[104]

Surviving Burgundian serpentines   A serpentine without its wooden bed would be just an open-ended iron barrel of which a number survive from the *Burgunderbeute*. These have been listed as crapaudeaux above as it the difference between the two types of gunpowder weapons is not at all clear. That serpentines were heavier seems certain, though whether this was due to them being longer or larger in diameter cannot be ascertained. The evidence that they fired *plommées* would indicate that the serpentine was, on the whole, of smaller bore than the crapaudeau and therefore possibly longer. The surviving piece catalogue no. 13 has a bore of just 35 mm and may be a serpentine.

---

[100]   Item pour mener cinq moïennes serpentines et quatre petites fault avoir assavoir aux moïennes serpentines, trois chevaulx et aux petites deux: font 23 chevaulx (Garnier, p. 179).

[101]   Payé 16 gros à un voiturier qui a vaqué deux jours avec ses quatre chevaux pour remener de Gray à Dijon la grosse serpentine du duc. Juin 1474.
Payé 2 f. à un autres dont les six chevaux ont ramené également trois des serpentines du duc (Garnier, p. 184).

[102]   Dix-huit chevaux, groupés par trois et une conducteur, trainaient les six serpentines blanches et rouges (Garnier, p. 193).

[103]   Charroi sur deux chers de six grosses pièces de bois d'orme dont on a fait les affusts des six serpentines dernièrement faites par Marion, 4 f. ½ (Garnier, p. 189).

[104]   . . . et de 450 pierres de fer servans a grosses coulovrines, serpentines et autres battons . . . (Garnier, p. 85).

Similarly the surviving pieces, catalogue no. 9, catalogue no. 11, and catalogue no. 12 are all quite heavy and also may be serpentines rather than crapaudeaux.

VEUGLAIRE

Summary

Like many types of early artillery the sources indicate that there is no obvious fixed size for a *veuglaire* – the term did not represent a size of gun as later names of guns came to be (for example a culverin of 18 lb shot, a demi culverin of 9 lb shot weight etc.). They range in size from the small, only 420 mm (16 in.) long, up to monsters weighing almost 4,000 kg (8,600 lb). However, it is clear that, although there were extreme examples, there was some consistency. As with some other types of early artillery, there are three different categories of veuglaires: small, ordinary (medium), and large. The inventory of artillery made by J. Quenot and delivered by him in 1446 lists pieces ranging from 3 to 5 *piez* long with bores from about 2 to 8.5 *polz*. Looking more closely at this list however does reveal a degree of uniformity: the small (*petit*) veuglaire weighing between 100 and 300 *livres*; the veuglaire with weights from 400 to 800 *livres*; finally the great (*grosse*) veuglaire with weights of over 1,000 *livres*. This same consistency is reflected in the length to bore ratios, summarised below:

	Length of barrel *piez*	Diameter of stone *polces*	Length to bore ratio
Petit vuelglaire	4	3	16.0
(Petit) vuelglaire	4	3	16.0
(Petit) vuelglaire	4	3	16.0
(Petit) vuelglaire	3.5	2.5	16.8
(Petit) vuelglaire	3.5	2.5	16.8
(Petit) vuelglaire	3.5	2.5	16.8
(Petit) vuelglaire	3.5	3	14.0
(Petit) vuelglaire	3.5	2.67	15.7
(Petit) vuelglaire	3	2.67	13.5
Petit vuelglaire	3.5	2	13.5
Petit vuelglaire	3.5	2	21
Canon vuelglaire	4.5	6.5	8.3
Canon vuelglaire	4.5	7	7.7
Gros vuelglaire	3.67	8.5	5.2
Vuelglaire	4.3	6	8.6
Vuelglaire	4.5	5.5	9.8
Vuelglaire	4	4.33	11.1
Vuelglaire	4.33	5.5	9.5
Vuelglaire	4.67	4.33	12.9
Vuelglaire	4.67	4.33	12.9
Vuelglaire	4	4	12.0
Vuelglaire	4.5	6	9.0
Vuelglaire	4.5	5.5	9.8
Vuelglaire	4.5	5.5	9.8
Vuelglaire	4.5	6.33	8.5
Vuelglaire	4.67	6.75	8.3
Vuelglaire	4.5	6	9.0
Grosse vuelglaire	5	7.25	8.3

Some definite patterns can be seen in these figures. First, it is clear that the length to bore ratio is, on the whole, quite low – ranging from 8 to 16 for the majority of pieces. Those outside this range have ratios greater than 16 and are listed as *petit* veuglaire. What is also worthy of note is that the different sizes of veuglaires have different length to bore ratios, summarised below:

Petit veuglaire: 13–16
Veuglaire: 8–13
Grosse veuglaire: 5–8

From the dimensions given in a delivery of veuglaires, supplied by J. Cambier in 1446, it is clear that the length is proportional to the bore and that the length to bore ratio is a constant 12:

Length *piez*	Diameter of stone shot *polx*	Ratio of length to bore
4	4	12
5	5	12
6	6	12
7	7	12
8	8	12

To sum up, it is clear that the size of the veuglaire was not fixed and could range very widely. However, the available information points to the conclusion that that it was a shorter gun with a lower length to bore ratio, in contrast to the length to bore ratio for the crapaudaux of approximately 15 to 30. Veuglaires are perhaps best categorised as medium-sized artillery between bombards and crapaudaux.

Supporting evidence

Name variants   Veuglaire, veulglaire, vinglaire, vueigloire, vueilglaire, vuelglaire, vuglaire, weghelaire, weughelaire, weuglaire weuguelaire, wglaire, wiglaire, petit veuglaire, petit vuelglaire, petit veuglelaire, petit weughelaire, veuglaire moyens, gros veuglaire, gros veuglelaire, gros vinglaire, gros vueiglaire, gran veuglaire, canon vuelglaire.
This name has a large number of variant spellings. However, the greater number of references is to veuglaire.

Date range   The name occurs from 1417 with the last reference made in 1467. The largest number of references is to the period between about 1430 and 1450 with the highest concentration in the 1440s – there are 217 references in the period 1430 to 1439 and 628 in the following decade.

Size   Of all the various types of fifteenth-century gunpowder weapons, veuglaires have the most information about their sizes. This includes not only lengths and weights but also calibre. For example in 1445:

Today the 3rd of August 1445 by MM. of the comptes of the Duke of Burgundy at Dijon. Present Berthelot Lambin, controller of the artillery of my said Lord, and Jacob Belledent, clerk of Philibert de Vauldrey, master of the said artillery. An agreement was made with Jehan Quenot, forger [smith], living in the said Dijon, to make well [faithfully] and loyally and to accomplish to the satisfaction of the parties of the artillery these things afterwards declared.

First, twelve iron *veuglaires*, each furnished with two chambers firing stone weighing twelve *livres* and each chamber holding three *livres* of powder, of the length of six and a half *piez*, including the length of the said chamber.

Item, 24 other *veuglaires*, furnished with two chambers each firing stone of eight *livres* and holding two *livres* of powder of the length of five and a half *piez* including the chamber.

Item, forty others furnished as those above, firing stone of six *livres*, holding a livre and a half of powder, and of the length of five *piez*.

Item, sixty others furnished as those above, firing stone of four *livres* and each holding five *quarterons* [1¼ *livres*] of powder, of the length of four and a half *piez*.

Item, seventy others furnished and of the length of the above ten, firing stone of two *livres* and holding one *livre* of powder.

All the parties of this artillery, the said J. Quenot must return perfectly made to my said Lord in the town of Dijon before the feast of Easter coming next or sooner if possible. The *livre* of all work at the price of 15 *deniers tournois*.

This present agreement settled the penultimate day of July. Present the said Berthelot and not present MM des Comptes and the said Jacot Belledent, present J. Vurry, clerk of J. de Visen, and Perrinet Dandel, clerk living in Dijon. Signed J. Boiset.[105]

---

105 Aujoud'huy 3e jour d'aout 1445 par MM. Des Comptes de M. le duc de Bgne à Dijon, Présens Berthelot Lambin, contreroleur de L'artillerie de mondit Sr et Jacob Belledent, clerc de Philibert de Vauldrey, maitre de ladite artillerie, marchié a esté fait avecques Jehan Quenot, forgeur, demorant audict Dijon, de faire bien deuement et leaulment et acomplir et assovyr les parties d'artilleries cy après déclarées.

Premièrement, douze veuglaires de fer, chacun garnis de deux chambres gectans Pierre de douze livres pesans et chacune chamber tenant trois livres de pouldre, de la longueur de six piedz et demi, comprins en la longueur ladite chamber.

Item vingt et quatre autres veuglaires, garnis de deux chambres gectans chacune Pierre de huit lives et portant deux livres de pouldre de la longueur de cinq piez et demi comprins, la chambre.

Item quadrante autres garnis comme dessus, gectans pierre de six livres tenant livre et demie de pouldre et de la longueur de cinq piez.

Item soixante autres garnis comme dessus, gectans pierre de quatre livres et tenans chacun cinq quaterons de pouldre, de la longueur de quatre piez et demi.

Item soixante et dix autres garnis et de la longueur des dessus diz, gectans pierre de deux livres et tenant une livre de pouldre.

Toutes lesquelles parties d'artillerie, ledit J. Quenot doit rendre faites parfaits à mondit sr en la ville de Dijon dedans la feste de Pasques charnels prouchainement venant au plustost se bonnement faire le peult, la livre de tout le dit ouvraige au pris de 15 deniers tournois.

Ce présent marchié accordé la pénultième jour de juillet. Présents ledit Berthelot et passé présens MM. Des Comptes et ledit Jacot Belledent, présens J. Vurry clerc de J de Visen et Perrinet Dandel, clerc demourans à Dijon. Signé J. Boiset (Garnier, pp. 71–72).

In summary this is:

Number of veuglaires	Material	Number of chambers	Weight of stone shot *livres*	Weight of powder *livres*	Length *piez*
12	Iron	2	12	3	6½
24	Iron	2	8	2	5½
40	Iron	2	6	1½	5
60	Iron	2	4	1¼	4½
70	Iron	2	2	1	4½
206					

At least a part of this enormous contract for veuglaires was ready the following year when J. Quenot delivered a group of 28 veuglaires to Philibert de Vauldrey, master of the artillery. These guns were itemized and this is summarized below:[106]

	Length of barrel *piez*	Diameter of stone *polces*	Number of chambers	Weight of powder *livres*	Weight of barrel *livres*	Weight of chamber *livres*	Weight altogether *livres*	Material
Petit vuelglaire	4	3	2	1			219.5	Iron
(Petit) vuelglaire	4	3	2	1			281.5	Iron
(Petit) vuelglaire	4	3	2	1			203	Iron
(Petit) vuelglaire	3.5	2.5	2	1			142	Iron
(Petit) vuelglaire	3.5	2.5	2	1			105	Iron
(Petit) vuelglaire	3.5	2.5	2	1			150	Iron
(Petit) vuelglaire	3.5	3	2	1			155	
(Petit) vuelglaire	3.5	2.67	2	1			190	
(Petit) vuelglaire	3	2.67	2	1			176	
Petit vuelglaire	3.5	2	2	0.5			109 (218)	Iron
Petit vuelglaire	3.5	2	2	0.5			109 (218)	Iron
Canon vuelglaire	4.5	6.5	2	4	765	277.5	1042.5	Iron
Canon vuelglaire	4.5	7	2	4	976	306	1284	Iron
*Gros vuelglaire**	3.67	8.5	1	12	700	356	1056	
Vuelglaire	4.3	6	2	4	712	268.5	980.5	
Vuelglaire	4.5	5.5	2	3			780	
Vuelglaire	4	4.33	2	3			418.5	
Vuelglaire	4.33	5.5	2	3			850	
Vuelglaire	4.67	4.33	2	3			538	
Vuelglaire	4.67	4.33	2	3			492	
Vuelglaire	4	4	2	3			550	
Vuelglaire	4.5	6	2	4	844	262	1106	Iron
Vuelglaire	4.5	5.5	2	3			728	
Vuelglaire	4.5	5.5	2	3			775	Iron
Vuelglaire	4.5	6.33	2	4	788	312	1100	Iron
Vuelglaire	4.67	6.75	2	4	818	312	1130	Iron
Vuelglaire	4.5	6	2	3	800	225	1025	Iron
Grosse vuelglaire	5	7.25	2	4	1151	430	1481	Iron
TOTAL							17178.5	

* Like a bombardelle

106 Extracted from Garnier, pp. 166–70.

A similar contract was made with Jehan Cambier, probably in 1446, to supply gunpowder weapons including the following veuglaires:[107]

Number	Diameter of stone shot *polx*	Length *piez*	Number of chambers	Notes
12	4	4	2	To put on ribaudequins
12	4	4	2	To be loaded at the rear
2	7	7	2	
2	6	6	2	
2	5	5	2	
2	8	8	2	

However, veuglaires could also be quite large. For example, in 1436:

> Item a large iron *veuglaire* furnished with two chambers holding about 25 *livres* of powder.[108]

And similarly:

> Item a large iron *veuglaire* with two chambers, for firing stone shot of eleven *polz* diameter weighing 7,895 *livres*.[109]

The stone shot that this huge piece fired, with a diameter of 11 *polz* (the equivalent to about 25 cm) would have weighed in the region of 22 kg (48 lb). There are also very small veuglaires, not only in the size of shot, but also very short, just 1½ *piez* in length (see below).

Type, material, etc.   Most veuglaires were made from iron, but there are a small number made from copper alloy. Unusually, very few were made from cast iron, for example, in 1440–41:

> A cast-iron *veuglaire* without *bolte*, encased in wood on two wheels, firing stone of five to six *livres*.
> Item, another very small *veuglaire*, firing stone of about three *livres*, encased as above.[110]

Almost all veuglaires were breech loading and supplied with chambers, the majority with two.

An interesting feature of veuglaires is that some of them are referred to in 1443 as being loaded at the rear "in the new fashion":

---

[107] Extracted from Garnier, p. 113.

[108] Item ung gros veuglaire de fer garnis de deux chambres tenant 25 livres de pouldre ou environ (Garnier, p. 163).

[109] Item ung veuglaire de fer à deux chambres, pour tirer onze polz de pierre en croisière pesant 7,895 livres (Garnier, p. 120).

[110] Ung veuglaire de fondue de fer sans bolte, enchassé en bois sur deux rouelles, gectant pierres de cinq à six livres.
Item ung autre plus petit veuglaire, gectant pierre de trois livres ou environ, enchassé comme dessus (Garnier, p. 45 note).

Item other three iron *veuglaires* to fire three and a half *polz* of size, and all six *piez* long, barrel and chamber together, and are of three sorts, each furnished with two chambers to fire two and a half *polz* and three *polz* of stone in lead, and all in the new fashion to load the shot at the rear.[111]

This very intriguing reference is supported by others, in 1445 on a Burgundian galley, for example:

Item five *veuglaires* carrying stone shot of four *poulces* in diameter, each with 3 chambers serving as well one *veuglaire* as another. And each *veuglaire* will be four *piez* long, barrel and chamber, and the stone shot is loaded at the rear.[112]

If the stone shot was loaded from behind this means that the internal diameter at the rear of the veuglaire was the same as that at the front. This is in contrast to some extant guns where there is an internal ring at the rear of the barrel, with the result that the bore at the rear is less than that at the front. This means that the shot could only have been loaded into these guns at the muzzle and not at the rear. That this is called "of the new fashion" appears to indicate that this was a change from muzzle to breech loading, even though it has been assumed that all pieces with separate powder chambers were loaded from the rear.

As well as breech-loading chambered pieces, there is also evidence that some veuglaires were all of one piece and did not have separate powder chambers. An example comes from artillery recorded to be in Luxembourg during the middle of Philip the Good's reign:

Item an iron *veuglaire* of one piece of one and a half *pié* in length encased in wood. Item another of a *pié* and a half long of little value without a chamber. Item two *veuglaires* all of one piece encased in wood.[113]

Intriguingly, there is also an occasional reference to *veuglaires* in more than one piece: Item a small iron *veuglaire* in two pieces, furnished with a chamber, called *le Mátin*.[114]

Makers, suppliers, etc.   The two major suppliers of veuglaires to the Burgundians were Jehan Cambier and J. Quenot.

---

[111]   Item trois autres veuglaires de fer pour tirer trois polz et demi de grosseur, à touz chacun six piez de long voulée et chambre ensemble et sont de trois sortes, chacun fourny de deux chambres pour tirer deux polz et demi et trois polz de pierre en plomb, et tout de la nouvelle façon a bouter la pierre par derrière (Garnier, p. 120).

[112]   Item cinq veuglaires portant pierre de quatre poulces en croixière chacun à 3 chambres servans aussi bien à l'ung des veuglaires que l'autre. Et aura chacun veuglaire quatre piez de long, volée et chambre et se boutera la pierre par derrière (Garnier, p. 176). See also Appendix 3, and Kelly DeVries, "A 1445 Reference to Shipboard Artillery," *Technology and Culture* 31 (1990), 818–29.

[113]   Item ung veuglaire de fer d'une piece d'un pié et demi de long enfusté en bois.
Item ung autre d'ung pié et demi de long qui ne vaut guères sans chambre.
Item deux veuglaires tout d'une pièce enfusté en bois (Garnier, p. 129).

[114]   Item ung petit veuglaire de fer de deux pièces, garni d'une chambre, nommée le Mátin (Garnier, p. 129).

Carriage, mounting, etc.   There are frequent references to veuglaires being encased in wood, and this probably refers to the bed on which a wrought-iron gun was secured with a cut-out at the rear to take a separate powder chamber. Some were mounted on wheels:

> Item another iron *veuglaire* of about two and one half *piez* in length in one piece encased in wood on three wheels.[115]

Like crapaudeaux, veuglaires could also be mounted on ribaudequins:

> And first, six *ribaudequins* equipped with six *veuglaires*, each with two chambers, furnished with pavises, wheels, shafts, wooden tiles.[116]

Ammunition   All veuglaires fired stone shot.

Loading and firing   An interesting account from 1443 refers to a veuglaire being fired continuously during the siege of Villy Castle:

> Item for four large *veuglaires* which fired continously during the said siege to knock down castles and the hoardings that those in the fortress have made, 120 *livres* of powder for firing 300 marble stones.[117]

These four veuglaires must only have used less than half a *livre* of powder per shot.

Surviving Burgundian veuglaires   There are probably only two pieces that can be described as veuglaires in the surviving *Burgunderbeute*:

In Part 4 below	Length		Bore		Booty status
Cat. no 26	66 cm	2 ft 2 in.	14.2 cm	5.6 in.	Murten
Cat. no 27	83 cm	2 ft 8 in.	7.4 cm	2.9 in.	? Booty

The length-to-bore ratios of these two pieces are 4.6 and 11.2, putting them within the range of *veuglaires* from the documentary sources. What is also interesting is that both had to be loaded from the muzzle, an internal ring at the breech preventing the insertion of the shot from the rear.

---

[115] Item ung autre veuglaire de fir d'environ deux piez et demi de long d'une piece enfuste en bois sur trois roes (Garnier, p. 129).

[116] Et premièrement, six ribaudequins estouffez de six veuglaires, chacun à deux chambres, garnis de pavaix, de roes, de limons, d'aisseulx (Garnier, p. 142).

[117] Item pour quatre gros veuglaires qui continuellement tiroient durent ledit siege pour abattre chastaux et estaudis que ceulx de la forteresse faisaient, 120 livres de pouldre pour avoir tiré 300 pierres de mabre (Garnier, p. 134).

RIBAUDEQUIN

Summary

Ribaudequins have attracted a great deal of attention from historians of early artillery. The problem of interpretation turns on whether the term refers to a type of gun or carriage on which guns were mounted.[118] The evidence from the Burgundian accounts supports the thesis that they were a type of carriage on which guns were mounted.

Supporting evidence

Name variants   Ribaudequins, ribeaudequins, baudequins.

Date range   The earliest reference to a ribaudequin is in 1414, with references to them occuring throughout the archives.

Type, materials, etc.   Most of the references in Garnier are to wooden carts, chariots or wheeled machines onto which gunpowder weapons were mounted. For example, in 1414:

> Four small copper *canons* for *ribaudequins* and a cask of cannon powder.[119]

Similarly, in 1446:

> Item fifty-five wooden carts called *ribaudequins*, furnished with shafts, wheels, tables, pavises, and other things which belong to them and also furnished with iron and also chains . . .[120]

And in 1443:

> Another contract made with Désir de Templon and the Perreau brothers living in Namur, carpenters, to make fifty-four *ribaudequins* of woodwork with mantlets furnished and dressed according to the form and manner which they were contracted by my said lord. Each *ribaudequin* made of their carpentry will carry three, four or five *crapaudeaux* whichever the master of artillery will advise to be best. Each *ribaudequin* of four *piez* in base length of good dry wood for the price of four *livres* of 40 *gros*. And my said lord will deliver them wood from his woods, near to the said Namur, in lieu of the dry wood that they deliver. Made the 5th day of November 1443.[121]

---

[118]   See A.V.B. Norman, "Notes on Some Early Representations of Guns and on Ribaudekins," *Journal of the Arms and Armour Society* 8 (1975), 234–27, for a detailed discussion of this question in which he asserts that they are the mount rather than a type of artillery.

[119]   Quatre petiz canons de coyre pour ribeaudequins et une kaque de poudre de canon (Garnier, p. 38).

[120]   Item cinquante cinq charrioz de bois appellés ribaudequins, garnis de limons, roes, tables, pavaix et autres choses qui y appartiennent et aussi garnis de ferrure et liéz ainsi . . . (Garnier, p. 112). [N.B. The manuscript is damaged and incomplete.]

[121]   Autre marchié fait à Désir de Templon et Perreau frères demourant à Namur charpentiers, de faire cinquante quatre ribaudequins de charpentaige avec les manteaux garnis et habillés selon la forme et

And, in 1465:

> . . . four carts, loaded with four *ribaudequins*, on which there are three furnished each
> with two *flaigeoz* and their chambers; as also of wedges and other ironwork necessary
> there and the fourth which has three *flaigeoz* similarly furnished with their chambers,
> wedges and all that is needed.[122]

Finally, in 1439:

> It is necessary to have 120 iron *crapaudeaux* to put on *ribaudequins* of four and a half
> *piez* in length firing stone of two *poulces* in diameter and each furnished with three
> chambers . . .[123]

On the other hand, there are some references that seem to suggest that the *ribaudequin*
is actually the gunpowder weapon itself. For example, in 1419:

> Five little copper-alloy *baudequins* encased in wood each holding a *livre*.[124]

And, again in 1474:

> Made at Dijon four chambers for the two *ribaudequins* at the said castle.[125]

However, these references could simply be shorthand of the scribe or secretary using
the term "for the *ribaudequins*," meaning "for the guns mounted on the *ribaudequins*."
Taking all the evidence together, it seems clear that a *ribaudequin* was a type of cart or
carriage onto which several small guns were mounted.

MATERIALS AND METALLURGY

Contained within the accounts of the Burgundian dukes' artillery there is a great deal
of information about what guns were made from. Basically, as with all artillery until the
nineteenth century, there were three materials from which they could be manufactured: wrought iron, copper alloy, or cast iron.

Wrought iron   Wrought iron contains a variable amount of a non-metallic material,
called slag. Medieval smiths were not able to make wrought iron molten and to pour it

---

manière qui leur a esté baillée par mondit s^r. Chacun ribaudequin fait de leur mestier de charpenterie
portant trois, quatre ou cinq crappaudaulx que par le maistre de L'artillerie leur sera devisé, lequel sera la
mieulx. Chacun ribaudequin de quatre piez de long d'assiette de bon bois sec pour le pris de quatre livres de
40 gros. Et mondit s^r leur doit bailer bois en ses bois, prez dudit Namur en lieu du bois sec qu'ils baillent.
Fait le 5e jour de Novembre 1443 (Garnier, p. 116).

[122]   . . . quatre charettes, chargées de quatre ribaudequins, dont il y en a trois garnis chacun de deux flaigeoz et de
leurs chambers; comme aussi de coings et d'autres ferrures y nécessaires et le quatrième qui est de trois
flaigeoz semblablement garnis de leurs chambres, de coings et de tout ce qu'il fault (Garnier, p. 80). Just
what *flaigeoz* are is unclear and there are only two references to them. Garnier suggests that they are small
pieces like "organ pipes," coulovrines or crapaudeaux for mounting on a ribaudequin (Garnier, p. 254).

[123]   C'est assavoir pour 120 crappaudeaulx de fer à mettre sur ribaudequins de quatre piez et demi de long
portans pierre de deux poulces en croisière et garnis chacun de trois chambres . . . (Garnier, p. 110).

[124]   Cinq petiz baudequins de metal enfustés de bois pourtant chacun une livre (Garnier, p. 67).

[125]   Facon à Dijon de quatre chambres pour les deux ribaudequins étant audit chatel (Garnier, p. 79).

into a mould as they could both copper alloys and cast iron. It is ductile material which possesses high tensile strength and elongation. This means that it can be easily, or relatively easily, worked both hot and cold into a wide variety of shapes and forms. It is also relatively easy to join pieces of wrought iron together by what is technically called pressure welding or, more usually, hammer welding. When heated to the correct temperature, in the region of 1100° C, two pieces of wrought iron can be welded together by simply hitting them with a hammer. In this process the slag in the iron melts and runs over the surface to be joined, preventing oxidation by the air which would otherwise prevent successful welding. If properly carried out the weld is almost as strong as the original metal and is virtually invisible. If not properly done the two pieces might appear to be welded together but the join will break open under stress.

The medieval smith quickly learned to make complex forms of gunpowder weapons from smaller pieces of iron. The technique seems to have been adopted from the very beginning of European gunpowder weapons – building up a barrel from staves of iron with hoops and bands slid over them at red heat so that on cooling they bound the staves together. The technique had enormous advantages for the smith. Complex and large forms could be built up from smaller pieces by the simple techniques that were part and parcel of the smith's repertoire of skills.[126]

Throughout the Burgundian accounts the term "de fer" is understood to mean wrought iron. Interestingly, there are occasional references to specific types of iron – for example, Spanish iron or iron from Lyon. It is clear that at least the iron from Spain was "special" in some way. Though it is not at all clear why, and there is currently no way of determining the reason for this selection of iron, the likeliest reason is better quality. An example is found in 1431:

> Item 5 barrels of Spanish iron.[127]

And in 1447:

> And first thirty *canons* of good Spanish iron, each four *piez* long, chamber and barrel, each furnished with three chambers carrying stone of four *polz* in diameter . . .[128]

Copper alloys Pure copper is relatively soft and not an ideal material for making gunpowder weapons. However, the addition of small amounts of other metals, tin or zinc, make it stronger and tougher. Today these alloys are called brass, made from copper and zinc, and bronze, copper and tin. A complicating factor is the addition of other metals, primarily lead, but also antimony and arsenic for example. In the late medieval and early modern period the difference between these various alloys and metals was not always clear and a number of names were used, the meanings of which are not obvious to us today. In English sources we find bronze and brass but also *latten*, *gun metal* and the word *metal* meaning a copper alloy. In the Burgundian archives we find *arain*, *mitaille*, *métal*, *cuivre* and variants of these words. Whether at the time they

---

[126] For a discussion of medieval wrought iron technology see Robert D. Smith, "The Technology of Wrought-Iron Artillery," *Royal Armouries Yearbook* 5 (2000), 68–79.

[127] Item 5 barreaulx de fer d'Espaigne (Garnier, p. 74).

[128] Et premièrement trente canons de bon fer d'Espaigne, chacun de quatre piez de long chamber et volée, garnis chacun de trois chambers portans pierre de quatre polz en croixère. (Garnier, p. 114).

were as clearly understood is unlikely. It is probable that there was a great deal of confusion both on the part of the founder and even more on the part of the scribe or clerk recording the details in the records. (Because of this uncertainty, the phrase "copper alloy" has been used for the entire range of copper-based alloys.) For example, in 1414:

First the large *bombard* of *coivre* or *arain*, called the *bombard* of Dijon . . .[129]

In 1421:

6 April, two *canons* of *métal* called *veuglaire*.[130]

And in 1422:

9 August, two *canons* of *mitaille* firing 6 or 7 *livres* of stone . . .[131]

Finally, in 1430:

A large *cuivre bombard* called *Prusse*, furnished with its cart and *engin*.[132]

Unlike wrought iron, copper alloys can be heated to the molten state and then poured into pre-prepared moulds, a method used since earliest times to make a very wide range of artefacts from axe heads and brooches to statues and bells. To cast a gun the founder would make an exact full size pattern from which a mould was made into which molten metal was poured. Both the pattern and the mould were destroyed in the process so that each individual gun was unique.

Cast iron   The third and most interesting material is cast iron. Unlike wrought iron, cast iron can easily be heated to the molten state and then poured into a pre-prepared mould like copper alloys. Although seemingly a simple material, basically just iron alloyed with 2–4% carbon, it is very complex and, depending on a number of factors, can exhibit widely different properties.

The widespread use of cast iron for artillery, though very desirable from an economic and strategic standpoint – it was both cheap and widely available – did not occur till the middle years of the sixteenth century when ways were discovered of ensuring that the metal was suitable for making gunpowder weapons. However, its use in gunpowder weapons before the 1540s, though known, is still not clearly understood nor well researched.

Throughout the accounts and records of the Dukes of Burgundy there are guns that are described as being made of *fer fondue*, cast iron, making it clear that cast-iron guns were being made and used in the fifteenth century. For example, in 1415:

6 November, two cast-iron *canons*, two other iron *canons*, throwing stone weighing 8½ *livres*. . .[133]

---

[129] Premièrement la grosse bombarde de coivre ou arain, dite la bombarde de Dijon . . . (Garnier, p. 37).
[130] 6 avril Deux canons de métal appelez Weghelaire (Garnier, p. 44).
[131] 9 août Deux canons de mitaille portant de 6 ou 7 livres de pierre . . . (Garnier, p. 41).
[132] Une grosse bombarde de cuivre appelée Prusse garnie de son cher et de son engine (Garnier, p. 55).
[133] 6 novembre Deux canons de fer de fondue, deux autres canons de fer, gectans pierre pesant 8 livres et demie . . . (Garnier, p. 51).

In 1417:

20 July, a cast-iron *canon*.[134]

In 1431:

Item a small cast-iron *bombardelle*, firing about six *livres* of iron.[135]

And, in 1442:

Item a cast-iron *canon*.[136]

The earliest method for making iron was the bloomery, or single stage, method. Ore was converted to iron in a solid-state process whereby the iron was never in the molten state and the product was wrought iron. During the fifteenth century the process was perfected whereby iron was produced from the ore in liquid form as cast iron, that is iron with a high carbon content. This cast iron was then either used as it was, cast into the shape required, or was reheated and treated to remove the carbon and produce wrought iron, the two stage process. As already outlined above, cast iron is a complex material and its strength and hardness is governed by a large number of variables ranging from the presence of impurities such as sulphur and phosphorus, the amount of carbon present, and the cooling rate of the casting itself. Without close control of these variables the iron produced can be extremely brittle and certainly not suitable for making gunpowder weapons, though it was ideal for making shot and for a wide range of domestic wares. Some time in the late fifteenth century the casting process was perfected and control was close enough to enable the founder to make gunpowder weapons routinely. It is also clear that the place where this technological change was taking place was in northwest France. The whole area of northwestern France and the area of the southern Low Countries was highly industrialised in the fifteenth century and many centres, such as Mons and Malines (Mechelen), had a long tradition of producing arms and artillery. In short, the manufacture of cast-iron gunpowder weapons in the fifteenth century would have been part of the most up-to-date manufacturing process and would probably have originated in the Burgundian lands of northwestern Europe.[137]

SURFACE TREATMENT AND COLOUR

It was not uncommon for pieces of gunpowder artillery at this time to be given a surface treatment, varnish of some kind, or to be coloured. For example, in 1413:

Ten iron *canons* varnished firing stone of 7 to 20 *livres*, 2 hundred [weight] of salt-petre, 1 hundred [weight] of sulphur.[138]

---

134   20 juillet Un canon de fer de fondue (Garnier, p. 40).
135   Item une petite bombardelle de fondue de fer, portant environ six livres de fer (Garnier, p. 73).
136   Item ung canon de fondue de fer (Garnier, p. 148).
137   See Brian G. Awty, "The Origin of the Blast Furnace: Evidence from Francophone Areas," *Historical Metallurgy* 21 (1987), 96–99, and Claude Gaier, *L'industrie et le commerce des armes dans les anciennes principautés Belges du XIIIme à la fin du XVe siècle* (Paris, 1963).
138   Dix canons de fer vernissiez gectans pierre de 7 à 20 livres, 2 cent de sale pester, 1 cent de souffre (Garnier, p. 42).

Again, in 1414:

> An iron *canon* varnished.[139]

Presumably this coating, which seems to have been only applied to iron pieces, was to prevent corrosion or rusting. An interesting reference in 1465 implies that the surface of a *coulovrine* was protected with tin foil or leaf:

> 20 June . . . Two iron coulevrines, one covered with tin leaf, the other painted red and 60 *livres* of powder, sent for the safekeeping of the castle.[140]

Red was not always the chosen colour, as in this reference to two different colours in 1465:

> A white *coulovrine*, one red . . .[141]

Similarly, in 1476–77:

> J. Chandelier, mirror maker, to mark and paint these *serpentines* white and red, 3 *fr.*[142]

Larger guns were also painted, as seen in 1443:

> Item a red iron *veuglaire* without a chamber.[143]

Other materials could also be used to prevent rusting. In 1473–74, for example:

> Purchase of 5 *livres* of grease to grease the four *serpentines*, 2½ *gr.*[144]

Although the number of references is not large it is clear that some guns, at least, were protected from the ravages of the environment by being given a protective coating of varnish or paint and even, in one case, a surface treatment of tin. Of course, today there is little left of these colours. However, it has been reported that when *Mons Meg* was cleaned in the 1980s, traces of red paint were discovered in cracks and crevices of the surface.[145]

MARKS

There are a few occasions when the artillery mentioned in the accounts and registers transcribed by Garnier is noted as having marks of some sort. The largest number of these occurs in 1445–46 when a number of veuglaires, made and delivered by J. Quenot, were received by Philibert de Vauldrey, master of the artillery. Each piece is described in some detail and there is then a note of the mark on the gun itself. These are

---

139   Ung canon de fer vernissié . . . (Garnier, p. 43).
140   20 juin . . . Deux coulevrines de fer, l'une couverte d'une feuille d'étain, l'autre paincturée de rouge et 60 livres de pouldre, envoyés pour la sureté du chateau (Garnier, p. 80).
141   Une couleuvrine blanche, une rouge . . . (Garnier, p. 82).
142   J Chandelier, mirolier, empreint et vernit ces serpentines en coleur blanche et rouge, 3 f. (Garnier, p. 190).
143   Item ung rouge veuglaire de fer sans chambre (Garnier, p. 123).
144   Achat de 5 livres de graisse pour engraisser les quatre serpentines, 2 gr ½ (Garnier, p. 184).
145   Personal communication with Richard Whelander.

all simple geometric forms of marks – simple crosses and combinations of straight or curved lines. For example:

There are also occasional notes of other pieces that were marked. For example, in 1458:

> Tuesday, the 14th day of December 1458. Present Guillaume de Ternay and Jehan de la Grange, of the ordnance of MM. of the Comptes at Dijon, were considering in the house of Phelippe Donet and by the said Phelippe a *canon* chamber belonging to J Quenot the which chamber is painted red and marked on the two ends of the neck, one a right cross at each end and marked at the opening where the fire [match] is placed is another mark, and it weighs 203 *livres* of iron.[146]

Again in 1465:

> One will send him equally a large iron *veuglaire*, furnished with a chamber which is about eight *pieds* long, signed and marked on the barrel just in front of the end and on the main ring of three large arrows of green or red. And on a nozzle attached to the chamber and in the middle of which, a St Andrew's cross was made with arrows of green and between the said cross are four shields stamped on the said neck.[147]

On the same date:

> . . . it is necessary that the barrel has the mark "<>" and the chamber has the sign "W."[148]

It is not uncommon for surviving pieces of wrought-iron artillery to have marks. These are almost exclusively of the very simple sort as described above – geometric forms frequently based on the figure 4 with additional strokes. These are similar to the types of marks on medieval wooden, stone or metal objects.[149] Occasionally these can be ascribed to individuals but, all too often, they are the marks of unknown individuals. It may be, of course, not always the case that these marks are those of the maker of the piece and could be just identifying marks as noted above.

---

[146] Le jeudi 14 jour de decembre 1458 présens Guillaume de Ternay et Jehan de la Grange, de l'ordonnance de MM. Des Comptes à Dijon fut pesée en l'ostel Phelippe Donet et par ledit Phelippe une chamber de canon appartenant à J Quenot, laquelle chamber est vernie de rouge et marquée sur les deux bouts de l'ance, de une croix droicte à chacun bout et emprès le pertuis ou se boute le feu une autre croix droitte et poise 203 livres de fer (Garnier, p. 77).

[147] On lui envoya également ung gros weuglaire de fer, garny de sa chamber qui a de longueur totale environ huit pieds, signé et marqué en la chasse au bout devant d'icelle et sur le principal sercle de trois gros traiz de lyme ou royes. Et sur une ance etant en la chamber et au milieu d'icelle, à une croix St Andrien faiz à traiz de lyme et entre ladite croiz quatre escussons estampés sur ladite ance (Garnier, pp. 80–81).

[148] . . . c'est assavoir la volée à ce saing <> et la chamber à ce saing W (Garnier, p. 81).

[149] F.A. Girling, *English Merchants' Marks: A Field Survey of Marks Made by Merchants and Tradesmen in England between 1400 and 1700* (London, 1964).

POWDER

Summary

References to gunpowder in the Burgundian archives are numerous. Although gunpowder is a simple mixture of saltpetre, sulphur and charcoal, its properties are dependent on a number of factors which, even today, are not clearly understood. In its simplest terms, not only is the actual proportional composition important but, equally vital, is the physical form of the various ingredients, their state and purity, the degree to which they have been ground and, most especially, any treatment to incorporate or corn them.[150] There is a wealth of data to be gleaned from the Burgundian sources and, though not all that might be desired for a more detailed understanding of the gunpowder used in the fifteenth century, it is very indicative of the situation.

As with so many of the terms used it is difficult to be sure just what the contemporary scribe or clerk meant when he used this or that word, so it is with gunpowder. In many references the term "powder" alone is used, but early in the fifteenth century the term "cannon powder" appears, and later, by the 1430s at least, "coulovrine powder" is also referred to. That these two powders were different is clear from the sources, but there is no indication of what this difference was.

---

[150] Recent work by, among others, Gerhard Kramer ("*Das Feuerwerkbuch*: Its Importance in the Early History of Black Powder," in *Gunpowder: The History of an International Technology*, ed. B. Buchanan [Bath, 1996], pp. 45–56) and Bert S. Hall (*Weapons and Warfare in Renaissance Europe: Gunpowder, Technology, and Tactics* [Baltimore, 1997]) has identified the various problems in our understanding of early gunpowder but, has as yet, not been able to push the boundary of our knowledge further. The two areas which seem to be important are the saltpetre and the degree of incorporation or corning. The question of saltpetre is just what the actual chemical composition was. Today we understand saltpetre to be potassium nitrate but nitrates produced in Europe are more likely to be the calcium salt which is highly deliquescent. However, this calcium salt can be easily converted to the potassium salt by the addition of potash in the form of wood ashes. Early treatises and sources make no mention of this step in the process of making saltpetre and it is still in doubt as to exactly when this step was introduced. Without it the saltpetre produced will, at best, spoil quickly and, at worst, not work at all, as recent experimentation has confirmed.

The degree of corning and where and when this step was introduced is also still problematic. Taking the ground mixture – saltpetre, charcoal, and sulphur – and mixing it with a liquid, usually alcohol, vinegar or water, and then drying it produces a more intimate mix of the ingredients and is purported to produce a more powerful propellant. However, corning can take two forms, the first is where the dried wet mixture is ground into a fine powder and the second is where it is formed into granules, corns, of a pre-determined size. The late medieval nomenclature is, as in so many areas, confusing, so the following modern terms will be used.

Rough powder:	Gunpowder made by the simple mixture of powdered saltpetre, sulphur and charcoal.
Meal powder:	Gunpowder made by first mixing the dry, powdered ingredients. These are then dampened by adding water or other liquid, for example alcohol, and further ground together. The resultant paste is then dried and finally ground up into a fine powder.
Fine incorporated powder:	Gunpowder made as for meal powder but when wet it is formed into small granules or corns before it is dried.
Coarse incorporated powder:	Gunpowder made as for meal powder but when wet it is formed into large granules or corns before it is dried.

Information in the Burgundian sources is not, unfortunately, detailed enough to enable us to decide which form of powder is being referred to.

The raw ingredients, saltpetre, sulphur and charcoal, to make powder are frequently noted though there are few direct references to charcoal. Why this is so is unclear and difficult to explain and, though a number of suppositions can be advanced there is no clear and logical reason.[151]

There are also occasional mentions of the equipment to make powder – for example sieves, pestles and mortars. Containers to store and transport powder are frequently noted, mostly various types and sizes of barrels, as well as leather bags or sacks. For loading into guns, there is considerable evidence that by the end of the fifteenth century powder was put into pre-prepared containers. Manuscript illustrations provide a wealth of information relating to the use of specially prepared bags of powder which were transported in boxes. These pre-measured containers could have been loaded into the gun by means of a ladle in the same way as loose powder, and would have considerably simplified and speeded up the process of loading the powder charge.

Supporting evidence

Gunpowder is usually referred to in the Burgundian sources simply as *poudre*. Some time early in the fifteenth century a distinction was made between cannon powder, *poudre à canon*, and powder for handguns, *poudre de coulevrine*.
For example, in 1411:

> Item two casks of cannon powder.[152]

In 1414:

> 6 August. Forty *livres* of powder.[153]

In 1415:

> 16 July. . . 15 *livres* of cannon powder.[154]

In 1436:

> Two casks of cannon powder, one of *coulovrine* powder . . .[155]

And in 1443:

> Item a thousand *livres* of cannon powder
> Item a small barrel which will hold forty *livres* of coulovrine powder.[156]

Some references give the cost of the different types of powder. For instance, in 1443:

---

151 The likeliest is that charcoal could be purchased readily and easily locally though it would still have to be paid for.
152 Item deux quaques de poudre de canon (Garnier, p. 38).
153 6 août. Quarante livres de poudre (Garnier, p. 39).
154 16 juillet . . . 15 livres de poudre à canon (Garnier, p. 39).
155 Deux quaques de poudre de canon, une de poudre de coulovrines . . . (Garnier, p. 160).
156 Item mille livres de poudre de canon
     Item ung petit tonnelet ou il avoit quarante livres de poudre de coulverine (Garnier, p. 124).

Item to Colard Deschamps 676 *livres* of cannon powder at 3 *sols* the *livre*.[157]

And in1447:

> . . . and three thousand six hundred *livres* of powder, half cannon [powder] and the other half coulovrine [powder], a *livre* of each at the price of six *gros* . . .[158]

Considerable quantities of gunpowder are sometimes noted. For example, in 1445:

> Item saltpetre, that found in Luxembourg, which was bought, 11,927 *livres*.
> Item sulphur likewise 8,080 *livres*.
> Item likewise cannon powder, 6,242 *livres*.
> Item likewise *coulovrine* powder 440 *livres*.[159]

And in 1476–77:

> Paid to P. Angelin, powder maker, the sum of 211 *f.*, 2 *gros*, 4 *engrognes* for having made since January 1476/7 to 30 June 14,080 *livres* of cannon powder at the price of 18 *gros* the hundred [weight].[160]

Although gunpowder was frequently bought ready made, its ingredients were also frequently purchased separately. In 1409–10:

> Paid 168 *fr* 10 *s* to Barth de Pietre, spice merchant of Paris, for 800 *livres* of saltpetre and 500 *livres* of sulphur bought in December and taken to the siege before Valexon.[161]

In 1411:

> The last day of September 1411 was discharged in the Chamber of Account at Dijon that M J Chousat, councillor of my Lord, had sent to Paris in three barrels 1,126 *livres* of saltpetre and 380 *livres* of sulphur, the which was delivered to Manus, cannoneer of My Lord, to make cannon powder.[162]

In 1447:

> Item yet again to deliver four thousand five hundred *livres* of saltpetre of Champagne,

[157] Item de Colard Deschamps 676 livres de pouldre de canon à 3 sols la livre (Garnier, p. 125).
[158] . . . et trois milles six cent livres de pouldre, moittié de canon et l'autre moittié de culouvrine, chacune livre l'une portant l'autre au pris de six gros . . . (Garnier, pp. 114–15).
[159] Item salepestre tant trouvé à Luxembourg que d'achat, 11,927 livres.
Item soulfre pareillement 8,080 livres.
Item pareillement pouldre de canon, 6,242 livres.
Item semblablement pouldre de coulverine 440 livres (Garnier, p. 172).
[160] Payé à P. Angelin, ouvrier de poudre, la somme de 211 f. 2 gros 4 engrognes, pour avoir fabriqué depuis le mois de janvier 1476/7 au 30 juin la quantité de 14,080 livres de poudre à canon au prix de 18 gros le cent (Garnier, p. 192).
[161] Payé 168 fr 10 s par à Barth de Pietre, espicier à Paris, pour 800 livres de salepestre et 500 livres de souffre achetées en décembre et menées au siège devant Valexon (Garnier, p. 26 note).
[162] Le derrier jour de septembre 1411 fut deschargée en la Chambre de Comptes à Dijon que M J Chousat, conseiller de Mᵍʳ y envoya de Paris en trois poinceons 1,126 livres de salepestre et 380 livres de soffre, lesquelles furent délivrées à Manus, cannonnier de Mᵍʳ pour en faire poudre de canon (Garnier, p. 37).

all refined and all pressed, to make powder at the price of 18 f the hundred [weight].
Item four thousand five hundred *livres* of sulphur, at the price of 8 *f* 4 *gros* the hundred [weight].
Item a thousand [weight] of charcoal.[163]

Finally, in 1476–77:

Bought 3,092 *livres* of sulphur at 4, 6 and 10 *f* the hundred [weight].
Bought 12,140 *livres* of saltpetre at 10 and 12 *francs* the hundred [weight].
Bought 2,879 *livres* of charcoal of willow and of lime at 20 *gros* the hundred [weight].
Making 3,920 *livres* of powder at the rate of 18 *gros* the hundred [weight].[164]

Utensils to make gunpowder are also mentioned. For example in 1421–22:

Paid different sums to Jacquemart Ladan of Arras for the purchase of cloth to be stretched out to dry the powder which was re-wetted – of two sieves and two tubs to sieve the said powder- and a mortar and two pestles to pound the said powder.[165]

And in 1480–85, for example:

Item a sieve to sift cannon powder.[166]

There are numerous references to powder being used to test guns, and this gives a useful insight into the quantities of powder used in each type of gun. For example, in 1413:

The 24 October 1413. Delivered to Germain de Givry, governor of the Duke's artillery, a cask of powder weighing 216 *livres*, to be taken to Auxonne to prove the *canons* and *bombards*, newly taken to the said place, which trial My Lord the Duke had commanded J Chousat, his councillor, to make. That is to say:
For the *bombard* of *Valecon* (Dijon), 36 *livres*
For *Gueriette*, 28 *livres*
For *Liete*, 24 *livres*
For the *bombard* called Sister *Gueriete* and her companion each 18 *livres*
For *Senelle*, 36 *livres*
For 10 *canons* with three chambers, 30 *livres*[167]

---

163 Item doit encore livrer quatre mille cinq cent livres de salepestre de Champaigne tout affiné et tout prest, pour faire pouldre audit pris de 18 f. le cent.
Item quatre mille cinq cent livres de soulfre, au pris de 8 f. 4 gros le cent.
Item ung millier de charbon (Garnier, p. 117).
164 Achat de 3,092 livres de souffre à 4, 6 et 10 f. le cent
Achat de 12,140 livres de saltpetre à 10 et 12 francs le cent
Achat de 2,879 livres de charbon de saulce et de thillot à 20 gros le cent.
Facon de 3,920 livres de poudre à raison de 18 gros le cent (Garnier, p 189)
165 Payé differentes sommes à Jacquemart Ladan d'Arras pour achat de toile destinée à estendre et seichier de la pouldre qui etoit remoistiée – de deux tamis et deux cuviers à tamiser ladite poudre – d'un mortier et de deux pesteaulx à estamper ladite poudre (Garnier, p. 91).
166 Item une saye à sasser pouldre de canon (Garnier, p. 230).
167 Le 24 octobre 1413. Il fut delivré à Germain de Givry, gouverneur de L'artillerie du duc, une caque de poudre, pesant 216 livres pour icelle mener à Auxonne, pour assaier les canons et bombardes nou vellement menées audit lieu et que Monseigneur le duc avait mandé a J Chousat, son conseiller, de faire traire. C'est

Powder was supplied in a variety of containers – barrels of various types and leather bags – as in 1392–93:

> Item a *poinson* full of cannon powder weighing about 9 *sextiers*.[168]

In 1433:

> 23 September. Six *livres* of powder in a bag of white leather which cost 43 *sols* 9 *d*.[169]

And in 1443:

> From Bernart d'Eschenon glover of Lille six large leather sacks in which to put cannon powder.[170]

The transportation of powder necessitated both carts and horses. In 1474, for example:

> Item to take thirty casks of powder at the rate of each cart five casks making six carts which need 24 horses.[171]

AMMUNITION

Summary

There are three basic types of ammunition referred to in the fifteenth century, stone, lead and iron. Of these the greatest number were made from stone. Smaller calibre guns, especially handguns, fired lead shot, called *plommées*. Cast-iron shot, sometimes called *plommées de fer*, only occurs towards the end of the century. There are also, although only very occasionally, references to composite shot, which was made of more than one material.

Stone shot

Name variants   Stone shot is generally referred to simply as *pierre* – stone. Sometimes this is qualified by the type of gunpowder weapon, as in *pierre de canon* or *pierre de bombard*, but it is more often just *pierre*.

---

assavoir:
Pour la bombarde de Valecon (Dijon), 36 livres
Pour Gueriette, 28 livres
Pour Liete, 24 livres
Pour la bombarde dite: Fille Gueriete et pur sa compaigne chacune 18 livres
Pour Senelle, 36 livres
Pour dix canons à trois chambres, 30 livres (Garnier, pp. 57–58).

[168] Item ung poinson plain de pouldre de canon tenant environ 9 sextiers (Garnier, p. 15).
[169] 23 septembre. Six livres de pouldre en un sac de cuir blanc qui content 43 sols 9 d. (Garnier, p. 44).
[170] De Bernart d'Eschenon gantier à Lille six grans sacs de cuir à mettre pouldre de canon (Garnier, p. 127).
[171] Item pour mener trente cacques de pouldre à compter sur chacum chariot cinq cacques feront six chariots qui font 24 chevaulx (Garnier, p. 179).

Date range Stone shot is referred to in all Burgundian sources and was used throughout the reign of the Valois dukes.[172]

Size Where the size of stone shot is stated, it is normally given not by weight, but by diameter. For example, in 1443:

> Item a great iron *veuglaire* with two chambers, for firing stone shot of eleven *polz* diameter weighing 7,895 *livres*.[173]

Manufacture Stone shot was made and prepared by stonemasons who used hammers, chisels and gauges, as in 1431:

> Three masons from Chalon who worked for three days to cut stone shot for *veuglaires* and *bombards*, at the cost of 10 *blancs* each per day.[174]

In 1419–20:

> Purchase of 8 hammers and six iron pecks to cut sandstone shot.[175]

And in 1431:

> Item 96 masons' hammers as many large as small.
> Item 55 iron masons' chisels.[176]

Carving stone shot to the correct diameter was, of course, very important and various gauges were used. In 1420–21:

> Paid 8 *sols* to J. Labbé, smith, for making three iron rings to take measurements of stone shot of *canon*.[177]

And, again in 1431:

> Item 6 iron gauges [moulds] to cut *bombard* stone shot.[178]

Not having the correct size of stone shot could damage the barrel of a gunpowder weapon, as shown by the following reference from the first decade of the fifteenth century:

> Eighteen masons were continually employed on cutting, rough-hewing, and

---

[172] In actual fact, stone was used as a material for making shot from the very earliest use of gunpowder artillery until well into the seventeenth century – particularly in some types of guns at sea.

[173] Item ung veuglaire de fer à deux chambres, pour tirer onze polz de pierre en croisière pesant 7,895 livres (Garnier, p. 120).

[174] Trois maçons de Chalon travaillèrent pendant trois jours à tailler les pierres des veuglaires et des bombardes, au prix de 10 blancs chacun par jour (Garnier, p. 54).

[175] Achat de 8 marteaulx et six becquoirs de fer, pour tailler pierres de grès (Garnier, p. 87).

[176] Item 96 marteaulx à macon que granz que petit.
Item 55 ciseaulx de fer à macon (Garnier, pp. 73–74).

[177] Payé 8 sols à J. Labbé fevre, pour la facon de trois cercles de fer à prendre mesures de pierres de canon (Garnier, p. 91).

[178] Item 6 moles de fer à tailler pierres de bombarde (Garnier, p. 74).

finishing stone shot for *bombards*, *canons*, and *engins*, which were brought from the adjacent quarries and which were only roughed out in long logs, reduced, and hit to fit well and cleanly, so that when they leave the said *bombards*, they do not break them. And in working from 2 October to 2 January, they made 1,600 stone shot, of which the three parts were cut to the patterns [gauges] of the large *bombards* of Bourgogne and of Chalon; to the two great *bombards* of Vergy which were broken, of which the one was of iron and the other of copper; of the *bombard* of Dijon and of Villars which were similarly broken, the one of Modon, of Pagny, and of other small *bombards*.[179]

This also indicates just how long it took to make shot. Assuming that the eighteen masons worked for six days each week then they must have made just over one shot per day.

Further information on making stone shot can be found in this reference from 1421:

Purchase of a hundred [weight] of iron, of which was made fourteen steel hammers with a *quarteron* of steel, to make round, and gauge the stone shot of *bombards*, *canons* and *veuglaires* at the siege of St.-Riquier.

Refacing, rehafting, and repairing the points of the said hammers 103 times from 6 to 29 August 1421.

Purchase and making of two planks to make the patterns [gauges] of stone shot for *canons*.

Purchase of twelve wheel hubs on which were made round the said stone shot.

Payment for ten masons for 21 days, cutting 250 stone *canon* shot of many sizes, at 4 *sols* per day.[180]

This account makes very clear just how stone shot were manufactured and confirms the rate at which they were made, just over one shot per day. The wheel hubs were presumably used as a form of simple turntable to enable the craftsman to ensure that the stone was made properly spherical. From the number of times that their tools needed re-sharpening and mending, it is also clear that the tools used were well used.

Occasionally, the cost of buying individual shot is given. For example, in 1431:

Making of 44 stone shot for the four *veuglaires*, 21½ *gr*.[181]

---

[179]   Dix-huit maçons furent continuelment employés pour taillier, effaitier et afflorer les pierres des bombardes, canons et engins, amenées des carrières voisines et qui n'étaient seulement qu'ébauchées en billes longues, les diminuer et batter à l'allée bien et nettement, affin que au partir desdites bombardes, elles ne les rompissent. Et en ont affaitié depuis le 2 octobre au 2 janvier, 1,600 pierres, dont les trois parts étaient taillliées aux patrons des grosses bombardes de Bourgogne et de Chalon, des deux grosses bombardes de Vergy qui furent despeciez, dont l'une estoit de fer et l'autre du cuivre; de la bombarde de Dijon et de Villars qui furent semblablement rompues, de celles de Modon, de Pagny et d'autres petites bombardes (Garnier, p. 29).

[180]   Achat d'un cent de fer, dont il a été fait quatorze marteaux acérés avec un quarteron d'acier, pour faire arondir et amoysonnir les pierres des bombardes, canons et veuglaires au siege de St-Riquier.
Reffacon, rechaussement et remise à point desdites marteaux par 103 fois depuis le 6 au 29 aout 1421.
Achat et facon de deux ais pour faire les patrons des pierres de canons.
Achat de douze moyeux de roués, sur les quels on a arrondi lesdites pierres.
Paiement des diz macons qui durent 21 jours, taillerent 250 pierres de canon de plusiers moisons, à 4 sols par jour (Garnier, p. 92).

[181]   Facon de 44 pierres pour les quatre veuglaires, 21 gr ½ (Garnier, p. 54).

The low cost of these shots might possibly indicate that they were already partly prepared and this payment was just for finishing.

There are also references to the stone from which these shot were made – mostly marble, though sandstone is also noted, as above. For example, in 1439–45:

> Item 10,075 marble stones for *veuglaires* and *crapaudeaux* mentioned above, at the price of 8 *d.* the piece, sum 339 *livres 7 sols 6 deniers*.[182]

Similarly, in 1443:

> Item 50 marble stone shot for great *bombards* which the said people of Bruges took to Sluys.[183]

Plommées

Lead shot, *plommée*, is the second most frequent type of ammunition mentioned in the Burgundian sources.

Name variants Lead shot are usually called *plommées*, *plomées*, or *plombées*. Occasionally they are referred to as *billettes de plomb* or as *perrettes*. For example, in 1443:

> Item *billettes de plomb* appertaining to the said *coulouvrines* and *crapaudeaux*.[184]

Date range The earliest reference is in 1368–69 when an account of Thevenin Vurry mentions *plommées* made from tin:

> Paid to Perrenin du Pont who supplied for two *canons* five *livres* of powder, fourteen *garroz*, and twelve *plommées* of tin which he made and delivered to the said siege, 4 *livres* 10 *sols*.[185]

From this time and throughout the fifteenth century *plommées* are continuously mentioned among artillery and other munitions. For example, in 1443:

> Item a thousand [weight] of *plommées* for *coulovrines*, as many large as small.[186]

Size On the whole, *plommées* were used in coulovrines and smaller gunpowder weapons though there are references to them also being used in larger pieces, as in 1444:

> Two iron *veuglaires* of about four *piez* long furnished with four chambers holding two *livres* of lead.[187]

---

182 Item 10,075 pierres de marbre pour servir aux veuglaires et crappaudeaulx dessus dits, au pris de 8 d. la piece, valent 339 livres 7 sols 6 deniers (Garnier, p. 120).
183 Item cinquante pierres de marbre de grosses bombardes que lesdits de Bruges menèrent devant l'Ecluse (Garnier, p. 122).
184 Item les billettes de plomb appartenant ausdites coulouvrines et crappaudeaulx (Garnier, p. 121).
185 Payé à Perrenin du Pont qui dehu lui estoient pour deux canons et cinq livres et demie de poudre, quatorze garroz et douze plombées d'estain qu'il fit avoir et bailla audit siege: 4 livres 10 sols (Garnier, p. 7).
186 Item ung millier de plombées pour coulouvrines que grans que petiz (Garnier, p. 123).
187 Deux Weuguelaires de fer d'environ quatre piez de long garnis de quatre chambres portans deux livres de plomb (Garnier, p. 50).

However, these references are unusual and the majority of *plommées* were made and supplied for smaller gunpowder weapons.

Individual weights of *plommées* are rarely, if ever, noted but occasionally it is possible to work out from the information given the weight of a single shot. For example, in 1432–33:

> Paid to J. de Champlitte, merchant of Dijon, the sum of 4½ f. for 25 *livres* of lead which were used to make 400 *plommées* for the *coleuvres* taken to Auxerre and for 50 *livres* of wax in candles taken with the said artillery.[188]

If the 25 *livres* of lead were used to make 400 *plommées* then each one weighed 0.0625 *livre* or about 30 g (1.1 oz). However, it is also clear that larger *plommées* were also made, as in 1473–74:

> Item 200 lead *plommées* . . . the said *plommées* weighing 505 *livres*.[189]

Each *plommée* in this case weighed just over 2½ *livres* each. However, the majority of references do not specify any weight. For instance, in 1431, there is this rather intriguing reference:

> Item 37 large iron *plombées* firing *plommées* of lead.[190]

Manufacture   Although *plommées* were purchased ready made, lead was often acquired in large quantities to be cast into *plommées*. For example, in 1443:

> . . . 1,600 *livres* of lead to make *plommées*.[191]

However, much smaller quantities are also noted, as in 1446–47:

> 10 *livres* of lead to make *plombées*.[192]

Frequently, coulovrines were purchased or noted with supplies of lead to make shot. For example, in 1430:

> Two iron *coleuvres* and 6 *livres* of lead.[193]

Plommées were made by pouring molten lead into a mould. Occasionally, there are references to these moulds, for example in 1443:

> Eight moulds to make *plommée* as many for *crapaudeaux* as for *coulovrines*.[194]

---

[188] Payé à J. de Champlitte, M^d à Dijon, la somme de 4 f. ½ pour 25 livres de plomb dont il a été fait 400 plombées pour les coleuvres menées au voyage d'Auxerre et pour 50 livres de suif en chandelled menées avec ladite artillerie (Garnier, p. 98).

[189] Item 200 plommées de plomb . . . lesdites plommées pesans 505 livres. (Garnier, p. 187)

[190] Item 37 grosses plombées de fer gectant plombées de plomb (Garnier, p. 73). Presumably *grosses plombées de fer* were iron guns which fired lead shot.

[191] . . . 1,600 livres de plomb a faire plombées (Garnier, p. 126).

[192] 10 livres de plomb pour faire les plombées (Garnier, p. 78).

[193] Deux coleuvres de fer et 6 livres de plomb (Garnier, p. 43).

[194] Huit moles a faire plombées, tant pour crappaudeaulx que pour coulovrines (Garnier, p. 126).

Again, in 1436:

> . . . nine stone moulds to make *plommées* for *coulovrines*.[195]

Other tools necessary for the casting of lead into shot are also sometimes noted, as at the siege of Crotoy in 1437:

> Item two large iron ladles to cast lead to make *plommées*.[196]

And again in 1436:

> Six iron ladles to melt lead to make *plommées* for *crapaudeaux* and *coulovrines*.[197]

An enigmatic reference implies that there were possibly two sorts of *plommées* though the difference is not explained:

> Item 600 small *plommées* of two sorts, for the *coulovrines* and 400 also of two sorts, for the *crapaudeaux*.[198]

Another intriguing reference to *plommées* in 1476–77 implies that a type of lead shot was being made with a piece of iron inside it:

> Making of 2,000 *plommées*, 6 *f.* and purchase of 600 *livres* of iron to make cubes to put in *plommées*.[199]

This may explain what is meant in this 1473–74 reference:

> Item 200 lead *plommées*, some of which have iron inside, for the said *serpentines*, the said *plommées* weighing 505 *livres*.[200]

The implication from this is that the lead was cast around a piece of iron. In the sixteenth century so-called composite shot is well known from both documentary sources and from archaeological excavation, most notably from the wreck of the *Mary Rose* of 1545.[201]

A further unusual lead shot was a composite of lead and stone, as seen in the following reference from 1443:

> Item other three iron *veuglaires* to fire three and a half *polz* of size . . . each furnished with two chambers to fire two and a half *polz* and three *polz* of stone in lead . . .[202]

---

[195] . . . neuf moles de pierre à faire ploⅿées pour coulovrines (Garnier, p. 154).

[196] Item deux grans louches de fer à faire fondre plomb, pour faire plombées (Garnier, p. 141).

[197] Six cuillers de fer à fonder plomb pour faire plombées à crappaudeaulx et coulovrines (Garnier, p. 154).

[198] Item de 600 de petites plombées de deux façons, selon les coulovrines et 400 aussi de deux façons, selon les crappaudeaulx (Garnier, p. 159).

[199] Façon de 2,000 de plombées, 6f. et achat de 600 livres de fer pour faire billes à mettre es plombées (Garnier, p. 194).

[200] Item 200 plommées de plomb esquelles a du fer deans, servans esdites serpentines, lesdites plommées pesans 505 livres (Garnier, p. 187).

[201] Robert Walker, Richard Dunham, Alexzandra Hildred, and Margaret Rule, "Analytical Study of Composite Shot from the Mary Rose," *Journal of Historical Metallurgy Society* 23.2 (1989), 84–90.

[202] Item trois autres veuglaires de fer pour tirer trois polz et demi de grosseur . . . chacun fourny de deux chambres pour tirer deux polz et demi et trois polz de pierre en plomb . . . (Garnier, p. 120).

Cast-iron shot

There are very few references to iron shot and most of these appear towards the end of the fifteenth century. However, there are a very few early references, for example in 1431:

> Item a small cast-iron *bombardelle*, firing about six *livres* of iron.[203]

It is not till the 1470s that there are frequent references to cast-iron shot. For example:

> 1474. Sixty iron shot made for the garrison at the castle.[204]

Similarly, in 1478–79:

> Paid to Simon Mahenard, master of the forge of Diénay, the sum of 36 *l.* for the delivery of 127 shot, shot of cast-iron for the great *colevrine* called *la Gouvernante* each of the said shot weighing 16 *livres* of iron.[205]

Again, in 1478–79:

> Paid to Anthoine de Maison, master iron forger of Beze, the sum of 140 *l.* for 43 large cast-iron shot, for the *canons* taken to the king, and 203 small cast-iron shot, for the great *coulovrines Gouvernante*, *Champaigne* and *Jonvelle*, which weigh all together 7,000 *livres* at the rate of 20 *l. t.* the thousand [weight].[206]

Moreover, it is only from this time that large quantities of iron shot were purchased. For example in 1478:

> Bought from J. Servant, merchant of Troyes, for 500 *l. t.* of 20,000 cast-iron shot for the *coulevrines*.[207]

Bolts

Although bolts, *garros*, were a common form of ammunition in the fourteenth century there are very few references to them in the Burgundian sources. In 1362, for example, guns to fire bolts were purchased at Troyes:

> . . . two *canons* to fire bolts.[208]

---

[203] Item une petit bombardelle de fondue de fer, portant environ six livres de fer (Garnier, p. 73).
[204] *1474. Soixante plombées de fer mises en garnison au chateau* (Garnier, p. 79).
[205] Payé à Simon Mahenard, maistre de la forge de Diénay, la somme de 36 l. pour la délivrance de 127 pierres, de boulets de fer de fondue pour servir à la grosse colevrine appelée la Gouvernante pesant chascune desdites pierres 16 livres de fer (Garnier, p. 198).
[206] Payé à Anthoine de Maison, maistre forgeron de Beze, la somme de 140 l. pour 43 gros boulets de fer fondu, servans aux canons amenés de devers le roi, et 203 petits boulets de fer fondu, servant aux grosses couleuvrines Gouvernante, Champaigne et Jonvelle, lesquels pèsant ensemble 7,000 livres au pris de 20 l. t. le millier (Garnier, p. 199).
[207] Achat de J. Servant, marchand à Troyes, moyennant 500 l. t. de 20,000 boulets de fer servant aux coulevrines (Garnier, p. 206).
[208] . . . deux quanons à gitter garroz (Garnier, p. 7).

And in 1368, an inventory lists:

> . . . two *canons* and five and a half pounds of powder, forty bolts and 12 *plommées* of "tin."[209]

From other sources, it is clear that gunpowder-propelled bolts were wooden arrows with iron tips and copper-alloy flights.[210]

Fusées

Although stone, lead, and cast iron were the main types of shot used there is one further type of ammunition that should be noted, the *fusée*. From the accounts and references it is clear that the *fusée* was a type of "shell" filled with combustible material and fired at the enemy. The first mention of them is in 1412 taken to the siege of Chinon:

> . . . 25 *fusées* to throw Greek fire . . .[211]

The actual shell itself, the *fusée*, was normally cast, as for example, noted in 1443:

> Item 10 cast shot with which to throw Greek fire to set on fire towns and castles. Item fifteen cast shot to throw Greek fire that the said people of Bruges took to Sluys.[212]

From these references it would appear that the *fusées* were filled with a combustible material, which was called Greek fire in the late Middle Ages. But in 1431 a recipe exists which describes what a *fusée* was filled with:

> Payment of 20 *t. s.* to J. Quenot, metalworker in Dijon, to make 26 *fers*, to make *fusées* for the use of the said artillery. Bought from Jacot de Roches, artilleryman, two *onces* of camphor, one *livre* of *eau de vie*, two *livres* of powder, two *livres* of saltpetre, four *livres* of sulphur and an ell of fustian to make 26 *fusées*.[213]

The cost of these *fusées* was quite high. In 1419–20, for example:

> To J. Regnaut for the material and making of 200 *fusées* . . . 46 f. 13 s. 8 d.[214]

---

[209] . . . *deux canons et cinq livres et demie de poudre, quatorze garroz et douze plombées d'estain* (Garnier, p. 7).

[210] An account for making bolts in Saint-Omer in 1342 is published in Napoleon and Favé, III:77–78, n. 1 (volume by Favé alone). See also Robert D. Smith, "The Reconstruction and Firing Trials of a Replica of a 14th-Century Cannon," *Royal Armouries Yearbook* 4 (1999), pp. 92–93.

[211] . . . *25 fusées à geter le feu grioiz* . . . (Garnier, p. 43).

[212] Item dix pierres de fondue dont on tire feu grégeois pour bruler villes et chasteaulx
Item quinze pierres de fondue à getter feu gregeois que lesdites de Bruges menèrent devant l'Ecluse (Garnier, p. 122).

[213] Paiement de 20 t. s. à J. Quenot, serrurier à Dijon, pour la facon de 26 fers, pour faire fusées pour le fait de ladite artillerie. Achat par Jacot de Roches, artilleur, de deux onces de canfre, une livre d'eau de vie, deux livres de poudre, deux livres de saltpêtre, quatre livres de souffre et une aune de futaine pour faire lesdits 26 fusées (Garnier, p. 74 note). It is worth noting that these constituents were normal at this period for making 'fireworks' and other combustible mixtures.

[214] A J. Regnaut pour les estoffes et facon de 200 fusées portans feu . . . 46 f. 13 s. 8 d. (Garnier, p. 87).

Just how large *fusées* were is never noted nor is the method by which they were thrown. It is possible that they were not meant to be fired from non-gunpowder artillery weapons but were thrown by hand or shot from crossbows.

CARRIAGES AND TRANSPORT

Summary

It is difficult from the archival sources transcribed by Joseph Garnier to gain any detailed picture of the form and construction of carriages during the fifteenth century. Although there are recorded many payments and references to parts and accessories for carriages, there is little from which a picture of carriages can be assembled. Again, the obscure medieval technical vocabulary is not easy to understand. There are other sources, some of a later date, which, together with Burgundian references, help to clarify the mounting and transport of early gunpowder weapons.

Bombards

It is clear that bombards were transported by means of special large carts. In 1411, for example:

> Bought at Besançon a large iron-bound cart on four great wheels on which was taken the said *bombard*, 15 *fr*. 9 *gr*.[215]

They were loaded onto and off these carts by means of a device called an *engin*. No details of the form of these devices are to be found in the Burgundian archives, but it is likely that they were similar to the three-legged cranes illustrated in various contemporary manuscripts and treatises. These devices were made from wood and used a rope and pulley arrangement. For example, in 1429–30:

> Purchase of four small iron chains for the *engin* of the *bombard*.
> Making of the *engin* of wood, 5 *fr*.
> Purchase of a rope for the *engin*, weighing 38 *livres* at 12 *d*. the *livre*, costing 24 *gros* 15 *d*. and of a copper pulley for the said rope, weighing 41 line, 2½ *fr*.[216]

These *engins* could be bound with iron, for example in 1433:

> A wooden *engin* to lift the great *bombards*, paid 6 *f* to J. Courtillem, carpenter of Dijon, the which was bound with iron by J. Quenot and the ironwork weighed a

---

[215] Achat à Besançon d'un gros char ferré a quatre grosses roes sur lequel on a mené ladite bombarde, 15 fr. 9 gr. (Garnier, p. 31).

[216] Achat de quatre petites chainnes de fer servant à l'engin d'icelle bombarde.
Facon de l'engin de bois, 5 fr.
Achat d'une corde servant à l'engin, pesant 38 livres à 12 d. la livre, valant 24 gros 15 d., et d'une polie de cuivre servant à ladite corde, pesant 41 l. 2 fr. ½ (Garnier, p. 64).

hundred and twenty *livres* of iron which cost 6 *francs*.
A great rope serving the above mentioned *engin* weighing fifty *livres*.[217]

However, just how the *engine* was constructed and operated is impossible to determine from the written sources, as the following from 1433 demonstrates:

> Item for a great iron peg and the key also of iron to put in the pulley of the *engin* of the said *bombard* and for two iron links which were seated the length of two pins and also for eight iron wheels which were put between the wheels and the *eusse* of the carts of the said *bombard*. For these three parts weighing together 98 *livres* of iron a 12 *s. tournois* the *livre*, by contract made by the said Jehan de Gray value 4 *fr.* 10 *gr* 3 *s*.[218]

Bombards apparently did not remain on their carriages during firing, but were laid on the ground and secured by means of wooden abutments. In 1429–30, for example:

> Purchase of a large wooden block to mount the *bombard* 16½ g, of one other piece of wood to put behind the said block.[219]

Other gunpowder weapons

Apart from the bombard, other gunpowder artillery pieces seem most often to have been mounted on wooden beds to which they were secured by iron bands. These were then commonly mounted on wheels or occasionally on a turning pivot. This occurred quite early, for example, in 1376–77:

> To Guiot Baudot of Chalon for the sale of a large block of wood where the one encases the said *canon*, 6 *gros*.[220]

And, in 1409:

> The making of a great wooden cart bound with large iron bands of iron of Lyon, each band weighing twelve *livres*, furnished with great double nails. – Bound the axles with iron all around, so that they are stronger. Made for the same great esses of iron. – Made for the cart a great iron peg called the *symosour*. – Two large transverse iron pegs. – Made for the four ends eight large iron links, so that they would not break off. – Made for the same cart four iron pegs called the four *ortours*, two pegs lengthwise, four great shafts for the use of the horses and all other things necessary to the said force.[221]

---

[217] Un engin de bois a lever les grosses bombardes, acheté 6 f. a J. Courtillem, charpentier à Dijon, lequel a été ferré par J. Quenot et pese la ferrure six vingt livres de fer qui a costé 6 francs.
Une grosse corde servant à l'engin ci-dessus pesant cinquante livres (Garnier, p. 66)

[218] Item pour une grosse cheville de fer et la clef aussi de fer pour mettre en la polie de l'engin de ladite bombarde et pour deux chenons de fer qui furent assiz du long des deux aissiz et aussi pour huit rouelles de fer qui furent mises entre les roes et l'eusse des charioz de ladite bombarde. Pour ces trois parties pesans ensemble 98 livres de fer a 12 s. tournois la livre, par marché fait par ledit Jehan de Gray valant 4 fr. 10 g. 3 s. (Garnier, p. 102)

[219] Achat d'un gros plot de bois pour affuter la bombarde 16 g ½, d'une antre piece de bois pour metre derrière ledit plot (Garnier, p. 64).

[220] A Guiot Baudot de Chalon pour la vendue d'ung gros plot de bois ou lon (a) enchassez ledit canon, 6 gros (Garnier, p. 9).

[221] Façon d'un gros char de bois ferré de grosses bandes de fer de Lyon, chacune bande pesant douze livres,

Carriages on which gunpowder weapons were mounted are occasionally noted to be able to be turned on pivots. For example, in 1443:

> Item four *crapaudeaux* with eight chambers, mounted on four wooden engines turning on pivots.[222]

That it is the wooden mountings that turn is made clear from the following reference, again from 1443:

> Item three wooden *engins* turning on pivots without *crapaudeaux*.[223]

LOADING, AIMING, AND FIRING

There is little direct evidence from the Burgundian archives about the loading, aiming, and firing of artillery in this period.

For breechloading gunpowder weapons, the powder chamber would have been filled with powder and the chamber sealed with a wooden tompion hammered into place. Either the chamber was then placed into the bed behind the barrel secured in place by a transverse wedge and the ball loaded from the muzzle, or the ball was first loaded into the rear of the barrel before the powder chamber was similarly secured in place. Around 1445 this latter sequence is referred to as "the new fashion," implying that the former was the normal method of loading before then.[224]

For muzzle-loading gunpowder weapons, the powder was either loaded loose with a ladle or in pre-measured "cartridges," again with the use of a ladle before the shot was loaded. Although it is likely that a tampion was also used, there is no evidence to support this assumption.

Early in their history there is little direct evidence for how gunpowder weapons were aimed at their targets. Late fifteenth-century illustrations show a variety of elevation devices as part of the carriage on which the gun was mounted. And, indeed, many extant gunpowder weapons have a rudimentary sight at the muzzle.

It is clear from the frequent references to mantlets and pavises accompanying gunpowder weapons that these were used to protect the weapon and its operators. Such is confirmed by contemporary illustrations.

Finally, there is little, if any, information about the method of ignition – whether by match or by hot iron. Pictorial evidence would suggest that a heated iron rod was the preferred method of firing, but this is pure conjecture. Again, the sources are silent.

garnies de granz cloux doubles. – Ferré les assis de grands fers prenans tout autour, affin qu'ils soient plus forts. Fait en iceulx quatre gros esses de fer. – Fait au char une grosse cheville de fer appellée le symosour. – Deux grandes chevilles de fer traversaines. – Fait es quatre bouts huit gros lyens de fer, affin qu'ils ne fandissent. – Fait en icellui chert quatre chevilles de fer appellées les quatre ortours, deux chevilles en la longe, quatre grosses escaleurs pour aployer les chevaulx et toutes autres choses nécessaires à la force d'icellui (Garnier, p. 27 note).

222 Item quatre crappaudaulx à huit chambres, estans sur quatre engines de bois tournans sur pivoz (Garnier, p. 121).

223 Item trois engins de bois tournans sur pivoz sans crappaudeaulx (Garnier, p. 122).

224 See, for example, Garnier, p. 120.

PERSONNEL

The Burgundian archival records transcribed by Garnier give a good impression of the various officials responsible for the artillery under the Burgundian dukes and many of these are named, though their exact function is often unclear and their titles often change throughout the years. Apart from the officials who compiled the inventories and accounts of the duke there is little information about the personnel who actually loaded and fired the guns on campaign. However, an indication of just what was required is contained in a list of the materiel and personnel ordered from the town of Lille as part of the first campaign to Lorraine of Charles the Bold, duke of Burgundy, in 1475. Lille was, at this time, the seat of the financial administration of Artois and thus one of the main administrative centres of the dukes of Burgundy. It also seems to have held the main arsenal of gunpowder weapons for the Burgundian lands in this area, especially as the southern Low Countries so frequently rose in rebellion.[225]

To fire the 6 *bombards*	6 master bombardiers
To fire the 6 *bombardelles*	6 other cannoneers or bombardiers
for the 6 *mortars*	6 cannoneers
for the 9 *courtaux* and the 15 large *serpentines*	20 others [cannoneers]
for the medium and small *serpentines*	40 others [cannoneers]
to fire the *arquebuses*	50 couloviniers
	14 cannoneers' aides and bombardiers

Bombardiers are listed to fire the bombards and cannoneers the other large guns though just what extra was needed to fire the bombards that a cannoneer could not do is not stated. Although not listed in the table above, this source makes clear that a great number of other men were needed to help with the gunpowder weapons, especially for their movement and transport, including carpenters, carters, armourers, tent erectors, pioneers, farriers, masons and founders.

SHIPS

Included in the various Burgundian archival documents are some that mention the armament of ships, making clear that at a fairly early date that various types of gunpowder weapons were being placed on board Burgundian naval vessels. In many cases the ships were used simply as transports, to take armaments, including gunpowder weapons to sieges – such as the ship bound from Sluys in 1440 – or to other destinations – such as the five galleys which carried the arms dowry from Duke Philip the Good to Scotland for the marriage of his grand-niece, Mary of Guelders, to James II.[226] However, one reference specifically records the gunpowder weapons to be used as

---

225 See Smith, "Good and Bold," pp. 98–105, where the full inventory and commentary are published.
226 On the ship departing from Sluys see Garnier, pp. 132–33, and on the arms dowry see Garnier, pp. 130–31,

artillery on board the vessel, a ship bound for the Mediterranean to fight the Ottomans in 1445:

> Item five *veuglaires*, firing stone of four *poulces* in diameter, each with 3 chambers, and the said chambers serving as well the one *veuglaire* as another. And each *veuglaire* will be four *piez* long, barrel and chamber, and the stone is to be loaded from the rear.
> Item two *coulovrine*, turning on pivots, each with three chambers, each chamber serving the one as another.
> Item twelve other *coulovrines* to be held by hand.[227]

and "A 15th-Century Weapons Dowry: The Weapons Dowry of Duke Philip the Good of Burgundy for the Marriage of Mary of Guelders and James II of Scotland in 1449," *The Royal Armouries Yearbook* 6 (2001), 22–31. The complete dowry is transcribed in Appendix 5.

227 On the 1445 ship into the Mediterranean see Garnier, pp. 175–76, and DeVries, "A 1445 Reference to Shipboard Artillery," pp. 818–29. It is also transcribed in full in Appendix 3.

4

Catalogue of the Surviving Guns

1

Collection/museum Historic Scotland, Edinburgh Castle

Short description Bombard (*Mons Meg*)   **Material** Wrought iron

Catalogue description A large wrought-iron gunpowder weapon. The barrel is made from 25 staves each approximately 60–70 mm wide and 25 mm thick, bound together with 37 hoops. The thickness of the hoops reduces from the rear to the muzzle which is formed from three hoops of increasing diameter. The staves extend about 10 mm beyond the front face of the muzzle hoop and are neatly rounded off. Two hoops at the rear of the barrel are damaged and broken, and the staves are clearly visible. The powder chamber is a large wrought-iron forging made from smaller pieces of iron hammer welded together to form an open-ended cylinder, the rear of which was plugged. The front of the powder chamber fits into the rear of the barrel and the two are locked together by means of a tongue and groove arrangement – a feature proved by x-radiography (Robert D. Smith and Ruth Rhynas Brown, *Mons Meg and her Sisters* (London, 1989), pp. 13–20). At the front and rear of the powder chamber are two bands with slots cut into their periphery. Accurate measurement of the weight of *Mons Meg* shows that its weighs 6040 kg (13,316 lb).

Date 1449

Dating evidence Dated from contemporary documents (Claude Gaier, "The Origin of Mons Meg," *Journal of the Arms and Armour Society* 5 (1967), 426).

Provenance/booty status Not applicable

Bore barrel 480 mm

Bore powder chamber 230 mm

Length overall 4040 mm

Length barrel 2880 mm

Literature Smith and Brown, pp. 39–45.

Notes This important bombard, preserved since the fifteenth century in Edinburgh Castle in Edinburgh, Scotland, is a key piece in the study of medieval artillery as contemporary documents have shown that it was made in 1449 in the workshop of Jehan Cambier in Mons. Its subsequent move to Scotland in 1457 as a gift to James II of Scotland, is also documented and its later history is very well known and published (for the latest information see Smith and Brown). The important analytical work carried out in the 1980s has also been instrumental in understanding its construction and manufacture and led to a re-appraisal of the construction and manufacture of wrought-iron artillery in general (Robert D. Smith, "The Technology of Wrought-Iron Artillery," *Royal Armouries Yearbook* 5 (2000), pp. 68–79). This work proved that the idea that the powder chamber was screwed into the rear of the barrel is completely false. The slots cut into the front and rear of the powder chamber were probably for inserting iron bars to manoeuvre the gun.

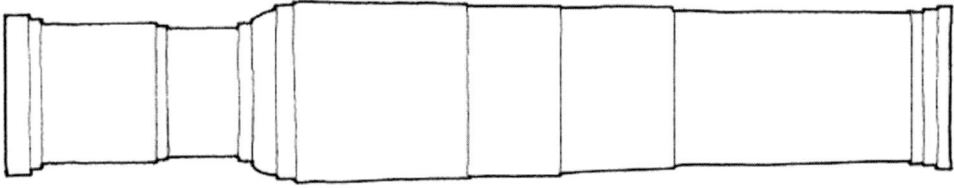

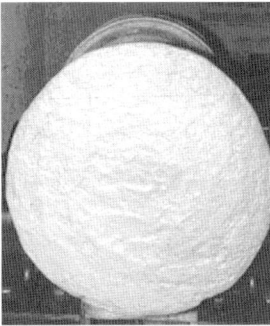

Rear face of powder chamber   Powder chamber

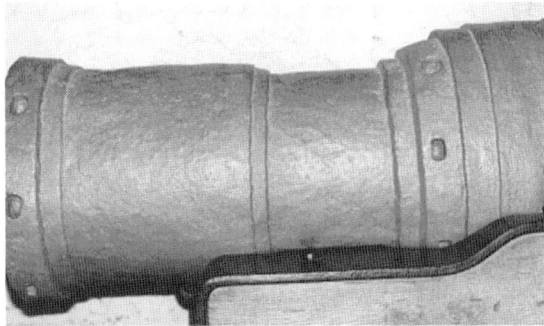

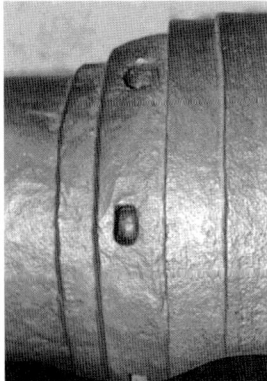

Powder chamber/barrel area   Detail of damage to barrel   Muzzle

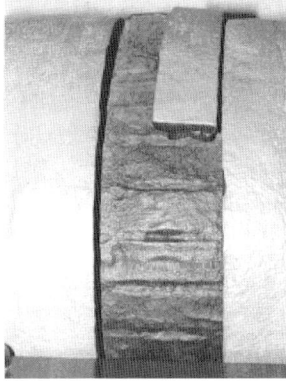

2

Collection/museum Historisches Museum, Basel, Switzerland

Accession number 1874–93

Short description Bombard   **Material** Wrought iron

Catalogue description A large wrought-iron bombard. The barrel is made from 20 staves, each approximately 50 to 55 mm wide, bound with hoops. The staves protrude slightly from the front face of the muzzle hoop and are neatly and carefully rounded. The muzzle is formed from three hoops of increasing diameter. Although the diameter of the hoops decreases from the rear to the front of the barrel, this is not a gradual, even decrease, but is achieved in discreet steps with groups of hoops of similar diameter. Near the rear of the barrel is a wide band of larger diameter which appears to be added over the top of the hoops, its ends being hammer-welded together at the bottom of the barrel. At the rear of the barrel are three hoops of decreasing diameter. The central hoop of this group has a series of rectangular slots cut into its outer edge. The powder chamber appears to be a single iron forging with few or no discernible features. It tapers outwards from the barrel to the rear. On its rear face there is a circular feature which is the plug that sealed the powder chamber. Just forward of the touch hole there is an engraved shield divided into small squares which are alternately plain and dot-punched.

Date c. 1450

Dating evidence By comparison with *Mons Meg*, made in 1449 (Gaier, "The Origins of Mons Meg," p. 426).

Provenance/booty status Booty from Murten

Bore barrel 340 mm

Bore powder chamber 150 mm

Length overall 2719 mm

Length barrel 1880 mm

Literature Florens Deuchler, *Die Burgunderbeute: Inventar der Beutestucke aus den Schlachten von Grandson, Murten und Nancy 1476/77* (Bern, 1963), no. 23; Smith and Brown, pp. 39–45.

Notes This important bombard has been extensively published, most recently by Smith and Brown. Their work shows that it very closely resembles *Mons Meg*, dated to 1449, and *Dulle Griet*, and from this can be dated to the mid-fifteenth century. Its extremely close resemblance to *Mons Meg* also strongly indicates that this gun was, like *Mons Meg*, made by Jehan Cambier of Mons in Hainault. The major difference between these three guns is the way that the powder chambers were made. That for *Dulle Griet* appears to be made by a stave-and-hoop type method while those of *Mons Meg* and the Basel bombard are made from massive iron forgings. In the past it has been suggested that the rectangular slots in the hoop at the front of the powder chamber were to insert bars so that the powder chamber could be unscrewed from the barrel. Smith and Brown have shown that this is not true for *Mons Meg* and it is clearly not true for this piece either. The wide band near the rear of the barrel is probably a later repair. Although it has been suggested that the shield may be part of the coat of arms of the d'Auxy family this device was used widely throughout Europe. However, Jean IV, lord of Auxy (1396–1474), was made a member of the Order of the Golden Fleece in 1445 (*Gulden Vlies, Het: Vijf eeuwen kunst en gescheidenis* (Bruges, 1962), p. 36) so it is likely that he was the owner of this gun and that it was taken to the Burgundian wars in Switzerland.

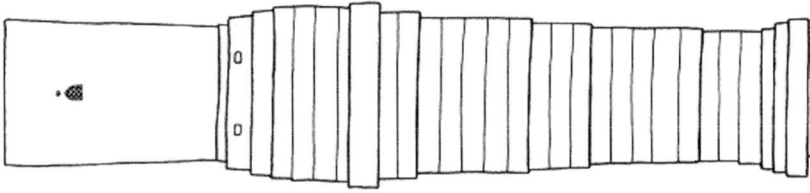

Front section and muzzle

Muzzle

Centre section

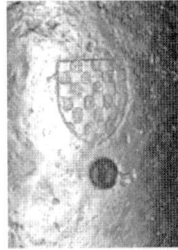

Shield and touch hole

Powder chamber

3

Collection/museum Ghent

Short description Bombard (*Dulle Griet*)　　　**Material** Wrought iron

Catalogue description A very large wrought-iron bombard. The barrel consists of 32 staves, each approximately 60 mm wide and 25 mm thick, bound together with 43 hoops. The hoops are arranged in groups with small reductions in diameter between them, giving the barrel a taper from rear to muzzle, which consists of 3 hoops of increasing diameter. The coat of arms of Philip the Good is cut into the top of the barrel. The powder chamber appears to be of the same stave-and-hoop construction though it is not possible to be absolutely certain. The rear is closed up with a plug. There is band with slots cut into its periphery at its front and rear.

Date c. 1450

Dating evidence By comparison with *Mons Meg*, made in 1449 (Gaier, "The Origin of Mons Meg," p. 426).

Provenance/booty status Not applicable

Bore barrel 640 mm

Length overall 5010 mm

Length barrel 3460 mm

Literature Smith and Brown, pp. 39–45, and Marc Beyaert, "Nieuwe historisch onderzoek van de Dulle Griet bombarde in Gent," *Handelingen der Maatschappij voor geschiedenis en oudheidkunde te Gent*, n.s. 53 (1999), 3–59.

Notes *Dulle Griet* is probably the largest complete surviving bombard in the world. Its remarkable similarity to *Mons Meg* (catalogue no. 1) has led to the conclusion that it was made by Jehan Cambier at about the same time – the middle of the fifteenth century. Though very close in overall design to *Mons Meg*, it differs in that its powder chamber appears to have been made from staves and hoops, unlike *Mons Meg* and the Basel bombard (catalogue nos. 1 and 2) which are large wrought-iron forgings.

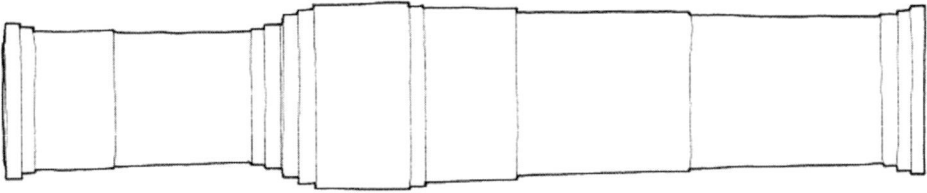

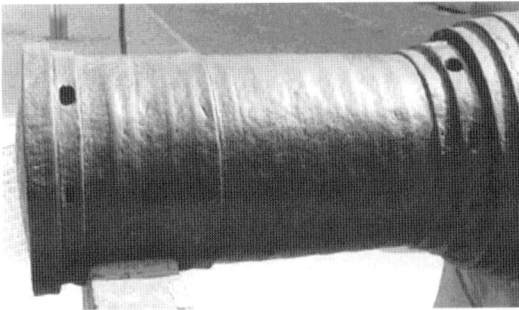

Powder chamber

Rear face of powder chamber

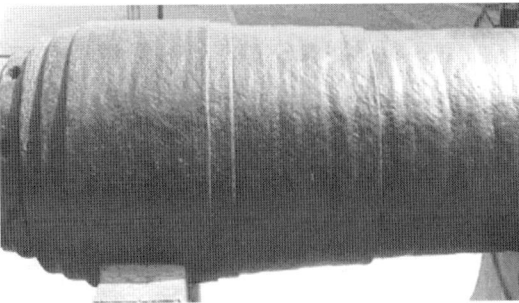

Rear section of barrel

Muzzle

Drawing of coat of arms on barrel (by courtesy of B. Ellis)

4

Collection/museum Musée de l'Armée, Paris

Accession number N55 (formerly N34)

Short description Coulovrine   **Material** Wrought iron

Catalogue description A small piece consisting of a barrel and smaller diameter powder chamber. The barrel, 190 mm long overall with a bore of 130 mm, has a narrow band at its rear and flares slightly from the rear to the muzzle. The powder chamber is tubular with a raised touch hole at the rear. The gun is attached to a wooden bed with an iron band, though whether these are original or modern is impossible to ascertain.

Date Deuchler dates this piece to the middle of the fifteenth century.

Dating evidence None

Provenance/booty status From St Ursanne, Switzerland; possibly booty from Murten.

Bore barrel 130 mm

Length overall 390 mm

Length barrel 190 mm

Literature Deuchler no. 233.

Notes This piece is very difficult to date and place – there are no comparable dated or datable pieces and just where this type of gun fits in the history of early gunpowder weapons is problematic. While it appears to be primitive and therefore early in date this is merely assumption and it is possible that it is later. It has also not been possible to ascertain whether the wooden mount on which it is presently attached is an original feature, though it appears not to be. While not easy to prove or substantiate, it is likely to be early in date – possibly mid-fifteenth century.

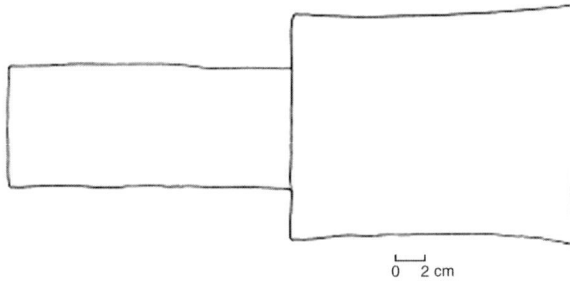

Powder chamber

5

Collection/museum Historisches Museum, Basel, Switzerland

Accession number 1905–4975

Short description Coulovrine   **Material** Copper alloy

Catalogue description The hexagonal copper-alloy barrel tapers from back to front. The muzzle is flared and is finely made with a small fillet. A small extension on top of the muzzle is probably a sight. An iron band incorporating trunnions has been added near the centre of the gun. The band has been hammered around the barrel and its ends fastened together with an iron pin, the end of which is bent back to secure it. On the lower facet, just behind the trunnion band, is a rectangular mark. Towards the rear are two shields containing coats of arms. The touch hole is set within a raised circular cup set on the top. At the rear there are two slightly larger diameter fillets. A small depression probably marks the position of the rear sight which has been removed. The rear face of the barrel shows evidence that it has been filled with a different material, possibly lead.

Date Deuchler dates this piece to about 1470.

Dating evidence None

Provenance/booty status Burgundian Booty

Bore barrel 29 mm

Length overall 985 mm

Literature Deuchler, no. 244.

Notes Although this barrel now has trunnions and is mounted on a ship's carriage it is clear that it was originally a hand gun or coulovrine. The trunnions have very definitely been added and the rectangular feature on the bottom facet is where a hook, or *croque*, has been removed. Comparison with other examples indicates that the barrel was hollowed out behind the touch hole to take a wooden stock and that this has been filled in at a later date – presumably when the hook was removed and the trunnions added. Deuchler states that this piece was already mounted on its carriage by 1709 (Deuchler, p. 324). Unfortunately, it has not been possible to trace the coat of arms or mark.

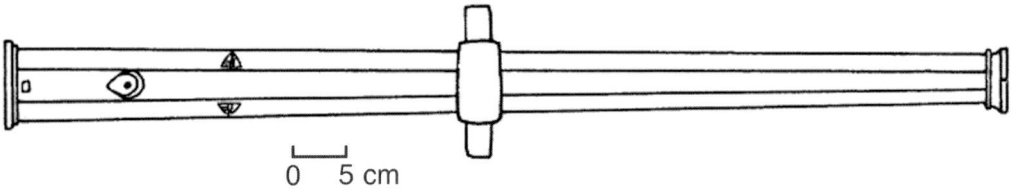

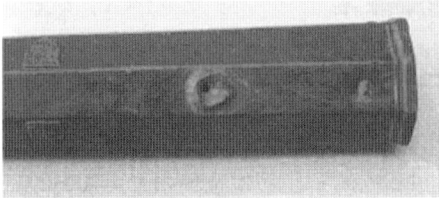

Rear section showing touch hole, mark, and
coat of arms

Detail of coat of arms

Rear showing filler in socket

Detail of added trunnions

6

Collection/museum Historisches Museum, Basel, Switzerland

Accession number 1874.95

Short description *Courtau*   **Material** Copper alloy

Catalogue description A parallel-sided barrel cast in copper alloy. The plain, smooth barrel is marked at regular intervals by ornate mouldings, those at the muzzle being of greater size and diameter. Behind the raised muzzle moulding is the inscription JEHAN DE MALINES MA FAYT LAN MCCCCLXXIIII. Behind this are the arms of Charles the Bold, duke of Burgundy, flanked by a flaming fire steel, to the left, and adorsed "Cs" entwined with rope to the right. Behind this a long band of greater diameter than the front and rear is undecorated and has two centrally placed trunnions. Behind this section the barrel decreases in diameter and is similar to the front section. The cascable is tubular, forming a socket 180 mm deep, and decorated with a beast's head with an open-toothed mouth and flaming mane. The touch hole is very small and, unusually, is formed in the edge of the rearmost raised moulding. Internally, the bore, 230 mm in diameter, reduces to form the powder chamber at the rear edge of the wide band.

Date 1474

Dating evidence Dated

Provenance/booty status Booty from Grandson

Bore barrel 230 mm

Length overall 2170 mm

Literature Deuchler, no. 232.

Notes This superb example of the cannon founder's art is in extraordinary condition, with barely a blemish. An almost identical piece, called Burgnderin is illustrated in the *Zeughaus Books* of the Emperor Maximilian I (Vienna, Österreichische Nationalbibliothek, Cod. 10824, f.).

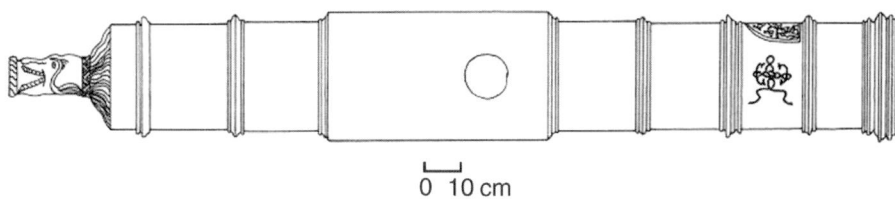

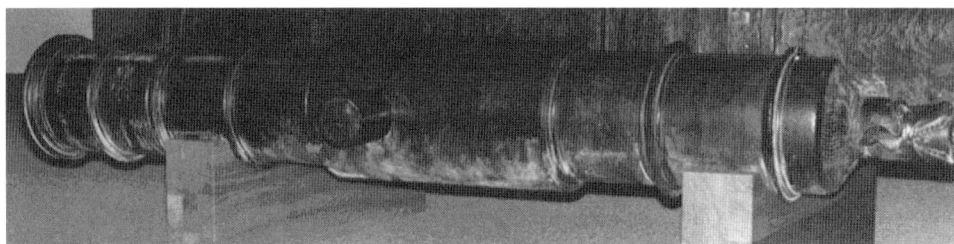

Muzzle

Cascable

Centre section with trunnions

Coat of arms

Fire steel emblem

Adorsed "Cs" emblem

7

Collection/museum Historisches Museum, St. Gallen, Switzerland

Accession number 16681

Short description Courtau ? – fragment   **Material** Copper alloy

Catalogue description A fragment, about 470 mm long, of the facetted barrel of a large bronze cannon, possibly a courtau. On one facet there is a shield containing the arms of the dukes of Burgundy, the Burgundian fire steel emblem on another, and adorsed "Cs" with an entwined rope motif on a third.

Date 1467–76

Dating evidence Dated by the coat of arms and adorsed "Cs" to the reign of Charles the Bold.

Provenance/booty status Found in the Blumenbergplatz in St. Gallen in 1953.

Bore barrel 120 mm (by calculation)

Literature Deuchler, no. 254; Hans-Peter Trenschel, "Drei Geschützfragmente aus der Bungunderbeute," *Jahrbuch des Bernischen Historischen Museums in Bern* 47–48 (1967–1968), 9–60.

Notes Although this is just a fragment, it has been possible to calculate the original bore of the gunpowder weapon from which it came as 120 mm (Trenschel, pp. 12–13). The decorative motifs are identical to those found on the courtau now in the Historisches Museum, Basel, inventory number 1874.95, dated 1474 (described above, catalogue no. 6).

Cross section

Burgundian coat of arms

Fire steel emblem

8

Collection/museum Musée de La Neuville, La Neuville, Switzerland

Short description Crapaudeau ?   **Material** Wrought iron

Catalogue description This breech-loading barrel is made from eight staves bound together with a series of hoops and bands. The hoops are between 11 mm and 17 mm in width, and the bands vary from 68 mm to 80 mm in width. The front and rear edges of each band have been carefully hammered to close up the gap between it and the adjacent hoop. The barrel is tapered: the external diameter of the bands increases from 310 mm to 345 mm while the bore increases from 69 mm to 78mm. The bands show some evidence that they were wrapped and their ends lap welded together. Originally this piece would have been mounted on a wooden bed and provided with a powder chamber.

Date Deuchler dates this piece to about 1460.

Dating evidence Dated by Burgundian Booty.

Provenance/booty status Booty from Grandson

Bore barrel 69 mm tapering to 78 mm

Length overall 1080 mm

Literature Deuchler, no. 239.

Notes This very simple barrel, basically an open-ended tube, would have been mounted on a wooden bed and was extremely common in the fifteenth and throughout much of the sixteenth century.

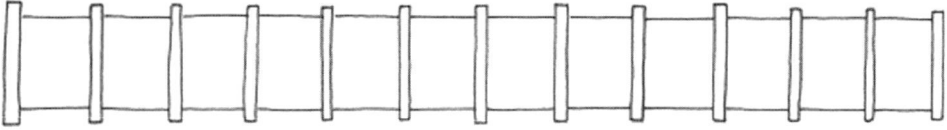

Detail of barrel

Muzzle

9

Collection/museum Musée de La Neuville, La Neuville, Switzerland

Short description Crapaudeau ?   **Material** Wrought iron

Catalogue description The barrel is made from ten staves, each approximately 25 mm wide by 10 mm thick, bound together with hoops and bands. The hoops are in groups of three, with a larger diameter central hoop, and range from approximately 17 mm to 23 mm wide. Some of the larger diameter hoops have a depression in their outer surface consistent with the remains of lifting ring lugs which have been removed. The bands are of smaller diameter than the hoops and range from 48 mm to 53 mm in width. The muzzle hoop is of considerably larger diameter and has been fitted over a narrow band leading to the conclusion that this has been added at some later stage and is not original to the piece. The breech end has a similar general appearance to the rest of the barrel but two of the bands are of similar diameter to the smaller of the three hoops. In addition, there is a curious band which fits round the barrel whose ends are bent outwards and a bolt fitted through as though to secure or reinforce one of the bands.

Date Deuchler dates this piece to 1460–70.

Dating evidence Burgundian Booty

Provenance/booty status Booty from Grandson

Bore barrel 72 mm

Length overall 1595 mm

Literature Deuchler, no. 235.

Notes The reinforcing band at the breech of this gunpowder weapon is a very unusual feature. Although it is unclear precisely what it is for, close examination of the piece leads to the conclusion that it might originally have been a muzzle-loading gun with a separate powder chamber, and at a later date its powder chamber was permanently secured to the rear of the barrel and held in place with this additional band, thus converting it to a muzzle loader with fixed powder chamber. Alternatively, it is possible that it was made originally as a muzzle-loading gun, and that this band is an additional reinforcement for the rear of the barrel. Unfortunately, the carriage and bed on which the barrel is now mounted obscures the situation. The added muzzle hoop and the way that the lifting ring hoops have been obliterated would seem to confirm the idea that the gun has undergone fairly radical change at some period. The carriage is probably nineteenth-century.

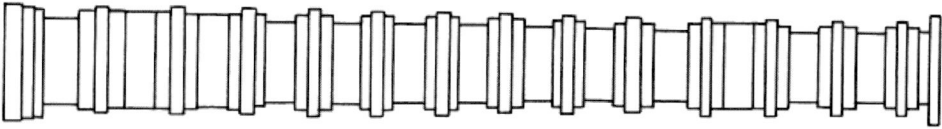

0   10 cm

Muzzle

Front of barrel

Rear showing how powder chamber has been inserted into rear of barrel and
clamped in place

10

Collection/museum Musée de La Neuville, La Neuville, Switzerland

Short description Crapaudeau ?   **Material** Wrought iron

Catalogue description This unusual muzzle-loading gun has a smooth outer surface without the hoop-and-band structure of many wrought-iron guns. The rear of the barrel has a smooth outer surface which tapers from the rear towards the trunnions. The back of the barrel is flat with a tapered projection of rectangular form. The touch hole is small and set within a deep rounded depression. The top of the barrel bears an incised mark of roughly V-shaped form. Between the rear of the barrel and the trunnions is a shallow groove and roll moulding. The trunnions project from a wide band which is of larger diameter than the barrel and which is flanked by roll mouldings and narrow bands of slightly smaller diameter. Forward of the trunnions the barrel is again smooth surfaced and tapers from the trunnions to the muzzle. Just forward of the trunnions there are double groove and roll mouldings marking a slight reduction in diameter. The muzzle consists of a hexagonal slightly flared band behind which is a small roll moulding.

Date Deuchler states that this is either Burgundian 1460–70 or possibly German about 1500.

Dating evidence None

Provenance/booty status Possibly Burgundian Booty

Bore barrel 58 mm

Length overall 2213 mm

Length barrel 2108 mm

Literature Deuchler, no. 245.

Notes This gun is extremely unusual and there are few, if any, comparative examples. Its closest resemblance is to a number of iron guns found in museums across Europe, also undated and unprovenanced, which have the same smooth outer appearance and which taper from back to front. It also somewhat resembles the two wrought-iron guns in this catalogue, nos. 14 and 15, as well as the two bronze pieces in Neuchâtel (Smith, "All Manner of Peeces," pp. 135–36). It is likely to date from the final decades of the fifteenth century and certainly might have been used by the Burgundian forces in the 1470s.

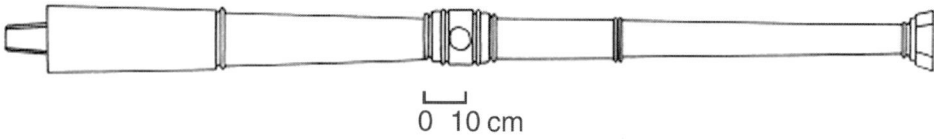

Front section

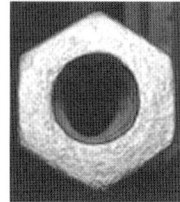

Muzzle

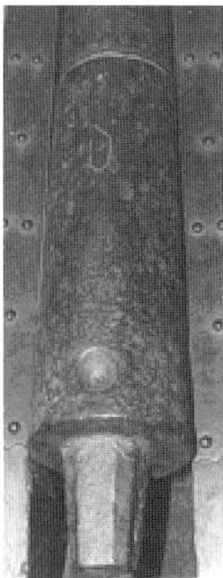

Rear

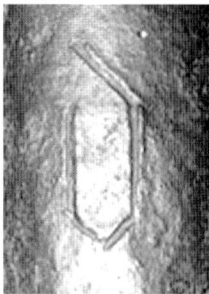

Mark

Trunnions

11

Collection/museum Musée de La Neuville, La Neuville, Switzerland

Short description Crapaudeau ?   **Material** Wrought iron

Catalogue description The ten staves which form the core of the barrel of this gun are each about 20 mm wide by 10 mm thick. The hoops are grouped in sets of three with a middle hoop of greater diameter than those on either side of it. The hoops are between 12 mm and 19 mm wide. The bands vary from 49 mm to 66 mm wide. At the muzzle there is a hoop of larger diameter from which the staves project slightly and are hammered into a smooth rounded shape. The trunnions, which are bent forward at a considerable angle, are formed from two pieces of iron joined horizontally and appear to have been added over the top of one of the bands. At the rear of the barrel there is a rounded square projection. The touch hole is small and blocked.

Date Deuchler dates this piece to 1460–70.

Dating evidence From association with the Burgundian Booty

Provenance/booty status Booty from Grandson

Bore barrel 70 mm

Length overall 1525 mm

Length barrel 1397 mm

Literature Deuchler, no. 234.

Notes Although it is now difficult to be sure, it is likely that this piece was formed from a muzzle-loading gun which has been plugged at the breech and had trunnions added. The hammered and rather rough appearance of the breech plug has all the appearance of being inserted at a later date. The way the trunnions have been added, being made from two pieces of iron, adds weight to this suggestion. The plug bears close resemblance to catalogue nos. 10 and 15.

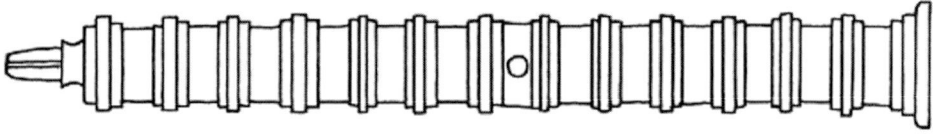

0 10 cm

Muzzle

Front

Trunnions

Rear of barrel

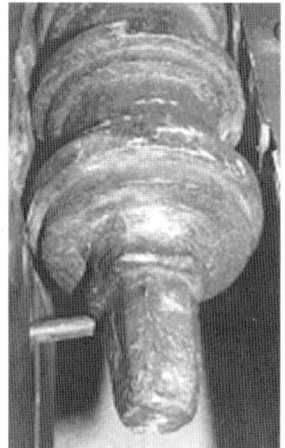

Rear

12

Collection/museum Musée de La Neuville, La Neuville, Switzerland

Short description Crapaudeau ?   **Material** Wrought iron

Catalogue description The barrel consists of six staves, each approimately 45 mm wide by 8 mm thick, bound with hoops and bands. At the muzzle there is, unusually, an added small fillet stave. The hoops are grouped in threes, the central hoop of larger diameter than the two outer ones. The muzzle hoop, of greater diameter than the other hoops, is octagonal and of scalloped form with incised decoration. Many of the central hoops also have incised decoration in the form of chevrons or arrows. Three of the hoops include lifting-ring loops though these are set lower down on the barrel. The trunnions have been made from two pieces of iron clamped over a band and rivetted together. The rear consists of two wide thick bands which have been clamped over the last two sections of the barrel. These bands are wrapped round and clamped together on the bottom of the gun with double rivets. The breech consists of a rounded disc of iron from which a flared projection extends. The touch hole is a small hole set within a circular dish.

Date Deuchler dates this piece to 1460–70.

Dating evidence Dated by association with the Burgundian Booty.

Provenance/booty status Booty from Grandson

Bore barrel 73 mm

Length overall 2190 mm

Length barrel 2075 mm

Literature Deuchler, no. 238.

Notes Several of the features of this piece indicate that it was originally a breech-loading gun which has been altered, at some time, to a muzzle-loading piece. The two unusual bands at the rear were clearly added at a later stage, as is evident from the way they have been joined by means of rivets. The lifting-ring lugs, which are offset and now near the bottom of the barrel and not near or at the top of the barrel, as is normal, also point to the same conclusion. Further evidence is also provided by the fact that the decoration on the hoops is much clearer underneath than at the top surface. Comparison with other pieces indicates that decoration is normally more finished and pronounced on the top surface leading to the conclusion that the barrel has been offset about 120°.

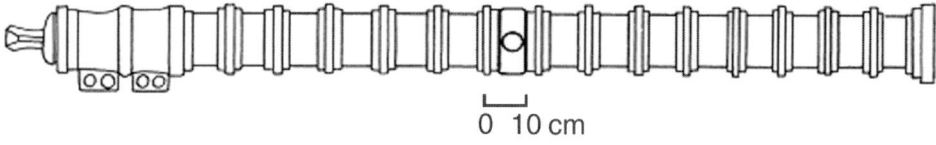

0 10 cm

Muzzle

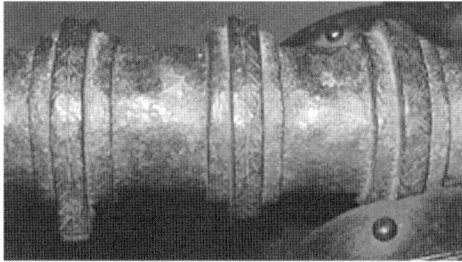

Detail of barrel

Trunnions

Rear showing added rear section

Detail of rivets securing added rear section

13

Collection/museum Historisches Museum, Murten, Switzerland

Accession number 111

Short description Crapaudeau ?   **Material** Wrought iron

Catalogue description The staves are bound with hoops and bands; the hoops are grouped in threes. The muzzle band is larger diameter and decorated with incised lines on its edge and on its front face. The hoops are approximately 9 mm to 12 mm wide and the bands vary from 56 mm to 74 mm in width. Lifting-ring lugs, complete with rings, are formed in the fifth hoop structure from the muzzle and the fourth from the breech. These are, unusually, both offset to one side. The diameter of the bands decreases from 96 mm at the breech end to 70 mm at the muzzle. The breech is very similar to the muzzle with three hoops of increasing diameter, with that at the very rear being the largest. The carriage obscures the rear face of the breech, making it impossible to be sure of its precise form. The touch hole, in the first band from the breech, is formed in a copper-alloy tube set within a circular depression with a groove running backwards towards the breech.

Date Deuchler dates this piece to the first half of the fifteenth century.

Dating evidence By association with the Burgundian Booty

Provenance/booty status Booty from Murten

Bore barrel 35 mm

Length barrel 1388 mm

Literature Deuchler, no. 241.

Notes Unfortunately, it proved impossible to examine closely the rear face of the breech so that it was not possible to ascertain whether this piece was a converted breech loader or was made as a muzzle loader. The conversion would have necessitated the insertion of a breech plug and the drilling of a touch hole. The offset lifting-ring lugs are unusual and may indicate that it was originally a breech loader with a separate powder chamber, in which case the lugs would have been placed centrally on top. The touch hole appears to have been repaired at some time by the insertion of a copper-alloy tube into an earlier touch hole.

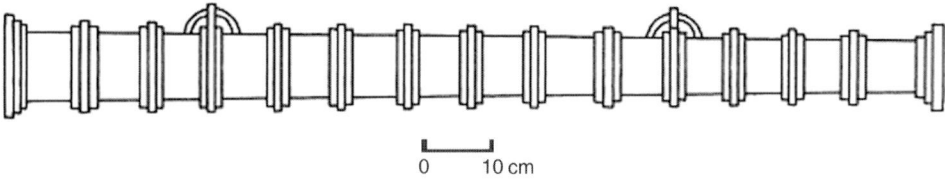

0   10 cm

Rear   Offset lifting-ring lug and ring   Muzzle

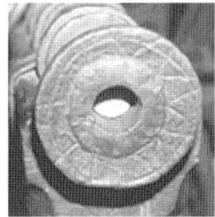

14

Collection/museum Chateau de Grandson, Switzerland (Collection of La Neuville)

Short description Crapaudeau ?   **Material** Wrought iron

Catalogue description The barrel of this piece is made from two staves bound together with hoops and bands. The muzzle consists of two hoops, the front hoop being of slightly greater diameter. The staves protrude slightly from the front of this muzzle hoop and are carefully rounded over. The trunnions divide the barrel into two unequal halves and mark a distinct reduction in diameter from back to front. The trunnions protrude from a band bordered front and back by a square-shaped hoop. The breech consists of a similar double-hoop form to that at the muzzle, the rear hoop being of slightly greater diameter. The cascable is flat and has a rectangular projection pierced horizontally by a hole. The touch hole is small and set within a small circular dish.

Date Deuchler dates this piece to the second half of the fifteenth century.

Dating evidence None

Provenance/booty status Burgundian wars

Bore barrel 50 mm

Length barrel 1350 mm

Literature Deuchler, no. 256.

Notes This muzzle-loading piece is very similar to catalogue no. 15. The rear projection would appear to be for adjusting the elevation of the barrel within a carriage. It is, as always, difficult to be sure what type of gun this is but its small bore and high length-to-bore ratio would point to it being a crapaudeau. The precise and very careful outer appearance of this piece is striking, as is the reduction in diameter behind and in front of the trunnions. Internally the barrel has only two staves, a feature paralleled on late sixteenth-century swivel guns (Robert D. Smith, "Wrought-Iron Swivel Guns," in *The Archaeology of Ships of War*, ed. M. Bound (Oxford, 1995), pp. 104–13). Taken overall this appears to be a very developed and sophisticated design. It can, perhaps, be compared with two bronze pieces in the collection of Neuchatel dated 1488. Although these do not have the hoop-and-band appearance they are tapered in a similar way, have trunnions and an extension at the rear which could be used for elevation (Robert D. Smith, " 'All Manner of Peeces': Artillery in the Late Medieval Period," *The Royal Armouries Yearbook* 7 (2002), 135–6). Taking the evidence overall, this piece, and the similar one, catalogue no.15, may date from the last decades of the fifteenth century.

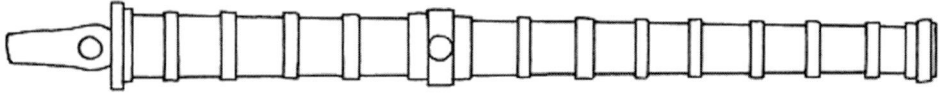

0   10 cm

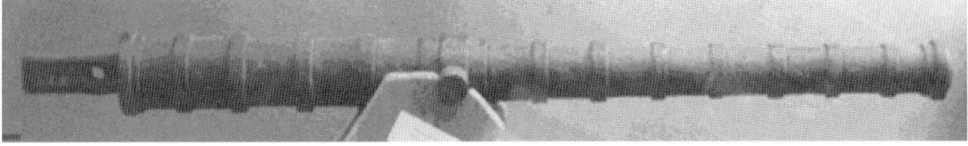

Rear   Trunnions   Muzzle

15

Collection/museum Musée de La Neuville, La Neuville, Switzerland

Short description Crapaudeau ?   **Material** Wrought iron

Catalogue description The barrel of this muzzle-loading piece is made from two staves bound together with hoops and bands. The muzzle consists of two hoops together, the front hoop being of slightly greater diameter. The staves protrude slightly from the front of this muzzle hoop and are carefully rounded over. The trunnions divide the barrel into two unequal halves and mark a distinct reduction in diameter from back to front. The trunnions protrude from a band bordered front and back by a small roll moulding. The breech consists of a similar double-hoop form to that at the muzzle, the rear hoop being of slightly greater diameter and bearing a simple incised mark in the form of an "N". The cascable is flat and has a rectangular projection pierced horizontally by a hole. The touch hole is small and set within a small circular dish.

Date Deuchler dates this piece to 1460–70.

Dating evidence Dated by Burgundian Booty

Provenance/booty status Booty from Grandson

Bore barrel 60 mm

Length barrel 1130 mm

Literature Deuchler, no. 236.

Notes See catalogue no. 14 for further notes.

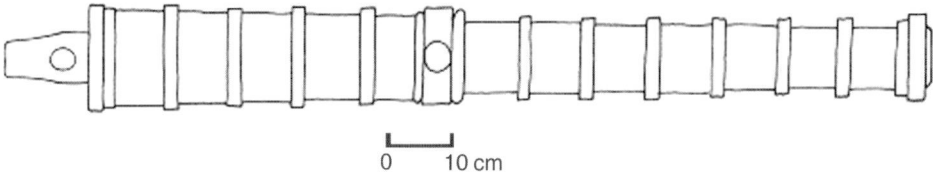

0   10 cm

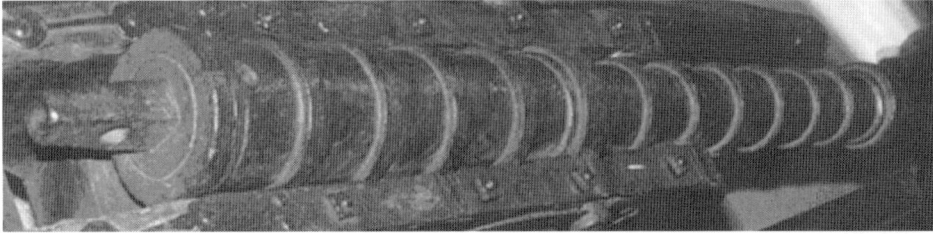

Rear   Trunnions   Muzzle

16

Collection/museum Musée de La Neuville, La Neuville, Switzerland

Short description Crapaudeau ?   **Material** Wrought iron

Catalogue description The barrel is made from four staves bound with hoops and bands. Very unusually, the hoops are not set at regular intervals down the length of the barrel. The muzzle consists of a double hoop, that at the front being very large in diameter, over the front face of which the staves have been hammered. Set on top of this hoop is a horizontal plate in the form of a shield beneath which is a rectangular slot. The hoops are very narrow and set in groups of three. Behind the muzzle the outer surface is smooth though it is clear that it consists of six narrow bands of similar diameter. A second group of three hoops, with lifting ring, is followed by a barrel section made from four bands. There follows a series of three triple hoops and three band structures. Behind this the next triple hoop has a flat plate set horizontally on a rectangular projection pierced with a slot, as at the muzzle. This plate has three punched "H" marks. Behind this the hoops are again in groups of three but the bands are double. The triple-hoop structure next to the breech has a similar lifting-ring loop and lifting ring to that near the muzzle. The breech consists of a triple-hoop structure, but the very end of the barrel is completely obscured by the carriage on which it is set. The touch hole is a small hole set within a shallow rectangular depression.

Date Deuchler dates this piece to about 1460.

Dating evidence Dated by Burgundian Booty

Provenance/booty status Booty from Grandson

Bore barrel 60 mm

Length overall 2925 mm

Literature Deuchler, no. 237.

Notes This gun is unique in the *oeuvre* of wrought-iron gunpowder weapons. Its non-regular structure and the use of very wide bands are not paralleled elsewhere. Uncommonly for a muzzle-loading piece, there are no trunnions. The flat shield-shaped plates are also unusual. Interestingly, the lifting-ring lugs are offset to either side of the centre line of the barrel and ensure that the slots in the hoops can be used as a sighting device. Dating it without any parallels is impossible, but there is no reason to doubt the attribution to the Burgundian wars and a date around 1470.

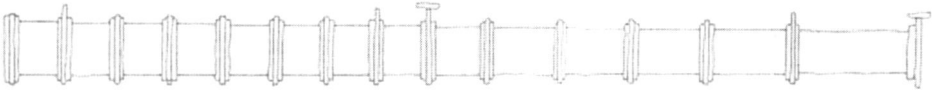

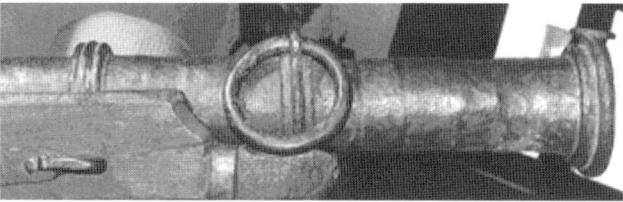

Front section

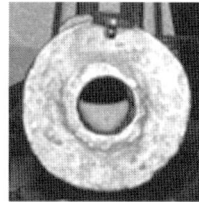

Muzzle

Breech and touch hole

Detail of shield with marks

17

Collection/museum Alte Zeughaus, Solothurn, Switzerland

Accession number AZ631

Short description Crapaudeau ? Fragment   **Material** Wrought iron

Catalogue description The broken breech of a muzzle-loading gunpowder weapon, consisting of the very rear and a short portion of barrel. The rear consists of two narrow bands. That at the rear, of larger diameter than the other, has the remains of a sight. The end face is slightly domed. The barrel itself appears to be made from three separate layers. The inner one probably consisted of staves, of which only a fragment of one remains. Around this is a single hoop, approximately 50 mm wide, surrounded by a series of three hoops, each 30 mm wide. The touch hole is in the rearmost hoop and consists of a raised circular iron feature into which the hole is formed.

Date Late fifteenth century

Dating evidence Association with Burgundian Booty

Provenance/booty status Burgundian Booty ?

Bore barrel 65 mm ?

Length overall 143 mm

Literature Deuchler, no. 255.

Notes This fragment looks like the rear of the gun in catalogue no. 16 from La Neuville.

Rear   Touch hole   Showing internal construction

18

Collection/museum Musée de La Neuville, La Neuville, Switzerland

Short description Pestereau ?   **Material** Wrought iron

Catalogue description The barrel is made up from fourteen staves, each approximately 40 mm wide, bound together with six hoops, five of which are roughly 50 mm to 60 mm wide while the fifth hoop from the front is only 30 mm wide. The hoops are lap welded together, each weld being over-lapped in the opposite way from that beside it, and each weld is placed diametrically opposite those on either side of it. The barrel tapers markedly from rear to front, both externally and internally, the bore being approximately 150 mm at the base and 190 mm at the muzzle. Attached to the fourth hoop is a lifting-ring lug complete with lifting ring. The powder chamber is of much smaller diam-eter and externally is reinforced with four hoops. It is not possible to see how the powder chamber was made internally. The rear face shows evidence of an inserted plug indicating that the powder chamber was made as a open-ended tube, a plug being inserted and welded into position to close it up. The touch hole is formed of a rectangular hole cut into the outer reinforcing hoop connecting with a round hole in the iron beneath. The join between the powder chamber and the rear of the barrel is covered with a flat plate obscuring all details of the method of attaching the two parts together.

Date Deuchler dates this piece to the fifteenth century.

Dating evidence None

Provenance/booty status Ascribed to Burgundian wars

Bore barrel 150 mm at rear, 190 mm at muzzle

Bore powder chamber 50 mm

Length overall 535 mm

Literature Deuchler, no. 252.

Notes This piece and the closely related pieces, below, form a very distinct group of guns. They are very similar to each other and very different from other guns. Their closest parallel are the mortars of the late fifteenth century and later. This similarity has led to the suggestion that these pieces are the pestereaux referred to in the Burgundian sources and which, towards the end of the fifteenth century, are described as "like a mortar." However there is some evidence, though the arguments are some-what circular, that this type of piece is very early in date – perhaps dating to the end of the fourteenth and the beginning of the fifteenth century. With our current knowledge this question is impossible to answer and their dating must remain open to question. Their appearance in the Burgundian Booty would suggest a later date. However, even his has been questioned. The suggestion is that, after the defeat at Grandson, Charles the Bold called up all the artillery in his lands, and that this meant that earlier pieces, not deemed worthy of inclusion in the first artillery train of Charles' campaign, were sent to him in Switzerland for his subsequent battle fought outside Murten. This argument, while superficially persuasive, is open to serious doubt. Charles would not have emptied his entire holdings of artillery to take on his campaigns. His holdings were enormous and would have meant that many pieces were left behind – a position reinforced by his need to leave behind sufficient forces, including artillery, to ensure that any outbreaks of trouble could have been dealt with effec-tively. To the argument that they are later in date must be added the cast-iron pieces which are so similar in form to these wrought-iron pieces. Cast iron, while not unknown in the earlier fifteenth century, was not common till the later decades of that century. It is clear that this type of gunpowder weapon is problematic but on balance the evidence would point to their dating to the second half of the fifteenth century.

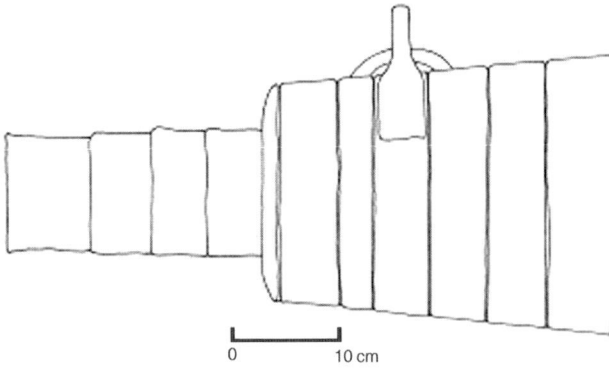

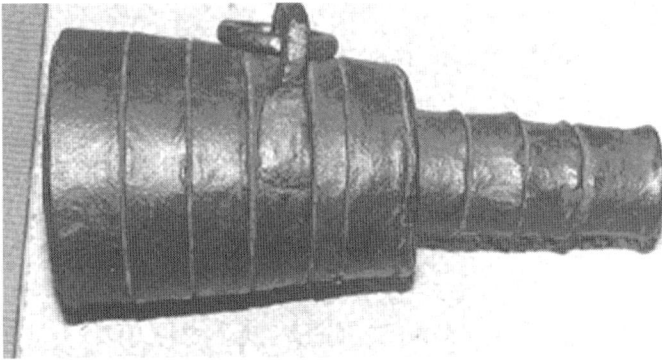

Powder chamber

Barrel

Muzzle showing interior

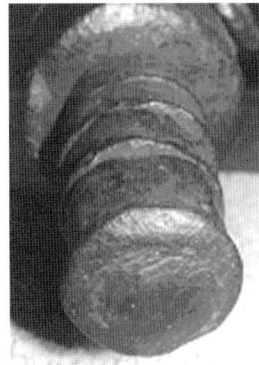

Rear of powder chamber

19

Collection/museum Musée de La Neuville, La Neuville, Switzerland

Short description Pestereau   **Material** Wrought iron

Catalogue description The barrel is not made from staves in the normal fashion but appears to be made of a single iron plate wrapped round to form a cylinder, the ends of which are overlapped. Whether the ends were welded is not clear, but there is no clear indication of a weld visible. Around this inner cylinder a series of hoops of varying width have been added. These reduce in external diameter towards the breech giving the barrel a stepped appearance. Internally the bore of the barrel tapers from the rear at 155 mm to the front at 175mm. The powder chamber is of considerably smaller diameter and, although at first glance it appears to be a uniform cylinder with a smooth exterior, it is made from three distinct sections. It is 250 mm long with a bore of 50 mm. The join between the barrel and powder chamber is marked by two hoops. The touch hole is a simple round hole placed at the back of the powder chamber.

Date

Provenance

Dimensions: overall

barrel bore

powder chamber bore

Literature

Notes See catalogue no. 18 above for a general discussion of this type of artillery. Though very close in overall form to that piece this example differs from it in its method of construction. Just what this means is unclear and it is not possible to draw any further conclusions about these enigmatic pieces.

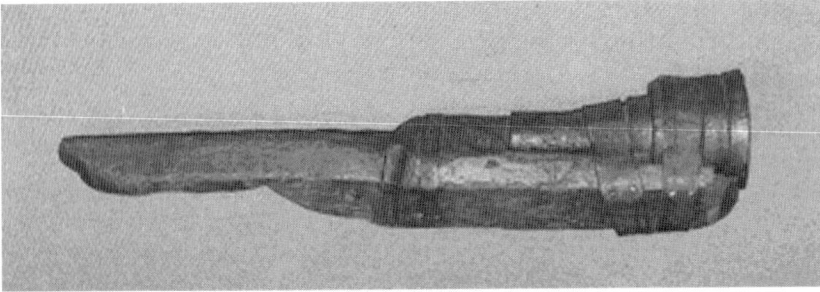

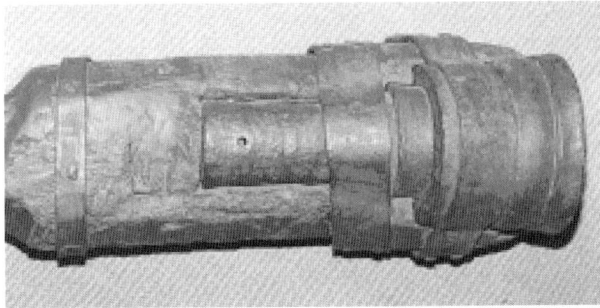

Gun set into bed

Rear showing gun set into bed

20

Collection/museum Musée de La Neuville, La Neuville, Switzerland

Short description Pestereau ?   **Material** Cast iron

Catalogue description A short muzzle-load gunpowder weapon made from cast iron. Externally the barrel is approximately parallel sided, 190 mm in diameter, with a shallow groove, 45 mm wide and 10 mm deep, near the muzzle. Forward of this groove the barrel flares slightly. The powder chamber tapers down from the rear of the barrel and, like the barrel, is roughly parallel sided, 130 mm in diameter. The rear of the powder chamber is formed as a band, 50 mm wide, of slightly larger diameter. The touch hole is approximately 10 mm in diameter and situated 65 mm from the rear of the powder chamber. The rear face is flat though hidden by the wooden bed into which it is attached. There is an integral semi-circular in-line lifting-ring hoop of rectangular cross section, complete with lifting ring, which bridges between the powder chamber and the barrel. The bore of the barrel is 180 mm long and tapers from 145 mm at the mouth to 130 mm at the base of the barrel. The bore of the powder chamber is approximately 45 mm in diameter and 250 mm long. The barrel is mounted on what appears to be an original wooden bed. Made from a single piece of wood the front is shaped and hollowed out to take the barrel, which is set approximately half into the bed. Two wrought-iron bands which wrap round the barrel and bed are secured by nails to the sides and bottom of the bed. The forward band is positioned just behind the groove in the front of the barrel while the rear band goes round the powder chamber. It is probable that these are not original: the sides of the bed have been cut to form a shallow groove into which it would appear the securing band would have fitted but the present band is positioned behind the cut-out; similarly it would seem likely that the groove round the front of the barrel was made to take the band which fixed it to the bed, but this band does not fit into the groove. On the underside of the bed there are two rectangular cut-outs. Behind the barrel the bed tapers to form a tiller-like projection. On the underside of this tiller, at its front, there is a narrow section with a transverse hole. This, together with two rectangular cut-outs just forward of it, appear to be the method by which the bed was supported, a suggestion confirmed by the reinforcing iron plate which covers the area around both features. The bed has been extensively repaired.

Date Deuchler dates this to fourteenth/fifteenth century.

Dating evidence None

Provenance/booty status Unknown. Ascribed to the Burgundian Booty.

Bore barrel 150 mm

Bore powder chamber 45 mm

Length overall Barrel 490 mm. Overall with bed 1670 mm.

Length barrel 190 mm

Literature Deuchler, no. 250.

Notes For a general discussion of this type of gun see catalogue no. 18. While that piece was made of wrought iron, this example is made from cast iron – though it must be stressed of exactly the same form. As has been discussed in Part 3 above, cast iron and its use in the fifteenth century is very problematic and still a subject of considerable debate. Though examples do occur in the earlier fifteenth-century records, its use was rare – see also the sections on ammunition in Part 3 – and it would be more appropriate to date these cast-iron examples to the later decades of the fifteenth century than earlier.

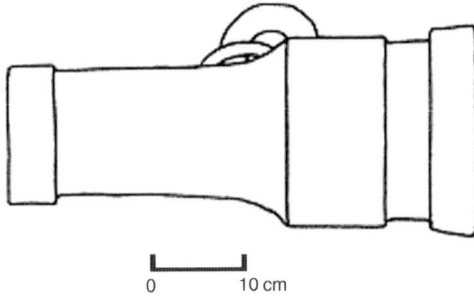

0   10 cm

Barrel and bed before repair

Bands holding barrel to bed

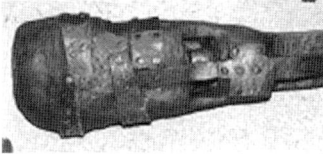

Underside of bed

Side of bed showing possible
method of supporting gun

Detail of possible support

21

Collection/museum Historisches Museum, Murten, Switzerland

Accession number 110

Short description Pestereau ?   **Material** Wrought iron

Catalogue description The thirteen staves, each approximately 50 mm to 60 mm wide and 10 mm thick, which comprise the barrel are bound together with six wide bands, each between 45 mm and 51 mm in width. The bands have not been fully hammered together and there are considerable gaps betwen them. The staves have been bent back, very crudely, over the front band. It is clear that this front band was made by hammering a bar of iron into a circle, overlapping its ends and hammer welding them together, the join being clearly visible. A lifting-ring loop, complete with ring, is welded to the fourth band from the front. Externally the barrel tapers from the rear to the mouth, but it proved impossible to measure the internal dimensions, including those of the powder chamber, as there is a stone ball stuck within the barrel. The powder chamber is of considerably smaller diameter than the barrel and, externally, consists of six bands ranging from 46 mm to 51 mm in width. The rearmost band is sightly smaller in diameter than the others and has a rounded cut-out in its forward edge corresponding to a small touch hole cut into the iron beneath the outer band. The rear face of the barrel is covered by an iron plate of rounded form which obscures the details of the join between the barrel and the powder chamber.

Date Unknown

Provenance/booty status Burgundian wars

Bore barrel 210 mm

Length overall 625 mm

Length barrel 325 mm

Literature Deuchler, no. 249.

Notes Deuchler dates this piece to the end of the fourteenth or beginning of the fifteenth century. He also suggests that it may be of Swiss or Burgundian origin (Deuchler, p. 326). However, if this piece is a pestereau, as we believe, it could be dated to the later part of the fifteenth century and therefore be more closely linked to the Burgundian Booty.

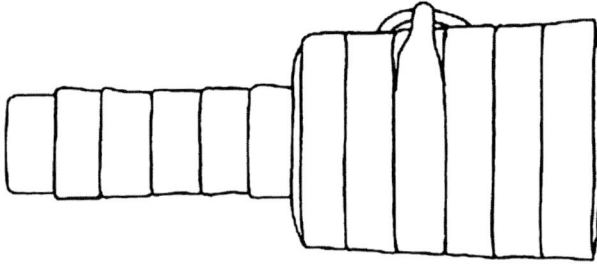

Barrel

Powder chamber

Junction of barrel and powder chamber

Detail of barrel showing staves

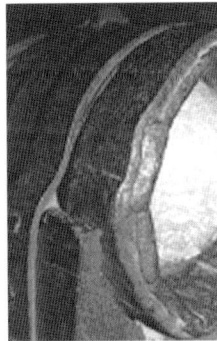

Detail of stave ends at muzzle

22

Collection/museum Historisches Museum, Murten, Switzerland

Accession number 113

Short description Pestereau   **Material** Wrought iron

Catalogue description The barrel is made from fourteen staves, bound together with six bands of between 46 mm and 56 mm in width. A stone ball is stuck inside the barrel making it impossible to investigate the bore of the barrel fully or the internal size of the powder chamber. The bands are not closed up one to another and there are considerable gaps between them. Externally the barrel tapers from 262 mm in diameter at the rear to 282 mm at the muzzle. The powder chamber is of much smaller diameter and it too tapers, from 132 mm in diameter at the rear to 156 mm at the front. It is made externally of six bands though these have been carefully fitted and hammered so that the joins between them are indistinct, unlike the barrel. The rear face of the barrel is considerably distorted, and it is clear that the staves have been hammered down over an iron ring which appears to be the front of the powder chamber. A lifting-ring lug, complete with ring, has been formed on the fourth band from the rear. At the very back of the powder chamber is a narrow hoop of larger diameter, but the rear face is obscured by the carriage. The touch hole is a 20 mm hole driven through the second band from the rear. There is a large lug with an in-line hole to the left of the touch hole and a corresponding rectangular feature on the right side.

Date Deuchler dates this to the late fourteenth or early fifteenth century.

Dating evidence None

Provenance/booty status Burgundian wars

Bore barrel 213 mm

Length overall 735 mm

Length barrel 333 mm

Literature Deuchler, no. 247.

Notes Although similar in many respects to other pestereaux, and especialy to catalogue no. 18, this piece has a number of unusual features: the lifting-ring lug is secured to the powder chamber and not to the barrel; the rear of the powder chamber is formed from a narrow hoop of larger diameter than the rest of the powder chamber; and there are lugs on either side of the touch hole. These latter are probably, by comparison with other guns, the fixings for a touch hole cover plate. The rectangular feature is the remains of the hinge, which has been removed, and the remaining lug is where the other end of the plate would have fitted, being secured by a pin placed through the hole in the lug. This feature is common on bronze guns of the late fifteenth and sixteenth centuries. The way the staves have been hammered down over the front of the powder chamber offer a clue to the method by which this was achieved in other guns where this detail is usually concealed beneath a cover plate, presumably missing in this instance.

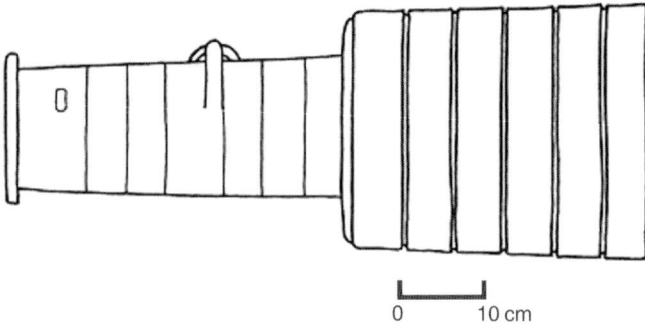

0   10 cm

Barrel

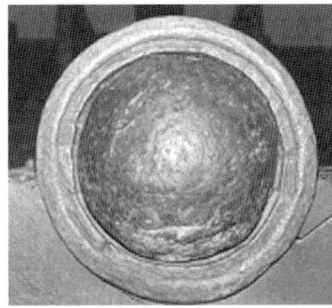

Muzzle with ball stuck in

Powder chamber

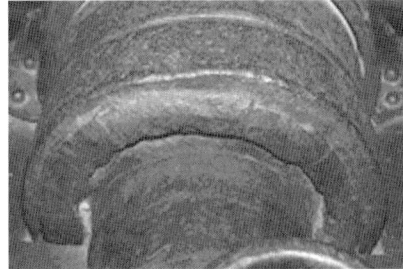

Junction between powder chamber and barrel

23

Collection/museum Historisches Museum, Murten, Switzerland

Accession number 115A

Short description Pestereau ?   **Material** Cast iron

Catalogue description Externally the barrel is smooth and tapers from a diameter of 200 mm at the rear to 230 mm at the muzzle. The bore is similarly tapered being 150 mm at the rear and 160 mm at the muzzle. The powder chamber has the same featureless outer surface as the barrel to which it is joined seamlessly. It is basically parallel sided with a bore of 55 mm. At the rear there is a slightly larger diameter band, though again there is no evidence of a join. The rear face is smooth and featureless. The touch hole is at the rear of the powder chamber. Between the powder chamber and the barrel is a single lifting-ring lug, roughly semi-circular in outline and square in cross section.

Date Deuchler dates this to the end of the fourteenth or the early fifteenth century.

Dating evidence None

Provenance/booty status Burgundian wars

Bore barrel 160 mm

Bore powder chamber 55 mm

Length overall 480 mm

Length barrel 220 mm

Literature Deuchler, no. 246 or 248.

Notes From its overall smooth appearance this gun is probably made from cast iron though no analyses have been carried out. The similarity between this gunpowder weapon and catalogue no. 24 is striking.

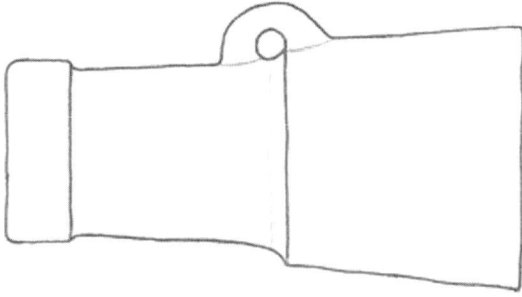

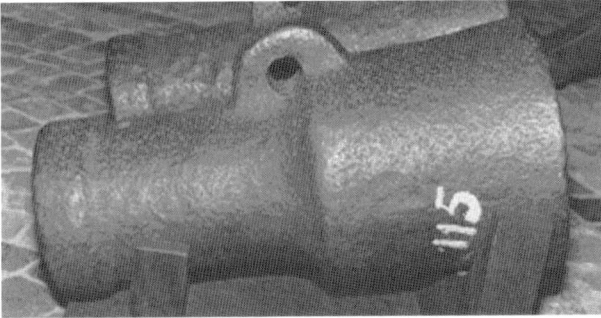

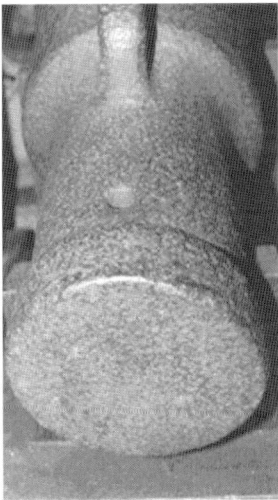

Rear   Muzzle

24

Collection/museum Historisches Museum, Murten, Switzerland

Accession number 115B

Short description Pestereau   **Material** Cast iron

Catalogue description Externally the barrel is smooth and tapers from a diameter of 205 mm at the rear to 235 mm at the muzzle. The bore is similarly tapered, being 140 mm at the rear and 165 mm at the muzzle. There is some damage to the front face of the barrel at the bottom edge. The powder chamber has the same featureless outer surface as the barrel to which it is joined seamlessly. It is basically parallel sided with a bore of 55 mm. At the rear there is a slightly larger diameter band, though again there is no evidence of a join. The rear face is smooth and featureless. The touch hole is at the rear of the powder chamber. Between the powder chamber and the barrel is a single lifting-ring lug, roughly semi-circular in outline and square in cross section.

Date Deuchler dates this to the end of the fourteeth or the early fifteenth century.

Dating evidence None

Provenance/booty status Burgundian wars

Bore barrel 165 mm

Bore powder chamber 55 mm

Length overall 480 mm

Length barrel 220 mm

Literature Deuchler, no. 246 or 248.

Notes From its overall smooth appearance this gun is probably made from cast iron though no analyses have been carried out. The similarity between this gunpowder weapon and catalogue 23 is striking.

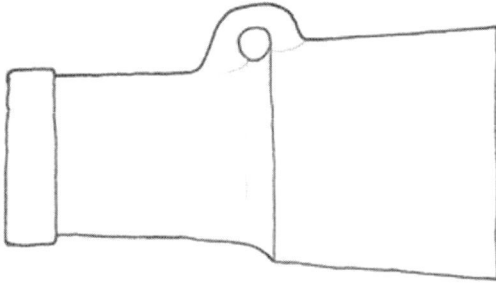

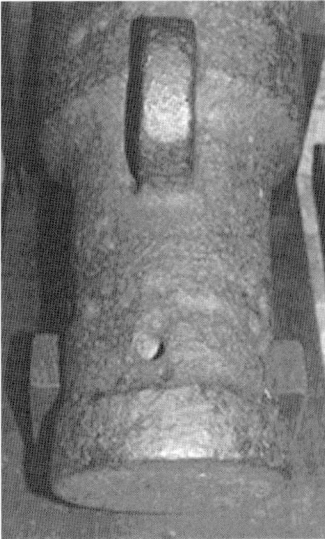

Rear   Muzzle

25

Collection/museum Zeughaus, Berlin, Germany ?

Short description Pestereau ?   **Material** Wrought iron

Catalogue description This gunpowder weapon has a barrel of large diameter with a smaller diameter powder chamber. There is a single lifting-ring lug at the rear of the barrel through which a ring survives. Unfortunately, much of the detail of the barrel and powder chamber are obscured by the iron bands securing the gun to its carriage.

Date Deuchler dates this piece to the fifteenth century.

Dating evidence None

Provenance/booty status Said to be booty from the battle of Nancy.

Bore barrel 180 mm

Bore powder chamber 50 mm

Length overall 805 mm

Length barrel 305 mm

Literature Deuchler, no. 253.

Notes It is unclear whether this piece still exists, but it was formerly in the collections of the Zeughaus in Berlin. The details of dimensions are taken from Deuchler, pp. 327–28.

26

Collection/museum Historisches Museum, Murten, Switzerland

Accession number 109

Short description Veuglaire ?   **Material** Wrought iron

Catalogue description A barrel made from ten staves bound with hoops and bands. The muzzle consists of a double hoop, with that at the end being of considerably larger diameter. Behind the muzzle are three triple-hoop structures, the first and third of which incorporate lifting-ring lugs and rings. The bands in this part of the barrel are very wide, approximately 100 mm. The rear of the gun is made of alternating bands and single hoops, the latter of differing sizes and at irregular spacing. Unusually, the very rear of the piece terminates with a narrow band, which flares outwards, rather than a hoop as in most other wrought-iron gunpowder weapons. The bore of the barrel is approximately 142 mm, but at the rear an additional, internal, ring has been inserted, the join between it and the rearmost band can be clearly seen, reducing the diameter of the breech to 76 mm. On the inside of the gun the staves have been bent inwards to follow the shape of the bore.

Date Deuchler dates this to 1450.

Dating evidence Dated by association with the booty of the battle of Murten.

Provenance/booty status Booty from Murten

Bore barrel 142 mm

Length overall 660 mm

Literature Deuchler, no. 240.

Notes The shape of the rear of this gun, both the irregular spacing and the varying size of the hoops, is unlike the majority of other wrought-iron pieces of similar form. However, more unusual is the way that the bore of the barrel has been drastically reduced at the rear to approximately half its width. The powder chamber neck which fitted this gunpowder weapon was therefore of quite small size. This affects the way in which this gun was loaded, as the ball would have to have been inserted into the muzzle rather than at the breech as is possible with most surviving guns of this type. A very similar-looking gun is shown on a tapestry, now in the Doria Pamphili Gallery in Rome, showing the siege of Rome and dated to 1459. It shows a barrel propped up on timber of similar size and proportions. Two soldiers are shown on either side. The one to the right is completing the loading of a powder chamber by hammering into its neck a wooden tompion. The soldier to the left is preparing to insert a second chamber into the barrel ready for firing. Several large cannon balls and a vase-shaped pot spouting flames from its mouth can be seen next to the gun and in front of the whole scene is a wooden hoarding, a mantlet, protecting the soldiers from enemy attack while they load the gun. Intriguingly, there is no wooden bed which might be expected to contain the barrel and powder chamber in position. A second similar gun is shown being fired in another part of the tapestry. While one soldier pulls down the rear edge of the mantlet to open it, another is shown holding a piece of lighted rope and applying it to the touch hole. Flames and a ball are seen coming from the mouth of the gun. In this scene, although the gun is not mounted on a wooden bed, there is a wooden structure at its rear against which it appears the gun is wedged. The tapestry, which depicts the story of Alexander the Great, was made by Pasquier Grenier in Tournai and is believed to have formed part of the '*chambre*' acquired by Philip the Good from Grenier in 1459.

0   10 cm

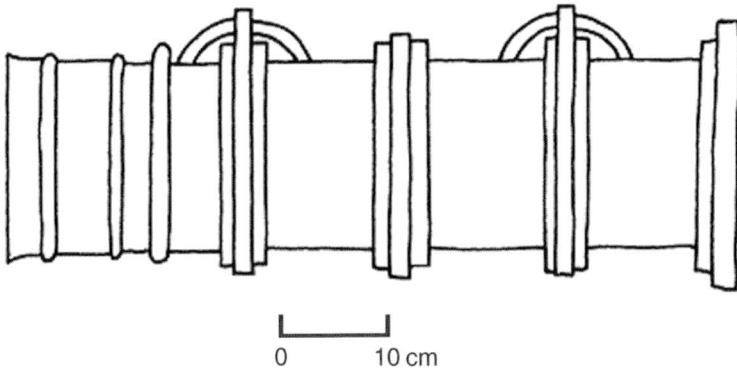

Detail of muzzle

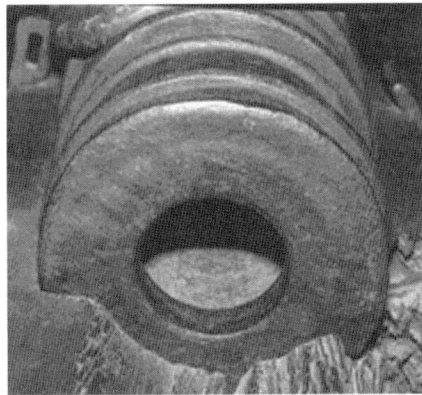

Detail of breech with the opening smaller than the bore of the barrel

27

Collection/museum Historisches Museum, Murten, Switzerland

Accession number 112

Short description Veuglaire ?   **Material** Copper alloy

Catalogue description This gunpowder weapon is cast in copper alloy and has a very pronounced casting line down either side. The muzzle flares out and its front face has been moulded to form a circular indentation. Outwardly, the barrel resembles a wrought-iron gunpowder weapon and has regular semi-circular mouldings in imitation of the hoops of wrought-iron guns. Two lifting-ring lugs, semi-circular with scalloped edges, have been cast into the top of the barrel and still retain their iron lifting rings. Cast into the top of the barrel are two raised circular discs. The opening at the rear of the barrel is slightly smaller, 70 mm in diameter, than the rest of the bore which is approximately 75 mm.

Date Deuchler dates this piece to about 1450.

Dating evidence None

Provenance/booty status Burgundian Booty ?

Bore barrel 75 mm

Length barrel 837 mm

Literature Deuchler, no. 243.

Notes This curious gunpowder weapon has no parallels as far as the authors are aware and, on first inspection, was assumed to be a modern copy due to the pronounced casting lines down either side. However, it is likely that it is original. Like, catalogue no. 26, the ball could only have been loaded at the muzzle.

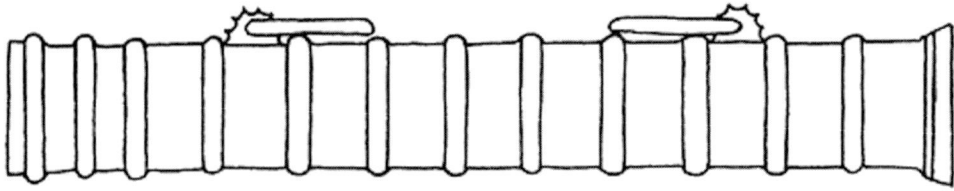

0   10 cm

Muzzle

Muzzle

Breech

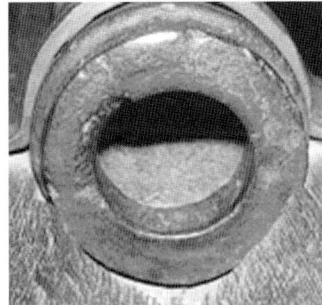

Breech

Conclusion

The history of medieval warfare before the invention and proliferation of gunpowder weapons is largely one based on only two types of combatants: cavalry and infantry, with the infantry broken into two branches, those fighting with static, hand-held weapons and those fighting with archery weapons. The operators of pre-gunpowder artillery were almost always few in number and seem to have been mustered from local populations or regular soldiers. The use of pre-gunpowder artillery was also mainly confined to sieges, and many besieging forces did not even use artillery. Artillery pieces of this sort could be fabricated before the siege, just as easily on site. Examples, such as the siege of Jerusalem in 1099, where the wood for siege machines was found in a nearby cave and from the dismantling of several ships, are frequently found in medieval annals. Medieval generals could react to the circumstances of their sieges and, in the short time it took to construct these engines, be throwing rocks of considerable size against the walls of the besieged fortifications.

As gunpowder weapons began to enter into military frameworks of the fourteenth and fifteenth centuries, there needed to be significant changes in military thinking, and not just in strategy and tactics, which the entry of gunpowder weapons into conflict obviously affected, but also in military administration, logistics, planning, and technology. In their essence, the traditional branches of military service, cavalry and infantry, did not change. But added to them was an entirely new branch: gunpowder artillery. And this was not just a question of new military personnel, nor even a question of a new weapon. Cavalry and infantry were largely self-contained. They could, and usually did, have assistants, varlets, squires, grooms, etc., but this personnel did not need specialist training, nor were they really required. If necessary, a cavalry soldier could take care of himself and his horse; and an infantry soldier generally took care of his own armour and weapons. They also could supply their own victuals, if necessary. On site, though, artillery personnel could do little for themselves and their weapons. While it is true that they did take care of their own personal protection and provided their own foodstuffs, their weapons, gunpowder weapons of all sizes, could not so easily be maintained. Gunpowder artillery personnel could not even carry their own artillery pieces, unless they were the smallest of weapons.

Gunpowder weapons themselves were also an entirely different matter. Gunpowder artillery could rarely be constructed on site. The general thus had to plan to take gunpowder weapons to a siege or battle in advance; he also had to plan what types, sizes, and how many needed to be gathered and transported. All of the ancillary equipment to operate these guns also had to be planned for, gathered, and transported. At the least, this meant gunpowder, ammunition, loading and firing accessories, mounts and beds, but could also include defensive shields – mantlets and pavises – smiths' forges, masons' tools, replacement parts, and fire, not to mention the extraordinarily large number of horses and carts needed to transport all of the guns and their equipment. (In 1475, for example, the whole artillery train needed over 5,000 horses and in excess of 1,000 carts.[1]) Of course, these too needed their personnel: carpenters, masons, smiths, farriers, grooms, pioneers, carters, joiners, tent builders and maintainers, ammunition founders, and their servants.

And this was only what was needed on site. Behind all of this were gunfounders and gunsmiths, gunpowder makers, and carpenters who constructed mounts, carriages, and shields. Moreover, to bring this together there needed to be a substantial increase in the administrative mechanisms to ensure that the gunpowder weapons required on the battlefield or at siege were available. Gunpowder weapons, their powder, and carriages needed to be purchased, made, and stored.

Naturally, there was also the effect of gunpowder weaponry on strategy and tactics: the speed and terrain of march, deployment of forces, order of fighting, position, timing, etc. What was the general trying to achieve and how was he trying to achieve it? What he was trying to achieve was, of course, victory at the lowest possible cost. To do this he had to make the crucial decisions about how and how quickly to arrive at a battlefield or siege and, once there, where to deploy what forces he had – cavalry, infantry, and artillery – in places which he hoped would provide him with a quick and convincing victory. We have already seen how, at Nicopolis, this was done poorly with cavalry and infantry forces alone. On the other hand, at Crécy and Agincourt the English had developed tactics, with only a limited addition of gunpowder weapons, against the French which led to overwhelming victories. Sometimes a general using gunpowder weapons could also fail in his tactics, such as at Beauvais in 1472, when Charles the Bold dragged a huge bombard to the town but failed to bring sufficient ammunition to achieve the conquest, or at the battle of Gavere in 1453, when a stray spark flying into an open gunpowder sack was so misunderstood that it caused the operators to flee and take others with them despite the fact that there was no real danger; the battle was lost. Elsewhere, at Odruik in 1379 and Melun in 1420, to name just two examples, tactics using gunpowder weaponry seem to have been decisive in determining victory.

What this all means is that gunpowder weapons alone were not the determining factor in victory or defeat. Victory still relied largely on the acumen, and sometimes the inventiveness, of the general – as well as on generous doses of luck in many cases. The general who could use gunpowder weapons well undoubtedly benefited from them, though not always. The question then is where and how did gunpowder artillery fit into the established order of things? One of the most interesting aspects of early artillery was the use, in the very earliest guns, of arrows or quarrels as ammunition. This seems at first a strange choice to the modern mind but looked at from another perspective clearly shows that, at a time when there was no way of knowing that spherical projectiles would become the norm for artillery, the gunpowder weapon user was merely copying what was already prevalent, the use of arrows as projectiles both in

---

[1] See Appendix 2.

longbows and crossbows, as well as *ballistae*. However, by the end of the fourteenth and beginning of the fifteenth century, the period concurrent with the beginning of the Valois Burgundian dukes, gunpowder artillery was well established as a weapon of war.

Appendix 1
Summary of Weapons, from
Joseph Garnier

KEY TO TABLE

No	Number
Metal	Material from which gun was made
	A *Arain* (a copper alloy – ?bronze)
	C *Cuivre* (a copper alloy)
	I Iron
	M *Mitaille* (a copper alloy)
	P *Plommée* (lead)
Mat	Method of manufacture
	C Cast
	F Forged
Wt	Weight of piece – in *livres*
Len	Length of piece – in *pieds*
Cal	Calibre of piece – in *pouces*
Ball	Material that ammunition was made of
	I Iron
	P *Plommée* (lead)
	S Stone
Ball wt	Weight of ball – in *livres*
Ch	Number of chambers
Ch wt	Weight of chamber – in *livres*
Pd wt	Weight of powder – in *livres*
Place	Where gun was noted and moved to
	> From
	< To

Bombard

Date	Artillery name	No	Metal	Mat	Wt	Len	Cal	Ball	Ball wt	Ch	Ch wt	Pd wt	Name	Place
1412	Bombard	10												Cuisery
1412	Grant Bombard	1							84.0					Cuisery
1412	Gros Bombard	1		C	16000.0							1.5	d'Auxonne	Dijon
1412	Gros Bombard	1		C								1.5	de Prusse	Dijon
1413	Bombard	1						I	12.0			9.0		Saint-Aubin
1413	Bombard	1											de Valecon	Dijon
1413	Bombard	1											Gueriette	Dijon
1413	Bombard	1											Fille Gueriete	Dijon
1413	Bombard	1											Compaigne	Dijon
1413	Bombard	1											Liete	Dijon
1413	Bombard	1											Senelle	Dijon
1414	Bombard	1											Cenelle	Villaines
1414	Bombard	1											Liete	Villaines
1414	Bombard	1											Compaigne	Villaines
1414	Gros Bombard	1	C/A										de Dijon	Auxonne > Valexon > Villaines
1417	Bombard	1											la fille Griete	Arras Flanders
1417	Grant Canon Bombard	1						S	100.0				La petite Liete	Chateauvilain
1419	Bombard	4												Noyers
1419	Petit Bombard	1		M								7.0		Dijon
1419	Petit Bombard	1		M								4.0		Dijon
1419	Petit Bombard	1		M								3.0		Dijon
1420	Bombard	2						I						Apremont
1420	Bombard	1						I					Cambray	Dijon
1420	Bombard	1						I					l'Ecluse	Dijon
1424	Bombard	1											Griete	Dijon > siege of La Buxiere
1424	Bombard	1											Katherine	Dijon > siege of La Buxiere
1424	Bombard	1											Cambray	Dijon > siege of La Buxiere
1424	Bombard	1											l'Ecluse	Dijon > siege of La Buxiere
1426	Bombard	1											Griete	Dijon > siege of Mailly-le-Duc
1426	Bombard	1											Katherine	Dijon > siege of Mailly-le-Duc
1430	Bombard	1											Prusse	Dijon?
1430	Gros Bombard	1											de Prusse	Dijon

1430–31	Bombard	1	C				S	80.0			*Prusse*	Dijon > Chalon
1431	Bombard	1	C								*Valexon*	Dijon
1431	Bombard	1	C									Dijon
1431	Bombard	1	C									Dijon
1431	Bombard	1	I				S	400.0			*Griete*	Dijon
1431	Bombard	1										Chalon
1431	Bombard	1									*Prusse*	Chalon
1431	Gros Bombard	1	M	C			S	600.0	1		*Bourgoinge*	Dijon
1433	Bombard	1	C							70.0		Besançon
1433	Gros Bombard	1					S				*Bourgoingne*	Dijon
1436	Bombard	2	I				S					Picardy
1436	Bombard	3	C				S					Burgundy
1436	Bombard	2	I				S	120.0				Abbeville
1436	Bombard	1							N			Abbeville
1436	Bombard	1	C								*Pruce*	St. Bertin monastery in St. Omer
1436	Bombard	1	C								*Pruce*	St. Bertin monastery in St. Omer
1436	Bombard	1	C								*Bergiere*	St. Bertin monastery in St. Omer
1436	Bombard Chamber	1	C						1		*Bourgoingne*	St. Bertin monastery in St. Omer
1436	Bombard	1	I									St. Bertin monastery n St. Omer
1436	Gros Bombard	3	I									Holland > siege of Calais
1436	Gros Bombard	3										Holland > siege of Calais
1442	Bombard	1	I								*Katherine*	Dijon
1442	Bombard Chamber	1	I						1		*Griete*	Dijon
1443	Bombard	1	C									St. Omer
1443	Bombard	1	I								*Artois*	St. Omer
1443	Bombard	1	I									Lille?
1443	Bombard	2	I						2		*Bergiere*	Damp > Namur
1443	Bombard	1	C						1		*Bergier*	> Peronne
1443	Bombard	1							N		*Bergier*	> Peronne
1445	Bombard	1	I		24000.0	14.0	S					Lille
1445	Bombard	1	I		24000.0	14.0	S					Lille
1445	Bombard	1	I		24000.0	14.0	S					Namur > Lille
1445	Bombard	1	C									Lille
1445	Bombard	2	I		22000.0	12.0	S		3		*Le damp*	Lille
1445	Bombard	1	I								*Bergier*	Lille
1445	Bombard	1	I									Lille

Date	Artillery name	No	Metal	Mat	Wt	Len	Cal	Ball	Ball wt	Ch	Ch wt	Pd wt	Name	Place
1445	Bombard	1	I											Namur > Lille
1445	Bombard	2											*Le damp*	Lille
1445	Bombard	1											*Bergier*	Lille
1445	Bombard	1											*Artois*	Lille
1445	Bombard	1											*Prusse*	Lille
1445	Gros Bombard	1	I		8200.0		13.0	S		N				Namur
1445	Gros Bombard	2	I		30000.0		22.0	S						Lille
1445	Gros Bombard	2	I											Lille
1446	Gros Bombard	1	I		12000.0	16.0		S	350.0	1		72.0		Tournai
1446	Petit Bombard	1				13.0	12.0							Dijon?
1447	Bombard barrel	1	A			12.0	28.0	S		1			*Luxembourg*	Luxembourg (founded there)
1474	Bombard	1	I											Dijon > Burgundy
1474	Gros Bombard	1	I					S						Dijon > siege of Sancenay
		106												
	Bombardelle													
1431	Petit Bombardelle	1	I	C				I	6.0					Dijon
1442	Bombardelle	3	I							N				Dijon
1443	Bombardelle	1								2			*Bergier*	Lille?
		5												
	Canon													
1410	Canon	1												Montot en Charollois
1410	Canon	3												Cuisery
1410	Canon	4												Cuisery
1411	Canon	4	I					S	20.0					Dijon
1411	Canon	4	I					S	12.0					Dijon
1411	Canon	12	I					S	5.0					Dijon
1411	Canon	7	I					P						Dijon
1411	Canon	1						P						Duesme
1411	Canon	1						S	5.0					Duesme
1411	Canon	1	I					S	5.0					Maisey
1411	Canon	2	I					P						Salmaise

1411	Canon	1	I		5.0	S	Salmaise
1411	Canon	1	I			P	Vielchastel
1411	Canon	1	I		5.0	S	Argilly
1411	Canon	2	I		5.0	S	Montbar
1411	Canon	2	I		5.0	S	Montreal
1411	Canon	1	I			P	Chastelgirard
1411	Canon	1	I		5.0	S	Brancion
1411	Canon	1	I			P	Brancion
1411	Canon	2	I		5.0	S	Châtillon-sur-Seine
1411–12	Canon	1	I			P	Châtillon-sur-Seine
1412	Canon	6					Cuisery
1412–13	Canon	23	I			S	Dole
1413	Canon	23	I			S	Dole
1413	Canon	4	I		10.5	S	Dole
1413	Canon	12	I		8.5	S	Dole
1413	Canon	8	I		7.5	S	Dole
1413	Canon	1	I		8.5	S	Chastelgirard
1413	Canon	2	I		12.0	S	Semur en Brionnois
1413	Canon	1	I		17.0	S	Montcenis
1413	Canon	1	I		11.0	S	Montcenis
1413	Canon	1	I			S	Brancion
1413	Canon	2	I			S	Sagy
1413	Canon	10	I			S	Places du Charollais
1413	Canon	1	I		7.0	S	La Colonne
1413	Canon	1	I		8.5	S	La Colonne
1413	Canon	1	I		24	S	Châtillon-les-Besançon
1413	Canon	1	I		7.5	S	Châtillon-les-Besançon
1413	Canon	10	I	3		S	Dijon
1413	Petit canon	1	I		17.0		Montbard
1413	Petit canon	1	I		10.5		Montbard
1413	Petit canon	1	I		7.5		Montbard
1414	Canon	1	I		16.0	S	Châtillon-sur-Seine
1414	Canon	2	I			P	Aignay
1414	Canon	1	I	C	12.0	S	Aigna
1414	Canon	2	I			P	Villaines
1414	Canon	1	I		10.0	S	Villaines

Date	Artillery name	No	Metal	Mat	Wt	Len	Cal	Ball	Ball wt	Ch	Ch wt	Pd wt	Name	Place
1414	Canon	1	I					S	8.5					Villaines
1414	Canon	6	I					P						"Jussey, Faucogney, Montjustin"
1414	Canon	3						S	10.0					"Jussey, Faucogney, Montjustin"
1414	Canon	3						S	8.0					"Jussey, Faucogney, Montjustin"
1414	Canon	6	I	C										Dijon
1414	Petit Canon	4		C										Artois
1415	Canon	2						P						Aisey
1415	Canon	2	I	C										"Belfort, county Ferrette"
1415	Canon	2	I		8.5									"Belfort, county Ferrette"
1415	Canon	4						P						"Belfort, county Ferrette"
1415	Canon	2			15.0									Pontarlier
1415	Canon	9			18.0									Pontarlier
1415	Gros Canon	1	I					C						Montmirey
1416	Gran Canon	2	I					S	15.0					Vignory
1417	Canon	1	I	C				S	20.0	N				Montbar; > siege of St.-Florentin
1417	Canon	2	P	C										Rouvre
1417	Canon	1	I											Rouvre
1417	Petit Canon	1	I					S	7.5					Châteauvillain
1417	Petit Canon	1	I											Siege of Nogent-le-Roi
1417	Petit canon	2						P						Siege de Nogent-le-Roi
1419	Canon	2						P						Aisey
1419	Gros Canon	1												Lille > Roye
1420	Canon	1											Weghelaire	Montcenis
1420	Canon	1	I					S	20.0					Cherlieu
1420	Gros Canon	1												Lille > Roye
1420	Gros Canon	1												Lille? > Roye
1420	Petit Canon	1						P						Saint-Seine-sur-Vingeanne
1422	Canon	2	M					S						Cuisery
1422	Canon	2	I		60.0			S	3.0					Cuisery
1422	Canon	6	M	C				S						Dijon
1422	Canon	2	M	C				S	6.0					Cuiserey Dijon
1422	Canon	1		C										Cuiserey Dijon
1422	Canon	2	M	C				S	7.0					Louhans Dijon
1422	Canon	2						S						Sagy Dijon

Year	Weapon	No.	Col.1	Col.2	Wt.1	Wt.2	Col.3	No.2	Col.4	No.3	Location
1426	Canon	1	I				P				Vielchastel
1429	Canon	1	I				S				Salmaise
1430	Canon	1	I				S	8.5			Chaussins
1431	Canon	57	I		31.0						Talant
1431	Meschant Canon	1	I	C		1.0	S	3.0	N		Dijon
1433	Canon	7	I				S	10.0			Aval
1433	Gros Canon	1	I				S	24.0			Aval? > Grancey-le-Château
1433	Gros Canon	2	I				S	16.0			Aval? > Grancey-le-Château
1433	Gros Canon	2	I				S	12.0			Aval? > Grancey-le-Château
1436	Gros Canon	3	I								St. Omer > Montraire Castle
1436	Petit Canon	2							7		Abbeville
1437	Canon	2					S		2		siege of le Crotoy
1437	Petit Canon	1	C						2		Vergy
1442	Canon	1	I	C							Dijon
1442	Canon	1	I	C							Dijon
1443	Canon	2	I			2.0			N		Luxembourg
1443	Canon	1	I			1.5			N		Luxembourg
1443	Canon	1	I			2.5					Luxembourg
1443	Petit Canon a main	1	I								Villy Castle
1443	Petit Canon	4	I			1.0					Villy Castle
1443	Petit Canon	1	I			1.0					Luxembourg
1443	Petit Canon	1	I			1.0					Luxembourg
1443	Petit Canon	1	I			1.0					Luxembourg
1445	Canon	1	I		976.0	4.5	S		2		Dijon
1446	Gros Canon	1	I			7.0	S	20.0	2	306.0	Tournai
1447	Canon	30	I			4.0	S		3	4.0	Dijon
1447	Canon	1	I		4000.0	8.0	S			8.0	Dijon
1459	Gros Canon	1	I			9.0					Dijon
1465	Canon	1	I		3.0	3.0	S		1		Saulx-le-Duc
		381									

Coulovrine

Year	Weapon	No.	Col.1	Col.2	Wt.1	Wt.2	Col.3	No.2	Col.4	No.3	Location
1420	Couleuvrine	6					P				Montreal
1420	Couleuvres	3									Sagy
1429	Coleuvre	6	I								Bar-sur-Seine

Date	Artillery name	No	Metal	Mat	Wt	Len	Cal	Ball	Ball wt	Ch	Ch wt	Pd wt	Name	Place
1430	Coleuvre	2	I					P						La Colonne
1430	Coleuvre	2	I											Germoles
1430	Coleuvre	3	I											siege of Sancenay
1430	Coleuvre	6	C											
1430	Coleuvre	26	I		14.3									
1430	Coleuvre	5	I		15.0									
1430	Coleuvre	16												
1430	Coleuvre	6			12.0									Chalon > siege of Sancenay
1430	Coleuvre a main	1												Saulx-le-Duc
1430	Couleuvre	4	I											Lanthenay
1430	Couleuvre	2												Talant
1430	Couleuvre	6	I					P						Châteaugirard
1430	Couleuvre	2												Dijon?
1430	Couleuvre	6			12.0									Châtillon-sur-Seine
1430	Couleuvres	6												Mirebeau
1430	Couleuvres	2	I											"Jussey, Faucogney, Montjustin"
1430	Couleuvres	2	I											Aisey
1430	Petit couleuvres	4												
1430–31	Coleuvre	8	I		9.8									Dijon
1430–31	Coleuvre	8			13.1									Dijon
1430–31	Coleuvre	16			14.9									Dijon
1430–31	Coleuvre	8			13.5									Dijon
1431	Coleuvre	8	I											
1431	Coleuvre	42	I											Dijon (Normandeaul hostel)
1431	Coleuvre	3	C	C										Dijon (Normandeaul hostel)
1431	Coleuvrine	48			13.9									
1431	Colevrine	11	I					S						Bracon
1431	Couleuvre	2												Le Riveaul d'Autun
1432–33	Coleuvre	26						P						Dijon
1433	Colovrine	4			51.5									Places du Charollais
1433	Couleuvre	2												Le Riveaul d'Autun
1433	Couleuvre	4												Dijon > siege of Avalon?
1433	Coulouvrine	3												Flanders > Burgundy
1433	Gros Coulovrine	7	I											Flanders > Burgundy

Year	Type	No.					Location
1433	Gros Coulovrine	6	C				Flanders > Burgundy
1433	Petit Coulovrine à main	6	C				Flanders > Burgundy
1436	Couleuvrine	24	C				Sluys
1436	Couleuvrine	40	I				> siege of Calais
1436	Couleuvrine	200	C	0.5	N		> siege of Calais
1436	Coulovrine à escappe	1	C		1		> siege of Calais
1436	Coulovrine à escappe	1	C		2		> siege of Calais
1436	Coulovrine	3	C		2		> siege of Calais
1436	Coulovrine à main	8	C				naval
1436	Coulovrine à escappe	1	C		1		naval
1436	Coulovrine à escappe	1	C		2		naval
1436	Coulovrine à escappe	1	C		2		naval
1436	Coulovrine	3	C				naval
1436	Coulovrine	100	C				St. Bertin Abbey in St. Omer
1436	Couleuvrine	39	I	0.5			St. Bertin Abbey in St. Omer
1436	Couleuvrine	5	C				Gravelines
1436	Couleuvrine	8	I				Sluys Castle
1436	Couleuvrine	33	C				Sluys
1436	Couleuvrine	8	C				Avesnes
1436	Couleuvrine	2					St. Omer > Montraire Castle
1436	Couleuvrine	9	I				St. Omer > Ardres
1436	Couleuvrine	30	C				St. Omer > Ardres
1436	Couleuvrine	24	I				siege of Calais
1436	Gros Coulovrine	4	I				siege of Calais
1436	Gros Coulovrine	24	I				Sluys
1436	Gros Coulovrine	24	I			N	siege of le Crotoy
1436	Petit Coulovrine	4	C			N	siege of le Crotoy
1437	Colouvrine	1	I			N	siege of le Crotoy
1437	Colouvrine	4	C				siege of le Crotoy
1437	Couleuvrine	21	I				siege of le Crotoy
1437	Couleuvrine	15					siege of le Crotoy
1437	Coulouvrine	3	C				siege of le Crotoy
1437	Coulovrine	23	I				St. Omer > siege of le Crotoy
1437	Coulovrine	28	C				St. Omer > siege of le Crotoy
1437	Coulovrine	3					St. Omer siege of le Crotoy
1437	Coulovrine	6	I				Abbeville > siege of le Crotoy
1437	Coulovrine	1	I				siege of le Crotoy

Date	Artillery name	No	Metal	Mat	Wt	Len	Cal	Ball	Ball wt	Ch	Ch wt	Pd wt	Name	Place
1437	Coulovrine	4	C											siege of le Crotoy
1437	Coulovrine	4	C											siege of le Crotoy
1437	Coulovrine	6	C					P	2.0					siege of le Crotoy
1437	Coulovrine	6	I											siege of le Crotoy
1437	Coulovrine	2												siege of le Crotoy
1437	Coulovrine	2	I											siege of le Crotoy
1437	Coulovrine	2	C											siege of le Crotoy
1437	Coulovrine	2	C					P						siege of le Crotoy
1437	Coulovrine	4												siege of le Crotoy
1437	Coulovrine	6												siege of le Crotoy
1437	Coulovrine	4	I											Abbeville > siege of le Crotoy
1437	Coulovrine	6	C											Abbeville > siege of le Crotoy
1437	Coulovrine	12	I											siege of le Crotoy
1437	Coulovrine	24												siege of le Crotoy
1437	Petit Coulovrine à main	12								2				Lille > Abbeville
1438	Colovrine	3	I											Chaussins
1440	Gros Coulovrine	25	I											siege of Villy
1440	Moyen Coulovrine	25	I											siege of Villy
1442	Coulovrine	6	C											Dijon
1442	Coulovrine	6	C											Dijon
1442	Coulovrine	6	C	C										Dijon
1442	Coulovrine	6	C											Dijon
1442	Coulovrine à main	1	C							3				Dijon
1442	Coulovrine	4	C	C										Dijon
1442	Coulovrine	6	C											Dijon
1442	Coulovrine chamber	27	C											Dijon
1442	Coulovrine	12	I/C											Flanders > Burgundy
1442	Grande Coulovrine	1	C											Dijon
1443	Colouvrine	122	I											Aire Castle
1443	Coulouvrine	4								4				Bruges > Aire Castle
1443	Coulouvrine	1												Bruges > Aire Castle
1443	Colouvrine à main	6												Bruges > Aire Castle
1443	Couleuvrine	2												Vergy
1443	Coulovrine	8	I											St. Omer

1443	Coulovrine	8	C	P			conquest of Luxembourg
1443	Coulovrine	8	I	P			conquest of Luxembourg
1443	Coulovrine	14	I			2	Bruges/Tournai > Luxembourg
1443	Coulovrine	12	I			1	Bruges/Tournai > Luxembourg
1443	Coulovrine	2	C				Aire Castle/St.Omer > Namur
1443	Coulovrine	8	C				Aire Castle/St.Omer > Namur
1443	Coulovrine	56	I				Aire Castle/St.Omer > Namur
1443	Coulovrine	3	I				Villy Castle
1443	Coulovrine	2					Luxembourg
1443	Coulovrine	6		P			siege of Villy
1443	Coulovrine	7					siege of Villy
1443	Coulovrine	2					siege of Villy
1443	Gran Coulovrine	25					Bruges
1443	Gran Coulovrine	25	C				Aire Castle & St. Omer > Namur
1443	Gran Coulovrine	3	C				Aire Castle & St. Omer > Namur
1443	Gros Coulovrine	18	C			2	Aire Castle & St. Omer > Namur
1443	Gros Coulovrine	1	C	P			Villy Castle
1443	Pesan Coulouvrine	18				2	Bruges
1443	Petit Coulovrine	2	C				Aire Castle/Lille > Namur
1444	Coulevrine	3	I		3.3	3	Mont-Saint-Vincent
1444	Coulovrine	2	I	P	2.3	3	Charolles
1444	Coulovrine	2	I	P	2.5	3	Dondain
1444	Coulovrine	1	I	P	2.5	3	Artus
1444	Coulovrine	2	I	P	2.5	3	Le Sauvement
1444	Gros Colovrine	4	I				Mont-Morot
1444	Gros Couleuvrine	2	I			2	"Jussey, Faucogney, Montjustin"
1444	Gros Couleuv-ine	2	I			1	"Jussey, Faucogney, Montjustin"
1445	Couleuvrine	2	I				Dueme
1445	Coulovrine	2	I				Vazage
1445	Coulovrine	8	I				Limburg Castle
1445	Coulovrine	4	I				Kerpen Castle
1445	Coulovrine	5	C				Luxembourg
1445	Coulovrine	4	I				Luxembourg
1445	Coulovrine	3	C	P			siege of Rochefort
1445	Coulovrine	4	I	P			siege of Rochefort
1445	Coulovrine à main	12	I				Oudenaarde/Courtrai

Date	Artillery name	No	Metal	Mat	Wt	Len	Cal	Ball	Ball wt	Ch	Ch wt	Pd wt	Name	Place
1445	Coulovrine	5	C					P		2				Lille
1445	Coulovrine	60	C					P						Lille
1445	Coulovrine	86	I					P						Lille
1445	Coulovrine	41	I					P						Lille
1445	Coulovrine	5	C					P						Lille
1445	Coulovrine	45	I											Lille
1445	Coulovrine	11	C											Lille
1445	Coulovrine	5	C							2				Lille
1445	Coulovrine	2								3				naval
1445	Coulovrine à main	12												naval
1445	Gros Couleuvrine	3	I											Pontailler-sur-Saône
1445	Gros Couleuvrine	6	C							2				Lille
1446	Colovrine	40												St. Omer?
1446	Colovrine	20												St. Omer?
1446	Coulouvrine	50	I							2				St. Omer?
1446	Coulouvrine	50	I							1				St. Omer?
1446	Coulouvrine	12	I							3				St. Omer?
1446	Coulouvrine à main	72	I											St. Omer?
1446	Coulouvrine	50	I											Tournai
1447	Coulouvrine	4	I											Cravant Castle
1449	Coulevrine	46	I											Antwerp > Scotland
1449	Coulevrine	1	I											> Namur
1449	Coulevrine à main	2	I											> Namur
1449	Coulevrine à main	4												> Namur
1451	Coulevrine à main	2	C											
1451	Coulevrine	1	I											
1465	Couleuvrines	1												> Villaines
1465	Couleuvrine	1												> Villaines
1465	Couleyrine	1	I											Saulx-le-Duc
1465	Couleyrine	1	I											Saulx-le-Duc
1465	Couleuvrine à main	4	I											Grancey-le-Château
1465	Coulovrine	2				2.5								Grancey
1465	Coulovrine	2				2.0								Grancey
1465	Coulovrine	2				2.5								Montbard

Year	Name	Count	Type	Weight		Num	Location
1465	Coulovrine	2		2.0			Montbard
1465	Petit Couleuvrine	2		2.0			Grancey
1472	Gros Coulovrine	4		4.0			Mont-Saint-Vincent
1474	Colevrine à crochet	6					Dijon
1474	Colevrine à main	4					Dijon
1474	Colovrine à croucher	1	M	44.0			
1474	Colovrine à croucher	1	M	41.0			
1474	Colovrine à croucher	1	M	37.0			
1474	Colovrine à croucher	1	M	47.0			
1474	Gros Coulevrine	16	I				
		2365					

Courtau

Year	Name	Count	Type	Weight		Num	Location
1474	Courtaul	2	M		S		Luxembourg
		2					

Crapaudeau

Year	Name	Count	Type	Weight		Num	Location
1433	Crappaudeaul	2	C			1	Flanders > Burgundy
1433	Crappaudeaul	1	I			7	Flanders > Burgundy
1436	Crappaudeau	12	I			2	> siege of Calais
1436	Crappaudeau	3					Abbeville
1436	Crappaudeau	5				2	Gravelines
1436	Crappaudeau	2	I			2	St. Omer > Ardres
1436	Petit Crappaudeau	2			S/P		
1437	Crapaudeau	1	I				Rue > siege of le Crotoy
1437	Crappaudeau	5	I			4	St. Omer > siege of le Crotoy
1437	Crappaudeau	1			S		LilleAbbeville
1437	Crappaudeau	2			P	2	siege of le Crotoy
1437	Crappaudeau	5	I			4	siege of le Crotoy
1437	Crappaudeaul	1	I			2	siege of le Crotoy
1437	Crappaudeaul	1				2	siege of le Crotoy
1440	Crappaudeau	1	I				siege of Villy
1440	Gros Crappaudeau	36				2	siege of Villy
1440	Gros Crappaudeau	4				2	siege of Villy
1442	Crappaudeau	34	I		P		Dijon

Date	Artillery name	No	Metal	Mat	Wt	Len	Cal	Ball	Ball wt	Ch	Ch wt	Pd wt	Name	Place
1442	Gros Crappaudeau	2	C											Dijon
1443	Crapaudeau	7	I											St. Omer
1443	Crappaudeau	2								2				Bruges
1443	Crappaudeau	2	C							2				Aire Castle & St. Omer > Namur
1443	Crappaudeau	74	I					S		2				Peronne
1443	Crappaudeau	29	C					S		2				Peronne
1443	Crapaudeau	4						S						siege of Villy
1443	Crappaudeaul	1	C					P		2				Villy Castle
1443	Crappaudeaul	1	C							2				Villy Castle
1443	Gran Crappaudeau	9								2				Bruges
1443	Gros Crappaudeau	9	C							2				Aire Castle & St. Omer > Namur
1443	Pesan Crappaudau	4								2				Bruges
1444	Crapaudine	1	I											Mont-Morot
1445	Crapaudeau	120	I				2.0	S		3				St. Omer
1445	Crapaudeau	50								3				St. Omer
1445	Crapaudeau	12	I				4.0	S		3				St. Omer
1445	Crapaudeau	115	I							0				Lille
1445	Crapaudeau	5	C							0				Lille
1445	Crappaudeau	3	I		175.0									siege of Rochefort/Harchimont
1445	Crapaudeau	2	I		132.0									siege of Rochefort/Harchimont
1445	Crappaudeau	6								2				Oudenaarde/Courtrai
1445	Crappaudeau	120	I		191.7		2.0	S		2				Lille
1445	Crappaudeau	50	C		140.0					3				Lille
1445	Crappaudeau	2	C							3				Lille
1445	Crappaudeau	5	I					P		2				Lille
1445	Crappaudeau	2	C							2				Lille
1445	Gros Crappaudeau	3								2				Lille
1445	Gros Crappaudeau	3	C											Lille
1446	Crappaudeau	87				5.0	2.0	S		2				St. Omer?
1446	Crappaudeau	15			106.7		2.0	S		2				Tournai
1446	Long Crapaudeau	24					2.0	S		2				St. Omer?
1449	Crappauldeau	1	I			4.5	1.0	S		2				Namur
1451	Crappaudeau	12	I			4.0	2.0	S		2				Ardre
		900												

Year	Name	Qty	Type	Weight	N	P	Location
Hacquebus							
1474	Hacquebus	4				P	Dijon
1475	Hacquebuss	5	I	44.2			Montreal
		9					
Miscellaneous							
1431	Gros Plombée	37	I			P	Dijon
1445	Perdrizau	14					Lille
1445	Perdrizau	14					Boulogne > Lille
		65					
Ribaudequin							
1419	Petit Baudequin	5	M		1.0		Dijon
1424	Petit Ribaudequin	4			2		Dijonsiege of La Buxiere
1474	Ribaudequin	2					Dijon
		11					
Serpentine							
1470	Gran Serpentire	2	I	5.0	2		Talant
1473–74	Serpentine	1	M	559.0		P	Dijon?
1474	Gros Serpentine	1					Dijon
1474	Gros Serpentire	1	M	1549.5			Dijon
1474	Moyen Serpen:ine	5					
1474	Petit Serpentire	4					
1474	Petit Serpentire	2	I				Arc-en-Barrois Castle
1474	Serpentine	3					Dijon
1474	Serpentine	2	I	332.0	1		Dijon
1474	Serpentine	1					Talaut
1474	Serpentine	1		547.0		P	Dijon?
		23					
Veuglaire							
1417	Veuglaire	2					Arras > Flanders
1417	Vueilglaire	2					Nogent-le-Roi

Date	Artillery name	No	Metal	Mat	Wt	Len	Cal	Ball	Ball wt	Ch	Ch wt	Pd wt	Name	Place
1420	Weughelaire	1												Saint-Seine-sur-Vingeanne
1421	Weghelaire	2	M											Saulx-le-Duc
1422	Veulglaire	1	I					S						Montréal
1423	Wguelaire	2							5.0					Dijon > siege of Cravant
1423	Vuelglaire	1	I					S						Montreal
1423	Veuglaire	1	I					S	4.0					Dijon
1423	Veuglaire	1	I					S	5.0					Dijon
1424	Gros Veuglaire	1							6.0					Dijon > siege of La Buxiere
1424	Veuglaire	4												Dijon > siege of La Buxiere
1426	Gros Veuglaire	1												Dijon > siege of Mailly-le-Duc
1429	Veuglaire	6												Bar-sur-Seine
1429	Vinglaire/Canon	1						S						Vielchatel
1430	WIglaire	1						S	25.0					Mirebeau
1431	Gros Veuglaire	2												Chalon > siege of Sancenay
1431	Gros Veuglelaire	1	I			1.5			24.0	1				Dijon
1431	Petit Veuglelaire	1	I						8.0	1				Dijon (Normandeaul hostel)
1431	Petit Veuglelaire	1	I						5.0	N				Dijon (Normandeaul hostel)
1431	Petit Weughelaire	1												Saint-Seine-sur-Vingeanne
1431	Veuglaires	3												siege of Sancenay
1431	Vuglaire	1	I											siege of Sancenay
1431	Weuglaire	2	M											Dijon
1433	Gros Vinglaire	1		F										
1433	WIglaire	4						S						Chalon
1436	Canon Veuglaire	23												Sluys
1436	Gros Veuglaire	1								2				Damp > siege of Calais
1436	Gros Veuglaire	3								1				> siege of Calais
1436	Gros Veuglaire	1								2				St. Bertin abbey in St. Omer
1436	Gros Veuglaire	4	I							N				St. Bertin abbey in St. Omer
1436	Gros Veuglaire	1								1				Graveline
1436	Gros Veuglaire	1								1				Gravelines
1436	Gros Veuglaire	4						S	5.0	2				naval
1436	Gros Veuglaire	3								3				naval
1436	Gros Veuglaire	1	I							1				Damp > Sluys
1436	Gros Veuglaire	1	I							2		25.0		St. Omer > Ardres

Year	Type	No.		Weight			Count	Location
1436	Gros Veuglaire	2	I	3000.0			2	> siege of Calais
1436	Petit Veuglaire	16					2	> siege of Calais
1436	Petit Veuglaire	4					3	> siege of Calais
1436	Petit Veuglaire	2		2.0				Abbeville
1436	Petit Veuglaire	3					1	
1436	Veuglaire	11					3	Holland > siege of Calais
1436	Veuglaire	2					0	Bruges > siege of Calais
1436	Veuglaire	4					2	
1436	Veuglaire	23					3	Bruges/Sluys > siege of Calais
1436	Veuglaire	10	I			s	2	
1436	Veuglaire	4	I			s	3	
1436	Veuglaire	5			_Anvers_		2	
1436	Veuglaire	1	I				0	Abbeville
1436	Veuglaire	2	I				1	Abbeville
1436	Veuglaire	1	I				5	Sluys
1436	Veuglaire	3	I				3	Sluys
1436	Veuglaire	2	I				3	Sluys
1436	Veuglaire	1	I				2	Sluys
1436	Veuglaire	2	I				1	Sluys
1436	Veuglaire	3					0	Sluys
1436	Veuglaire chamber	4	I				4	Sluys
1436	Veuglaire	2	I				3	Sluys
1436	Veuglaire	2	I				2	Sluys
1436	Veuglaire	2	I				2	on the barge Eliment Faye
1436	Veuglaire	10	I			s	2	Sluys Castle
1436	Veuglaire	4	I			s	2	On a galley made at Sluys
1436	Veuglaire	2	I				2	Avennes
1436	Veuglaire	4	I	8.0			2	Sluys (Tour de Bourgogne)
1436	Veuglaire	1	I				1	St. OmerArdres
1437	Gran Veuglaire	2	I				2	St. Omer
1437	Gran Veuglaire	2	I				2	siege of le Crotoy
1437	Gros Veuglaire	2				s	2	le Crotoy
1437	Gros Veuglaire	1				s	2	le Crotoy
1437	Petit Veuglaire	2	I				2	St. Omer > siege of le Crotoy
1437	Petit Veuglaire	2	I				2	siege of le Crotoy
1437	Veuglaire	2	I				2	St. Omer > siege of le Crotoy

Date	Artillery name	No	Metal	Mat	Wt	Len	Cal	Ball	Ball wt	Ch	Ch wt	Pd wt	Name	Place
1437	Veuglaire chamber	2	I							2				St. Omer > siege of le Crotoy
1437	Veuglaire	6								2				Lille > Abbeville
1437	Veuglaire	2	I							2				siege of le Crotoy
1437	Veuglaire chamber	1								1				siege of le Crotoy
1440	Gros Veuglaire	1	I		3300.0		8.5	S		2				siege of Villy
1440	Veuglaire	2	C					S/P		6				siege of Villy
1442	Gran Veuglaire	2					6.0	S		1				Dijon
1442	Veuglaire chamber	1	I											Dijon
1443	Gros Veuglaire	1	I		4600.0		9.0	S		2				St. Omer > Aire Castle
1443	Gros Veuglaire	1	I		3926.0		9.5	S		2				St. Omer > Aire Castle
1443	Gros Veuglaire	1	C							2				Luxembourg
1443	Gros Veuglaire	4						S						siege of Villy
1443	Petit Veuglaire	3	C			1.0				N				Luxembourg
1443	Petit Veuglaire	1	I							1				> Peronne
1443	Veuglaire	2	I			8.0		S					*le Matin*	Tournai > Aire Castle
1443	Veuglaire	2	I			6.0	4.0	S		2				Tournai > Aire Castle
1443	Veuglaire	2	I			4.0	4.0	S		2				Tournai > Aire Castle
1443	Veuglaire	3	I			6.0	3.0	P		2				Tournai > Aire Castle
1443	Veuglaire	1	I		7895.0		11.0	S		2				Tournai > Aire Castle
1443	Veuglaire	1	I		3349.0		8.5	S		2				Tournai > Aire Castle
1443	Veuglaire	2								2				Bruges > Aire Castle
1443	Veuglaire	2	I				8.0	S		2				Bruges
1443	Veuglaire	2	I				8.0	S		0				Bruges
1443	Veuglaire	1	I							0				St. Omer
1443	Veuglaire	1								0				St. Omer
1443	Veuglaire	1								0				St. Omer
1443	Veuglaire	3	I							2				Bruges/TournaiNamur
1443	Veuglaire	1	I							1				Villy Castle
1443	Veuglaire	6	I							2				Villy Castle
1443	Veuglaire	1	I							1				Villy Castle
1443	Veuglaire	2	I							1				Luxembourg
1443	Veuglaire	1	C			3.0				N				Luxembourg
1443	Veuglaire	1	C			2.5				N				Luxembourg
1443	Veuglaire	1	C							N				Luxembourg

Year	Name	No.	Cl.	Wt.	L.	cal.	P/S	shot	N	Wt.2	cost	Location
1443	Veuglaire	3	C						N			Luxembourg
1443	Veuglaire	1	I						N			Luxembourg
1443	Veuglaire	1							0			Luxembourg
1443	Veuglaire	2							N			Luxembourg
1443	Veuglaire	1	I						N			Luxembourg
1443	Veuglaire	1							N			Luxembourg
1443	Weuguelaire	2	I		1.5		P	2.0	4			"Jussey, Faucogney, Montjustin"
1444	Wglaire	1	I		1.5		S	8.0	2			Faucogney Castle
1444	Canon Vuelglaire	1	I	765.0	4.5	6.5	S		2	277.5	4.0	Dijon
1445	Gros Veuglaire	1				7.0	S		2			Oudenaarde/Courtrai
1445	Gros Veuglaire	1	I	4500.0		10.0	S		1			Lille
1445	Gros Veuglaire	4		1056.0	3.0	8.5	S		2	356.0	12.0	Dijon
1445	Gros Vueiglaire	1	I						2			Lille
1445	Petit Vuelglaire	2		219.5	4.0	3.0	S		2		1.0	Dijon
1445	Petit Vuelglaire	4	I	218.5	3.5	2.0	S		2		0.5	Dijon
1445	Veuglaire	12	I		6.5		S	12.0	2		3.0	Peronne
1445	Veuglaire	24	I		5.5		S	8.0	2		2.0	Dijon
1445	Veuglaire	40	I		5.0		S	6.0	2		1.5	Dijon
1445	Veuglaire	60	I		4.5		S	4.0	2		1.3	Dijon
1445	Veuglaire	70	I		4.5		S	2.0	2		1.0	Dijon
1445	Veuglaire	2	I		5.0	5.0	S		2			St. Omer?
1445	Veuglaire	3	I		3.0	3.0	S		2			St. Omer?
1445	Veuglaire	2	?F	985.0					2			siege of Rochefort/Harchimont
1445	Veuglaire	1	F		2.5	5.0	S		2			Luxembourg
1445	Veuglaire	1	I		2.5	5.0	S		2			Luxembourg
1445	Veuglaire	6	I			3.0	S		2		1.0	Oudenaarde/Courtrai Castles
1445	Vuelglaire	1	I	281.5	4.0	3.0	S		2		1.0	Dijon
1445	Vuelglaire	1	I	203.0	4.0	3.0	S		2		1.0	Dijon
1445	Vuelglaire	1	I	142.0	3.5	2.5	S		2		1.0	Dijon
1445	Vueiglaire	1	I	105.0	3.5	2.5	S		2		1.0	Dijon
1445	Vuelglaire	1	I	150.0	3.5	2.5	S		2		1.0	Dijon
1445	Vuelglaire	1	I	155.0	3.5	3.5	S		2		1.0	Dijon
1445	Vuelglaire	1	I	190.0	3.5	2.0	S		2		1.0	Dijon
1445	Veuglaire	3	I	176.0	3.0	10.0	S		2		1.0	Lille

Date	Artillery name	No	Metal	Mat	Wt	Len	Cal	Ball	Ball wt	Ch	Ch wt	Pd wt	Name	Place
1445	Veuglaire	5	I		800.0		5.0	S						Lille
1445	Veuglaire	2	I		2250.0		7.0	S						Lille
1445	Veuglaire	12	I		500.0		5.0	S		3				Lille
1445	Veuglaire	2	I							2				Lille
1445	Vuegloires	2	I											Lille
1445	Vuegloires	22	I											Lille
1445	Vuelglaire	1	I		846.3	4.1	6.0	S		2	134.3	4.0		Dijon
1445	Vuelglaire	1	I		780.0	4.5	5.5	S		2		3.0		Dijon
1445	Vuelglaire	1	I		418.5	4.0	4.0	S		2		3.0		Dijon
1445	Vuelglaire	1	I		850.0	4.1	5.5	S		2		3.0		Dijon
1445	Vuelglaire	1	I		538.0	4.4	4.1	S		2		3.0		Dijon
1445	Vuelglaire	1	I		492.0	4.0	4.1	S		2		3.0		Dijon
1445	Vuelglaire	1	I		550.0	4.5	4.0	S		2		4.0		Dijon
1445	Vuelglaire	1	I		728.0	4.5	5.5	S		2		3.0		Dijon
1445	Vuelglaire	1	I		775.0	4.5	5.5	S		2		3.0		Dijon
1445	Vuelglaire	1	I		1100.0	4.5	6.1	S		2	312.0	4.0		Dijon
1445	Vuelglaire	1	I		1130.0	4.2	6.8	S		2	312.0	4.0		Dijon
1445	Vuelglaire	1	I		1025.0	4.5	6.0	S		2	225.0	3.0		Dijon
1445	Vuelglaire	1	I		1366.0	5.0	7.3	S		2	215.0	4.0		Dijon
1446	Veuglaire	5				4.0	4.0	S		3				on galley
1446	Veuglaire	12				4.0	4.0	S		2				St. Omer?
1446	Veuglaire	6				7.0	7.0	S		2				St. Omer?
1446	Veuglaire	2				6.0	6.0	S		2				St. Omer?
1445	Vuelglaire	1	I		971.3	4.5	6.0	S		2	131.3			Dijon
1446	Veuglaire	2				5.0	5.0	S		2				St. Omer?
1446	Veuglaire	2				8.0	8.0	S		2				St. Omer?
1446	Veuglaire	1				8.0	10.0	S		2				St. Omer?
1446	Veuglaire	24	I					S	12.0	2		3.0		St. Omer?
1446	Veuglaire	40						S	7.0	2		2.0		St. Omer?
1446	Veuglaire	60						S	6.0	2		1.5		St. Omer?
1446	Veuglaire	70						S	5.0	2		1.3		St. Omer?
1446	Veuglaire	2						S	2.0	2		1.0		St. Omer?
1447	Veuglaire	2						S	4.0					Cravant Castle
1449	Veuglaire	22	I					S		3				Made at Antwerp for Scotland

Year	Name	No.		Wt. 1	Wt. 2	S	No.	Location
1449	Veuglaire	2	I	4.0		S	2	Namur
1449	Veuglaire	7			3.0	S	3	> Rhodes
1451	Moyen Veuglaire	3						Ardre
1451	Petit Veuglaire	2						
1465	Gros Weuglaire	1	I	8.0	8.0	S	2	Saulx-le-Duc
1465	WIglaire	1	I	5.0	4.0	S	1	Grancey
1467	Veuglaire	1		4.5	6.0	S	2	Fouvent Castle
		879						
	GRAND TOTAL	4746						

Appendix 2
A Burgundian Artillery Train of 1475[1]

The following document from the late fifteenth century, preserved in the archives of Lille in France, sheds some light on the equipment of an artillery train of the period. It is a list of the materiel and personnel ordered from the town of Lille as part of the campaign to Lorraine of Charles the Bold, duke of Burgundy, in 1475.

État de ce que pourra monter la despence de l'artillerie que mon très-redoubté et souverain seigneur le Duc entend présentement mener avec lui, selon qu'il a ordonné par ses lettres>, consistant en 6 bombardes tant de fer comme de métal, 6 manteaux pour lesdites bombardes, 6 poulains servant auxdits manteaux, 12 pierres de bombardes, 6 bombardelles, 6 manteaux moyens 7 poulains y servant, 12 pierres de bombardelle, 6 mortiers, 12 pierres de mortier, la serpentine Lambillon, 100 boulets y servant, manteaux d'approche pour mines, 10 courtaux, 2,000 pierres pour lesdits courtaux, 10 grosse serpentines, 3 serpentines de l'hòtel, 2 serpentines de Jacquin et une serpentine de Montlhéry, 36 serpentines moyennes, 48 petites serpentines, 200 arquebuses, 40,000 livres de plomb tant en plummets comme en saumon et 600 galets de fer fondu pour grosses serpentines, 200 pavois à potences, 250 pavois nervés, 400 targettes, 8000 arcs à main, 10,000 douzaines de flèches, 4,000 douzaines de cordes d'arc, 12,000 traits d'arbalète, 10,000 traits de crenequin, les caques de poudre et de fil d'Anvers, 500 youges, 600 épieux, 4,500 maillets de plomb, 6,000 piques, 1,200 fûts de lance, 1,000 fûts de demi-lance, 1,200 bâtons chargois (chargeoirs), 1,000 fûts de javeline, 400 jacques pour pionniers, 300 salades ou bonnets de fer, 1,000 louchets, 600 pelles

State of that which could make the expense of the artillery that my very redoubtable and sovereign lord the Duke intends to take with him at the present time, as he prescribes in his letters> consisting of 6 *bombards*, as many of iron as of copper alloy, 6 mantlets for the said bombards, 6 sleds serving to the said mantlets, 12 stone balls for *bombards*, 6 *bombardelles*, 6 medium mantlets, 7 sleds for them, 12 stone balls for *bombardelles*, 6 *mortars*, 12 mortar stones, the *serpentine Lambillon*, 100 stones for it, mantlet for miners and trench work, 10 *courtaux*, 2000 stone balls for the said *courtaux*, 10 large *serpentines*, 3 *serpentines de l'hotel*, 2 *serpentines* of Jacquin and a *serpentine* of Montlhéry, 36 medium *serpentines*, 48 small *serpentines*, 200 *arquebuses*, 40,000 *livres* of lead as much in balls as in salmon and 600 *galets* of cast iron for *great serpentines*, 200 pavises with a rest, 250 ridged pavises, 400 shields, 8,000 hand bows, 10,000 dozen arrows, 4000 dozen bow strings, 12,000 crossbow bolts, 10,000 bolts of *crenequin*, barrels of powder and rope of Anvers, 500 *youges*, 600 spears, 4,500 lead mallets, 6,000 pikes, 1,200 lance shafts, 1,000 shafts of demi-lances, 1,200 batons *chargois*, 1,000 javelin shafts, 400 jacks for pioneers, 300 sallets or iron bonnets, 1,000 spades, 600 iron shod shovels, 400 bill hooks, 300 wooden

[1] This was originally translated and published as part of Robert D. Smith, "Good and Bold: A Late 15th-Century Artillery Train," *The Royal Armouries Yearbook* 6 (2001), 98–105. The original is transcribed in *Inventaire sommaires des archives départementales antérieures à 1790. Nord. Série B*, ed. J. Finote (Lille, 1895), VIII:160–61.

ferrées, 400 serpes, 300 pelles de bois, 1,000
pics, 500 hoyaux, 1,000 cognées, 1,000
fermans (faucilles), un Moulin à vent, 1,200
moulins à bras, 1,000 pieds de pont consistant,
en <fustaillière, ouzieres, cherchles, ferrailles,
corail, gistes, sommiers et autres choses servans
pour ledit pont> et nécessitant au moins 100
chariots, cordial, ferraille et menuités servant
pour les charpentiers, cordial servant aux
carreliers, suif de provision, la forge étoffee,
falots, leviers de fer, saltpêtre, soufre et harpoi,
feuilles de fer, fil d'archal, sacs de cuir, clous,
lanterns et soufflets, moules pour les serpentines et fers de lance, bagues et outils des
charpentiers, bagues et outils des carreliers,
bagues des canonniers, les maisons du Duc
pour lesquelles il faudra 7 chariots, 3 pavillons
et une tente pour le Duc, 400 pavillons pour
les companies d'ordonnance et les gens de
l'hôtel du Duc, 350 etables neves, 26 tentes à 2
mâts, 7 pièces de tentes pour l'écurie du Duc, 2
tentes de guet, 16 autres pièces de tentes et
pavillons servant pour les maîtres, lieutenants,
receveur, contrôleur et aides de ladite artillerie,
cannevas de garnison, cordal, brocques,
vireulles, fil, mâts et environ 2,000 chevilles de
tentes, échelles, bateaux de cuir, hocqs
(grappins), le bochus (blockhaus) fait à
Malines, bagues des maîtres, lieutenants,
receveur, contrôleur et nobles hommes aides en
ladite artillerie. Pour le transport de toute cette
artillerie, il sera bon d'avoir 5,245 chevaux,
sans compter ceux nécessaires pour l'amenage
des poudre; à raison de 4 sols par jour par
cheval, la déspense pour le transport de
l'artillerie sera de 1,049 livres par jour. Gens
nécessaires pour le fait et conduite de cette
artillerie: 6 maitres bombardiers, 6 autres
canonniers ou bombardiers pour jouer des six
bombardelles, 6 canonniers pour les 6 mortiers,
20 autres pour les 9 courtaux et les 15 grosses
serpentines, 40 autres pour les serpentines
moyennes et petites, 50 coulevriniers pour
jouer des arquebuses, 14 aides de canonniers et
bombardiers, Amand Millon, maitre
charpentier, 8 charpentiers à cheval, 95
charpentiers à pied, maître Wouters Teytin,
maître carrelier, 20 carreliers a pied, 50
cuveliers, 45 compagnons harnesqueurs, un
maître huchier pour les maisons du Duc, 4
huchiers sous ses orders, 2 autres compagnons
pour porter l'aisselin (le bois), 4 tendeurs de
tentes, 20 charpentiers pour tentes et pavillons,

shovels, 1,000 pickaxes, 500 mattocks, 1,000
axes, 1,000 sickles, a windmill, 1,200 hand
mills, 1,000 feet of bridge consisting of
<*fustailliere* (wood), *ouzieres, cherchles*, iron
work, rails, *gistes, sommiers* and other things
serving to the said bridge> and needing at least
100 carts, rope, *ferraille* and *menuités* for the
carpenters, rope for the carters, tallow of provision, the forge stuff, large hand lanterns, iron
crowbars, saltpetre, sulphur and *harpoi*, sheets
of iron, copper wire, leather sacks, nails,
lanterns and bellows, patterns for the serpentines and lance heads, bags and tools of the
carpenters, bags and tools of the carters, bags
of the cannoniers, the houses of the Duke for
which is needed 7 carts, 3 pavilions, and a tent
for the Duke, 400 pavilions for the companies
of the ordinance and the attendants of the
hotel of the Duke, 350 new sheds/stables, 26
tents with 2 poles, 7 pieces of tents for the
Duke's stable, 2 tents for the watch, 16 other
pieces of tents and pavilions serving for the
masters, lieutenants, receiver, controller and
aides of the said artillery, canvas of the
garrison, rope, nails, screws, wire, poles and
about 2,000 tent pegs, ladders, leather boats,
grappling irons, the blockhouse made at
Malines, bags of masters, lieutenants, receiver,
controller and nobles helping with the said
artillery. For the transport of all this artillery, it
will be useful to have 5,245 horses, without
counting those necessary for the transport of
the powder, at the rate of 4 sols per day per
horse, the expense for the transport of the artillery will be 1,049 *livres* per day. Men necessary
for the making and moving of this artillery: 6
master bombardiers, 6 other cannoneers or
bombardiers to fire the 6 *bombardelles*, 6
cannoneers for the 6 *mortars*, 20 others for the
9 *courtaux* and the 15 large *serpentines*, 40
others for the medium and small *serpentines*, 50
coulovriniers to fire the *arquebuses*, 14 cannoneers aides and bombadiers, Amand Millon,
master carpenter, 8 carpenters on horseback,
95 carpenters on foot, master Wouters Teytin,
master carter, 20 carters on foot, 50 servants,
45 *compagnons harnesqueurs*, a master joiner for
the houses of the Duke, 4 joiners under his
orders, 2 other companions to carry wood, 4
stretchers of tents, 20 carpenters for tents and
pavilions, 200 other stretchers of tents, 400
pioneers, 2 master farriers, 4 farriers, 1 master
cutter of stone, 6 companion stone cutters, 3

200 autres tendeurs de tentes, 400 pionniers, 2 maîtres maréchaux, 4 maréchaux, 1 maîitre-tailleur de pierre, 6 compagnons tailleurs de pierre, 3 compagnons fondeurs de plummets, 8 navieurs pour les bateaux, 4 meuniers, 50 mineurs, 24 compagnons à cheval aides de l'artillerie. Total des gages des gens nécessaries au services de l'artillerie: 201 livres, 9 sols par jour. Total général avec les frais de charriage: 1250 livres, 9 sols par jour.

companion founders of plummets, 8 sailors for the boats, 4 millers, 50 miners, 24 companions on horse back aides of the artillery. Total of the wages of the men necessary to service the artillery: 201 *livres* 9 *sols* per day. General total with the expenses for carriage: 1250 *livres* 9 *sols* per day.

Appendix 3
A Burgundian Ship's Inventory of Arms from 1445[1]

Only one of the documents transcribed by Joseph Garnier listed weapons specifically for the arming of a naval vessel. The obvious conclusion might be to suggest that the Valois dukes were not concerned with ships and naval warfare. However, recent evidence has proven the opposite,[2] and the following document shows that not only were they clearly outfitting ships for fighting at sea, but that these ships often had gunpowder weapons designed specifically for their use at sea.

Cy après sensuit l'artillerie qu'il convient avoir pour fournir une gallée oultre et par dessus autres menues choses qu'il y convient avoir qu'il la vouldroit entierement armer.

Et premierement: Douze grosses arbalestes d'acier pour monter à guindaulx.

Item douze guindaulx, c'est assavoir huit sangles et quatre doubles.

Item douze autres arbalestes d'acier pour monter à croc et les porter à pie.

Item pour les grosses arbalestes, 1,800 de trait, moitié dondainnes et demi dondainnes qui se mettront en six cases.

Item pour les petites arbalestes à crocq, sept vingt cinq cent de trait commun – 200 livres de fil d'Anvers.

Item cinq veuglaires portant pierre de quatre poulces en croxière, chacun à 3 chambres et lesdites chambres servans aussi bien à l'ung des veuglaires que à l'autre and chacune chambre

Hereafter follows the artillery which is suitable to have for furnishing a galley beyond and above other things taken which it is fitting to have there when you want to be fully armed.

First: Twelve large steel crossbows to shoot with windlasses.

Item Twelve windlasses, that is eight singles and four doubles.Item twelve other steel crossbows to shoot with a hook and to be carried on foot.

Item for the large crossbows, 1,800 bolts, half *dondainnes*, and [half] *demi dondainnes* which are stored in six cases.

Item for the little crossbows with a hook, 17,500 common bolts – 200 *livres* of rope from Antwerp.

Item five *veuglaires*, firing stone of four *poulces* in diameter, each with 3 chambers, and the said chambers serving as well the one *veuglaire* as another. And each *veuglaire* will be four *piez*

1 This document was originally discussed in Kelly DeVries, "A 1445 Reference to Shipboard Artillery," *Technology and Culture* 31 (1990), 818–29. The Original is in Joseph Garnier, *L'artillerie des ducs de Bourgogne d'après les documents conservés aux archives de la Côte d'Or* (Paris, 1895), pp 175–76.

2 C.G. Roelofsen, "L'évolution de la flotte 'Bouguignonne' aux XVe et XVIe siècles: quelques remarques sur l'introduction du canon dans la guerre maritime et son influence," *Publication du centre Européen d'études Bourguignonnes (XIVe–XVIe s.)* 26 (1986), 87–95; A.G. Jongkees, "Armement et action d'une flotte de guerre: la contribution des comtés maritimes à l'armée générale des pays de Par-Deçà en 1477," *Publications du centre Européen d'études Bourguignonnes (XIVe–XVIe s.)* 26 (1986), 71–86; Jacques Paviot, *La politique navale des ducs de Bourgogne, 1384–1482* (Lille, 1995); and, in particular, Jacques Paviot, "Les navires du duc de Bourgogne Philippe le Bon (vers 1440–1465)," in *Atti del v convegno internazionale di studi colombiani: "Navi e navigazione nei secoli XV e XVI"* (Genoa, 1990), I:167–95.

servant autant à l'ung qu'à l'autre. Et aura chacun veuglaire quatre piez de long, volée et chambre et se boutera la pierre par derrière.

Item deux coulovrines pour tirer sur chevalez, chacun à trois chambres, chacun chambre servant autant à ung qu'à l'autre.

Item douze autres coulovrines pour tirer à main.

Item 600 livres de pouldre, moitié pour canon, l'autre pour coulovrine.

Item 36 juisarmes legières et bien forgiées, – 150 lances ferées – 50 demies lances ferrées.

Item 32 pavaix de popelier, pour faire rambades, lesquels convienent estre de six piez à seule de hault et quatre de large.

Item 120 pavais à main, bien garnis et bien estoffez comme il appartient de six pieds à seule de hault et de deux piez et demi de large.

Item 12 carquons tous de popelier et les plus legières que faire se pourront.

Item une quaque de chaussetrappes.

long, barrel and chamber, and the stone is to be loaded from the rear.

Item two *coulovrine*, turning on pivots, each with three chambers, each chamber serving the one as another.

Item twelve other *coulovrines* to be held by hand.

Item 600 *livres* of powder, half for *canon*, the other for *coulovrine*.

Item 36 gisarmes, light and well made – 150 iron-bound lances – 50 half iron-bound lances.

Item 32 pavises of poplar, to make a shield wall, which ought six *piez* tall and four wide.

Item 120 hand pavises, well furnished and of good quality and ought to be six *pieds* high and two and a half *piez* wide.

Item 12 quivers all of poplar and the lightest they can be made.

A cask of caltrops.

Appendix 4
The Manufacture of Iron Guns in 1376[1]

The following account of the making of iron guns in the fourteenth century is full of detail on the various materials needed and the wide range of people who contributed. Unfortunately, it includes no details about how these gunpowder weapons were actually constructed, but it gives some fascinating glimpses into the process – including the use of moulds and patterns. Also, of interest is that one of the suppliers of iron in Chalon was a woman, Perrenotte Lajolie!

Et premierement pour la fasceon d'ung canon de fer getant le pesant de 60 livres.

A Jehan Pourterat, bourgeois de Chalon, pour la vendue de 320 livres de fer au pois de Chalon, le cent au feur de 2 fr. 10 gros val. 9 t. un gros.

Item de quatre taulles de fer pesant 16 livres et demie, la livre au feur d'un gros, valant 16 gros et demi. Lequel fer a esté emploié entièrement en la fasceon dudit canon et es appartenances d'icellui. Pour ce 10 fr. 5 gros et demi.

A Jehan Levrat de la Forest, pour la vendue de certaine quantité de charbon desduit entièrement pour la firge et fasceon dudit canon, 4 f. 3 g.

A Jaquet, de Paris, serrurier et a quatre ouvriers avec lui qui ont fait ledit canon et y ont ouvré continuelment depuis le mercredi 22° jour d'octobre qu'ils commencèrent à forgier ledit canon jusques au samedi avant le feste de St Martin d'yver ensuivant que, il fut fait et assuiz entièrement ou quel terme sont 13 jours touz enclouz au feur de 16 gros par jour; marchié fait audit Jaquet par ledit receveur et les dessuz diz maistres de canons et parmi ce il a administré, hostel, forges, enclumes et touz utils de forge. Pour ce pour les diz 17 jours, 17 f. 4 gros.

And first for the making of an iron *canon* firing [shot] weighing 60 *livres*.

To Jehan Pourterat, burgher of Chalon, for the sale of 320 *livres* of iron [*au pois*] of Chalon, the hundred [weight] at the price of 2 *fr*. 10 *gros* costing 9 *t.* one *gros*.

Item for four pieces of iron weighing 16½ *livres*, the *livre* at the price of one *gros*, costing 16½ *gros*. Which iron was employed entirely in the making of the said *canon* and its. For this 10 *fr*, 5½ *gros*.

To Jehan Levrat de la Forest, for the sale of a certain quantity of charcoal destined entirely for the forge and the making of the said *canon*, 4 *f.* 3 *g.*

To Jaquet, of Paris, metal worker and to four labourers with him who had made the said *canon* and who had worked continually from Wednesday 22nd October when they commenced to forge the said *canon* until the Saturday before the feast of St Martin the following winter, it was made and bound entirely during which period are 13 days inclusive at the cost of 16 *gros* per day; contract made with the said Jaquet by the said receiver and the said masters of cannons under him and among whom the lodging, forges, anvils and all tools of the forge were organised. For this for the said 17 days, 17 *f.* 4 *gros*.

---

[1] Original is transcribed in Joseph Garnier, *L'artillerie des ducs de Bourgogne d'après les documents conservés aux archives de la Côte-d'Or* (Paris, 1895), pp. 9–11.

Pour une livre et demi de poudre à faire geter ledit canon. Laquelle poudre li diz Jacquet de Mallorques ala achater à Lion quar à Chalon non povoit lon trouver, ne faire aucune qui fut bonne, si comme disoient lesdiz maistres, 2 s. ½.

A Guiot Baudot de Chalon pour la vendue d'ung gros plot de bois ou lon (a) enchassez ledit canon, 6 gros.

A Jaquelin le Chapuis pour en chasser ledit plot et ycellui mettre à point et charpente, 6 gros.

A Huet Bordelli pour le loyer de sa charette a deux chevaux pour mener ledit canon ensemble les estoufes d'icellui, c'est assavoir deux pierres rondes pesant 120 livres, de Chalon à Dijon par devers mondit seigneur, 18 gros.

Somme 38 fr. 10 gros ½.

Item autres deniers paiez pour le fasceon de cinq canons de fer dont l'iung gete le pesant de 130 livres.

l'autre le pesant de 100 livres.

l'autre le pesant de 90 livres.

et les autres deux le pesant de 50 livres. C'est assavoir l'un 30 livres, et l'autre 20.

A André Bonin de Lion pour la vendue de 32 quintaulx de fer au pois de Chalon, le quintal au feur de 60 sols tournoi, lequel fer a esté tournez et convertiz en louvrage et fasceon desdiz canons, 97 l.

A Perrenotte Lajolie de Chalon pour la vendue de quatre quintalx et trios livres de fer au pois qui dessous, le quintal au même priz, 12 l. 21 d.

A elle pour la vendue d'une pièce de fer de chièvre, 10 s. t.

A Guillaume Chaudot pour la vendue de 3 quintalx 37 livres de fer, le quintal au feur de 60 sols, val. 9 l. 10 s. 9 d.

A lui pour la vendue d'ung carreal d'acier, mis et employé en l'ouvrage desdiz canons, 12 d.

A Guillaume Broé pour la vendue d'ung plot de bois dont lon a fait le mole de l'un desdiz canons.

A Symon le Roy de Dycone et pluseurs autres pour la vendue de certaine quantité de charbon, achetée à raison de 14 deniers le sac, ou 7 sols 6 deniers le charette, 15 l.

A Jacquet de Paris pour l'achat d'une grosse piece de fer pesant 34 livres au feur, 5 d. tournois la livre, 10 s.

A deux chapuiz pour faire les traitealx sur quoi

For one and a half *livres* of powder to fire the said *canon*. Which powder the said Jaquet de Mallorques had to buy in Lyon because it was not possible to find it in Chalon, nor could any good enough be made, as determined by the said masters, 2½ *s.*

To Guiot Baudot of Chalon for the sale of a large piece of wood in which to mount the said *canon*, 6 *gros.*

To Jaquelin le Chapuis to mount the said wood and shape and cut it, 6 *gros.*

To Huet Bordelli for the hire of his two horsed cart to take the said *canon* together with its equipment, that is to say two round stones weighing 120 *livres*, from Chalon to Dijon by order of my said lord, 18 *gros.*

Sum 38 *fr.* 10½ *gros.*

Item other monies paid for the making of five iron *canon* one of which will fire weighing stone [shot] of 130 *livres*,

another [firing shot] weighing 100 *livres*

another [firing shot] weighing 90 *livres*,

and the other to [firing shot] weighing 50 livres. That is to say the one 30 *livres*, and the other 20.

To André Bonin of Lyon for the sale of 32 *quintals* of iron [*au pois*] of Chalon, the *quintal* to cost 60 *sols tournoi*, which iron is to be turned and converted in working and making the said *canons*, 97 *l.*

To Perrenotte Lajolie of Chalon for the sale of four quintals and three *livres* of iron [*au pois*] below, the quintal at the same price, 12 *l.* 21 *d.*

To her for the sale of a piece of scrap iron, 10 *s. t.*

To Guillaume Chaudot for the sale of 3 quintals 37 *livres* of iron, a quintal at the price of 60 *sols*, costing 9 *l.* 10 *s.* 9 *d.*

To him for the sale of a block of steel, made and employed for the work of the said *canons*, 12 *d.*

To Guillaume Broé for the sale of a piece of wood from which was made the mould of one of the said *canons.*

To Symon le Roy of Dycone and many others for the sale of a certain quantity of charcoal, bought for this reason at 14 *deniers* the sack, or 7 *sols* 6 *deniers* the cart [full], 15 *l.*

To Jacquet of Paris for the purchase of a large piece of iron weighing 34 livres at the price of 5 *d. tournois* the *livre*, 10 *s.*

To two carpenters to make the trestles on

les sofflez de la forge desdiz canons sont assis, 4
s. 2 d.
A Fulminet le fernier pour la vendue d'une
bicorne de fer sur quoi lon forge les poz desdiz
canons, 40 s.
Audit Jacquet de Paris pour les journées de lui et
de quatre ouvriers, depuis le lundi 15 décembre
1376 jusques au mercredi veille de Noel, ou
sont 9 jours ouvrables au feur de 26 sols 8
deniers par jour, marchié fait à lui par lesdiz
maistres de canons, 11 l.
A Perrenotte Lajolie pour une certaine quantité
de fer, 41 s. 8 d. t.
A J. Levrat pour charroier et amener à Chalon
ung plot pour enchascier et enfuster l'un desdiz
canons, 3 s. 4 d.
A Gauchier Remondat pour la vendue dudit
plot, 16 s. 8 d.
A Rolant le serrurier, pour ferrer ledit plot en
deux morceaux, 20 d. t.
A André de Cusane, charpentier, demourant à
Chalon, pour trios journées par lui employees à
curier et vuidier ledit plot ou quell est enfustez
l'un ds diz canons, 6 s. 6 d.
A Jacques de Paris pour les journées de lui et de
quatre ouvriers avec lui, qui font 25 jours
entiers, la journée au pris de 26 sols 8 deniers,
23 l. 6 s. 3 d.
Au même pour 22 jours entiers que il et sesdiz 4
vallez ont ouvré esdiz canons au mois de mars,
29 l. 6 s. 8 d.
A Philibert le serrurier et à deux autres, ses
compaignons, pour ferrer ung gros plot pour
enfuster ung autre desdiz canons et pour ferrer
certaines autres pièces de bois à ce nécessaries,
5 s.
A Perronet de S\t-Martin, Philibert Rosset et
Michaut Martin, charpentiers, pour 6 journées
faites par chacun d'eux, en la charpenterie du
bois nécessaire pour emparer les diz canons, la
jounnée au feur de 2 gros, 60 s.
Audit Michaut Martin pour la vendue d'ung
tronceon de bois ron pour faire le mole et
patron du grant canon, 10 s.
A maistre Robert Michaut, pour 15 journées
que il et son valet ont ouvré à leurs despens,
pour faire les chasciz desdiz canons et pour faire
et mettre sus avec les autres chapuiz cy dessus
nommés, la charpenterie appurtenant esdiz
canons, la journée d'un chascun au feur de 3 s. 4
d. 100s.
A lui pour la vendue d'ung gros plot de bois ron,
pour faire ung mole pour l'un des diz canons, 20 s.

which the bellows of the forge for the said
canons were seated, 4 *s.* 2 *d.*
To Fulminet the harness maker for the sale of
an iron anvil on which is forged the chambers
of the said *canons*, 40 *s.*
To the said Jacquet of Paris for the days of him
and his four labourers, from Monday 15th
December 1376 until Wednesday Christams
Eve, 9 working days at the price of 26 *sols* 8
deniers per day, contracted with him by the
said master of *canons*, 11 *l.*
To Perrenotte Lajolie for a certain quantity of
iron, 41 *s.* 8 *d. t.*
To J. Levrat for carting and taking to Chalon a
piece of wood for the encasing and mounting
of one of the said canons, 3 *s.* 4 *d.*
To Gauchier Remondat for the sale of the said
piece, 16 *s.* 8 *d.*
To Rolant the metal worker, for binding the
said piece in two pieces, 20 *d. t.*
To André de Cusane, carpenter, living in
Chalon, for three days by him employed to
clean and remove waste from the said piece on
which one of these *canons* is mounted, 6 *s.* 6 *d.*
To Jacques of Paris for the days for himself and
his four labourers with him which were 25
complete days, the day at the price of 26 *sols*, 8
deniers, 23 *l.* 6 *s.* 3 *d.*
To the same for 22 complete days that he and
the said 4 valets had worked on the said *canons*
in the month of March, 29 *l.* 6 *s.* 8 *d.*
To Philibert the metal worker and to two
others, his companions, for binding a large
piece to mount one of the other *canons* and to
bind certain other pieces of wood as necessary,
5 *s.*
To Perronet of S\t-Martin, Philibert Rosset, and
Michaut Martin, carpenters, for 6 days worked
by each of them, in the working of the wood
necessary for the securing of the said *canons*,
the day at the price of 2 *gros*, 60 *s.*
To Michaut Martin for the sale of a round log
to make the mould and pattern of the large
canon, 10 *s.*
To master Robert Michaut, for 15 days that he
and his valet had worked at their expense, to
make the chassis of the said *canons* and to
make and put them with the other carpenters
named above, the carpentry appertaining to
the said *canons*, the day of each at the price of
3 *s.* 4 *d.* 100 *s.*
To him for the sale of a large round log, to
make a mould for one of these *canons*, 20 *s.*

A Hugonet Larcher pour la vendue d'ung plot de bois à faire les couvertures des diz canons et pour iceulx enchascier, 20 s. t.

A Jehan Frogier pour bois prins de lui pour l'emparement que dessus, 13 s. 4 d.

A Perronet de St-Martin et à Philibert Rousset, charpentiers, pour 10 journées que il ont vacqué à faire la charpenterie des emparemenz desdiz canons, la journée d'ung chascun au pris de 2 gros, val. 23 s. 4 d.

Audit M. Martin pour une journée faite en l'emparement des diz canons, 3 s. 4 d.

Au Roisseaul, gaignedenier, et à cinq autres, qui ont pourté lesdiz 5 canons dois la forge où ils ont esté faiz jusques en l'une des chambres de l'Espicererie pour les garder en ladite chambre, 5 s.

A Guillaume le Royer, pour la vendue de 4 petites rouez sur quoi le plu grant des diz canons, ensemble l'emparement d'icellui est assi et loigié, pour icellui plus aisiment mener là ou besoing seroit, 22 s. 4 s.

To Hugonet Larcher for the sale of a piece of wood to make the covers of these canons and for encasing them, 20 *s. t.*

To Jehan Frogier for wood of him for securing the above, 13 *s.* 4 *d.*

To Perronet of St-Martin and to Philibert Rousset, carpenters, for 10 days during which they devoted themselves to the carpentry of the securing the said *canons*, the day of each one at the price of 2 *gros*, costing 23 *s.* 4 *d.*

To M. Martin for a day spent in the securing of the said canons, 3 *s.* 4 *d.*

To Roisseaul, common labourer, and to five others, who had carried the said 5 *canons* from the forge where they had been made to one of the rooms of the *l'Espicererie* for keeping them in the said chamber, 5 *s.*

To Guillaume le Royer for the sale of 4 small wheels on which the largest of these *canons*, all together securely on that which it is mounted and lodged, on which it is more easily taken wherever necessary, 22 *s.* 4 *s.*

Appendix 5
A Burgundian Weapons Dowry from 1449[1]

One of the most interesting records of early gunpowder weapons transcribed by Joseph Garnier is a dowry given to James II, the king of Scotland, at his marriage to Mary of Guelders, the grand-niece of Philip the Good, in 1449. For not only did this dowry contain all of the usual monetary payments, in this case 60,000 crowns plus all wedding expenses, it also contained a large number of weapons which Philip the Good sent to Scotland from his own arsenal. Not only were the more usual arms and armour sent to the Scottish king as part of this "arms dowry," shipped on five galleys especially constructed for the purpose, but so too were a large number of gunpowder weapons, veuglaires and coulovrines, powder for both types, and ammunition – stone balls – for the veuglaires.

Cy après s'ensuit l'artillerie qui a esté mise en cinq galées, que M. le duc fist faire à Anvers es années 1448 et 1449, et lesquelles enmenerent la royne d'Escosse, Marie de Guelders, femme de Jacques II, en Escosse. Le duc Philippe avait lui-même négocié ce mariage.

Et premièrement.
Cinquante bringandines couvertes de futaine noire.
Trente-trois garde-bras de même couleur.
Quatre-vingt-seize bringandines pour galoz.
Item pour les dis galots, 649 salades.
Item 480 espées pour lesdis galots.
Item 126 arbalestes d'acier.
Item 36 martinots nommés baudry à tendre lesdites arbaletes.
Item 428 lances avecques estaisseurilles et rommeignolles.
Item 81 jusarmes.
Item 130 pavais tant gros que petis.
Item 115 casses de viretons contenant trente milliers de vireton.

Hereafter follows the artillery which was sent in five galleys, which the duke had built in Antwerp in the years 1448 and 1449, and which were taken to the queen of Scotland, Mary of Guelders, wife of James II, in Scotland. The Duke Philip himself had negotiated this marriage.

Firstly.
50 brigandines covered in black fustian.

33 garde-bras of the same color.
87 brigandines for the Scots.
Item for the Scots, 649 salades.
Item 480 swords for these Scots.
Item 126 steel crossbows.
Item 36 martinets called *haudré* to hold those crossbows.
Item 428 lances with stops and points.

Item 81 gisarmes.
Item 130 pavises, both large and small.
Item 115 cases of crossbow bolts, containing 30,000 crossbow bolts.

---

1   Previously discussed and translated in Kelly DeVries, "A 15th-Century Weapons Dowry: The Weapons Dowry of Duke Philip the Good of Burgundy for the Marriage of Mary of Guelders and James II of Scotland in 1449," *The Royal Armouries Yearbook* 6 (2001), 22–31. The original is transcribed in Joseph Garnier, *L'artillerie des ducs de Bourgogne d'après les documents conservés aux archives de la Côte-d'Or* (Paris, 1895), pp. 130–31.

Item 5,000 de dondainnes et 5,000 de demie dondainnes.
Item dix casses d'arcs, contenant 400 arcs.
Item 17 casses de flesches, containent 800 douzaines.
Item 22 veuglaires de fer et 64 chambres pour lesdiz veuglaires.
Item 46 coulovrines de fer.
Item cinq barilles de pouldre tant pour coulovrine que veuglaires
Item cinq barilles de fil d'Anvers.
Item 16 guindaulx.
Item 400 pierres de veuglaires.
Item 6,000 de chaussetrappes.

Item 5,000 large crossbow bolts and 5,000 half-size large crossbow bolts.
Item 10 cases of bows, containing 400 bows.
Item 17 cases of arrows, containing 9,600.
Item 22 iron *veuglaires* and 64 chambers for those *veuglaires*.
Item 46 iron *coulovrines*.
Item 5 barrels of powder, as much for *coulovrines* as for *veuglaires*.
Item 4 barrels of Antwerp rope.
Item 16 winches.
Item 400 stones for the *veuglaires*.
Item 6,000 caltrops.

Appendix 6
The Transport of Artillery in 1474[1]

When weights are given for most of the artillery pieces listed in the Burgundian archival records they are given in *livres*. In this rather intriguing order for arms to be transported to Dijon from Luxembourg at a time when Charles the Bold was preparing his artillery train for the unsuccessful siege of Neuss, the gunpowder weapons, their equipment and the arms accompanying them are listed with the number of horses needed to transport them.

Estat de ce qui semble ester necessaire pour la fait et conduit de l'artillerie que mon très redoubté seigneur M. le duc de Bourgoingne a ordonné estre menée en Bourgoingne, de celle qui se doit prendre en son dit pays de Bourgoingne à la conduit de Estienne Ferroux par lui commis au gouvernement et exercité de d'icelle.

Primo

A mondit seigneur ordonné ester méné deux courtaulx de metal estans presentement à Luxembourg et convient pour iceulx mener, 16 chevaulx.

Item pour mener cinq moiennes serpentines et quatre petites, fault avoir assavoir aux moiennes serpentines, trois chevaulx et aux petites deux; font 23 chevaulx.

Item pour mener trente cacques de pouldre à compter sur chacun chariot cinq cacques feront six chariots qui font 24 chevaulx.

Pour mener deux cent pierres de courtaulx à compter 40 pierres sur chacun (charriot) à quatre chevaulx font 20 chevaulx.

Pour mener les plomets servans ausdites 9 serpentines ung chariot et demi, 6 chevaulx.

Item pour mener 2,500 arcs, 2,700 douzaines de flesches, 6,000 cordes, 11 charriots qui feroient 44 chevaulx.

Pour mener picqs, horeaulx, lochets, ung chariot à 4 chevaulx.

State of that which seems to be necessary for the making and conducting of the artillery that our most redoubtable lord, M. the duke of Burgundy has ordered to be taken into Burgundy, the which ought to be taken into his said land of Burgundy under the direction of Estienne Ferroux by his commission to his government and army.

First

To my said lord it is ordered to be taken two copper alloy *courtaux* presently at Luxembourg and for which it is suitable to take, 16 horses.

Item to take five medium and four small *serpentines*, that is to say that for the medium *serpentines*, three horses and for the small [ones] two, making 23 horses.

Item to take thirty casks of powder at the rate of five casks on each cart making six carts which makes 24 horses

To take two hundred stone [shot] for *courtaux* at the rate of 40 stones on each (cart) of four horses making 20 horses.

To take the *plommées* for the said 9 serpentines one and a half carts, 6 horses.

Item to take 2,500 bows, 2,700 dozen arrows, 6,000 strings, 11 carts which make 44 horses.

To take picks, *horeaulx*, spades, a cart with 4 horses.

---

[1] Original is in Joseph Garnier, *L'artillerie des ducs de Bourgogne d'après les documents conservés aux archives de la Côte-d'Or* (Paris, 1895), pp. 179–80.

Pour mener oingt de garnison, les baghes du carrelleur et du cuvelier, ung chariot, 4 chevaulx

Pour mener les baghes de Estienne Ferroux et ses aides par un commis du receveur de l'artillerie, 6 chevaulx.

Prendre en Bourgogne une bombarde à Dijon et pour mener celle convient du moins avoir 24 chevaulx.

Pour mener ung manteau servant icelle, convient dix chariots qui font 40 chevaulx.

Pour mener ung affusts, 4 chevaulx.

Pour mener du moins cent pierres servans à ladite bombarde à dix pierres, ung chariot à quatre chevaulx, font 40 chevaulx.

Convient mener les baghes des charpentiers leurs hostiz et harnaix, 4 chevaulx.

Pour mener les baghes des harnesqueurs et autres menues gens de ladite artillerie, 4 chevaulx.

Pour mener les baghes des cannoniers deux chariots, 4 chevaulx.

To take grease, the bags of the saddler and of the cooper, a cart, 4 horses.

To take the bags of Estienne Ferroux and his aides by a commission of the receiver of the artillery, 6 horses.

To take into Burgundy a *bombard* to Dijon and to take which is needed no less than 24 horses.

To take a mantlet for this [bombard], ten cart are needed which makes 40 horses.

To take one carriage, 4 horses.

To take no less than one hundred stone [shot] for the said bombard at ten stones per cart with four horses making 40 horses.

It is necessary to take the bags of the carpenters their baskets and equipment, 4 horses.

To take the bags of the carters and other men of the said artillery, 4 horses.

To take the bags of the cannoniers two cart, 4 horses.

Bibliography

Original Sources

Analectes historiques, iii. Ed. L.P. Gachard. In: *Bulletin de la commission royale d'histoire*, ser. 2, 7 (1855).

Basin, Thomas. *Histoire de Charles VII*. 2 vols. Ed. C. Samaran. Paris, 1933–44.

———. *Histoire de Louis XI*. 3 vols. Ed. C. Samaran. Paris, 1963–72.

Basler Chroniken. Vol. 2. Ed. W. Vischer and H. Boos. Leipzig, 1880.

Berchen, Willem van. *Gelderse kroniek*. Ed. A.J. de Mooy. Arnhem, 1950.

Borgnet, Jules, ed. *Cartulaire de la commune de Bouvignes*. 2 vols. Namur: A. Wesmael-Legros, 1862.

Brusthem, Jean de. *Chronique*. In: *Chronique Liègeoises*, 2. Ed. S. Balau. Brussels, 1931.

The Brut, or the Chronicles of England. 2 vols. Ed. F.W.D. Brie. London, 1906–08.

Budt, Adrien de. *Chronique*. In: *Chroniques relatives à l'histoire de la Belgique sous la domination des ducs de Bourgogne (texts latins)*. Ed. Kervyn de Lettenhove. Brussels, 1870.

Cagny, Perceval de. *Chroniques*. Ed. H. Moranville. Paris, 1902.

Chants historiques et populaires du temps de Charles VII et de Louis XI. Ed. L. Roux de Lincy. Paris, 1857.

Chartier, Jean. *Chronique de Charles VII*. 3 vols. Ed. Vallet de Viriville. Paris, 1858.

Chastellain, Georges. *Œuvres*. Ed. Kervyn de Lettenhove. 8 vols. Brussels, 1863–66.

Chronicon comitum Flandriae. In: *Corpus chronicorum Flandriae*, 1. Ed. J.J. de Smet. Brussels, 1837.

Chronijk der landen van Overmaas en der aagrenzende gewesten. Ed. J. Habets. In: *Publications de la société archéologique et historique dans le duché de Limbourg* 7 (1870), 1–231.

Chronique de Flandre. In: *Istore et croniques de Flandres*. 2 vols. Ed. Kervyn de Lettenhove. Brussels, 1879–80.

Chronique de Lorraine. Ed. L. Marchal. In: *Recueil de documents sur l'histoire de Lorraine*, V. Nancy, 1859.

Chronique des cordeliers. In: Enguerran de Monstrelet, *Chronique*. Ed. L. Douet-d'Arcq. Vol. 6. Paris, 1857–62.

Chronique des Pays-Bas, de France, d'Angleterre et de Tournai. In: *Corpus chronicorum Flandriae*, 3. Ed. J.J. de Smet. Brussels, 1856.

Chronique des quatre premiers Valois (1327–1393). Ed. S. Luce. Paris, 1862.

Chronique des règnes de Jean II et de Charles V. 4 vols. Ed. R. Delachenal. Paris, 1910–20.

Chronique du bon duc Loys de Bourbon. Ed. A.-M. Chazaud. Paris, 1876.

Chronique du religieux de Saint-Denis. Ed. L. Bellaguet. 6 vols. Paris, 1839–52.

Chronographia regum Francorum. 3 vols. Ed. H. Moranville. Paris, 1891–97.

Clercq, Jacques du. *Memoires*. In: *Collection complète des memoires relatifs à l'histoire de France*, 11. Ed. M. Petitot. Paris, 1826.

———. *Memoires*. Ed. J.A.C. Buchon. In: *Choix de chroniques et memoires relatifs à l'histoire de France: Jacques du Clercq, Memoires*. Paris, 1875.

Collection de documents inédits concernant l'histoire de la Belgique. Ed. L.P. Gachard. 3 vols. Brussels, 1833–35.

Commynes, Philippe de. *Mémoires*. 3 vols. Ed. J. Calmette and G. Durville. Paris, 1924–25.

———. *Mémoires*. Ed. Dupont. 3 vols. Paris, 1840–47.

———. *The Memoirs of Philippe de Commynes*. 2 vols. Ed. Samuel Kinser. Trans. Isabelle Cazeaux. Columbia, 1969.

Compte du clos de galées de Rouen au XIVe siècle, Le. Ed. C. Bréard. Rouen, 1893.

Correspondance de la mairie de Dijon. Ed. J. Garnier. 3 vols. Dijon, 1868–70.

Cosneau, Eugène, ed. *Les grandes traités de la guerre de cent ans*. Paris, 1889.

Dépêches des ambassadeurs Milanais en France sous Louis XI et Francois Sforza. 4 vols. Ed. B. de Mandrot and C. Samaran. Paris, 1916–23.

Deschamps, Eustace. *Œuvres complètes*. 11 vols. Ed. Q. de Saint Hilaire and G. Raynaud. Paris, 1878–1903.

Deutsche Reichstagsakten. Ed. J. Weizsäcker et al. Munich, 1867– .

Diesback, Ludwig von. *Chronik und Selbstbiographie*. In: *Schweizerische Geschichtsforscher* 8 (1830), 161–215.

Discours du siège de Beauvais en 1472. Ed. L. Cimber. In: *Archives curieuses de l'histoire de France*, I. Paris, 1834, pp. 111–35, and in: *Album historique et paléographique beauvaisien*. Beauvais, 1913.

Dixmude, Jan van. *Kronyk*. In: *Corpus chronicorum Flandriae*, 3. Ed. J.J. de Smet. Brussels, 1856.

Dixmude, Oliver van. *Merkwaerdige gebeurtenissen vooral in Vlaenderen en Brabant van 1377 tot 1443*. Ed. J.J. Lambin. Ypres, 1835.

Doren, P.J. van. *Inventaire des archives de la ville de Malines*. 8 vols. Mechelen, 1859–94.

Eidgenössischen Abscheide aus dem Zeitraume von 1421 bis 1477, Die. In: *Amtliche sammlung der älteren Eidgenossichen Abscheide*, II. Ed. A.P. Segresser. Luzern, 1863.

Entreprises du duc de Bourgogne contre les Suisses. Ed. A. Schnegg. Quellen zur Schweizer Geschichte, new series, vol. 3. Basel, 1948.

Escouchy, Mathieu d'. *Chronique*. Ed. G. du Fresne de Beaucourt. 3 vols. Paris, 1863–64.

Etterlin, Peterman. *Kronica von der loblichen Eydtgnoschaft*. Basel, 1507.

Fris, V., ed. "Oorkonden betreffende den opstand van Gent tegen Philips den Goede (1450–53)," *Handelingen der Maatschappij voor Geschiedenis en Oudheidkunde te Gent* 4 (1901–1902), 55–146.

Froissart, Jean. *Chroniques*. 14 vols. Ed. S. Luce et al. Paris, 1869–1967.

———. *Chroniques*. In: *Œuvres de Froissart*. 29 vols. Ed. Kervyn de Lettenhove. Brussels, 1867–77.

Fudge, Thomas A., ed. and trans. *The Crusade against Heretics in Bohemia, 1418–1437: Sources and Documents for the Hussite Crusades*. Aldershot, 2002.

Garnier, Joseph. *L'artillerie des ducs de Bourgogne d'après les documents conservés aux archives de la Côte-d'Or*. Paris, 1895.

Gesta Henrici quinti. Ed. and trans. F. Taylor and J.S. Roskell. Oxford, 1975.

Ghinzoni, P. "La battaglia di Morat," *Archivio storico lombardo*, 2nd ser., 9 (1892), 102–09.

Guicciardini, Francesco. *The History of Italy*. 2 vols. Trans. Chevalier Austin Parke Goddard. London, 1754.

Hanserecesse: Die Recesse und andere Akten der Hansetage von 1431 bis 1476. Ed. G. von der Rupp. 7 vols. Leipzig, 1876–92.

Hassenstein, Wilhelm, ed. *Das Feuerbuch von 1420*. Munich, 1941.

Haynin, Jean de. *Mémoires*. 2 vols. Ed. R. Chalon. Mons, 1842.

Herbenus, Mathieu. "Deux écrits de Mathieu Herbenus sur la destruction de Liège par Charles-le-Téméraire." Ed. E. Bacha. In: *Bulletin de la commission royale l'histoire de Belgique* 76 (1907), 385–90.

Inventaire sommaire des archives départementales antérieures à 1790. Nord. Série B. Ed. A. le Glay et al. 10 vols. Lille, 1863–1906.

James, Montague Rhodes, ed. *The Treatise of Walter de Milemete*. London, 1913.

Journal d'un bourgeois de Paris, 1405–49. Ed. A. Teutey. Paris, 1881.

Juvenal des Ursins, Jean. *Histoire de Charles VI*. In: *Nouvelle collection des mémoires relatifs à l'histoire de France*, 2. Ed. M. Michaud. Paris, 1857.

Klinefelter, Ralph A., ed. " 'The Siege of Calais': A New Text," *Publications of the Modern Language Association* 67 (1952), 888–95.

Knebel, Johann. *Diarium*. Ed. W. Vischer and H. Boos. In: *Basler Chroniken*, II–III. Leipzig, 1880, 1887.

Knighton, Henry. *Knighton's Chronicle*. Ed. and trans. Geoffrey Martin. Oxford, 1995.

Königshoven, J. von. *Chronicke*. Ed. J. Schiltern. Strasbourg, 1698.

Kramer, Gerhard W., ed., and Klaus Leibnitz, trans. *The Firework Book: Gunpowder in Medieval Germany (Das Feuerwerkbuch, c. 1440)*. In: *Journal of Arms and Armour Society* 17 (Mar. 2001).

Kronyk van Vlaenderen van 580 tot 1467. 2 vols. Ed. P. Bloomaert and C.P. Serriere. Ghent, 1839–40.

Kuphal, E., ed. "Der Neusser Kugelbrief von 1475." In: *Aus Mittelalter und Neuzeit: Festschrift Gerhard Kallen*. Bonn, 1957, pp. 155–57.

La Marche, Oliver de. *Mémoires*. In: *Collection complète des mémoires relatifs à l'histoire de France*, 9–10. Ed. M. Petitot. Paris, 1820.

La Marche, Olivier de. *Mémoires*. Ed. Henri Beaune and J. d'Arbaumont. 4 vols. Paris, 1883–88.

Laborde, J. de. *Les ducs de Bourgogne. Études sur les lettres, etc.* 3 vols. Paris, 1849–52.

Lannoy, Guillebert de. *Oeuvres*. Ed. C. Potvin. Leuven, 1878.

Le Fevre, Jean. *Chronique*. 2 vols. Ed. F. Morand. Paris, 1876–81.

Légende Bourguignonne. In: *Recueil de pièces historiques imprimées sous le règne de Louis XI*. Ed. E. Picot and H. Stein. Paris, 1923.

Letters and Papers Illustrative of the Wars of the English in France during the Reign of Henry VI. 2 vols in 3. Ed. J. Stevenson. London, 1861–64.

Lettres de Louis XI roi de France. 12 vols. Ed. J. Vaesen and E. Charavay. Paris, 1883–1909.

Liber de virtutibus sui genitoris Philippi Burgundiae ducis. In: *Chroniques relatives à l'histoire de la Belgique sous la domination des ducs de Bourgogne (texts latins)*. Ed. Kervyn de Lettenhove. Brussels, 1876.

Livre des fais du bon messire Jehan le Maingre, dit Bouciquaut, mareschal de France et gouverneur de Jennes, Le. Paris, 1985.

Livre des trahisons de France envers la maison de Bourgogne, Le. In: *Chroniques relatives à l'histoire de la Belgique sous la domination des ducs de Bourgogne (texts Français)*. Ed. Kervyn de Lettenhove. Brussels, 1873.

Looz, Jean de. *Chronicon*. In: *Documents relatifs aux troubles du pays de Liège sous les princes-éveques Louis de Bourbon et Jean de Horne, 1455–1505*. Ed. P.F.X. de Ram. Brussels, 1844.

Louis XI. *Lettres choises*. Ed. Henri Dubois. Paris, 1996.

Magnum chronicon Belgicum, 54–1474. Ed. B.G. Struve. In: *Rerum germanicarum scriptores*, III. Regensburg, 1726.

Margny, Jean de. *L'aventurier*. Ed. J.R. de Chevanne. Paris, 1938.

Mémoires pour servir à l'histoire de France et de Bourgogne. 2 vols. Paris, 1852–64.

Merica, Henri de. *De cladibus Leodensium*. In: *Documents relatifs aux troubles du pays de Liège sous les princes-éveques Louis de Bourbon et Jean de Horne, 1455–1505*. Ed. P.F.X. de Ram. Brussels, 1844.

Merlin-Chazelas, A., ed. *Documents relatifs au clos des galées de Rouen*. Collection de documents inédits sur l'histoire de France, Section de philologie et d'histoire jusqu'a 1610. 2 vols. Paris, 1977.

Mézières, Philippe de. *Letter to King Richard II: A Plea Made in 1395 for Peace between England and France*. Ed. and trans. G.W. Coopland. Liverpool, 1975.

Molinet, Jean. *Chroniques*. Ed. G. Doutrepont and O. Jodogne. 3 vols. Academie royale de Belgique. Brussels, 1935–37.

Monstrelet, Enguerran de. *Chronique*. Ed. L. Douet-d'Arcq. 6 vols. Paris, 1857–62.

Morosini, Antonio. *Chronique: Extraits relatifs à l'histoire de France*. Trans. and ed. L. Dorez. 4 vols. Société de l'histoire de France. Paris, 1898–1902.

Musch, Walter, and E.A. Gessler, ed. *Die schweizer Bilderchroniken des 15/16 Jahrhunderts*. Zurich, 1941.

Narratio de morte Caroli ducis Burgundiae. In: *Chroniques relatives à l'histoire de la Belgique sous la domination des ducs de Bourgogne (texts latins)*. Ed. Kervyn de Lettenhove. Brussels, 1876.

Nederman, Cary J., ed. and trans. *Political Thought in Early Fourteenth-Century England: Treatises by Walter of Milemete, William of Pagula and William of Ockham*. Tempe, 2002.

Onofrio de Santa Croce. *Mémoire*. Ed. S. Bormans. Brussels, 1885.

Oudenbosch, Adrien d'. *Chronique*. Ed. C. de Borman. Liège, 1902.

Pauli, Theodoricus. *De rebus actis sub de ducibus Burgundiae*. In: *Chroniques relatives à l'histoire de la domination des ducs de Bourgogne (texts latins)*. Ed. Kervyn de Lettenhove. Brussels, 1876.

Peter of Bethlehem. *Chronica*. In: *Chroniques relatives à l'histoire de la Belgique sous la domination des ducs de Bourgogne (texts latins)*. Ed. Kervyn de Lettenhove. Brussels, 1876.

Petri, S. *Gesta pontificum Leodiensium a Joanne de Bavaria usque ad Evrardum a Marcka*. Ed. J. Chapeaville. In: *Gesta pontificum Leodiensium*, iii. Liège, 1616.

Pfettisheim, Conrad. *Chronique rimée des guerres de Bourgogne*. In: *Recueil de pièces historiques imprimées sous le règne de Louis XI*. Ed. E. Picot and H. Stein. Paris, 1923.

Pisan, Christine de. *The Book of Deeds of Arms and of Chivalry*. Ed. Charity Cannon Willard. Trans. Sumner Willard. State College, 1999.

———. *Le livre des fais et bonnes meurs du sage roy Charles V.* 2 vols. Ed. S. Solente. Paris, 1936–40.

Pius II. *The Commentaries of Pius II.* Trans. F.A. Gragg. Northampton, 1937, 1940, 1947, 1951, 1957.

Quicherat, Jules, ed. *Procès de condamnation et de réhabilitation de Jeanne d'Arc dite la Pucelle.* Société de l'histoire de France. Paris, 1841–49.

Recueil de choses advenues du temps et gouvernement de très haulte mémoire feu Charles, duc de Bourgogne, estant le seigneur du Fay gouverneur au pays de Luxembourg. In: *Publications de la Société pour la recherché et la conservation des monuments historiques dans le Grand-Duché de Luxembourg* 3 (1847), 85–153.

Régestes de la cité de Liège. Ed. E. Fairon. 4 vols. Liège, 1933–40.

Registres des comptes municipaux de la ville de Tours. Vol. 1. Ed. J. Delaville le Roulx. Tours, 1878.

Registres du conseil de Genève. Ed. E. Rivoire et al. 13 vols. Geneva, 1900–40.

"Règlement pour la défense du château de Bioule, 18 mars 1347," *Bulletin archéologique* 4 (1846–47), 490–95.

Rijmkroniek van Vlaenderen. In: *Corpus chronicorum Flandriae*, 4. Ed. J.J. de Smet. Brussels, 1865.

Robbins, Rossell Hope, ed. *Historical Poems of the XIVth and XVth Centuries.* New York, 1959.

Roye, Jean de. *Chroniques.* In: *Collection complète des mémoires relatifs à l'histoire de France*, 13–14. Ed. M. Petitot. 2 vols. Paris, 1820.

Rymer, Thomas, ed. *Foedera, conventiones, litterae. et cujuscunque generis acta publica inter reges Angliae et alios quosvis imperatores, reges, pontifices, principes, vel communitates (1101–1654).* London, 1709.

Schaumberg, W. von. *Die Geschichten und Taten.* Ed. A. von Keller. Stuttgart, 1859.

Schilling, Diebold. *Die Berner-Chronik, 1468–1484.* Ed. G. Tobler. 2 vols. Bern, 1897, 1901.

Schiltberger, Johannes. *Bondage and Travels of Johann Schiltberger, a Native of Bavaria, in Europe, Asia, and Africa (1396–1427).* Ed. K.F. Neumann. Trans. J.B. Telfer. London, 1879.

Stavelot, Jean de. *Chronique latine.* In: *Chroniques Liègeoises.* 1. Ed. S. Balau. Brussels, 1913.

Stolles, Konrad. *Thuringische-Erfurtische Chronik.* Ed. L.F. Hess. Stuttgart, 1854.

Straszburgische Archiv-Chronik. Ed. L. Schneegans and A. Strobel. In: *Code historique et diplomatique de la ville de Strasbourg.* Strasbourg, 1843, I.2:131–220.

Thielmans, Marie-Rose, ed. "Une lettre missive inédité de Philippe le Bon concernant le siège de Calais," *Bulletin de la commission royale d'histoire de Belgique* 115 (1950), 285–96.

Tuesch, Hans Erhart. *Chronique rimée des guerres de Bourgogne.* In: *Recueil de pièces historiques imprimées sous le règne de Louis XI.* Ed. E. Picot and H. Stein. Paris, 1923.

Unrest, J. *Oesterreichische Chronik.* Ed. K. Grossmann. Monumenta Germaniae historica scriptores (N.F.), XI. Weimar, 1957.

Walsingham, Thomas. *Historia Anglicana.* 2 vols. Ed. H.T. Riley. London, 1863–64.

Waurin, Jehan de. *Récueil des croniques et anchiennes istories de la Grant Bretaigne.* Ed. W. and E.L.C.P. Hardy. 5 vols. London, 1864–91.

The Westminster Chronicle, 1381–1394. Ed. and trans. L.C. Hector and Barbara F. Harvey. Oxford, 1982.

Wierstrait, C. *Historij des belegs van Nuys.* Ed. K. Meisen. Bonn, 1926.

Secondary Sources

Alberts, W. Jappe. "De eerste Bourgondische bezetting van Gelre, 1473–7," *Bijdragen van het Instituut voor middeleeuwsche geschiedenis der Rijksuniversiteit te Utrecht* 27 (1954), 49–82.

Allmand, Christopher T. *Henry V.* Berkeley and Los Angeles, 1992.

———. *The Hundred Years War: England and France at War c. 1300–c. 1450.* Cambridge, 1988.

Arnold, Thomas. *The Renaissance at War.* London, 2001.

Aston, Margaret. "The Impeachment of Bishop Despenser," *Bulletin of the Institute of Historical Research* 38 (1965), 127–48.

Atiya, Aziz Suryal. *The Crusade in the Later Middle Ages.* London, 1938.

———. *The Crusade of Nicopolis.* London, 1934.

Autrand, Françoise. *Charles VI: La folie du roi*. Paris, 1986.

———. "La paix impossible: les négociations franco-anglaises à la fin du 14e siècle," in Actes du colloque Nicopolis 1396–1996, *Annales de Bourgogne* 68 (1997), 11–22.

Awty, Brian G. "The Origin of the Blast Furnace: Evidence from Francophone Areas," *Historical Metallurgy* 21 (1987), 96–99.

Ayalon, David. *Gunpowder and Firearms in the Mamluk Kingdom: A Challenge to a Mediaeval Society*. London, 1956.

Bachrach, David S. "A Military Revolution Reconsidered: The Case of the Burgundian State Under the Valois Dukes," *Essays in Medieval Studies* 15 (1999), 9–17.

Ballard, Mark. "An Expedition of English Archers to Liège in 1467, and the Anglo-Burgundian Marriage Alliance," *Nottingham Medieval Studies* 34 (1990), 152–74.

Bartier, J. *Charles le Téméraire*. Brussels, 1944.

Benecke, Gerhard. *Maximilian I (1459–1519): An Analytical Biography*. London, 1982.

Bertin, J. "Le siège du château de Vellexon en 1409," *Bulletin de la société d'agriculture, science, commerce et arts du département de la Haute-Saône* 3rd ser. 31 (1900), 1–190 (also published as *Le siège du château de Vellexon en 1409* (Vesoul, 1901)).

Bertin, Pierre. "Le siège du chateau de Vellexon dans l'hiver 1409–1410," *Revue historique des armées* 27 (1971), 7–18.

Beyaert, Marc. "Nieuwe historisch onderzoek van de Dulle Griet bombarde in Gent," *Handelingen der Maatschappij voor geschiedenis en oudheidkunde te Gent*, n.s. 53 (1999), 3–59.

Binet, Sylvie. *Jeanne Hachette: l'héroine de Beauvais*. Paris, 1995.

Blackmore, Howard L. *The Armouries of the Tower of London*. I: *Ordnance*. London, 1976.

———. "The Boxted Bombard," *Antiquaries Journal* 67 (1987), 86–96.

———. "Master Jacobo's Culverin, 1517," *Journal of the Arms and Armour Society* 12 (1986–88), 312–44.

———. "The Oldest Dated Gun," *Canadian Journal of Arms Collecting* 34.2 (May 1996), 39–47.

Blockmans, Wim and Walter Prevenier. *The Promised Lands: The Low Countries Under Burgundian Rule, 1369–1530*. Ed. Edward Peters. Trans. Elizabeth Fackelman. Philadelphia, 1999.

Bonenfant, Paul. *Du meurtre de Montereau au traité de Troyes*. Brussels, 1958.

Brackenbury, Henry. "Ancient Cannon in Europe. Part I: From their First Employment to A.D. 1350," *Proceedings of the Royal Artillery Institution* 4 (1865), 287–308.

———. "Ancient Cannon in Europe. Part II: From A.D. 1351 to A.D. 1400," *Proceedings of the Royal Artillery Institution* 5 (1867), 1–37.

Brauner, Alois. *Die Schlacht bei Nikopolis, 1396*. Breslau, 1876.

Brusten, Charles. *L'armée bourguignonne de 1465 à 1468*. Brussels, 1954.

———. "L'armée Bourguignonne de 1465 à 1477," *Revue internationale d'histoire militaire* (1959), 452–66.

———. "La bataille de Morat," *Publications du centre européen d'études burgundo-médianes* 10 (1968), 79–84.

———. "Les campagnes Liègeoises de Charles de Téméraire." In: *Liège et Bourgogne. Actes de colloque tenu à Liège les 28, 29 et 30 Octobre, 1968*. Liège, 1972, pp. 81–99.

———. "Charles le Téméraire et la camp de Lausanne, mars–mai 1476," *Publications du centre européen d'études burgundo-médianes* 14 (1972), 71–81.

———. "Charles le Téméraire et la campagne de Neuss, 1474–75," *Publications du centre européen d'études burgundo-médianes* 13 (1971), 67–73.

———. "Les compaignies d'ordonnance dans l'armée Bourguignonne," *Revue internationale d'histoire militaire* 40 (1978), 112–69; and in: *Grandson 1476: Essai d'approche d'une action militaire du XVe siècle*. Ed. D. Reichel. Lausanne, 1976, pp. 112–69.

———. "La fin des compaignies d'ordonnance de Charles le Téméraire." In: *Cinq-centième anniversaire de la bataille de Nancy (1477): Actes du Colloque organisé par l'institut de recherche régionale en sciences sociales, humaines et économiques de l'Université de Nancy II (Nancy, 22–24 septembre 1977)*. Nancy, 1979, pp. 363–75.

————. "Les itinéraires de l'armée Bourguignonne de 1465 à 1478," *Publications du centre europeen d'études burgundo-medianes* 2 (1960), 55–67.

————. "A propos des campagnes bourguignonnes, 1475–78," *Publications du centre européen d'études burgundo-médianes* 9 (1967), 79–87.

Burne, Alfred H. *The Agincourt War: A Military History of the Latter Part of the Hundred Years War from 1369 to 1453*. London, 1956.

————. *The Crecy War: A Military History of the Hundred Years War from 1337 to the Peace of Bretigny, 1360*. London, 1955.

Camp, P. *Histoire d'Auxonne au moyen âge*. Dijon, 1961.

Carolus-Barre, Louis. "Compiegne et la guerre, 1414–1430." In: *111e Congres national des Sociétés savantes, Poitiers, 1986, Histoire médiévale, T. I: "La France Anglaise"*, pp. 383–92.

Caron, Marie-Thérèse. "17 février 1454: le Banquet du Voeu du Faisan, fête de cour et stratégies de pouvoir," *Revue du nord* 78 (1996), 269–88.

———— and Denis Clauzel, ed. *Le Banquet du Faisan*. Arras, 1997.

Carrier, Hubert. "*Si vera est fama*: Le retentissement de la bataille d'Othée dans la culture historique au XVe siècle," *Revue historique* 305 (2001), 639–70.

Caruana, Adrian B. *The History of English Sea Ordnance*, I: *The Age of Evolution, 1523–1715*. Rotherfield, 1994.

Cauchies, Jean-Marie. "Charles le Hardi à Neuss (1474/75): Folie militaire ou contrainte politique," *Publication du centre européen d'études bourguignonnes (XIVe–XVIe siècles)* 36 (1996), 105–15.

————. *Louis XI et Charles le Hardi: De Péronne à Nancy (1468–1477): le conflit*. Brussels, 1996.

Champion, Pierre. *Guillaume de Flavy: Captaine de Compiègne: Contribution à l'histoire de Jeanne d'Arc et à l'étude de la vie militaire et privée au XVe siècle*. Paris, 1906.

————. *Louis XI*. Trans. Winifred Stephens Whale. London, 1929.

Le Château de Grandson. Colmar, 1980.

Chevanne, J. Robert de. *Les guerres en Bourgogne de 1470 à 1475*. Paris, 1934.

Clauzel, Denis, Charles Giry-Deloison, and Christophe Leduc, ed. *Arras et la diplomatie européenne, xve–xvie siècles*. Centre de Recherches Historiques: "Des Anciens Pays-Bas à l'Eurorégion" (Université d'Artois–Arras). Arras, 1999.

Clephan, R. Coltman. "The Military Handgun of the Sixteenth Century," *Archaeological Journal* 67 (1910), 109–50.

————. "The Ordnance of the Fourteenth and Fifteenth Centuries." *Archaeological Journal* 68 (1911), 49–138.

————. *An Outline of the History and Development of Hand Firearms, from the Earliest Period to about the End of the Fifteenth Century*. London, 1906.

Clin-Meyer, Marie-Véronique. *Isabeau de Bavière, La Reine calomniée*. Paris, 1999.

Cockshaw, Pierre. "L'assassinat du duc Jean de Bourgogne à Montereau: Études des sources." In: *Les Pays-Bas bourguignons: Histoire et institutions. Mélanges André Uyttebrouck*. Ed. J.-M. Duvosquel, J. Nazet, and A. Vanrie. Brussels, 1996, pp. 145–62.

———— and Christiane Van den Bergen-Pantens, ed. *L'ordre de la Toison d'or, de Philippe le Bon à Philippe le Beau (1430–1505): Idéal ou reflet d'une société?* Brussels, 1996.

Collins, Hugh. "Sir John Fastolf, John Lord Talbot and the Dispute over Patay: Ambitions and Chivalry in the Fifteenth Century." In: *War and Society in Medieval and Early Modern Britain*. Ed. Diana Dunn. Liverpool, 2000, pp. 114–40.

Contamine, Philippe. "L'artillerie royale Française à la veille des guerres d'Italie," *Annales de Bretagne* 71 (1964), 221–61.

————. *La guerre de Cent Ans*, 3rd ed. Paris, 1977.

————. "La guerre de siège au temps de Jeanne d'Arc," *Dossiers de archéologie* 34 (May 1979), 11–20.

————. *Guerre, état et société à la fin du moyen âge: Études sur les armées des rois de France, 1337–1494*. Paris, 1972.

————. "Les industries de guerre dans la France de la Renaissance: l'exemple de l'artillerie." *Revue historique* 271 (1984), 249–80.

————. *L'oriflamme de Saint-Denis aux XIVe et XVe siècles*. Nancy, 1975.

————. *War in the Middle Ages.* Trans. Michael Jones. London, 1984.

Coville, A. *Les cabochiens et l'ordonnance de 1413.* Paris, 1888.

Curry, Anne. "English Armies in the Fifteenth Century." In: *Arms, Armies and Fortifications in the Hundred Years War.* Ed. A. Curry and M. Hughes. Woodbridge, 1994, pp. 39–68.

Daris, J. *Histoire du diocèse et de la principauté de Liège pendant le XVe siècle.* 3 [?] vols. Liège, 1887.

Decamps, Gonzalès. *L'artillerie montoise, ses origines.* Mons, 1906.

Delbrück, Hans. *History of the Art of War Within the Framework of Political History, vol. III: Medieval Warfare.* Trans. W.J. Renfroe, Jr. Westport, 1984.

Delisle, Leopold. *Histoire du chateau et des sires de Saint-Sauveur-le-Vicomte.* 2 vols. Paris, 1867.

Deuchler, Florens. *Die Burgunderbeute: Inventar der Beutestucke aus den Schlachten von Grandson, Murten und Nancy 1476/77.* Bern, 1963.

De Vos, Luc. "La bataille de Gavere le 23 juillet 1453. La victoire de l'organisation." In: *XXII. Kongreß der Internationalen Kommission für Militärgeschichte* Acta 22: *Von Crécy bis Mohács Kriegswesen im späten Mittelalter (1346–1526).* Vienna, 1997, pp. 145–57.

DeVries, Kelly. "A 1445 Reference to Shipboard Artillery," *Technology and Culture* 31 (1990), 818–29.

————. "The Effectiveness of Fifteenth-Century Shipboard Artillery," *The Mariner's Mirror* 84 (1998), 389–99.

————. "Facing the New Military Technology: Non-*Trace Italienne* Anti-Gunpowder Weaponry Defenses, 1350–1550." In: *Colonels and Quartermasters: War and Technology in the Old Regime.* Ed. Brett Steele. Cambridge, 2005, pp. 37–71.

————. "The Failure of Philip the Good to Fulfill His Crusade Promise of 1454." In: *Medieval Crusade.* Ed. Susan Ridyard. Woodbridge, 2004, pp. 157–70.

————. "A 15th-Century Weapons Dowry: The Weapons Dowry of Duke Philip the Good of Burgundy for the Marriage of Mary of Guelders and James II of Scotland in 1449," *The Royal Armouries Yearbook* 6 (2001), 22–31.

————. "The Forgotten Battle of Bevershoutsveld, May 3, 1382: Technological Innovation and Military Significance." In: *Armies, Chivalry and Warfare: Harlaxton Medieval Studies, VII.* Ed. Mathew Strickland. Stamford, 1998, pp. 280–94.

————. "Gunpowder and Early Gunpowder Weapons." In: *Gunpowder: The History of an International Technology.* Ed. Brenda Buchanan. Bath, 1996, pp. 121–36.

————. "Gunpowder Weaponry and the Rise of the Early Modern State," *War in History* 5 (1998), 127–45.

————. "Gunpowder Weaponry at the Siege of Constantinople, 1453." In: *War, Army and Society in the Eastern Mediterranean, 7th–16th Centuries.* Ed. Yaacov Lev. Leiden, 1996, pp. 343–62.

————. "Hunger, Flemish Participation and the Flight of Philip VI: Contemporary Accounts of the Siege of Calais, 1346–47," *Studies in Medieval and Renaissance History* n.s. 12 (1991), 129–81.

————. "The Impact of Gunpowder Weaponry on Siege Warfare in the Hundred Years War." In: *Medieval City Under Siege.* Ed. Ivy A. Corfis and Michael Wolfe. Woodbridge, 1995, pp. 227–44.

————. *Infantry Warfare in the Early Fourteenth Century: Discipline, Tactics, and Technology.* Woodbridge, 1996.

————. *Joan of Arc: A Military Leader.* Stroud, 1999.

————. "The Lack of a Western European Military Response to the Ottoman Invasions of Eastern Europe from Nicopolis (1396) to Mohács (1526)," *Journal of Military History* 63 (1999), 539–59.

————. *Medieval Military Technology.* Peterborough, 1992.

————. "The Reasons for the Bishop of Norwich's Attack on Flanders in 1383." In: *Fourteenth Century England III.* Ed. W.M. Ormrod. Woodbridge: The Boydell Press, 2004, pp 155–65.

————. "A Reassessment of the Gun Illustrated in the Walter de Milemete and Pseudo-Aristotle Manuscripts," *Journal of the Ordnance Society* 15 (2003), 5–17.

————. "The Rebellions of the Southern Low Countries' Towns during the Fourteenth and Fifteenth Centuries." In: *Power and the City in the Netherlandic World, 1000–2000.* Ed. W. TeBrake and W. Kibler. Leiden: Brill (forthcoming).

————. "Was There a Renaissance in Warfare? Humanism and Technological Determinism, 1300–1560" (forthcoming).

Dickinson, Joyceline Gledhill. *The Congress of Arras, 1435: A Study in Medieval Diplomacy*. Oxford, 1955.

Dubled, H. "L'artillerie royale Française à l'époque de Charles VII et au début du règne de Louis XI (1437–1469): Les frères Bureau," *Memorial de l'artillerie Française* 50 (1976), 555–637.

Dumolyn, Jan. *De Brugse opstand van 1436–1438*. Courtrai-Heule, 1997.

Eltis, David. *The Military Revolution in Sixteenth-Century Europe*. London, 1995.

Engel, Pál. "János Hunyadi: The Decisive Years of his Career, 1440–1444." In: *War and Society in Eastern Central Europe*. Vol III: *From Hunyadi to Rákóczi: War and Society in Late Medieval and Early Modern Hungary*. Ed. J.M. Bak and B.K. Király. New York, 1982, pp. 103–23.

Favier, Jean. *La guerre de cent ans*. Paris, 1980.

Finó, J.-F. "L'artillerie en France à la fin du moyen âge," *Gladius* 12 (1974), 13–31.

———. *Forteresses de la France médiévale*. Paris, 1967.

Finot, Jules. *L'artillerie bourguignonne à la bataille de Montlhéry*. Lille, 1896.

———. *La paix d'Arras, 1414–15*. Nancy, 1906.

———. "Projet d'expedition contre les Turcs préparée par les conseillers du duc de Bourgogne Philippe le Bon," *Mémoires de la société des sciences de Lille* 4th ser. 21 (1895), 161–206.

———. *Projet d'expédition contre les turcs préparé par les conseillers du duc de Bourgogne Philippe-le-Bon (janvier 1457)*. Lille, 1890.

Fredericq, Paul. *Essai sur le rôle politique et social des ducs de Bourgogne dans les Pays-Bas*. Ghent, 1875.

Fris, V. "La bataille de Gavre," *Bulletin de la société d'histoire et d'archéologie de Gand* 18 (1910), 185–233.

Fromont, A. and A. de Meunynck. *Histoire de canonniers de Lille*. 2 vols. Lille, 1892.

Fuhrer, Hans-Rudolf and Benjamin Geiger. *Les guerres de Bourgogne*. Trans. Christophe Eck. 2nd ed. Zurich: Ecole militaire supérieur, 1996.

Gaier, Claude. *Art et organisation militaires dans la principauté de Liège et dans le comté de Looz au moyen âge*. Brussels, 1968.

———. *Grandes batailles de l'histoire Liegéoise au moyen âge*. Liege, 1980.

———. *L'industrie et le commerce des armes dans les anciennes principautés Belges du XIIIme à la fin du XVe siècle*. Paris, 1963.

———. "The Origin of Mons Meg," *Journal of the Arms and Armour Society* 5 (1967), 425–31.

———. "Le rôle des armes à feu dans les batailles Liègeoises au XVe siècle," *Le musée d'armes* 51 (1986), 1–12 and *Publication du centre Européen d'études Bourguignonnes (XIVe–XVIe s.)* 26 (1986), 31–37.

Gaillard, Philippe. *La bataille d'Anthon: 11 juin 1430*. Annecy-le-Vieux, 1998.

Gautier, Paul. "Un récit inédit du siège de Constantinople par les turcs (1394–1402)," *Revue des études byzantines* 23 (1965), 100–17.

Gay, Victor. *Glossaire archéologique du moyen âge et de la renaissance*. 2 vols. Paris, 1887, 1928.

Gérard, Édouard. *Analectes pour servir à l'histoire de la ville de Dinant*. Namur, 1901.

——— and Gabrielle Gérard. *Histoire de la ville de Dinant*. Dinant, 1988.

Gibbons, Rachel. "Isabeau of Bavaria, Queen of France (1385–1422). The Creation of an Historical Villainess," *Transactions of the Royal Historical Society*, 6th ser., 6 (1996), 51–73.

Gille, Bertrand. *Engineers of the Renaissance*. Cambridge, 1966.

Gillet, C. and M. Lefebvre. "Quelle etait la puissance de feu de la 'Mons Meg', bombard Bourguignonne conservée à Edimourg?" *Le musée d'armes* 28.98–99 (Dec. 2000), 2–22.

Girling, F.A. *English Merchants' Marks: A Field Survey of Marks Made by Merchants and Tradesmen in England between 1400 and 1700*. London, 1964.

Goodman, Anthony. *The Wars of the Roses: Military Activity and English Society, 1452–97*. London, 1981.

Grosjean, George. *La bataille de Morat selon trios enluminures d'anciennes chroniques suisses*. Zurich, 1975.

———. "Die Murtenschlacht: Analyse eines Ereignisses." In: *Actes du Ve centenaire de la bataille de Morat*. Fribourg and Berne, 1976, pp. 35–90.

Guenée, Bernard. *Un meutre, une société: L'assassinat du Duc d'Orléans, 23 novembre 1407*. Paris, 1992.

Guillaume, M. *Histoire de l'organisation militaire sous les ducs de Bourgogne*. Academie royale de Belgique mémoires couronnes et mémoires des savantes étrangers, 12, n. 8. Brussels, 1848.

Guilmartin, John Francis, Jr. "Ballistics in the Black Powder Era." In: *British Naval Armaments*. Ed. Robert D. Smith. London, 1989, pp. 73–98.

———. "The Early Provision of Artillery Armament on Mediterranean War Galleys," *Mariner's Mirror* 59 (1973), 257–80.

———. *Gunpowder and Galleys. Changing Technology and Mediterranean Warfare at Sea in the Sixteenth Century*. Cambridge, 1974.

Gulden Vlies, Het: Vijf eeuwen kunst en gescheidenis. Tentoonstelling ingericht door het Ministerie van Nationale Opvoeding en Cultuur en de Stad Brugge in het Stedelijk Museum voor Schone Kunsten, 14 juli – 30 September 1962. Bruges, 1962.

Hachez, Henri. *Histoire de Dinant*. Brussels, 1932.

Haigh, Philip A. *The Military Campaigns of the Wars of the Roses*. Stroud, 1995.

Hall, Bert S. "The Corning of Gunpowder and the Development of Firearms in the Renaissance." In: *Gunpowder: The History of an International Technology*. Ed. Brenda Buchanan. Bath, 1996, pp. 87–120.

———. *Weapons and Warfare in Renaissance Europe: Gunpowder, Technology, and Tactics*. Baltimore, 1997.

Hammond, P.W. *The Battles of Barnet and Tewkesbury*. New York, 1990.

Held, Joseph. *Hunyadi: Legend and Reality*. Boulder, 1985.

Henneman, John Bell. *Olivier de Clisson and Political Society under Charles V and Charles VI*. Philadelphia, 1996.

Hennessy, N. St. John. "The Dublin Breech-Loading Swivel Gun," *Journal of the Ordnance Society* 3 (1991), 1–4.

Henrard, Paul. *Les campagnes de Charles les Téméraire contre les Liégeois (1465–1468)*. Brussels, 1867.

———. "Documents pour servir à l'histoire de l'artillerie en Belgique. Les fondeurs d'artillerie," *Annales de l'academie d'archéologie de Belgique* 45 (1889).

———. *Histoire de l'artillerie en Belgique depuis son oringe jusqu'au règne d'Albert et d'Isabelle*. Brussels, 1865.

Héricourt, A. d'. *Les sièges d'Arras*. Arras, 1844.

Hintzen, Johanna Dorina. *De Kruistochtplannen van Philips den Goede*. Rotterdam, 1918.

Hoch, Charles. *Morat et Charles-le-Téméraire, 1476–1876*. Neuchatel, 1876.

Hogg, O.F.G. *Artillery: Its Origin, Heyday and Decline*. London, 1970.

———. *English Artillery, 1326–1716*. London, 1963.

Housley, Norman. "The Bishop of Norwich's Crusade, May 1383," *History Today* 33 (1983), 15–20.

———. *The Later Crusades, 1274–1580: From Lyons to Alcazar*. Oxford, 1992.

Huyttens, Jules. "Recherches sur l'organisation militaire de la ville de Gand au moyen-âge," *Messager des sciences historiques*, 6th ser., 26 (1858), 413–52.

Jacob, E.F. "The Collapse of France, 1419–20," *Bulletin of the John Rylands Library* 26 (1941–42), 307–26.

———. *The Fifteenth Century, 1399–1485*. The Oxford History of England. Oxford, 1961.

———. *Henry V and the Invasion of France*. London, 1947.

Jones, Michael. "The Defence of Medieval Brittany: A Survey of the Establishment of Fortified Towns, Castles and Frontiers from the Gallo-Roman Period to the End of the Middle Ages," *Archaeological Journal* 138 (1981), 149–204.

Jones, Michael K. "John Beaufort, Duke of Somerset and the French Expedition of 1443." In: *Patronage, the Crown and the Provinces in Later Medieval England*. Ed. Ralph A. Griffiths. Gloucester, 1981, pp. 79–102.

———. "The Relief of Avranches (1439): An English Feat of Arms at the End of the Hundred Years War." In: *England in the Fifteenth Century: Proceedings of the 1992 Harlaxton Symposium*. Ed. N Rogers. Stamford, 1994, pp. 42–55.

Jongkees, A.G. "Armement et action d'une flotte de guerre: la contribution des comtés maritimes à l'armée générale des pays de Par-Deçà en 1477." *Publications du centre Européen d'études Bourguignonnes (XIVe–XVIe s.)* 26 (1986), 71–86; and in: *Burgundica et Varia*. Hilversum, 1990, pp. 302–18.

Jorga, N. *Philippe de Mézières (1327–1405) et la croisade au XIVe siècle*. Paris, 1896.

Keen, Maurice H. "The Changing Scene: Guns, Gunpowder, and Permanent Armies." In: *Medieval Warfare: A History*. Ed. Maurice Keen. Oxford, 1999, pp. 273–91.

Kendall, Paul Murray. *Louis XI: ". . . the Universal Spider . . ."*. London, 1974.

Kling, Gustav. *Die Schlacht bei Nikopolis im Jahre 1396*. Berlin, 1906.

Köhler, Gustav. *Die Entwickelung des Kriegswesens und der Kriegführung in der Ritterzeit von Mitte des 11. Jahrhunderts bis zu de Hussitenkriegen*. 2 vols. Breslau, 1886.

———. *Die Schlachten von Nicopoli und Warna*. Breslau, 1882.

Kramer, Gerhard. *Berthold Schwarz: Chemie und Waffentechnik im 15. Jahrhundert*. Munich, 1995.

———. "*Das Feuerwerkbuch*: Its Importance in the Early History of Black Powder." In: *Gunpowder: The History of an International Technology*. Ed. B. Buchanan. Bath, 1996, pp. 45–56.

Kupelweiser, L. *Die Kämpfe Ungarns mit den Osmanen bis zur Schlacht bei Mohács*. 2nd ed. Vienna, 1899.

Kurth, G. *La cité de Liège au Moyen Age*. 3 vols. Brussels, 1910.

Kurz, Hans-Rudolf. "Grandson – 2 Mars 1476 – le déroulement de la bataille." In: *Grandson 1476*. Centre d'histoire et de prospectives militaires. Serie recherches de sciences comparées, T. II. Lausanne, 1976, pp. 201–13.

La Fons-Meliococq, A. de. *De l'artillerie de la ville de Lille aux XIVe, XVe et XVIe siècles*. Lille, 1854.

Lacabane, L. "De la poudre à canon et de son introduction en France," *Bibliothèque de l'école de chartes*, 2nd ser., 1 (1844), 28–57.

Lacaze, Yvon. "Politique 'Méditerranéenne' et projets de croisade chez Philippe le Bon: De la chute de Byzance à la victoire chrétienne de Belgrade (mai 1453 – juillet 1456)," *Annales de Bourgogne* 41 (1969), 81–132.

Lachauvelaye, J. de. "Les armées des trois premiers ducs de Bourgogne," *Mémoires de l'academie des sciences, arts et belles-lettres de Dijon*, ser. 3, 6 (1880), 19–335.

———. "Mémoire sur la composition des armées de Charles le Téméraire dans les deux Bourgognes d'après les documents originaux," *Mémoires de l'academie des sciences, arts et belles-lettres de Dijon* 3rd ser., 6 (1880), 139–369.

Lafortune-Martel, Agathe. *Fête noble en Bourgogne au XVe siècle. Le banquet du Faisan (1454): Aspects politiques, sociaux et culturels*. Montreal,1984.

Lange, Joseph. "Pulchra Nussia: Die Belagerung der Stadt Neuss, 1474/75." In: *Neuss, Burgund und das Reich*. Neuss, 1975, pp. 9–190.

Lecoy de la Marche, Albert. *Le roi René*. 2 vols. Paris, 1875.

Leguai, André. "La conquête de la Bourgogne par Louis XI," *Annales de Bourgogne* 49 (1977), 7–12.

———. "Dijon et Louis XI," *Annales de Bourgogne* 17 (1945), 16–37, 103–15, 145–69, 239–63.

Libois, Raoul, Jacques Jeanmart, and Philippe Jaumin. *Houx (Yvoir) en zijn middeleeuws kasteel van Poilvache*. 2nd ed. Everhailles-Yvoir, 1993.

Lombarès, Michel de. "Castillon (17 juillet 1453), dernière bataille de la guerre de Cent Ans, première victoire de l'artillerie," *Revue historique des armées* (1976), 7–31.

Lot, Ferdinand. *L'art militaire et les armées au moyen-âge en Europe et dans le proche orient*. 2 vols. Paris, 1946.

Magee, James. "Sir William Elmham and the Recruitment for Henry Despenser's Crusade of 1383," *Medieval Prosography* 20 (1999), 181–90.

Marot, Pierre. "Le Duc de Lorraine René II et la Bataille de Nancy dans l'historiographie et la tradition lorraines." In: *Cinq-centième anniversaire de la bataille de Nancy (1477): Actes du Colloque organisé par l'institut de recherche régionale en sciences sociales, humaines et économiques de l'Université de Nancy II (Nancy, 22–24 septembre 1977)*. Nancy, 1979, pp. 83–126.

McNeill, William H. *The Pursuit of Power: Technology, Armed Force, and Society since A.D. 1000*. Chicago, 1982.

Monteuuis, Gustave. "Le siège de Bourbourg en 1383," *Annales du comité flamand de France* 22 (1895), 259–313.

Müller, Heribert. *Kreuzzugspläne und Kreuzzugspolitik des Herzogs Philipp des Guten von Burgund*. Gottingen, 1993.

Napoleon-Bonaparte, Louis and Ildéfonse Favé. *Études sur le passé et l'avenir de l'artillerie*. 6 vols. Paris, 1846–71.

Necipoglu, N. "Economic Conditions in Constantinople during the Siege of Bayezid I (1394–1402)." In: *Constantinople and Its Hinterland*. Ed. C. Mango and G. Dagron. Aldershot, 1995, pp. 157–67.

Newhall, Richard Ager. *The English Conquest of Normandy, 1416–1424: A Study in Fifteenth Century Warfare*. New Haven, 1924.

Nicholas, David. *Medieval Flanders*. London, 1992.

———. *The Van Arteveldes of Ghent: The Varieties of Vendetta and the Hero in History*. Ithaca, 1988.

Nicolle, David. *Nicopolis, 1396: The Last Crusade*. London, 1999.

Norman, A.V.B. "Notes on Some Early Representations of Guns and on Ribaudekins," *Journal of the Arms and Armour Society* 8 (1975), 234–27.

Ochsenbein, G.F. *Die Akten der Belagerung und Schlacht von Murten*. Freiburg, 1876.

Offenstadt, Nicolas. "Le paix d'Arras, 1414–15: un paroxysme rituel?" In: *Arras et la diplomatie européenne, xve–xvie siècles*. Ed. Denis Clauzel, Charles Giry-Deloison, and Christophe Leduc. Centre de Recherches Historiques: "Des Anciens Pays-Bas à l'Eurorégion" (Université d'Artois–Arras). Arras, 1999, pp. 65–80.

Oman, Charles. *A History of the Art of War in the Middle Ages*. 2 vols. London, 1905.

Palmer, J.J.N. *England, France and Christendom, 1377–99*. Chapel Hill, 1972.

Paravicini, Werner. *Karl der Kühne: Das Ende des Hauses Burgund*. Göttingen, 1976.

Parker, Geoffrey. *The Army of Flanders and the Spanish Road, 1567–1659*. Cambridge Studies in Early Modern History. Cambridge, 1972.

———. *The Military Revolution: Military Innovation and the Rise of the West, 1500–1800*. Cambridge, 1988.

Partington, J.R. *A History of Greek Fire and Gunpowder*. Cambridge, 1960; rpt. Baltimore, 1998.

Paviot, Jacques. "Les navires du duc de Bourgogne Philippe le Bon (vers 1440–1465)." In: *Atti del v convegno internazionale di studi colombiani: "Navi e navigazione nei secoli XV e XVI"*. Genoa, 1990, I:167–95.

———. *La politique navale des ducs de Bourgogne, 1384–1482*. Lille, 1995.

———, ed. *Portugal et Bourgogne au XVe siècle: Recueil de documents extraits des archives bourguignonnes*. Lisbon and Paris, 1995.

——— and M. Chauney-Bouillot, ed. "Nicopolis, 1396–1996: Actes du Colloque international," *Annales de Bourgogne* 68 (1996).

Pepper, Simon. "Castles and Cannon in the Naples Campaign of 1494–95." In: *The French Descent into Renaissance Italy, 1494–95: Antecedents and Effects*. Ed. D. Abulafia. Aldershot, 1995, pp. 263–93.

Pernoud, Régine, and Marie-Véronique Clin. *Joan of Arc: Her Story*. Trans. and rev. J.D. Adams. New York, 1998.

Perrin, Noel. *Giving Up the Gun: Japan's Reversion to the Sword, 1543–1879*. Boston, 1979.

Perroy, Edouard. *L'Angleterre et le grand schisme d'occident: étude sur la politique religieuse de l'Angleterre sous Richard II (1378–1399)*. Paris, 1933.

———. "L'artillerie de Louis XI dans la campagne d'Artois," *Revue du Nord* 26 (1943), 171–96, 293–315.

———. "L'artillerie royale à la bataille de Montlhery (10 juillet 1465), *Revue historique* 149 (1925), 187–89.

———. *The Hundred Years War*. Trans. W.B. Wells. London, 1951.

Pirenne, Henri. *Histoire de Belgique*. Vol. 2: *Du commencement du XIVe siècle à la mort de Charles le Téméraire*. Brussels, 1903.

Plancher, U. *Histoire générale et particulaire de Bourgogne*. 4 vols. Dijon, 1793–81.

Pocquet du Haut Jussé, Barthélemy-Amédée. *François II, duc de Bretagne, et l'Angleterre (1458–1488)*. Paris, 1929.

Puype, Jan Piet. "Het embleem van Lodewijk van Gruuthuse." In: *Lodewijk van Gruuthuse: Mecenas en europees diplomaat, ca. 1427–1492*. Ed. Maximiliaan P.J. Martens. Bruges, 1992, pp. 93–108.

Quicke, F. *Les Pays-Bas à la veille de la periode Bourguignonne, 1356–1384: Contribution à l'histoire politique et diplomatique de l'Europe occidentale dans la seconde moitié du XIVe siècle*. Brussels, 1947.

Rathgen, Bernhard. *Das Aufkommen der Pulverwaffe*. Munich, 1925.

———. "Feuer- und fernwaffen des 14. jahrunderts in Flandern." *Zeitschrift für historisches Waffenkunde* 7 (1915–17), 275–306.

———. *Die feuer- und fernwaffen in Naumburg von 1348–1449.* Naumburg: H. Sielings Buchdruckerei, 1921.

———. *Das Geschütz im mittelalter: Quellenkritische untersuchungen.* Berlin: VDI-Verlag GMBH, 1928.

——— and Karl Heinrich Schäfer. "Feuer- und fernwaffen beim päpstlichen Heere im 14. Jahrhundert." *Zeitschrift für historisches Waffenkunde* 7 (1915–17), 1–15.

Richard, Jean. "La croisade bourguignonne dans la politique européen," *Publications du centre européen d'études burgundo-médianes* 10 (1968), 41–44.

———. "Quelques idées de François de Surienne sur la défense des villes à propos de la fortification de Dijon (1461)," *Annales de Bourgogne* 16 (1944), 36–43.

Roelofsen, C.G. "L'évolution de la flotte 'Bouguignonne' aux XVe et XVIe siècles: quelques remarques sur l'introduction du canon dans la guerre maritime et son influence," *Publication du centre Européen d'études Bourguignonnes (XIVe–XVIe s.)* 26 (1986), 87–95.

Rogers, Clifford J. "The Military Revolutions of the Hundred Years War," *Journal of Military History* 57 (1993), 241–78.

Rogers, H.C.B. *Artillery through the Ages.* London, 1971.

Roland, C. "L'artillerie de la ville de Binche, 1362–1420," *Bulletin de la société royale paléontologique et archéologique de l'arrondissement judicaire de Charleroi* 23 (1954), 17–38.

Ropp, Theodore. *War in the Modern World.* 2nd ed. New York, 1962.

Rosetti, R. "Notes on the Battle of Nicopolis (1396)," *Slavonic and East European Review* 15 (1936–37), 629–38.

Roulet, Louis-Edouard. "Le duc René à la bataille de Morat." In: *Cinq-centième anniversaire de la bataille de Nancy (1477): Actes du Colloque organisé par l'institut de recherche régionale en sciences sociales, humaines et économiques de l'Université de Nancy II (Nancy, 22–24 septembre 1977).* Nancy, 1979, pp. 415–28.

———. "Formation de la Suisse." In: *Actes du Ve centenaire de la bataille de Morat.* Fribourg and Berne, 1976, pp. 163–69.

———. "Présence et engagement des combattants Anglais à Grandson et à Morat." In: *L'Angleterre et les pays Bourguignons: Relations et comparaisons (Xve–XVIe siècles).* Neuchâtel, 1995, pp. 107–22.

———. "La route Berne-Genève et les guerres de Bourgogne," *Publication du Centre européen d'études burgundo-médianes* 23 (1983), 43–51.

———. "Le Téméraire à Morat: plaidoyer pour une rehabilitation," *Publication du centre Européen d'études Bourguignonnes (XIVe–XVIe s.)* 26 (1986), 39–56.

Runciman, Steven. *The Fall of Constantinople, 1453.* Cambridge, 1965.

Salamagne, Alain. "L'attaque des places-fortes au XVe siècle à travers l'exemple des guerres anglo et franco-bourguignonnes," *Revue historique* 289 (1993), 65–113.

Saul, Nigel. *Richard II.* New Haven, 1997.

Savage, Henry L. "Enguerrand de Coucy VII and the Campaign of Nicopolis," *Speculum* 14 (1939), 423–42.

Scherff, Bruno. "Die Ordonnanz Karls des Kühnen von Burgund aus dem Jahre 1473," *Militärgeschichtliche Mitteilungen* 57 (1998), 319–31.

Schmidtchen, Volker. *Die Feuerwaffen des deutschen Ritterordens bis zur Schlacht bei Tannenberg 1410.* Lüneberg, 1977.

Schmitz, F. *Der Neusser Krieg, 1474–75.* Bonn, 1896.

Schnerb, Bertrand. *Les Armagnacs et les Bourguignons: La maudite guerre.* Paris, 1988.

———. "La bataille rangée dans la tactique des armées Bourguignonnes au début du 15e siècle: essai de synthèse," *Annales de Bourgogne* 61 (1989), 5–32.

———. *Bulgnéville (1431): L'état bouguignon prend pied en Lorraine.* Paris, 1993.

———. *L'état Bourguignon, 1363–1477.* Paris, 1999.

———. "Troylo da Rossano et les Italiens au service de Charles le Téméraire," *Francia* 26 (2000), 103–28.

Scrive-Bertin, M. "Les canonniers Lillois avant 1483," *Bulletin de la commission historique du departement du nord* 19 (1890), 119–91.

Setton, Kenneth M. *The Papacy and the Levant (1204–1571).* Vol I: *The Thirteenth and Fourteenth Centuries.* Philadelphia, 1976.

Seward, Desmond. *Henry V as Warlord.* London: Sidgwick and Jackson, 1987; rpt. London: Penguin Books, 2001.

Simmons, Joe J., III. "Lidded-breech Wrought-iron Swivel Gun at Southsea Castle, Portsmouth, England," *Journal of the Ordnance Society* 1 (1989), 63–68.

Šišić, Ferdinand von. "Die Schlacht bei Nikopolis (25. September 1396)," *Wissenschaftliche mitteilungen aus Bosnia und der Hercegovina* 6 (1899), 291–327.

Smith, Robert D. " 'All Manner of Peeces': Artillery in the Late Medieval Period," *The Royal Armouries Yearbook* 7 (2002), 130–38.

———. "Good and Bold: A Late 15th-Century Artillery Train," *The Royal Armouries Yearbook* 6 (2001), 98–105.

———. "Port Pieces: The Use of Wrought-Iron Guns in the Sixteenth Century," *Journal of the Ordnance Society* 5 (1993), 1–10.

———. "The Reconstruction and Firing Trials of a Replica of a 14th-Century Cannon," *Royal Armouries Yearbook* 4 (1999), 86–94.

———. "The Technology of Wrought-Iron Artillery," *Royal Armouries Yearbook* 5 (2000), 68–79.

———. "Towards a New Typology for Wrought Iron Ordnance," *International Journal of Nautical Archaeology and Underwater Exploration* 17 (1988), 5–16.

———. "Wrought-Iron Swivel Guns." In: *The Archaeology of Ships of War.* Ed. M. Bound. Oxford, 1995, pp. 104–13.

——— and Ruth Rhynas Brown. *Mons Meg and Her Sisters.* London, 1989.

——— and Kelly DeVries. "Breech-Loading Guns with Removable Chambers: A Long-Lived Military Technology." In: *Gunpowder, Explosives, and the State: A Technological History.* Ed. Brenda Buchanan. (forthcoming).

Sommé, Monique. "L'armée Bourguignonne au siège de Calais de 1436." In: *Guerre et société en France, en Angleterre et en Bourgogne XIVe–XVe siècle.* Ed. P. Contamine et al. Lille, 1991, pp. 197–219.

———. "Les mesures dans l'artillerie Bourguignonne au XVe siècle," *Cahiers de metrologie* 7 (1989), 43–53.

Steel, Anthony. *Richard II.* Cambridge, 1941.

Stein, Henri. *Charles de France, frère de Louis XI.* Paris, 1919.

Szakály, F. "Phases of Turco-Hungarian Warfare before the Battle of Mohács," *Acta orientalia academia scientia Hungarensis* 33 (1979), 65–111.

Taveneaux, René. *Histoire de Nancy.* Toulouse, 1978.

Terlinden, Charles. *Histoire militaire des Belges.* Brussels, 1931.

Thielmans, Marie-Rose. *Bourgogne et Angleterre: relations politiques et économiques entre les Pays-Bas Bourguignonnes et l'Angleterre, 1435–1467.* Brussels, 1966.

Thiry, Claude. "Les poèmes de langue Française relatifs aux sacs de Dinant et de Liège." In: *Liège et Bourgogne. Actes du colloque tenu à Liège les 28, 29 et 30 Octobre 1968.* Liège, 1972, pp. 101–27.

Tipton, Charles L. "The English at Nicopolis," *Speculum* 37 (1962), 528–40.

Tittmann, Wilfried. "Die Eltzer Büchsen pfeile von 1331/2," *Waffen-und Köstumkunde* 36 (1994), 117–28; 37 (1995), 53–64.

Tout, T.F. "Firearms in England in the Fourteenth Century," *English Historical Review* 26 (1911), 666–702; rpt. *Firearms in England in the Fourteenth Century.* London, 1968.

Trenschel, Hans-Peter. "Drei Geschützfragmente aus der Bungunderbeute," *Jahrbuch des Bernischen Historischen Museums in Bern* 47–48 (1967–1968), 9–60.

T'Sas, Francois. "Dulle Griet. La grosse bombarde de Gand, et ses souers." *Armi antiche* 1969, 13–57.

Vale, M.G.A. "The Last Years of English Gascony, 1451–1453," *Transactions of the Royal Historical Society* 5th ser., 19 (1969), 119–38.

———. "New Techniques and Old Ideals: The Impact of Artillery on War and Chivalry at the End of the

Hundred Years War." In: *War, Literature and Politics in the Late Middle Ages: Essays in Honour of G.W. Coopland*. Ed. C.T. Allmand. Liverpool: University of Liverpool Press, 1975, pp. 57–72.

———. "Seigneurial Fortification and Private War in Late Medieval Gascony." In: *Gentry and Lesser Nobility in Late Medieval Europe*. Ed. Michael Jones. Gloucester, 1986, pp. 133–58.

———. *War and Chivalry: Warfare and Aristocratic Culture in England, France and Burgundy at the End of the Middle Ages*. London, 1981.

Vallière, P.E. de. *Morat: Le siège et la bataille, 1476*. Lausanne, 1926.

Vandermaesen, M. and M. Ryckaert. "De Genste opstand (1379–1385)." In: *De witte Kaproenen: De Gentse opstand en de geschiedenis van de Brugse Leie*. Ed. Maurice Vandermaesen, Marc Ryckaert, and Maurits Coornaert. Kultureel Jaarboek Oost-Vlaanderen bijdragen, n.s., 10. Ghent: Provinciebestuur Oost-Vlaanderen Eksemplaren te verkrijgen bij de Provinciale Kulturele Dienst, 1979. pp. 7–31.

Van Praet, L. *Recherches sur Louis de Bruges: Seigneur de la Gruythuse*. Paris, 1831.

Vaughan, Richard. "500 Years after the Great Battles," *Bijdragen en mededelingen betreffende de geschiedenis der Nederlanden* 95 (1980), 377–90.

———. *Charles the Bold: The Last Valois Duke of Burgundy*. London, 1973.

———. *John the Fearless: The Growth of Burgundian Power*. London, 1966.

———. *Philip the Bold: The Formation of the Burgundian State*. London, 1962.

———. *Philip the Good: The Apogee of Burgundy*. London, 1970.

———. "Quelques observations sur la Bataille de Nancy." In: *Cinq-centième anniversaire de la bataille de Nancy (1477): Actes du Colloque organisé par l'institut de recherche régionale en sciences sociales, humaines et économiques de l'Université de Nancy II (Nancy, 22–24 septembre 1977)*. Nancy, 1979, pp. 23–32.

———. *Valois Burgundy*. London, 1975.

Vedrès, G. *Chateaux de Bourgogne*. Paris, 1948.

Verbruggen, J.F. *De slag bij Guinegate, 7 augustus 1479: De verdediging van het graafschap Vlaanderen tegen de koning van Frankrijk, 1477–1480*. Brussels, 1993.

———. "Un plan de bataille du duc de Bourgogne (14 september 1417) et la tactique de l'époque," *Revue internationale d'histoire militaire* 20 (1959), 443–51.

Vercauteren, Fernand. *Luttes sociales à Liège, XIIIe et XIVe siècles*. 2nd ed. Brussels, 1946.

Wailly, Henri de. *Crecy, 1346: Anatomy of a Battle*. Poole, 1987.

Walker, Robert, Richard Dunham, Alexzandra Hildred, and Margaret Rule. "Analytical Study of Composite Shot from the Mary Rose," *Journal of Historical Metallurgy Society* 23.2 (1989), 84–90.

Wattelet, Hans. *Die Schlachten bei Murten: historische-kritische Studie*. Freiburg, 1894.

Wille, Erich. *Die Schlacht von Othée, 23 septembre 1408*. Berlin, 1908.

Winkler, Albert Lynn. "The Swiss at War: The Impact of Society on the Swiss Military in the Fourteenth and Fifteenth Centuries." Unpublished dissertation. Provo: Brigham Young University, 1982.

Wrong, George M. *The Crusade of 1383 Known as That of the Bishop of Norwich*. London, 1892.

Index

Page numbers in **bold** are to sections dealing with the topic